TAKING SIDES

Clashing Views
on Controversial Issues
in American History

Volume I
The Colonial Period to Reconstruction

4th edition

Edited, Selected, and with Introductions by

Larry Madaras
Howard Community College

and

James M. SoRelle
Baylor University

The Dushkin Publishing Group, Inc.

To Eugene Kuzirian (1939–1987),
coeditor of the first two editions of
Taking Sides: Clashing Views on
Controversial Issues in American
History, *whose devotion to good*
teaching and critical thinking still
permeates this text

Library of Congress Catalog Card Number:
90-84857
Manufactured in the United States of America
Fourth Edition, First Printing
ISBN: 0-87967-934-4

 Printed on Recycled Paper

The Dushkin Publishing Group, Inc.
Sluice Dock, Guilford, CT 06437

PREFACE

The success of the past three editions of *Taking Sides: Clashing Views on Controversial Issues in American History* has encouraged us to remain faithful to its original objectives, methods, and format. Our aim has been to create an effective instrument to enhance classroom learning and to foster critical thinking. Historical facts presented in a vacuum are of little value to the educational process. For students, whose search for historical truth often concentrates on *when* something happened rather than on *why*, and on specific events rather than on the *significance* of those events, *Taking Sides* is designed to offer an interesting and valuable departure. The understanding that the reader arrives at based on the evidence that emerges from the clash of views encourages the reader to view history as an *interpretive* discipline, not one of rote memorization.

As in previous editions, the issues are arranged in chronological order and can be easily incorporated into any American history survey course. Each issue has an issue *introduction*, which sets the stage for the debate that follows in the pro and con selections and provides historical and methodological background to the problem that the issue examines. Each issue concludes with a *postscript*, which ties the readings together, briefly mentions alternative interpretations, and supplies detailed *suggestions for further reading* for the student who wishes to pursue the topics raised in the issue.

Changes to this edition In this edition we have continued our efforts to move beyond the traditionally ethnocentric and male-oriented focus of American history, both in terms of the issues and the authors selected to represent the clashing viewpoints. This edition depicts a society that benefited from the presence of Native Americans, African Americans, and women of various racial and ethnic origins. With this in mind, we present four entirely new issues: *Did Racism Cause the Conflict Between Native Americans and Colonists?* (Issue 2); *Did Capitalist Values Motivate the American Colonists?* (Issue 4); *Did Slaves Exercise Religious Autonomy?* (Issue 13); and *Reconstruction: Could It Have Given Blacks Full Equality?* (Issue 17). For the issues on colonial culture (Issue 1), the Constitution (Issue 7), and antebellum reform (Issue 11), the issues have remained the same, but the NO readings have been changed to give the debate a fresh perspective. In all, there are nine new readings in this fourth edition.

Supplements An *Instructor's Manual with Test Questions* (multiple-choice and essay) is available through the publisher for the instructor using *Taking Sides* in the classroom. Also available is a general guidebook, *Using Taking Sides in the Classroom*, which discusses methods and techniques for integrating the pro-con approach into any classroom setting.

i

Acknowledgments Many individuals have contributed to the successful completion of this edition. We appreciate the evaluations submitted to the Dushkin Publishing Group by those who have used *Taking Sides* in the classroom. Special thanks go to those who responded with specific suggestions for the fourth edition: W. Dionisio, Sacramento City College; Nancy Zens, Central Oregon Community College. We particularly are indebted to Maggie Cullen, Cindy SoRelle, Barry A. Crouch, Virginia Kirk, Helen Mitchell, and Jean Soto, who shared their ideas for changes, pointed us toward potentially useful historical works, and provided significant editorial assistance. Finally, Lynnette Geary (Baylor University) and Marsha Madigan (Howard Community College) performed indispensable typing duties connected with this project.

James M. SoRelle
Baylor University

Larry Madaras
Howard Community College

CONTENTS IN BRIEF

CONTENTS

Professor of history Gary B. Nash argues that colonial American culture emerged from a convergence of three broad cultural traditions—European, Native American, and African—which produced a unique triracial society in the New World. Professor of history David Hackett Fischer contends that the cultural traditions of colonial America and the United States were derived from English folkways transported by migrants from four different regions in the British Isles.

Professor of history Alden T. Vaughan presents the Native American as a victim of color symbolism, racial differences, and nonconformity to European culture. Professor of history Karen Ordahl Kupperman insists that the English colonists' efforts to exercise unrestricted power over Native Americans, not racism, provided the catalyst for conflict between these two groups in early America.

Professor Lois Green Carr and Lorena S. Walsh, a fellow with the Colonial Williamsburg Foundation, identify several factors that coalesced to afford women in seventeenth-century Maryland a higher status with fewer restraints on their social conduct than those experienced by women in England. Lyle Koehler, an administrator at the University of Cincinnati, contends that the division of labor that separated work into male and female spheres and Puritan attitudes towards rights of inheritance severely limited opportunities for upward mobility among New England women.

Professor of geography James T. Lemon argues that the liberal, middle-class, white settlers of southeastern Pennsylvania placed individual freedom and material gain at a higher priority than that of the public interest. Professor of American history James A. Henretta claims that the colonial family determined the character of agrarian life because it was the primary economic and social unit.

Professor of history Allan Kulikoff claims that Chesapeake slaves developed their own social institutions and a distinct indigenous culture in the years between 1740 and 1790. Associate professor of history Jean Butenhoff Lee emphasizes the difficult and often unsuccessful efforts of slaves to create a stable family and community life in eighteenth-century Maryland.

Professor of history William G. McLoughlin claims that the Great Awakening, by promoting religious revitalization, intercolonial unity, and democracy, paved the way for the American Revolution. Professor of religious studies Jon Butler challenges the validity of the term "Great Awakening" and argues that a link between the eighteenth-century colonial religious revivals and the American Revolution was virtually nonexistent.

Political scientist Michael Parenti argues that the Constitution was framed by financially successful planters, merchants, and creditors in order to protect the rights of property rather than the rights and liberties of individuals. Professor of history Gordon S. Wood views the struggle for a new constitution in 1787–1788 as a social conflict between upper-class Federalists who desired a stronger central government and the "humbler" Anti-Federalists who controlled the state assemblies.

Pulitzer Prize-winning historian Richard Hofstadter argues that Thomas Jefferson was a moderate, practical politician who followed a course of action which eventually co-opted the major policies of the Federalists. Professor of history Forrest McDonald believes that President Jefferson attempted to replace Hamiltonian Federalist principles with a Republican ideology and that he wanted to restore America's agrarian heritage.

Nancy Woloch, a fellow of the National Endowment for the Humanities, describes the exercise of autonomy in the domestic life of middle-class wives. Professor of history Gerda Lerner considers a spectrum of women's roles, emphasizing the subservient position of female industrial workers.

Professor of history Robert V. Remini argues that the 1828 presidential election symbolized the people's arrival at political responsibility and began a genuine, nationally organized, two-party system that came of age in the 1830s. Professor of history Richard P. McCormick maintains that voting statistics demonstrate that a genuine political revolution did not take place until the presidential elections of 1840, when fairly well balanced political parties had been organized in virtually every state.

Professor of history Alice Felt Tyler argues that American reformers in the antebellum period were products of evangelical religion and frontier democracy who accepted the mission of perfecting human institutions. Professor of history David J. Rothman contends that antebellum reformers established orphan asylums and reformatories primarily to enforce strict discipline and to inculcate respect for authority and order among those seeking refuge in these institutions.

Professor of history Ramon Eduardo Ruiz argues that, for the purpose of conquering Mexico's northern territories, the United States waged an aggressive war against Mexico from which Mexico never recovered. Professor of diplomatic history Robert Hugh Ferrell believes that, although the American government waged an aggressive war in Mexico, it remained the Manifest Destiny of the United States to possess Texas, New Mexico, and California.

Professor of history Albert J. Raboteau claims that the religious activities of American slaves were characterized by institutional and personal independence, which undermined the ability of the masters to exercise effective control over their chattel property. Professor of history John B. Boles recognizes that slaves often worshiped apart from their masters, but he asserts that the primary religious experience of Southern slaves occurred within a biracial setting in churches dominated by whites.

PART 4 CONFLICT AND RESOLUTION

Professor of history Avery Craven believes that the fanaticism of the abolitionist crusade created an atmosphere of crisis that resulted in the outbreak of the Civil War. Professor of American studies Irving H. Bartlett differentiates between agitation and fanaticism and claims that abolitionists like Wendell Phillips were deeply committed to improving the quality of life for all Americans, including those blacks held as slaves.

Professor of history Eugene D. Genovese believes "that slavery gave the South a social system and a civilization with a distinct class structure, political community, economy, ideology and set of psychological patterns." Professor of history Edward Pessen argues that a comparison of Northern and Southern states in the three decades before the Civil War reveals common political, economic, and social practices.

Professor of history Stephen B. Oates insists that Abraham Lincoln's greatness as president of the United States stemmed from a moral vision that had as its goal the protection and expansion of popular government. Professor of English literature M. E. Bradford characterizes Lincoln as a cynical politician whose abuse of authority as president and commander in chief during the Civil War marked a serious departure from the republican goals of the Founding Fathers and established the prototype for the "imperial presidency" of the twentieth century.

Professor of history Eric Foner believes that, although Reconstruction was nonrevolutionary and conservative, it was a splendid failure because it offered blacks a temporary vision of a free society. Professor of history C. Vann Woodward argues that there was very little hope that African Americans would receive their basic freedoms when we compare our Reconstruction with the treatment accorded slaves in other societies, as well as the failure of our own land distribution policies toward poor whites and Native Americans.

INTRODUCTION

The Study of History

James M. SoRelle
Larry Madaras

In a pluralistic society such as ours, the study of history is bound to be a complex process. How an event is interpreted depends not only on the existing evidence but also on the perspective of the interpretor. Consequently, understanding history presupposes the evaluation of information, a task that often leads to conflicting conclusions. An understanding of history, then, requires the acceptance of the idea of historical relativism. Relativism means that redefinition of our past is always possible and desirable. History shifts, changes, and grows with new and different evidence and interpretations. As is the case with the law and even medicine, many beliefs that were unquestioned one or two hundred years ago have been discredited or discarded since.

Relativism, then, encourages revisionism. There is a maxim that "the past must remain useful to the present." Historian Carl Becker argued that every generation should examine history for itself, thus assuring constant scrutiny of our collective experience through new perspectives. History, consequently, does not remain static, in part because historians cannot avoid being influenced by the times in which they live. Almost all historians commit themselves to revising the views of other historians, synthesizing theories into macrointerpretations, or revising the revisionists.

SCHOOLS OF THOUGHT

Four predominant schools of thought have emerged in American history since the first graduate seminars in history were given at The Johns Hopkins University in Baltimore in the 1870s. The *progressive* school dominated the professional field in the first half of the twentieth century. Influenced by the reform currents of Populism, Progressivism, and the New Deal, these historians explored the social and economic forces that energized America. The progressive scholars tended to view the past in terms of conflicts between groups, and they sympathized with the underdog.

The post–World War II period witnessed the emergence of a new group of historians who viewed the conflict thesis as overly simplistic. Writing against the backdrop of the Cold War, these *neoconservative* or *consensus* historians argued that Americans possess a shared set of values and that the areas of agreement within our nation's basic democratic and capitalistic framework were more important than the areas of disagreement.

In the 1960s, however, the civil rights movement, women's liberation, and the student rebellion (with its condemnation of the war in Vietnam) fragmented the consensus of values upon which historians and social scientists of the 1950s had centered their interpretations. This turmoil set the stage for the emergence of another group of scholars. *New Left* historians began to reinterpret the past once again. They emphasized the significance of conflict in American history and they resurrected interest in those groups ignored by the consensus school. In addition, New Left scholars critiqued the expansionist policies of the United States and emphasized the difficulties confronted by Native Americans, African Americans, women, and urban workers in gaining full citizenship status.

Progressive, consensus, and New Left history is still being written. The most recent generation of scholars, however, has focused upon social history. Their primary concern is to discover what the lives of "ordinary Americans" were really like. These new social historians have employed previously overlooked court and church documents, house deeds and tax records, letters and diaries, photographs, and census data to reconstruct the everyday lives of average Americans. Some have employed new methodologies such as quantification (enhanced by advancing computer technology) and oral history, while others have borrowed from the disciplines of political science, economics, sociology, anthropology, and psychology for their historical investigations.

The proliferation of historical approaches, which are reflected in the issues debated in this book, has had mixed results. On the one hand, historians have become so specialized in their respective time periods and methodological styles that it is difficult to synthesize the recent scholarship into a comprehensive text for the general reader. On the other hand, historians know more about the American past than at any other time in our history. They have dared to ask new questions or ones which previously were considered to be germane only to scholars in other social sciences. Although there is little agreement about the answers to these questions, the methods employed and intriguing issues explored make the "new history" a very exciting field to study.

The topics that follow represent a variety of perspectives and approaches. Each of these controversial issues can be studied for its individual importance to our nation's history. Taken as a group, they interact with one another to illustrate larger historical themes. The issues, when grouped thematically, reveal continuing motifs in the development of American history.

NEW SOCIAL HISTORY: RED, WHITE, AND BLACK

Some of the most innovative historical research over the last 20 years has dealt with the colonial period (1607–1763) and reflects the interests of the new social historians. The work of several representatives of this group appear in this volume. For example, in Issue 1, Gary B. Nash sets the tone for the readings on early America when he suggests that colonial society must be studied from the perspective of the cultural convergence of three broad groups in North America—Native Americans, Europeans, and African Americans. He takes issue with David Hackett Fischer, who insists that American culture originated solely from the British Isles.

Issue 2 discusses the nature of the early conflicts between Native Americans and European colonizers. Alden T. Vaughan relies on the concept of historical change to explain how Europeans initially thought Native Americans were Caucasians like themselves but later assigned American Indians to an inferior racial status as "redskins." Karen Ordahl Kupperman, on the other hand, blames the colonists' attempts to dominate the Native Americans for the conflicts.

Issues 3 and 9 cover the field of women's history. One question frequently asked is whether or not the colonial period was a "golden age" for women in America. Lois Green Carr and Lorena S. Walsh argue that "the four characteristics of the seventeenth-century population—immigrant predominance, early death, late marriage, and sexual imbalance" gave women in early Maryland power in the household which English women did not enjoy. Yet Lyle Koehler finds that women in seventeenth-century New England were similar in status to their English counterparts and did not possess legal or political rights or control the affairs within the household.

Issue 9 explores a similar question for a later time period. In the early nineteenth century, society became more settled and the family's role was defined more clearly. The home took on a new significance, and women were in charge of preserving the moral climate of the family. Nancy Woloch believes that acceptance of the "cult of motherhood" enabled women to achieve greater power in the new nation. But the well-known feminist scholar Gerda Lerner challenges this interpretation.

Within the past three decades our perception of blacks in American history has changed dramatically. More consideration has been given to African Americans as active participants in American history, not simply as "victims" or "problems." In Issue 5, Allan Kulikoff concludes from his analysis of probate inventories, runaway advertisements, court depositions, and several diaries and account books kept by whites that slaves in late eighteenth-century Maryland and Virginia had begun to develop a distinct African American culture. Jean Butenhoff Lee, however, thinks that Kulikoff overstates his case.

Issue 13 deals with a similar question in the context of the nineteenth century. Most scholars have offered generalizations about slavery based on an examination of the records of large plantation owners in the antebellum Deep South. Several have considered the impact of the slave system on black community institutions, such as their religious practices. Albert J. Raboteau believes that slaves were able to maintain their own systems of religion without interference from their masters. John B. Boles, on the other hand, insists that the white slave owners controlled where, when, and how their slaves could worship.

RELIGION, REVOLUTION, REFORM, RECONSTRUCTION

Beyond suggesting that much of the colonizing experiment in British North America was motivated by a search for religious freedom, many textbooks avoid extended discussions of religion as a force in history. In the last half century, however, professional historians have assumed that the religious revivals in the middle of the eighteenth century, known as the "Great Awakening," played a major role in the political and social evolution of colonial society. In Issue 6, the well-known religious historian William G. McLoughlin argues that the criticism of mainstream theology that many laymen and clergy made during the Great Awakening set the stage for later challenges to British political authority. Historian Jon Butler disputes the interpretation by McLoughlin and others who view the Great Awakening as the first "intercolonial movement." In fact, Butler denies that any great unified revival movement existed in the eighteenth century at all.

During the 1830s and 1840s, a wave of reformism swept across America. Various individuals and groups sought to strengthen the democratic experiment in the United States by ridding the society of its imperfections. There were health faddists and spiritualists, as well as advocates for peace, temperance, public education, special education for the deaf and blind, and communal living experiments. Issue 11 explores the motivations behind these antebellum reforms. In *Freedom's Ferment*, the classic treatment of this subject, Alice Felt Tyler insists that humanitarian goals underlay antebellum reform impulses. David J. Rothman notes that, by the 1850s, institutions such as schools, prisons, and hospitals for the mentally ill were established to control the behavior of the nation's citizens. Rothman sees the emerging poorhouses as an attempt by the middle- and upper-class elite to control the social behavior of the masses and to maintain moral order in the United States.

The major and most controversial reform effort in the pre–Civil War period was the movement to abolish slavery. Issue 14 also deals with the complexities of motivation. Avery Craven, a well-known Southern historian, believed that the Civil War had been caused unnecessarily by extremists in both the North and the South. In particular, Craven denounced the abolitionists as irresponsible fanatics who filled their propagandistic literature and speeches with lies about lazy, aristocratic plantation owners who constantly brutalized their slaves. By the early 1960s, the brutalities accorded civil rights workers in the South made Craven's pro-Southern interpretation of abolitionism unacceptable to most historians. Irving H. Bartlett reflects a new approach to · abolitionists in his sympathetic portrayal of Wendell Phillips.

The debate over slavery worked to isolate the South from the rest of the nation, but just how different was Dixie? Issue 15 poses the question: *Was the Antebellum South a Unique Section in American History?* Marxist historian Eugene D. Genovese believes "that slavery gave the South a social system and a civilization with a distinct class structure, political community, economy, ideology, and set of psychological patterns." A more recent analysis by social historian Edward Pessen takes issue with Genovese. Summarizing much of the recent scholarship on the antebellum social and economic structure in the North and South, Pessen finds more similarities than differences between the two sections.

Perhaps no period of American history has been subjected to more myths than the Reconstruction era. It has been only within the past 25 years that the older, pro-Southern interpretation has been revised in high school and college texts. In Issue 17, C. Vann Woodward compares Reconstruction in the United States to the relatively generous treatment of slaves in other societies. Also, by examining U.S. policies of land distribution to poor whites and Indians, Woodward concludes that blacks had very little hope of achieving their basic freedoms. Eric Foner, searching for an interpretation which places the event within the context of an era of tremendous economic change, concedes that Reconstruction was not very radical, much less revolutionary. Reconstruction was, nevertheless, a splendid failure because it offered blacks a vision of what a free society should look like.

POLITICS IN AMERICA

The American people gave legitimacy to their revolution through the establishment of a republican form of government. The nation has existed under two constitutions: the first established the short-lived confederation from 1781 to 1789; the second constitution was written in 1787 and remains in effect over two hundred years later. Ever since Charles Beard wrote *An Economic Interpretation of the Constitution of the United States* in 1913, historians have been debating the motivations of the Founding Fathers. In Issue 7, Michael Parenti restates Beard's thesis by arguing that the Constitution is an elitist document framed by a group of financially successful planters, merchants, and creditors in order to protect the rights of property over the rights and liberties of persons. Gordon S. Wood concludes that the struggle associated with creating the new constitution stemmed from the conflict between the Federalists' desire for a stronger central government and the Anti-Federalists, who feared losing power at the state level.

According to the Constitution, an election is held every four years to choose our president. Political scientists have designated those elections which mark a significant change in the distribution of power as "key" or "realigning" elections. In Issue 10, Professor Robert V. Remini argues that the 1828 election both symbolized the people's arrival at political responsibility and began a genuine, nationally organized two-party system that came of age in the 1830s. In contrast, Richard P. McCormick employs a clever statistical analysis of voter participation in state and local, as well as presidential, elections from 1812 through 1840. Based on this analysis, McCormick claims that a genuine political revolution did not take place until the presidential election of 1840.

No discussion of American politics is complete without examining the lives of some of the key presidents. Two of the greatest (and among the most controversial) were Thomas Jefferson (see Issue 8) and Abraham Lincoln (see Issue 16).

THE UNITED STATES AND THE WORLD

A discussion of early nineteenth-century foreign policy in Issue 12 concerns both our diplomatic relations with the rest of the world and our self-perception within the world of nations. Did the United States government conceive of its power as continental, hemispheric, or worldwide? Ramon Eduardo Ruiz argues that the United States waged a racist and imperialistic war against Mexico for the purpose of conquering what became the American Southwest. Robert Hugh Ferrell, however, believing that U.S. possession of the southwestern region was inevitable and unalterable, cites Manifest Destiny as the reason for the Mexican War.

CONCLUSION

The process of historical study should rely more on thinking than on memorizing data. Once the basics (who, what, when, where) are determined, historical thinking shifts to a higher gear. Analysis, comparison and contrast, evaluation, and explanation take command. These skills not only increase our knowledge of the past but they also provide general tools for the comprehension of all the topics about which human beings think.

The diversity of a pluralistic society, however, creates some obstacles to comprehending the past. The spectrum of differing opinions on any particular subject eliminates the possibility of quick and easy answers. The variety of thought demands thorough comparison and contrast. In the final analysis, conclusions often are built through a synthesis of several different interpretations, but, even then, they may be partial and tentative.

The study of history in a pluralistic society allows each citizen the opportunity to reach independent conclusions about the past. Since most, if not all, historical issues affect the present and future, understanding the past becomes necessary if society is to progress. Many of today's problems have a direct connection with the past. Additionally, other contemporary issues may lack obvious direct antecedents, but historical investigation can provide illuminating analogies. At first, it may appear confusing to read and to think about opposing historical views. In the end, however, the survival of our democratic society will depend on such critical thinking by acute and discerning minds.

PART 1

From Settlement to Revolution

Colonial settlement took place in the context of conditions that were unique to that time and place. The ethnic identity of the colonists affected their relations with Native Americans and with each other and influenced the nature of the institutions that developed. Many of the institutions and ideals that grew out of the colonial experience served the early settlers well and are still emulated today. Others, such as slavery, have left a less positive legacy.

Was Colonial Culture Uniquely American?

Did Racism Cause the Conflict Between Native Americans and Colonists?

Was the Colonial Period a "Golden Age" for Women in America?

Did Capitalist Values Motivate the American Colonists?

Did American Slaves Develop a Distinct African American Culture in the Eighteenth Century?

Was the Great Awakening a Key to the American Revolution?

ISSUE 1

Was Colonial Culture Uniquely American?

YES: Gary B. Nash, from *Race, Class, and Politics: Essays on American Colonial and Revolutionary Society* (University of Illinois Press, 1986)

NO: David Hackett Fischer, from *Albion's Seed: Four British Folkways in America* (Oxford University Press, 1989)

ISSUE SUMMARY

YES: Professor of history Gary B. Nash argues that colonial American culture emerged from a convergence of three broad cultural traditions—European, Native American, and African—which produced a unique triracial society in the New World.
NO: Professor of history David Hackett Fischer contends that the cultural traditions of colonial America and the United States were derived from English folkways transported by migrants from four different regions in the British Isles.

Michel-Guillaume Jean de Crevecoeur was a French immigrant who became a naturalized subject of the colony of New York in 1764. He married an American woman, and the couple settled on a comfortable estate in New York. In 1782, Crevecoeur published a volume entitled *Letters from an American Farmer* in which he attempted to analyze the culture and national character of his adopted land. In probing the unique quality of the American, Crevecoeur wrote: "What then is the American, this new man? He is either an European, or the descendent of an European, hence that strange mixture of blood, which you will find in no other country. . . . *He* is an American who, leaving behind him all his ancient prejudices and manners, receives new ones from the new mode of life he has embraced, the new government he obeys, and the new rank he holds. He becomes an American by being received in the broad lap of our great *Alma Mater*. Here individuals of all nations are melted into a new race of men, whose labors and posterity will one day cause great changes in the world." A half century later another Frenchman, the aristocratic Alexis de Tocqueville, explored the distinctiveness of America by emphasizing the twin components of democracy and equality. But it was an American historian, Frederick Jackson Turner, who captured the attention of generations of scholars and students by characterizing the unique qualities of life in America and distinguishing that life from Old World culture. For Turnerians, it was the American frontier experience that was most responsible for Crevecoeur's "new man."

Historians continue to express interest in the nature of American culture as they explore the Old World and New World roots of the American people and the society they created beginning in the seventeenth century. Just how new was that early American culture? How much did it depart from the cultural heritage of those tens of thousands of immigrants who arrived in England's North American colonies prior to the American Revolution? Modern-day students who are unfamiliar with the writings of Crevecoeur, Tocqueville, and Turner should find it worthwhile to explore the basic components of the American culture that emerged in the colonial period. By understanding the nature of that culture, Americans obtain a better grasp of who they are.

For Gary B. Nash, the main problem in developing a clear picture of colonial American culture has been the tendency of past generations of scholars to operate from a male-dominated and highly ethnocentric framework. In Nash's view, those who ignore important segments of the population that played significant roles in colonial social development fail to describe that development accurately. His essay makes clear that while white male Europeans were prominent in carving a cultural base for the American people, they were assisted by their female counterparts, as well as Native Americans and Africans of both sexes. That culture was unique, he suggests, primarily because it was a triracial composite, not one simply transferred intact from Europe.

Not all scholars, however, agree with this notion of American distinctiveness. In the nineteenth century, historian Herbert Baxter Adams and his followers insisted that American culture was best understood as an extension of England or Europe. Contemporary historian David Hackett Fischer presents an intriguing modification of this so-called germ theory. According to Fischer, American society was germinated by four waves of British immigrants, each of which brought with them the shared characteristics of the English as well as the distinctive folkways of their respective regions. These four different sets of folkways, he concludes, account for the distinctiveness of regional cultures in the New World colonies, but each remains a direct product of English culture. In his essay, Fischer focuses upon the different ways in which the concept of freedom is defined in American society. These differences, says Fischer, reflect the varying "freedom ways" of immigrants from eastern England, the southern and western counties, the North Midlands, and the borders of North Britain and northern Ireland, who settled in British North America between 1629 and 1775.

YES
Gary B. Nash

THE SOCIAL DEVELOPMENT OF COLONIAL AMERICA

The history of social development in colonial America—portrayed in this paper primarily as the history of social relations between groups of people defined by race, gender, and class—is in glorious disarray. Disarray because all of the old paradigms have collapsed under the weight of the last generation of scholarship. Glorious because a spectacular burst of innovative scholarship, the product of those who have crossed disciplinary boundaries, transcended filiopietism, and been inspired in the best sense by the social currents of their own times, has left us with vastly more knowledge of the first century and a half of American history than we ever had before. . . .

So much creative work has been done during the last generation that it may seem that the time has arrived to build new models of social development. Yet this still may be premature because in spite of their many virtues, the innovative studies of the past two decades are so male-centered and oblivious to the black and native American peoples of colonial society that any new synthesis would necessarily be constructed with materials that present a skewed and incomplete picture of the social process in the prerevolutionary period.

If social development is defined as changing social relations between different groups in society, then the foundation of any such study must be rigorous analysis of the structural arrangements that did not strictly govern most human interaction but set the boundaries for it in the preindustrial period, as between masters and slaves, men and women, parents and children, employers and employees. Those relationships, moreover, must be examined within the context of a triracial society. This marks a fundamental difference between social development in England and America or in France and America. Of course other differences existed as well, but perhaps none was so great as that produced by the convergence of three broad cultural groups on the North American coastal plain in the seventeenth and eighteenth centuries. Some of the best work in colonial social history has been unmindful of this, drawing conceptually on European historical studies as if

From Greene and Pole, eds., *Colonial British America: Essays in the New History of the Early Modern Era* (The Johns Hopkins University Press, 1984), pp. 233–261. Reprinted by permission of The Johns Hopkins University Press.

4

the colonies were pure offshoots of English society. . . . We must regard the social development of colonial America as *sui generis* because of the triracial environment in which most colonists lived their lives. This racial intermingling had profound effects on the social formation of the colonies. . . .

NATIVE AMERICANS

Ideally, a discussion of the role of native American societies in the social development of eastern North America should be regionally organized because there was no unified "Indian" experience and the various tribal histories that ethnohistorians have reconstructed are closely related to the histories of European colonizers in particular areas. But space limitations permit only some general remarks about the underdeveloped field of native American history and its connection to the history of the colonizers. It is important to differentiate between coastal and interior tribes: even though disease and warfare thoroughly ravaged the numerous seaboard tribes by the third generation of settlement in every colony, these small societies profoundly affected the shaping of settler communities.

The process of decimation, dispossession, and decline among the Indian societies of the coastal areas occurred in different ways during the first century of European colonization. Everywhere that Europeans settled, a massive depopulation occurred as the invaders' diseases swept through biologically defenseless native societies. Yet this rarely broke the resistance of the native peoples. In New England that occurred only after the stronger coastal tribes, such as the Wampanoags and Narragansetts, finally succumbed in a long war of attrition to an enemy who sought no genuine accommodation. In Virginia and Maryland the tidewater tribes genuinely strove for accommodation following their unsuccessful resistance movements of 1622 and 1644. But, as in New England, their inability to function in any way that served European society finally led to conflict initiated by whites. Even as friendly colonized people they were obstacles in the path of an acquisitive and expanding plantation society. In South Carolina it was not dead Indians but Indians alive and in chains that benefited the white settlers. The build-up of the colonizer population was slow enough, and the desire among the Indians for trade goods intense enough, that the white Carolinians, most of them transplanted from Barbados, where they had learned to trade in human flesh, could lure the coastal tribes into obliterating each other in the wars for slaves.

The result was roughly the same in all the colonies along the seaboard. By the 1680s in the older colonies and by the 1720s in the new ones the coastal tribes were shattered. Devastated by disease and warfare, the survivors either incorporated themselves as subjects of stronger inland groups or entered the white man's world as detribalized servile dependents. Their desire for European trade goods, which kept them in close contact with European colonizers, and the persistence of ancient intertribal hostilities, which thwarted pan-tribal resistance, sealed their fate once the growth of the settler population made it apparent that their value as trading partners was incidental in comparison with the value of the land that their destruction would convert to European possession.

Although they were defeated, the coastal cultures served a crucial function for tribes farther inland. Their prolonged resistance gave interior societies time to adapt to the European presence and to devise strategies of survival as the white societies grew in size and strength. "People like the Iroquois," T.J.C. Brasser has pointed out, "owed a great deal to the resistance of the coastal Algonkians, and both peoples were well aware of this." The coastal tribes provided a buffer between the interior Indians and the Europeans, and when the coastal tribes lost their political autonomy, their remnants were often incorporated into the larger inland tribes. This was important in the much stronger opposition that the Iroquois, Cherokees, and Creeks offered to European encroachment—a resistance so effective that for the first century and a half of European settlement the white newcomers were restricted to the coastal plain, unable to penetrate the Appalachians, where the interior tribes, often allied with the French, held sway.

During the first half of the eighteenth century the interior Indian societies demonstrated their capacity for adapting to the presence of Europeans and for turning economic and political interaction with them to their own advantage. Drawing selectively from European culture, they adopted through the medium of the fur, skin, and slave trade European articles of clothing, weapons, metal implements, and a variety of ornamental objects. To some extent this incorporation of material objects robbed the Indians of their native skills. But agriculture, fishing, and hunting, the mainstays of Indian subsistence before the Europeans came, remained so thereafter. European implements such as the hoe only made Indian agriculture more efficient. The knife and fishhook enabled the natives to fish and trap with greater intensity in order to obtain the commodities needed in the barter system. However, pottery making declined, and the hunter became more dependent upon the gun.

Yet, interaction with European societies over many generations sowed seeds of destruction within tribal villages. It is not necessary to turn Indians into acquisitive capitalists to explain their desire for trade goods. They did not seek guns, cloth, kettles, and fishhooks out of a desire to become part of bourgeois culture, accumulating material wealth from the fur trade, but because they recognized the advantages, within the matrix of their own culture, of goods fashioned by societies with a more complex technology. The utility of the Europeans' trade goods, not the opportunities for profit provided by the fur trade, drew native Americans into it, and from the Indian point of view, trade was carried on within the context of political and social alliance.

Nonetheless, the fur trade required native Americans to reallocate their human resources and reorder their internal economies. Subsistence hunting turned into commercial hunting, and consequently males spent more time away from the villages trapping and hunting. Women were also drawn into the new economic organization of villages, for the beaver, marten, or fox had to be skinned and the skins scraped, dressed, trimmed, and sewn into robes. Among some tribes the trapping, preparation, and transporting of skins became so time-consuming that food resources had to be procured in trade from other tribes. Ironically, the reorientation of tribal economies toward the fur trade dispersed villages and weakened the localized basis of clans and lineages. Breaking up in order to be nearer the widely dispersed trapping grounds, Indian villages moved closer to the nomadic woodland existence that Europeans had charged them with at the beginning of contact.

Involvement in the fur trade also altered the relationship of native Americans to their ecosystem. The tremendous destruction of animal life triggered by the advent of European trade undermined the spiritual framework within which hunting had traditionally been carried out and repudiated the ancient emphasis on living in balance with the natural environment. Trade also broadened vastly the scale of intertribal conflict. With Europeans competing for client tribes who would supply furs to be marketed throughout Europe, Indian societies were sucked into the rivalry of their patrons. As furs became depleted in the hunting grounds of one tribe, they could maintain the European trade connection only by conquering more remote tribes whose hunting grounds had not yet been exhausted or by forcibly intercepting the furs of other tribes as they were transported to trading posts. Thus, the Iroquois decimated the Hurons of the Great Lakes region in the mid-seventeenth century as part of their drive for beaver hegemony.

While the interior tribes were greatly affected by contact with the colonizers, they nonetheless rejected much of what the newcomers presented to them as a superior way of life. Tribes such as the Iroquois, Creeks, and Cherokees were singularly unimpressed with most of the institutions of European life and saw no reason to replace what they valued in their own culture with what they disdained in the culture of others. This applied to the newcomers' political institutions and practices, system of law and justice, religion, education, family organization, and child-

rearing practices. Many aspects of Indian life were marked by cultural persistency in the long period of interaction with Europeans. Indian societies incorporated what served them well and rejected what made no sense within the framework of their own values and modes of existence.

Despite their maintenance of their traditional culture in many areas of life, the native Americans' involvement in the European trade network hastened the spread of epidemic diseases, raised the level of warfare, depleted ecozones of animal life, and drew Indians into a market economy that over a long period of time constricted their economic freedom. The interior tribes reorganized productive relations within their own communities to serve a trading partner who, through the side effects of trade, became a trading master.

Social development within the British mainland colonies proceeded in some unexpected ways because of the Indian presence. Unable to coordinate themselves militarily and politically in the first 150 years of settlement, English colonizers were unable to conquer or dislodge from their tribal homelands—as did their Spanish counterparts to the south—the powerful interior native American societies. Hence, the settler's societies, restricted to the coastal plain, developed differently than if they had been free to indulge their appetite for land and their westward yearning. Higher mortality rates associated with the spread of epidemic diseases in more densely settled areas, the rise of tenantry in rural areas, underemployment in the cities at the end of the colonial period, the decline of indentured servitude because of the growing pool of landless free laborers, and the rise of class tensions in older seaboard communities are some of the social phenomena that may be attributed in part to the limitations placed upon westward movement by the controlling hand of the major eastern tribes in the trans-Allegheny and even the Piedmont region. The native American was also of primary importance in forging an "American" identity among English, Scotch-Irish, German, and other European immigrants in North America. In their relations with the native people of the land the colonizers in British North American served a long apprenticeship in military affairs. Far more populous than the settlers of New France and therefore much more covetous of Indian land, they engaged in hundreds of military confrontations ranging from localized skirmishes to large-scale regional wars. The allegiance of the diverse immigrants to the land, the annealing of an American as distinct from an English identity, had much to do with the myriad ways in which the colonists interacted with a people who were culturally defined as "the others" but were inextricably a part of the human landscape of North America.

AFRO-AMERICANS

Unless we wish to continue picturing some one million Africans brought to or born in America before the Revolution as mindless and cultureless drones, it will be necessary to push forward recent work on the social development of black society and then to incorporate this new corpus of scholarship into an overall analysis of colonial social development. It bears noting that a large-majority of the persons who crossed the Atlantic to take up life in the New World in the three hundred years before the American Revolution were Africans. Their history is still largely untold because so much attention has been paid to the kind of slave systems Europeans fashioned in the New World—the black codes they legislated, their treatment of slaves, the economic development they directed—that the slaves themselves, as active participants in a social process, are often forgotten.

In attempting to remedy this gap, historians have borrowed heavily from the work of anthropologists. The encounter model of Sidney Mintz and Richard Price, developed with reference to the Caribbean world, is especially useful because it explores how Africans who found themselves in the possession of white masters five thousand miles from their homeland created institutions and ways of life that allowed them to live as satisfactorily as possible under the slave regimen imposed upon them by the master class. In their New World encounter with European colonizers the problem was not one of merging a West African culture with a European culture, because the human cargoes aboard slave ships were not a single collective African people but rather a culturally heterogenous people from many tribes and regions. Hence, arriving slaves did not form "communities" of people at the outset but could only become communities through forging a new life out of the fragments of many old cultures combined with elements of the dominant European culture that now bounded their existence. "What the slaves undeniably shared at the outset," according to Mintz and Price, "was their enslavement; all—or nearly all—else had to be created by them."

Major strides have been taken in tracing this process of social adaptation in the Chesapeake region and along the rice coast of South Carolina and Georgia, though much remains to be done. Already, it is apparent that in this process of adaptation there was a premium on cultural innovations and creativity, both because slaves had to adjust rapidly to the power of the master class and because of the initial cultural heterogeneity of the Africans. Unlike the European colonizers, Africans were immediately obliged "to shift their primary cultural and social commitment from the Old World to the New." This required rapid adaptation, learning new ways of doing things that would ensure survival. It is not surprising, therefore, that Africans developed local slave cultures rather than a unified Afro-American culture. In adapting to North American slavery, they adopted "a general openness to ideas and usages from other cultural traditions, a special tolerance (within the West African context) of cultural differences." Of all the people converging in seventeenth- and eighteenth-century North America, the Africans, by the very conditions of their arrival, developed the greatest capacity for cultural change.

The complexity of black culture in America cannot be understood without considering the evolution of distinct, regional black societies as they developed over the long course of slavery. One of the accomplishments of the new social historians of the colonial South is to have broken much new ground on the life cycle, family formation, and cultural characteristics of the black population, which was increasingly creole, or American-born, as the eighteenth century progressed. This work makes it possible already to go beyond earlier studies of slave life in the colonies, which were based largely on studies of nineteenth-century sources, when discussing the development of Afro-American society in the eighteenth-century colonies.

How much of African culture survived under eighteenth-century slavery is an oft-debated question. There can be little doubt that slave masters were intent on obliterating every Africanism that reduced the effectiveness of slaves as laborers and that they had some success in this. It is also true that slavery eliminated many of the cultural differences among slaves, who came from a wide variety of African cultural groups—Fulanis, Ibos, Yorubas, Malagasies, Ashantis, Mandingos, and others. At the same time, it must be remembered that throughout the eighteenth century, unlike the nineteenth, large numbers of new Africans arrived each year. Slave importations grew rapidly in the eighteenth century, so that probably never more than half the adult slaves were American-born. This continuous infusion of African culture kept alive many of the elements that would later be transmuted almost beyond recognition. Through fashioning their own distinct culture within the limits established by the rigors of the slave system, blacks were able to forge their own religious forms, their own music and dance, their own family life, and their own beliefs and values. All of these proved indispensable to survival in a system of forced labor. All were part of the social development of black society. And all affected the social development of white society as well.

WOMEN

One final aspect of social development, occasionally alluded to in this essay but indispensable to the work that lies ahead, concerns social relations defined by gender. In the last ten years, and especially in the last four or five, a wave of new work has appeared, some of it defined as women's history and some as demographic or family history. This work shows how rich the possibilities are for those who wish to study the lives of women and female-male relationships. It is crucial to the construction of new paradigms of social development that these studies of women's productive and reproductive lives, which need to be studied with class, racial, and regional differences in mind, be pushed forward at an accelerated pace and then integrated with the studies of the much better understood male half of the population. It is out of the convergence of the already completed demographic and community studies and the studies of women, blacks, and native Americans still remaining to be done that a new understanding of the social development of colonial America will emerge.

NO

David Hackett Fischer

ALBION'S SEED

In Boston's Museum of Fine Arts, not far from the place where English Puritans splashed ashore in 1630, there is a decidedly unpuritanical painting of bare-breasted Polynesian women by Paul Gauguin. The painting is set on a wooded riverbank. In the background is the ocean, and the shadowy outline of a distant land. The canvas is crowded with brooding figures in every condition of life—old and young, dark and fair. They are seen in a forest of symbols, as if part of a dream. In the corner, the artist has added an inscription: "D'ou venons nous? Qui sommes nous? Ou allons nous?"

That painting haunts the mind of this historian. He wonders how a Polynesian allegory found its way to a Puritan town which itself was set on a wooded riverbank, with the ocean in the background and the shadow of another land in the far distance. He observes the crowd of museumgoers who gather before the painting. They are Americans in every condition of life, young and old, dark and fair. Suddenly the great questions leap to life. Where do *we* come from? Who are we? Where are we going?

The answers to these questions grow more puzzling the more one thinks about them. We Americans are a bundle of paradoxes. We are mixed in our origins, and yet we are one people. Nearly all of us support our republican system, but we argue passionately (sometimes violently) among ourselves about its meaning. Most of us subscribe to what Gunnar Myrdal called the American Creed, but that idea is a paradox in political theory. As Myrdal observed in 1942, America is "conservative in fundamental principles . . . but the principles conserved are liberal and some, indeed, are radical."

We live in an open society which is organized on the principle of voluntary action, but the determinants of that system are exceptionally constraining. Our society is dynamic, changing profoundly in every period of American history; but it is also remarkably stable. The search for the origins of this system is the central problem in American history. . . .

The organizing question here is about what might be called the determinants of a voluntary society. The problem is to explain the origins and stability of a social system which for two centuries has remained stubbornly democratic in its politics, capitalist in its economy, libertarian in its laws, individualist in its society and pluralistic in its culture.

Much has been written on this subject—more than anyone can possibly read. But a very large outpouring of books and articles contains a remarkably small number of seminal ideas. Most historians have tried to explain the determinants of a voluntary society in one of three ways: by reference to the European culture that was transmitted to America, or to the American environment itself, or to something in the process of transmission.

During the nineteenth century the first of these explanations was very much in fashion. Historians believed that the American system had evolved from what one scholar called "Teutonic germs" of free institutions, which were supposedly carried from the forests of Germany to Britain and then to America. This idea was taken up by a generation of historians who tended to be Anglo-Saxon in their origins, Atlantic in their attitudes and Whiggish in their politics. Most had been trained in the idealist and institutional traditions of the German historical school.

For a time this Teutonic thesis became very popular—in Boston and Baltimore. But in Kansas and Wisconsin it was unkindly called the "germ theory" of American history and laughed into oblivion. In the early twentieth century it yielded to the Turner thesis, which looked to the American environment and especially to the western frontier as a way of explaining the growth of free institutions in America. This idea appealed to scholars who were middle western in their origins, progressive in their politics, and materialist in their philosophy.

In the mid-twentieth century the Turner thesis also passed out of fashion. Yet another generation of American historians became deeply interested in processes of immigration and ethnic pluralism as determinants of a voluntary society. This third approach was specially attractive to scholars who were not themselves of Anglo-Saxon stock. Many were central European in their origin, urban in their residence, and Jewish in their religion. This pluralistic "migration model" is presently the conventional interpretation.

Other explanations have also been put forward from time to time, but three ideas have held the field: the germ theory, the frontier thesis, and the migration model.

This [essay] returns to the first of those explanations, within the framework of the second and third. It argues a modified "germ thesis" about the importance for the United States of having been British in its cultural origins. The argument is complex, and for the sake of clarity might be summarized in advance. It runs more or less as follows.

During the very long period from 1629 to 1775, the present area of the United States was settled by at least four large waves of English-speaking immigrants. The first was an exodus of Puritans from the east of England to Massachusetts during a period of eleven years from 1629 to 1640. The second was the migration of a small Royalist elite and large numbers of indentured servants from the south of England to Virginia (ca. 1642–75). The third was a movement from the North Midlands of England and Wales to the Delaware Valley (ca. 1675–1725). The fourth was a flow of English-speaking people from the borders of North Britain and northern Ireland to the Appalachian backcountry mostly during the half-century from 1718 to 1775.

These four groups shared many qualities in common. All of them spoke the English language. Nearly all were British Protestants. Most lived under British laws and took pride in possessing British liberties. At the same time, they also differed from one another in many other ways: in their religious denominations, social ranks, historical generations, and also in the British regions from whence they came. They carried across the Atlantic four different sets of British folkways which became the basis of regional cultures in the New World.

By the year 1775 these four cultures were fully established in British America. They spoke distinctive dialects of English, built their houses in diverse ways, and had different methods of doing much of the ordinary business of life. Most important for the political history of the United States, they also had four different conceptions of order, power and freedom which became the cornerstones of a voluntary society in British America.

Today less than 20 percent of the American population have any British ancestors at all. But in a cultural sense most Americans are Albion's seed, no matter who their own forebears may have been [Albion was the first recorded name for the island of Britain]. Strong echoes of four British folkways may still be heard in the major dialects of American speech, in the regional patterns of American life, in the complex dynamics of American politics, and in the continuing conflict between four different ideas of freedom in the United States. The interplay of four "freedom ways" has created an expansive pluralism which is more libertarian than any unitary culture alone could be. That is the central thesis of this [essay]: the legacy of four British folkways in early America remains the most powerful determinant of a voluntary society in the United States today. . . .

MASSACHUSETTS FREEDOM WAYS: THE PURITAN IDEA OF ORDERED LIBERTY

The public life of New England was . . . shaped by an idea of liberty which was peculiar to the Puritan colonies. To understand its nature, one might begin with the word itself. From the generation of John Winthrop (1558–1649) to that of Samuel Adams (1722–1803), the noun "liberty" was used throughout New England in at least four ways which ring strangely in a modern ear.

First, "liberty" often described something which belonged not to an individual but to an entire community. For two centuries, the founders and leaders of Massachusetts wrote of the "liberty of New England," or the "liberty of Boston" or the "liberty of the Town." This usage continued from the great migration to the War of Independence and even beyond. Samuel Adams, for example, wrote more often about the "liberty of America" than about the liberty of individual Americans.

This idea of collective liberty, or "publick liberty" as it was sometimes called, was thought to be consistent with close restraints upon individuals. In Massachusetts these individual restrictions were numerous, and often very confining. During the first generation, nobody could live in the colony without approval of the General Court. Settlers even of the highest rank were sent prisoners to England for expressing "divers dangerous opinions," or merely because the Court judged them to be "persons unmeet to inhabit here." Others were not allowed to move within the colony except by special permission of the General Court. For a time, the inhabitants of Dedham, Sudbury and Concord were forbidden to move out of their towns, because the General Court believed that those frontier settlements were dangerously under-populated. . . .

New Englanders also used the word "liberty" in a second way which is foreign to our own time. When it referred to individuals, it often became a plural noun—"liberties" rather than "liberty." These plural liberties were understood as specific exemptions from a condition of prior restraint—an idea which had long existed in East Anglia and in many other parts of the western world. In the manor of Hengrave (Suffolk), for example, tenants were granted a specific "liberty" of fishing in the river Lark. Such a liberty was not universal or absolute; the river was closed to all other people. There were a great many of these liberties in East Anglian communities during the early seventeenth century. A person's status was defined by the number and nature of liberties to which he was admitted.

The idea of plural liberties as specific exemptions from a condition of prior constraint was carried to Massachusetts. The General Court, for example, enacted laws which extended "liberties and privileges of fishing and fowling" to certain inhabitants, and thereby denied them to everyone else. One persons's "liberty" in this sense became another's restraint. In Massachusetts, as in England, a person's rank was defined by the liberties that he possessed, and vice versa.

The laws of the Bay Colony granted some liberties to all men, others to all free men, and a few only to gentlemen. For example, a "true gentleman" and "any man equal to a gentleman," was

granted the liberty not to be punished by whipping "unless his crime be very shameful, and his course of life vicious and profligate." Other men had a lesser liberty, not to be whipped more than forty stripes. Other liberties were assigned not to individuals at all, but to churches and towns and other social groups. . . .

New England Puritans also used the word "liberty" in a third meaning, which became urgently important to the founders of Massachusetts. This was the idea of "soul liberty," or "Christian liberty," an idea of high complexity. Soul liberty was freedom to serve God in the world. It was freedom to order one's own acts in a godly way—but not in any other. It made Christian freedom into a form of obligation.

The founding generation in Massachusetts often wrote of "soul liberty," "Christian liberty" or "liberty of conscience." Many moved to the New World primarily in hopes of attaining it. What they meant was not a world of religious freedom in the modern sense, or even of religious toleration, but rather of freedom for the true faith. In their minds, this idea of religious liberty was thought to be consistent with the persecution of Quakers, Catholics, Baptists, Presbyterians, Anglicans and indeed virtually everyone except those within a very narrow spectrum of Calvinist orthodoxy. Soul liberty also was thought to be consistent with compulsory church attendance and rigorous Sabbath laws. Even the Indians were compelled to keep the Puritan Sabbath in Massachusetts. To the founders of that colony, soul freedom meant that they were free to persecute others in their own way. . . . To others of different persuasions, the Puritans' paradoxical idea of "soul freedom" became a cruel and bloody contradiction. But to the Puritans themselves "soul liberty" was a genuinely libertarian principle which held that a Christian community should be free to serve God in the world. Here was an idea in which the people of Massachusetts deeply believed, and the reason why their colony was founded in the first place.

The words "liberty" and also "freedom" were used in yet a fourth way by the builders of the Bay Colony. Sometimes, the people of Massachusetts employed the word "freedom" to describe a collective obligation of the "body politicke," to protect individual members from the tyranny of circumstance. This was conceived not in terms of collective welfare or social equality but of individual liberty. It was precisely the same idea that a descendant of the Massachusetts Puritans, Franklin Roosevelt, conceived as the Four Freedoms. That way of thinking was not his invention. It appeared in Massachusetts within a few years of its founding. The Massachusetts poor laws, however limited they may have been, recognized every individual should be guaranteed a freedom from want in the most fundamental sense. The General Court also explicitly recognized even a "freedom of fear." Its language revealed a libertarian conception of social problems (and solutions) that was characteristic of English-speaking people as early as the seventeenth century.

These four libertarian ideas—collective liberty, individual liberties, soul liberty and freedom from the tyranny of circumstance—all had a common denominator. They were aspects of a larger conception which might be called ordered liberty. This principle was deeply embedded in Puritan ideas and also in East Anglian realities. It came to be firmly established in Massachusetts even before the end of the great migration. For many years it continued to distinguish the culture of New England from other parts of British America. Even today, in much modified forms, it is still a living tradition in parts of the United States. But this principle of "ordered liberty" is also opposed by other libertarian ideas, which were planted in different parts of British America. . . .

VIRGINIA FREEDOM WAYS: THE ANGLICAN IDEA OF HEGEMONIC LIBERTY

"How is it," Dr. Samuel Johnson asked, "that we hear the loudest yelps for liberty among the drivers of negroes?" That famous question captured a striking paradox in the history of Virginia. Like most other colonists in British America, the first gentlemen of Virginia possessed an exceptionally strong consciousness of their English liberties, even as they took away the liberty of others. Governor William Berkeley himself, notwithstanding his reputation for tyranny, wrote repeatedly of "prized liberty" as the birthright of an Englishman. The first William Fitzhugh often wrote of Magna Carta and the "fundamental laws of England," with no sense of contradiction between his Royalist politics and libertarian principles. Fitzhugh argued that Virginians were both "natural subjects to the king" and inheritors of the "laws of England," and when they ceased to be these things, "then we are no longer freemen but slaves."

Similar language was used by many English-speaking people in the seventeenth and eighteenth century. The fine-spun treatises on liberty which flowed so abundantly from English pens in this era were rationales for political folkways deeply embedded in the cultural condition of Englishmen.

These English political folkways did not comprise a single libertarian tradition. They embraced many different and even contradictory conceptions of freedom. The libertarian ideas that took root in Virginia were very far removed from those that went to Massachusetts. In place of New England's distinctive idea of ordered liberty, the Virginians thought of liberty as a hegemonic condition of dominion over others and—equally important—dominion over oneself. . . .

Virginia ideas of hegemonic liberty conceived of freedom mainly as the power to rule, and not to be overruled by others. Its opposite was "slavery," a degradation into which true-born Britons descended when they lost their power to rule. . . .

It never occurred to most Virginia gentlemen that liberty belonged to everyone. It was thought to be the special birthright of free-born Englishmen—a property which set this "happy breed" apart from other mortals, and gave them a right to rule less fortunate people in the world. Even within their own society, hegemonic liberty was a hierarchical idea. One's status in Virginia was defined by the liberties that one possessed. Men of high estate were thought to have more liberties than others of lesser rank. Servants possessed few liberties, and slaves none at all. This libertarian idea had nothing to do with equality. Many years later, John Randolph of Roanoke summarized his ancestral creed in a sentence: "I am an aristocrat," he declared, "I love liberty; I hate equality."

In Virginia, this idea of hegemonic liberty was thought to be entirely consistent with the institution of race slavery. A planter demanded for himself the liberty to take away the liberties of others—a right of *laisser asservir*, freedom to enslave. The growth of race slavery in turn deepened the cultural significance of hegemonic liberty, for an Englishman's rights became his rank, and set him apart from others less fortunate than himself. The world thus became a hierarchy in which people were ranked according to many degrees of unfreedom, and they received their rank by the operation of fortune, which played so large a part in the thinking of Virginians. At the same time, hegemony over others allowed them to enlarge the sphere of their own personal liberty, and to create the conditions within which their special sort of libertarian consciousness flourished. . . .

Hegemonic liberty was a dynamic tradition which developed through at least three historical stages. In the first it was linked to Royalist cause in the English Civil War. The Virginia gentleman Robert Beverley boasted that the colony "was famous, for holding out the longest for the Royal Family, of any of the English Dominions." Virginia was the last English territory to relinquish its allegiance to Charles I, and the first to proclaim Charles II king in 1660 even before the Restoration in England. Speeches against the Stuarts were ferociously punished by the county courts. The Assembly repeatedly expressed its loyalty to the Crown, giving abundant thanks for "his Majesty's most gracious favors towards us, and Royal Condescensions to anything requisite."

In the second stage, hegemonic liberty became associated with Whiggish politics, and with an ideology of individual independence which was widely shared throughout the English-speaking world. In Virginia, many families who had been staunch Royalists in the seventeenth century became strong Whigs in eighteenth century; by the early nineteenth century they would be Jeffersonian Republicans. Their principles throughout tended to be both elitist and libertarian—a clear expression of a cultural ethic which was capable of continuing expansion. . . .

In the nineteenth and twentieth centuries, the tradition of hegemonic liberty entered a third stage of development, in which it became less hierarchical and more egalitarian. Such are the conditions of modern life that this idea is no longer the exclusive property of a small elite, and the degradation of others is no longer necessary to their support. The progress of political democracy has admitted everyone to the ruling class. In America and Britain today, the idea of an independent elite, firmly in command of others, has disappeared. But the associated idea of an autonomous individual, securely in command of self, is alive and flourishing. . . .

DELAWARE FREEDOM WAYS:
THE QUAKER IDEA OF
RECIPROCAL LIBERTY

Quakers believed in an idea of reciprocal liberty that embraced all humanity, and was written in the gold rule.

This Christian idea was reinforced in Quaker thinking by an exceptionally strong sense of English liberties. As early as 1687, William Penn ordered the full text of the Magna Carta to be reprinted in Philadelphia, together with a broad selection of other constitutional documents. His purpose was to remind the freeholders of Pennsylvania to remember their British birthright. . . .

On the subject of liberty, the people of Pennsylvania needed no lessons from their Lord Proprietor. Few public questions were introduced among the colonists without being discussed in terms of rights and liberties. On its surface, this libertarian rhetoric seemed superficially similar to that of Massachusetts and Virginia. But the founders of Pennsylvania were a different group of Englishmen—a later generation, from another English region, with a special kind of Christian faith. Their idea of liberty was not the same as that which came to other parts of British America.

The most important of these differences had to do with religious freedom— "liberty of conscience." William Penn called it. This was not the conventional Protestant idea of liberty to do only that which is right. The Quakers believed that liberty of conscience extended even to ideas that they believed to be wrong. Their idea of "soul freedom" protected every Christian conscience.

The most articulate spokesman for this idea was William Penn himself. Of nearly sixty books and pamphlets that Penn wrote before coming to America, half were defenses of liberty of conscience. Some of these works were among the most powerful statements ever written on this subject. One ended with a revealing personal remark: " . . . tis a matter of great satisfaction to the author that he has so plainly cleared his conscience in pleading for the liberty of other men's." . . .

William Penn's personal experience of religious persecution gave him other reasons for believing in religious liberty. His own sufferings convinced him that the coercion of conscience was not merely evil but futile, and deeply dangerous to true faith. "They subvert all true religion," Penn wrote, " . . . where men believe, not because 'tis false, but so commanded by their superiors."

These memories and experiences were not Penn's alone. In the period from 1661 to 1685, historians estimate that at least 15,000 Quakers were imprisoned in England, and 450 died for their beliefs. As late as the year 1685, more than 1,400 Quakers were still languishing in English jails. Most "books of sufferings" recorded punishments that continued well into the eighteenth century—mostly fines and seizures for nonpayment of tithes. . . .

Many Quaker immigrants to Pennsylvania had experienced this religious persecution; they shared a determination to prevent its growth in their own province. The first fundamental law passed in Pennsylvania guaranteed liberty of conscience for all who believed in "one Almighty God," and established complete freedom of worship. It also provided penalties for those who "derided the religion of others." The Quaker founders of Pennsylvania were not content merely to restrain government from interfering with rights of conscience. They also made it an instrument of positive protection. Here was a reciprocal idea of religious liberty which they actively extended to others as well as themselves.

Liberty of conscience was one of a large family of personal freedoms which Quakers extended equally to others. William Penn recognized three secular "rights of an Englishman": first, a "right and title to your own lives, liberties and estates; second, representative government; third, trial by jury." In Pennsylvania, these liberties went far beyond those of Massachusetts, Virginia and old England itself. . . .

The Quakers of the Delaware Valley also differed from other English-speaking people in regard to race slavery. The question was a difficult one for them. The first generation of Quakers had been deeply troubled by slavery, but many were not opposed outright. The problem was compounded in the Delaware Valley by the fact that slavery worked well as an economic institution in this region. Many Quakers bought slaves. Even William Penn did so. Of the leaders of the Philadelphia Yearly Meeting for whom evidence survives, 70 percent owned slaves in the period from 1681 to 1705.

But within the first decade of settlement a powerful antislavery movement began to develop in the Delaware Valley. As early as 1688, the Quakers of Germantown issued a testimony against slavery on the ground that it violated the golden rule. In 1696, two leading Quakers, Cadwalader Morgan and William Southeby, urged the Philadelphia Yearly Meeting to forbid slavery and slave trading. The meeting refused to go that far, but agreed to advise Quakers "not to encourage the bringing in of any more Negroes." As antislavery feeling expanded steadily among Friends, slaveowning declined among leaders of the Philadelphia yearly meeting—falling steadily from 70 percent before 1705, to only 10 percent after 1756.

The Pennsylvania legislature took action in 1712, passing a prohibitive duty on the importation of slaves. This measure was disallowed by the English Crown, which had a heavy stake in the slave trade. In 1730 the Philadelphia yearly meeting cautioned its members, but still a few Friends continued to buy slaves. Other Quaker antislavery petitions and papers followed in increasing number. . . . The argument came down to the reciprocal principle of the gold rule. Quakers argued that if they did not wish to be slaves themselves, they had no right to enslave others. . . .

The Quakers radically redefined the "rights of Englishmen" in terms of their

Christian beliefs. But they never imagined that they were creating something new. Penn and others in the colony wrote always of their rights as "ancient" and "fundamental" principles which were rooted in the immemorial customs of the English-speaking people and in the practices of the primitive church.

In the conservative cast of their libertarian thinking, the Quakers were much the same as Puritans and Anglicans. But in the substance of their libertarian thought they were very different. In respect to liberty of conscience, trial by jury, the rights of property, the rule of representation, and race slavery, Quakers genuinely believed that every liberty demanded for oneself should also be extended to others. . . .

BACKCOUNTRY FREEDOM WAYS: THE BORDER IDEA OF NATURAL LIBERTY

The backsettlers, no less than other colonists in every part of British America, brought with them a special way of thinking about power and freedom, and a strong attachment to their liberties. As early as the middle decades of the eighteenth century their political documents contained many references to liberty as their British birthright. In 1768, the people of Mecklenberg County, North Carolina, declared, "We shall ever be more ready to support the government under which we find the most liberty."

No matter whether they came from . . . England or Scotland or Ireland, their libertarian ideas were very much alike—and profoundly different from notions of liberty that had been carried to Massachusetts, Virginia and Pennsylvania. The traveler Johann Schoepf was much interested in ideas of law and liberty which

he found in the backcountry. "They shun everything which appears to demand of them law and order, and anything that preaches constraint," Schoepf wrote of the backsettlers. "They hate the name of a justice, and yet they are not transgressors. Their object is merely wild. Altogether, natural freedom . . . is what pleases them."

This idea of "natural freedom" was widespread throughout the southern back settlements. But it was not a reflexive response to the "frontier" environment, nor was it "mere wild," as Schoepf believed. The backcountry idea of natural liberty was created by a complex interaction between the American environment and a European folk culture. It derived in large part from the British border country, where anarchic violence had long been a condition of life. The natural liberty of the borderers was an idea at once more radically libertarian, more strenuously hostile to ordering institutions than were the other cultures of British America. . . .

A leading advocate of natural liberty in the eighteenth century was Patrick Henry, a descendant of British borderers, and also a product of the American backcountry. Throughout his political career, Patrick Henry consistently defended the principles of minimal government, light taxes, and the right of armed resistance to authority in all cases which infringed liberty. . . .

Patrick Henry's principles of natural liberty were drawn from the political folkways of the border culture in which he grew up. He imbibed them from his mother, a lady who described the American Revolution as merely another set of "lowland troubles." The libertarian phrases and thoughts which echoed so strongly in the backcountry had earlier been heard in the borders of North Britain. When the backcountry people celebrated the supremacy of private interests they used the same thoughts and words as William Cotesworth, an English borderer who in 1717 declared: " . . . you know how natural it is to pursue private interest even against that Darling principle of a more general good. . . . It is the interest of the Public to be served by the man that can do it cheapest, though several private persons are injured by it."

This idea of natural liberty was not a reciprocal idea. It did not recognize the right of dissent or disagreement. Deviance from cultural norms was rarely tolerated; opposition was suppressed by force. One of Andrew Jackson's early biographers observed that "It appears to be more difficult for a North-of-Irelander than for other men to allow an honest difference of opinion in an opponent, so that he is apt to regard the terms opponent and enemy as synonymous."

When backcountrymen moved west in search of that condition of natural freedom which Daniel Boone called "elbow room," they were repeating the thought of George Harrison, a North Briton who declared in the borderlands during the seventeenth century that "every man at nature's table has a right to elbow room." The southern frontier provided space for the realization of this ideal, but it did not create it.

This libertarian idea of natural freedom as "elbow room" was very far from the ordered freedom of New England towns, the hegemonic freedom of Virginia's county oligarchs, and the reciprocal freedom of Pennsylvania Quakers. Here was yet another freedom way which came to be rooted in the culture of an American region, where it flourished for many years to come.

POSTSCRIPT

Was Colonial Culture Uniquely American?

Although Nash and Fischer approach the issue of American exceptionalism from different perspectives, both recognize a certain uniqueness in American society. Fischer's America is the product of an Old World English cultural heritage. However, by emphasizing the impact on America of the distinct folkways of peoples migrating from four different geographical regions in the British Isles, Fischer reinforces the notion of a unique quality to American culture, one grounded in British customs. Unfortunately, this Anglocentric argument leaves no room for cultural contributions from either Native Americans and Africans, or Germans, Dutch, and Swedes. Nash, on the other hand, suggests that we examine the numerous non-English and non-European elements of American culture. His appreciation of cultural pluralism is developed in greater detail in *Red, White, and Black: The Peoples of Early America*, 2d ed. (Prentice Hall, 1974).

Another significant issue in the study of our cultural origins is the question of their impact on the American character. Frederick Jackson Turner's "The Significance of the Frontier in American History," a paper read at the annual meeting of the American Historical Association in 1893, reflects the views of Crevecoeur and Tocqueville by asserting that a unique national character developed out of America's frontier experience. The Turner thesis remained a hot topic of historical debate for three quarters of a century as Turnerians and anti-Turnerians debated the fine details of the impact of the frontier on American national character. The staunchest disciple of Turner was Ray Allen Billington, whose *The Far Western Frontier, 1830–1860* (Harper & Row, 1956), *The Frontier Heritage* (Holt, Rinehart, 1966), and *Frederick Jackson Turner* (Oxford University Press, 1973) should be examined. An important extension of the Turner thesis is offered in David M. Potter, *People of Plenty: Economic Abundance and the American Character* (University of Chicago, 1954), which identifies another factor contributing to the distinctive American character. Michael Kammen's *People of Paradox: An Inquiry Concerning the Origins of American Civilization* (Knopf, 1972) argues that American distinctiveness is derived from the contradiction produced by a culture created from an interaction of Old and New World patterns. Students interested in pursuing these questions of culture and character should examine Michael McGiffert, ed., *The Character of Americans: A Book of Readings*, rev. ed. (Dorsey Press, 1970), and David Stannard, "American Historians and the Idea of a National Character," *American Quarterly* (May 1971).

ISSUE 2

Did Racism Cause the Conflict Between Native Americans and Colonists?

YES: Alden T. Vaughan, from "From White Man to Redskin: Changing Anglo-American Perceptions of the American Indian," *The American Historical Review* (October 1982)

NO: Karen Ordahl Kupperman, from *Settling With the Indians: The Meeting of English and Indian Cultures in America, 1580–1640* (Rowman & Littlefield, 1980)

ISSUE SUMMARY

YES: Professor of history Alden T. Vaughan presents the Native American as a victim of color symbolism, racial differences, and nonconformity to European culture.
NO: Professor of history Karen Ordahl Kupperman insists that the English colonists' efforts to exercise unrestricted power over Native Americans, not racism, provided the catalyst for conflict between these two groups in early America.

Relations between Native Americans and Europeans were marred by the difficulties arising from people of very different cultures encountering each other for the first time. These encounters led to inaccurate perceptions, misunderstandings, and failed expectations. While at first the American Indians deified the explorers, experience soon taught them to do otherwise. European opinion ran the gamut from admiration to contempt; for example, some European poets and painters expressed admiration for the Noble Savage while other Europeans accepted as a rationalization for genocide the sentiment that "the only good savage is a dead one."

Spanish, French, and English treatments of Native Americans differed and were based to a considerable extent on each nation's hopes about the New World and how it could be subordinated to the Old. The Spanish exploited the Indians most directly, taking their gold and silver, transforming their government, religion, and society, and even occasionally enslaving them. The French posed a lesser threat than did the others because there were fewer of them and because many French immigrants were itinerant trappers and priests rather than settlers. In the long run, emigration from England was the most threatening of all. Entire families came from England, and they were determined to establish a permanent home in the wilderness.

The juxtaposition of Native Americans and English settlers from the Atlantic to the Appalachians resulted sometimes in coexistence, other times in enmity. English settlers depended on the Indians' generosity in sharing the techniques of wilderness survival. Puritan clergymen tried to save their neighbors' souls, going so far as to translate the Bible into dialects, but they were not as successful at conversion as were the French Jesuits and Spanish Franciscans. Attempts at coexistence did not smooth over the tension between the English and the Indians. They did not see eye to eye, for example, about the uses of the environment. To the English settlers, Indian agriculture was neither intense nor efficient. Native Americans observed that white settlers consumed large amounts of food per person and cultivated crops not only for themselves but also for towns and villages that bought the surplus. Subsistence farming collided with the market economy.

Large-scale violence erupted in the 1670s. In the Virginia piedmont, frontiersmen led by Nathaniel Bacon attacked tribes living in the Appalachian foothills, while throughout New England the Wampanoags, Narragansetts, Mohegans, Podunks, and Nipmunks united to stop the encroachments into their woodlands and hunting grounds. King Philip's War erupted in June 1675 and lasted until September 1676, with isolated raids stretching on until 1678. Casualties rose into the hundreds and Anglo-Indian relations deteriorated.

In the next century Spain, France, and England disputed each other's North American claims and Native Americans joined sides, usually allying with France against England. These great wars of the eighteenth century ended in 1763 with England claiming the victory, but disputes over territorial expansion continued. Colonial officials objected to the Proclamation of 1763 by which King George III's imperial government forbade his subjects from settling west of the Appalachian watershed. The area from those mountains to the Mississippi River, acquired by the British from France under the terms of the peace negotiated in Paris in 1763, was designated as an Indian reservation. From 1763 to 1783, as Anglo-colonial relations moved from disagreement to combat to independence, the London government consistently sided with the Native Americans.

In the following selections, Alden T. Vaughan explores the relations between Native Americans and European colonists by focusing upon color consciousness as an important explanation for European racism. Eighteenth-century racial theories, Vaughan contends, combined with frustration over Indian rejections of Christianity, inflated Anglo-American hostilities toward the Indians. Karen Ordahl Kupperman, on the other hand, argues that English settlers attempted to shape the Indians' culture to conform to the English model. The conflict that followed was caused by fear and guilt on the part of the English colonists, which led to hostile overreaction in the face of Indian unwillingness to conform to European ways.

YES

Alden T. Vaughan

FROM WHITE MAN TO REDSKIN: CHANGING ANGLO-AMERICAN PERCEPTIONS OF THE AMERICAN INDIAN

Documenting the shifts in the Anglo-American perceptions of Indian color is easier than explaining them. Contemporary authors were oblivious to the changes; they were too close to the phenomena and too involved in them. To a large extent, of course, the reasons for changing attitudes can only be surmised, for they reflect a vast and complicated alteration in millions of disparate individuals whose perceptions of the Indian cannot be precisely recontructed. Nonetheless, Anglo-American writings of the eighteenth century offer important clues to the psychological imperatives that encouraged "white" Americans to believe that Indians were significantly and irrevocably darker than themselves. At least three major interrelated and mutually reinforcing influences are apparent: the Anglo-Americans' anger at Indian hostility, their frustration over Indian rejection of Christianity and "civility," and their adoption of eighteenth-century racial theories.

First, chronologically, was the transformation of the Indian in English eyes from potential friend to inveterate enemy. That change took place gradually and unevenly, occurring at different times in different places, as military conflict increasingly characterized Indian-English contact. From the standpoint of Anglo-American attitudes, the causes of conflict were irrelevant: Englishmen at home or in America almost invariably blamed the Indians for hostilities and, hence, came to think of them as incorrigibly aggressive and ruthless. It was only a short step from regarding the Indians as bloodthirsty foes to perceiving them as naturally inferior in morality and humanity, and eventually in color.

The initial Anglo-American view of the Indians was largely amiable and optimistic. Most of the "savages," imperial spokesmen contended, would be friendly. They would also be eager for commerce and the gospel, partly because it would be in their own self-interest but mainly because the English professed to come peacefully, offering voluntary acceptance of English culture and religion. (By contrast, English imperialists viewed Spanish settlement as a model of how to alienate and exterminate the natives.) The Indians would therefore welcome English outposts, willingly sell surplus land, engage in mutually profitable trade, and enthusiastically embrace Protestantism. Yet, from the earliest days of English colonialism, its champions predicted—judging from a century of European experience in America—that some natives would oppose settlement no matter how fairly they were treated. And Indians who persisted in hostility or obstinately rejected free trade and proselytizing, the imperialists argued, deserved no quarter; the English never seriously questioned their own right to occupy part of America, by force if necessary. England's deeply ingrained ethnocentrism (a characteristic other European nations possessed, but apparently to a lesser degree), and England's determination to make profits and converts, which it hoped would emulate Spanish success but not Spanish methods, would brook no native opposition. Even the usually benign younger Hakluyt minced no words on this point: "To handle them gently, while gentle courses may be found to serve . . . be without comparison the best: but if gentle polishing will not serve, then we shall not want hammerours and rough masons enow, I meane our old soldiours trained up in the Netherlands, to square and prepare them to our Preachers hands." With the few recalcitrants chastised, colonization would proceed peacefully, to the benefit of settlers and Indians alike.

Such expectations died early. At Roanoke Island in the 1580s, most of the Indians turned against the colonists, for justifiable reasons, and the neighboring Powhatans probably exterminated the "Lost Colony" of 1587. In Virginia, settlers and natives clashed almost incessantly from 1607 to 1613, often in open warfare, sometimes in sporadic skirmishes, occasionally in bloodless but hostile negotiations. Nearly a decade of relative calm followed the captivity and conversion of Pocahontas in 1613; the brief and imperfect respite from hostilities ended suddenly with the massacre of 1622, which almost exterminated the colony. Even though responsibility for the massacre ultimately belonged with the English, as their own accounts unwittingly reveal, the Anglo-American attitude toward the Indians quickly shifted from contempt to hatred—a sentiment intensified by the ensuing decade of blatant carnage and by a similar massacre in 1644.

New England's experience offers some parallels and some marked contrasts to Virginia's. Unlike Virginia, the New England colonies had generally peaceful relations with the local tribes until 1675. To a considerable extent that reflected New England's unusual population ratio: epidemics in 1616-17 and 1633-34 greatly reduced the natives while barely touching the colonists, which lessened Indian resistance and further encouraged Puritan immigrants to believe that God intended them to create a New English Zion. So did the Pequot War of 1637, which briefly threatened New England's view of the Indians as potential friends and converts. The decisive victory over the Pequots further reduced Indian numbers, and, when most of the tribes remained neutral or actively supported the colonists, the Puritans' confidence in their own invincibility and in the Indians' vulnerability was reinforced rather than un dermined. By contrast, early Virginians faced an Indian population that vastly outnumbered them and that had enough political cohesion to use its numerical strength effectively.

But numbers do not tell the whole story. Important too was the strong missionary impulse among New England's founders, an impulse that eventually enjoyed a quarter-century of modest achievement. New England's missionary activity began belatedly in the 1640s, but its success from then until King Philip's War seemed to justify earlier expectations. The uprisings of 1675—once again an Indian response to colonial encroachment and abuses—dashed Puritan assumptions about the eventual transformation of the Indians into proper Englishmen. Henceforth, the British colonists in New England joined those in the Chesapeake and elsewhere in a growing conviction that Indians in general were their enemies. That conviction hardened in the late seventeenth century and throughout the eighteenth as the British colonial frontier became a vast English-Indian battleground, often exacerbated by troops or agents from other colonial powers. Even Pennsylvania, after the effective withdrawal of the Quakers from political control and after the influx of a predominantly non-Quaker population, had its share of racial conflict.

Frequent and ferocious hostilities, regardless of who was at fault, inevitably corroded the earlier Anglo-American view of the Indians and reshaped its vocabulary. References to the Indians, never especially flattering, now became almost universally disparaging. In the aftermath of 1622, Anglo-American spokesmen portrayed the Virginia native as "having little of Humanitie but shape," "more brutish than the beasts they hunt," and "naturally born slaves." New Englanders reacted similarly to King Philip's War. The Indians were "Monsters shapt and fac'd like men," wrote one New England poet, and most of his compatriots undoubtedly agreed. Even book titles reflect the shift in attitude. In 1655 John Eliot could write hopefully of the Indians' progress toward conversion in *A Late and Further Manifestation of the Progress of the Gospell amongst the Indians in New England: Declaring Their Constant Love and Zeal to the Truth, with a Readiness to Give Account of Their Faith and Hope, as of Their Desire to Be Partakers of the Ordinances of Christ.* Twenty years later, in the midst of New England's struggle for survival, an anonymous pamphleteer suggested a far different view of the Indians in a *Brief and True Narration of the Late Wars Risen in New-England, Occasioned by the Quarrelsome Disposition, and Perfidious Carriage of the Barbarous, Savage, and Heathenish Natives there.* As warfare increasingly became the dominant mode of English-Indian contact, the image of the Indian as vicious savage made deep inroads on the Anglo-American psyche. Cotton Mather, whose rhetorical flights often exaggerated but seldom misrepresented colonial sentiments, gave revealing advice to New England's soldiers in King William's War: "Once you have but got the Track of those Ravenous howling Wolves, then pursue them vigorously; *Turn not back till* they *are consumed.* . . . Beat them small as the *Dust before the Wind* . . . *Sacrifice them to the Ghosts of Christians whom they have Murdered.* . . . *Vengance, Dear Country-men! Vengance upon our Murderers.*" The culmination of a century and a half of military escalation came in 1776 in the Declaration of Independence's only reference to the Indians: The king "has endeavored to bring on the inhabitants of our frontiers, the merciless Indian savages, whose known rule of warfare is an undistinguished destruction of all ages, sexes and conditions." Nearly a decade of border warfare exacerbated the revolutionaries' fear and hatred of the Indians. "The white Americans," observed a British traveler in 1784, "have the most rancorous antipathy to the whole race of Indians; and nothing is more common than to hear them talk of extirpating them totally from the face of the earth, men, women, and children."

War-bred animosities did not require a difference in color perception, but the unconscious temptation to tar the Indian with the brush of physical inferiority—to differentiate and denigrate the enemy—appears to have been irresistible. Wartime epithets have often invoked outward appearance, however irrelevant (witness the "yellow Japs" of World War II), and British Americans frequently resorted to pejorative color labels. In the late seventeenth and early eighteenth centuries, as war raged along the northern New England frontier, Cotton Mather castigated "those Tawny Pagans, than which there are not worse Divels Incarnate upon Earth," and "a *swarthy* Generation of *Philistines* here; the *Indian* Natives, I mean, whom alone we are like to have any *Warrs withal.*" Nearly a century later, when the bulk of the Indians sided with Great Britain during the American Revolution, Henry Dwight complained of "copper Colour'd Vermine" and hoped that an American army would "Massacre those Infernal Savages to such a degree that [there] may'nt be a pair of them left, to continue the Breed upon the Earth." Logically enough, "redskins" eventually emerged as the epithet for enemies who usually used red paint on the warpath. Not coincidentally, perhaps, the first reported use of that term appears in a passage about Indian assaults on frontier settlements. In a sentence that suggests the impact of war on changing English attitudes, Samuel Smith of Hadley, Massachusetts, recalled in 1699 that several decades earlier his father had endured Indian raids in the Connecticut Valley. "My Father ever declardt," Smith remembered, "there would not be so much to feare iff ye Red Skins was treated with suche mixture of Justice & Authority as they cld understand, but iff he was living now he must see that wee can do nought but *fight* em & that right heavily."

The Indians' refusal to adopt English concepts of civility and religion poisoned Anglo-American attitudes as thoroughly as did warfare. Sixteenth- and seventeenth-century expectations of rapid and wholesale anglicization met constant rebuff; by the end of the seventeenth century it must have been clear to all but the more optimistic missionaries that most Indians would never be Christian in faith or English in allegiance and customs. Converts in the southern and middle colonies numbered only a handful; most of John Eliot's "praying towns" had been scuttled by King Philip's War and its aftermath; and even the Quakers in Pennsylvania, despite a commendable effort to treat the Indians fairly, had won few to English ways or beliefs. Occasional successes notwithstanding, the missionary movement had failed. Even less successful was the broader mission of eliminating customs that Englishmen subsumed under the heading of "savagery," such as nakedness, scarification, tribal law and government, hunting instead of herding, and, perhaps most important of all, an exclusively oral language. Some technological assimilation had occurred, as had some imaginative blending of religious ideas, but the overwhelming majority of Indians steadfastly held to their traditional ways and rejected most of the alien culture's offerings.

Who was to blame? The most obvious scapegoat was the Indian himself. He stubbornly resisted spiritual and material improvement, his critics charged, and they eventually concluded that his resistance stemmed either from a deeply ingrained antipathy to "civilization" or from a natural incapacity for improvement. Benjamin Franklin explained to a correspondent in 1753 that "Little Success . . . has hitherto attended every attempt to Civilize our American Indians in their present way of living. . . . When an Indian Child has been brought up among us, taught our language and habituated to Our Customs, yet if he goes to see his relations and make one Indian Ramble with them, there is no perswading him ever to return." Franklin did not consider the Indians inherently incapable of adopting English ways; they simply and obstinately preferred their own. Many of Franklin's contemporaries were less charitable. The editor of the 1764 edition of William Wood's *New England's Prospect*, for example, thought the Indians incurably barbarian and pagan. "The christianizing the Indians," he noted,

> scarcely affords a probability of success; for their immense sloth, their incapacity to consider abstract truth . . . and their perpetual wanderings, which prevent a steady worship, greatly impede the progress of Christianity, a mode of religion adapted to the most refined temper of the human mind. . . . The feroce manners of a native Indian can never be effaced, nor can the most finished politeness totally eradicate the wild lines of his education.

Almost predictably, the editor believed that Indians were not born white: with few exceptions, contempt for Indians correlated highly with a belief in their innate darkness.

A third major influence toward perceiving the Indians as inherently tawny or red came from eighteenth-century naturalists. Few of them had first-hand information about the American Indians—most were European scholars who never visited the New World—but in their frantic attempt to classify systematically all plant and animal life, including the principal divisions of mankind, they contributed directly to the notion of Indians as inherently red and indirectly at least to the belief in their inferiority.

Initially, the naturalists' categories had no hierarchical intent. Their taxonomies were horizontal, not vertical, and each branch of humanity enjoyed equality with all others. Before long, however, the subdivisions of *homo sapiens* acquired descriptive judgments that suggest a relative superiority in Europeans and corresponding inferiority in other races. Such a view meshed perfectly with the eighteenth century's emphatic belief in natural order, mataphorically expressed as a "Great Chain of Being," in which all creatures from microorganisms to angels had permanent places on a hierarchical continuum. The idea of an orderly chain of life had existed for centuries; it flourished in the fifteenth century, for example, when Sir John Fortescue recorded a classic description: "In this order angel is set over angel, rank upon rank in the Kingdom of Heaven; man is set over man, beast over beast, bird over bird, and fish over fish . . . so that there is no worm that crawls upon the ground, no bird that flies on high, no fish that swims in the depths, which the chain of this order binds not in most harmonious concord." Not until the eighteenth century, however, did ranks *within* humankind receive much attention. Then, because natural scientists almost invariably chose skin color as the principal criterion of racial identity, darkness of hue became "scientifically" linked to other undesirable qualities. As Winthrop Jordan has pointed out, for Africans the "Great Chain of Being" soon became a "Great Chain of Color" on which whites regarded blacks as divinely relegated to a lesser rank of humanity. In the eighteenth century, American Indians also became victims, though not quite so pejoratively, of the color chain's invidious implications. . . .

American racial thought in the post-Revolutionary era underwent subtle but significant changes. Ever since the sixteenth century, Europeans had viewed Africans and Indians as fundamentally different from each other in postdiluvian biological development and in their prospects for absorption into British-American society. In the eighteenth century, the gap gradually closed as the Indian became, in the eyes of most white observers, inherently tawny. As earlier, most Anglo-Americans considered Africans immutably black; in the late eighteenth and early nineteenth centuries some writers further debased the Afro-American by contriving polygenic theories to explain what they believed to be the black race's irredeemable physical and behavioral inferiority. Indians, by contrast, were sometimes lauded for superior appearance, virtue, or ability, yet increasingly they too suffered the stigma that white America attached to peoples of darker skin.

That the Indian was, in fact, inherently darker than the European, and that his pigmentation was the sign of a separate branch of mankind, had become axio-matic by the outbreak of the American Revolution. What remained for the Jeffersonian generation and its early nineteenth-century successors was to determine the Indians' proper color label and to reach a rough consensus on the implications of a racial status that was clearly inferior to the white man's but also superior to the black's. . . .

Once red became a viable designation, it seems to have satisfied everyone. To the Indians' bitterest critics, red could signify ferocity, blood, and anger; to their most avid supporters and to the Indians themselves, red could suggest bravery, health, and passion; to those who fell between the judgmental extremes, red could mean almost anything or nothing. In short, red was sufficiently flexible and ambiguous to meet the metaphysical imperatives of a society that did not wholly agree about the Indian's basic character or social and political fate. . . .

Even among their supposed supporters, however, the Indians fared badly, as a host of examples from Jefferson through Thomas McKenney and Lewis Cass amply illustrate. Such "friends" of the Indians contended that in the long run the Indian must be incorporated into the American mainstream, but increasingly in the nineteenth century the number of such advocates declined and the duration of the Indians' expected tutelage expanded. The Indians, assimilationists argued, must become farmers, landowners, and citizens; they must adopt "white" America's language, laws, and customs. They must cease to be Indians—even if it took centuries to reach that end. Along the way, Indian desires were rarely considered. Although the overwhelming majority wanted to retain their land and their culture, the Eastern tribes had little choice. In the first half of the nineteenth century, the basic options were assimilation or extermination, with removal to the West as a temporary stage in either case.

Some assimilationists advocated miscegenation as the surest path to de-Indianization. Ironically, the biological solution emerged almost simultaneously with laws in many states against Indian-white intermarriage. Such laws hint at hypocrisy and racial intransigence among the majority of Americans and reveal the implausibility of intermarriage as a solution to race relations in nineteenth-century America. But whatever the solution—miscegenation, allotment of farmlands in the East, removal to the West, or education in white-controlled boarding schools—the Indian was marked for gradual extinction by the uneasy coalition of his friends and foes. For both groups, as well as for the bulk of Americans who were neither friend nor foe but merely indifferent, the conviction that the Indians were innately and ineradicably "redmen" underlay their concern, or lack of it, for the Indians' fate. And to most white observers—certainly to the Indians' foes and almost certainly to the millions who scarcely cared—the stereotypical color carried a host of unfavorable associations that prevented the Indians' full assimilation into the Anglo-American community and simultaneously precluded their acceptance as a separate and equal people. Although a few dissenters resisted the prevailing color taxonomy and its correlative racial policies, the surviving literature, both factual and fictional, shows that the Indian was no longer considered a member of the same race; he remained forever distinct in color and character. Even relatively sympathetic spokesmen now believed the Indians to be permanently different. "No

Christianizing," declares Natty Bumppo in Cooper's *Pathfinder* (1840), "will ever make even a Delaware [Indian] a white man, nor any whopping and yelling convert a paleface into a redskin." Bumppo earlier—in *The Prairie* (1827)—puts the same idea more succinctly: "Red natur' is red natur'."

NO

Karen Ordahl Kupperman

SETTLING WITH THE INDIANS

THE NATURE OF THE RELATIONSHIP

The ideal version of the English-Indian relationship involved a tutelary relationship similar to that of older brother to younger and husband to wife. Reports to and from America constantly refer to the Indians as "our kinsmen and younger brethren." The colonists, as the older brothers, would instruct and shape the Indians and their culture. Indian tuition could mean nothing short of the destruction of their culture and religion and their replacement by European civilization and Christianity. People in superior positions naturally assumed the right and necessity to shape and instruct in England as well as America. That such instruction involved the priceless gift of Christianity enhanced the obligation to assume the tutelary role.

English theorists willfully deluded themselves when they translated this tutelary image into policy. They assumed that the process of getting the natives to accommodate themselves to English settlement would be much easier than in fact it was. The English were let down by their own preconceptions and wishful thinking. English writers commonly foresaw a two-step approach: gentleness to be followed, if necessary, by severity. The elder Richard Hakluyt is the first of a long series of advisers who urge the importance of maintaining peaceful relations with the Indians by using "humanitie and curtesie and much forbearing of revenge."

In fact it was clear from the beginning that the second Step, the use of severity, would dominate. Early colonial leaders were chosen for their experience in chastising recalcitrant populations. The younger Hakluyt first enunciated the idea that the English could draw on experience gained in the cruel European and Irish wars in handling the American natives. In his preface to de Soto's *Virginia Richly Valued* he advocated treating the Indians with gentleness, but "if gentle polishing will not serve, then we shall not want hammerours and rough masons enow, I meane our old soldiours trained up in the Netherlands, to square and prepare them to our Preachers

From Karen Ordahl Kupperman, *Settling With the Indians: The Meeting of English and Indian Cultures in America, 1580–1640* (Rowman & Littlefield, 1980). Copyright © 1980 by Rowman & Littlefield. Reprinted by permission. References omitted.

hands." The policy of treating the Indians as a conquered population originated with Ralph Lane, the governor of the first large-scale colony at Roanoke. Lane, with military experience in Ireland, like John Smith and the long line of Virginia governors whose prior experience was military, saw the problem of organizing both settlers and Indians as essentially martial. All the early governors in Virginia followed a policy of intimidation, certainly insofar as it meant requisitioning food for the colonists and using whatever methods were necessary to ensure this food supply. Small excuses were sought to justify actions calculated to impress the Indians. Ralph Lane and John Smith found it useful to kidnap children to use as hostages when they entered Indian Villages. Smith endorsed this policy in a marginal note: "How to deale with the Salvages." Colonists and theorists in England alike understood that the Indians must be overawed if the colonies were to be safe. People in England believed that English weapons and technology were so obviously superior that overawing the Indians would be natural, and that the Indians could be dominated through fear.

In fact the early colonists were extremely vulnerable. Despite the frequently friendly first meetings between new colonists and natives, English writers assumed that Indians would be fundamentally hostile to the settlements. This was not because the Indians were seen as savage and treacherous, but because they were human beings. All men have dignity and pride in their identification with their own land. Hakluyt believed so strongly that the Indians would necessarily fight for their birthright that he warned the first Jamestown settlers that war would be inevitable. Therefore he urged the colonists to trade for corn and supplies before the Indians realized a permanent settlement was planned. The Virginia Company's instructions to its governors and Matthew Cradock's letter of instructions to Massachusetts Bay draw on the same assumptions about Indian behavior toward the colonies. The colonists are always warned to treat Indians justly but to expect hostility even from those natives who appear friendly. In 1609 the Virginia Company wrote "it is Clere even to reason" that the Indians would not like "our neighbourhood," and that they would be helpful to the colonists either out of fear or because they thought the English could be helpful to them in their intertribal wars. The Ancient Planters of Virginia later attested that fear had been the only source of loyalty in the Indians. John Smith recorded the Indian belief that "we were a people come from under the world to take their world from them." . . .

The colonists' awareness of their own vulnerability combined with their feelings of guilt at the mistreatment of those Indians they could dominate to produce the rage and hostility which is characteristic of many of their actions. Colonists acknowledged a sense of guilt from the beginning of colonization. Thomas Hariot ascribed the change in relations with the Indians at Roanoke to English mistreatment of the Indians. The English had "shewed themselves too fierce . . . upon causes that on our part, might easily enough have bene borne withall." Richard Hakluyt in England made a dramatic assessment of the same evidence. He described the storm and the resultant haste with which the colony packed and left Roanoke, "as if they had bene chased from thence by a mightie armie, and no doubt so they were, for the hande of God came upon them for the crueltie, and outrages committed by some of them against the native inhabitantes of that Countrie." John Smith said he would need soliders to lead an expedition to New England "because of the abuses which have been offered the poore Salvages." Many writers acknowledged that the spreading of the Virginia colony and the false dealings of the colonists were the root cause of bad relations with Indians in the Chesapeake area: "Wee our selves have taught them to bee trecherous by our false dealinge . . ." The Virginia Company acknowledged that fear of dispossession inspired the Indian attack on the Virginia plantations in 1622. John Penreis testified that perfidious dealing with friendly Indians continued after 1622 and continued to trouble the consciences of some colonists. Penreis said killing and seizing corn under pretence of friendship was "contrarie to ye equity of God & natures lawes, whereby ye name of God, our King & Cuntry are all dishonored, we being formerly for our Justice and vertuous Government Called Gods, but now through treacherous & inhumaine Cruelty esteemed worse then Divels for which (I feare me) Gods punishment is & wilbe uppon us."

Philip Vincent and John Underhill of Massachusetts Bay admitted, when writing of their burning an Indian fort with its 400 inhabitants of both sexes and all ages, that conditions in America have caused them to do things which are outside their own code. They both say they would have been moved to pity but for the bad actions of the Pequots. Vincent says "severe justice" was substituted for pity. Underhill's *Newes from America* refers those who think they were too cruel to the story of David's war: "but we will not dispute it now. We had sufficient light from the word of God for our proceedings."

Guilt and vulnerability reinforced each other in the American colonies. Colonists' fear caused them to overreact to small provocations or to make pre-emptive strikes as in the Pequot War. Their dependence on Indians for food led to bullying when they could get by with it. Their feelings of guilt and vulnerability generated rage and hostility against those who caused them to have these feelings. . . .

In the case of the colonists, their guilt and conviction that the Indians must fight for their land combined with their very real appreciation of their vulnerability to produce the truism that Indians are treacherous. This could then justify retribution in advance of any real evidence of such treachery. In fact this psychological mechanism is clearly at work when we find so many of the writers saying they know Indians are treacherous even though they have never seen any evidence of it, even though they find the Indians trustworthy and praiseworthy in every other respect. More importantly guilt reinforced the reaction of rage when open Indian attacks made the colonists too aware of just how vulnerable they were.

The massacre of 1622 signalled the failure of Virginian attempts to conciliate and dominate their Indian neighbors. It was certainly the most important event in Indian-English relations during the first period of colonization, especially in its psychological effects. . . .

Immediately following the massacre, the Virginia Company moved to explain it to the English public. Edward Waterhouse wrote the authorized version of the events and their cause in 1622. His account was reprinted by Samuel Purchas in his compilation *Hakluytus Post-*

humus or Purchas his Pilgrimes and by John Smith in his *Generall Historie.* Waterhouse denounced the Virginia Indians as resembling beasts more than men. He stressed the barbarity of their attack in the massacre, which was successful not because of their strength, but because of their perfidy. Purchas, in a separate essay, "Virginia's Verger," went further, saying the Indians were "more brutish then the beasts they hunt." Waterhouse and Purchas agreed that the Virginia natives were now unworthy of consideration and could therefore be enslaved, thus making the massacre a blessing in disguise for Virginia. Even in the midst of these denunciations, however, Waterhouse demonstrated the organized political life of the Indians. Not only do they live by planting corn, but the massacre was done "at one instant of time, though our severall Plantations were an hundred and forty miles up one River on both sides." Clearly it was not the work of people who range over the land like beasts. . . .

Documents from the colony reveal, as is to be expected, enormous hostility after 1622, but this is hostility toward a formidable enemy, not denunciation of cultureless animals. Published works about Virginia fall off rapidly following the massacre largely because the Virginia Company was involved in its final struggle, which culminated in Virginia's being made a royal colony in 1625. Between 1625 and 1640 published works about Virginia stop altogether. Therefore, the documentary evidence offers the only source about the plans and attitudes of the colonists following the massacre. All the plans for dealing with the Indians demonstrate the competence of the Indians and the fear of the settlers. One animal comparison occurs, but it is obvi-

ously meant as a figure of speech. William Capps, angry that a decisive blow had not been struck against the Indians, wrote of them as "the Heathen kennell of dogges," but in the same passage he said the English were "weatherbeaten Crowes" and compared English cultivation of tobacco to the rooting of hogs. Plans for revenge were not written, except perhaps in the safety of London, in a spirit of exhilaration that the inhibitions were now off, and even those plans which came from London reminded the colonists of the duty of converting the young Indians. Rather those plans that proceeded from the colonists were tinged with desperation and real fear. When they were warned by the Virginia Company to drive away their enemies fairly and in accordance with justice and truth, the colonists answered that they could not win unless they adopted treacherous tactics. The colonists planned to lull the Indians into a false sense of security by "A perfidious treatye" and then strike when they least expected it, "that wee may followe their Example in destroying them." This willingness to adopt unworthy tactics proceeded not from contempt for the enemy, but respect for his ability. George Wyatt, advising his son Sir Francis, who was governor in Virginia, offered the most realistic assessment of the colonists' situation from England. His main message was against underestimating the enemy. "Yet I doe not with contempt reccon of them as cowards, as our common opinions esteemes. Neither did this their enterprise or execution, either want politie or corage." He went on to say that their striking and running away was an intelligent strategy and that they had an efficient intelligence system. His best advice was to follow the example of the Indians in understanding all about the enemy and being always prepared for war. He sent his son several stratagems to use, the art of which is "a politie of war by wils of wit rather then force to make benefit of an Enimise Error." The Indians also make use of stragagems "as you have felt."

Virginian plans for conquering the Indians not only reveal them as formidable opponents, but also emphasize the civil and organized nature of Indian life. When Waterhouse was arguing that the massacre would ultimately be beneficial to Virginia, one reason he gave was that it would enable colonists to seize Indian cornfields "(which are situate in the fruitfullest places of the land.)" Virtually every serious plan involved striking at the Indians through their cornfields. It was agreed that the Indians must be starved out rather than vanquished in a direct attack. Even that was more difficult than it seemed, because the Indians could plant in secret and hidden places. Thus, what was required, according to the Council of State in Virginia, was a false peace, so when the Indians "grow secure uppon the treatie, we shall have the better Advantage both to surprise them, & cutt downe theire Corne, by knowinge where they plant, which otherwise they will plant in such Corners, as it will nott be possible for us to finnde owte." That Indian life was sedentary and based on agriculture is revealed by the colonists' conviction that, if their attack were delayed until late summer, the Indians would be unable to leave the area of their cornfields and, once their fields were burned, it would be impossible for them to find food for the winter. There is no attempt to hide the fact that the perfidious treaty, a device to which the English had been driven by desperation, was essential to these plans. Though

the revenge tactics were not notably successful, the colonists continued to believe in them. In 1626, 1627, and 1628 similar plans were announced for expeditions against the enemy. In progress reports, the colonists reveal the large-scale planting of the Indians. In January 1623/4, the Council reported that they had "Cut downe theire Corne in all places which was planted in great abundance, uppon hope of a fraudulent peace . . ." and in one expedition the governor carried away "a marvelous quantitie of Corne." In December of the same year a report of a victory over the Pamunkeys includes the statement that they cut down corn "Sufficyent to have Sustayned fower Thousand men for a Twellv mounthe." The colonists were particularly pleased by this victory because they hoped it would diminish the reputation of the Pamunkeys with Indians to the north, one tribe of whom had sent an observer.

One point made by many historians is that when the Indians were helpful or loving in their relationships with the English, they were not given the credit for it, rather the credit for their actions was given to God for moving their hearts. This is certainly true in all the records as well as the published reports. What is also true is that the harm the Indians did to the colonists was also attributed to God. Virtually every reference to the massacre of 1622 in the Virginia records spoke of the Indian attack and the subsequent scarcity and mortality from famine and disease as God's punishment on them for their sins. The Indians were frequently referred to specifically as God's instruments. While this looks like simple rhetoric, a few of the writers offered an explanation of the connection between their sins and the massacre which made it a convincing explanation.

Chief among their sins was greed, which manifested itself in cultivating tobacco to the exclusion of all else. This in turn made the settlers dependent on the Indians for their food supply. Tobacco cultivation required large amounts of land, so the colonists were forced to live dispersed and this made them more vulnerable. Further, those lands which were best for tobacco cultivation were said to be the most unhealthy for men. Greed was not the only sin being punished. George Sandys said the desire to live dispersed was fed by the colonists' wanting to "lyve like Libertines out of the eye of the Magistrate." He said that even if they had had ample warning of the Indians' plans, they were too dispersed to help each other.

Finally, the relative positions of the English and the Indians following the massacre are clearly shown by the fact that the colonists continued to be dependent on native suppliers for corn, and therefore continued to be vulnerable. In the months following the massacre, different types of expeditions were sent out for corn. Some were sent to territories defined as enemy and they were authorized to simply seize whatever they could. Others were sent to trade, but authorized to fight if "occasion shall be given by the Indians." Ralph Hamor in May, 1622, was authorized to take corn from the Indians if they would not trade, but his commission added parenthetically "(if he be able)." By 1623 the necessity to become self-sufficient in corn was clearly understood. Here begins a pattern of commanding the settlers to plant corn, and forbidding trading in corn. As often as these proclamations are made, exemptions are granted in the form of special licenses. In 1623 trading was forbidden partly because the governor believed Indians ostensibly trading actually came "to spy and observe the weaknes of our plantationes." In May Governor Wyatt commanded the colonists to plant corn because it was dishonourable and dangerous to rely on "these base Salvages" for "our most necessarie food." Three days later he gave Gilbert Peppet a commission to trade for corn. In September, 1623, trading for corn was absolutely forbidden because it had devalued the English trading goods and kept people from planting corn. In November of the same year, Wyatt himself led an expedition to settle trade in the bay area. By January, 1624, the Council was saying that the food shortages were temporary and to be expected after such a massacre, and they pointed to a basic problem. The colonists could not make war on the Indians according to their basic strategy and be home tending their own corn. What they wanted was to be left free to cultivate their own fields, not to burn those of the Indians. Also in January Ralph Hamor was given a license to carry on trade for the public benefit of the country. He was cautioned not to compel the Indians to trade, unless he suspected treachery on their part. On March 5, 1624, the Council and Assembly in Virginia ordered that all trading in corn with the "Savages" would be ended after June, 1624, and everyone was ordered to plant sufficient corn for his own family, with the price of corn being allowed to float. On March 16 Rawleigh Croshawe was given a commission to trade similar to Hamor's. In December of 1624 Robert Poole reported on his trading voyage, saying that they stayed at "Pocotanck" for "23 or 24 days in hope the Indyans would have furnisht them with Corne." The pattern of forbidding trading and punishing people who traded illegally and commanding planting of corn while making constant exceptions and sending out trading parties continued for many years. In 1638 George Donne felt he could sum up the cause of Virginia's troubles best by quoting Samuel Purchas's judgment after the massacre, which included: "Injuries to and from the savaldges and yet A necessity of their use and helpe."

New England's policy of vengeance paralleled that of Virginia. In addition to urging good treatment as the most intelligent approach to Indian relations, the New England colonists also attempted to win native support by manipulation of rivalries between tribes. But every provocation, they felt, must be met with a show of force. The settlers felt they had almost constant reinforcement for their idea that overawing the natives was the only proper approach to them. Again and again, the journal-keepers speak of the many tribes who came to them and sued for peace or alliance after a punitive expedition. Confirmation also came from the example of the improvident Wessagusset colonists who, according to the Plymouth historians, became utterly dependent on the Indians and were treated with extreme contempt by them. Thomas Dudley said the Indians "oppressed these weak English." So important was this policy of overawing the natives that the colonists considered revenge even when they clearly acknowledged that the Indians' acts against individual Englishmen were justified by extreme provocation on the Englishmen's parts.

It was not the policy but the degree of vengeance exacted that troubled some writers. The Plymouth colony's move against the Indians at Wessagusset was criticized by their Leyden pastor, John Robinson, in one of the most famous letters of this literature:

> On, how happy a thing had it been, if you had converted some before you had killed any! Besides, where blood is once begun to be shed, it is seldom staunched of a long time after. You will say they deserved it. I grant it; but upon what provocations and invitements by those heathenish Christians? Besides, you being no magistrates over them were to consider not what they deserved but what you were by necessity constrained to inflict.

Robinson goes on to say that at most they should have killed one or two principals as an example, "according to that approved rule, The punishment to a few, and the fear to many."

In the Pequot War the justification was the conviction of the colonists that the Pequots were too dangerous to ignore. Massachusetts Bay took the lead in a policy which aimed at nothing less than the elimination of the Pequots as a tribal entity. Large numbers of Pequots were either killed or taken prisoner. Women and children were sometimes among those killed, as in the burning of the Pequot fort, and in one case, Winthrop admits, a captive was tortured to death by the Saybrook men in retaliation for torture deaths of some of their men. Those who were taken prisoner were dispersed among the towns of Massachusetts Bay and Connecticut and their status can only be guessed. Two women and 15 boys who were sent to Old Providence in the West Indies were almost certainly made slaves. Plymouth was a reluctant ally in the Pequot War. Bradford wrote to Winthrop his conviction that it was Massachusetts which had occasioned the war. Winthrop's complex answer revolved around his conviction that if even 100 were left alive, they could do as much harm as the entire tribe was ever likely to do. Thus, as in Virginia after the massacre, a policy of vengeance was based on or justified by the right of self-preservation. In 1640 the plantations in Connecticut wrote jointly to Massachusetts "wherein they declared their dislike of such as would have the Indians rooted out, as being of the cursed race of Ham, and their desire of our mutual accord in seeking to gain them by justice and kindness . . ." Winthrop wrote back "our consent" but Massachusetts refused to join in any pact with Aquiday, a dissident plantation.

John Winthrop and the leaders of Massachusetts felt they were acting on a recognized principle in exacting extreme vengeance for wrongs done. This was not lawless justice justified by the fact that the enemy was racially or culturally inferior. There is one clear statement of the principle of vengeance in this literature and in it John Winthrop is justifying Indian vengeance against Englishmen. . . .

Each colony learned for itself that the Indians could not and would not accept the role of the younger brethren of the English. European culture was not the powerful magnet for Indians which colonization promoters assumed it would be, so Indians were not willing to submerge or forsake their own culture in favor of the "civilization" offered by the English. Nor was English technology at first the powerful instrument for forcing Indian cooperation which promoters assumed. The technology and culture of Indians on America's east coast were genuine rivals to those of the English and the eventual outcome of the rivalry was not at first clear. In these circumstances, whatever those comfortable people who remained in England wrote, colonists were faced with the necessity of coping with a formidable people on whom they were encroaching and on whom they, intermittently at least, were dependent. Much of what is taken for contempt in their writings is really the voice of vulnerability speaking. One can only speculate what the outcome of the rivalry would have been if the impact of European diseases on the American population had not been so devastating. If colonists had not been able to occupy lands already cleared by Indian farmers who had vanished, colonization would have proceeded much more slowly. If Indian culture had not been devastated by the physical and psychological assaults it had suffered, colonization might not have proceeded at all in the 16th and 17th centuries. European diseases did more than European technology to vanquish the American Indian in the early years of colonization.

One of the conclusions which English people derived from the wealth of information sent home was that the Indians had an interesting culture and one that clearly fulfilled the requirements of civil life. This realization was reinforced by the conclusion that American Indians were in no fundamental way different from Europeans, that they were racially similar and that they would soon be indistinguishable from Europeans. Despite the military clashes and exploitation, this line of reasoning about the Indians continues in some writers throughout the period. Some of the most enthusiastic descriptions of Indian culture come from the end of the period.

Just at the end of the period, though, those people who admire Indian culture begin to diverge from the earlier themes in one way; that is, they begin to see Indian culture as something which Europeans might respect and leave alone at least in some of its aspects. No writer could assume that Christianity should not be imposed on Indians, but observers such as Thomas Morton and William Wood begin in a very tentative way to suggest that the Indians need not become indistinguishable from Europeans. Though this seems to underly much of what they write, it is stated clearly only when they discuss Indian clothes. Clothes . . . were of primary importance as a badge of identity. To accept that the Indians should continue to dress in their traditional way was to accept a continuation of their separate identity. Yet, this is just what Morton and Wood proposed.

Unfortunately, this new idea that the Indians should be viewed as permanently separate from the English contained the seeds of racism. As long as the English believed that the Indians were their "younger brothers," that the Americans were different in no fundamental way, they could not be viewed as inherently inferior to Europeans. Once the differences between the two groups came to be seen as important and continuing, it would be a short step to seeing the different life of the Indians as less valuable than the European way of life, and to attributing their different patterns of development to qualities inherent in each group. Both of these traditions developed through the remainder of the 127th century, though the attitude of respect grows much rarer. When English colonists later in the century began to rely massively on African slaves as a labor supply and to categorize servants purely on the basis of race, this could meld with the idea that Indians were permanently different from Europeans to make them co-victims of racism. The criteria by which people were classified shifted from manipulable cultural traits to theoretically inherent racially bound traits.

The belief that expropriation and enslavement of the Indians was legitimate grew as a result of experiences in America. The fact that the precedent of the Israelites' war against the Canaanites was used so sparingly and so carefully points to the assumption that there was no intention in the beginning to sweep away the Indians in America. The American experience allowed, in the absence of the normal constraints of English society, unrestricted power over the other human beings. It was the ultimate powerlessness of the Indians, not their racial inferiority, which made it possible to see them as people without rights.

Europeans of the late 16th and early 17th centuries were capable of acting with barbarity toward those who were powerless, whether these were Indians, Africans, or fellow Europeans. The civilization of which they were so proud and so confident was not fully internalized. When they were outside their normal society and its constraints, their deviations from the standards of civilization could be enormous. This was especially true if, as in the case of colonization, the condition of being separated meant personal risk and the possibility of great power over other human beings. It was the effect of unrestricted power, not preconceived racism, which caused the English to treat the American Indians as they did. If, in the period after 1640, the American Indians were the subjects of racism by English people, the conclusion must be that this racism was a product of, not the cause of, the treatment of Indians by colonists.

POSTSCRIPT

Did Racism Cause the Conflict Between Native Americans and Colonists?

The complexities associated with the relations between Native Americans and colonists from Europe are evident from the foregoing essays by Vaughan and Kupperman. Together they suggest the difficulty of trying to generalize about the clash of cultures that occurred on New World shores. A case in point is the history of Indian-white relations in early Virginia. The colonists participating in the Jamestown expedition, for example, were attacked by a group of Indians almost as soon as they set foot on American soil. A few months later, however, Powhatan, the dominant chief in the region, provided essential food supplies to the Jamestown residents who were suffering from disease and hunger. By the latter part of 1608, however, the colonists, under the leadership of John Smith, had begun to take an antagonistic stance toward Powhatan and his people. Smith attempted to extort food supplies from the Indians by threatening to burn their villages and canoes. These hostilities continued long after Smith's departure from Virginia and did not end until the 1640s, when colonial leaders signed a formal treaty with the Powhatan Confederacy.

Extensive literature addresses the relationship between Native Americans and Europeans in the seventeenth and eighteenth centuries. Gary Nash, *Red, White, and Black: The Peoples of Early America*, 2d ed. (Prentice Hall, 1982), is an excellent survey for the colonial period. Robert Berkhofer, *The White Man's Indian: Images of the American Indian From Columbus to the Present* (Random House, 1978), provides a panoramic consideration of the Indian stereotypes developed by Europeans and white Americans. Three works by James Axtell—*The European and the Indian: Essays in the Ethnohistory of British America, 1607–1789* (Oxford University Press, 1981); *The Invasion Within: The Contest of Cultures in Colonial North America* (Oxford University Press, 1985);

and *After Columbus: Essays in the Ethnohistory of Colonial North America* (Oxford University Press, 1988)—are indispensable. The themes of coexistence and coercion in relation to contacts between Native Americans and Englishmen in New England are assessed in Neal E. Salisbury, *Manitou and Providence: Indians, Europeans, and the Beginnings of New England* (Oxford University Press, 1982), and Francis Jennings, *The Invasion of America: Indians, Colonialism, and the Cant of Conquest* (University of North Carolina Press, 1975). Douglas E. Leach, *Flintlock and Tomahawk: New England in King Philip's War*, rev. ed. (Norton, 1966), is a well-written study of that momentous clash. Every student interested in the history of Native American societies should read Anthony F. C. Wallace's classic anthropological and historical work *The Death and Rebirth of the Seneca* (Alfred A. Knopf, 1970).

ISSUE 3

Was the Colonial Period a "Golden Age" for Women in America?

YES: Lois Green Carr and Lorena S. Walsh, from "The Planter's Wife: The Experience of White Women in Seventeenth-Century Maryland," *William and Mary Quarterly* (October 1977)

NO: Lyle Koehler, from *A Search for Power: The "Weaker Sex" in Seventeenth-Century New England* (University of Illinois Press, 1980)

ISSUE SUMMARY

YES: Professor Lois Green Carr and Lorena S. Walsh, a fellow with the Colonial Williamsburg Foundation, identify several factors that coalesced to afford women in seventeenth-century Maryland a higher status with fewer restraints on their social conduct than those experienced by women in England.
NO: Lyle Koehler, from the University of Cincinnati, contends that the division of labor that separated work into male and female spheres and Puritan attitudes towards rights of inheritance severely limited opportunities for upward mobility among New England women.

Students in American history classes have for generations read of the founding of the colonies in British North America, their political and economic development, and the colonists' struggles for independence without ever being confronted by a female protagonist in this magnificent historical drama. The terms "sons of liberty" and "founding fathers" reflect the end result of a long tradition of gender-specific myopia. In fact, only in the last two decades have discussions of the role of women in the development of American society made their appearance in standard textbooks. Consequently, it is useful to explore the status of women in colonial America.

The topic, of course, is quite complex. The status of colonial women was determined by the cultural attitudes that were exported to the New World from Europe, by the specific conditions confronting successive waves of settlers—male and female—in terms of labor requirements, and by changes produced by colonial maturation over time. It would be impossible to pinpoint a single, static condition in which *all* colonial women existed.

What was the status of women in the British North American colonies? To what degree did the legal status of women differ from their *de facto* status? A half century of scholarship has produced the notion that colonial women enjoyed a more privileged status than either their European contemporaries or their nineteenth-century descendants. This view, developed in the writings of Richard B. Morris, Elizabeth Dexter, and Mary Beard, was reinforced in the 1970s by John Demos and Roger Thompson. For example, Demos contends that despite the fact that Plymouth Colony was based on a patriarchal model in which women were expected to subordinate themselves to men, women still shared certain responsibilities with their husbands in some business activities and in matters relating to their children. At the same time, however, women were closed off from any formal public power in the colony even when they performed essential economic functions within the community. They not only performed all the household duties but also assisted the menfolk with agricultural duties outside the home when the necessity arose. Still, society as a whole viewed women as "weaker vessels."

Women were crucial to the economic success of the colonial experiments and performed numerous functions in various occupations and professions. Women in colonial America and during the American Revolution practiced law, pounded iron as blacksmiths, trapped for furs and tanned leather, made guns, built ships, and edited and printed newspapers. At the same time, colonial society viewed women as subordinate beings. They held no political power within the individual colonies and still were suspect as the transmitters of evil, simply because they were women. Nor was it a coincidence that most suspected witches were female. As Carol F. Karlsen has argued recently, 78 percent of 344 alleged witches in New England were female. Many of those accused were older women who had inherited land that traditionally would have gone to males. Such patterns of inheritance, she contends, disrupted the normative male-dominated social order. Witchcraft hysteria in colonial America, then, was a by-product of economic pressures *and* gender exploitation.

The following essays explore the status of women in seventeenth-century America. Lois Green Carr and Lorena S. Walsh assess this issue against the backdrop of four factors in colonial Maryland: the predominance of an immigrant population; the early death of male inhabitants; the late marriages of women due to their indentured servitude; and the sexual imbalance in which men greatly outnumbered women. As a result of these conditions, Maryland women experienced fewer restraints on their social conduct and enjoyed more power than did their English counterparts. Most who survived became planter's wives, enjoyed considerable freedom in choosing their husbands, and benefited from a substantial right to inherit property.

Lyle Koehler argues that Puritan views limited the economic independence of New England women by preventing fathers and husbands from providing their daughters and wives with an inheritance. Despite labor shortages in the colonies, women did not benefit by taking on traditionally male jobs. Hence, upward mobility for the New England woman could be achieved only through a fortuitous marriage.

YES

Lois Green Carr and
Lorena S. Walsh

THE PLANTER'S WIFE: THE EXPERIENCE OF WHITE WOMEN IN SEVENTEENTH-CENTURY MARYLAND

Four facts were basic to all human experience in seventeenth-century Maryland. First, for most of the period the great majority of inhabitants had been born in what we now call Britain. Population increase in Maryland did not result primarily from births in the colony before the late 1680s and did not produce a predominantly native population of adults before the first decade of the eighteenth century. Second, immigrant men could not expect to live beyond age forty-three, and 70 percent would die before age fifty. Women may have had even shorter lives. Third, perhaps 85 percent of the immigrants, and practically all the unmarried immigrant women, arrived as indentured servants and consequently married late. Family groups were never predominant in the immigration to Maryland and were a significant part for only a brief time at mid-century. Fourth, many more men than women immigrated during the whole period. These facts—immigrant predominance, early death, late marriage, and sexual imbalance—created circumstances of social and demographic disruption that deeply affected family and community life.

We need to assess the effects of this disruption on the experience of women in seventeenth-century Maryland. Were women degraded by the hazards of servitude in a society in which everyone had left community and kin behind and in which women were in short supply? Were traditional restraints on social conduct weakened? If so, were women more exploited or more independent and powerful than women who remained in England? Did any differences from English experience which we can observe in the experience of Maryland women survive the transformation from an immigrant to a predominantly native-born society with its own kinship networks and community traditions? The tentative argument put forward here is that the answer to all these questions is Yes. There were degrading aspects of servitude, although these probably did not characterize the lot of most women; there were fewer restraints on social conduct, especially in courtship, than in England; women were less protected but also more powerful than those who remained at home; and at least some of these changes survived the appearance in Maryland of New World creole communities. . . .

Whatever their status, one fact about immigrant women is certain: many fewer came than men. Immigrant lists, head-right lists, and itemizations of servants in inventories show severe imbalance. On a London immigrant list of 1634-1635 men outnumbered women six to one. From the 1650s at least until the 1680s most sources show a ratio of three to one. From then on, all sources show some, but not great, improvement. Among immigrants from Liverpool over the years 1697-1707 the ratio was just under two and one half to one.

Why did not more women come? Presumably, fewer wished to leave family and community and venture into a wilderness. But perhaps more important, women were not as desirable as men to merchants and planters who were making fortunes raising and marketing tobacco, a crop that requires large amounts of labor. The gradual improvement in the sex ratio among servants toward the end of the century may have been the result of a change in recruiting the needed labor. In the late 1660s the supply of young men willing to emigrate stopped increasing sufficiently to meet the labor demands of a growing Chesapeake population. Merchants who recruited servants for planters turned to other sources, and among these sources were women. They did not crowd the ships arriving in the Chesapeake, but their numbers did increase.

To ask the question another way, why did women come? Doubtless, most came to get a husband, an objective virtually certain of success in a land where women were so far outnumbered. The promotional literature, furthermore, painted bright pictures of the life that awaited men and women once out of their time; and various studies suggest that for a while, at least, the promoters were not being entirely fanciful. Until the 1660s, and to a less degree the 1680s, the expanding economy of Maryland and Virginia offered opportunities well beyond those available in England to men without capital and to the women who became their wives.

Nevertheless, the hazards were also great, and the greatest was untimely death. Newcomers promptly became ill, probably with malaria, and many died. What proportion survived is unclear; so far no one has devised a way of measuring it. Recurrent malaria made the woman who survived seasoning less able to withstand other diseases, especially dysentery and influenza. She was especially vulnerable when pregnant. Expectation of life for everyone was low in the Chesapeake, but especially so for women. A woman who had immigrated to Maryland took an extra risk, though perhaps a risk not greater than she might have suffered by moving from her village to London instead.

The majority of women who survived seasoning paid their transportation costs by working for a four- or five-year term of service. The kind of work depended on the status of the family they served. A female servant of a small planter—who through about the 1670s might have had a servant—probably worked at the hoe.

Such a man could not afford to buy labor that would not help with the cash crop. In wealthy families women probably were household servants, although some are occasionally listed in inventories of well-to-do planters as living on the quarters—that is, on plantations other than the dwelling plantation. Such women saved men the jobs of preparing food and washing linen but doubtless also worked in the fields. In middling households experience must have varied. Where the number of people to feed and wash for was large, female servants would have had little time to tend the crops.

Tracts that promoted immigration to the Chesapeake region asserted that female servants did not labor in the fields, except "nasty" wenches not fit for other tasks. This implies that most immigrant women expected, or at least hoped, to avoid heavy field work, which English women—at least those above the cottager's status—did not do. What proportion of female servants in Maryland found themselves demeaned by this unaccustomed labor is impossible to say, but this must have been the fate of some. . . .

The woman who immigrated to Maryland, survived seasoning and service, and gained her freedom became a planter's wife. She had considerable liberty in making her choice. There were men aplenty, and no fathers or brothers were hovering to monitor her behavior or disapprove her preference. This is the modern way of looking at her situation, of course. Perhaps she missed the protection of a father, a guardian, or kinfolk, and the participation in her decision of a community to which she felt ties. There is some evidence that the absence of kin and the pressures of the sex ratio created conditions of sexual freedom in court-ship that were not customary in England. A register of marriages and births for seventeenth-century Somerset County shows that about one-third of the immigrant women whose marriages are recorded were pregnant at the time of the ceremony—nearly twice the rate in English parishes. There is no indication of community objection to this freedom so long as marriage took place. No presentments for bridal pregnancy were made in any of the Maryland courts.

The planter's wife was likely to be in her mid-twenties at marriage. An estimate of minimum age at marriage for servant women can be made from lists of indentured servants who left London over the years 1683-1684 and from age judgments in Maryland county court records. If we assume that the 112 female indentured servants going to Maryland and Virginia whose ages are given in the London lists served full four-year terms, then only 1.8 percent married before age twenty, but 68 percent after age twenty-four. Similarly, if the 141 women whose ages were judged in Charles County between 1666 and 1705 served out their terms according to the custom of the country, none married before age twenty-two, and half were twenty-five or over. When adjustments are made for the ages at which wives may have been purchased, the figures drop, but even so the majority of women waited until at least age twenty-four to marry. Actual age at marriage in Maryland can be found for few seventeenth-century female immigrants, but observations for Charles and Somerset counties place the mean age at about twenty-five.

Because of the age at which an immigrant woman married, the number of children she would bear her husband was small. She had lost up to ten years of her childbearing life—the possibility of perhaps four or five children, given the usual rhythm of childbearing. At the same time, high mortality would reduce both the number of children she would bear over the rest of her life and the number who would live. One partner to a marriage was likely to die within seven years, and the chances were only one in three that a marriage would last ten years. In these circumstances, most women would not bear more than three or four children—not counting those stillborn— to any one husband, plus a posthumous child were she the survivor. The best estimates suggest that nearly a quarter, perhaps more, of the children born alive died during their first year and that 40 to 55 percent would not live to see age twenty. Consequently, one of her children would probably die in infancy, and another one or two would fail to reach adulthood. Wills left in St. Mary's County during the seventeenth century show the results. In 105 families over the years 1660 to 1680 only twelve parents left more than three children behind them, including those conceived but not yet born. The average number was 2.3, nearly always minors, some of whom might die before reaching adulthood.

For the immigrant woman, then, one of the major facts of life was that although she might bear a child about every two years, nearly half would not reach maturity. The social implications of this fact are far-reaching. Because she married late in her childbearing years and because so many of her children would die young, the number who would reach marriageable age might not replace, or might only barely replace, her and her husband or husbands as child-producing members of the society. Consequently, so long as immigrants were heavily predominant in the adult female population, Maryland could not grow much by natural increase. It remained a land of newcomers. . . .

A hazard of marriage for seventeenth-century women everywhere was death in childbirth, but this hazard may have been greater than usual in the Chesapeake. Whereas in most societies women tend to outlive men, in this malaria-ridden area it is probable that men outlived women. Hazards of childbirth provide the likely reason that Chesapeake women died so young. Once a woman in the Chesapeake reached forty-five, she tended to outlive men who reached the same age. . . .

However long they lived, immigrant women in Maryland tended to outlive their husbands—in Charles County, for example, by a ratio of two to one. This was possible, despite the fact that women were younger than men at death, because women were also younger than men at marriage. Some women were widowed with no living children, but most were left responsible for two or three. These were often tiny, and nearly always not yet sixteen.

This fact had drastic consequences, given the physical circumstances of life. People lived at a distance from one another, not even in villages, must less towns. The widow had left her kin 3,000 miles across an ocean, and her husband's family was also there. She would have to feed her children and make her own tobacco crop. Though neighbors might help, heavy labor would be required of her if she had no servants, until—what admittedly was usually not difficult—she acquired a new husband.

In this situation dying husbands were understandably anxious about the welfare of their families. Their wills reflected their feelings and tell something of how they regarded their wives. In St. Mary's and Charles counties during the seventeenth century, little more than one-quarter of the men left their widows with no more than the dower the law required—one-third of his land for her life, plus outright ownership of one-third of his personal property. If there were no children, a man almost always left his widow his whole estate. Otherwise there were a variety of arrangements.

During the 1660s, when testators begin to appear in quantity, nearly a fifth of the men who had children left all to their wives, trusting them to see that the children received fair portions. Thus in 1663 John Shircliffe willed his whole estate to his wife "towards the maintenance of herself and my children into whose tender care I do Commend them Desireing to see them brought up in the fear of God and the Catholick Religion and Chargeing them to be Dutiful and obedient to her." As the century progressed, husbands tended instead to give the wife all or a major part of the estate for her life, and to designate how it should be distributed after her death. Either way, the husband put great trust in his widow, considering that he knew she was bound to remarry. Only a handful of men left estates to their wives only for their term of widowhood or until the children came of age. When a man did not leave his wife a life estate, he often gave her land outright or more than her dower third of his movable property. Such bequests were at the expense of his children and showed his concern that his widow should have a maintenance which young children could not supply.

A husband usually made his wife his executor and thus responsible for paying his debts and preserving the estate. Only

11 percent deprived their wives of such powers. In many instances, however, men also appointed overseers to assist their wives and to see that their children were not abused or their property embezzled. Danger lay in the fact that a second husband acquired control of all his wife's property, including her life estate in the property of his predecessor. Over half of the husbands who died in the 1650s and 1660s appointed overseers to ensure that their wills were followed. Some trusted to the overseers' "Care and good Conscience for the good of my widow and fatherless children." Others more explicit made overseers responsible for seeing that "my said child . . . and the other [expected child] (when pleases God to send it) may have their right Proportion of my Said Estate and that the said Children may be bred up Chiefly in the fear of God." A few men—but remarkably few—authorized overseers to remove children from households of stepfathers who abused them or wasted their property. On the whole, the absence of such provisions for the protection of the children points to the husband's overriding concern for the welfare of his widow and to his confidence in her management, regardless of the certainty of her remarriage. Evidently, in the politics of family life women enjoyed great respect.

We have implied that this respect was a product of the experience of immigrants in the Chesapeake. Might it have been instead a reflection of the English culture? Little work is yet in print that allows comparison of the provisions for Maryland widows with those made for the widows of English farmers. Possibly, Maryland husbands were making traditional wills which could have been written in the communities they left behind. However, Margaret Spufford's recent study of three Cambridgeshire villages in the late sixteenth century and early seventeenth century suggests a different pattern. In one of these villages, Chippenham, women usually did receive a life interest in the property, but in the other two they did not. If the children were all minors, the widow controlled the property until the oldest son came of age, and then only if she did not remarry. In the majority of cases adult sons were given control of the property with instructions for the support of their mothers. Spufford suggests that the pattern found in Chippenham must have been very exceptional. On the basis of village censuses in six other counties, dating from 1624 to 1724, which show only 3 percent of widowed people heading households that included a married child, she argues that if widows commonly controlled the farm, a higher proportion should have headed such households. However, she also argues that widows with an interest in land would not long remain unmarried. If so, the low percentage may be deceptive. . . .

Remarriage was the usual and often the immediate solution for a woman who had lost her husband. The shortage of women made any woman eligible to marry again, and the difficulties of raising a family while running a plantation must have made remarriage necessary for widows who had no son old enough to make tobacco. One indication of the high incidence of remarriage is the fact that there were only sixty women, almost all of them widows, among the 1,735 people who left probate inventories in four southern Maryland counties over the second half of the century. Most other women must have died while married and therefore legally without property to put through probate.

One result of remarriage was the development of complex family structures. Men found themselves responsible for stepchildren as well as their own offspring, and children acquired half-sisters and half-brothers. Sometimes a woman married a second husband who himself had been previously married, and both brought children of former spouses to the new marriage. They then produced children of their own. The possibilities for conflict over the upbringing of children are evident, and crowded living conditions, found even in the households of the wealthy, must have added to family tensions. Luckily, the children of the family very often had the same mother. In Charles County, at least, widows took new husbands three times more often than widowers took new wives. The role of the mother in managing the relationships of half-brothers and half-sisters or stepfathers and stepchildren must have been critical to family harmony.

Early death in this immigrant population thus had broad effects on Maryland society in the seventeenth century. It produced what we might call a pattern of serial polyandry, which enabled more men to marry and to father families than the sex ratios otherwise would have permitted. It produced thousands of orphaned children who had no kin to maintain them or preserve their property, and thus gave rise to an institution almost unknown in England, the orphans' court, which was charged with their protection. And early death, by creating families in which the mother was the unifying element, may have increased her authority within the household.

When the immigrant woman married her first husband, there was usually no property settlement involved, since she was unlikely to have any dowry. But her remarriage was another matter. At the very least, she owned or had a life interest in a third of her former husband's estate. She needed also to think of her children's interests. If she remarried, she would lose control of the property. Consequently, property settlements occasionally appear in the seventeenth-century court records between widows and their future husbands. Sometimes she and her intended signed an agreement whereby he relinquished his rights to the use of her children's portions. Sometimes he deeded to her property which she could dispose of at her pleasure. Whether any of these agreements or gifts would have survived a test in court is unknown. We have not yet found any challenged. Generally speaking, the formal marriage settlements of English law, which bypassed the legal difficulties of the married woman's inability to make a contract with her husband, were not adopted by immigrants, most of whom probably came from levels of English society that did not use these legal formalities.

The wife's dower rights in her husband's estate were a recognition of her role in contributing to his prosperity, whether by the property she had brought to the marriage or by the labor she performed in his household. A woman newly freed from servitude would not bring property, but the benefits of her labor would be great. A man not yet prosperous enough to own a servant might need his wife's help in the fields as well as in the house, especially if he were paying rent or still paying for land. Moreover, food preparation was so time-consuming that even if she worked only at household duties, she saved him time he needed for making tobacco and corn. The corn, for example, had to be pounded in the mortar or ground in a handmill before it could be used to make bread, for there were very few water mills in seventeenth-century Maryland. The wife probably raised vegetables in a kitchen garden; she also milked the cows and made butter and cheese, which might produce a salable surplus. She washed the clothes and made them if she had the skill. When there were servants to do field work, the wife undoubtedly spent her time entirely in such household tasks. A contract of 1681 expressed such a division of labor. Nicholas Maniere agreed to live on a plantation with his wife and child and a servant. Nicholas and the servant were to work the land; his wife was to "Dresse the Vitualls milk the Cowes wash for the servants and Doe allthings necessary for a woman to doe upon the s[ai]d plantation." . . .

Historians have only recently begun to explore the consequences of the shift from an immigrant to a predominantly native population. We would like to suggest some changes in the position of women that may have resulted from this transition. It is already known that as sexual imbalance disappeared, age at first marriage rose, but it remained lower than it had been for immigrants over the second half of the seventeenth century. At the same time, life expectancy improved, at least for men. The results were longer marriages and more children who reached maturity. In St. Mary's County after 1700, dying men far more often than earlier left children of age to maintain their widows, and widows may have felt less inclination and had less opportunity to remarry.

We may speculate on the social consequences of such changes. More fathers were still alive when their daughters married, and hence would have been able to exercise control over the selection of their sons-in-law. What in the seventeenth century may have been a period of comparative independence for women, both immigrant and native, may have given way to a return to more traditional European social controls over the creation of new families. . . .

We may also find the wife losing ground in the household polity, although her economic importance probably remained unimpaired. Indeed, she must have been far more likely than a seventeenth-century immigrant woman to bring property to her marriage. But several changes may have caused women to play a smaller role than before in household decision-making. Women became proportionately more numerous and may have lost bargaining power. Furthermore, as marriages lasted longer, the proportion of households full of stepchildren and half-brothers and half-sisters united primarily by the mother must have diminished. Finally, when husbands died, more widows would have had children old enough to maintain them and any minor brothers and sisters. There would be less need for women to play a controlling role, as well as less incentive for their husbands to grant it. The provincial marriage of the eighteenth century may have more closely resembled that of England than did the immigrant marriage of the seventeenth century.

If this change occurred, we should find symptoms to measure. There should be fewer gifts from husbands to wives of property put at the wife's disposal. Husbands should less frequently make bequests to wives that provided them with property beyond their dower. A wife might even be restricted to less than her dower, although the law allowed her to choose her dower instead of a bequest.

At the same time, children should be commanded to maintain their mothers.

St. Mary's County wills show some of these symptoms. Wives occasionally were willed less than their dower, an arrangement that was rare in the wills examined for the period before 1710. More important, there was some decrease in bequests to wives of property beyond their dower, and a tendency to confine the wife's interest to the term of her widowhood or the minority of the oldest son. On the other hand, children were not exhorted to help their mothers or give them living space. Widows evidently received at least enough property to maintain themselves, and husbands saw no need to ensure the help of children in managing it. Still, St. Mary's County women lost some ground, within the family polity. Evidently, as demographic conditions became more normal, St. Mary's County widows began to lose ground to their children, a phenomenon that deserves further study.

NO   Lyle Koehler

WOMEN IN WORK AND POVERTY: THE DIFFICULTIES OF EARNING A LIVING

For some time now, many scholars of early American history have asserted that the absence of sufficient manpower resulted in extensive economic freedom for the "weaker sex." As Page Smith puts it, "There were, in the early years, very few negative definitions—that this or that activity was unsuitable or inappropriate for a woman to engage in. In consequence colonial women moved freely into most occupations in response to particular needs and opportunities rather than abstract theories of what was proper." Eleanor Flexner has more emphatically concluded, "In a struggling society in which there was a continuous labor shortage, no social taboos could keep a hungry woman idle." Barbara Mayer Wertheimer enthusiastically catalogues many of the jobs held by colonial women, and asserts that the earliest female settlers possessed "power and responsibility such as they had never known in seventeenth-century England or on the European continent . . . [They] labored at] many kinds of work outside the home from which they were later barred."

Despite such assertions, there has been no systematic effort to determine the exact occupations available to women, and the extent to which these utilized skills *not* focused strictly around the domesticity and nurturance of the conventional female role. Moreover, we do not know how many women worked at some occupation other than that of housewife and mother, or how much they earned. Because the characterization of woman as the weaker sex affected Puritan views of sexual behavior, intelligence, and social privilege, we might suspect that it also deterred women from supporting themselves. In fact, as we shall see, economic factors discouraged productive, independent activity on the part of women.

LIMITATIONS ON SEARCHING OUT A CALLING

Puritans certainly believed in the efficacy of work. Detesting those who lived "idle like swine," they felt that labor brought "strength to the body, and

From Lyle Koehler, *A Search for Power: The "Weaker Sex" in Seventeenth-Century New England* (University of Illinois Press, 1980). Copyright © 1980 by Lyle Koehler. Reprinted by permission.

vigour to the mynde," thereby providing an outlet for energies which could other-wiselead one to sin. The authorities encouraged each person to search out a suitable calling through apprenticeship, self-training, or hiring out. Boys had considerably more options than girls; apprenticeship contracts specified that the latter be taught only housewifely duties like cooking and sewing, while boys could learn the "secrets" of any number of trades, including blacksmithing, husbandry, shop management, milling, carpentry, and seamanship. It is unlikely that those daughters who never served as apprentices learned any of the male occupational "secrets," because limited opportunities for occupational training, as well as denial of access to public schools, put at a disadvantage any "strong-minded" woman who wished to advance in the world of work. Even if she could overcome the limits of her socialization for domesticity, or use that training to hire herself out in a female vocation, a young woman still could not readily accrue the funds necessary to set herself up in a business or trade; besides, she was unable to earn very much at women's jobs.

Moreover, fathers neglected to give their daughters a portion of the family estate as a nest egg, while they did sometimes convey realty to sons. . . . The daughter who inherited very much from her father's estate was quite a rarity in seventeenth-century Connecticut; only the daughter of a very wealthy man could actually have taken steps to become economically self-sufficient after her father's demise. Furthermore, daughters tended to receive their share in personalty, not realty which could be converted into a permanent productive income, whereas for sons the reverse was true. In fact, daughters inherited proportionally smaller legacies than had been customary in late medieval England.

The mean and median (£22) values of daughters' inheritances yielded some immediate purchasing power, but did little to increase their occupational possibilities. The average inheritance did not allow a daughter money enough to purchase a home lot near the town's center, which sold for £80 or £100. Nor could she rent a shop and stock it with goods. While the young man could work at a trade and save a tidy sum by his late twenties, the young women possessed no similar option. Hartford County records indicate that seventeenth-century inheritance patterns made it virtually impossible for a maiden, whose access to employment was already limited by her training and lack of education, to become part of the property-holding group which ran New England affairs.

THE SINGLE WOMAN AS SERVANT

While her parents were still alive, or after she inherited too little to buy her own financial independence, a single woman could strive to earn money at only one occupation before 1685. Domestic servitude did little more than insure that the young woman would continue to exist as a member of the submissive, inferior, financially dependent class. Female servants assisted with household duties, child care, and garden maintenance—but always under the supervision of a "mistress" or "master," whose orders had to be obeyed unless they violated criminal law. Servants received meals, clothing, and a place to sleep, but generally earned no financial remuneration in return for their valuable work. The few women who hired themselves out (unlike those invariably single ones who served as apprentices, redemptioners, indentured domestics, and even slaves) enjoyed a small measure of economic reward. Their typical annual salary was just £3 or £4, only 50 to 60 percent of the male hired servant's wage. Even with the addition of a sum for the room and board furnished by the master, the female domestic drew one of the lowest annual incomes of any working person.

Since before 1650 domestic servitude was considered an honorable occupation for a woman, some newly arrived single women sought employment in that capacity. These females, whose mean age was 20.7 years, often lived briefly in Puritan households under conditions of relative equality, and then married into the best families. Still, their actual numbers were few; in addition, male domestics migrating to New England outnumbered females three to one. . . .

In the first three decades of settlement, then, a handful of women used servitude as a vehicle for marital advancement, although not as a means to accumulate money for future investment. Since such women labored as indentured servants or redemptioners (usually for seven years, in return for the cost of their passage), before 1650 there is no instance of a female hiring out her own time. After that date, however, the image of the servant deteriorated so remarkably that only a severely impoverished single woman would want to become a domestic. Scottish, Irish, Indian, black, and poor English servants soon replaced the earlier "most honourable" English. . . .

The deterioration of servant status after 1650 made domestic work no longer a realistic option for the "middling" and "better sorts." Because women of those classes no longer became servants, op-portunities for them to leave home and hire out their labor decreased. Nor did the poor English, Scottish, Irish, black, and Indian women who became servants and slaves gain even a small measure of control over their own lives. For sustenance, every woman had to rely on a father, master, or husband; marriage became literally basic to survival for many New England women.

As a result, housewifery served as the chief "occupation" for almost all New England women, and it no more facilitated financial independence than had other forms of domestic servitude. Women certainly contributed to the productivity of the family farm. Although they did not often work outdoors planting and harvesting crops, as English farm wives did, many spent a good deal of time cleaning house, spinning flax, dipping candles, canning preserves, roasting meat, caring for children, and performing untold other tasks. Some spun and made stockings, shirts, or breeches, which they sold to neighbors for an occasional shilling. Goodwives also sold poultry, butter, cheese, and garden produce, or bartered such items for desired commodities in the informal village trade networks. However, woman's work in the home was assumed to be less dangerous and time-consuming than men's—a conclusion which may have rankled Puritan women as much as it has irritated housewives in more modern times. Above all else, the wife was not to use her presumed "free time" to exceed her ordained station by taking an interest in commercial activities or any other "outward matters." She could contract for rents and wages, sell goods, and collect debts only when her husband had so authorized. The records from seventeenth-century civil cases reveal that

New England husbands granted their wives such privileges in only 6 or 7 percent of all families. The wife's access to experience in "outward matters" which could have provided her with some income in either marriage or widowhood was, therefore, much circumscribed.

THE NURTURANT CALLINGS OF WET NURSE, TEACHER, DOCTOR, AND MIDWIFE

Of course, Puritans did allow married women to labor at activities other than housewifery; but those activities also centered around the female's assumed nurturance, and were unremunerative and part-time. Serving as a wet nurse was one such activity, even though its short-term and low-demand characteristics made it a very insubstantial "occupation." Wet nurses enjoyed some popularity because, despite the strong cultural ideal affirming maternal breast-feeding, Puritan mothers sometimes found it impossible to perform that "duty." Puerperal fever or other serious illnesses incapacitated mothers and, it was believed, could be transmitted through the milk. Sore or inverted nipples, breast inflammations, and scanty milk also necessitated the occasional use of a wet nurse. Fear of the presumed toxic effects of colostrum caused mothers to observe a taboo on suckling infants for three or four days after delivery, which increased possibilities for wet nursing. Still, wet nurses rarely received more than temporary employment, and the payment for that service was probably never very great. In fact, such short-term help may have been freely given, much the way neighboring wives helped out during measles or other epidemics. There is no record of New Englanders "farming out" babies to wet nurses for anywhere from ten to nineteen months, as was common in England. Indeed, Puritan women who wet nursed infants probably did not even think of themselves as being employed at an occupation.

Like wet nurses, teachers maternally provided for the needs of the young. At dame schools, where a wife or "poor patient widow sits/And awes some twenty infants as she knits," the female teacher instructed her neighbor's younger offspring for 10s. to £2 per year, 1/10th to 1/120th of the salary for male teachers in the public schools. As early as 1639 Mistress Jupe taught pupils at the Ipswich dame school; before the century's end, twenty-three or twenty-four other women assisted young scholars in reading, writing, and religion at fourteen different New England locales. These schoolmarms were expected to rely upon their husbands' or ex-husbands' estates for sustenance, not upon any salary for their own work. Moreover, they were barred from working with the upper grades (over age nine or ten), lest the difficulty of the material studied at those levels overtax a woman's "weak" intellectual ability. They constituted only 12.6 percent (25 of 199) of all schoolteachers this researcher could locate in the seventeenth-century Puritan records.

The practice of medicine was another nurturant occupational activity open to married women. Many English housewives and their American counterparts learned "chirurgery"—the use of herbs, potions, and poultices to cure any number of maladies. Knowledge of the medicinal properties of wild herbs passed through the female line in some families for generations. Alice Apsley, Lady Fenwick, one of the first women to settle at Ft. Saybrook, Connecticut, distributed homegrown herbs to sick callers at her residence from 1639 until her departure from the colony in 1645. Mistress Field of Salem prepared a green "sympathetic oynment" which purportedly healed sprains, aches, cramps, scaldings, cuts, mange in cattle, stench blood, tumors, the bites of "Venomous Beasts," and "old Rotten Sores." Doctor Margaret Jones of Charlestown, Massachusetts, secured some reputation as a witch because the aniseed, liquors, and small doses of herbs she administered produced "extraordinary violent effects." Hannah Bradford of Windsor, Connecticut, was such a capable physician that she reputedly "taught the first male doctor much of his medical lore." At least three women proved to be able surgeons. Henry Winthrop's widow reportedly "hath very good successe" in her "Surgerye"; Mistress Allyn patched up wounded soldiers as any army surgeon during King Philip's War; and, on Martha's Vineyard, Mistress Blande dispensed "Phisicke and Surgery" to many sick Indians.

Altogether, women comprised 24 percent (42 of 175) of New England's medical practitioners. These female doctors, nurses, and midwives earned the respect of their neighbors, but evidence suggests that they received little income for their services. Medicine in the seventeenth century lacked the financial advantages of ministry, governorship, or commerce; not until the 1690s did physicians begin to achieve some recognition as highly paid, self-conscious professionals. Before that, almost all doctors practiced medicine as a second profession, spending the bulk of their working hours in the ministry, the magistracy, husbandry, or housewifery. . . .

In the 1690s, the professionalization of medicine had severe consequences for female physicians. Men trained through apprenticeship to male doctors began displacing local female chirurgeons. One can search the colonial records in vain for some mention of female physicians during that decade. For the first time, particularly in urban areas, Puritans began distinguishing between male "doctors" and female "nurses," even though such "nurses" assisted Boston wives in recovering from childbirth, cared for infants' ailments, and treated cases of smallpox. Sam Sewall mentions seven different male physicians in his diary for the years 1674 to 1699, but all women who treat illnesses are referred to either as midwives or as nurses.

Throughout the seventeenth century both sexes dispensed medical advice, but one realm of experience, midwifery, remained the exclusive province of women. (In fact, the York County authorities fined one man fifty shillings "for presuming to Act the Part of a Midwife.") Women learned midwifery from personal experience, from other midwives, or from standard obstetrical texts like Nicholas Culpeper's *Directory for Midwives* (1651). There were no medical examinations to pass in New England, nor did a prospective midwife take out a license to practice, as was required in England and in nearby New Amsterdam.

Midwives occupied a position of some influence. They were given the important function of examining women accused of premarital pregnancy, infanticide, or witchcraft; often the guilt or innocence of the accused rested on the findings of these female juries. In return for this necessary service, the town selectmen sometimes issued grants of land to widowed midwives. However, that happened only in a few instances, and it is significant that this researcher has found no account book or other record which mentions a midwife receiving any reward for her services. . . .

WOMEN IN BUSINESS

Limitations on daughters' inheritances and the lack of remunerative work for single women meant that few could join the property-holding group which controlled capital investment in land. So, too, did the paltry wages of midwives, physicians, teachers, and wet nurses, along with husbandly control over their incomes, prevent working wives from acquiring the economic security which would have enabled them to become property owners. As urbanization increased, especially late in the century, working women were generally unable to accumulate the capital necessary to participate in the Commercial Revolution enveloping New England.

Of course, some women who possessed both money and prestige also maintained small-scale businesses. As early as 1640 Philippa Hammond operated a shop at Boston. So did Widow Howdin (1645), Alice Thomas (before 1672), Ann Carter (1663), Jane Bernard (1672-76), Abigail Johnson (1672-73), Mistress Gutteridge (1690), Elizabeth Connigrave (1672-74), Rebecca Windsor (1672-74), and Mary Castle (1690). Almost all of these women ran coffee or cook shops, thereby utilizing their domestic training. Mary Avery and Susanna Jacob kept shop between 1685 and 1691, but whether they were owners or merely employees is unknown. Esther Palmer, a merchant, located in the metropolis in 1683, and Florence Mackarta, in partnership with two men, constructed a slaughterhouse on Peck's Wharf in 1693. A 1687 Boston tax list gives the names of forty-eight different women who derived some income from a trade or their estates—11.4 percent of all such persons rated. But businesswomen were rarer than the initial impression suggests. For example, it is not actually specified how many of the women on the 1687 list owned businesses and how many merely drew income from the estates of their deceased husbands. What *is* clear is that fully 85.4 percent of these women were widows.

Businesswomen, whether married or widowed, were few throughout New England. The paucity of early businesswomen can be readily demonstrated by searching through transcriptions of courtroom proceedings, town records, and other sources. . . . In all of New England outside Boston there are records of only nine women who worked at a trade or who ran a business other than innkeeping. By late century Margaret Barton of Salem, a chair frame maker, had accrued a fortune in "ventures at sea." In Hartford County, Elizabeth Gardner, Mary Phelps, and Mary Stanly owned interests in (respectively) an iron mill, a grist mill, and a shop. Jane Stolion appeared in court in 1645-46, accused of charging excessive prices at her New Haven dress and cloth shop. Mistress Jenny came before the Plymouth General Court in 1644 for not keeping the mortars at her mill clean, nor the bags of corn there from spoiling. Elizabeth Cadwell operated her husband's ferry across the Connecticut River at Hartford after his death in 1695. One Maine widow, Elizabeth Rowdan, maintained a blacksmith shop and mill. Other women may have worked in their husband's bakery, cook, or apparel shops, or may have tailored clothing for sale; but the records observe a rigorous silence on that score, mentioning only one female baker at Salem (1639). Altogether, only 2.3 percent (23 of 988) of all tradespeople-merchants (again excluding innkeepers) were members of the "weaker sex."

An examination of those licensed to keep inns or sell alcoholic beverages indicates that few women supported themselves in this occupation, at least before the 1690s. Since all innkeepers had to secure licenses from the authorities, the records are quite complete. The first female innkeeper does not appear until 1643. Between 1643 and 1689 at least fifty-seven other women operated inns; however, they constituted but 18.9 percent of Boston's innkeepers and only 5 percent of those in the remainder of New England. On Ebenezer Peirce's *Civil, Military, and Professional Lists of Plymouth and Rhode Island Colonies* just three of seventy Plymouth innkeepers are female. In the 1690s, with large numbers of men away fighting in the Maine Indian wars, the New England total increased sharply, to eighty-four women—eight in Maine, twenty-four in New Hampshire, and fifty-two in the Bay Colony. Women then comprised over half of the tavernkeepers in Boston and approximately 20 percent of those in other locales. . . .

Although innkeeping or some other business may have given the individual woman some measure of personal satisfaction and self-sufficiency, the Boston tax list of 1687 suggests that businesswomen fared less well than businessmen. An occasional woman like the Widow Kellond might derive an annual income as high as £80 from her trade and estates, but she was much the exception. Only nineteen members of the "weaker sex"— 39.6 percent of all tradeswomen—earned £10 or more from their trades and estates, while 74 percent of all tradesmen earned

that much. The forty-eight female traders made £580 over the previous year, an average of £12, whereas the 373 male traders made £7,383, or £20 each.

There were several reasons why tradeswomen, when they managed to open shops, earned only 60 percent as much as tradesmen. Since the women possessed little training, their businesses tended to accent service in a way that was compatible with female sex-role stereotyping. Distributing beer, maintaining a cook shop, keeping an inn, and operating a millinery shop utilized talents common to housewives, but ones which returned little profit. Women in such businesses could not easily attract customers on the open market, for they lacked the mobility of carpenters, bricklayers, blacksmiths, and coopers. They could not advertise in newspapers, for none existed. They could not reap the benefits of an international trade, since they lacked ties to the great English trading houses and familiarity with foreign markets. Even credit was a problem. As milliner Hannah Crowell complained in 1696, "being a Woman [I] was not able to ride up and down to get in debts."

Women also lacked the capital necessary to establish large scale businesses. Only after her husband died did the typical woman strike out on her own, with the help of her widow's portion. Of all women who were licensed to sell spirituous liquors, some 71.1 percent were widows. Innkeeping was a ready source of sustenance for any widow whose husband left her house and little else. Working at a trade became an acceptable means of support for widows of artisans, but even they could only rarely increase the net value of their estates over the amounts they inherited. Age, decreased mobility, and a lack of appropriate training or education each took a toll. Moreover, husbands were often reluctant to provide for their wives by leaving them a full or part interest in their trade tools or their shops. Only two of fifty-seven Hartford County artisans, merchants, and shopkeepers bequeathed their widows interest in their businesses. Another man left a shop at Hartford to his sister.

Even those few widows who enjoyed some occupational independence were expected to restrict their activities to nurturant, housewifely, and comparatively low-status occupations. High-status positions such as public grammar-school teaching, the ministry, and major public offices were limited to men. Elizabeth Jones, appointed the Boston pound-keeper in 1670, 1676, and 1689, was the only woman to serve as a public official on even a minor level.

The woman who wished to work "by her own hand," whether widowed, married, or single, faced still other disadvantages. Before 1647 the Maine General Court forbade any woman from inhabiting the Isles of Shoales, thereby making it impossible for females to help out with the fishing or to operate stores at which the fishermen might buy provisions. Perhaps deterred by the sentiment expressed in Maine law, no woman of record ever fished at sea for a profit. Nor could women become sailors—when one dressed as a man and left Massachusetts on a vessel, her fellow seamen, upon discovering her sex, tarred and feathered her in a nearly fatal maltreatment. The presence of working women on the Atlantic was so inconceivable to Puritans that when a mysterious "Shallop at Sea man'd with women" was reported, men attributed the phenomenon to witchcraft.

WEALTH AND POVERTY

The limited, poorly paid, comparatively low status employment opportunities available to early New England women meant that they could not really participate in the expanding possibilities opened by the Commercial Revolution. Despite such disabilities, some observers might argue that dependent wives were rewarded in the end, by inheriting sizable properties (although not businesses) from their deceased husbands. Such widows could enjoy some independence in their later years. The tax lists seem to provide some evidence for this view; women appear as heads of families approximately 6 percent of the time, and fare well when their estates are compared to those of male family heads. . . .

It would be incorrect to assume, however, that as a group widows in Puritan New England were comparatively well-to-do, for most never appeared on a tax list. . . . Many husbands, well aware that their wives might have difficulty maintaining an estate, specified that their widows live with one or more sons in the family dwelling unit. Such men usually reserved one room, a garden, a cow, and some household goods for their widow's use. In one-tenth of all wills (30 of 282) fathers directed children to maintain their mother with annual supplies or a monetary allotment. The annual maintenance payment rarely amounted to much, however, averaging £9 13s.; most widows received less that £7. . . .

Although one-sixth or one-fifth of all widows (those of the middling and better sorts) enjoyed limited affluence, many more suffered poverty. . . .

The appointment of "keepers" for the indigent, or lodging them in the alms-house under a male attendant's supervision, blatantly reinforced female dependence. Such control angered some poor women, and at least two of them entirely rejected the dependence entailed in any form of relief. Mary Webster, a "wretched woman" of Hadley, Massachusetts, protested the efforts of church deacon Philip Smith to mitigate her indigence, expressing herself so sharply "that he declared himself apprehensive of receiving mischief at her hands" (ca. 1684). Jane Bourne of Cambridge refused to accept an allotment from the town for her food and lodging, instead moving out of town to secure employment elsewhere as a servant (1663). A third woman, Abigail Day, was "full of Discontent" and "Impatience under her Afflictions" while at the Boston almshouse. She would "thank neither God nor man" for the objectionable diet there, and she complained that her keeper "had several times made attempts upon her chastity" (1697).

The dissatisfaction of poor women like Abigail Day, Jane Bourne, and Mary Webster is readily understandable, for the paternalism of the Puritan system of poor relief too easily reflected women's difficulties in searching for gainful employment or starting businesses. Wherever they turned, women encountered the fruits of Puritan sexism—in low pay, lack of education and job training, decreased opportunities to secure the funds needed to open a business, and limitations on the kinds of employment available. . . . The great majority of women in early New England worked under a condition of dependence, whether as servants under the control of masters, poor women under the control of almshouse attendants or other keepers, widows under the relative control of their children, or (in the most common occupation of all) housewives under the control of their husbands.

The circumstances of life in seventeenth-century Puritan New England hardly had an emancipating effect. New England wives sometimes maintained family businesses in their husband's absence, or occasionally ran shops of their own; but so did English women. In fact, Alice Clark's research indicates that English women, as members of a more urbanized society, labored at many more occupations than did their New England counterparts. . . . While all of the information is not yet in, it is striking that 40 percent of New England's adult population comprised just 25 percent of all servants, 24 percent of all medical practitioners (if nurses and midwives are subtracted, the percentage drops to 9.6), 12.6 pecent of all schoolteachers, 18 percent of all innkeepers, and 2.3 percent of all tradespeople-merchants. Moreover, these women received much less remuneration than their male counterparts. Although labor shortages were frequent in the first few decades of settlement, such times did not lead to more women on the job market, or to women doing men's work. Inheritance patterns in agrarian locales made it virtually impossible for daughters and wives to exercise much control over capital investment in land. All but a few urban women were similarly unable to acquire real estate or capital which would have enabled them to expand their incomes. The only way for women to experience any upward mobility was to marry well. Seventeenth-century New England was a "Garden of Eden" only for the woman who pursued economic opportunity dependently, as the rib of a (hopefully) prospering and generous Adam.

POSTSCRIPT

Was the Colonial Period a "Golden Age" for Women in America?

The Koehler and Carr and Walsh studies focus upon two different regions in the seventeenth century. Their respective essays indicate that what might have been true for women in colonial New England might not hold true for women who migrated from Europe to the Chesapeake region. Moreover, there is no guarantee that the status of women remained constant throughout the colonial period.

Changes in the status of colonial women have been explored in Mary Beth Norton, "The Evolution of White Women's Experience in Early America," *American Historical Review* (June 1984). Norton surveys the basic elements of the "golden age theory" and perceptively pronounces that theory to be "simplistic and unsophisticated" because it concentrates primarily upon the economic function of women in colonial society. The experiences of early American women, she asserts, are best explored within three chronological divisions: 1620 to 1660; 1660 to 1750; and 1750 to 1815.

Surveys of American women's history that address the colonial period include June Sochen, *Herstory: A Woman's View of American History* (Alfred Publishing Company, 1974); Mary P. Ryan, *Womanhood in America: From Colonial Times to the Present* (New Viewpoints, 1975); and Nancy Woloch, *Women and the American Experience* (Knopf, 1984). Support for the "golden age theory" can be found in Richard B. Morris, *Studies in the History of American Law*, 2d ed. (Octagon Books, 1964); Elizabeth Anthony Dexter, *Colonial Women of Affairs*, 2d ed. (Houghton Mifflin, 1931); Mary Ritter Beard, *Woman as Force in History* (Macmillan, 1946); Eleanor Flexner, *Century of Struggle* (Belknap Press, 1959); Roger Thompson, *Women in Stuart England and America: A Comparative Study* (Routledge and Kegan, 1974); and Page Smith, *Daughters of the Promised Land: Women in American History* (Little, Brown, 1977). For the relationship between women and witchcraft, see John Putnam Demos, *Entertaining Satan: Witchcraft and the Culture of Early New England* (Oxford University Press, 1982), and Carol F. Karlsen, *The Devil in the Shape of a Woman: Witchcraft in Colonial New England* (Norton, 1987). Women in the age of the American Revolution are treated in Mary Beth Norton, *Liberty's Daughters: The Revolutionary Experience of American Women, 1750–1800* (Little, Brown, 1980), and Linda K. Kerber, *Women of the Republic: Intellect and Ideology in Revolutionary America* (University of North Carolina Press, 1980). N. E. H. Hull's *Female Felons: Women and Serious Crime in Colonial Massachusetts* (University of Illinois Press, 1987) is a work which concludes that men and women received equal justice in the colonial period.

ISSUE 4

Did Capitalist Values Motivate the American Colonists?

YES: James T. Lemon, from *The Best Poor Man's Country: A Geographical Study of Early Southeastern Pennsylvania* (Johns Hopkins University Press, 1972)

NO: James A. Henretta, from "Families and Farms: *Mentalité* in Pre-Industrial America," *William and Mary Quarterly* (October 1978)

ISSUE SUMMARY

YES: Professor of geography James T. Lemon argues that the liberal, middle-class, white settlers of southeastern Pennsylvania placed individual freedom and material gain at a higher priority than that of the public interest.
NO: Professor of American history James A. Henretta claims that the colonial family determined the character of agrarian life because it was the primary economic and social unit.

Studies completed during the past 80 years that examine the colonies and earliest local communities can be classified according to three major schools of though: (1) Progressive historians who emphasize the *conflicts* between aristocrats and lower-middle elements; (2) neoconservatives who view the colonists as primarily *middle-class* democrats; and (3) new social historians who stress *family history* through the use of semidemographic models based upon the behavioristic theories of other social scientists.

Whether they acknowledge it or not, most historians are influenced by the political and intellectual currents of the times in which they live. During the first half of the twentieth century, American society underwent profound changes as the nation was transformed from a rural and agricultural society into an urban and industrial one. It was also a time when many progressive American reformers focused on rooting out the corruption they perceived in the country's economic and political institutions and worked to bring about change. Professional historians active during the Progressive Era read the social and economic conflicts of their own time back into the nation's past. Rejecting the patriotic views of earlier writers, these progressive historians saw the past in terms of continual conflicts between the forces of liberalism and conservatism, aristocracy and democracy, and the rich and the poor.

There was little doubt as to which side the progressive historians favored. In his study *The Founding of New England* (1921), James Truslow Adams blasted the Puritan establishment for being undemocratic because its religious leaders denied its followers the basic rights of free speech and religious tolerance. Puritans like Roger Williams and Anne Hutchinson who dissented from the repressive views of the Puritan oligarchy were, by necessity, banished from Massachusetts Bay Colony.

After World War II, a new generation of historians began to tear down the progressive view of history. There were two reasons for this change. First, the times were better. America had emerged from the Depression and the war eras as the strongest nation in the world. Conflicts between the rich and the poor appeared settled; the majority of Americans were middle-class homeowners who shared a common heritage; a capitalist economy and a democratic government were values in which all Americans seemingly shared. A cold war had also been declared. The American system needed to be defended against Russia, an old-fashioned imperialistic nation that now wanted to spread socialism instead of capitalism and replace democracy with communism.

A second and more important reason for the breakdown of the progressive synthesis was that it often oversimplified the conflict of our past and could not withstand the rigors of contemporary scholarship. Robert and Katherine Brown became two of the leading consensus or neoconservative scholars of the 1950s. In a series of separate studies on Massachusetts and in a joint effort, *Virginia 1705–1786: Democracy or Aristocracy?* (Michigan State University Press, 1964), the Browns concluded that "what now passes in this country as middle-class, representative democracy was well-entrenched in the Old Dominion long before the American Revolution."

A third group of scholars has attempted to rid itself of the ideological biases of its predecessors. Relying upon the attempts of the behavioral sciences to fashion new methodological approaches to the study of the human race, a number of recent scholars have undertaken the study of family history. These new social historians approach history from the bottom up instead of the top down. They attempt to reconstruct the histories of the average colonial family by exploring such quantitative materials as land titles, house deeds, marriage and divorce records, wills, inventories, church listings, voter registrations, and, of course, local and national census data. A number of such studies in 1970 centered upon New England.

In the following selections, historical geographer James T. Lemon supports the middle-class consensus view of history. According to Lemon, the citizens of southeastern Pennsylvania were of "liberal middle-class orientation" who sought the freedom to pursue "better opportunities for themselves and their families." Using a different approach, James A. Henretta attempts to synthesize the *mentalité* or mindset of the eighteenth-century settlers. Contrary to Lemon, Henretta denies the importance of the entrepreneurial spirit and argues that the need to maintain a viable family structure determined the character of agrarian life in colonial America.

YES
James T. Lemon

THE BEST POOR MAN'S COUNTRY

Early Pennsylvania was, in many respects, the prototype of North American development. Its style of life presaged the mainstream of nineteenth-century America; its conservative defense of liberal individualism, its population of mixed national and religious origins, its dispersed farms, county seats, and farm-service villages, and its mixed crop and livestock agriculture served as models for much of the rural Middle West.

To many western Europeans of the late seventeenth and eighteenth centuries Pennsylvania was a veritable paradise and refuge from oppression. Indeed, many commentators referred to it as "the best poor man's country in the world." Without doubt the area was one of the most affluent agricultural societies anywhere. For these reasons as well as for its contribution to the American style of life that followed, early Pennsylvania deserves a great deal more scrutiny than it has hitherto received.

This study in historical geography considers a number of issues bearing on the interplay of society and land in early Pennsylvania and centering on the Pennsylvanians' attachment to the land. . . .

One central conceptual matter needs to be mentioned: the interpretation. In this study a wide range of variables is used to explain the material. Traditionally, students of rural America have tended to present either the cultural background of settlers, or the natural environment, or the frontier as the key to understanding what people did. In Pennsylvania's case the emphasis has been on national or ethnic traditions.

In particular, the "Pennsylvania Dutch" (Germans) have been lauded since Benjamin Franklin's time as better farmers than those from the British Isles. Poor Richard admired the "habitual industry and frugality" of the Germans. Dr. Benjamin Rush, another influential Philadelphian, asserted that German farms could be distinguished "by the fertility of their Fields; the luxuriance of their meadows, and a general appearance of plenty and neatness in everything that belongs to them." Later commentators elaborated the theme until it became a commonplace in the literature. A parallel assertion has been that Ulstermen (usually called Scotch-Irish), though poor

From James T. Lemon, *The Poor Man's Country: A Geographical Study of Early Southeastern Pennsylvania* (The Johns Hopkins University Press, 1972). Copyrigh © 1972 by The Johns Hopkins University Press. Reprinted by permission.

farmers, were the "toughest, most adventurous pioneers" on the frontier.

Such a stance accentuates the habitual behavior and the persistence of presumed customs and virtues of these groups. Proponents of national cultural traditions have, therefore, underplayed other cultural, environmental, and social factors. They have not recognized that western Europeans generally shared, for example, a diet emphasizing pork, beef, and small grains. They have not recognized the importance of the new environment.

As is well known, others have used the frontier, or climate, or topography to explain the course of American development. I suspect that some historians think that geographers should talk about the role of, say, mountains in determining the course of settlement, as did Ellen Churchill Semple in her *American History and Its Geographic Conditions*, published in 1903. That is not the perspective taken in this study because it does not give enough due to the people. If cultural determinists made people into pre-programmed automatons who followed custom, then environmentalists imagine people like Pavlovian dogs able only to react to external stimuli.

This study does not deny the power of tradition and environment; but it considers more centrally the decisions of the people and their more immediate social situation. The many decisions that shaped life on the land in early Pennsylvania were the result of how people perceived their situation. Inputs did come from the environment and cultural traditions, but they were interpreted in the light of what people expected to do and what they were able to do. In other words, their ideology (or less strongly, their goals) and their practices determined their actions. So we have to consider the political and economic structures they operated in, the constraints of population growth, developments in western Europe and the Atlantic world, and the status and beliefs of the people who came to the region.

A basic stress in these essays is on the "liberal" middle-class orientation of many of the settlers who elected to leave their European communities. "Liberal" I use in the classic sense, meaning placing individual freedom and material gain over that of public interest. Put another way, the people planned for themselves much more than they did for their communities. Communities, like governments, were necessary evils to support individual fulfillment. This is not to say that the settlers were "economic men," single-minded maximizing materialists. Few could be, or even wanted to be. Nevertheless, they defended their liberal propensities in a tenacious manner. The conservative supporters of individualism were not only the more affluent citizens but also those who moved elsewhere to seek better opportunities for themselves and their families. Undoubtedly their view was fostered by a sense that the environment was "open." As individualists, they were ready in spirit to conquer the limitless continent, to subdue the land. As we now struggle in a "closed" system to find community and to learn to live with a finite nature, we must look at our ancestors to learn how they operated in their environment. We can see the early signs of liberal North America in Pennsylvania as much as anywhere. The interpretation presented here leads us closer, I believe, to an understanding of what the people were doing than either the cultural or the environmental or the economic deterministic perspectives can alone. . . .

SOCIETY AND ENVIRONMENT OF EARLY PENNSYLVANIA

Frederick Brown was a typical (if hypothetical) early Pennsylvanian. Brown came from the Rhineland in 1725 as a boy of ten. With his parents and siblings he settled in Lancaster County near people from Germany and the British Isles. Brown's family was Lutheran; they shared the township with a wide variety of Protestant groups—Quakers, Mennonites, Scotch-Irish Presbyterians, and others. Brown's father established a reasonably successful farm that produced most of the materials needed for a comfortable if not affluent life. When his father retired in 1750 Frederick was married. He took over part of the family farm, carrying on much as his father had, but with increasing economic dependence on the Atlantic world through Lancaster and Philadelphia. As his own sons matured all but one left home, one to a nearby township, the other to the west. Eventually Brown, too, retired from farming in 1780 and became dependent on the support of his eldest son. In 1790 he was buried in the cemetery by the church.

Frederick Brown's life was quite ordinary—ordinary in the sense that he did the sorts of things that many rural Americans did in the eighteenth and nineteenth centuries. But the commonplace qualities of his life and the lives of his fellow Pennsylvanians should not keep us from trying to understand their structure and rhythm, for they stood as a model for later Americans.

The activities of Brown and others grew out of a range of factors including western European cultural traditions, the social characteristics of Pennsylvania life, and the natural qualities of the area. Pennsylvania was a part of western European society, and many of its traditions—the patriarchal family and Christian doctrines, for example—were carried across the Atlantic. Yet the migrants did not represent a cross section of western European life. They were neither the richest nor the poorest Europeans, most were skilled, and perhaps most importantly, most were the kind of people who sought individual satisfaction. To some extents they were entrepreneurs, though not maximizing materialists. Their descendants shared this concern and some imprinted Pennsylvania with a "liberal" image. Pennsylvanians nevertheless were marked by different origins and belonged to different religious groups that helped shape their style of life. The rate of population growth exerted an influence. In their government, they erected structures based on English precedents. They participated in an economic system marked by a strong subsistence component but also by Atlantic trading patterns. Their preindustrial technology used animal and human rather than inanimate sources of energy. These structures affected them all. Moreover, the people had to deal with the Indians and a distinctive set of resources—the climate, the terrain, soil, and forests—that encouraged new methods of land utilization.

These characteristics of tradition, society, and environment combined to create the distinctive Pennsylvanian modes of life. They will be utilized in varying degrees to explain the processes on the land's surface. . . .

In stressing the middle class origins of immigrants and character of Pennsylvania society, the degree of social stratification that developed in the region should not be understated. The inhabitants were conscious of the categories "better," "middling," and "poorer sorts." The distribution of wealth, the number of landless people toward the end of the century, and direct references to poverty tend to support this ranking. By 1800 a fairly wide spread in wealth had arisen between the most affluent and those at the bottom in Chester County. At that time the wealthiest 10 per cent paid 38 per cent of the taxes and the poorest 30 per cent paid only 4 per cent. This was a sharper difference than existed in the 1690s, when the upper 10 per cent held less than 24 per cent of the wealth. Considering that the richer were probably undertaxed, the stratification was probably more marked than the tax lists suggest. In one of the few extant quantitative references to stratification, the assessor of relatively backward and predominantly German Brecknock Township in Lancaster County in 1750 recorded 27 per cent of the people "poor," compared with 40 per cent "middling" and 33 per cent "able," in their capacity to pay taxes. But this is not altogether helpful. The various categories of wealth suggest that probably only three or four persons would be classed as "better sort"; most of 73 per cent called "middling" and "able" were probably "middling." It seems unlikely that most of the "poor" were destitute, but their circumstances are harder to determine. In 1782 nonlandowners in Chester and Lancaster counties totaled about 30 per cent of the population. This category included tenant farmers and "inmates," a designation that might refer to indentured and apprenticed persons, many of whom were born in Pennsylvania and some of whom were married. The most that can be said with certainty, however, is that inmates lived in someone else's house and were craftsmen and laborers rather than farmers. Whatever the facts, the number of landless persons

in Lancaster and Chester counties seems to have been high if we presume, as did some in the eighteenth century and later, that land was freely available and that America was a nation of freeholders.

In Pennsylvania, according to reports, poverty was not uncommon, at least in times of recession. In 1747 an observer in Philadelphia noted: "It is remarkable what an increase of the number of Beggars there is about this town this winter, many more than I have before observed." Soon after this, when conditions were quite good, an item in the Lancaster County Commissioners' Book stated that the poor were suffering because the appropriation for squirrel bounties had been curtailed. In the early 1760s redemptioners were little in demand, and money was given to paupers. Agents of the Hamilton family, which owned the town of Lancaster, reported that quit-rents could never be collected from the poor of the town, who were idle "for want of employment," except during harvest time. Mortgages were foreclosed on poorer farmers during difficult times. Toward the end of the century, an Englishman who had expected to see few beggars reported a "great" many in Pennsylvania, and about that time poor houses were established, suggesting either that an endemic situation had finally been recognized or that conditions had recently become worse.

Despite these references to poverty and the acceptance of a tripartite division of society by early Pennsylvanians, we can still affirm that Pennsylvanians were predominantly middle class. Except during times of depression, wages were probably higher throughout the century than in Europe. Even at the end of the century, few tax lists record destitute persons. "Poor tax" records have few entries. If the "holy experiment" did not bring bounty for all, it allowed many to improve their material lot—and if not even if there were many needy, as there were in Pennsylvania in recent years when about 25 per cent of the population could be classed as poor, Pennsylvanians believed that hard work would bring success. In the last analysis, the middle class faith in the right to seek success was the hallmark of Pennsylvania society and distinguished it somewhat from western Europe, where the landed aristocracy still remained powerful and the many peasants had extremely limited aspirations. Yet it was from western Europe that this liberal philosophy had been carried to fulfillment in America, perhaps most clearly in Pennsylvania.

If the settlers and their descendants were similar in social and economic status, they were varied in language, national origin, and religion. These have contributed to the impression of the society as a pluralistic "mosaic." Many commentators on life in early Pennsylvania have stressed language and national origin, but, these were less relevant to people's action on the land than was previously thought. Religious distinctions, however, were of considerable importance.

On the basis of surname analysis (admittedly an uncertain technique) and other data, the proportions of persons in national groups in 1790 can be estimated. The major groups were Germans and German-speaking Swiss, Englishmen, and Ulstermen, the last called "Irish" by contemporaries and "Scotch-Irish" since the nineteenth century. Even though the distinctiveness of the Scotch-Irish as a cultural group can be questioned, as can that of any English-speaking Celts, in this study I have tried to separate them

from the English largely for the sake of argument. . . .

In 1790 persons of German and Swiss background constituted a larger proportion of the population in southeastern Pennsylvania (40 per cent) than in the state as a whole (33 per cent). The English were more numerous in the state than in the region (35 per cent as compared with less than 30), as were the Scotch-Irish and Scots (23 per cent compared with 18 per cent). These proportions can be attributed to continued immigration from the British Isles after 1755, particularly in the early 1770s, and to a dearth of German-speaking migrants after 1755. Estimates of numbers in national groups earlier than 1790 are speculative. Before 1725 the "English" predominated and the Welsh and Swedes were considerably more numerous than they were later. In 1750 the proportion of Germans was probably higher than in 1790.

Language is valid only to distinguish German-speaking from English-speaking persons. Yet many Germans Anglicized themselves. . . . Some Germans, including Mennonites, anxious to have their children learn English, set up schools with English teachers. Although a differentiating characteristic, language was less significant as an influence on social and especially economic processes than has often been stated.

Differences in customs and practices associated with national groups have also been misstated or exaggerated far out of proportion to their significance. . . . The economic status of various national groups did not diverge greatly. A sample of estate inventories, excluding land values, in Lancaster and Chester counties between 1713 and 1790, though an imprecise measure, suggests that differences were not great. The average assessment within a number of townships with substantial numbers in each national group, probably a better yard-stick than inventories, shows that in half of eighteen townships the "English" had the edge, but distinctions were not sharp. In 1782 the most affluent were divided among national groups in Lancaster County; only the few Welsh were proportionately more wealthy. In lower income levels differences were not great. Economic status, then, appears to have been much the same among national groups. . . .

Most Pennsylvanians were Protestants, or at least non-Catholic. But denominational affiliations divided the people into groups, and this pluralism was a distinctive mark of the society. Although use of the word "denomination" implies tolerance and an easing of sharp theological conflicts, and although it is clear that groups experienced varying degrees of doctrinal and social metamorphosis throughout the period, some differences remained clear enough to have a significant effect. The critical distinction was between "sects" and "churches." Sectarian "plain folk," notably Friends and Mennonites, were much more prominent than in Europe. Because their values and organizations favored cooperation and discipline, these groups acted on the land in a somewhat different fashion than did Lutheran, Reformed, Anglican, and Presbyterian members. A substantial number of persons were not related to any denomination.

The Friends (mostly from the west of England, the London area, and Wales) and Mennonites (mostly from the lower and middle Rhine Valley and Switzerland) were the most important "sects." During the first forty years of the province these groups, especially the Quakers,

were in the majority. In 1790, when Quakers and Mennonites were easily outnumbered by others, they remained substantial minorities in some counties, including Chester, Lancaster, Bucks, and Montgomery. Although the term "sect" is not fully adequate for describing these "plain folk" or others such as the Dunkers, Schwenkfelders, and Moravians, who lived communally for a generation, certain social values set them apart from "church" groups. The Quakers at first stressed the goal of perfecting rather than ignoring the world and encouraged other groups to share in the wealth of the land. But rural Friends and the Mennonites were markedly selective in membership, and as the century passed they relied more on "birthright" than voluntary confession to define membership. This exclusiveness was fostered by a strong sense of self-righteousness, and among the Quakers the notion of perfectibility shifted from the "holy experiment" and society at large to the group. This desire for perfection encouraged a drive for material well-being, possibly to prove their salvation to the world. Paradoxically, then, worldly success for individual members of the group became a goal for those who officially eschewed worldliness. To this end strong local leaders, especially in rural areas, exhorted members to purity of doctrine, society, domestic responsibility, hard work, and mutual help. Thus for the sake of gain, both material and social, Mennonites and Quakers formed societies of discipline, emulation, and mutual aid.

Because of these characteristics, reinforced by their early arrival and their somewhat greater initial affluence, Quakers and Mennonites possessed throughout the period a higher average economic status than members of other denominational groups. In 1782 in Lancaster County, among the sixty Germans paying taxes of £ 40 or more, thirty-five were Mennonites, a proportion of 58 per cent compared with a Mennonite share of 37 per cent of the German population. In Chester County Quakers headed many tax lists. The tax data are corroborated by contemporary comments. For example, the Anglican clergyman William Smith considered the Mennonites "the most considerable and wealthy sect among the Germans," and another observer asserted, "almost all the Quakers are wealthy people, who never let anyone belonging to their sect be reduced to poverty." Although some poor Quakers and Mennonites lived in the area and members of other groups acquired wealth, the sectarians were generally the most affluent people in rural Pennsylvania.

In spite of the sectarian views held by Quakers and Mennonites, William Penn welcomed other Protestants to Pennsylvania, and Roman Catholics were admitted. This permissive attitude eventually undercut the goal of a clearly structured society based on Quaker principles; but far from making Pennsylvania a failure, as Penn finally felt it might have, this policy resulted in the immigration of many persons who contributed to the growth of the region.

The prominent "church" groups were Presbyterian, Lutheran, Reformed, and Anglican, and to a lesser degree Baptist, Roman Catholic, and eventually Methodist. Their members submitted to looser disciplines and were less inclined to mutual help than the sectarians, partly because they relied on an uncertain supply of ministers from Europe or at least from other communities. In rural areas their average economic status was lower despite the affluence of some. . . .

Because these "church" people, especially the larger Presbyterian, Lutheran, and Reformed memberships, mainly arrived between 1725 and 1755, their influence on the initial patterns of action on the land was less marked than that of Quakers and Mennonites. Without doubt the "church" groups markedly influenced life during the third and subsequent generations. As first arrivals, Quakers and Mennonites were free to choose sites near Philadelphia or on the best soils. Even though substantial numbers of Quakers lived in towns, the many rural Quakers and the Mennonites were more tightly clustered geographically and were less mobile than "church" people. The greater wealth of Quakers and Mennonites and other data suggest that on the whole they were better farmers than others. Unlike the communitarian Moravians, however, Quakers and Mennonites lived on family farms rather than in agricultural villages, and most "church" people followed this practice.

Pennsylvanians thus were divided in varying degrees by nationality and language and denomination as well as somewhat by economic status. The divisions varied in importance. Antagonisms among groups and also within groups led to such times of trouble as the debates over the Great Awakening, the controversy over defense against the French and Indians, and the Revolution. . . .

Not only the people's characteristics but their numbers were important in directing their actions on the land. Given limitations in the economic system and backward technologies in agriculture and transportation, the density of population and the rate of growth exerted considerable influence on availability of land and thus on farming opportunities in the areas of initial and later settlement.

The population of the region expanded from about 9,000 in 1690 to more than 300,000 a century later. The rate of growth was most rapid before 1700 and was quite marked between 1730 and 1760, a time of substantial immigration. Considerably slower increases occurred in the last third of the century, when fewer immigrants arrived, the birth rate probably was lower, and the region had virtually been occupied, so that many people moved beyond rather than within southeastern Pennsylvania. . . .

Pennsylvanians were involved in two economic systems, the subsistence economy and the Atlantic trading empire centered in London. Few persons were completely self-reliant; few depended entirely on others. Many townsmen kept gardens, orchards, and a cow or two, and remote frontiersmen and laborers bought and sold goods and services in the market. The eighteenth century witnessed an elaboration of the commercial network within the area and with other provinces, Great Britain, and foreign areas, so that Pennsylvania economically was well developed for the time and compared with most areas in Europe. By the third generation, after 1740, farmers of "middling" status sold between a third and a half or more of their production, at least during peacetime. The pattern was preindustrial, however, and farmers did not specialize to the degree they would after 1820 or 1830 when manufacturing and urbanization increased demands for farm products.

The credit and marketing system in the Atlantic world involved many links that gave rise to urban places and a degree of commercial agricultural production. Rural Pennsylvanians were connected by a chain of credit through Philadelphia and Baltimore and through merchants, millers, and shopkeepers in smaller places with London merchants. Although the Atlantic world's economic center was in London, and Pennsylvania exported mostly unprocessed or little-processed agricultural and forest products, Pennsylvania was not locked into a bilateral and dependent pattern to the degree the "staple"-producing southern colonies were. Autonomous connections with other mainland colonies, the West Indies, and southern Europe provided income that helped to compensate for the persistent adverse balance of trade with England. Success in trading encouraged even longer extensions of credit by London merchants confident of Pennsylvania's future growth. Rural Pennsylvanians, especially those west of the Susquehanna River, had the option of dealing with Maryland as well as Philadelphia. In both cases farmers received goods from back-country shopkeepers and merchants, delivered or had delivered their products to Philadelphia or other points, and requested the buyers to credit their dealers' accounts with importers. Even though cash was scarce and banks did not appear until 1783, business was not on a barter level. All commodities carried monetary value, and merchants and other wealthy persons acted as bankers. These structures contributed to the development of urban places as the centers of regional activity. Philadelphia, Baltimore, and county seats especially became important.

Pennsylvania's customers were responsible for the kinds of commodities that entered its export trade. The West Indies, New England, southern Europe, Ireland, and ship provisioners demanded flour, bread, and wheat, and to a lesser extent corn, lumber, flaxseed, and many other goods. Because the West Indies opened as a market at about the time Pennsylvania was founded, the Quaker colony was spared the limitations placed on southern colonies by the demands of England for tobacco, rice, and indigo. From the outset it was able to trade outside this bilateral system. Although Pennsylvania supplied England with iron after 1750 and wheat after 1765, encouragement of hemp and silk production as "staples" failed partly because of Pennsylvania's success with other commodities. External markets had a significant bearing on shaping the agricultural system and regional patterns of land use.

Despite the complex commercial connections, internal and external markets were limited by later standards, communication and transport facilities were inadequate, processing operations were unsophisticated, and agricultural tools were primitive. These deficiencies contributed to a continuation of the subsistence aspect of the economy, to a limited specialization of agriculture, and to the existence of the family farm as the chief unit of production.

Information on market conditions outside Pennsylvania was vital for profitable decisions. But four weeks was the minimum travel time from London, so that when prices changed rapidly in Europe and elsewhere Pennsylvanians often could not react as quickly as they might have wished. Within the colonies, even in the late eighteenth century, the overland stage trip between Philadelphia and New York took a minimum of one day. Horse-drawn wagons, the chief means of transporting goods, were slow and costly. Thirty miles was the maximum distance a loaded wagon could cover in a day under favorable weather conditions. Ferriage was also expensive, especially across the Susquehanna. Water transport complemented wagon transportation only to a small extent in Pennsylvania. By 1770 some Pennsylvanians were displeased with their transportation facilities. Yet it appears that more were satisfied with the rate of return from the economy, and therefore not until the early 1790s did the legislature finance the construction of the Lancaster Turnpike. Canals were built even later than this.

The preindustrial character of the economy was nowhere more apparent than in the manufacturing sector. It lacked the diversification, corporate enterprise, and concentration. Many more craftsmen lived in rural areas than scholars have recognized, and Pennsylvania at the time did not trail many parts of Europe in implementing new processing methods. Still, many goods were fabricated by farmers, and most industrial organizations were small and owned by proprietors. Only ironmaking and, toward the end of the century, flour milling and cotton milling foreshadowed nineteenth century corporate structures. Craftsmen and farmers who integrated many operations were the chief manufacturers. The British policy of restriction laws and government subsidies in the wrong areas, such as hemp and silk production, contributed to this state of affairs. But more fundamental factors were the attractions of land investment and of agriculture and other primary production. Investors in England and Pennsylvania were attracted by the certain or higher rates of return in these sectors. The slow development of textile manufacturing in the eighteenth century and well into the nineteenth resulted basically from the diversion of energies and capital to primary production, notably farming, and speculation in land.

Finally, the tools of agriculture limited productivity and encouraged reliance upon the family farm as the basic unit of production. Relatively few innovations—such as the Dutch fan for blowing away chaff—appeared in harvesting and threshing equipment despite recurrent labor shortages and higher labor costs than in Europe. Reformers tried to inform farmers of English methods of improving yields, but aside from perhaps the more affluent sectarians concerned with status, new ideas were not welcomed. Not until the nineteenth century did the agricultural technological revolution occur that has led to the highly capitalized corporate farming of today in many areas. In the eighteenth century, technical limitations both on and off the farm restrained commercialization and caused a large share of production to be consumed at home. Combined with the desire of most settlers to be captains of their own destiny and with the kinds of markets farmers sold to outside the region, these technical constraints encouraged the family farm to thrive as the cornerstone of this agrarian economy. . . .

By the last decade of the eighteenth century the European occupation had dramatically transformed the southeastern Pennsylvania landscape. In 1680 the area was lightly populated by Indians and a few Europeans along the Delaware. In 1800 there were more than 300,000 persons of European descent here, and many others had moved on to other areas. In this 120 years the people organized the space into farms, arrayed their social and political institutions and physical facilities over the area, built towns that became the centers of regional and local activity, and exploited the land's resources for forestry, mining, and especially agriculture.

Yet in spite of the marked alteration of the surface of the land the Pennsylvanians' mode of living had changed very little. Though their average standard of living had risen, the prosperity, paradoxically, had been achieved through traditional ways. There were few technological advances. Pennsylvanians were perhaps the most liberal people in the world—they believed implicitly, some even explicitly, in individual material success. Yet because many were successful, liberalism (in the traditional sense) became enshrined as a style of life. Many of those who were not so fortunate or were dissatisfied repeated the original movement across the Atlantic by moving to the frontier. They, too, shared the hope of achieving success. Vast resources lay out beyond the settled area, and few persons felt actually limited. (The least stable and successful were sustained by another variation: individual immortality on another frontier.) The openness contributed to making these people conservative, not in the sense of espousing community but in preserving their freedom and privacy. What structures there were, and they were minimal by today's standards, existed for the individual and his family. This can be said even for the more disciplined Quakers and Mennonites. And so the paradox deepens. Their authoritarianism and ideology of hard work existed to prove not only that their groups were viable but that they as individuals were justified in seeking perfection. In this resource-rich environment, what better way could they achieve this than through exploitation of the land?

NO
James A. Henretta

FAMILIES AND FARMS: *MENTALITÉ* IN PRE-INDUSTRIAL AMERICA

The history of the agricultural population of pre-industrial America remains to be written. As a result of quantitative investigations of wealth distribution and social mobility; of rates of birth, marriage, and death; and of patterns of inheritance, officeholding, and church membership, there is an ever-growing mass of data that delineates the *structures* of social existence in the small rural communities that constituted the core of American agricultural society in the North before 1830. But what of the *consciousness* of the inhabitants, the mental or emotional or ideological aspects of their lives? And what of the relationship between the two? Can a careful statistical analysis of people's lives—a precise description of their patterns of social actions—substantiate at least limited statements as to their motivations, values, and goals?

A number of historians have attempted to establish a connection between the subsistence activities of the agricultural population and its institutional, ideological, and cultural existence. Consider, for example, the entrepreneurial interpretation implicit in James T. Lemon's highly regarded quantitative analysis of the eighteenth-century agricultural society of Southeastern Pennsylvania:

> A basic stress in these essays is on the "liberal" middle-class orientation of many of the settlers. . . . "Liberal" I use in the classic sense, meaning placing individual freedom and material gain over that of public interest. Put another way, the people planned for themselves much more than they did for their communities. . . . This is not to say that the settlers were "economic men," single-minded maximizing materialists. Few could be, or even wanted to be. Nevertheless, they defended their liberal propensities in a tenacious manner. . . . Undoubtedly their view was fostered by a sense that the environment was "open." As individualists, they were ready in spirit to conquer the limitless continent, to subdue the land.

However overburdened with reservations and qualifications, the general thrust of this depiction of values and aspirations is clear enough. Lemon's settlers were individualists, enterprising men and women intent upon the pursuit of material advantage at the expense of communal and non-economic goals.

Can the "consciousness" with which Lemon has endowed these early Pennsylvanians be verified by historical evidence? The question is important, for many of the statistical data presented by Lemon do not support this description of the inhabitants' "orientation," "spirit," or "propensities." Take the pattern of residence. It is true that the predominance of isolated farmsteads—rather than nucleated villages—suggests that these men and women were planning "for themselves much more than . . . for their communities." But what of the presence of clusters of ethnic and religious groups? Such voluntary concentrations of like-minded settlers indicate the importance of *communal* values, of people who preferred to share a religious or ethnic identity. Here the author's evidence contradicts his conclusion. "Most of the people who came during this period," Lemon writes of the years between 1700 and 1730, "settled together in areas and communities defined by nationality or denomination. . . . Language and creed thus exerted considerable influence on the whereabouts of people. Yet groups were mixed in several areas, for example on the Lancaster Plain."

This exception only confirms the rule. Nearly every historian who has studied ethnic settlement patterns in the colonial period has stressed the existence of communal concentrations. In the Middle Colonies, for example, patterns of spatial segregation appeared among the Dutch in Newark, New Jersey, and to some extent among Quakers and Seventh Day Baptists in the same area. Most of the German immigrants who arrived in Lan-caster, Pennsylvania, in 1744 settled on the lots laid out by Dr. Adam Simon Kuhn, the leading German resident, rather than on land offered by the English proprietor, Alexander Hamilton. These linguistic and religious ties extended beyond settlement patterns to encompass economic relationships. Every one of the one hundred names inscribed in the account book of Henry King—shoemaker, butcher, and currier of Second River, in New Jersey in 1775—was of Dutch origin; and the main business connections of the merchants of Lancaster, whether they were Jewish or Quaker or German, were with their coreligionists in Philadelphia.

Is an individualist spirit fully compatible with these communal settlement patterns and this religiously determined economic activity? It is possible, of course, that these ethnic or linguistic preferences facilitated the pursuit of individual economic gain, and that the patronage of the shop of a fellow church member brought preferred treatment and lower prices. But the weight of the evidence indicates that these decisions were not made for narrowly economic or strictly utilitarian reasons: the felt need to maintain a linguistic or religious identity was as important a consideration as the fertility of the soil or the price of the land in determining where a family would settle. The "calculus of advantage" for these men and women was not mere pecuniary gain, but encompassed a much wider range of social and cultural goals.

These ethnic, linguistic, or religious ties did not reflect a coherent ideological system, a planned *communitarian* culture similar to the highly organized Moravian settlement at Bethlehem, Pennsylvania. These bonds among families, neighbors, and fellow church members were informal; nonetheless, they circumscribed the range of individual action among the inhabitants of Pennsylvania and laid the foundations for a rich and diverse cultural existence. These community-oriented patterns of social interaction emerge clearly from Lemon's quantitative data, yet they do not figure prominently in his conclusion. He has not explained the complexity of the settlers' existence but has forced their lives into the mold of a timeless, placeless concept of "liberal individualism."

A similar discrepancy between data and interpretation appears in Lemon's analysis of the economic goals and achievements of the inhabitants of eighteenth-century Pennsylvania. What becomes of the open environment and the conquering spirit when "tenant farming was much more frequent than we might expect. . . . In 1760 and 1782 about 30 per cent of Lancaster's and Chester's married taxpayers were landless" and an additional 15 percent of the total number of taxpayers in Chester County were single freemen—mostly young men without landed property. With nearly 45 percent of the members of the adult white male population without land of their own, the gap between evidence and conclusion is so obvious that it must be confronted; and what better way than by evoking the spirit of Frederick Jackson Turner? "As long as the frontier was open . . .," Lemon writes, "many people were able to move, and as a result frustrations were dampened and the liberal values of the original inhabitants of the colony were upheld."

This is an appealing interpretation, especially since it admits the necessary connection between the structure of opportunity offered by a given environment and the consciousness of the inhabitants, but it is not completely satisfactory. It assumes that the migrants came with "liberal" values, with an expectation that most adult males would own a freehold estate and that anything less than this would generate anger and frustration. Neither the basic proposition nor its corollary is acceptable, for both fail to convey the settlers' conception of social reality, their understanding of the structural components of age and wealth.

To be "young" in this agricultural society (as in most) was either to be landless or without sufficient land to support a family. As Philip J. Greven, Daniel Scott Smith, and Robert A. Gross have shown, male parents normally retained legal control of a sizable portion of the family estate until death, in order to ensure their financial well-being in old age, and the economic security of their widows was carefully protected by dower rights. Nor were these cultural restraints on the transmission of improved property the only, or even, the main, obstacle to the economic prospects of the next generation. For the high rate of natural increase constantly threatened to overwhelm the accumulated capital resources of many of these northern farm families. There was never sufficient cleared and improved property, or livestock, or farm equipment, or adequate housing to permit most young men and women to own a farm. In five small agricultural towns in New Jersey in the 1770s, for example, one half of all white males aged eighteen to twenty-five were without land, while another 29 percent of this age group owned fifty acres or less. And in Concord, Massachusetts, the percentage of landless males (many of whom were young) remained at 30 percent from 1750 to 1800. This correlation between age and wealth persisted throughout the life-cycle; all of the males in the lowest quintile of the taxable population in East Guilford, Connecticut, in 1740 were below the age of forty, while every person in the highest quintile was that age or above.

The accumulation of financial resources by aging men brought them higher status and political power. In Concord, between 1745 and 1774, the median age of selectmen at the time of their first election to office was forty-five, a pattern that obtained in Dedham and Watertown as well. Indeed, the correlation among age, wealth, status, and power in these agricultural communities indicates the profound importance of age as a basic principle of social differentiation. And so it appeared to the Reverend William Bentley of Salem on a visit to Andover in 1793; the country people, he noted, assembled to dance "in classes due to their ages, not with any regard to their condition, as in the Seaport Towns." In such an age-stratified society economic "success" was not usual (and not expected) until the age of thirty-five, forty, or even forty-five. Propertied status was the product of one or two decades of work as a laborer or tenant, or of the long-delayed inheritance of the parental farm. The ownership of a freehold estate was the *goal* of young male farmers and their wives; it was not—even in the best of circumstances—a universal condition among adult males at any one point in time. Age stratification thus constituted an important aspect of what Michael Zuckerman has neatly conceptualized as the "social context" of political activity in these small and ethnically homogeneous agricultural settlements. The economic dependence and powerlessness of young adults was a fact of life, the proper definition of social reality.

If cultural norms legitimated an age-stratified society in the minds of most northern farmers, then the character of social and economic life accustomed them to systematic inequalities in the distribution of wealth. Consider the evidence. In southeastern Pennsylvania in 1760 and again in 1782, the top 40 percent of the taxable population owned 70 percent of the assessed wealth, while the top 10 percent controlled 33 percent. On the 1784 tax list of Newtown, Long Island, the proportions were nearly identical, with the top 40 percent owning 73 percent of the wealth, and the richest 10 percent holding 37 percent. In both places, inequality increased steadily from the end of the seventeenth century even as the rate of natural population growth declined—a clear indication of advancing social differentiation (and not simply age stratification). And in Newtown, at least, the bulk of the poor population in 1784 was composed not of "younger sons or older men" but of workers in the prime of their productive lives.

The westward migration of this excess farm population was of crucial importance, although not for the precise reasons suggested by Turner and Lemon. Young men and women without a landed inheritance moved to newly settled communities not as yeomen but as aspirants to that status; they hoped to make the difficult climb up the agricultural "ladder" from laborer to tenant to freeholder. This geographical movement, in turn, helped to maintain social stability in long-settled agricultural towns. One-third of all adult males in Goshen, Connecticut, in 1750 were without land; but two decades later a majority of these men had left the town and 70 percent of those who remained had obtained property through marriage, inheritance, or the savings from their labor. A new landless group of unmarried sons, wage laborers, and tenant farmers had appeared in Goshen by 1771, again encompassing one-third of the adult males. A similar process of out-migration and property accumulation would characterize many of the lives of this landless group, but throughout the northern region there was a steady increase in the number of permanent tenant farmers as the century progressed.

The renewed expropriation of aboriginal lands during the early nineteenth century brought a partial reversal of this trend. Massive westward migration enabled a rapidly growing Euro-American population to *preserve* an agricultural society composed primarily of yeoman freeholding families in many eastern areas, and to *extend* these age and wealth-stratified communities into western regions. This movement did not, however, produce less stratified communities in the Northwest states, nor did it assure the universal ownership of land. Within a few decades of settlement the wealth structure of the frontier states was nearly indistinguishable from that in the agricultural areas of the more densely settled east. In Trempealeau County, Wisconsin, in 1870 the poorest 10 percent of the properties population owned less than 1 percent of all assessed wealth, while the most affluent 10 percent controlled 39 percent. This distribution was almost precisely the same as that in those regions of Vermont from which many of the inhabitants of this farming county had recently migrated. "On no frontier," Neil McNall concludes from an intensive study of the settlement of the rich Genesee Valley in upstate New York between 1790 and 1860, "was there an easy avenue to land ownership for the farmer of limited means."

Evidence from a variety of geographic locations indicates, therefore, that Lemon has presented an overly optimistic description of the agricultural economy of early America and has falsely ascribed a "liberal" consciousness to the inhabitants of eighteenth-century Pennsylvania. His analysis is not unique. A number of historians of colonial New England have offered similar interpretations of an entrepreneurial mentality among the majority of the agricultural population. Sometimes the ascription is implicit and perhaps inadvertent, as in the case of Philip Greven's path-breaking analysis of Andover, which focuses attention on the single economic variable of land transmission. Was the preservation of a landed inheritance the concern of *most* Andover families or only that of the very select group of substantially endowed first settlers and their descendants whom Greven has studied? The pattern of family life, geographic mobility, and economic values may have been very different among later arrivals to Andover—those who had less land to pass on to the next generation—yet this group constituted a majority of the town's population by the eighteenth century. Or what of the pervasive entrepreneurial outlook among Connecticut farmers which is posted by Richard L. Bushman in his stimulating examination of the transition *From Puritan To Yankee*? Bushman's interpretation of the Great Awakening is predicated upon the emergence of an accumulation-oriented pattern of behavior, and yet little—if any—evidence is presented to demonstrate its existence among the mass of the population. . . .

Even in the most market-oriented areas of the Middle Colonies, many farmers participated in the commercial capitalist economy in a much more limited way and with rather different goals. Lacking slaves or indentured servants and unwilling to bid for wage labor, they planted only 8 to 10 acres of wheat each year, a crop that could conveniently be harvested by the farmer, one or two growing sons, and (in some cases) his wife. Of the normal yield of 80 to 100 bushels, 60 would be consumed by the family or saved for seed; the surplus of 20 to 40 bushels would be sold on the Philadelphia market, bringing a cash income in the early 1770s of £ 5 to £ 10 sterling. The ordinary male farmer, Lemon concludes, was content to produce "enough for his family and . . . to sell a surplus in the market to buy what he deemed necessities." There was little innovative, risk-taking behavior; there was no determined pursuit of profit. Indeed, the account books of these farm families indicate that they invariably chose the security of diversified production rather than hire labor to produce more wheat or to specialize in milk production. Economic gain was important to these men and women, yet it was not their dominant value. It was subordinate to (or encompassed by) two other goals: the yearly subsistence and the long-run financial security of the family unit.

Thus, the predominance of subsistence or semi-subsistence productive units among the yeoman farming families of the northern colonies was not only the result of geographic or economic factors—the ready access to a reliable, expanding market. These men and women were enmeshed also in a web of social relationships and cultural expectations that inhibited the free play of market forces. Much of the output of their farms was consumed by the residents, most of whom were biologically or legally related and who were not paid wages for their labor. A secondary group of consumers consisted of the inhabitants of the local area, members of a community often based on ties of kinship, language, religion, or ethnicity. An impersonal price system figured prominently in these transactions, but goods were often bartered for their exchange value or for what was considered a "just price." Finally, a small (but growing) proportion of the total production of these farms was "sold" on an external market through a series of formal commercial transactions.

If freehold ownership and participation in these urban and international markets meant that northern agriculture did not have many of the characteristics of a closed peasant or a pre-capitalist economy, they do not imply that this system of production and exchange was modern or that its members were motivated primarily by liberal, entrepreneurial, individualist, or capitalist values. Nor is it sufficient to describe these farming communities as "transitional" between the ideal-types of traditional and modern or pre-capitalist and capitalist. To adopt such an idealist approach is to substitute typology for analysis, to suggest a teleological model of historical development, and to ignore the specific features of this social and economic system. Rather, one must point to its central features: the community was distinguished by age- and wealth-stratification and (usually) by ethnic or religious homogeneity, while on the family level there was freehold property ownership, a household mode of production, limited economic possibilities and aspirations, and a safety-first subsistence agriculture within a commercial capitalist market structure. And then one must seek an understanding of the "coping strategies" used by individuals, groups, and governments to reconcile the competing demands, the inherent tensions, and the immanent contradictions posed by this particular configuration of historical institutions and cultural values.

It would be premature, at this point, to attempt a complete analysis of the *mentalité* of the pre-industrial yeoman population. Yet a preliminary examination may suggest both a conceptual framework for future research and the character of certain widely accepted values, goals, and behavioral norms. An important, and perhaps controversial, premise should be made explicit at the beginning. It is assumed that the behavior of the farm population constitutes a crucial (although not a foolproof) indicator of its values and aspirations. This epistemological assumption has an interpretive implication, for it focuses attention on those activities that dominated the daily lives of the population—in the case of this particular society, on the productive tasks that provided food, clothing, and shelter.

This process of production and capital formation derived much of its emotive and intellectual meaning from the cultural matrix—from the institutional character of the society. Work was arranged along familial lines rather than controlled communally or through a wage system. This apparently simple organizational fact was a crucial determinant of the historical consciousness of this farming population. For even as the family gave symbolic meaning and emotional significance to subsistence activities, its own essence was shaped by the character of the productive system. There was a complex relationship between the agricultural labor and property system of early America and its rural culture; and it is that matrix of productive activities, orga-

nizational structures, and social values which the following analysis attempts (in a very preliminary fashion) to reconstruct.

Because the primary economic unit—the family—was also the main social institution, production activities had an immense impact on the entire character of agrarian life. Family relationships could not be divorced from economic considerations; indeed, the basic question of power and authority within the family hinged primarily on legal control over the land and—indirectly—over the labor needed to work it. The parents (principally the husband) enjoyed legal possession of the property—either as freeholders, tenants or sharecroppers—but they were dependent on their children for economic support in their old age. Their aim, as Greven has pointed out, was to control the terms and the timing of the transfer of economic resources to the succeeding generation.

The intimate relationship between agricultural production and parental values, between economic history and family history, is best approached through a series of case studies. The first of these small family farms began in 1739 with the arrival in Kent, Connecticut, of Joseph Fuller. At one time or another Fuller was an investor in an iron works, a "typical speculative proprietor," and a "rich squatter" who tried to deceive the Connecticut authorities into granting him (and his partner Joshua Lassell) 4,820 acres of provincial land. Fuller's energy, ambition, and activities mark him as an entrepreneur, even a "capitalist." Yet his behavior must be seen in the widest possible context, and the motivation assessed accordingly. When this restless man arrived in Kent at the age of forty (with his second wife), he was the father of seven sons, aged two to sixteen; thirteen years later, when his final petition for a land grant was rejected, he had nine sons, aged eleven to twenty-nine years, and five daughters. With fourteen children to provide with land, dowries, or currency, Fuller *had* to embark on an active career if he wished to keep his children (and himself and his wife in their old age) from a life of landless poverty.

In the event, fecundity overwhelmed the Fullers' financial ingenuity. None of the children of Joseph Fuller ever attained a rating on the tax list equal to the highest recorded for their father, and a similar pattern prevailed among the sons of the third generation. The total resources of the Fuller "clan" (for such it had become) grew constantly over time—with nine second- and twelve third-generation males appearing on the tax lists of Kent—but their per capita wealth declined steadily. The gains of one generation, the slow accumulation of capital resources through savings and invested labor, had been dispersed among many heirs.

Such divisions of limited resources inevitably roused resentment and engendered bitter battles within farm families. Ultimately, the delicate reciprocal economic relationship between parents and children might break down completely. Insufficiency of land meant that most children would have to be exiled—apprenticed to wealthier members of the community or sent out on their own as landless laborers—and that parents would have to endure a harsh old age, sharing their small plot with the remaining heir. High fertility and low mortality threatened each generation of children with the loss of class status; the unencumbered inheritance of a freehold estate was the exception, not the rule.

Even in these circumstances—as a second example will suggest—the ideal for many dispossessed children remained property ownership and eventual control of the transfer process with regard to their own offspring. "My parents were poor," an "Honest Farmer" wrote to the *Pennsylvania Packet* in 1786,

> and they put me at twelve years of age to a farmer, with whom I lived till I was twenty one . . . I married me a wife— and a very working young woman she was—and we took a farm of forty acres on rent. . . . In ten years I was able to buy me a farm of sixty acres on which I became my own tenant. I then, in a manner, grew rich and soon added another sixty acres, with which I am content. My estate increased beyond all account. I bought several lots of outland for my children, which amounted to seven when I was forty-five years old.
>
> About this time I married my oldest daughter to a clever lad, to whom I gave one hundred acres of my out-land.

Was this "success story" typical? Did the "Honest Farmer" minimize the difficulties of his own ascent and exaggerate the prospects of his seven children, each of whom would have to be provided with land, livestock, or equipment? It is clear, at any rate, that this Pennsylvanian enjoyed a crucial advantage over Joseph Fuller; he could accumulate capital through the regular sale of his surplus production on the market, and offer economic assistance to his children. His grandchildren, moreover, would grow up in the more fully developed commercial economy of the early nineteenth century. Ten years of work as a farm laborer—and an intense commitment to save— would now yield a capital stock of five hundred dollars. With this sum invested in equipment, livestock, and supplies, it would then be feasible to rent a farm, "with the prospect of accumulating money at a rate perhaps double that possible by wage work." To begin with less than five hundred dollars was to increase dependence on the landlord—to accept a half-and-half division of the produce rather than a two-third share. In either case, there was a high financial and psychological price to be paid. For many years these young adults would be "dependent," would work as wage laborers without security, as sharecroppers without land, or as mortgagors without full independence; their labor would enrich freeholders, landlords, and bankers even as it moved them closer to real economic freedom.

The process is readily apparent in a third case study, an archetypical example of the slow but successful accumulation of productive agricultural property in the mid-nineteenth century. In 1843 a young farmer in Massachusetts bought an old farm of 85 acres for $4,337; "in order to pay for it, I mortgaged it for $4,100, paying only $237, all that I had, after buying my stock." Nine years later it was clear that some progress had been made, for he had "paid up about $600 on the mortgage, and laid out nearly $2,000 in permanent improvements on my buildings and farm." This hard-working farmer was "a little nearer the harbor than I was when I commenced the voyage," but he was still $3,500 in debt and had interest payments of $250 to make each year. These obligations might be met in ten or fifteen years, but by then new debts would have to be incurred in order to provide working capital for his children. This farmer would die a property owner, but . . . some of his offspring would face a similarly time-consuming and difficult climb up the agricultural ladder.

Two features of the long-term process of capital formation through agricultural production revealed by these case studies stand out as particularly important, one static and the other dynamic. The recurrent factor was the continual pressure of population on the existing capital stock; the rate of natural increase constantly threatened to outstrip the creation of new productive resources: cleared land, machinery, housing, and livestock. This danger is demonstrable in the case of the Fuller clan, and its specter lurks in the prose of the "Honest Farmer" and his younger accumulation-oriented counterpart in Massachusetts. Economic prosperity was the result of unremitting labor by each generation. Only as farm parents began consciously to limit their fertility were they able to pass on sizable estates to their children—and this occurred primarily after 1830.

What changed—from the seventeenth to the early nineteenth century—was the increased rate of capital formation stemming from the expansion of the market economy; the growing importance of "unearned" profits because of the rise in the value of land and of other scarce commodities; and the extent to which middlemen dominated the processes of agricultural production and of westward migration. These three developments were interrelated. All were aspects of an increasingly important system of commercial agriculture that generated antagonistic social relationships and incipient class divisions. These alterations brought greater prosperity to those farmers whose geographic locations and cultural values were conducive to market activity. . . .

The lineal family—not the conjugal unit and certainly not the unattached individual—thus stood at the center of economic and social existence in northern agricultural society in pre-industrial America. The interlocking relationship between the biological life cycle and the system of agricultural (and domestic) production continued to tie the generations together even as the wider economic structure was undergoing a massive transformation and as the proportion of farming families in the population was steadily declining. Most men, women and children in this yeoman society continued to view the world through the prism of family values. This cultural outlook—this inbred pattern of behavior—set certain limits on personal autonomy, entrepreneurial activity, religious membership, and even political imagery. Lineal family values did not constitute, by any means, the entire world view—the *mentalité*—of the agricultural population, but they did define a central tendency of that consciousness, an abiding core of symbolic and emotive meaning; and, most important of all, they constituted a significant and reliable guide to behavior amid the uncertainties of the world.

POSTSCRIPT

Did Capitalist Values Motivate the American Colonists?

Both Henretta and Lemon defend their arguments on the basis of their own research into primary sources. Their opposing interpretations stem from the differing assumptions both historians make. In the first place, Lemon believes that the settlers of southeastern Pennsylvania placed "individual freedom and material gain over that of public interests. Put another way, the people planned for themselves much more than they did for their communities." Henretta, on the other hand, argues that Lemon has been unduly influenced by the principles of neo-Whig historians writing in the 1950s and has imposed these twentieth-century values onto eighteenth-century settlers. Synthesizing a number of recent studies about the colonial family, Henretta concludes that "an intimate relationship 'existed' between agricultural production and parental values, between economic history and family history." Henretta turns Lemon's entrepreneurial argument against him when Lemon admits that language and religious beliefs often exerted a considerable influence on the location and actions of a number of the ethnic groups that settled in southeastern Pennsylvania. Lemon, however, strongly disagrees with this criticism. In his "Comment on James A. Henretta's 'Family and Farms,' " *William and Mary Quarterly* (October 1980), Lemon accuses Henretta of "detaching families from society" and retreating "toward a nostalgic populism of self-sufficient families."

Another area of disagreement in the two readings centers on "the timing of historical change." Lemon argues that a middle-class society of expectant capitalists based on the "accumulation of property is central from the first settling of America onward." But Henretta views colonial America as a precapitalist society, possessing a *mentalité* of traditional old world religious, family, and agrarian values. He believes that the transition to a bourgeois industrial society started after 1750 and gradually expanded until it encompassed America in the 1820s and 1830s.

In the survey "The Social Development of Colonial America," *Race, Class and Politics* (University of Illinois Press, 1986), colonial scholar Gary Nash shrewdly observes that the argument between Henretta and Lemon may be false because Henretta's evidence comes from his portrait of New England families while Lemon's theory is based upon an intensive study of one portion of a major Pennsylvanian colony. But Nash comes up with an astute geographical explanation of his own that is neglected by both authors. He notes that the geographical differences between thin-soiled New England and the rich, alluvial soil of Pennsylvania may explain why the Middle colonists may have been more entrepreneurial as commercial farmers than their New England counterparts. This, Nash says, may be due to the fact that in pre-Columbian times the Native Americans of the mid-Atlantic left far greater amounts of tillable soil to the future European emigrants than the Algonquians did in the New England area.

A major study synthesizing the past two decades of research on the social structure of colonial America is needed. Jackson Turner Main's *The Social Structure of Revolutionary America* (Princeton, 1965) emphasizes mobility in frontier regions and the subsistence of farming communities, as well as the economic inequalities within the towns and most commercial regions. Main's work is a good starting point, but it is dated, narrow in its time frame, and probably optimistic in its conclusions. More critical and with an excellent introduction to a collection of primary sources and interpretative essays is Gary Nash's *Class and Society in Early America* (Prentice Hall, 1970).

Most research on the class structure of colonial America focuses on case studies of local communities. Nearly everyone agrees that the middle-class democracy thesis perpetuated by neo-Whig historians underestimates income inequalities among the settlers. But the issue is a complex one. Recent research points out how tenancy can be interpreted in a variety of ways. Studies of dissatisfied tenants scorned as the "idle and dissolute" who fall in status and live in permanent poverty can be found in Stephen Innes, "Land Tenancy and Social Order in Springfield, Massachusetts, 1652 to 1702," *William and Mary Quarterly* (October 1978); Gregory Stiverson, *Poverty in a Land of Plenty: Tenancy in Eighteenth-Century Maryland* (Johns Hopkins, 1977); and Edward Countryman, *A People in Revolution: The American Revolution and Political Society in New York, 1760–1790* (Johns Hopkins, 1981). A more favorable view, which argues that tenants had rights, often achieved mobility, and were able to extract favorable terms from their landlords, can be found in Sung Bok Kim, *Landlord and Tenant in Colonial New York: Manorial Society, 1664–1775* (University of North Carolina Press, 1978). Lucy Siler reworked some of the same data as Lemon in a very sophisticated analysis of the subject, "Tenancy in Colonial Pennsylvania: The Case of Chester County," *William and Mary Quarterly* (October 1986). She distinguishes among three groups of tenants: *householders* who were real tenants who rented and occupied the lands or buildings of another, and *inmates* and *freemen* who were not only nonland*owners* but also nonland*holders*.

Finally, both Lemon and Henretta have written broader essays that substantiate their original premises. See, for example, Lemon's "Early Americans and their Social Environment," *Journal of Historical Geography,* 2 (1980). Sharon V. Salinger has also addressed in great detail the labor question and the shift from lineal to entrepreneurial values near the end of the eighteenth century. As she argues in *To Serve Well and Faithfully: Labor and Indentured Servants in Pennsylvania, 1682–1800* (Cambridge University Press, 1987), "The traditional outlook, in which this mutuality and communal spirit dominated, [began to collapse during the late colonial period] and was replaced by the 'entrepreneurial spirit.' "

ISSUE 5

Did American Slaves Develop a Distinct African American Culture in the Eighteenth Century?

YES: Allan Kulikoff, from *Tobacco and Slaves: The Development of Southern Cultures in the Chesapeake, 1680–1800* (University of North Carolina Press, 1986)

NO: Jean Butenhoff Lee, from "The Problem of Slave Community in the Eighteenth-Century Chesapeake," *William and Mary Quarterly* (October 1986)

ISSUE SUMMARY

YES: Professor of history Allan Kulikoff claims that Chesapeake slaves developed their own social institutions and a distinct indigenous culture in the years between 1740 and 1790.
NO: Associate professor of history Jean Butenhoff Lee emphasizes the difficult and often unsuccessful efforts of slaves to create a stable family and community life in eighteenth-century Maryland.

The arrival at Jamestown, Virginia, in 1619 of a Dutch frigate carrying 20 Africans marked a momentous event for the future development of England's North American colonies. The introduction of a new racial component generated political, economic, and social repercussions that are still felt in modern America. With the development of black slavery, American colonists set the stage for a long-term moral dilemma that ultimately produced the bloodshed and destruction of civil war.

In the last 30 years, historians have given considerable attention to colonial American slavery. Their research, however, has left unresolved a question regarding those first Africans in Jamestown: Were the first blacks in England's North American colonies immediately bound out as slaves? While the evidence is inconclusive, there is strong reason to believe that the first Africans brought to Jamestown became indentured servants and were freed after fulfilling their contracts to their masters. These individuals formed the basis for the nation's free black population, which by 1860 would number approximately five hundred thousand.

If slavery did not originate with those first Africans, when did the institution appear? The process was remarkably gradual in the Chesapeake where the first slave codes were not enacted by the Virginia and Maryland legislatures until the 1660s. Some extant records, however, suggest that the status of "slave" was being given to black servants at least 20 years prior to the appearance of a *de jure* system. In 1640, John Punch, a black servant, was arrested with two white fellow servants for running away. All were found guilty, and the two white men were whipped and given additional time to serve on their indentures. Punch, however, was only whipped. The court record revealed that since he was already serving his master for life, no time could be added on. In other words, John Punch was a slave.

By 1750, the institution of slavery had emerged in all the British colonies in North America. The preponderance of male bondsmen, however, prevented American slave populations from expanding naturally. Masters, therefore, depended upon shipments from Africa for new slaves until the sex ratio achieved greater parity. In addition, heavy concentrations of slaves did not appear until the rise of large plantations. In New England, such plantations were limited to Rhode Island's Narragansett Valley; in the Middle colonies, New Yorkers and Pennsylvanians acquired some extensive lands worked by slaves; and in the South, large plantations cultivating tobacco and rice appeared in the eighteenth century.

This, however, tells us little about the slaves themselves. How did they live? What was the scope of their lives? Was there a slave community in the colonial period?

In the following essays, Allan Kulikoff contends that only with a more equal sex ratio, large plantations, and concentrated numbers of bondsmen could slaves develop a community life apart from that of their masters. These characteristics emerged in the Chesapeake area between 1740 and 1790 and permitted slaves to establish a recognizable, autonomous African American culture. Jean Butenhoff Lee agrees that the development of African American slave community life was a gradual process, but she challenges Kulikoff's conclusions regarding the emergence of an autonomous slave community. By focusing on a single county, Lee determines that African American family and communal life was quite fragile and subject to constant disruption. The contacts among slaves on a single plantation or on adjacent plantations, she asserts, were so limited as to preclude the kind of community life Kulikoff describes.

YES
Allan Kulikoff

ORIGINS OF BLACK SOCIETY

Although the eighteenth-century Chesapeake planter looked upon newly enslaved Africans as strange and barbaric folk, he knew that American-born slaves could be taught English customs. Hugh Jones, a Virginia cleric, commented in 1724 that "the languages of the new Negroes are various harsh jargons" but added that slaves born in Virginia "talk good English, and affect our language, habits, and customs." How readily did slaves in Maryland and Virginia accept English ways? Did the preponderance of whites in the region's population and their power force slaves to accept Anglo-American beliefs, values, and skills? Or did slaves succeed in creating their own institutions despite white repression? . . .

How readily slaves could form their own culture depended upon both the pattern of forced African immigration to the Americas and the economic and demographic environment that awaited new slaves. Black forced immigrants came from hundreds of different communities and did not have a common culture. Their religious beliefs, kinship systems, and forms of social organization differed substantially. Nevertheless, West Africans did share some values and experiences. For example, each West African group developed different kinship practices, but throughout the region each person located his place in society by his position in his kin group and lineage. When Africans arrived in the New World, their cultural differences were initially of greater significance than the values they shared. They shared only their experience as slaves and labored to make a new society out of their common beliefs and values. The features of the society they formed depended upon the demands of the white masters, the characteristics of the economy, the demography of slave and white populations, and the extent of ethnic division among blacks. As they interacted daily, slaves learned to cope with ordinary problems of working, eating, marrying, and child rearing under the adverse conditions of slavery. The social institutions they developed were neither imposed by Europeans nor directly taken from African communities, but were a unique combination of elements borrowed from the European enslavers and from the common values of various African societies. As soon as slaves formed social institutions, internal conflict diminished, and blacks could place a new Afro-American culture into a settled social context.

The size of working units that masters organized, the number of Africans they bought from slavetraders, and the crops they grew, as well as the rules they required their slaves to follow, influenced the kind of communities their slaves could form. Economic decisions by thousands of masters determined both the density of the black population and the proportion of whites in the population, and these demographic patterns in turn set limits on the intensity of slave community life. The choice of crops was crucial. Some crops required large plantations; others could be grown on small farms. Since large plantations needed more slaves than small farms, large planters purchased greater numbers of African slaves, and consequently, regions dominated by large plantations had greater concentrations of slaves and a larger proportion of Africans in their slave population than regions dominated by farms. Slaves who lived on a large plantation in a region where a substantial majority of the people were enslaved and the density of the slave population was high probably had more opportunities to worship their gods, begin stable families, and develop their own communities than did slaves who lived on small quarters in a preponderantly white country. A slave who lived with many Africans in a place where continual heavy importation of blacks kept the proportion of Africans high was more likely to adopt African customs than the slave who lived where

importation was sporadic, the proportion of immigrants among black adults low, and the number of whites great.

This model explains the development of black society in the Chesapeake colonies quite well. African and Afro-American slaves developed a settled life there very slowly. Three stages of community development can be discerned. From roughly 1650 to 1690, blacks assimilated the norms of white society, but the growth of the number of blacks also triggered white repression. The period from 1690 to 1740 was an era of heavy slave imports, small plantation sizes, and social conflicts among blacks. The infusion of Africans often disrupted newly formed slave communities. Finally, from 1740 to 1790, imports declined and then stopped, plantation sizes increased, the proportion of blacks in the population grew, and divisions among slaves disappeared. Consequently, native blacks formed relatively settled communities. . . .

TOWARD AFRO-AMERICAN SLAVE COMMUNITIES

The demographic conditions that prevented blacks from developing a cohesive social life before 1740 changed during the quarter of a century before the Revolution, as immigration of Africans to the Chesapeake declined sharply. Only 17 percent of Virginia's adult blacks in 1750 and 15 percent in 1755 had arrived within the previous ten years, and these newcomers went in relatively greater numbers to newer piedmont counties than had their predecessors. . . .

As the number of enslaved Africans in tidewater declined, the internal division among blacks diminished. These recent arrivals were under greater pressure than their predecessors to acquire the language, values, and beliefs of the dominant native majority. Like new Negroes before them, they sometimes ran away, but with less success. On arrival, they found themselves isolated and alone. Olaudah Equiano, for example, was brought to Virginia in 1757 at age twelve. "I was now exceedingly miserable," he later wrote, "and thought myself worse off than any . . . of my companions; for they could talk to each other, but I had no person to speak to that I could understand. In this state I was constantly grieving and pining, and wishing for death." But once slaves like Equiano learned English, they became part of the Afro-American community. Bob, twenty-nine, and Turkey Tom, thirty-eight, were new Negroes who lived on the home plantation of Charles Carroll of Carrollton in 1773. Since Bob and Tom were apparently the only two recent immigrant slaves on any of Carroll's many plantations, they both could participate fully in plantation life. Bob was a smith, a position usually reserved for natives; he married the daughter of a carpenter and lived with her and their two children. Tom, a laborer, also found a place in the plantation's kinship networks: his wife was at least a third-generation Marylander. Very few Africans probably ever became artisans, but so few Africans were imported that most Africans in tidewater could find wives among the native majority. . . .

The size of quarters increased after 1740 throughout tidewater, providing greater opportunities for slaves to develop a social life of their own. The proportion who lived on units of more than twenty slaves doubled in St. Mary's County, increased by half in York and Anne Arundel counties, and grew, though more slowly, in Prince George's.

In the 1780s, one-third to two-thirds of the slaves in eleven tidewater counties lived on farms of more than twenty slaves, and only a sixth to a tenth lived on units of fewer than six. If these counties were typical, 44 percent of tidewater's blacks lived on farms of more than twenty slaves, and another 26 percent lived on medium-sized units of eleven to twenty. The number of very large quarters also grew. Before 1740 few quarters housed more than thirty slaves, but by the 1770s and 1780s the wealthiest gentlemen ran home plantations with more than one hundred slaves and quarters with thirty to fifty. . . .

Because plantation sizes increased, more lived on quarters away from the master's house and his direct supervision. On small plantations the quarter could be located in an outbuilding or in a single dwelling. On large plantations, the quarters resembled small villages. Slave houses and the yards that surrounded them were centers of domestic activity. The houses were furnished with straw bedding, barrels for seats, pots, pans, and usually a grindstone or handmill for beating corn into meal. Agricultural tools and livestock were scattered outside the houses, and the quarter was surrounded by plots of corn and tobacco cultivated by the slaves.

Afro-Americans made the quarters into little communities, usually organized around families. Because the African slave trade largely ceased, the adult sex ratio decreased. Almost all men and women could marry, and by the 1770s many slaves had native grandparents and great-grandparents. The quarter was the center of family activity every evening and on Sundays and holidays, for except during the harvest, slaves had these times to themselves. Nonresident fathers visited their wives and children; runaways stayed with friends or kinfolk. In the evenings native men sometimes traveled to other quarters, where they passed the night talking, singing, smoking, and drinking. On occasional Sundays they held celebrations at which they danced to the banjo and sang bitter songs about their treatment by the master. . . .

After 1740, the density of the black population and the proportion of slaves in the population of tidewater both increased, and, as a result, the area's slave society gradually spread out to embrace many neighboring plantations in a single network. Ironically, masters provided slaves with several tools they could use to extend these cross-quarter networks. Slave sales tore black families asunder, but as masters sold and transferred their slaves, more and more kinfolk lived on neighboring quarters, and naturally they retained ties of affection after they were separated. Whites built numerous roads and paths to connect their farms and villages, and their slaves used these byways to visit friends or run away and evade recapture. By the 1770s and 1780s, Afro-Americans numerically dominated many neighborhoods and created many cross-plantation networks. . . .

Quarters were connected by extensive networks of roads and paths, which grew remarkably complex during the eighteenth century. For example, Prince George's County had about 50 miles of public roads in 1700, but 478 in 1762, or one mile of public road for every square mile of taxed land in the county. This elaboration of roads made it easier for slaves to visit nearby plantations. Whites could not patrol all these roads, let alone private paths not maintained by the county, without a general mobilization of the white population. . . .

The Afro-Americans made good use of these opportunities to create their own society. In the years before the Revolution, they developed a sense of community with other slaves both on their own plantations and in the neighborhood. This social solidarity can be shown in several ways. In the first place, Afro-Americans often concealed slaves from within the neighborhood on their quarters. Since masters searched the neighborhood for runaways and placed notices on public buildings before advertising in a newspaper, many runaways, especially truants who were recaptured or returned voluntarily after a few days' absence, were not so advertised. The increasing appearance of such advertisements in the *Maryland Gazette* during the thirty years before the Revolution suggests that slaves were becoming more successful in evading easy recapture. The numbers of runaways in southern Maryland rose in each five-year period between 1745 and 1779, except the years 1765-1769, and the increase was especially great during the Revolution, when some escaped slaves were able to reach British troops. . . .

The slave community, of course, had its share of conflicts, and on occasion a slave assaulted or stole from another slave. Nonetheless, accounts of several of these incidents suggest that the rest of the slave community united against the transgressors. Slaves sometimes refused to testify against their fellows, especially when blacks stole goods from whites, but when a member of the black community was hurt, slaves testified against the guilty person to protect themselves or their property. In May 1763 Jack poisoned Clear with a mixture of rum and henbane; she became ill and died the following February. Six slaves who belonged to Clear's master informed him of the act and testified against Jack in Prince George's court. They were joined by three slaves who lived on nearby plantations. The jury found Jack guilty, and he was sentenced to hang. Similarly, when Tom (owned by Richard Snowden, a prominent ironmaker) broke into Weems's quarter (near the Snowden ironworks) in Anne Arundel County and took goods belonging to Weems's slaves, six men and women owned by James and David Weems testified against him. He was found guilty and hanged.

There were limits to slave solidarity. Though native-born slaves often remained loyal to immediate kinfolk and friends on their own quarters, to more distant kinfolk, and to slaves on nearby or distant plantations, these loyalties sometimes clashed with each other or with the demands of the master. Then slaves had to choose sides in intricate master-slave conflicts. The development of these alliances can be seen in the response of Landon Carter and of his slaves when Simon, Carter's ox-carter, ran away in March 1766. Carter had Simon outlawed, and joined the militia to hunt for him. Simon was aided directly by at least six residents of his quarter, including an uncle, a brother, and a sister-in-law. Nonetheless, several other kinfolk, who lived on other quarters, were forced by Carter to inform against him. Finally, after two weeks, Talbot (another of Carter's slaves who lived some distance from Simon) shot Simon in the leg and, with the aid of several other slaves, recaptured him.

THE ORIGINS OF AFRO-AMERICAN CULTURE

Slaves in the Chesapeake, unlike those in the West Indies, took several generations to form a semiautonomous Afro-American culture. West Africans needed settled communities to develop the bundle of common values and beliefs they brought over with them into a syncretic culture, but the demographic environment of the early eighteenth-century Chesapeake was extremely hostile to the formation of settled communities. Heavily white populations, high black sex ratios, continually declining proportions of Africans among slaves, conflicts between African and creole slaves, and small unit sizes all made the development of both slave communities and slave culture difficult. African forced migrants did not forget these values, however, but used behavioral symbols of them whenever they could. These Africans practiced their beliefs in disconnected and often private episodes, not in daily social interaction with many other slaves. African slaves in the Chesapeake made tribal drums, strummed on their banjos, poisoned their enemies as did African witches and cunning men, passed on a few African words to their descendants, and sometimes engaged in private devotions to Allah or their tribal gods.

Afro-American slaves had developed strong community institutions on their quarters by the 1760s and 1770s, but the values and beliefs they held are difficult to ascertain. Since blacks in the Chesapeake region did not achieve a settled social life until after a heavy African slave trade stopped and since whites continued to live in even the most densely black areas, one would expect slave culture in the region to reflect white values and beliefs. Even native-born slaves had little choice either about their work or about the people who lived with them in their quarters. Nevertheless, they had a small measure of self-determination in their family life, in their religion, and in the ways they celebrated and mourned. When they could choose, Afro-American slaves simultaneously borrowed from whites and drew on the values and beliefs their ancestors brought from West Africa to form a culture not only significantly different from that of Anglo-Americans but also different from the culture of any West African group or any other group of North American slaves.

The ways Afro-American slaves organized their family life indicates most clearly how they used both African and Euro-American forms to create a new institution compatible with their life under slavery. By the time of the Revolution, most slaves lived in families, and slave households were similar to those of their white masters. About as many creole slaves as whites lived in two-parent and extended households. Whites lived in monogamous families, and only scattered examples of the African custom of polygyny can be found among creole blacks. Slavery forced the kinfolk of extended families to live very close to one another on large plantations, where they played and worked together. By contrast, whites only occasionally visited their extended kinfolk and worked in the fields only with their children, not with adult brothers and sisters. This closeness fostered a sense of kin solidarity among Afro-Americans. They named their children after both sides of the family (but interestingly enough, daughters were not often named after their mothers). And they sometimes refused to marry within the plantation even when sex ratios were equal: many of the available potential partners were first cousins, and black slaves apparently refused to marry first cousins. This may have represented a transformation of African marriage taboos that differed from tribe to tribe but tended to be stricter than those of Chesapeake whites, who frequently married first cousins.

West African religions varied remarkably among themselves, yet enslaved Africans shared a similar way of viewing the world, which they passed on to their native black children. All activities, Africans believed, were infused with sacredness, each in its own particular way. Religion was not universal but was practiced only within a communal context. God, spirits, animals, and plants were all seen in relation to people in the community, and certain men—rainmakers, medicine men, priests, sorcerers—had special powers over spirits or material life not available to most people.

In contrast, the Anglican faith practiced by most slaveholders in the Chesapeake before the Revolution radically separated the sacred from the secular: Anglicans attended church services in isolated buildings on Sundays but often ignored religious ceremonies the rest of the week. Although native slaves occasionally accepted the outward signs of Christian belief, few became convinced Protestants. Their children were baptized, and sometimes they received religious instruction. All three Anglican clergymen of Prince George's County reported in 1724 that they baptized slave children and adults (especially native-born adults) and preached to those who would listen. In 1731 one Prince George's minister baptized blacks "where perfect in their Catechism" and "visit[ed] them in their sickness and married them when called upon." Similar work continued in Virginia and Maryland in the generation before the Revolution. Nonetheless, Thomas Bacon, a Maryland cleric and publisher of a compendium of the colony's laws, believed that these baptized slaves were often "living in as profound Ignorance of what Christianity really is, (except as to a few outward Ordinances) as if they had remained in the midst of those barbarous Heathen Countries from whence their parents had been first imported."

Native-born slaves continued to observe African forms of mourning and celebrating, but they did not place these forms within the structure of Anglican religion, nor did masters give them time enough to expand these occasional ceremonies into an indigenous Afro-American religion. Whites sometimes observed these strange practices. Thomas Bacon, for instance, preached to blacks on Maryland's Eastern Shore in the 1740s at services they directed "at their *funerals* (several of which I have attended)—and to such small congregations as their *marriages* have brought together." Two early nineteenth-century observers connected similar services they saw to the slaves' remote African past. Henry Knight, who traveled to Virginia in 1816, explained that masters permitted slaves a holiday to mourn the death of a fellow slave. The day of the funeral, "perhaps a month after the corpse is interred, is a jovial day with them; they sing and dance and drink the dead to his new home, which some believe to be in old Guinea," the home of their grandparents and great-grandparents. A Charlotte County, Virginia, cleric saw more solemn but equally emotional services. He contended that there were "many remains . . . of the savage customs of Africa. They cry and bawl and howl around the grave and roll in the dirt, and make many expressions of the most frantic grief . . . sometimes the noise they make may be heard as far as one or two miles."

The slaves' music and dance, though often unconnected to their religion, displayed a distinctly African character. Afro-American slaves continued to make and to play two instruments (the banjo and balafo) of African origin. In 1774 Nicholas Cresswell, a British visitor, described slave celebrations in Charles County, Maryland. On Sundays, he wrote, the blacks "generally meet together and amuse themselves with Dancing to the Banjo. This musical instrument . . . is made of a Gourd something in the imitation of a Guitar, with only four strings." "Their poetry," Cresswell reported, "is like the music—Rude and uncultivated. Their Dancing is most violent exercise, but so irregular and grotesque. I am not able to describe it." Cresswell's reaction to the dancing suggests that it contained African rhythms unknown in European dance. If the form was African, it was placed in an American context: the slave songs Cresswell heard "generally relate the usage they have received from their Masters or Mistresses in a very satirical stile and manner."

Native slaves retained folk beliefs that may have been integral parts of West African religions. Slaves sometimes turned to magic, sorcery, and witchcraft to resolve conflicts within their own community or to strike back at harsh or unreasonable masters. Some African medicine men, magicians, sorcerers, and witches migrated and passed on their skills to other slaves. These men were spiritual leaders (or powerful, if evil men) in many African communities, including those of the Ibos, and they continued to practice among creole slaves who believed in their powers. Several examples suggest the prevalence of these beliefs. William Grimes was born in King George County, Virginia, in 1784; his narrative of his life as a runaway suggests that he was terrified by a woman he thought was a witch, that he feared sleeping in the bed of a dead man, and that he consulted fortune-tellers. Dissatisfied slaves might consult conjurers to discover how to poison their masters. In 1773, for instance, Sharper was accused by his master, Peter Hansbrough of Stafford County, Virginia, of "Endeavouring to Procuring Poison from a Negroe Doctor or Conjurer as they are Call'd" for an unknown but dangerous purpose after Hansbrough had "discovered Some behaviour in . . . Sharper which occasioned [him] to be more Strict in inquiring into . . . where he Spent his time in his absent hours." Similarily, two slave blacksmiths in Spotsylvania County were convicted of attempting to poison their master in 1797, but seventy-six local residents petitioned the state for clemency because the slaves had been influenced by "a Negro Wench, or conjurer of Mr. James Crawford."

Afro-American slaves did not transform these disparate fragments of African cultures into a new slave religion until the development of white evangelical religion during the decades before and after the Revolution. Revivalist preachers permitted and even encouraged slaves to adapt African forms to the Christian faith. The most intensive black religious activity was in southside and central piedmont Virginia, areas with the Chesapeake's highest concentrations of new Negroes. The first evangelical mission to slaves began in 1755, when two white Baptists organized a black congregation on William Byrd's plantation in Mecklenburg County; that group of Christians lasted until the Revolution. Samuel Davies, a Presbyterian clergyman who practiced in Hanover County, and several of his colleagues converted as many

as a thousand slaves to evangelical Protestantism in the 1750s. Davies thought that these blacks were true Christians, not only acquainted with "the important doctrines of the Christian Religion, but also a deep sense of things upon their spirits, and a life of the strictest Morality and Piety." They placed African music into Protestant liturgy: "The *Negroes,*" Davies commented, "above all of the human species that ever I knew, have an ear for Music, and a kind of delight in Psalmody." Some of his converts even "lodged all night in my kitchen; and sometimes, when I have awakened about two or three a-clock in the morning, a torrent of sacred harmony poured into my chamber, and carried my mind to heaven."

The numbers of Afro-Americans attracted to evangelical Protestantism rose slowly in the 1770s and then increased rapidly during the awakenings of the 1780s and 1790s. By 1790, about 7 percent of Virginia's black adults were members of Baptist or Methodist churches, and far more were affected by the revivals in both piedmont and tidewater counties. Slave work patterns and the authority of masters might be affected by this new and all-encompassing religiosity. For instance, some members of the Episcopal church in King George County complained in the mid-1780s that "Preachers or Exhorters" daily gathered "together Multitudes of People in the Woods most of them Slaves, alienating their minds from their Daily Labour and their Masters Interest."

Blacks accepted the exhortations of Baptist and Methodist preachers in the 1780s and 1790s far more enthusiastically than did whites. They answered the preacher's call with crying, shouting, shaking, and trembling. Their reaction was perhaps in part dictated by their African past: the ceremonies of revivals were similar to those of some African religions, and African forms meshed well with the emerging theology of evangelical Protestantism. Revivals, unlike the liturgy of rational religion, allowed slaves to reduce the distinctions between sacred and secular and return to a holistic, African kind of religiosity.

Afro-American slaves developed their own social institutions and indigenous culture during the second half of the eighteenth century. A period of great disruptions among blacks early in the century was followed by a time of settled communities. Newly enslaved Africans came to the Chesapeake colonies in large enough numbers to cause conflicts between native slaves and new Negroes, but the migration was too small to allow Africans to develop syncretic communities and cultures. It was only when native adults began to predominate that earlier conflicts among blacks were contained and families and quarter communities began to emerge. The culture these creole slaves forged put African forms of behavior into Euro-American familial and religious structures. Creole slaves by that time were two or three generations removed from Africa and (except in southside Virginia) infrequently saw Africans. They may not have been aware of the complicated origins of their behavior.

For the slaves, the origins of their culture were less important than its autonomy. White observers agreed that the music, dance, and religiosity of black slaves differed remarkably from those of whites. The emergence of black culture, and especially the beginnings of Afro-Christianity, played an important role in the development of slave solidarity. Slaves possessed little power over their lives: they suffered the expropriation of the fruits of their labor by their masters; they could be forced to move away from family and friends at a moment's notice; they were subject to the whip for any perceived transgressions. The practice of a distinctive culture within their own quarters gave them some small power over their own lives and destinies they otherwise would not have possessed.

The development of an indigenous black community life and culture had a great impact upon the social structure of the entire region. Afro-Americans became both an enslaved working class and a racial caste, separate from their white masters. They had their own system of social relations among themselves, within the context of slavery. Even though whites continued to possess remarkable power over blacks, they had to relate to slaves as a group with a structure and culture they could not entirely control. Afro-American communal life and culture, then, set minimal bounds on white behavior and encouraged black solidarity.

NO

Jean Butenhoff Lee

THE PROBLEM OF SLAVE COMMUNITY IN THE EIGHTEENTH-CENTURY CHESAPEAKE

In the spring of 1774, a young Englishman named Nicholas Cresswell crossed the Atlantic, entered Chesapeake Bay, and came to safe anchorage on the Rappahannock River. From there, three black oarsmen rowed him north on the bay as far as the broad mouth of the Potomac River, then upriver along the shores of St. Mary's and Charles counties, Maryland. On the afternoon of May 21, Cresswell reached his destination, the tiny village of Nanjemoy in southwestern Charles County.

A week later, as he was becoming acquainted with the sights and sounds of the Tobacco Coast, Cresswell attended what he called a "Negro Ball" near Nanjemoy. "Sundays being the only days these poor creatures have to themselves," he wrote, "they generally meet together and amuse themselves with Dancing to the Banjo," a four-stringed gourd "something in the imitation of a Guitar." Some of the slaves also sang "very droll music indeed," songs in which "they generally relate the usage they have received from their Masters or Mistresses in a very satirical stile and manner." The newcomer pronounced the music and verse "Rude and uncultivated," the dancing "most violent excercise . . . irregular and grotesque." With a hint of disbelief he concluded that the slaves "all appear to be exeedingly happy at these merry-makings and seem as if they had forgot or were not sensible of their miserable condition."

Cresswell's account is the kind of infrequent literary evidence that historians of the black experience in early America cherish for its clues to social intercourse among the enslaved, to their distinctive and expressive folk art, their use of leisure hours, and their resistance to the slave labor system, if only in lyrical satire. That Sunday in 1774 the Englishman observed a manifestation of what several scholars have argued was a recent development in the Chesapeake tidewater: stable Afro-American communities, a distinctive amalgam forged in the demographic experience of blacks during

From Jean Butenhoff Lee, "The Problem of Slave Community in the Eighteenth-Century Chesapeake," *William and Mary Quarterly*, 3rd ser., vol. 43 (July 1986). Reprinted by permission.

the preceding century. By the era of the American Revolution, it is argued, slave population growth had proceeded far enough that many blacks could exercise substantial control over their labor and leisure. They maintained reasonably stable family lives, extensive kin networks, and social intercourse that transcended plantation boundaries. The present article describes this interpretation more fully, offers a general critique of it, and employs quantifiable and narrative sources to examine slave life in the heavily black tidewater county that Cresswell observed. The evidence from Charles County does not deny that slaves sought to create communal life but emphasizes what a difficult—and often unsuccessful—effort it must have been.

RELYING ON PROBATE INVENTORIES COMpiled between 1658 and 1730 in Charles and three adjacent counties on Maryland's lower Western Shore, Russell R. Menard has suggested that the few slaves who lived there in the seventeenth century must have endured an isolated and dehumanizing existence. Most were adult males. Housed mainly on small plantations, they lived out their brief lives in a dreary round of clearing land, tending livestock, and growing tobacco and corn. They were cut off from their African culture, no longer part of kin groups through which African societies were organized, and often unable to find wives and form families. Importation of large numbers of Africans during the late seventeenth and early eighteenth centuries exacerbated the sexual imbalance among blacks, for adult males predominated in slave cargoes.

Allan Kulikoff hypothesizes that skewed sex ratios, small plantations, and the presence of many Africans persisted un-til about 1740. These conditions, he holds, impeded the development of a distinctive Afro-American culture because the experiences of Chesapeake and African slaves were different. Blacks who were born in the Chesapeake or who lived there for some time presumably were more or less assimilated to life in the white-dominated society of the Tobacco Coast. Periodically their lives were disrupted by the arrival of newcomers fresh from Africa, people of many ethnic groups who spoke a babel of languages, worshiped an array of deities, were bereft of family ties, and had to learn new ways of life and labor. Successive infusions of Africans, Kulikoff argues, therefore delayed formation of a society that was distinctively Afro-American.

Menard and Kulikoff agree that important demographic changes in the eighteenth century heralded the emergence of more settled social conditions and greater cultural homogeneity among slaves. First, the black population began to grow by natural increase, and importations from Africa declined. As a result, the proportion of children increased, and the ratio of men to women improved. In other words, as the slave population changed from largely immigrant to native-born, it gradually acquired more normal demographic characteristics. Second, slave population density increased, as did the number of large plantations. These factors allegedly led to widened opportunities within bondage. Some slaves escaped wearisome toil in the fields to become artisans or domestics. Others gained a measure of autonomy over their lives by being assigned to quarters where whites were not regularly present. For many more, a growing, sexually balanced, and largely native-born population clustered on large plantations was conducive, in Menard's words, to "social contact, intimate personal relationships, and a stable family life." By 1790, Kulikoff contends, "native blacks formed relatively settled communities," both within and among plantations. The linchpin of this argument is demographic change: as a native-born, sexually balanced black population experienced natural growth, and as population density and plantation size also increased, these conditions provided the basis for family and community life, occupational diversity, and autonomy.

Kulikoff has located this important transition in the years 1740 to 1790. He has also attempted to establish the distribution of the Chesapeake slave population and to explore some of the social and cultural consequences. He cautions that research on the region is incomplete, that his conclusions are based at least partly on unprovable assumptions, and that relationships between demographic and economic conditions, on the one hand, and slave society and culture, on the other, are "difficult to determine." He nevertheless believes that between 1740 and the American Revolution, in the area from "just north of the Patuxent" River in Anne Arundel and Prince George's counties, Maryland, "to just south of the James" River in Virginia, "plantations were large, black population density was high, few whites were present," and "well developed" road networks linked plantations. Slaves in this broad region "could create a rudimentary cross-plantation society," a process whites facilitated by selling slaves within their neighborhoods. Whereas blacks rarely lived in groups of more than thirty before 1740, "by the 1770s and 1780s the wealthiest gentlemen ran home plantations with more than one hundred slaves and quarters with thirty to fifty." By the 1780s, Kulikoff

argues, perhaps 44 percent of the enslaved resided on large quarters (those with more than twenty blacks); another 4 percent were men on smaller units located near "many large quarters." Yet another 26 percent lived on middling plantations, in groups of eleven to twenty, "and could participate in the family and community activities of their quarters." Composing the last one-fourth of the slaves, he contends, were "women and children who lived on small plantations . . . [and] usually did not travel from quarter to quarter but had to wait for husbands and fathers to visit them."

Kulikoff holds that, before the Revolution, slaves "developed strong community institutions on their quarters" and formed complex, cross-plantation kin networks. Balanced sex ratios enabled most men and women to marry, and by the 1770s the majority of Afro-Americans lived in families and had households "similar to those of their white masters. About as many creole slaves as whites lived in two-parent and extended households." Grandparents and even great-grandparents were common. A family or two usually inhabited the small plantations, while "extended families in which most residents were kinfolk" occupied the large units. Because slave dwellings on large plantations usually were located, Kulikoff claims, at some distance from the master's house, their occupants spent many hours of their lives free of direct white supervision. By the 1780s, one-half to three-fourths of the slaves living in the Chesapeake tidewater "enjoyed some sort of social life not controlled by their masters." Slaves socialized with one another, tended gardens located in the yards surrounding their quarters, sang and danced at gatherings like the one Nicholas Cresswell witnessed in 1774, traveled from one plantation to another to visit friends and relatives, gave food and other help to runaways, and protected themselves from harm at the hands of fellow bondsmen and bondswomen.

THIS CONCEPTION OF BLACK LIFE NOW DOMinates discussion of slavery in the eighteenth-century Chesapeake. Yet it remains unproven. The obscurity in which most slaves lived obstructs historians' efforts to reconstruct their lives, nor have scholars made full use of the sources that are available. Information on the number of Africans carried to Maryland and Virginia—blacks who allegedly intruded upon existing slave communities—is incomplete. Data on their dispersal are fragmentary. Historians have little notion who purchased the Africans, whether they were bought singly or in groups, and whether they joined preexisting black households. The rate at which Africans reproduced, when natural increase began, and when a largely native-born black population emerged in the Chesapeake have not been determined with any precision.

Attempts to identify Afro-American family connections, moreover, often prove futile. Marriage and birth registers are rare for slaves. Masters' wills and inventories of estates only occasionally reveal kinship ties among a decedent's human chattels; when they do, these sources often link only a mother and her youngest child. The disruptions to which slaves were subjected—assignment to outlying quarters, hiring out, sale, and dispersal through gift or bequest—preclude any confident expectation that blacks who lived near one another were necessarily related. Nor does procreation by itself signify marriage or other enduring family commitments. The best evidence for slave families comes from the papers of a few great planters, but it is questionable whether kin connections that can be identified on some of the largest units were duplicated elsewhere, especially on smaller plantations.

The ruling interpretation leaves many questions to be answered with greater specificity. One would expect that growing population densities enhanced blacks' abilities to interact, find spouses, raise families, and create an Afro-American culture. But how dense was the slave population in the eighteenth-century Chesapeake? How many tidewater planters managed home plantations with more than one hundred blacks and quarters with thirty to fifty? How distant, typically, were slave dwellings from the master's house? If one-half to three-fourths of the blacks had "some sort of social life not controlled by their masters," is it believable that masters entirely controlled the lives of the rest of the enslaved?

Another problem concerns slaves' ability to interact across plantation boundaries. Road networks, high black population densities, and the practice of selling or otherwise disposing of slaves—especially relatives and friends—within neighborhoods obviously increased opportunities for contact. How often contacts were actually made is, of course, another matter. As yet we know little about how slaves were dispersed geographically, about the extent of road and path networks across the Chesapeake, or about how easily slaves could travel—either furtively or with their masters' permission—from one plantation to another. We shall never know how many mothers walked through the night in order to lie with their children for a few hours, as Frederick Douglass remembered his mother doing in the nineteenth century. Nor shall we ever know how often a slave hurried to a neighboring plantation to warn a relative of imminent danger, as Charles Ball's grandfather did in the late eighteenth century when he learned that his son was about to be sold to a slave dealer. But we can be reasonably certain that most of the black laborers of the Chesapeake spent no more than a small part of their time en route to or visiting friends and relatives who were not housed on their own quarters. For most of their lives, slaves' chances for social interaction were limited to the fields and meadows, the quarters and woods, of their home plantations.

It is to the groups in which slaves passed most of their daily lives, then, that we need to look for whatever *regular* occasions existed for family life and social interaction. The first Federal census of 1790, which is extant for Maryland but not Virginia, offers an opportunity to glimpse the spatial distribution of blacks. The returns show that, for the end of the eighteenth century, generalizations about large plantations, high slave density, and the presence of few whites are overdrawn. Whites were not few; they outnumbered slaves by 43,091 to 42,681 in the five lower Western Shore counties of the Maryland sector of the Patuxent-to-James region. The average number of whites in slaveholding families was 5.2 to 5.5 by county; these families possessed an average of 7.8 to 11.4 blacks. Nor were large plantations the norm: the proportion of slaveholding families with 20 or more slaves was less than one in ten in three of the four counties for which such data are extant. In the other, Prince George's, 15.5 percent of the plantations can be classified as large. When families that did not have slaves are included, the percentages fall below 10 percent in all four counties. These figures hardly convey the impression that few whites and large plantations characterized the Maryland portion of the region. Before drawing conclusions, then, about opportunities for family formation and the development of Afro-American society and culture in the eighteenth-century Chesapeake, the spatial distribution of slaves deserves closer attention. Here is a subject for which many data exist, in the form of tax lists, censuses, and estate inventories. In fact, for the majority of blacks who toiled in the Chesapeake before 1800, the most common, often the only, documentary record we have of their existence, is their aggregate numbers. We need to get these numbers straight.

Charles County, in the heart of the region, is an advantageous place to examine the distribution of slaves. Its planters were heavily committed to tobacco production and slave labor. Furthermore, during the eighteenth century the number of large plantations, the proportion of slaves whose masters owned more than twenty blacks, and the ratio of blacks to whites in the whole population and in slaveholding households all increased. By 1790, black slaves were approaching a majority, and the county ranked third in Maryland in the number of black inhabitants, second in percentage of blacks, and first in the proportion of slaveowning families. . . .

For Charles County, the extant list enumerated two-thirds of both the white and slave populations. The distribution of slaves in 1782 exhibited some marked similarities to that of the 1750s. So far as can be documented, the proportion of households with adult slave laborers was about the same at the end of the War for Independence as it had been thirty years earlier. The highest concentration of blacks was still found in the lower hundred of William and Mary Parish, the lowest in Durham Parish in the western part of the country. In Pomonkey Hundred, slaveholding still hovered around 50 percent. Yet if the proportion of slaveholders and the concentration of blacks in the civil subdivisions of the county look much alike in the 1750s and early 1780s, the distribution of blacks among households does not. The taxable labor force became more heavily black during the intervening years. Moreover, the proportion of slaves whose masters owned more than ten taxable blacks increased, while the proportion whose masters held five or fewer declined. We also find that 81.4 percent of plantations had five taxable slaves or fewer in 1758, but that figure fell to 57.4 percent a generation later. And while less than 1 percent . . . of the plantations accounted for in the earlier set of tax records had adult slave labor forces in excess of twenty men and women, in 1782 the percentage stood at 5.8. . . .

During the era of the Revolution, then, Charles County slaves were experiencing the kind of demographic change that Menard predicted and Kulikoff has affirmed for the Chesapeake—a movement toward larger plantations where the possibilities for communal ties, family formation, and the sharing of tribulation and joy, of dreams and despair, presumably were significantly greater than in the period before 1730 when plantations were small and the average slave population density was much lower. How does the 1782 distribution of slaves in the ten hundreds of the county compare with what Kulikoff believes likely for the Chesapeake tidewater generally by the 1780s? First, notwithstanding the growth of the slave population, whites remained numerically dominant, 6,457 to 5,411. Second, Kulikoff's conjectures on plantation size, if applied to Charles County, consistently exaggerate the extent to which basic spatial distribution enhanced opportunities for slave family and communal life. His figures appreciably underestimate the proportion of slaves living in small groups of ten or fewer (44.9 percent in the county, 26 percent according to Kulikoff), are closer to the mark for the percentage living in groups of eleven to twenty (30.2 versus 26 percent), and significantly overestimate the proportion living on large plantations (25 percent versus 44 percent). Finally, no slaveowner held one hundred or more persons in bondage. Rather, the largest holding was sixty.

The 1782 assessment itself probably *overstates* the size of some slave groups because of the way it was taken. If a master had slaves in more than a single hundred of the county, they were counted for the hundred where they lived. But the tax lists do not reveal whether or how masters divided their slaves *within* hundreds. Owners of large tracts of land or separate tracts may well have stationed blacks on several quarters. In addition, slaves who were hired out were nevertheless credited to the master. Thus slaves were probably more scattered and less able to maintain regular contact with one another than the records disclose.

The wealth of data in the 1782 assessment enables one to move beyond generalizations about the number of slaves per master and to scrutinize at closer range 776 groups containing a total of 5,411 persons. Every slave, whether living in daily isolation from other blacks or in the largest group, can be placed in one of five age categories, and those in the most productive years of life can be distinguished by gender. From this evidence of the distribution of the youngest children and those who survived early childhood, of the comparative numbers of women and men of reproductive age, and of the proportion of slaves whose age and condition reduced their economic value, the most elementary boundaries of slave life emerge. . . .

Only on plantations with slaves in all five age/gender categories could the full range of daily contacts occur, between young and old, male and female, parent and child and perhaps grandparents. More than one-half of the slaves . . . tallied in the tax lists did *not* have that opportunity. Among the rest . . . , the opportunity was realized only if none of the groups was fragmented among quarters or through hiring out—a highly improbable circumstance. When one examines the age and gender groups plantation by plantation, moreover, it becomes obvious that many blacks endured a truncated existence of one kind or another, even if masters kept them all together. Examination of the holdings of masters who owned slaves in up to three of the age/gender categories reveals some distinctly constricted living arrangements in Charles County. On some quarters, children were without regular parental supervision and guidance. On others, men and women returning from the fields did not hear the voices of black children. Older slaves had no audience of young listeners to whom they could pass along memories of Africa, religious instruction, or advice about making the most of bondage. Women and children or, less commonly, men and children were the only occupants of some quarters; there young Afro-Americans lacked continuous contact not only with one parent but with any black adult of the absent gender who could serve as a model. . . .

The tax records demonstrate constraints that plantation agriculture placed upon blacks' ability to live in groups that, although not of their own choosing, at least included friends and relatives, males and females, young and old. The drawback of these records is that they yield a static picture. They reveal nothing about the experiences of slaves at other times in their lives, and they cannot even hint at the dislocations slaves endured at the whim of masters who hired or loaned them out, used them to satisfy debts, gave them away, or sold them for financial reasons or because they were recalcitrant. As probate records disclose, dislocation also occurred when masters died—a point deserving attention. In Charles County during the eighteenth century, slaves and land were the most valuable forms of wealth. Of these, the former were movable and easily more divisible. When a master died intestate, Maryland law prescribed that the slaves in the estate be divided among the widow, the surviving children, and the lineal descendants of children who had predeceased the parent. When masters wrote wills, they, too, customarily adopted partible inheritance of slave property. Significantly, among all parent-testators whose wills were filed for probate in the county between 1740 and 1784, daughters received a higher proportion of slave bequests than did sons. And it was daughters who, at marriage, usually moved to their husbands' land and took their slaves with them. Thus, for numerous reasons, no slave family or community escaped the threat of being torn apart. . . .

Many owners probably broke up slave groups with no more disquietude than merchant Thomas Howe Ridgate expressed when he wrote, "so adieu to [the] Negro's." When the tobacco crop was in the shed, when funds had to be raised to satisfy a debt or pay for a child's education, when children came of age, daughters married, or a widow died, when a slave mother weaned her infant, or when "any of the negroes shou'd misbehave, or . . . my Executors shou'd think it more to the advantage of my children that some of the negroes should be sold," then blacks who had endured bondage together were torn apart. In 1768 Roger Smith bequeathed to his wife a lifetime estate in two slave families, a couple with seven children and a woman with two. When Mrs. Smith remarried, her blacks came under the mastery of her new husband, though he could not sell or mortgage them. At her death these families descended intact to her brother-in-law, Basil Smith; but when he died in 1774, just six years after the initial bequest, the two slave families were parceled out in four lots. Another testator, Ann Dent, in 1764 gave mulatto Tom to one married daughter, Tom's wife Cate to a second married daughter, and the couple's son to a granddaughter. Whether or how often this slave family thereafter was allowed to reunite, even briefly, thus depended upon the location and decision of three different masters. Such parceling out, repeated again and again through several generations, certainly established dispersed kin networks, but how successful Afro-Americans were in using those networks, or how often they simply lost contact with parents, siblings, and spouses, is unknown.

The 1782 tax assessment lists and testamentary evidence show that it was not uncommon for children to be separated from their mothers, even at an early age. Sometimes masters planned to dispose of children still in the womb; at other times they deliberated what to do with a woman's "future increase." Ann Cornish decided that "as she had not a negroe apiece for each of her Grand Children she wou[ld] give them as they came into the World." Cebberamous, a bondswoman of Elizabeth Askin, was destined to lose "the first Child that . . . [she] shall bring to good." Theodocia Speake's slave Sue was similarly to be stripped of "the first Child that . . . [she] Brings that liveth a year & if in Case it Dieth in a year then the next Child the aforesaid negro Sue bringeth." Mothers—and fathers, too, if they were present—whose children remained with them only a year abruptly lost them just as they were beginning to explore the world on foot. Richard Maston's pregnant slave Venus kept her infant until it could babble and toddle but then had to relinquish it to a white couple who were to "take the Child . . . under their own immediate Care so soon as it . . . shall arrive at the Age of two years." Almost as if he were dealing out cards, Maximillion Matthews of Durham Parish in 1770 gave the first child of his slave woman Henny to his daughter, the second to his wife, and the third to his son, "and so Alternatively and respectively for all the increase that the said negro Henny may have."

Members of slave communities who were allocated among masters' wives, sons, daughters, and grandchildren could hope to see one another at least occasionally. And blacks who were temporarily hired out could look forward to returning to their home plantations at the termination of their contracts. Slave sales, especially public auctions, were a different matter. Masters who had a surplus of blacks or needed to raise funds, and executors who needed to clear an estate of debt, could not afford to be much concerned about ties among blacks.

Nor would they have gone to the trouble and expense of advertising in the *Maryland Gazette* and Virginia newspapers had they expected to dispose of slaves entirely in the immediate neighborhood.

Dispersal of Benjamin Fendall's blacks illustrates what could happen among even the largest slaveholders. Fendall owned a well-developed plantation on the Potomac River, rented some of his lands to tenants, and operated several mills and a bakery that sold ship bread to passing vessels. In addition to field hands, his slaves included a blacksmith, an "ingenious fellow" who "is a Carpenter, Cooper, Shoemaker, and Tanner," a waiter, and "a fine Cook Wench, who is a good Seamstress, and can do any Kind of House-work." During his lifetime Fendall gave some of his slaves to his adult children. At his death in 1764, twenty-nine remained. These he willed to be sold, with the rest of his estate, to pay his debts and provide legacies for two children who were minors. Sale of the slaves was not swift: it was accomplished in two public auctions held six months apart. At the first, in the midst of the growing season in July 1764, seven males aged fourteen and above, one woman, and three children were sold. Then in January 1765 the executors disposed of all but one of the remaining slaves: eight males aged fourteen and above, six women, and four children. The twenty-nine slaves went to seventeen different masters. . . .

UNTIL RECENTLY, HISTORIANS HAVE PORtrayed North American slavery with too little sensitivity to time or place, so that it appeared a static rather than dynamic institution. They have also studied slavery mainly at what Ira Berlin has called its point of maturity: the antebellum years, which composed less than one-quarter of the time the institution existed in North America. Recent scholarship has helped to redress that imbalance by focusing on the preceding, formative centuries, and in that regard a paradigm based on Chesapeake demographic conditions is valuable. For most blacks in the Chesapeake before 1800, the only documentary evidence of their existence is their aggregate numbers set down in census and tax records and—for those listed in estate inventories—their names, gender, and age. The eighteenth-century data from Charles County suggest that it is time to refine and clarify the paradigm—to examine Chesapeake slave distribution more fully at the plantation level, to be sensitive to regional variations, and to establish more precisely the timing of demographic change.

In Charles County, the development of stable slave communities proceeded much more slowly than Menard or Kulikoff hypothesized in their pioneering work. Demographic encouragement of stability, moreover, never seems to have been as favorable as the current paradigm would suggest. True, the number of large plantations, the proportion of slaves living on those plantations, and the proportion of slaves in the county's population increased during the eighteenth century. Nonetheless, it would distort reality to apply to the county the prevailing interpretation of slave distribution in the Chesapeake tidewater. As late as 1782, large plantations, few whites, and high black population densities did not characterize Charles County. Rather, 45 percent of the enslaved were held by masters who owned ten or fewer slaves, and another 30 percent by masters who had eleven to twenty. Whites continued to outnumber blacks, as they had throughout the eighteenth century. These demographic factors need to be considered in relation to masters' treatment of slaves as property, to be acquired and disposed of at pleasure. The result was an Afro-American family and communal life that was markedly fragile and subject to disruption.

POSTSCRIPT

Did American Slaves Develop a Distinct African American Culture in the Eighteenth Century?

The essays by Kulikoff and Lee both suggest that the emergence of a cohesive African American community life was a gradual process that occurred over the course of two centuries. They differ not on the question of whether slaves attempted to create a communal life for themselves in the Chesapeake, but rather on the degree of success achieved by bond servants in gaining control over their community institutions. Kulikoff's conclusions are supported by Russell Menard, whose demographic studies provide a wealth of information on the colonial Chesapeake region. See "The Maryland Slave Population, 1658 to 1730: A Demographic Profile of Blacks in Four Counties," *William and Mary Quarterly* (January 1975) and "From Servants to Slaves: The Transformation of the Chesapeake Labor System," *Southern Studies* (Winter 1977). Although attention has focused largely on colonial Virginia and Maryland, you can examine further support for the Kulikoff thesis in William D. Piersen, *Black Yankees: The Development of an Afro-American Subculture in Eighteenth-Century New England* (University of Massachusetts, 1988).

How much African American culture was inspired by African survivers? How much cultural baggage did Africans bring with them to the New World? Anthropologist Melville Herskovits argued in *The Myth of the Negro Past* (1941) that numerous elements of West African culture survived the "middle passage" and were adapted by slaves to their New World environment.

Despite the fact that historians of slavery have generally focused upon the antebellum period, there is a significant body of literature pertaining to the colonial period. The details of the Atlantic slave trade are treated best in Basil Davidson, *Black Mother: The African Slave Trade: Precolonial History, 1450–1850* (Little, Brown, 1961); Daniel P. Mannix, *Black Cargoes: A History of the Atlantic Slave Trade, 1518–1865* (Viking Press, 1962); and Philip D. Curtin, *The Atlantic Slave Trade: A Census* (University of Wisconsin, 1969). The origins of slavery in the British mainland colonies are debated in Oscar and Mary Handlin, "The Origins of the Southern Labor System," *William and Mary Quarterly* (April 1950); Carl N. Degler, "Slavery and the Genesis of American Race Prejudice," *Comparative Studies in History and Society* (October 1959); and Winthrop Jordan, "Modern Tensions and the Origins of American Slavery," *Journal of Southern History* (February 1962). The development of black slavery in various British mainland colonies is treated in Mechal Sobel, *The World They Made Together: Black and White Values in Eighteenth-Century Virginia* (Princeton University Press, 1987), and Peter H. Wood, *Black Majority: Negroes in Colonial South Carolina from 1670 Through the Stono Rebellion* (Knopf, 1974).

ISSUE 6

Was the Great Awakening a Key to the American Revolution?

YES: William G. McLoughlin, from " 'Enthusiasm for Liberty': The Great Awakening as the Key to the Revolution," in Jack P. Greene and William G. McLoughlin, *Preachers and Politicians: Two Essays on the Origins of the American Revolution* (American Antiquarian Society, 1977)

NO: Jon Butler, from "Enthusiasm Described and Decried: The Great Awakening as Interpretative Fiction," *Journal of American History* (September 1982)

ISSUE SUMMARY

YES: Professor of history William G. McLoughlin claims that the Great Awakening, by promoting religious revitalization, intercolonial unity, and democracy, paved the way for the American Revolution.

NO: Professor of religious studies Jon Butler challenges the validity of the term "Great Awakening" and argues that a link between the eighteenth-century colonial religious revivals and the American Revolution was virtually nonexistent.

Although generations of American school children have been taught that the British colonies in North America were founded by persons fleeing religious persecution in England, the truth is that many of those early settlers were motivated by other factors, some of which had little to do with theological preferences. To be sure, the Pilgrims and Puritans of New England sought to escape the proscriptions established by the Church of England. Many New Englanders, however, did not adhere to the precepts of Calvinism and, therefore, were viewed as outsiders. The Quakers who populated Pennsylvania were mostly fugitives from New England, where they had been victims of religious persecution. But to apply religious motivations to the earliest settlers of Virginia, South Carolina, or Georgia is to engage in a serious misreading of the historical record. Even in New England the religious mission of (the first governor of the Massachusetts Bay Colony) John Winthrop's "city upon a hill" began to erode as the colonial settlements matured and stabilized.

Although religion was a central element in the lives of the seventeenth- and eighteenth-century Europeans who migrated to the New World, proliferation of religious sects and denominations, emphasis upon material gain in all parts of the colonies, and the predominance of reason over emotion that is associated with the Deists of the Enlightenment period all contributed to a gradual but obvious movement of the colonists away from the church and clerical authority. William Bradford (the second governor of Plymouth Colony), for example, expressed grave concern that many Plymouth residents were following a path of perfidy, and William Penn (founder of Pennsylvania) was certain that the "holy experiment" of the Quakers had failed. Colonial clergy, fearful that a fall from grace was in progress, issued calls for a revival of religious fervor. The spirit of revivalism that spread through the colonies in the 1730s and 1740s, therefore, was an answer to these clerical prayers.

The episode known as the First Great Awakening coincided with the Pietistic movement in Europe and England and was carried forward by dynamic preachers such as Gilbert Tennent, Theodore Frelinghuysen, and George Whitefield. They promoted a religion of the heart, not of the head, in order to produce a spiritual rebirth. Although the degree to which the Great Awakening influenced the colonies is disputed, several consequences can be firmly established. The revivals, for example, reinvigorated American Protestantism. Many new congregations were organized as a result of irremediable schisms between "Old Lights" and "New Lights." Skepticism about the desirability of an educated clergy sparked a strong strain of anti-intellectualism. Also, the emphasis on conversion was a message to which virtually anyone could respond, regardless of age, sex, or social status.

For some historians, the implications of the Great Awakening extend beyond the religious sphere into the realm of politics and the American Revolution. To what extent is the argument suggesting a relationship between religion and revolution valid?

In the following selections, William G. McLoughlin contends that the roots of the War for Independence were clearly imbedded in the Great Awakening. He argues that the democratic ideals associated with the American Revolution were spawned by the itinerant preachers who encouraged greater democracy in the religious lives of their listeners, making the Revolution nothing less than a political revitalization of a people whose religious regeneration began with the Great Awakening. Jon Butler claims that the link between the revivals and the American Revolution was virtually nonexistent. This period of revivalism, he argues, generated democracy only minimally and provided little focus for intercolonial unity. He concludes with the suggestion that historians abandon the concept of the "Great Awakening" because, in reality, the mid-eighteenth-century revivals did not produce the kinds of dramatic changes, religious or political, frequently ascribed to them.

YES   William G. McLoughlin

THE GREAT AWAKENING AS THE KEY
TO THE REVOLUTION

No one doubts that the Americans were basically a very religious people. The First Great Awakening in the 1730s (which we associate with the preaching of Jonathan Edwards, George Whitefield, Theodore Frelinghuysen, Samuel Davies, and Gilbert Tennet) and the Second Great Awakening in the early nineteenth century (which we associate with the frontier camp meetings) prove that. It can also be shown that American patriots (with the possible exception of Thomas Jefferson) intended to create, and did so, not a secular nation but a Christian nation (with paid chaplains for Congress and the military, tax exemption for all church property, and 'In God We Trust' on our coinage). But the intransigent problem continues to plague us when we seek precisely for any implicit or overt religious aspects of the Revolution.

One way to solve this puzzle is to define religion in such a broad way as to describe the Revolution itself as a quasi-religious movement. . . . But there is another strategy which I am convinced is equally important and which I shall utilize here. That is to demonstrate that the roots of the Revolution as a political movement were so deeply imbedded in the soil of the First Great Awakening forty years earlier that it can be truly said that the Revolution was the natural outgrowth of that profound widespread religious movement.

The anthropologist Kenelm Burridge has said, "All religions are basically concerned with power. . . . Religions are concerned with the systematic ordering of different kinds of power": the power of God over life and death, disease and health; the power of the parent over the child or the husband over the wife; the power of the law over the criminal or the state over the citizen. "No religious movement," Burridge argues, "lacks a political ideology." That is to say, no religious movement can avoid having some assumptions about the right and wrong ways in which power and authority can be used. What we call "politics" is really our agreement as groups or nations as to how we wish to enforce a particular code of behavior (which is assumed to be godly) upon those who dissent from it.

From William G. McLoughlin, " 'Enthusiasm for Liberty': The Great Awakening as the Key to the Revolution," in Greene and McLoughlin, *Preachers and Politicians: Two Essays on the Origins of the American Revolution* (American Antiquarian Society, 1977). Copyright © 1977 by the American Antiquarian Society. Reprinted by permission.

If we accept this broad anthropological definition of religion, we can begin to understand why the Great Awakening of 1735 to 1765 was so important, and why it had such a profound impact upon the Revolution. During this generation the British colonists revised in very drastic ways their conception of how God's power should and would operate in North America—and, by extension, how it ought to operate everywhere in the world. In the end the Founding Fathers were fighting, as they said, not just for the rights of Englishmen but for the rights of mankind. . . .

The central feature of the great revivals of the 1730s and 1740s was the experience of individual conversion. New Light ministers (Whitefield, Edwards, Davies, Tennent, Frelinghuysen) told their congregations that men and women did not gain favor or forgiveness from God simply by learning or by conforming to the man-made creeds of a church or to the prevailing moral standards of their community. God demanded a higher standard of spiritual commitment than that. He demanded total submission to his will, complete repentance for sins and utter obedience to his commands. And for a variety of reasons multitudes of Americans felt the need for such forgiveness and submission.

Historians have now shown pretty convincingly that Americans in the early years of the eighteenth century were very uncertain of their relationship to God as well as of their relations with one another. The original zeal of the earlier generations of pious settlers, struggling to win a beachhead on the stern frontier along the coast, had worn thin. In all the colonies the people were badly divided over questions of mercantile and land development. Times were prosperous.

There were many opportunities to grow rich. Neighbor began to vie with neighbor, merchant with merchant, in aggressive, competitive ways, scrambling to make the most of the New World's fabulous resources. Normally decent people began to cut moral corners, to abuse their offices, to slight their social responsibilities in order to engage in sharp dealing for private profit. This in turn produced an increasing number of lawsuits over alleged frauds or violations of contract. Town meetings became bitter, quarrelsome affairs and frequently one part of a town or county petitioned the legislature to settle problems which the local judicial or political system could not. Parish ministers were unable to appeal effectively to conscience, moral law, or communal harmony to reconcile angry factions within their congregations and were themselves often at odds with their parishioners over salaries or religious taxes. The poor began to accuse the rich of oppression and to attack the learned clergy for siding with the upper class against the common interest. Though few acknowledged it, increasing social and economic tensions produced increasing guilt feelings and pangs of conscience. People seemed to have lost that close relationship with God and each other which had marked the earlier generations of settlers.

Looking back, the historian can see these anxieties as part of the growing pains of the colonies as they adjusted to the New World environment and began to abandon the old ways they had known in Europe. As towns matured and land became scarce and expensive, the old patriarchal relationships and community spirit gave way to change and migration. The rapid expansion of seaports and market towns and the growing size of the population and its rapid movement westward in search of cheaper land and greater opportunities could not help but affect loyalty, the ties of friendship, the covenant of the church, and the respect for the parish minister. As these institutional constraints failed to preserve order, the more devout churchgoers began to lose faith in the authority of the church and the state. Somehow the old system seemed to be breaking down. The old ways of acting and believing, sharing and trusting no longer carried authority. The institutions of the old corporate social order were suffering what the sociologists call a crisis of cultural legitimacy. But no one knew what to do about it.

In this uneasy state of affairs the emergence of revival ministers preaching a doctrine of immediate repentance from sin and immediate conversion to God aroused an inordinate amount of attention after 1735. Pious people were anxious to know why God was angry with them and seemed to have departed from their midst. They wanted to regain their standing in God's good graces. When the Reverend George Whitefield arrived from England in 1739, he had already established a reputation as a successful revivalist in the old country. Americans found his style of preaching strikingly different from what they had been hearing in their local parish churches. Many were caught up in the enthusiasm aroused by this twenty-three-year-old evangelist as he traveled from town to town along the whole Atlantic coast of North America. Even Benjamin Franklin, who went to hear him with considerable skepticism in Philadelphia, was so excited by his words that he emptied his pockets into the collection plate. Jonathan Edwards's wife in Massachusetts said that it is "wonderful to see what a

spell he casts over an audience. . . . I have seen upwards of a thousand people hang on his words with breathless silence, broken only by an occasional half-suppressed sob." One ordinary farmer in Connecticut who saddled his horse, hoisted his wife up behind him, and rode madly into town to hear Whitefield said that when the preacher mounted the platform erected for him on the village green, "He lookt almost angellical, a young, slim, slender youth before some thousands of people & with a bold, undaunted countenance, & my hearing how god was with him everywhere as he came along, it solumnized my mind & put me in a trembling fear before he began to preach, for he looked as if he was Cloathed with Authority from the great god." Americans believed in God, in heaven and hell, in damnation, and in miracles. Their suppressed guilt and anxiety were overwhelmed when they were persuaded that Whitefield was a prophet of God, a man sent as God's messenger to arouse a sinful people from their wicked ways. And not only did God raise up Whitefield, but he raised up a host of other eloquent young revivalists to call the people back to the ways of God.

In describing the kinds of feelings which swept over them in these revival meetings or in retrospect afterwards, most converts agreed that what struck them most forcefully was not God's anger but his concern, his interest in helping them to mend their ways. The revivalists preached hellfire for the wicked but they also promised rewards to the repentant. . . .

What this kind of conversion experience seemed to be telling Americans as it swept over the colonies was that God does not work through kings and bishops, through a learned clergy or an upper class of the rich and wellborn, but through the people themselves. Out of the death of the old covenanted ideal of the corporate community was born the new republican ideal of government by consent. . . . It was fortunate perhaps that after 1765 the king and Parliament began to tighten imperial control over the colonies, for in doing so it allowed the new force unleashed by the Awakening to turn against this outside, alien foe rather than against the internal authorities in the colonies. The guilt which had been internalized prior to 1735 and which had caused such turmoil during the Awakening was projected outward after 1765 upon a common enemy. New Light religion absorbed social anxiety and private guilt into a political reformation which, the colonists told themselves, was as much for the purification of old England as for the reformation of New America. . . . Religious and political regeneration merged in a triumphant effort to realize the rising glory of God in America.

In addition to changing American social and ecclesiastical institutions the Awakening brought about a very critical turning point in American theology. As a result of the Awakening American pietists came to believe that they had a special role to play in God's providential plan for the redemption of mankind. By 1765 the whole significance of millennialism had been transformed in America. Prior to the Awakening theologians in America had universally preached that the millennium would occur only when Christ returned to earth to set right the wicked ways of this world. The second coming had to precede the millennium because men themselves were too wicked ever to create a perfect social and moral order. Increase Mather had been so fearful of the barbarous influence of the frontier environment that he predicted "that in the glorious times promised to the Church on Earth, America will be Hell." But by 1745 the glorious showers of blessing spread by God throughout the colonies had caused a far different and more optimistic interpretation to arise. American theologians began to argue that perhaps God meant to convert all the people of America and then to enlist them to help prepare the way for Christ's return by creating a perfect social order in the New World. No less a theologian than Jonathan Edwards expounded this new postmillennial optimism in a series of sermons in 1742. Christ will not return to earth before the millennium, he said, but after it. What was more, the New Jerusalem would not be accomplished all at once "by some miracle" but will be "gradually brought to pass" through the work of man. "It is not unlikely that this work of God's Spirit [the Awakening], so extraordinary and wonderful, is the dawning, or at least a prelude of that glorious work of God so often foretold in Scripture which, in the progress and issue of it, shall renew the world of mankind. . . . We cannot reasonably think otherwise than that the beginning of this great work of God must be near. And there are many things that make it probable that this work will begin in America." In this postmillennial view of American destiny it was manifest that Americans were the successors of the Jewish nation, the chosen people of God, God's New Israel. As such they had a mission to serve as the avant-garde of God's millennial kingdom on earth.

As this opinion spread after 1742 throughout the colonies, many came to believe that Americans could not effectively fulfill this mission so long as they were tied to a corrupt, oppressive, and tyrannical monarch and Parliament in England. In the years 1765 to 1775 those imbued with this new light God had shed during the Awakening became convinced that God was trying to show them how much more important it was to adhere to his higher laws than to the man-made laws of Parliament. Regardless of a man's denomination, this post-millennial optimism influenced many colonists to believe in 1775 that God had ordained, planned, and guided the British colonies to that moment when they must take their destiny into their own hands. Only in a purified and perfect republican social order, which guaranteed political and religious liberty to all men, could their mission to the world be accomplished. Thereafter the rights of Englishmen became the inalienable rights of mankind and the Americans felt obliged to bring the blessings of liberty to the rest of the world. . . .

[W]hen the crisis of institutional authority began in the colonies in the 1730s and when the old hierarchical, corporate order seemed unable to provide harmony and leadership, the common folk began to have serious doubts about its validity. The efforts of the "authorities" to oppose the religious enthusiasm of the Great Awakening only contributed . . . to the downfall of the old order. The upper orders in church and state insisted that the revivalists were fanatical demagogues causing disorder in the parishes and invading the rights and privileges of the settled parish ministers; by causing schisms in the churches and disputes over religious taxes they were undermining the laws. So itinerant preachers were fined, jailed, and banished, and when their converts accused the parish ministers of being enemies to God and oppo-

nents of his divine outpouring of grace, many of them were put in jail for refusing any longer to pay taxes to support such sadducees and pharisees. In Anglican Virginia the Baptists were regularly jailed and mobbed right up until 1775 on the grounds that their revivals disturbed the civil peace and their churches were not properly licensed by the state.

The Awakening also produced bitter quarrels and schisms in the Middle Colonies where there was no established church system but where conservative ministers in the Dutch Reformed and Presbyterian churches opposed the fervent religious enthusiasm of the revival. It is significant that even George Whitefield and Gilbert Tennent (though not Jonathan Edwards) encouraged pious converts to leave their parish churches and go to hear New Light preaching if their parish ministers were not converted and therefore could not support God's work. Over 125 parishes in New England were split between New Lights and Old Lights by the 1750s and many more such schisms took place in the middle and southern colonies.

These decisions, made by thousands upon thousands of individuals, thinking and acting entirely upon their own responsibility and risking their livelihood, their status, and the welfare of their families, constitute the religious foreshadowing of the political decisions taken in 1775 for or against separation from the empire. The New Light nonconformists would not contribute in person or in purse to the continued support of corrupt religious institutions which opposed God's law, denied the freedom of conscience of individuals, and utilized the power of the state to oppress those who did God's will. These dissenters from the established order in parishes and counties across the colonies were taken to jail, fined, or had their household goods sold at auction by the local sheriff for engaging in civil disobedience to the powers that be. But they chose to obey God rather than man. Having done so once, they were fortified to do so again after 1765 in protest against the injustices of the Stamp Act, the Coercive Acts, the Admiralty laws, and the tea tax. Something crucial happened in the Awakening: in that great religious upheaval the colonists learned to judge for themselves and to act out of their own consciences. By 1776 it had become axiomatic that "disobedience to tyrants is obedience to God."

Fortunately for the Christian churches in the colonies the great majority of their ministers eventually came to agree with the New Lights. They concluded that the Great Awakening was truly a work of God. Hence America was spared that anticlericalism which wreaked such havoc in the French and Russian revolutions where the clergy allied themselves with the old order. By 1765 the New Lights had come to predominate in most of the Protestant denominations and even had strongly influenced the young Catholic churches in the colonies. Only, as might be expected, in a hierarchy where church appointments derived directly from the secular authority of the king, that is, in the Anglican Church, did the parish priests side with the ancien régime.

The Awakening also helped the colonies to develop a new kind of intercolonial unity. Some historians have seen this unity deriving essentially from the interdenominational concert among non-Anglican ministers after 1760 to oppose the appointment of an Anglican bishop for the colonies. Actually intercolonial unity preceded rather than followed this plan for "Christian Union" (as Ezra Stiles called it). The true basis for intercolonial unity lay in the system of itinerant preaching which played so important a part in spreading the New Light revival spirit after 1735. Itinerant preachers of all denominations, lay and clerical, followed Whitefield's example and toured from one colony to another gathering converts for their particular denominations or for all denominations. As the dissenting churches grew in number, the itinerants helped to unite them throughout the colonies. From these informal ties came the formal nationalization of the major Protestant denominations. Out of seeming disunity emerged a new order of union. The Revolutionary motto, "e pluribus unum," had its practical beginning in the religious unity of the New Light preachers. Although each particular Christian persuasion devoutly believed that its way of faith and practice was the one true way prescribed by God, all of them agreed that God's truth would prevail through religious freedom and did not need coercive uniformity. . . .

Less attention has been paid to the equally important fact that the itinerant revivalism of the generation of the Awakening fostered a new system of mass communication in America. Much has been made of the importance of colonial newspapers in spreading the word of republic ideology. Professor Harry Stout has recently noted that we must give equal attention to the role of itinerant preachers in spreading the word of God's New Light ideology which was its spiritual counterpart. When Stout argues that itinerancy must be studied in terms of Marshall McLuhan's axiom that 'the medium is the message,' he does not mean to denigrate the religious or doctrinal content of the New Light preachers. He does mean that itinerants conveyed a message of free and voluntary individual choice in religious affairs simply by offering their message in village squares or private homes as an alternative to the official word from the parish, tax-supported, church. But equally as important was the way in which the itinerants preached that message of free choice. Not being cloaked with the authority of the state or with the familiarity of the local community, the itinerant spoke simply as one individual to another; he spoke outside of any temporal or territorial location. And in doing so he freed Americans forever from the Old World view that religious stability relied on having roots in a fixed place or parish. Itinerant preaching freed the individual to travel where he would by assuring him that wherever he went the word of God through divinely ordained messengers would reach him. And since itinerant preachers played down doctrinal and ecclesiastical differences in order to lay stress upon individual repentance and conversion, mobile Americans could rest assured that whatever denominational exhorter followed them to the frontier or from rural farm to coastal city the essential spiritual message he would hear would be the same: repent, throw yourself on God's mercy, and he will save and protect you personally by sending his spirit to dwell in your heart wherever you may roam or whatever community you may temporarily reside in.

At the same time, the itinerant, who frequently lacked any formal education and almost never had a college education, spoke to other men as equals. Not only did he eschew the parish church but he stood on the same ground as the people to whom he spoke; he lived at their level and spoke in their language.

Itinerancy democratized America's religion before the Revolution democratized its government. In preaching, the itinerant did not, because he knew he could not, order or command his hearers to conform. He was clothed only with spiritual authority and his power was based solely on his ability to persuade the individual listener to act upon his own free will. People who were rebellious against parental authority, or that of town fathers or legislators or royal governors or Parliament or their royal father in Buckingham Palace, could nevertheless accept attacks upon their sins and salvation for their guilt from an equal who had experienced the same psychological and spiritual problems. . . . Out of the Awakening came an individualized, non-theological, voluntary, and migratory ecclesiastical order perfectly suited to the needs of a people who had to shake off the institutional restrictions of an Old World order if they were ever to spread across the New World continent. . . .

Much has been made by social historians of the fact that the Enlightenment ushered in an era of concern for the benevolent care of the poor, the sick, the orphan, and the criminal. Philanthropic effort seemed to go hand-in-hand with the belief that science was teaching men better ways to heal and to rehabilitate those who had previously been considered inveterate sinners or children of the devil. Yet we can also credit the Great Awakening with a very similar impulse toward humanitarian reform. Jonathan Edwards defined true Christian virtue in 1756 as "interested benevolence to Being in general." Edwards's pupil Samuel Hopkins interpreted disinterested benevolence to mean devout Christian concern for the care and freedom of our fellow human beings. In 1773 Hopkins joined with Ezra Stiles (a minister who had not been overly friendly toward the New Light movement) in attacking the slave trade. And that same year some New Light Baptists in Boston, joined by others in the remote town of Ashfield, issued public broadsides against slavery itself. Here again we can see how the rationalists and pietists, starting from different parts of the republican-Christian world view, had arrived by 1775 at very similar positions. Jefferson, for his part, wrote into the Declaration of Independence a clause justifying rebellion on the grounds that George III had forced slavery upon his colonies.

Finally we can note that John Adams, though a Unitarian, and the Reverend John Witherspoon, a New Light Presbyterian, shared the same concern for the importance of public virtue in the new republic. Adams spoke of the United States of America as a "Christian Sparta"—a nation whose citizens should be as willing to sacrifice themselves for the good of their country as the Spartans at Thermopylae and at the same time as dedicated to God as the Christians who were thrown to the lions by the Emperor Nero. Witherspoon, who served in the Continental Congress while at the same time remaining president of the New Light college in Princeton, New Jersey, said, "In free States where the body of the people have the supreme power properly in their own hands and must be ultimately resorted to on all great matters if there be a general corruption of manners there can be nothing but confusion. So true is this that civil liberty cannot long be preserved without virtue. A monarchy may subsist for ages, and be better or worse under a good or bad prince; but a republic once equally poised must either preserve its virtue or lose its liberty." Adams and Witherspoon, the rationalist and the pietist, represent the two sides of the Revolutionary coin, the connection between the Awakening and the Revolution. The Enlightened rationalist provided Americans with a theory of political science which stated that it was a natural law that government must be by the consent of the governed, that it must preserve inalienable natural rights, that it must have checks and balances, but that it must depend ultimately upon the willingness of the individual citizen to sacrifice his own comfort and welfare for the good of the commonwealth. The pietist provided Americans with a religious ideology which said that God's power inhered essentially in the free and voluntary consent of the individual, that Americans were God's chosen people, that true virtue required disinterested benevolence toward all mankind, and that without total commitment to God's higher law as expressed in his holy word no nation could save itself from corruption and tyranny.

. . . [T]he Revolution can be described as the political revitalization of a people whose religious regeneration began in the Great Awakening. Regeneration or cultural rebirth was the key which unlocked the door to the new household of the republic.

NO   Jon Butler

THE GREAT AWAKENING

How do historians describe "the Great Awakening"? Three points seem especially common. First, all but a few describe it as a Calvinist religious revival in which converts acknowledged their sinfulness without expecting salvation. These colonial converts thereby distinguished themselves from Englishmen caught up in contemporary Methodist revivals and from Americans involved in the so-called Second Great Awakening of the early national period, both of which imbibed Arminian principles that allowed humans to believe they might effect their own salvation in ways that John Calvin discounted. Second, historians emphasize the breadth and suddenness of the Awakening and frequently employ hurricane metaphors to reinforce the point. Thus, many of them describe how in the 1740s the Awakening "swept" across the mainland colonies, leaving only England's Caribbean colonies untouched. Third, most historians argue that this spiritual hurricane affected all facets of prerevolutionary society. Here they adopt [Jonathan] Edwards's description of the 1736 Northampton revival as one that touched "all sorts, sober and vicious, high and low, rich and poor, wise and unwise," but apply it to all the colonies. Indeed, some historians go farther and view the Great Awakening as a veritable social and political revolution itself. Writing in the late 1960s, [Richard] Bushman could only wonder at its power: "We inevitably will underestimate the effect of the Awakening on eighteenth-century society if we compare it to revivals today. The Awakening was more like the civil rights demonstrations, the campus disturbances, and the urban riots of the 1960s combined. All together these may approach, though certainly not surpass, the Awakening in their impact on national life."

No one would seriously question the existence of "the Great Awakening" if historians only described it as a short-lived Calvinist revival in New England during the early 1740s. Whether stimulated by Edwards, James Davenport, or the British itinerant George Whitefield, the New England revivals between 1740 and 1745 obviously were Calvinist ones. Their sponsors vigorously criticized the soft-core Arminianism that had reputedly

From Jon Butler, "Enthusiasm Described and Decried: The Great Awakening as Interpretative Fiction," *Journal of American History*, vol. 69 (September, 1982). Copyright © 1982 by the Organization of American Historians. Reprinted by permission.

overtaken New England Congregational-ism, and they stimulated the ritual renewal of a century-old society by rein-troducing colonists to the theology of distinguished seventeenth-century Puri-tan clergymen, especially Thomas Shep-ard and Solomon Stoddard.

Yet, Calvinism never dominated the eighteenth-century religious revivals ho-mogenized under the label "the Great Awakening." The revivals in the middle colonies flowed from especially disparate and international sources. . . . The re-vivals among English colonists in Virginia also reveal eclectic roots. Presbyterians brought Calvinism into the colony for the first time since the 1650s, but Arminian-ism underwrote the powerful Methodist awakening in the colony and soon crept into the ranks of the colony's Baptists as well.

"The Great Awakening" also is diffi-cult to date. Seldom has an "event" of such magnitude had such amorphous beginnings and endings. In New Eng-land, historians agree, the revivals flour-ished principally between 1740 and 1743 and largely ended by 1745, although a few scattered outbreaks of revivalism oc-curred there in the next decades. Estab-lishing the beginning of the revivals has proved more difficult, however. Most historians settle for the year 1740 because it marks Whitefield's first appearance in New England. But everyone acknowl-edges that earlier revivals underwrote Whitefield's enthusiastic reception there and involved remarkable numbers of col-onists. Edwards counted thirty-two towns caught up in revivals in 1734–1735 and noted that his own grandfather, Stod-dard, had conducted no less than five "harvests" in Northampton before that, the earliest in the 1690s. Yet revivals in Virginia, the site of the most sustained

such events in the southern colonies, did not emerge in significant numbers until the 1750s and did not peak until the 1760s. At the same time, they also contin-ued into the revolutionary and early na-tional periods in ways that make them difficult to separate from their prede-cessors.

Yet even if one were to argue that "the Great Awakening" persisted through most of the eighteenth century, it is ob-vious that revivals "swept" only some of the mainland colonies. They occurred in Massachusetts, Connecticut, Rhode Is-land, Pennsylvania, New Jersey, and Vir-ginia with some frequency at least at some points between 1740 and 1770. But New Hampshire, Maryland, and Geor-gia witnessed few revivals in the same years, and revivals were only occasionally important in New York, Delaware, North Carolina, and South Carolina. The re-vivals also touched only certain seg-ments of the population in the colonies where they occurred. The best example of the phenomenon is Pennsylvania. The revivals there had a sustained effect among English settlers only in Presby-terian churches where many of the laity and clergy also opposed them. The Bap-tists, who were so important to the New England revivals, paid little attention to them until the 1760s, and the colony's taciturn Quakers watched them in per-plexed silence. Not even Germans im-bibed them universally. At the same time that Benjamin Franklin was emptying his pockets in response to the preaching of Whitefield in Philadelphia—or at least claiming to do so—the residents of Ger-mantown were steadily leaving their churches, and Stephanie Grauman Wolf reports that they remained steadfast in their indifference to Christianity at least until the 1780s. . . .

Historians also exaggerate the cohesion of leadership in the revivals. They have accomplished this, in part, by overstressing the importance of Whitefield and Edwards. Whitefield's early charismatic influence later faded so that his appearances in the 1750s and 1760s had less impact even among evangelicals than they had in the 1740s. In addition, Whitefield's "leadership" was ethereal, at best, even before 1750. His principal early importance was to serve as a personal model of evangelical enterprise for ministers wishing to promote their own revivals of religion. Because he did little to organize and coordinate integrated colonial revivals, he also failed to exercise significant authority over the ministers he inspired.

The case against Edwards's leadership of the revivals is even clearer. Edwards defended the New England revivals from attack. But, like Whitefield, he never organized and coordinated revivals throughout the colonies or even throughout New England. Since most of his major works were not printed in his lifetime, even his intellectual leadership in American theology occurred in the century after his death. Whitefield's lack of knowledge about Edwards on his first tour of American in 1739-1740 is especially telling on this point. Edwards's name does not appear in Whitefield's journal prior to the latter's visit to Northampton in 1740, and Whitefield did not make the visit until Edwards had invited him to do so. Whitefield certainly knew of Edwards and the 1734-1735 Northampton revival but associated the town mainly with the pastorate of Edwards's grandfather Stoddard. As Whitefield described the visit in his journal: "After a little refreshment, we crossed the ferry to Northampton, where no less than three hundred souls

were saved about five years ago. Their pastor's name is Edwards, successor and grandson to the great Stoddard, whose memory will be always precious to my soul, and whose books entitled 'A Guide to Christ,' and 'Safety of Appearing in Christ's Righteousness,' I would recommend to all."

What were the effects of the prerevolutionary revivals of religion? The claims for their religious and secular impact need pruning too. One area of concern involves the relationship between the revivals and the rise of the Dissenting denominations in the colonies. Denomination building was intimately linked to the revivals in New England. There, as C. C. Goen has demonstrated, the revivals of the 1740s stimulated formation of over two hundred new congregations and several new denominations. This was accomplished mainly through a negative process called "Separatism," which split existing Congregationalist and Baptist churches along prorevival and antirevival lines. But Separatism was of no special consequence in increasing the number of Dissenters farther south. Presbyterians, Baptists, and, later, Methodists gained strength from former Anglicans who left their state-supported churches, but they won far more recruits among colonists who claimed no previous congressional membership.

Still, two points are important in assessing the importance of revivals to the expansion of the Dissenting denominations in the colonies. First, revivalism never was the key to the expansion of the colonial churches. Presbyterianism expanded as rapidly in the middle colonies between 1710 and 1740 as between 1740 and 1770. Revivalism scarcely produced the remarkable growth that the Church of England experienced in the eighteenth century unless, of course, it won the favor of colonists who opposed revivals as fiercely as did its leaders. [Edwin] Gaustad estimates that between 1700 and 1780 Anglican congregations expanded from about one hundred to four hundred, and Bruce E. Steiner has outlined extraordinary Anglican growth in the Dissenting colony of Connecticut although most historians describe the colony as being thoroughly absorbed by the revivals and "Separatism."

Second, the expansion of the leading evangelical denominations, Presbyterians and Baptists, can be traced to many causes, not just revivalism or "the Great Awakening." The growth of the colonial population from fewer than three hundred thousand in 1700 to over two million in 1770 made the expansion of even the most modestly active denominations highly likely. This was especially true because so many new colonists did not settle in established communities but in new communities that lacked religious institutions. As Timothy L. Smith has written of seventeenth-century settlements, the new eighteenth-century settlements welcomed congregations as much for the social functions they performed as for their religious functions. Some of the denominations reaped the legacy of Old World religious ties among new colonists, and others benefited from local anti-Anglican sentiment, especially in the Virginia and Carolina backcountry. As a result, evangelical organizers formed many congregations in the middle and southern colonies without resorting to revivals at all. The first Presbyterian congregation in Hanover County, Virginia, organized by Samuel Blair and William Tennent, Jr., in 1746, rested on an indigenous lay critique of Anglican theology that had turned residents to the works of

Martin Luther, and after the campaign by Blair and Tennent, the congregation allied itself with the Presbyterian denomination rather than with simple revivalism.

The revivals democratized relations between ministers and the laity only in minimal ways. A significant number of New England ministers changed their preaching styles as a result of the 1740 revivals. [Alan] Heimert quotes Isaac Backus on the willingness of evangelicals to use sermons to "insinuate themselves into the affections' of the people" and notes how opponents of the revivals like [Charles] Chauncy nonetheless struggled to incorporate emotion and "sentiment" into their sermons after 1740. Yet revivalists and evangelicals continued to draw sharp distinctions between the rights of ministers and the duties of the laity. Edwards did so in a careful, sophisticated way in *Some Thoughts concerning the Present Revival of Religion in New England*. Although he noted that "disputing, jangling, and contention" surrounded "lay exhorting," he agreed that "some exhorting is a Christian duty." But he quickly moved to a strong defense of ministerial prerogatives, which he introduced with the proposition that "the Common people in exhorting one another ought not to clothe themselves with the like authority, with that which is proper for ministers." Gilbert Tennent was less cautious. In his 1740 sermon *The Danger of an Unconverted Ministry*, he bitterly attacked "Pharisee-shepherds" and "Pharisee-teachers" whose preaching was frequently as "unedifying" as their personal lives. But Gilbert Tennent never attacked the ministry itself. Rather, he argued for the necessity of a *converted* ministry precisely because he believed that only preaching brought men and women to Christ and that only ordained ministers could preach. Thus, in both 1742 and 1757, he thundered against lay preachers. They were "of dreadful consequence to the Church's peace and soundness in principle. . . . [F]or Ignorant Young Converts to take upon them authoritatively to Instruct and Exhort publickly tends to introduce the greatest Errors and the greatest anarchy and confusion." . . .

Did itinerants challenge this ministerial hegemony? [William G.] McLoughlin has framed such an argument in exceptionally strong terms. He has argued that the itinerant significantly changed the early American social and religious landscape because he usually lacked formal education, "spoke to other men as equals" in a traditionally deferential society, "eschew[ed] the parish church," refused to "order or command his hearers to conform," and was "clothed only with spiritual authority [so that] his power was based solely on his ability to persuade the individual listener to act upon his own free will."

Actually, itinerancy produced few changes in colonial American society and religion and is frequently misunderstood. Although some itinerants lacked institutionally based formal educations, none are known to have been illiterate. The most famous itinerant of the century, Whitefield, took an Oxford degree in 1736, and the most infamous, Davenport, stood at the top of his class at Yale in 1732. Itinerants usually bypassed the local church only when its minister opposed them; when the minister was hospitable the itinerants preached in the church building. One reason itinerants eschewed the coercive instruments of the state was that they never possessed them before the Revolution. But after the Revolution the denominations they represented sought and received special favors from the new state governments, especially concerning incorporation, and won the passage of coercive legislation regarding morality and outlawing blasphemy. Finally, itinerants seldom ventured into the colonial countryside "clothed only with spiritual authority." Instead, itinerants acknowledged the continuing importance of deference and hierarchy in colonial society by stressing denominational approbation for their work. Virtually all of them wore the protective shield of ordination—the major exceptions are a few laymen who itinerated in New England in the early 1740s and about whom virtually nothing is known—and nearly all of them could point to denominational sponsorship. Even Virginia's aggressive Samuel Davies defended himself to the Bishop of London, Gov. William Gooch, and the sometimes suspicious backcountry settlers to whom he preached by pointing to his ordination and sponsorship by the Presbytery of New Castle. Only Davenport ventured into the countryside with little more than the spirit (and his Yale degree) to protect him. But only Davenport was judged by a court to have been mentally unstable.

In this context, it is not surprising that the eighteenth-century revivals of religion failed to bring significant new power—democracy—to the laity in the congregations. Although Gilbert Tennent argued that the laity had an obligation to abandon unconverted, unedifying ministers in favor of converted ones, it is not possible to demonstrate that the revivals increased the traditional powers that laymen previously possessed or brought them new ones. Congregations throughout the colonies had long exercised considerable power over their ministers through their effective control of church spending and fund raising as well as through the laity's ability simply to stop attending church services at all. As examples, witness alone the well-known seventeenth-century disputes between ministers and their listeners in Sudbury and Salem Village in Massachusetts and the complaints against ministers brought by the laity to the Presbytery of Philadelphia between 1706 and 1740. Yet, although the revivals should have increased this lay willingness to complain about ministerial failings, no historian ever has demonstrated systematically that this ever happened. . . .

What, then, of the relationship between the revivals and the American Revolution? Obviously, the revivals provided little focus for intercolonial unity in the way some historians have described. They appeared too erratically in too few colonies under too many different auspices to make such generalizations appropriate. The eighteenth-century colonial wars are more appropriate candidates for the honor. They raised significant legislative opposition to the crown in many colonies and cost many colonists their lives, especially in the last and most "successful" contest, the French and Indian War. Nor is it possible to demonstrate that specific congregations and denominations associated with the revivals originated anti-British protest that became uniquely important to the Revolution. Nathan O. Hatch has noted that Andrew Crosswell's revivalist congregation in Boston had all but collapsed by 1770, and no historian ever has demonstrated that similar congregations elsewhere served as isolated cells of anti-British protest. The connection is equally difficult to make with denominations. Connecticut New Lights and Pennsylvania Presby-

terians played important roles in the colonial protests, but their activity does not, in itself, link revivals to the Revolution in any important way. First, the revivals in both places occurred a quarter of a century before the Revolution began. Second, neither group expanded in the 1740s or sustained its membership later exclusively because of the revivals. Third, the British probably angered laymen of both groups because the latter were important politicians rather than because they were New Lights and Presbyterians. Or, put another way, they were political leaders who happened to be New Lights and Presbyterians rather than Presbyterians and New Lights who happened to be politicians.

This is not to say that colonial revivalism did not reinforce anti-British protest in some way. Heimert has argued that the Calvinism of the revivals "provided pre-Revolutionary America with a radical, even democratic, social and political ideology" and contained millennialist themes that bore equally dangerous implications for British rule. But the secret to the success of anti-British and revolutionary protests lay in the expanse of their ideological foundations. Millennialism was indeed important to the American revolutionaries because, as Hatch as argued, it crossed Old Light-New Light boundaries, while Bernard Bailyn has demonstrated in his capsule biographies of the New England clergymen Andrew Eliot, Jonathan Mayhew, and Stephen Johnson that both Calvinism and theological liberalism produced positive responses on questions of democracy and the Revolution. And, of course, some historians still argue for the importance of the secular Enlightenment in shaping revolutionary ideology, whether it be in the thought of John Locke, John Trenchard, and Thomas Gordon, or in new-found Scottish philosophers.

Some historians have argued that the eighteenth-century revivals had a more subtle, yet still profound, effect on the colonies in fostering a new system of mass communications among settlers. Stout has written that itinerancy and extemporaneous preaching—but specifically not the intellectual content of the sermons reached—stimulated social and political egalitarianism in the colonies. They created a "spirit of liberty" that tore at traditional social and political deference and fitted Americans superbly for the contests of the 1760s and 1770s. Here again problems of timing and effect intrude. The political ramifications of extemporaneous sermons delivered by itinerant or resident preachers were unclear at best and were delayed for as long as twenty-five years. Moreover, the Revolution they presumably underwrote made only the most modest contributions to social egalitarianism and democracy, of which they probably were not the sole cause.

Yet the real Achilles heel of Stout's interpretation may center on the extent of extemporaneous preaching itself. Stout—and McLoughlin, who has echoed him—did not study the frequency of extemporaneous preaching in the revivals. They built their argument on the assumption that it was the key to the revivals and the dominant mode of revival preaching, just as revival critics claimed. This may not be the case, however. As used in the eighteenth century, the term "extempore preaching" did not mean preaching without preparation. Rather, it meant preaching without a written text or notes in a way that, according to Stout, allowed the minister greater flexibility in shaping his subject and communicating with his au-dience. Although extemporaneous preaching was notorious at the height of the 1740 revivals, not all revival ministers engaged in the practice. Edwards probably never gave extemporaneous sermons despite the fact that he relaxed his sermon style after 1740. Gilbert Tennent, who appears to have preached extemporaneously through about 1743, apparently reduced this practice in the next decade. In 1762, Gilbert Tennent opposed the appointment of a man who preached extemporaneously as an assistant minister in Tennent's Philadelphia congregation, and he attacked extemporaneous preaching in an important but unpublished treatise he wrote in the same year. In the surviving draft of this document, Gilbert Tennent argued that ministers who favored extemporaneous preaching frequently overstressed emotion and that, ideally, ministers ought to mix their preaching styles by preaching with notes "in the morning to inform the mind" and by preaching extemporaneously "in the afternoon to affect the Heart." But in an observation obviously meant to deflate proponents of extemporaneous preaching, he also commented that in his own experience "the Difference between the two modes of preaching with or without notes is So Small, that if you Shutt your eyes or Sit where you don't See the Speaker, you will be often at a Loss to Distinguish which mode is used."

The caution of Edwards and Gilbert Tennent in eschewing or abandoning extemporaneous preaching and the fact that nearly all reports about its frequency come from revival critics raise important questions about its real influence in the colonies. Did Whitefield, for example, memorize texts, speak from brief notes, or simply begin preaching without previously having given the sermon extended thought? Did other ministers speak extemporaneously on some occasions but revert, on others, to reading their sermons or delivering them from extensive notes? And between 1730 and 1770 did ministers adopt or abandon extemporaneous preaching in different denominations at different times? Since we do not yet have the answers to these questions, generalizations about the political implications of extemporaneous preaching in the revivals are premature.

What, then, ought we to say about the revivals of religion in prerevolutionary America? The most important suggestion is the most drastic. Historians should abandon the term "the Great Awakening" because it distorts the character of eighteenth-century American religious life and misinterprets its relationship to prerevolutionary American society and politics. In religion it is a deus ex machina that falsely homogenizes the heterogeneous; in politics it falsely unites the colonies in slick preparation for the Revolution. Instead, a four-part model of the eighteenth-century colonial revivals will highlight their common features, underscore important differences, and help us assess their real significance.

First, with one exception, the prerevolutionary revivals should be understood primarily as regional events that occurred in only half the colonies. Revivals occurred intermittently in New England between 1690 and 1745 but became especially common between 1735 and 1745. They were uniformly Calvinist and produced more significant local political ramifications—even if they did not democratize New England—than other colonial revivals except those in Virginia. Revivals in the middle colonies occurred primarily between 1740 and 1760. They had remarkably eclectic theological ori-

gins, bypassed large numbers of settlers, were especially weak in New York, and produced few demonstrable political and social changes. Revivals in the southern colonies did not occur in significant numbers until the 1750s, when they were limited largely to Virginia, missed Maryland almost entirely, and did not occur with any regularity in the Carolinas until well after 1760. Virginia's Baptist revivalists stimulated major political and social changes in the colony, but the secular importance of the other revivals has been exaggerated. A fourth set of revivals, and the exception to the regional pattern outlined here, accompanied the preaching tours of the Anglican itinerant Whitefield. These tours frequently intersected with the regional revivals in progress at different times in New England, the middle colonies, and some parts of the southern colonies, but even then the fit was imperfect. Whitefield's tours produced some changes in ministerial speaking styles but few permanent alterations in institutional patterns of religion, although his personal charisma supported no less than seven tours of the colonies between 1740 and his death in Newburyport, Massachusetts, in 1770.

Second, the prerevolutionary revivals occurred in the colonial backwaters of Western society where they were part of a long-term pattern of erratic movements for spiritual renewal and revival that had long characterized Western Christianity and Protestantism since its birth two centuries earlier. Thus, their theological origins were international and diverse rather than narrowly Calvinist and uniquely American. Calvinism was important in some revivals, but Arminianism and Pietism supported others. This theological heterogeneity also makes it impossible to isolate a single overwhelmingly important cause of the revivals. Instead, they appear to have arisen when three circumstances were present—internal demands for renewal in different international Christian communities, charismatic preachers, and special, often unique, local circumstances that made communities receptive to elevated religious rhetoric.

Third, the revivals had modest effects on colonial religion. This is not to say that they were "conservative" because they did not always uphold the traditional religious order. But they were never radical, whatever their critics claimed. For example, the revivals reinforced ministerial rather than lay authority even as they altered some clergymen's perceptions of their tasks and methods. They also stimulated the demand for organization, order, and authority in the evangelical denominations. Presbyterian "New Lights" repudiated the conservative Synod of Philadelphia because its discipline was too weak, not too strong, and demanded tougher standards for ordination and subsequent service. After 1760, when Presbyterians and Baptists utilized revivalism as part of their campaigns for denominational expansion, they only increased their stress on central denominational organization and authority.

Indeed, the best test of the benign character of the revivals is to take up the challenge of contemporaries who linked them to "outbreaks of enthusiasm" in Europe. In making these charges, the two leading antirevivalists in the colonies, Garden of Charleston and Chauncy of Boston, specifically compared the colonial revivals with those of the infamous "French Prophets" of London, exiled Huguenots who were active in the city between 1706 and about 1730. The French Prophets predicted the downfall of English politicians, raised followers from

the dead, and used women extensively as leaders to prophesy and preach. By comparison, the American revivalists were indeed "conservative." They prophesied only about the millennium, not about local politicians, and described only the necessity, not the certainty, of salvation. What is most important is that they eschewed radical change in the position of women in the churches. True, women experienced dramatic conversions, some of the earliest being described vividly by Edwards. But, they preached only irregularly, rarely prophesied, and certainly never led congregations, denominations, or sects in a way that could remotely approach their status among the French Prophets.

Fourth, the link between the revivals and the American Revolution is virtually nonexistent. The relationship between prerevolutionary political change and the revivals is weak everywhere except in Virginia, where the Baptist revivals indeed shattered the exclusive, century-old Anglican hold on organized religious activity and politics in the colony. But, their importance to the Revolution is weakened by the fact that so many members of Virginia's Anglican aristocracy also led the Revolution. In other colonies the revivals furnished little revolutionary rhetoric, including even millennialist thought, that was not available from other sources and provided no unique organizational mechanisms for anti-British protest activity. They may have been of some importance in helping colonists make moral judgments about eighteenth-century English politics, though colonists unconnected to the revivals made these judgments as well.

In the main, then, the revivals of religion in eighteenth-century America emerge as nearly perfect mirrors of a regionalized, provincial society. They arose erratically in different times and places across a century from the 1690s down to the time of the Revolution. Calvinism underlay some of them, Pietism and Arminianism others. Their leadership was local and, at best, regional, and they helped reinforce—but were not the key to—the proliferation and expansion of still-regional Protestant denominations in the colonies. As such, they created no intercolonial religious institutions and fostered no significant experiential unity in the colonies. Their social and political effects were minimal and usually local, although they could traumatize communities in which they upset, if only temporarily, familiar patternsof worship and social behavior. But the congregations they occasionally produced usually blended into the traditional social system, and the revivals abated without shattering its structure. Thus, the revivals of religion in prerevolutionary America seldom became proto-revolutionary, and they failed to change the timing, causes, or effects of the Revolution in any significant way.

Of course, it is awkward to write about the eighteenth-century revivals of religion in America as erratic, heterogeneous, and politically benign. All of us have walked too long in the company of Tracy's "Great Awakening" to make our journey into the colonial past without it anything but frightening. But as Chauncy wrote of the Whitefield revivals, perhaps now it is time for historians "to see that Things have been carried too far, and that the Hazard is great . . . lest we should be over-run with *Enthusiasm*."

POSTSCRIPT

Was the Great Awakening a Key to the American Revolution?

Even if McLoughlin's thesis (that the revivals of the mid-eighteenth century were a "key" that helped open the door to the War for Independence) is not valid, there is room to argue that the Revolution was not without its religious elements. In his book *Religion in America: Past and Present* (Prentice Hall, 1961), Clifton E. Olmstead argues for a broader application of religious causes to the origins of the American Revolution. First, and consistent with McLoughlin, Olmstead contends that the Great Awakening did foster a sense of community among American colonists, thus providing the unity required for an organized assault on England. Moreover, the Awakening further weakened existing ties between colonies and Mother Country by drawing adherents of the Church of England into the evangelical denominations that expanded as a result of revivalistic Protestantism. Second, tensions were generated by the demand that an Anglican bishop be established in the colonies. Many evangelicals found in this plan evidence that the British government wanted further control over the colonies. Third, the Quebec Act, enacted by Parliament in 1774, not only angered American colonists by nullifying their claims to western lands, but also heightened religious prejudice in the colonies by granting tolerance to Roman Catholics. Fourth, ministers played a significant role in encouraging their parishioners to support the independence movement. Olmstead claims that this revolutionary movement in the colonies was defended overwhelmingly by Congregationalist, Presbyterian, Dutch Reformed, and Baptist ministers. Finally, many of the revolutionaries, imbued with the American sense of mission, believed that God was ordaining their revolutionary activities.

Further support for the views expressed by William McLoughlin can be found in Alan Heimert, *Religion and the American Mind from the Great Awakening to the Revolution* (Cambridge University Press, 1966); William Warren Sweet, *The Story of Religion in America* (New York, 1950); Cedric B. Cowing, *The Great Awakening and the American Revolution: Colonial Thought in the Eighteenth Century* (University of Chicago, 1971); Richard Hofstadter,

America at 1750: A Social Portrait (Knopf, 1973); Rhys Isaac, *The Transformation of Virginia, 1740–1790* (University of North Carolina Press, 1982); Ruth H. Bloch, *Visionary Republic* (Cambridge University Press, 1985); Harry S. Stout, *The New England Soul: Preaching and Religious Culture in Colonial New England* (Oxford University Press, 1986); and Patricia U. Bonomi, *Under the Cope of Heaven: Religion, Society, and Politics in Colonial America* (Oxford University Press, 1986). Alan Heimert's views have been challenged by Sidney Mead and Bernard Bailyn. Students interested in the Great Awakening should consult Edwin Scott Gaustad, *The Great Awakening in New England* (Peter Smith, 1957); David S. Lovejoy, *Religious Enthusiasm and the Great Awakening* (Prentice Hall, 1969); and Marilyn J. Westerkamp, *Triumph of the Laity: Scots-Irish Piety and the Great Awakening, 1625–1760* (Oxford University Press, 1987). George Athan Billias, ed., *The American Revolution: How Revolutionary Was It?* (Holt, Rinehart & Winston, 1965), offers different perspectives on the war for independence, as does Bernard Bailyn in *Ideological Origins of the American Revolution* (Harvard University Press, 1967).

PART 2

The New Nation

As America grew and became more established, its people and leaders struggled to fully implement the ideals that had sparked the Revolution. What had been abstractions before the formation of the new government had to be applied and refined in day-to-day practice. The nature of post-revolutionary America, government stability, the transition of power, the reality of citizens' civil rights, and the role of women had to be worked out.

The Constitution: Was It an Economic Document?

Did President Jefferson Outfederalize the Federalists?

Did Women Achieve Greater Autonomy in the New Nation?

ISSUE 7

The Constitution: Was It an Economic Document?

YES: Michael Parenti, from *Democracy for the Few,* 5th ed. (St. Martin's Press, 1988)

NO: Gordon S. Wood, from "Democracy and the Constitution," in Robert A. Goldwin and William A. Schambra, eds., *How Democratic Is the Constitution?* (American Enterprise Institute for Public Policy Research, 1980)

ISSUE SUMMARY

YES: Political scientist Michael Parenti argues that the Constitution was framed by financially successful planters, merchants, and creditors in order to protect the rights of property rather than the rights and liberties of individuals.

NO: Professor of history Gordon S. Wood views the struggle for a new constitution in 1787–1788 as a social conflict between upper-class Federalists who desired a stronger central government and the "humbler" Anti-Federalists who controlled the state assemblies.

The United States possesses the oldest written constitution of any major power. The 55 men who attended the Philadelphia Convention in 1787 could scarcely have dreamed that 200 years later the nation would venerate them as the most "enlightened statesmen" of their time. James Madison, the principal architect of the document, may have argued that the Founding Fathers had created a system that might "decide forever the fate of Republican Government which we wish to last for ages," but Madison also told Jefferson in October 1787 that he did not think the document would be adopted, and if it was, it would not work.

The enlightened statesmen view of the Founding Fathers, presented by nineteenth-century historians like John Fiske, became the accepted interpretation among the general public until the Progressive Era. In 1913, Columbia University professor Charles A. Beard's *An Economic Interpretation of the Constitution of the United States* (1913, Reprint, The Free Press, 1986) caused a storm of controversy because it questioned the motivations of the Founding Fathers. The Founding Fathers supported the creation of a stronger, central government, argued Beard, not for patriotic reasons, but because they wanted to protect their own economic interests. Beard argues his thesis in a dull, pedestrian manner, but more than 75 years later it remains perhaps the most influential book ever written in American history.

Beard's research method was fairly simple. Drawing upon a collection of old, previously unexamined treasury records in the National Archives, he discovered that a number of delegates to the Philadelphia Convention and, later, the state ratifying conventions, held substantial amounts of continental securities that would sharply increase in value if a strong national government were established. In addition to attributing economic motives to the Founding Fathers, Beard included a Marxist class conflict interpretation in his book. Those who supported the Constitution, he said, represented "personalty interests which had been adversely affected under the Articles of Confederation: money, public securities, manufactures, and trade and shipping." Those who opposed ratification of the Constitution were the small farmers and the debtors.

Beard's socioeconomic conflict interpretation of the supporters and opponents of the Constitution raised another issue. How was the Constitution ratified if the majority of Americans opposed it? Beard's answer was that most Americans could not vote because they did not own property. Therefore, the entire process, from the calling of the Philadelphia Convention to the state ratifying conventions, was nonrepresentative and nondemocratic.

An Economic Interpretation was a product of its times. Economists, sociologists, and political scientists had been analyzing the conflicts that resulted from the Industrial Revolution, which America had been experiencing at the turn of the twentieth century. Beard joined a group of progressive historians who were interested in reforming the society in which they lived, and who also shared his discontent with the old-fashioned institutional approach. The role of the new historians was to rewrite history and discover the real reason why things happened. For the progressive historians, reality consisted of uncovering the hidden social and economic conflicts within society.

In the years between the world wars, the general public held steadfastly to the enlightened statesmen view of the Founding Fathers, but Beard's thesis on the Constitution became the new orthodoxy in most college texts on American history and government.

A good example of Beard's influence lasting into the 1980s can be found in the first selection. Michael Parenti argues that the Constitution is an elitist document framed by financially successful planters, merchants, and creditors in order to protect the rights of property over the rights and liberties of individuals. In the second selection, Gordon S. Wood accepts part of Beard's class conflict model but emphasizes the social and political conflicts between provincial local leaders and the more cosmopolitan national elites. He argues that the Federalists distrusted the provincial outlook held by the majority of members in the state legislatures and desired a stronger national government run by the "better sort" of men.

YES

Michael Parenti

A CONSTITUTION FOR THE FEW

To help us understand the American political system, let us investigate its origins and its formal structure, the rules under which it operates, and the interests it represents, beginning with the Constitution and the men who wrote it. Why was a central government and a Constitution created? By whom? And for what purposes?

It is commonly taught that in the eighteenth and nineteenth centuries men of property preferred a laissez-faire government, one that kept its activities to a minimum. In actuality, while they wanted government to leave them free in all matters of trade and commerce, not for a moment did they desire a weak, inactive government. Rather, they strove to erect a civil authority that worked *for* rather than against the interests of wealth, and they frequently advocated an extension rather than a diminution of state power. They readily agreed with Adam Smith, who said that government was "instituted for the defense of the rich against the poor" and "grows up with the acquisition of valuable property."

CLASS POWER AND CONFLICT IN EARLY AMERICA

During the period between the Revolution and the Constitutional Convention, the "rich and the wellborn" played a dominant role in public affairs.

> Their power was born of place, position, and fortune. They were located at or near the seats of government and they were in direct contact with legislatures and government officers. They influenced and often dominated the local newspapers which voiced the ideas and interests of commerce and identified them with the good of the whole people, the state, and the nation. The published writings of the leaders of the period are almost without exception those of merchants, of their lawyers, or of politicians sympathetic with them.

The United States of 1787 has been described as an "egalitarian" society free from the extremes of want and wealth that characterized the Old World, but there were landed estates and colonial mansions that bespoke an

From Michael Parenti, *Democracy for the Few,* 5th ed. (St. Martin's Press, 1988). Copyright © 1988 by Michael Parenti. Reprinted by permission of St. Martin's Press, Inc.

impressive munificence. From the earliest English settlements, men of influence had received vast land grants from the crown. By 1700, three-fourths of the acreage in New York belonged to fewer than a dozen persons. In the interior of Virginia, seven persons owned a total of 1,732,000 acres. By 1760, fewer than 500 men in five colonial cities controlled most of the commerce, banking, mining, and manufacturing on the eastern seaboard and owned much of the land.

As of 1787, property qualifications left perhaps more than a third of the White male population disfranchised. Property qualifications for holding office were so steep as to prevent most voters from qualifying as candidates. Thus, a member of the New Jersey legislature had to be worth at least 1,000 pounds, while state senators in South Carolina were required to possess estates worth at least 7,000 pounds, clear of debt. In addition, the practice of oral voting, rather than use of a secret ballot, and an "absence of a real choice among candidates and programs" led to "widespread apathy." As a result, men of substance monopolized the important offices. Not long before the Constitutional Convention, the French *chargé d'affaires* wrote to his Foreign Minister:

Although there are no nobles in America, there is a class of men denominated "gentlemen." . . . Almost all of them dread the efforts of the people to despoil them of their possessions, and, moreover, they are creditors, and therefore interested in strengthening the government, and watching over the execution of the law. . . . The majority of them being merchants, it is for their interest to establish the credit of the United States in Europe on a solid foundation by the exact payment of debts, and to grant to Congress powers extensive enough to compel the people to contribute for this purpose.

The Constitution was framed by financially successful planters, merchants, and creditors, many linked by kinship and marriage and by years of service in Congress, the military, or diplomatic service. They congregated in Philadelphia in 1787 for the professed purpose of revising the Articles of Confederation and strengthening the powers of the central government. They were aware of the weaknesses of the United States in its commercial and diplomatic dealings with other nations. There were also problems among the thirteen states involving trade, customs duties, and currency differences, but these have been exaggerated and in fact, some reforms were being instituted under the Articles.

Most troublesome to the framers of the Constitution was the increasingly insurgent spirit evidenced among the people. Fearing the popular takeover of state governments, the wealthy class looked to a national government as a means of protecting their interests. Even in states where they were inclined to avoid strong federation, the rich, once faced with the threat of popular rule "and realizing that a political alliance with conservatives from other states would be a safeguard if the radicals should capture the state government . . . gave up 'state rights' for 'nationalism' without hesitation."

The nationalist conviction that arose so swiftly among men of wealth during the 1780s was not the product of inspiration; it was not a "dream of nation-building" that suddenly possessed them. (If so, they kept it a secret in their public and private communications.) Rather, their newly acquired nationalism was a practical response to material conditions affecting them in a most immediate way. Their like-minded commitment to federalism was born of a common class interest that transcended state boundaries.

The populace of that day has been portrayed as irresponsible and parochial spendthrifts who never paid their debts and who believed in nothing more than timid state governments and inflated paper money. Most scholars say little about the actual plight of the common people, the great bulk of whom lived at a subsistence level. Most of the agrarian population consisted of poor freeholders, tenants, and indentured hands (the latter lived in conditions of servitude). Small farmers were burdened by heavy rents, ruinous taxes, and low incomes. To survive, they frequently had to borrow money at high interest rates. To meet their debts, they mortgaged their future crops and went still deeper into debt. Large numbers were caught in that cycle of rural indebtedness which is today still the common fate of agrarian peoples in many countries.

Throughout this period, newspapers complained of the "increasing numbers of young beggars in the streets." Economic prisoners crowded the jails. In 1786, one county jail in Massachusetts held eighty-eight persons of whom eighty-four were incarcerated for debts or nonpayment of taxes. Among the people there grew the feeling that the revolution against the English crown had been fought for naught. Angry armed crowds in several states began blocking foreclosures and forcibly freeing debtors from jail. Disorders of a violent but organized kind occurred in a number of states. In the winter of 1787, debtor farmers in western Massachusetts led by Daniel Shays took up arms. But their rebellion was forcibly put down by the state militia after several skirmishes that left eleven men dead and scores wounded.

CONTAINING THE SPREAD OF DEMOCRACY

The specter of Shays' Rebellion hovered over the delegates who gathered in Philadelphia three months later, confirming their worst fears. They were determined that persons of birth and fortune should control the affairs of the nation and check the "leveling impulses" of the propertyless multitude that composed "the majority faction." "To secure the public good and private rights against the danger of such a faction," wrote James Madison in *Federalist* No. 10, "and at the same time preserve the spirit and form of popular government is then the great object to which our inquiries are directed." Here Madison touched the heart of the matter: how to keep the *spirit* and *form* of popular government with only a minimum of the *substance*; how to construct a government that would win some popular support but would not tamper with the existing class structure, a government strong enough to service the growing needs of an entrepreneurial class while withstanding the democratic egalitarian demands of the popular class.

The framers of the Constitution could agree with Madison when he wrote in the same *Federalist* No. 10 that "the most common and durable source of faction has been the various and unequal distribution of property. Those who hold and those who are without property have ever formed distinct interests in society" and "the first object of government" is "the protection of different and unequal faculties of acquiring property." The framers were of the opinion that democracy was "the worst of all political evils," as Elbridge Gerry put it. Both he and Madison warned of "the danger of the leveling spirit." "The people," said Roger Sherman, "should have as little to do as may be about the Government." And according to Alexander Hamilton, "All communities divide themselves into the few and the many. The first are the rich and the well-born, the other the mass of the people. . . . The people are turbulent and changing; they seldom judge or determine right."

The delegates spent many weeks debating their interests, but these were the differences of merchants, slave owners, and manufacturers, a debate of haves versus haves in which each group sought safeguards within the new Constitution for its particular concerns. Added to this were disagreements about how best to achieve agreed-upon ends. Questions of structure and authority occupied a good deal of the delegates' time: How much representation should the large and small states have? How might the legislature be organized? How should the executive be selected? What length of tenure should exist for the different officeholders? Yet questions of enormous significance, relating to the new government's ability to protect the interests of property, were agreed upon with surprisingly little debate. On these issues, there were no dirt farmers or poor artisans attending the convention to proffer an opposing viewpoint. The debate between haves and have-nots never occurred. Thus Article I, Section 8 of the Constitution, which gives the federal government the power to support commerce and protect the interests of property, was adopted within a few days with little debate. It empowered Congress to:

1. Regulate commerce among the states and with foreign nations and Indian tribes
2. Lay and collect taxes and impose duties and tariffs on imports but not on commercial exports
3. Establish a national currency and regulate its value
4. "Borrow Money on the credit of the United States"—a measure of special interest to creditors
5. Fix the standard of weights and measures necessary for trade
6. Protect the value of securities and currency against counterfeiting
7. Establish "uniform Laws on the subject of Bankruptcies throughout the United States"
8. "Pay the Debts and provide for the common Defence and general Welfare of the United States"

Congress was limited to powers specifically delegated to it by the Constitution or implied as "necessary and proper" for the performance of the delegated powers. Over the years, under this "implied power" clause, federal intervention in the private economy grew to an extraordinary magnitude.

Some of the delegates were land speculators who expressed a concern about western holdings. Accordingly, Congress was given the "Power to dispose of and make all needful Rules and Regulations respecting the Territory or other Property belonging to the United States." Some delegates speculated in highly inflated and nearly worthless Confederation securities. Under Article VI, all debts incurred by the Confederation were valid against the new government, a provision that allowed speculators to make enormous profits when their securities, bought for a trifling, were honored at face value.

By assuming this debt, the federal government—under the policies of the first Secretary of the Treasury, Alexander Hamilton—"monetarized" the economy, using the public treasury to create a vast amount of credit for a propertied class that could then invest further in commerce and industry. The eventual payment of this assumed debt would come out of the pockets of the general public. In effect, the government helped greatly to finance the early process of capital accumulation. In assuming the debt, Hamilton was using the federal power to bolster not only the special interests of speculators and creditors but also the overall interest of an emerging capitalist class.

In the interest of merchants and creditors, the states were prohibited from issuing paper money or imposing duties on imports and exports or interfering with the payment of debts by passing any "Law impairing the Obligation of Contracts." The Constitution guaranteed "Full Faith and Credit" in each state "to the Acts, Records, and judicial Proceedings" of other states, thus allowing creditors to pursue their debtors across state lines.

Slavery—another form of property— was afforded special accommodation in the Constitution. Three-fifths of the slave population in each state were to be counted when calculating representation in the lower house. The importation of slaves was given constitutional protection for another twenty years. And slaves who escaped from one state to another had to be delivered up to the original owner upon claim, a provision that was unanimously adopted at the Convention.

The framers believed the states acted with insufficient force against popular uprisings, so Congress was given the task of "organizing, arming, and disciplining the Militia" and calling it forth, among other reasons, to "suppress Insurrections." The federal government was empowered to protect the states "against domestic Violence." Provision was made for "the Erection of Forts, Magazines, Arsenals, dock-Yards and other needful Buildings" and for the maintenance of an army and navy for both national defense and to establish an armed federal presence within the potentially insurrectionary states—a provision that was to prove a godsend to the industrial barons a century later when the army was used repeatedly to break strikes by miners and railroad and factory workers.

In keeping with their desire to contain the majority, the founders inserted "auxiliary precautions" *designed to fragment power without democratizing it.* By separating the executive, legislative, and judicial functions and then providing a system of checks and balances among the various branches, including staggered elections, executive veto, Senate confirmation of appointments and ratification of treaties, and a bicameral legislature, they hoped to dilute the impact of popular sentiments. They contrived an elaborate and difficult process for amending the Constitution, requiring proposal by two-thirds of both the Senate and the House, and ratification by three-fourths of the state legislatures. (Such strictures operate with anti-majoritarian effect to this day. Thus, although national polls show a substantial majority of Americans supports the Equal Rights Amendment, the proposal failed to make its way through the constitutional labyrinth.) To the extent that it existed at all, the majoritarian principle was tightly locked into a system of minority vetoes, making swift and sweeping popular action less likely.

The propertyless majority, as Madison pointed out in *Federalist* No. 10, must not be allowed to concert in common cause against the established social order. First, it was necessary to prevent a unity of public sentiment by enlarging the polity and then compartmentalizing it into geographically insulated political communities. The larger the nation, the greater the "variety of parties and interests" and the more difficult it would be for a majority to find itself and act in unison. As Madison argued, "A rage for paper money, for an abolition of debts, for an equal division of property, or for any other wicked project will be less apt to pervade the whole body of the Union than a particular member of it." An uprising of impoverished farmers may threaten Massachusetts at one time and Rhode Island at another, but a national government will be large and varied enough to contain each of these and insulate the rest of the nation from the contamination of rebellion.

Second, not only must the majority be prevented from finding horizontal cohesion, but its vertical force—that is, its upward thrust upon government—should be blunted by interjecting indirect forms of representation. Thus, senators from each state were to be elected by their respective state legislatures. The chief executive was to be selected by an electoral college voted by the people but, as anticipated by the framers, composed of political leaders and men of substance who would gather in their various states and choose a president of their own liking. It was believed that they would usually be unable to muster a majority for any one candidate, and that the final selection would be left to the House,

with each state delegation therein having only one vote. The Supreme Court was to be elected by no one, its justices being appointed to life tenure by the president and confirmed by the Senate. In time, of course, the electoral college proved to be something of a rubber stamp, and the Seventeenth Amendment, adopted in 1913, provided for popular election of the Senate—demonstrating that the Constitution is modifiable in democratic directions, but only with great difficulty.

The only portion of government directly elected by the people was the House of Representatives. Many of the delegates would have preferred excluding the public entirely from direct representation: John Mercer observed that he found nothing in the proposed Constitution more objectionable than "the mode of election by the people. The people cannot know and judge of the characters of Candidates. The worst possible choice will be made." Others were concerned that demagogues would ride into office on a populist tide only to pillage the treasury and wreak havoc on all. "The time is not distant," warned Gouverneur Morris, "when this Country will abound with mechanics [artisans] and manufacturers [industrial workers] who will receive their bread from their employers. Will such men be the secure and faithful Guardians of liberty? . . . Children do not vote. Why? Because they want prudence, because they have no will of their own. The ignorant and dependent can be as little trusted with the public interest."

When the delegates finally agreed to having "the people" elect the lower house, they were referring to a select portion of the population. Property qualifications disfranchised the poorest White males in various states. Half the adult population was denied suffrage because they were women. American Indians had no access to the ballot. About one-fourth, both men and women, had no vote because they were held in bondage, and even of the Blacks who had gained their legal freedom, in both the North and the South, none was allowed to vote until the passage of the Fourteenth Amendment, after the Civil War.

PLOTTERS OR PATRIOTS?

The question of whether the framers of the Constitution were motivated by financial or national interest has been debated ever since Charles Beard published *An Economic Interpretation of the Constitution* in 1913. Beard believed that the "founding fathers" were guided by their class interests. Arguing against Beard are those who say that the framers were concerned with higher things than just lining their purses. True, they were moneyed men who profited directly from policies initiated under the new Constitution, but they were motivated by a concern for nation building that went beyond their particular class interests, the argument goes. To paraphrase Justice Holmes, these men invested their belief to make a nation; they did not make a nation because they had invested. "High-mindedness is not impossible to man," Holmes reminds us.

That is exactly the point: high-mindedness is a common attribute among people even when, or especially when, they are pursuing their personal and class interests. The fallacy is to presume that there is a dichotomy between the desire to build a strong nation and the desire to protect wealth and that the framers could not have been motivated by both. In fact, like most other people, they be-

lieved that what was good for themselves was ultimately good for the entire society. Their universal values and their class interests went hand in hand, and to discover the existence of the "higher" sentiment does not eliminate the self-interested one.

Most persons believe in their own virtue. The founders never doubted the nobility of their effort and its importance for the generations to come. Just as many of them could feel dedicated to the principle of "liberty for all" and at the same time own slaves, so could they serve both their nation and their estates. The point is not that they were devoid of the grander sentiments of nation building but that *there was nothing in their concept of nation that worked against their class interest and a great deal that worked for it.*

People tend to perceive issues in accordance with the position they occupy in the social structure; that position is largely—although not exclusively—determined by their class status. Even if we deny that the framers were motivated by the desire for personal gain that moves others, we cannot dismiss the existence of their class interest. They may not have been solely concerned with getting their own hands in the till, although enough of them did, but they were admittedly preoccupied with defending the wealthy few from the laboring many—for the ultimate benefit of all, as they understood it. "The Constitution," as Staughton Lynd noted, "was the settlement of a revolution. What was at stake for Hamilton, Livingston, and their opponents, was more than speculative windfalls in securities; it was the question, what kind of society would emerge from the revolution when the dust had settled, and on which class the political center of gravity would come to rest."

The small farmers and debtors, who opposed a central government that was even farther beyond their reach than the local and state governments, have been described as motivated by self-serving, parochial interests—unlike the supposedly higher-minded statesmen who journeyed to Philadelphia and others of their class who supported ratification. How and why the wealthy became visionary nation-builders is never explained. Not too long before, many of them had been proponents of laissez-faire and had opposed a strong central mercantile government. In truth, it was not their minds that were so much broader but their economic interests. Their motives were neither higher nor lower than those of any other social group struggling for place and power in the United States of 1787. They pursued their material interests as might any small freeholder. But possessing more time, money, information, and organization, they enjoyed superior results.

How could they have acted otherwise? For them to have ignored the conditions of governance necessary for the maintenance of the social order that meant everything to them would have amounted to committing class suicide—and they were not about to do that. They were a rising bourgeoisie rallying around a central power in order to develop the kind of national powers that would (a) better provide for the growing needs of a national commercial economy, (b) protect their overseas trading and diplomatic interests, and (c) defend their class interests from the competing claims of other classes within their own society. Some of us are quite willing to accept the existence of such a material-based nationalism in the history of other countries, but not in our own.

Finally, those who argue that the founders were motivated primarily by high-minded objectives consistently overlook the fact that the delegates repeatedly stated their intention to erect a government strong enough to protect the haves from the have-nots. They gave voice to the crassest class prejudices and never found it necessary to disguise the fact—as have latter-day apologists—that their concern was to diminish popular control and resist all tendencies toward class equalization (or "leveling," as it was called). Their opposition to democracy and their dedication to moneyed interests were unabashedly and openly avowed. Their preoccupation with their class interests was so pronounced that one delegate, James Wilson of Pennsylvania, did finally complain of hearing too much about how the sole or primary object of government was property. The cultivation and improvement of the human mind, he maintained, was the most noble object—a fine sentiment that evoked no opposition from his colleagues as they continued about their business.

If the founders sought to "check power with power," they seemed chiefly concerned with restraining mass power, while assuring the perpetuation of their own class power. They supposedly had a "realistic" opinion of the rapacious nature of human beings—readily evidenced when they talked about the common people—yet they held a remarkably sanguine view of the self-interested impulses of their own class, which they saw as inhabited largely by virtuous men of "principle and property." According to Madison, wealthy men (the "minority faction") would be unable to sacrifice "the rights of other citizens" or mask their "violence under the forms of the

Constitution." They would never jeopardize the institution of property and wealth and the untrammeled uses thereof, which in the eyes of the framers constituted the essence of "liberty."

AN ELITIST DOCUMENT

More important than to conjecture about the framers' motives is to look at the Constitution they fashioned, for it tells us a good deal about their objectives. The Constitution was consciously designed as a conservative document, elaborately equipped with a system of minority checks and vetoes, making it easier for entrenched interests to endure. It provided ample power to build the services and protections of state needed by a growing capitalist class but made difficult the transition of rule to a different class. The Constitution was a historically successful ruling-class undertaking whose effects are still very much with us. . . .

The Constitution championed the rights of property over the rights and liberties of persons. For the founders, liberty meant something different from and antithetical to democracy. It meant liberty to invest, speculate, trade, and accumulate wealth and to secure its possession without encroachment by sovereign or populace. The civil liberties designed to give all individuals the right to engage in public affairs won little support from the delegates. When Colonel Mason recommended that a committee be formed to draft "a Bill of Rights," a task he said could be accomplished "in a few hours," the other convention members offered little discussion on the motion and voted unanimously against it.

If the Constitution was so blatantly elitist, how did it manage to win ratifica-

tion? Actually, it did not have a wide backing, initially being opposed in most of the states. But the same superiority of wealth, organization, and control of political office and the press that allowed the rich to monopolize the Philadelphia Convention enabled them to orchestrate a successful ratification campaign. The Federalists also used bribes, intimidation, and other discouragements against opponents of the Constitution. What's more, *the Constitution never was submitted to a popular vote.* Ratification was by state convention composed of delegates drawn mostly from the same affluent strata as the framers. Those who voted for these delegates were themselves usually subjected to property qualifications.

DEMOCRATIC CONCESSIONS

For all its undemocratic aspects, the Constitution was not without its historically progressive features. Consider the following:

1. The very existence of a written constitution with specifically limited powers represented an advance over more autocratic forms of government.

2. No property qualifications were required for any federal officeholder, unlike in England and most of the states. And salaries were provided for all officials, thus rejecting the common practice of treating public office as a voluntary service, which only the rich could afford.

3. The president and all other officeholders were elected for limited terms. No one could claim a life tenure on any office.

4. Article VI reads: "no religious Test shall ever be required as a Qualification to any Office or public Trust under the United States," a feature that represented a distinct advance over a number

of state constitutions that banned Catholics, Jews, and nonbelievers from holding office.

5. Bills of attainder, the practice of declaring by legislative fiat a specific person or group of people guilty of an offense, without benefit of a trial, were made unconstitutional. Also outlawed were ex post facto laws, the practice of declaring an act a crime and punishing those who had committed it *before* it had been unlawful.

6. As noted earlier, the framers showed no interest in a Bill of Rights, but supporters of the new Constitution soon recognized their tactical error and pledged the swift adoption of such a bill as a condition for ratification. So, in the first session of Congress, the first ten amendments were swiftly passed and then adopted by the states; these rights included freedom of speech and religion; freedom to assemble peaceably and to petition for redress of grievances; the right to keep arms; freedom from unreasonable searches and seizures, self-incrimination, double jeopardy, cruel and unusual punishment, and excessive bail and fines; the right to a fair and impartial trial; and other forms of due process.

7. The Constitution guarantees a republican form of government and explicitly repudiates monarchy and aristocracy; hence, Article I, Section 9 states: "No title of Nobility shall be granted by the United States. . . ." According to James McHenry, a delegate from Maryland, *at least twenty-one of the fifty-five delegates favored some form of monarchy.* Yet few dared venture in that direction out of fear of popular opposition. Furthermore, delegates like Madison believed that stability for their class order was best assured by a republican form of government. The time had come for the bour-geoisie to rule directly without the baneful intrusions of kings and nobles.

Time and again during the Philadelphia Convention, this assemblage of men who feared and loathed democracy found it necessary to show some regard for popular sentiment (as with the direct election of the lower house). If the Constitution was going to be accepted by the states and if the new government was to have any stability, it had to gain some measure of popular acceptance; hence, the founders felt compelled to leave something for the people. While the delegates and their class dominated the events of 1787–1789, they were far from omnipotent. The class system they sought to preserve was itself the cause of marked restiveness among the people.

Land seizures by the poor, food riots, and other violent disturbances occurred throughout the eighteenth century in just about every state and erstwhile colony. This popular ferment spurred the framers in their effort to erect a strong central government *but it also set a limit on what they could do.* The delegates "gave" nothing to popular interests, rather—as with the Bill of Rights—they reluctantly made concessions under the threat of democratic rebellion. They kept what they could and grudgingly relinquished what they felt they had to, driven not by a love of democracy but by a fear of it, not by a love of the people but by a prudent desire to avoid popular uprisings. The Constitution, then, was a product not only of class privilege but of class struggle—a struggle that continued and intensified as the corporate economy and the government grew.

NO

Gordon S. Wood

DEMOCRACY AND THE CONSTITUTION

THE DEBATE OVER THE CONSTITUTION

The historical debate over the Constitution and democracy continues, for the debate is rooted in the original controversy that surrounded the creation of the Constitution in 1787–1788. In fact, all the historical debates over the democratic nature of the Constitution are essentially reverberations of this original dispute at the time of the framing. The creators and supporters of the Constitution, the Federalists as they called themselves, argued strenuously that the Constitution was a fulfillment, not a repudiation, of the Revolution and that it provided for a thoroughly republican and popular government. The opponents of the Constitution, the Antifederalists, charged that the Constitution was a denial of the principles of 1776 and that it was an aristocratic document calculated to create an undemocratic government benefiting the few at the expense of the many. It is essentially these two contrasting viewpoints of 1787–1788 that have been echoing through our historical writing on the origins of the Constitution ever since. We are forever trying to decide in these debates who was more right in their interpretation of the Constitution, the Federalists or the Antifederalists.

Cast in this way, the question will inevitably force us to take sides and argue that either the Federalists or the Antifederalists had a more "correct" view of the "real" Constitution. But there was and is no "real" Constitution against which we can measure the conflicting statements of the Federalists and Antifederalists. The only Constitution that existed in 1787–1788 was the one men at the time believed in and described; and these beliefs and descriptions were very different.[1] Instead of asking whether the Constitution was democratic, we should be asking what the historical participants were up to and why they described the Constitution in such different ways. When the questions are posed in this way, the answers will show that neither the Federalists nor the Antifederalists were more right in their interpretation of the Constitution; both had good reason to think as they did about the Constitution.

From Gordon S. Wood, "Democracy and the Constitution," in Goldwin and Schambra, eds., *How Democratic Is the Constitution?* (American Enterprise Institute, 1980). Copyright © 1980 by the American Enterprise Institute for Public Policy Research, Washington, D.C. Reprinted by permission.

From the vantage point of 1776, which was generally the perspective of the Antifederalists, the Constitution of 1787 looms as an extraordinary, even unbelievable, creation. None of the revolutionary leaders at the time of independence even contemplated, let alone suggested, the possibility of erecting over all America such a strong, overarching national government as the Constitution provided. Such a powerful central government operating directly on individuals was diametrically opposed to all the principles of the Revolution. More than anything else, the Revolution intended to reduce the overweening power of the government, particularly far-removed central government associated with the British imperial system. Any revolutionary in 1776 suggesting a national government resembling the one eventually created by the Constitution of 1787 would have been branded a lunatic or, worse, a British monarchist.

THE ARTICLES OF CONFEDERATION

Of course, some Americans in 1776 wanted a stronger central government than that provided by the Articles of Confederation. But even the most fervent advocates in 1776–1777 of a stronger confederation, like John Dickinson, never envisioned a national government like that of 1787. For most revolutionaries, the confederation was a simple political response to the need for union against Britain. They were interested less in creating an enduring nation-state than in legitimizing the resistance movement and the activity of the Continental Congress. At most, they wanted a strong union of the separate states that would have substantial authority over matters of general concern such as war, trade, interstate disputes, and western lands. However substantial such a confederation might be, it was still to be a confederation—a union of separate and remarkably independent states. The actual Articles of Confederation that emerged from the congressional discussions of 1776–1777 were weaker than some had wanted, but this limited union represented the views of most Americans at the time.[2]

Given these American fears of far-removed central power, explaining the adoption of the Constitution of 1787–1788 becomes quite a problem. Indeed, the formation of the Constitution seems to be such an unexpected and unprecedented event that historians of all persuasions have felt compelled to rely on some version of a "great men" explanation to account for it. Some have followed [Charles] Beard [author of *An Economic Interpretation of the Constitution*] and stressed the conspiratorial character of the movement for the Constitution by a dynamic minority of nationalists who "conjured up" a crisis.[3] Others writing against a Beardian view have also emphasized the youthful energy and political effectiveness of a small group of farsighted Federalist leaders. In fact, the adulation of recent historians for the Federalists' élan and dash has become so great—one called them "giants in the earth"—that we may be returning to the nineteenth-century image of the Founding Fathers as demigods.[4] Apparently the formation of the Constitution is so inexplicable that it cannot be accounted for except in terms of the heroic actions of a few great men.

Of course, many historians have described the accumulating problems of the confederation in order to explain the writing of the Constitution. Although no one today endorses John Fiske's view that the decade of the 1780s was "the most critical moment in all the history of the American people"—a time of near chaos and anarchy—historians have pointed out that the confederation was suffering from a number of visible weaknesses.[5] In international affairs, the confederation was hard-pressed to maintain its territorial integrity. Great Britain refused to vacate the Northwest posts; Spain claimed a huge chunk of the Southwest and closed the Mississippi to traffic. The Barbary pirates were seizing American ships and crews because Congress had no money to pay the necessary tributes. Lacking any taxing power, the United States government could not even pay the interest on its debt to its creditors at home or abroad. Congress had no authority to regulate commerce and thus had no way of forcing any openings in the European mercantile empires for American traders. Efforts to get even limited taxing and commercial regulatory powers foundered on the requirements for the unanimous consent of all the states for amendment of the Articles of Confederation.

Pressing and serious as these problems of the confederation were, they cannot by themselves explain the formation of the Constitution. The Constitution created a national government whose strength and character were out of proportion to the obvious and acknowledged weaknesses of the confederation. Indeed, by 1787 almost everyone recognized the debility of the Articles and was prepared to grant additional powers to Congress. They were not prepared for what came out of the Philadelphia Convention of 1787—a revolutionary transformation of the entire American political system including a radical diminishing of the independence and power of the states. This was no invigorated league of states that the Constitution created. This totally new and extraordinarily powerful national government operating directly on individuals went well beyond what the difficulties of credit and commerce and the humiliations in foreign affairs demanded in additional central powers.

THE PROBLEM OF DEMOCRACY IN THE STATES

Something besides the obvious debility of the confederation lay behind such a radical political transformation. Only political conditions in the states—political conditions of the most threatening kind—can ultimately explain the creation of the Constitution. There in the states, the political entities the revolutionaries cared about most, the problem of democracy was revealed; and it is that problem the Constitution sought to solve.

The state republics created in 1776 were at the heart of the Revolution. Winning the war and forming the Articles of Confederation were crucial, no doubt, but creating new state constitutions, as Thomas Jefferson said in 1776, was "the whole object of the present controversy." In their new commonwealths, Americans aimed to test all that they had learned about tyranny and liberty from their colonial experience and their debate with Britain in the 1760s and 1770s. Republicanism and popular government in America, and indeed in the world, would live or die by what happened in these individual states.[6]

In 1776 Americans as yet did not call their new governments democracies; it is important for our understanding of the Constitution's relationship to democracy to know why they did not. It is true that the new state governments were very popular, more popular surely than any other government in the eighteenth-century world. In the American states, a greater proportion of people could vote and a greater proportion of government officials were elected than in any other country. The most popular part of the state governments, the lower houses of the legislatures, were given an extraordinary amount of power, including many prerogatives, like the granting of pardons and the appointment of judges, that were traditionally exercised only by magisterial authority in other countries. Still, these new governments were not called democracies because, as the eighteenth century commonly understood the term, they were *not* democracies.

Americans in 1776 thought of democracy in a traditionally classical manner. Democracy was not what it has become for us—a general set of values embracing popular government, equality, and liberty. It was still a rather technical term of political science used much as Aristotle had used it. It meant literally government by the people, referring in the strictest sense to political gatherings of the people in person in town meetings and the like. Since such pure democracy was impractical for most governmental affairs, Americans recognized as democratic the modern refinement of representation, which allowed elected agents to participate in government in place of the people. Representation was not yet equated, as it is now, with mere popular election. The representatives of the people were exclusively those elected members of the lower houses of the legislatures—the houses of representatives. The officials of the other branches of the government—whether governors or senators—even though elected by the people, were not yet considered to be in any way "representatives" of the people.

They stood "for" the people but were not "of" them. Thus, any state that possessed a governor and a senate, although popularly elected, could not be a democracy. Americans in 1776 therefore saw themselves creating mixed republics, with the democratic element, the lower assemblies, playing a very dominant role.

By the 1780s, many American leaders realized that these state assemblies were abusing their extraordinary powers. The annually elected legislatures, beset by hosts of various interests, were constantly changing their membership and were making legislation chaotic. As James Madison pointed out, more laws were enacted by the states in the decade following independence than in the entire colonial period. Many of these laws were unjust: paper money acts, stay laws, and other forms of debtor relief legislation hurt various creditor groups in the society and violated individual property rights. To some, the legislatures seemed more frightening than the former royal governors. It did not matter that the legislators were supposedly the representatives of the people and annually elected by them. "173 despots would surely be as oppressive as one," wrote Jefferson. "An *elective despotism* was not the government we fought for."[7]

These legislative abuses, many American leaders believed, flowed from too much democracy. The legislators were too susceptible to various narrow and parochial interests and had become merely spokesmen for their local constituents. "A spirit of locality" in the state legislatures, said Madison, was destroying "the aggregate interests of the Community," and this localist spirit was "inseparable" from elections by small districts or towns. Each representative, said Ezra Stiles, president of Yale, was concerned only with the special interests of his electors. At the reading of a bill in the legislature, "every one instantly thinks how it will affect his constituents."[8] In short, the representatives of the people—the democratic parts of the mixed constitutions—were responding too readily to the wishes of the people they represented. When the Federalists in 1787 came to complain of "the turbulence and follies of democracy," this is what they meant.[9]

American leaders tried several approaches to these democratic abuses in the states. Some attempted to reform the revolutionary state constitutions by reducing the power of the popular assemblies and enhancing that of the governors and senates. The Massachusetts constitution of 1780 embodied many of these second thoughts, and during the 1780s other states sought to remake their constitutions in Massachusetts' image. Others tried to use the judiciary against what were thought to be unconstitutional acts of the legislatures; there were scattered and rudimentary expressions of what would become judicial review. Many leaders, however, thought such judicial overturnings of law enacted by popularly elected legislatures smacked of despotism and were contrary to republican government.

By the mid-1780s, men were increasingly disillusioned with these reforms and devices at the state level. Finally, when even Massachusetts with its supposedly model constitution experienced popular excesses, including Shays' Rebellion and the subsequent legislative "tyranny" of Shaysite sympathizers, many leaders were ready to shift the arena of constitutional change from the states to the nation. It seemed to many that only by modifying the structure of the central government could America find an answer to its democratically caused problems within the states.

What happened in 1786–1787, in brief, was the coalescing of two different and hitherto separate reform movements. The previously frustrated attempts of various groups—public creditors, merchants, and others—to amend the Articles of Confederation were reinforced by the efforts of those alarmed by majoritarian tyranny within the states. Heightened concern with the implications of state politics overwhelmed the state particularism and the fear of far-removed central power that had prevented earlier reform of the Articles of Confederation and forced a recasting of the terms of the problem facing Americans. Since the legislative abuses of the states flowed from the revolutionary aim of increasing the participation of the people in government, the very success of the revolutionary experiment in popular government was at stake. Thus, changing the central government was no longer a matter of standing firm in foreign affairs or of satisfying particular creditor or mercantile interests. It was now a matter, as Madison said, that would "decide forever the fate of republican government."[10]

AN ENLARGED AND ELEVATED REPUBLIC

No one saw this linkage between reform of the central government and reform of the states more clearly and used it more effectively than Madison. Nearly everyone is familiar with Madison's central role in planning for the Philadelphia Convention and in drafting the Virginia plan, which was the convention's working proposal. But not everyone is equally familiar with what Madison wanted from the new central government and how disappointed he was with the final Constitution. Madison's proposals were truly radical; they were designed not to solve particular problems of the confederation but to remedy the deficiencies of republicanism itself. The evidence is strong that Madison and other nationalists who thought like him wanted greater consolidation and a correspondingly greater weakening of the states than they got. Madison wanted a national government that not only would have "a positive and compleat authority in all cases where uniform measures are necessary," as in commerce and foreign policy, but would have "a negative in all cases whatsoever on the Legislative Acts of the States as the King of Great Britain heretofore had." This veto power over all state legislation seemed to Madison "to be absolutely necessary, and to be the least possible encroachment on the State jurisdictions."[11] Without it, he believed, none of the great objects which led to the convention—neither the need for more central authority nor the desire to prevent instability and injustice in state legislation—would be met. When the convention eventually set aside this national veto power, Madison initially thought that the Constitution was doomed to failure.[12]

Although deeply disappointed with the Constitution, Madison and other nationalists aimed to make the best of what they had, a greatly enlarged and elevated republic. All scholars now know how ingeniously Madison made theoretical sense of the new national system. Seizing on David Hume's radical suggestion that a republican government might operate better in a large territory than in a small one, Madison reversed the traditional assumptions about the appropriate size of a republic. Since experience in

America from 1776 had demonstrated that no republic could be made small enough to avoid the clashing of rival parties and interests (tiny Rhode Island was the most faction-ridden of all), the republican state, said Madison in a series of notable letters, essays, and speeches climaxing with his *Federalist* No. 10, must be enlarged "without a departure from the elective basis of it." In this way "the propensity in small republics to rash measures and the facility of forming and executing them" by overbearing factional majorities would be stifled. "In a large Society," said Madison, "the people are broken into so many interests and parties, that a common sentiment is less likely to be felt, and the requisite concert less likely to be formed, by a majority of the whole."[13]

All this may be common knowledge to scholars, but it has led to great misunderstanding of Madison's meaning. Some have pictured Madison as the originator of what has come to be called an "interest-group" theory of politics. But Madison was not a forerunner of Arthur Bentley, David Truman, or Robert Dahl. Despite his keen appreciation of the multiplicity of interests in a commercial society, Madison was not presenting a pluralist conception of politics. He did not envision public policy or the common good emerging naturally from the give-and-take of hosts of competing interests.[14] Instead he hoped that these competing parties and interests in an enlarged republic would neutralize themselves, which in turn would allow rational men to promote the public good. It had worked that way in America's religious situation, which was a common analogy for Madison. The multiplicity of religious sects in America prevented any from dominating the state and permitted the enlightened reason of *philosophes* like Jefferson and himself to shape public policy and church-state relations. Madison did not want the new national government to be an integrator and harmonizer of different interests in the society; instead he wanted it to be a "disinterested and dispassionate umpire in disputes" between these different interests.[15] In other words, Madison was not as modern as we often make him out to be. He hoped the national government might play the same role the British king had been supposed to play in the empire.

COSMOPOLITANISM vs. LOCALISM

If the new government were to be monarchlike with its own "dispassionate and disinterested" authority, how was it to work in republican America? "It may be asked," Madison said, "how private rights will be more secure under the Guardianship of the General Government than under the State Governments, since they are both founded on the republican principle which refers the ultimate decision to the will of the majority."[16] What, in other words, was really different about the new federal Constitution from the state constitutions that would enable it to lessen the effects of tyrannical majorities and keep it from succumbing to the same popular pressures besetting the state governments in the 1780s?

The answer the Federalists gave to these questions cut to the heart of the new system and reveals clearly the problem of the Constitution's relation to democracy. The Federalists, Madison included, were not as much opposed to governmental power per se as to the character and outlook of the people wielding it. They thought that the vices of the state assemblies in the 1780s flowed essentially from the kinds of people being elected to these assemblies. Such legislators were too often too much like the people they represented.

The Revolution had democratized the state assemblies by increasing the number of representatives and by altering their social character. Men of more humble, more rural origins, less educated, and with more parochial interests than those in the colonial legislatures became state representatives after 1776. These nongentry elements formed what Jackson Turner Main has called "localist parties" in all the state legislatures.[17] Although the turnover of membership among these groups was perhaps too great to permit such a rigid classification as "party," these legislative blocs took consistently localist positions on many issues that their cosmopolitan elite opponents criticized as "illiberal," "interested," and "unprincipled." Madison and other gentlemen believed that these ordinary men lacked the "enlarged" and "liberal" outlooks of the more cosmopolitan "natural aristocracy" that Jefferson, for one, had expected to dominate government. These ordinary men were the ones winning elections to the state legislatures and enacting most of what the Federalists described as the confused, unjust, and narrowly based legislation of the 1780s. What the Federalists wanted from the Constitution was a structure of government that would inhibit such localist kinds of men from gaining power.

They proposed to do this by enlarging the arena of politics. Raising important governmental decision making to the national level would expand the electorate and at the same time would reduce the number of those elected. This expanded electorate and elevated government would then act as a kind of filter, refining the kind of men who would become national leaders. In a larger arena with a smaller number of representatives, only the most notable and most socially established were likely to gain political office. If the people of a state, New York, for example, had to select only ten men to the federal Congress in contrast to the sixty-six they elected to their state assembly, they were more apt in the case of the few representatives in the national government to ignore obscure ordinary men with local reputations and elect those who were well bred, well educated, and well known. Election by the people in large districts would inhibit demagoguery and crass electioneering and would therefore, as Madison's closest ally in the convention, James Wilson, said, "be most likely to obtain men of intelligence and uprightness."[18]

What was the meaning of all this Federalist talk of keeping out of government "men of factious tempers, of localist prejudices, or of sinister designs?" Who were the men possessing "the most attractive merit and most diffusive and established characters?"[19] If anyone today used those terms to describe political leaders, we would be understandably suspicious. We might even say that these are "code words" for distinct social types. The Federalist diagnosis of the problems of state politics in the 1780s was at bottom social. Prior to the Revolution, the colonists, like all eighteenth-century Englishmen, had less need for such circumlocutions; they then talked more candidly about the distinction between gentlemen and ordinary people and were much more blunt in designating some as aristocrats and most as not. Since the Revolution, however, the distinction between gentlemen and common people was becoming blurred; aristocracy, even a republican "natural aristocracy," had become a pe-

jorative term in many parts of the country. It is perhaps anachronistic and crude to refer to this gentry sense of difference from obscure ordinary people as a "class" distinction, for it was a distinction that belonged to the older hierarchically and vertically organized society of ranks and degrees and not to the economically based class and horizontally organized society of the future. Yet, it is surely more accurate to describe the controversy over the Constitution in these anachronistic and crude "class" terms than to suggest that it had no social implications whatsoever. The Federalists knew well the social significance of their enlarged republic. They had a shrewd sociological insight into American politics, and they aimed to use it in transforming the social character of American government.

It is a sociological insight that was exploited time and again in later American history. The Progressive period, for example, was marked by the reforming efforts of cosmopolitan types, often liberal, upper-income professionals and businessmen, to wrest the reins of government out of the hands of "corrupt" and "undesirable" localist elements. The Progressive reformers often did this by shifting the level of governmental decision making from wards, towns, and counties to the states and the nation. Commissions of "experts" at the state and federal level supplanted parochial politicians who could not see beyond their own neighborhoods.[20] Changing the level of decision making continues to have social implications; much of our national politics still swirls around this cosmopolitan-localist dichotomy. What do we mean socially when we refer to "establishment types," "limousine liberals," "Middle America," or "Archie Bunkers"?

A REPUBLICAN REMEDY FOR REPUBLICAN DISEASES

Whether such cosmopolitan efforts to create political structures that deliberately excluded the ordinariness of ordinary people are undemocratic was precisely the issue raised at the framing of the Constitution. The Antifederalists, speaking for a populist localist tradition, certainly thought the Constitution was undemocratic. They immediately saw the social implications of the elevated federal government, where only certain "high-toned" and "great men" would hold office and consequently attacked it as "aristocratic" and contrary to the aim of the Revolution.

Yet, the issue has always been complicated by the fact that the Federalists did not allow themselves to be pictured as opposed to the people or republicanism. They had good reason to know that the Constitution would be seen as undemocratic. "When this plan goes forth," John Dickinson warned the Philadelphia Convention, "it will be attacked by the popular leaders. Aristocracy will be the watchword; the Shibboleth among its adversaries." Precisely because the Antifederalists, as Alexander Hamilton observed in the New York ratifying convention, did talk "so often of an aristocracy," the Federalists were compelled in the ratifying debates and in their publications to minimize, even to disguise, the elitist elements of the Constitution.[21] Much of *The Federalist*, for example, was devoted to demonstrating just how "strictly republican" the new system was.[22] The Federalists emerged from the debates, if we take their public statements at face value, as the great defenders of the supremacy of the people in politics. They said over and over again that the new national government, unlike the old confederation, was fully derived from the people. The states could not stand in the way of what the people wanted, and the Constitution was only fulfilling at the national level what the Revolution in 1776 had begun. In effect, the Federalists usurped the popular revolutionary language that rightfully belonged to their opponents and, in the process, helped to further the extraordinary changes taking place in the American conception of politics and democracy.

By the end of the debate over the Constitution, it was possible for the Federalists to describe the new national government, even with its indirectly elected president and Senate, as "a perfectly democratical form of government."[23] Already by 1787–1788 democracy had come to be identified by some Americans simply as a representative government derived from the people. In other words, republicanism and democracy were becoming equated. The houses of representatives lost their exclusive connection with the people. Representation was now identified simply with election; thus, all elected officials, and, for some, even those not elected, such as judges, were considered somehow "representative" of the people. Consequently, the older classical ideas of democracy and mixed government that went back to Aristotle became irrelevant in describing the new American political system. Democracy rapidly became a generic label for all American government.

The changes in language and thought that made this new, more modern definition of democracy possible were not as easily reached as suggested here. Nor was the Federalist use of populism to defend the Constitution as self-conscious or calculating as here implied. Ideas and words are not manipulated or transformed quite that crudely. But, in sum, the Federalists did seek to cover their aristocratic document with a democratic mantle. The state problems of the 1780s they hoped to solve were those of excessive democracy; yet, the solution, they said, or felt compelled to say, was likewise democratic. As Madison, who was somewhat less willing than other Federalists to distort language and indulge the people, put it, the Constitution was "a republican remedy for the diseases most incident to republican government."[24] Whatever the terms used, the Federalists in their public statements were not able to say candidly what at least some had said within the secrecy of the Philadelphia Convention: that the source of their difficulties came from too much local democracy, and that the solution was to limit this local democracy by erecting a more aristocratic structure over it.

In the end, the Federalists had little choice in their rhetoric. If they were to get the Constitution ratified, they had to work within the egalitarian and populist currents flowing from the Revolution. Despite the suggestion of disingenuousness, there is no denying their achievement. They thought and acted more creatively than any other generation in American history. They not only convinced the country to accept a national government inconceivable a decade earlier but they did so without repudiating the republicanism and the popular basis of government that nearly all devoutly believed in. The Federalists of 1787–1788 were not the Federalists of the 1790s; they were alarmed by the abuses of popular power, but they were not, like the later Federalist party, actually fearful of the people. They remained confident that, if only the people's choice could be undisturbed by ambitious local demagogues and crass electioneering, the people would "choose men of the first character for wisdom and integrity," men very much like themselves.[25] It was an achievement that transcended their intentions and one that has rightly earned them the admiration of subsequent generations. Somehow for a moment they reconciled aristocracy with democracy and gave us, as John P. Roche has said, "a classic example of the potentialities of a democratic elite."[26]

Nevertheless, great as the Federalists' achievement was, the cost to the future of American politics was high. By using the most popular and democratic rhetoric available to explain and justify their aristocratic system, the Federalists helped to foreclose the development of an American intellectual tradition in which differing ideas of politics would be intimately and genuinely related to differing social interests. In other words, the Federalists of 1787 furthered the American disavowal of any sort of aristocratic conception of politics and encouraged the American belief that the ills of democracy can be cured by more democracy. From the creation of the Constitution, as the Federalist party of the 1790s eventually discovered to its dismay, democracy in America was no longer something to be discussed skeptically and challenged but a faith to which all Americans and all American institutions must unquestioningly adhere.

NOTES

1. The assertion that "there was and is no 'real' Constitution" is open to misunderstanding and criticism, which I would like to forestall. I am arguing that there was not in 1787 a single "true" or "correct" interpretation of the Constitution. The Constitution was what people thought it was; hence, the disagreement over its meaning. The continuing struggle over the

meaning of the Constitution, . . . only substantiates my point. That struggle will never end because the "true" meaning, the "true reality" of the Constitution will never be finally discovered; no such animal exists.

It should not be thought that I am saying we haven't had a Constitution at all to debate. The Constitution is a very different thing from what it was in 1787, and not just because of the amendments. It can be argued that many, if not all, of these changes and additions are "illegitimate," but, if the political culture generally comes to hold them as legitimate, then for most people this changed Constitution becomes the "real" Constitution. It is because of this process of constant accretion and change that we have continuous arguments among ourselves over the meaning of the Constitution. The participants in the struggle obviously have to believe that their particular contesting interpretations are more "true" or "right" than others.

2. For the most recent and most persuasive account of the Confederation Congress, see Jack N. Rakove, The Beginnings of National Politics: An Interpretive History of the Continental Congress (New York: Knopf, 1979).

3. See E. James Ferguson, The Power of the Purse: A History of American Public Finance, 1776-1790 (Chapel Hill: University of North Carolina Press, 1961), p. 337; Merrill Jensen, The New Nation: A History of the United States, 1781-1789 (New York: Knopf, 1950), pp. 348-49; and Jackson Turner Main, The Antifederalists: Critics of the Constitution, 1781-1788 (Chapel Hill: University of North Carolina Press, 1961), pp. 177-78.

4. See Stanley Elkins and Eric McKitrick, "The Founding Fathers: Young Men of the Revolution," Political Science Quarterly, vol. 76 (1961), pp. 181-216; John P. Roche, "The Founding Fathers: A Reform Caucus in Action," American Political Science Review, vol. 55 (1961), pp. 799-816; Robert A. Rutland, Ordeal of the Constitution: The Antifederalists and the Ratification Struggle of 1787-1788 (Norman: University of Oklahoma Press, 1966); and Forrest McDonald, E Pluribus Unum: The Formation of the American Republic, 1776-1790 (Boston: Houghton Mifflin, 1965), p. 236.

5. John Fiske, The Critical Period of American History (New York: Houghton Mifflin, 1888), p. 55.

6. For the importance of the state constitutions to the Revolution of 1776, see Gordon S. Wood, The Creation of the American Republic, 1776-1787 (Chapel Hill: University of North Carolina Press, 1969), pp. 127-255.

7. Thomas Jefferson, Notes on the State of Virginia, ed. William Peden (Chapel Hill: University of North Carolina Press, 1955), p. 120.

8. Madison's observations on Jefferson's draft of a constitution for Virginia (1788), Julian P.

Boyd, ed., The Papers of Thomas Jefferson (Princeton: Princeton University Press, 1950-), vol. 6, pp. 308-09; Ezra Stiles, "The United States Elevated to Glory and Honor . . ." (New Haven, 1783), in John W. Thornton, ed., The Pulpit of the American Revolution . . . (Boston: Gould and Lincoln, 1860), p. 420.

9. Edmund Randolph in Max Farrand, ed., The Records of the Federal Convention (New Haven: Yale University Press, 1937), vol. 1, p. 51.

10. Madison quoted in Charles Warren, The Making of the Constitution (Cambridge, Massachusetts: Harvard University Press, 1947), p. 82.

11. Madison to Edmund Randolph, April 8, 1787, Robert A. Rutland et al., eds., The Papers of James Madison (Chicago: University of Chicago Press, 1962-), vol. 9, p. 370; Madison to George Washington, April 16, 1787, ibid., vol. 9, p. 383.

12. For a recent discussion of Madison's national veto, see Charles F. Hobson, "The Negative on State Laws: James Madison and the Crisis of Republican Government," William and Mary Quarterly, 3rd ser., vol. 36 (1979), pp. 215-35.

13. The Federalist, ed. Jacob E. Cooke (Middletown, Connecticut: Wesleyan University Press, 1961), No. 10; Madison to Jefferson, October 24, 1787, Rutland et al., eds., Madison Papers, vol. 10, p. 214.

14. On this point, see Robert J. Morgan, "Madison's Theory of Representation in the Tenth Federalist," Journal of Politics, vol. 36 (1974), pp. 852-85; and Paul F. Bourke, "The Pluralist Reading of James Madison's Tenth Federalist," Perspectives in American History, vol. 9 (1975), pp. 271-95.

15. Madison to Washington, April 16, 1787, Rutland et al., eds., Madison Papers, vol. 9, p. 384.

16. Madison to Jefferson, October 24, 1787, Rutland et al., eds., Madison Papers, vol. 10, p. 212.

17. Jackson Turner Main, Political Parties before the Constitution (Chapel Hill: University of North Carolina Press, 1973).

18. Wilson in Farrand, ed., Records of the Federal Convention, vol. 1, p. 154. The first Congress had only sixty-five representatives, smaller than most of the state assemblies at that time.

19. The Federalist No. 10.

20. See especially Samuel P. Hays, "Political Parties and the Community-Society Continuum," in William Nisbet Chambers and Walter Dean Burnham, eds., The American Party Systems: Stages of Political Development (New York: Oxford University Press, 1967), pp. 152-81.

21. Dickinson in Farrand, ed., Records of the Federal Convention, vol. 2, p. 278; Hamilton in Jonathan Elliot, ed., The Debates of the Several State Conventions on the Adoption of the Federal Constitution (Philadelphia: Lippincott, 1876), vol. 2, p. 256.

22. See especially Martin Diamond, "Democracy and *The Federalist:* A Reconsideration of the Framers' Intent," *American Political Science Review,* vol. 53 (1959), pp. 52–68, and Diamond, "The Federalist, 1787–1788," in Leo Strauss and Joseph Cropsey, eds., *History of Political Philosophy* (Chicago: Rand McNally, 1963), pp. 573–93.

23. Nathaniel Gorham (Massachusetts) in Elliot, ed., *Debates,* vol. 2, p. 69.

24. *The Federalist* No. 10. Madison's careful distinction between a republic, "in which the scheme of representation takes place," and a democracy, where the people "assemble and administer the government in person," was not supported by many Federalists. Before long all American governments were being called "representative democracies." See Wood, *Creation of the American Republic,* pp. 593–96.

25. *Hartford, Connecticut Courant,* February 5, 1787.

26. Roche, "The Founding Fathers," p. 816.

POSTSCRIPT

The Constitution: Was It an Economic Document?

Parenti is a radical political scientist. In *Democracy for the Few,* he extends the underlying assumptions of Beard's *An Economic Interpretation* throughout his own examination of the operations of our present-day American government. Like Beard, Parenti assumes that the Constitution was written to protect the economic interests of the upper classes. The checks and balances system, he argues, was designed to protect the property of the elite while pretending to give some political power to the masses.

Wood agrees with the class conflict theories of Beard and Parenti regarding the supporters and opponents of the Constitution, but he stresses social and ideological, not economic, motivations. Wood argues that the Federalists were upper-class aristocrats who believed that the national government, which they controlled, provided a more cosmopolitan and enlightened outlook than the local and provincial interests of the "humbler sort" who ran the state assemblies. In a clever manner, says Wood, the Federalists at both the Philadelphia and the state ratifying conventions argued falsely that the new national government was as democratic as the Confederation government it would replace. In truth, the new national government was a republic (indirect representation), not a democracy (direct ruling by the people). Only members of the House of Representatives were directly elected by the people; the president, U.S. senators, and Supreme Court justices were chosen by indirect means.

In a manner also reminiscent of Beard's conspiratorial thesis, Wood believes that the Founding Fathers argued for the new government in "democratic" language to avoid charges of setting up an "aristocratic" government. He also distinguishes between the Federalists of the 1780s, who feared abuses of power, and the 1790s Federalists, who distrusted the masses.

Students wishing to pursue his "republican" thesis should read Wood's *The Creation of the American Republic, 1776–1789* (North Carolina University Press, 1969). Attempts to move beyond Wood can be found in the *William and Mary Quarterly* (July 1987), which contains the papers presented by a dozen historians at a symposium that treated Wood's major work. A devastating critique of the methodological fallacies of Wood and other intellectual writers on this period can be found in Ralph Lerner's "The Constitution of the Thinking Revolutionary," in Richard Beeman et al., eds., *Beyond Confederation: Origins of the Constitution and American National Identity* (University of North Carolina Press, 1987).

The bicentennial celebration of the Constitution witnessed the publication of numerous works on this period. Edmund S. Morgan reviews 19 of them in *The New Republic* (June 29, 1987). Richard B. Morris, *The Forging of the Union,*

1781–1789 (Harper & Row, 1987), summarizes a lifetime of scholarship by one of the most knowledgeable historians of this period. Michael Kammen, *A Machine That Would Go Of Itself: The Constitution in American Culture* (Knopf, 1986), elaborates on the place the Constitution has occupied "in the public consciousness and symbolic life of the American people."

Beard's work has been heavily criticized for its antidemocratic tone and faulty arguments by neoconservative historian Robert E. Brown, in *Charles Beard and the Constitution* (Princeton, 1956), and for oversimplifying political ideologies and economic interest groups in Forrest McDonald, *We The People: The Economic Origins of the Constitution* (Chicago, 1958), and more recently, *Novus Seclorum: The Intellectual Origins of the Constitution* (Kansas, 1985). The two most important interpretative essays are Stanley Elkins and Eric McKitrick, "The Founding Fathers: Young Men of the Revolution," *Political Science Quarterly* (June 1961), an older but outstanding article which summarizes the neoconservative attacks on Beard and attempts its own synthesis, and James H. Hutson, "The Constitution: An Economic Document?" in Leonard W. Levy and Dennis J. Mahoney, eds., *The Framing and Ratification of the Constitution* (New York, 1987). Finally, Peter S. Onaf's "Reflections on the Founding: Constitutional Historiography in Bicentennial Perspective," *William and Mary Quarterly* (April 1989) is essential for advanced students because of its sophisticated analysis and voluminous references.

ISSUE 8

Did President Jefferson Outfederalize the Federalists?

YES: Richard Hofstadter, from *The American Political Tradition and the Men Who Made It* (Random House, 1948)

NO: Forrest McDonald, from *The Presidency of Thomas Jefferson* (The University Press of Kansas, 1976)

ISSUE SUMMARY

YES: Pulitzer Prize-winning historian Richard Hofstadter argues that Thomas Jefferson was a moderate, practical politician who followed a course of action which eventually co-opted the major policies of the Federalists.

NO: Professor of history Forrest McDonald believes that President Jefferson attempted to replace Hamiltonian Federalist principles with a Republican ideology and that he wanted to restore America's agrarian heritage.

"Jefferson still lives," stated John Adams as he died on July 4, 1826, the 50th anniversary of Independence Day. Unknown to Adams, Jefferson had passed away a few hours earlier that same day. But Jefferson never really died. He was one of the few heroes of history to become a living legend.

There are two Jeffersons. One was the true Renaissance man who knew a little about everything. "Not a sprig of grass shoots uninteresting to me," he once wrote to his daughter. As a philosopher who spoke to posterity, he waxed eloquent in his letters about civil liberties, the rights of man, states' rights, strict construction of the Constitution, and the virtues of the agrarian way of life. A practical man, he was an architect of the nation's capital, the University of Virginia, and his own home. Visitors to his Monticello plantation are amazed by the elaborate pulley and drainage systems that he devised. A respected member of the Virginia aristocracy who owned about 10,000 acres and from 100 to 200 slaves, Jefferson ran his farm in a self-sufficient manner and carefully studied the efficiency of employing slave labor. When he traveled, he recorded everything he observed in detailed journals. The newest inventions—steam engines, thermometers, elevators—fascinated him.

The other Jefferson was the man who has been ranked among the top half-dozen U.S. presidents in every major poll taken by historians in the last 35 years. Does Jefferson deserve such an honor? It depends on how the functions of the presidency are perceived. One role that Jefferson disdained more than any other president in our history was the function of chief of state. So important to the modern presidency, the ceremonial role could have been played by the tall, dignified Virginia aristocrat as well as it was by George Washington, had he so desired. But Jefferson hated formalities. He walked to his inauguration and refused to wear a hat. Because he was a widower, he abandoned the practice of holding large, formal parties. He also felt they smacked too much of monarchy. He preferred small, intimate dinners with his intellectual friends and political cronies. A shy, soft-spoken individual with a slight speech impediment, the author of the Declaration of Independence did not campaign for office. He also refused to deliver an annual address to Congress, preferring to send them a written message. In short, if one uses modern terminology, Jefferson was not "mediagenic." In 1988, Jefferson might not have even been nominated by his party, much less elected to the presidency.

In the following selections, Richard Hofstadter rejects the notion that Jefferson was an impractical visionary who thought that a rebellion every 20 years was an excellent idea. He believes that Jefferson was a cautious, practical politician with policies appealing to moderate Federalists and what today would be called Middle Americans. By 1820 Jefferson and his successors had totally eliminated the Federalist Party "but only at the cost of taking over its program." Forrest McDonald, on the other hand, sees Jefferson as a man staunchly opposed to Alexander Hamilton's Federalist programs and his philosophy of government. In his view, Jefferson wanted to take government away from the mercantile classes and return it to the farmers.

YES

Richard Hofstadter

THOMAS JEFFERSON:
THE ARISTOCRAT AS DEMOCRAT

Jefferson was a complex person who must be measured in whole, not in part, in action as well as thought. There were deep ambiguities in his thinking, which made any effort at consistency impossible. Although Federalist historians have cited these ambiguities as evidence of a moral taint, a constitutional shiftiness of mind, they may in fact be traced to a continuously ambivalent personal and political history. He valued much more highly the achievements of his father, whom he intensely admired, than the social status of his mother, whose influence he never acknowledged; but from the beginning he was aware of both the assurance of the aristocracy and the real merits and talents of men who came from unknown families. In his autobiography he remarked dryly of the Randolph genealogy: "They trace their pedigree far back in England and Scotland, to which let everyone ascribe the faith and merit he chooses." When he came to maturity, Jefferson was a slaveowner and yet a revolutionist, who could say that man's rights were "unalienable" at the very moment when he owned several dozen souls. All his life he circulated among men of wealth, learning, and distinction, and as befitted one who disliked acrimony he learned to accommodate himself to them—but he also absorbed the most liberal and questionable opinions of his age and associated on congenial terms with men like Thomas Paine and Joel Barlow. In American politics he became a leader of yeomen farmers—but also of great planters. He was the head of a popular faction that stood against the commercial interests—but it was also a propertied faction with acquisitive aspirations of his own. Well read in the best philosophical literature of his century, he accepted broad cosmopolitan ideas, but he was also an ardent American patriot. He was a pacifist in personal temperament and philosophy, a nationalist by training, and yet a Virginian with strong parochial loyalties. He wanted with all his heart to hold to the values of agrarian society, and yet he believed in progress. Add to all this the fact that he lived an unusually long life, saw many changes, and tried to adapt his views to changing circumstances.

Jefferson had warm impulses. His cosmopolitan mind refracted the most advanced and liberating ideas of his time. He believed in those ideas, and rephrased and reiterated them in language that has become classic; he was not in the habit of breaking lances trying to fulfill them. The generous and emancipating thoughts for which his name is so justly praised are to be found almost entirely in his *private* correspondence; after he wrote the Declaration of Independence and the Virginia Statute for Religious Freedom he avoided expressing his more unacceptable ideas in public. He understood that in the workday world of public activity his most lofty ideals were chiefly valuable to indicate the direction in which society should be guided. He never really expected them to be realized in his time and preferred to place his hopes in progress, in the promise that mankind would consummate his ideals in some magnificent future. ("Your taste is judicious," John Adams once taunted him, "in liking better the dreams of the future than the history of the past.")

Jefferson's practical activity was usually aimed at some kind of minimum program that could be achieved without keen conflict or great expenditure of energy. He hated vigorous controversy, shrank from asserting his principles when they would excite the anger of colleagues or neighbors. He tried to avoid a wide circulation of his *Notes on Virginia* because he did not want Virginians to read his bitter remarks on slavery and a few tart observations on the province's Constitution. Jefferson did not lack courage—his futile embargo policy, carried out under bitter protest from every part of the country, proves that—but rather that hardihood of spirit which makes a political fight bearable. Although he had

strong political prejudices and sometimes violent animosities, he did not enjoy power and could not bear publicity. He was acutely sensitive to criticism, admitting to Francis Hopkinson in 1789: "I find the pain of a little censure, even when it is unfounded, is more acute than the pleasure of much praise." Abnormally shy and troubled by a slight speech defect, he found it impossible to read his messages in person to Congress as Washington and Adams had done. He had not the temperament of an agitator, hardly even of a leader in the qualities that leadership requires under modern democracy. Not once did he deliver an exciting speech. His private life was one of enormous variety and interest, and there were many times when he would have been happy to desert public service to enjoy is farm, his family, and his books.

Jefferson's Federalist opponents feared, above all, power lodged in the majority. Jefferson feared power lodged anywhere else. In his First Inaugural Address he asked concerning the common observation "that man cannot be trusted with the government of himself": "Can he, then, be trusted with the government of others?" He would have agreed with Madison that power is "of an encroaching nature," and he was sure that power corrupts those who possess it. "If once the people become inattentive to the public affairs," he wrote Edward Carrington from Paris, "you and I and Congress and Assemblies, Judges and Governors, shall all become wolves. It seems to be the law of our general nature, in spite of individual exceptions."

Admitting that a majority will often decide public questions wrongly, Jefferson argued that "the duperies of the people are less injurious" than the self-interested policies of kings, priests, and aristocrats. He refused to be alarmed by popular uprisings like the Shays Rebellion. In the safety of his private correspondence he felt free to say that "honest republican governments" should be "so mild in their punishment of rebellions as not to discourage them too much." "A little rebellion now and then is a good thing, and as necessary in the political world as storms in the physical." The people are not always well informed, but it is better that they have misconceptions that make them restless than that they be lethargic—for lethargy in the people means death for republics.

Again and again Jefferson urged that the people be educated and informed through a broad common-school system and a free press. Although he had small faith in the power of republics to resist corruption and decay, he hoped that mass education would stem this degenerative process. Education not only would give stability and wisdom to the politics of a commonwealth, but would widen opportunities, bring out the natural talents that could be found in abundance among the common people. Throughout Jefferson's life there runs this humane concern for "the pursuit of happiness," for the development of the individual without regard to limitations of class.

By and large, however, when Jefferson spoke warmly of the merits and abilities of "the people" he meant "the farmers." He did not see a town until he was almost eighteen, and he believed deeply that rural living and rural people are the wellspring of civic virtue and individual vitality, that farmers are the best social base of a democratic republic. "Those who labor in the earth are the chosen people of God, if ever he had a chosen people," he proclaimed in his Notes on *Virginia*. "Corruption of morals in the mass of cultivators is a phenomenon of which no age nor nation has furnished an example."

> . . . generally speaking, the proportion which the aggregate of the other classes of citizens bears in any State to that of its husbandmen, is the proportion of its unsound to its healthy parts, and is a good enough barometer whereby to measure its degree of corruption. While we have lands to labor then, let us never wish to see our citizens occupied at a work bench or twirling a distaff. . . . Let our workshops remain in Europe

The American economy, then, should be preserved in its agricultural state. Manufacturers, cities, urban classes, should be held at a minimum. So Jefferson believed, at any rate, until the responsibilities of the White House and the conduct of foreign policy caused him to modify his views. He once went so far as to say that he hoped the United States would remain, with respect to Europe, on the same economic footing as China. Commerce he would encourage—it supplied the needs of agriculture—but this was the extent of his early concessions to the urban classes.

Thus far Jefferson, with his faith in the farmers, his distrust of the urban classes, and his belief in the long-range value of rebellions and social disturbances, seems at the opposite pole from the Constitution-makers—and so he might have been if his political theory had been elaborated into a coherent system. But he had more in common with the conservative thinkers of his age than is usually recognized. His differences with the political theory of the Constitution-makers were differences of emphasis, not of structure. He shared their primary fears. He did not think that political constitutions could safely rely on man's virtue. In a letter to Mann Page in 1795 he declared that he could not accept the idea of the Rochefoucaulds and Montaignes that "fourteen out of fifteen men are rogues." "*But I have always found that rogues would be uppermost*, and I do not know that the proportion is too strong for the higher orders and for those who, rising above the swinish multitude, always contrive to nestle themselves into the places of power and profit." . . .

Jefferson, of course, accepted the principle of balanced government and the idea that the people must be checked. "It is not by the consolidation, or concentration of powers, but by their distribution that good government is effected," he wrote in his autobiography. He designed a constitution for Virginia in 1776 which employed the principle of checks and balances and required property qualifications of voters. Of the two houses of the legislature, only the lower was to be elected by the people; the senate was to be chosen by the house, as was the governor, so that two of the three parts of the lawmaking body were at once removed from the citizens. Five years later, criticizing the Constitution that had been adopted by Virginia instead of his own, he complained primarily of its lack of checks: the Senate and the House of Delegates were too much alike because both were chosen by the voters in the same way. *"The purpose of establishing different houses of legislation is to introduce the influence of different interests or different principles."* he continued:

> All the powers of government, legislative, executive, and judiciary, result to the legislative body. The concentrating these in the same hands is precisely the definition of despotic government. It will be no alleviation that these powers will be exercised by a plurality of hands and not by a single one. One hundred and seventy-three despots would surely be as oppressive as one. . . . As little will it avail us that they are chosen by ourselves. An *elective despotism* was not the government we fought for, but one which should not only be founded on free principles, but in which the powers of government should be so divided and balanced among several bodies of magistracy, as that no one could transcend their legal limits without being effectually checked and restrained by the others.

This would have been accounted sound doctrine at the Philadelphia Convention of 1787. A government that does not divide and balance powers in a system of checks is precisely what Jefferson means by despotic; the fact that the governing body is chosen by the people does not qualify his complaint; such a government, without checks, is merely "an elective despotism." Jefferson, then, refused to accept simple majority rule, adopting instead the idea that "different interests or different principles" should be represented in government.

All this sounds close to the theories of Madison and Adams. In fact, Jefferson did not differ with them strongly enough to challenge their conservative writings of the constitutional period. In 1788 he wrote to Madison praising the *Federalist* as "the best commentary on the principles of government which ever was written." Two years later, advising his nephew Thomas Mann Randolph on a course of reading, Jefferson praised Locke's work as being "perfect as far as it goes," and then added: "Descending from theory to practice, there is no better book than the Federalist." In 1787 he told John Adams that he had read his *Defence* "with infinite satisfaction and improvement. It will do great good in America. Its learning and its good sense will, I hope, make it an institute for our politicians, old as well as young."

When the text of the federal Constitution of 1787 reached him in France, Jefferson confessed to Adams that he was staggered at what had been attempted, but soon recovered his composure. He informed Madison that he saw many good features in it, but objected strongly to two things: the absence of a bill of rights (later included in the first ten amendments), and the eligibility of the president for more than one term. In the end he gave it a substantial endorsement: "It is a good canvas, on which some strokes only want retouching." His regard for it grew with the years.

As much as Madison or Morris, Jefferson disliked the idea of city mobs—"the panders of vice and the instruments by which the liberties of a country are generally overturned"—but he believed that they would not emerge in the calculable future because America's lands would be open to make substantial farmers of the ragged and discontented. In his First Inaugural he said that the land would last the American people "to the hundredth and thousandth generation"! The United States would be a nation of farmers, tilling their own soil, independent, informed, unexcitable, and incorruptible. Such a national destiny, he must have felt, would be secured by the Louisiana Purchase.

The future, then, would be founded on a propertied class in a propertied nation. Jefferson leaned strongly to the idea that a propertied interest in society is necessary to a stable political mentality. In 1800 he wrote a friend that he had always favored universal manhood suffrage; but

this was one of those theoretical notions to which he was not firmly wedded. "Still I find some very honest men," he added, "who, thinking the possession of some property necessary to give due independence of mind, are for restraining the elective franchise to property." His 1776 draft of a constitution for Virginia had required that voters own either a freehold estate of twenty-five acres in the country or one fourth of an acre in town, or pay taxes within two years of the time of voting. Never did Jefferson try to introduce universal manhood suffrage anywhere.

The outstanding characteristic of Jefferson's democracy is its close organic relation to the agrarian order of his time. It seems hardly enough to say that he thought that a nation of farmers, educated, informed, and blessed with free institutions, was the best suited to a democratic republic, without adding that he did not think any *other* kind of society a good risk to maintain republican government. In a nation of large cities, well-developed manufactures and commerce, and a numerous working class, popular republicanism would be an impossibility—or at best an improbability.

Certainly the balance of Jefferson's good society is a tenuous thing: the working class is corrupt; merchants are corrupt; speculators are corrupt; cities are "pestilential"; only farmers are dependably good. Sunder human nature from its proper or "natural" nourishment in the cultivation of the soil and the ownership of real property, and he profoundly distrusts it. Sunder democracy from the farm and how much more firmly does he believe in it than John Adams? Yet this is just what the relentless advance of modern industrial capitalism has done: it has sundered four fifths of society from the soil, has separated the masses from their property, and has built life increasingly on what Jefferson would have called an artificial basis—in short, has gradually emptied the practical content out of Jefferson's agrarian version of democracy. This process had its earliest beginnings during Jefferson's lifetime, and, as we shall see, he yielded a good part of his agrarian prejudices (like the pragmatic, undoctrinaire soul that he was) without sacrificing his democratic preferences. But although he clung to his humane vision of democracy, he left it without the new economic rationale that it required.

In after years Jefferson declared that the struggle between his party and the Federalists was one between those who cherished the people and those who distrusted them. But he had been associated with a number of men like Elbridge Gerry, Pierce Butler, Charles Pinckney, and Edmund Randolph who did not cherish the people in the least, and the differences in abstract principle were hardly intense enough to account for the fierceness of the conflict or for the peculiar lines along which it was drawn. Although democratically minded Americans did stand with Jefferson, the line of division was essentially between two kinds of property, not two kinds of philosophy.

The Federalists during Hamilton's service as Secretary of the Treasury had given the government a foundation of unashamed devotion to the mercantile and investing classes. Through his method of funding the national debt, through his national bank, and through all the subsidiary policies of the government, Hamilton subsidized those who invested in manufactures, commerce, and public securities, throwing as much of the tax burden as possible on planters and farmers. The landed interests, however, were in a majority, and it was only a matter of time before they could marshal themselves in a strong party of their own. Jefferson's party was formed to defend specific propertied interests rather than the abstract premises of democracy, and its policies were conceived and executed in the sober, moderate spirit that Jefferson's generation expected of propertied citizens when they entered the political arena.

When Jefferson was elected in 1800, the more naïve Federalists, frightened to the marrow by their own propaganda, imagined that the end of the world had come. Fisher Ames anticipated that he would soon scent "the loathsome steam of human victims offered in sacrifice." Among those who knew the President-elect, however, there was no such hysteria—especially not among insiders who had private knowledge of the circumstances under which he had been chosen.

The election of 1800 was unique in American history. Because no distinction had yet been made in the Constitution between ballots cast for presidential and vice-presidential candidates, Jefferson and his running mate, Aaron Burr, won the same number of votes in the electoral college. The tied contest was thrown into the House of Representatives, where it fell to Federalist Congressmen to choose between two Republicans. To some this seemed merely a choice of executioners; others, looking upon Jefferson as their supreme enemy, gravitated naturally toward Burr. Not so Alexander Hamilton, who had long been Burr's political rival in New York. In a remarkable letter to a Federalist Representative, Hamilton gave a shrewd estimate of Jefferson's character. He admitted that his old foe's views were "tinctured with fanaticism; that he is too much in earnest with his democracy." But it is not true, he continued, in an appraisal that is as penetrating in substance as it is unfair in phrasing,

> that Jefferson is zealot enough to do anything in pursuance of his principles which will contravene his popularity or his interest. He is as likely as any man I know to temporize—to calculate what will be likely to promote his own reputation and advantage; and the probable result of such a temper is the preservation of systems, though originally opposed, which, being once established, could not be overturned without danger to the person who did it. To my mind a true estimate of Mr. Jefferson's character warrants the expectation of a temporizing rather than a violent system. . . . Add to this that there is no fair reason to suppose him capable of being corrupted, which is a security that he will not go beyond certain limits

Not entirely satisfied with Hamilton's advice, Federalist leaders sought for assurance from Jefferson. The Virginian refused to commit himself in response to direct approach, but a friend who sounded him out informally was able to convey to the Federalists the comforting knowledge that Jefferson's intentions were moderate. That Jefferson abandoned any of his original plans, and in that sense bargained away any principles to win the office, is extremely unlikely; but when he entered the White House it was after satisfying the Federalists that he and they had come to some kind of understanding.

A little thought on the difficult position in which Jefferson now found himself should convince anyone that for a man of his moderate temperament there was small choice in fundamental policy. The Hamiltonian system, now in operation for twelve years, had become part of the American economy. The nation was faring well. To unscramble Hamilton's system of funding, banks, and revenues would precipitate a bitter struggle, widen the breach between the classes, and drive moderates out of the Republican ranks; it might bring depression, perhaps even rend the Union. And when the strife was over, there would always be the need of coming to terms with the classes that carried on commerce and banking and manufactures. Further, even if the landed interests were charged with the burden of Hamilton's debts, there was always the probability that they were better off when the system was working smoothing than they would be after a ruinously successful assault upon it. Jefferson, in short, found himself in a position much like that of modern social-democratic statesmen who, upon attaining power, find themselves the managers of a going concern that they fear to disrupt. Just as they have been incapable of liquidating capitalism, so Jefferson found himself unable to keep it from growing and extending its sway over the agrarian masses. Instead he wisely confined himself to trimming carefully at the edges of the Hamiltonian system.

Jefferson's First Inaugural Address was a conciliatory document contrived to bind up the wounds of the bitter period from 1798 to 1800 and to attract moderate Federalists to his support. "We are all republicans—we are all federalists," he declared. Soon the President was writing to Dupont de Nemours in words that show how well Hamilton had taken his measure:

> When this government was first established, it was possible to have kept it going on true principles, but the contracted, English, half-lettered ideas of Hamilton destroyed that hope in the

bud. We can pay off his debts in 15 years: but we can never get rid of his financial system. It mortifies me to be strengthening principles which I deem radically vicious, but this vice is entailed on us by the first error. In other parts of our government I hope we shall be able by degrees to introduce sound principles and make them habitual. What is practicable must often control what is pure theory

Jefferson kept his promises to friends and enemies alike. So successfully did he whittle away at the Federalist machinery by reducing expenditures that he was able to abolish the hated excise duties that stirred up the Whisky Rebellion and still make great inroads on the public debt. He tried hard to tame the federal judiciary—the last arm of the national government still under Federalist control—but to little effect. Through the Louisiana Purchase he widened the area for agrarian expansion. In 1811, two years after his terms were over, his party also allowed the First Bank of the United States to die upon the expiration of its charter.

But no attack was made upon other vital parts of the Hamiltonian system. No attempt was made to curb such abuses as speculation in public lands; nor did the well-organized Republican machines try hard to democratize the mechanics of government in the states or the nation. Limitations on the suffrage, for example, were left untouched. Professor Beard observes that the Republican states were "no more enamored of an equalitarian political democracy" than the Federalist states. Had Jefferson suggested a broad revision of the suffrage, many of his state leaders who had no use for theoretical democracy would have looked at him askance; if he had been the crusading democrat of Jeffersonian legend he could not have been so successful a machine leader.

Since his policies did not deviate too widely from those of the Federalists, Jefferson hoped to win over the moderates from their ranks and planned to use the patronage in doing so. "If we can hit on the true line of conduct which may conciliate the honest part of those who were called federalists," he wrote to Horatio Gates soon after taking office, "and do justice to those who have so long been excluded from [the patronage], I shall hope to be able to obliterate, or rather to unite the names of federalists and republicans."

In politics, then, the strategy was conciliation; in economics it was compromise. Soon the Republican machines began flirting with the financial interests they had sworn to oppose. Republican state legislatures issued charters liberally to local banks, which, in turn, tended to cleave to the Republican Party in politics. Jefferson gave his benediction to this process of mutual accommodation. When the Bank of Baltimore applied to the administration for assistance, he wrote to Secretary of the Treasury Albert Gallatin:

It is certainly for the public good to keep all the banks competitors for our favors by a judicious distribution of them and thus to engage the individuals who belong to them in support of the reformed order of things or at least in an acquiescence under it.

And:

. . . I am decidedly in favor of making all the banks Republican by sharing deposits among them in proportion to the disposition they show. . . . It is material to the safety of Republicanism to detach the mercantile interest from its enemies and incorporate them into the body of its friends. A merchant is naturally a Republican, and can be otherwise only from a vitiated state of things.

John Adams, in the quiet of his retirement at Quincy, might have been amused to see a new elite, closely linked to the fiscal interests, emerging in the heart of the Republican Party, but the militant agrarian John Taylor was deeply discouraged. In 1811 he wrote:

> . . . those who clearly discerned the injustice and impolicy of enriching and strengthening the federalists by bank or debt stock, at the publick expense, will seldom refuse to receive a similar sinecure. In short, a power in the individuals who compose legislatures, to fish up wealth from the people, by nets of their own weaving . . . will corrupt legislative, executive and judicial publick servants, by whatever systems constituted.

The inability of the Republicans to follow a pure policy of democratic agrarianism was matched by their inability to fashion a positive theory of agrarian economics. The predominant strain in their economic thinking was laissez-faire, their primary goal essentially negative—to destroy the link between the federal government and the investing classes. Acute and observant, their economic writing was at its best in criticism, but it offered no guide to a specific agrarian program. They had no plan; indeed, they made a principle of planlessness.

Jefferson has been described as a physiocrat by many writers—among them V. L. Parrington—but there is little more substance to this notion than there is to the preposterous idea that he was influenced chiefly by French thought. He was naturally content to remain an eclectic in economics. "No one axiom," he wrote to J. B. Say in 1815, "can be laid down as

wise and expedient for all times and circumstances." Their defense of free trade was responsible for whatever appeal the physiocrats had for Jefferson; but after he read *The Wealth of Nations* he became a convert to the doctrines of Adam Smith.

Like other theorists of the "natural law" era, Jefferson was quite ready to believe that the "natural" operations of the system of self-seeking private enterprise were intrinsically beneficent and should not normally be disturbed by government. In his First Inaugural he called for "a wise and frugal government, which shall restrain men from injuring one another, *which shall leave them otherwise free to regulate their own pursuits of industry and improvement*, and shall not take from the mouth of labor the bread it has earned." In a letter to Joseph Milligan, April 6, 1816, in which he discussed the proper limits of taxation, he concluded that the state ought not be aggressive in redistributing property:

> To take from one, because it is thought his own industry and that of his fathers has acquired too much, in order to spare to others, who, or whose fathers have not exercised equal industry and skill, is to violate arbitrarily the first principle of association, "the *guarantee* to everyone a free exercise of his industry and the fruits acquired by it."

John Taylor, perhaps the cleverest of the agrarian writers, likewise believed that "it is both wise and just to leave the distribution of property to industry and talents."

This conception of state policy was not anti-capitalist but anti-mercantilist. Jefferson and his followers had seen the unhappy effects of British governmental interference in American economic affairs, and they regarded Hamilton's system of state economic activity ("the contracted, English, half-lettered ideas of Hamilton") as merely a continuation at home of English economic ideas. Hamilton had set the government to helping the capitalists at the expense of the agrarians. The Jeffersonian response was not to call for a government that would help the agrarians at the expense of the capitalists, but simply for one that would let things alone. Where modern liberals have looked to government interference as a means of helping the poor, Jefferson, in common with other eighteenth-century liberals, thought of it chiefly as an unfair means of helping the rich through interest-bearing debts, taxation, tariffs, banks, privileges, and bounties. He concluded that the only necessary remedy under republican government would be to deprive the rich of these devices and restore freedom and equality through "natural" economic forces. Because he did not usually think of economic relationships as having an inherent taint of exploitation in them, he saw no necessity to call upon the state to counteract them. It was not the task of government to alter the economic order: the rich were not entitled to it and the poor would not find it necessary.

Jefferson rejected from his political philosophy the idea that one man has any intrinsic superiority over another; but he implicitly and perhaps unwittingly took it back again when he accepted competitive laissez-faire economics with its assumption that, so long as men were equal in law, and government played no favorites, wealth would be distributed in accordance with "industry and skill." Such a philosophy seemed natural enough to American farmers and planters who were in their own rights entrepreneurs, businessmen, exporters, and often, in a

small way, speculators with a weather eye on land values—men accustomed to stand on their own feet.

In due time, of course, Jeffersonian laissez-faire became the political economy of the most conservative thinkers in the country. Fifty years after Jefferson's death men like William Graham Sumner were writing sentences exactly like Jefferson's and John Taylor's to defend enterprising industrial capitalists and railroad barons from government regulation and reform. And one hundred years after the Jeffersonians first challenged John Adams at the polls, William Jennings Bryan, leading the last stand of agrarianism as an independent political power, was still striving to give his cause the color of respectability by showing that, after all, the farmer too was a businessman!

The practical conduct of foreign relations forced the Jeffersonians into a position no less frustrating than the maintenance of Hamilton's domestic system. In the East they found themselves almost as dependent on foreign commerce as were the sea traders of New England; their cheapest manufactured goods were bought abroad, and abroad their surplus was sold. In the West, where they looked about hungrily for new lands, fear of the Indians and of the closure of their trade outlet at New Orleans intensified their expansionist appetites. Expansion of their export market on the land and defense of it on the sea finally started them on a headlong retreat from Jeffersonian principles.

Jefferson himself was both a fierce patriot and a sincere pacifist. During the Napoleonic Wars, when England and France began to prey upon American commerce, he tried to retaliate by a pacifistic policy of economic coercion. In December 1807 Congress passed his drastic

Embargo Act, which simply confined American ships to port. His aim was to bring both sides to terms by withholding food and other supplies. This was the one doctrinaire and impractical measure of his career, and it proved a miserable failure. The Embargo not only failed to force Britain and France to respect American rights on the high seas, but also brought economic paralysis to the trading cities of the Northeast and the farms and plantations of the West and South. Jefferson finally admitted that the fifteen months of its operation cost more than a war. At the close of his second term the Embargo was replaced by a Nonintercourse Act, which opened trade with the rest of Europe but continued the costly ban on England and France.

Although Jefferson's successor, James Madison, continued to be harried by the maritime controversy, it was expansionism—what John Randolph called "agrarian cupidity"—rather than free trade that in the end brought the War of 1812. Southern planters wanted the Floridas and Northern farmers wanted Canada. Jefferson, always an ardent expansionist, approved of both aims and accepted the popular clichés with which expansion was justified. ("The possession of Canada," he wrote Adams in the summer of 1812, "secures our women and children forever from the tomahawk and scalping knife, by removing those who excite them.") As Julius W. Pratt has shown, enthusiasm for war with England raged along the broad arc of the frontier; resistance to war was hottest in the old Federalist and mercantile sections.

But if the United States was to withdraw from Europe economically, as under Jefferson, or to lose its best market through war, as under Madison, it had to find a way of employing its energies and

supplying its people with manufactured goods. Accordingly, capital, cut off from its normal investment outlet in overseas commerce, began to turn to manufacturing. The period of the Embargo and the War of 1812 proved to be the seedtime of American industrialism; Henry Adams remarked on the ironic fact that "American manufactures owed more to Jefferson than to northern statesmen who merely encouraged them after they were established."

Jefferson, of course, realized the immediate implications of his desire to pursue an independent economic course and as early as 1805 became a convert to the development of manufactures. "The spirit of manufacture has taken deep root among us," he wrote Dupont in 1809, "and its foundations are laid in too great expense to be abandoned." "Our enemy," he wailed to William Short in 1814, "has indeed the consolation of Satan on removing our first parents from Paradise: from a peaceable and agricultural nation he makes us a military and manufacturing one." To another he wrote; "We must now place the manufacturer by the side of the agriculturist." If the United States was to be peaceful, it must be self-sufficient, must end its dependence on foreign goods and overseas trade. The Napoleonic Wars destroyed the Jeffersonian dream of an agrarian commonwealth. Since Jeffersonian democracy, as embodied in measures of public policy, was entirely dependent upon the agrarian order, these wars also erased the practical distinction between Republicans and Federalists.

Manufactures, if they were to be maintained, needed tariffs, especially when British capitalists, hoping to crush their new competitors at once, began dumping goods in the American market at the close of the war. In 1816 the Republicans passed a much higher tariff than Hamilton's. They, not the Federalists, began the American protective system.

And war must be financed. Hard hit by the economic drain of military operations and the financial sabotage of the Northeast, the Republicans were confronted with a bitter dilemma: either they must go begging to the fiscal interests for support, or they must charter a new national bank to fill the vacuum they had created by letting Hamilton's bank expire. They chose the second course—and soon Republican newspapers were reprinting Alexander Hamilton's arguments in favor of the constitutionality of the First Bank of the United States! In vain did Jefferson rage in his letters against the banking system. A second bank, similar in structure to Hamilton's, was chartered by the Republicans in 1816. By the end of that year Jefferson's party had taken over the whole complex of Federalist policies—manufactures, bank, tariffs, army, navy, and all—and this under the administration of Jefferson's friend, neighbor, and political heir, James Madison. As Josiah Quincy complained, the Republicans had "out-Federalized Federalism." By 1820 they had driven the rival party completely off the field, but only at the cost of taking over its program. Federalism, Jefferson wrote to Albert Gallatin in 1823, "has changed its name and hidden itself among us . . . as strong as it has ever been since 1800." Nathaniel Macon, one of the last of the intransigent agrarians, lamented: "The opinions of Jefferson and those who were with him are forgot."

NO

Forrest McDonald

THE FAITHFUL AND
THE CRISIS OF FAITH

By most objective criteria, the Americans of 1800 had abundant cause to be proud, confident, even smug. . . .

And yet a sense of decadence had plagued the land for five years and more. From the pulpit rang cries of despair and doom; dishonesty as well as panic had invaded the marketplace; liars and libelers made a travesty of freedom of the press; violence, hysteria, and paranoia infested the public councils. Those Americans who called themselves Federalists felt betrayed by an ungrateful people for whom they had labored long and well, and feared that the horrors of Jacobinism and anarchy were hourly imminent. Those who called themselves Republicans felt betrayed by the twin evils of money and monarchy, and feared that liberty was about to breathe its last. Many who embraced neither political sect, whether from apathy or disgust, nonetheless shared the general feeling that the nation was in an advanced state of moral rot.

What the Federalists thought was actually of little consequence, for they were soon to expire, in what Thomas Jefferson called the Revolution of 1800. Almost miraculously, with their demise—though not because of it—despair suddenly gave way to euphoria. The new optimism, like the pervasive gloom and the defeat of Federalism that preceded it, stemmed from an interplay of social, religious, ideological, and economic forces and institutions, and from certain ingrained American characteristics. If one would understand the Jeffersonian revolution—how it happened and how it affected the nation's destiny—one must seek first to understand those forces, institutions, and characteristics.

One of the tenets of Republicanism in America was that, contrary to the teachings of Montesquieu and other theorists, republican government was best adapted to large territories, since in an area as vast as the United States the very diversity of the people would prevent an accumulation of power inimical to liberty. If the principle, was sound, the Americans were truly blessed, for their culture was nothing if not plural. At first blush that

From Forrest McDonald, *The Presidency of Thomas Jefferson* (University Press of Kansas, 1976). Copyright © 1976 by the University Press of Kansas. Reprinted by permission.

generalization might appear strong, or indeed entirely unfounded. Overwhelmingly, Americans were farmers or traders of British extraction and the Protestant faith; and even in politics, as Jefferson said in his inaugural address, "we are all republicans, we are all federalists." But the mother country itself was scarcely homogeneous, despite the amalgamation that financial and governmental power had brought to Great Britain in the eighteenth century; it comprised a host of different Celtic peoples—the Irish, the Welsh, the Cornish, and three distinct varieties of Scots—as well as Englishmen who differed from one another from north to south and east to west. Americans had proved slow to cast off the cultural baggage that they or their ancestors had brought with them; and a generation of independence, though building some sense of nationhood, had erased neither their original ethnic traits nor the intense localism that complemented and nourished those traits. As to differences in political principles, Jefferson was right in regarding them as largely superficial; yet they were substantive enough to lead many men to fight, and some to kill, one another. . . .

It should not be surprising that those who were saved through revivalism were also supporters of Jeffersonian Republicanism, for the theology of the one was psychologically akin to the ideology of the other. In part, to be sure, religious dissenters supported Jefferson because of his well-known championship of the cause of religious liberty. New England Baptists, for instance, having fought long and vainly for disestablishment, virtually idolized Jefferson. South and west of New England, however, establishment had long since ceased to be a live issue, and in much of that area Jefferson's religious views, to the extent that they were fully known, were if anything a political handicap. Rather, it was the compatibility of outlooks that made it possible for southern and western revivalists simultaneously to embrace evangelical Arminianism in religion and Republican ideology in politics.

Anglo-Americans, like the English themselves, were by and large nonideological people, but in 1800 the country was divided into two fiercely antagonistic ideological camps. In a loose, general sort of way, and with allowance for a number of exceptions, it can be said that the revival ideologies derived from contrasting views of the nature of man. The first view, that associated with the Hamiltonian Federalists, was premised upon the belief that man, while capable of noble and even altruistic behavior, could never entirely escape the influence of his inborn baser passions—especially ambition and avarice, the love of power and the love of money. The second, that espoused by the Jeffersonian Republicans, held that man was born with a tabula rasa, with virtually boundless capacity for becoming good or evil, depending upon the wholesomeness of the environment in which he grew. From the premise of the first it followed that government should recognize the evil drives of men as individuals, but check them and even harness them in such a way that they would work for the general good of society as a whole. From the premise of the second it followed that government should work to rid society of as many evils as possible—including, to a very large extent, the worst of evils, government itself. The one was positive, the other negative; the one sought to do good, the other to eradicate evil.

But the ideological division was more specifically focused than that. The High Federalists believed in and had fashioned a governmental system modeled upon the one that began to emerge in England after the Glorious Revolution of 1688 and was brought to maturity under the leadership of Sir Robert Walpole during the 1720s and 1730s. In part the system worked on the basis of what has often, simple-mindedly, been regarded as the essence of Hamiltonianism: tying the interests of the wealthy to those of the national government, or more accurately, inducing people of all ranks to act in the general interest by making it profitable for them to do so. But the genius of Hamilton's system ran much deeper. He erected a complex set of interrelated institutions, based upon the monetization of the public debt, which made it virtually impossible for anyone to pursue power and wealth successfully except through the framework of those institutions, and which simultaneously delimited and dictated the possible courses of government activity, so that government had no choice but to function in the public interest as Hamilton saw it. For instance, servicing the public debt, on which the whole superstructure rested, required a regular source of revenue that was necessarily derived largely from duties on imports from Great Britain. For that reason the United States could not go to war with Britain except at the risk of national bankruptcy, but could fight Revolutionary France or France's ally Spain, which were owners of territories that the United States avidly desired. Hamilton regarded this as the proper American foreign policy, at least for a time; and should circumstances change, he was perfectly capable of redefining the rules and rerigging the institutions so

as to dictate another policy. In domestic affairs, a wide range of implications of his system was equally inescapable.

The Jeffersonian Republicans regarded this scheme of things as utterly wicked, even as the English opposition had regarded Walpole's system. Indeed, though the Jeffersonians borrowed some of their ideas from James Harrington and other seventeenth-century writers and some from John Locke, their ideology was borrowed *in toto* from such Oppositionists as Charles Davenant, John Trenchard, Thomas Gordon, James Burgh, and most especially Henry St. John, First Viscount Bolingbroke. As a well-rounded system, it is all to be found in the pages of the *Craftsman*, an Oppositionist journal that Bolingbroke published from 1726 to 1737. The Republicans adjusted the ideology to fit the circumstances, to fit the United States Constitution and the "ministry" of Alexander Hamilton rather than the British constitution and the ministry of Robert Walpole; but that was all, and astonishingly little adjustment was necessary.

The Bolingbroke-Oppositionist *cum* Jeffersonian Republican ideology ran as follows. Corruption was everywhere, it was true; but given a proper environment, that need not be the way of things. Mankind could be rejuvenated through education and self-discipline, but that was possible only in the context of a life style that exalted living on, owning, and working the land. Only the land could give people the independence and unhurried existence that were prerequisite to self-improvement.

In some Edenic past, "the people"—which both Bolingbroke and Jefferson understood to mean the gentry and the solid yeomanry, and not to include aristocrats, money jobbers, priests, or the scum in the cities—had enjoyed the proper atmosphere, and therefore had been happy. Relationships were based upon agriculture and its "handmaiden" commerce, upon ownership of land, honest labor in the earth, craftsmanship in the cities, and free trade between individuals. All men revered God, respected their fellows, deferred to their betters, and knew their place. Because they were secure in their sense of place, they were also secure in their identities and their sense of values; and manly virtue, honor, and public spirit governed their conduct.

Then a serpent invaded the garden. To Bolingbroke, the evil started with the Glorious Revolution, which begat two bastard offspring: the Financial Revolution and the system of government by ministry, rather than the system of separation of powers that had been embodied in the ancient English constitution. To Jefferson, things were slightly more complex. America had been spared the corruption that had poisoned England until the accession of George III, and when it began to infest America, the spirit of 1776 had saved the day. Yet the American Revolution, because of the Hamiltonians, was ultimately undermined in just the way the English revolution had been: both were waged to check executive power, and both ended in the worst form of executive tyranny, ministerial government. The instrument of corruption in both instances was money—not "real" money, gold and silver, but artificial money in the form of public debt, bank notes, stocks, and other kinds of paper—the acquisition of which had nothing to do with either land or labor. Government ministers assiduously encouraged people to traffic in such paper, and with that stimulus the pursuit of easy wealth proved irresistible. A frenzy

for gambling, stock-jobbing, and paper shuffling permeated the highest councils of state and spread among the people themselves. Manly virtue gave way to effeminacy and vice; public spirit succumbed to extravagance, venality, and corruption.

Jefferson never tired of telling a story which, to him, epitomized what had gone wrong. Early in Washington's first administration, Jefferson recalled, he had been engaged in a friendly discussion of political principles with Hamilton and Vice-President Adams. Jefferson had maintained that an agrarian republic was most conducive to human happiness. Adams disagreed and, to Jefferson's horror, said that monarchy was better, that if the British government were purged of corruption it would be the best system ever devised. Hamilton, to the astonishment of both his listeners, declared that if the British system were urged of corruption it would not work: it was, he said, the most perfect system of government as it stood, for corruption was the most suitable engine of effective government.

In the matter of foreign relations, Republicans opposed the corrupt new order on two interrelated sets of grounds, with the same logic and often the same language that the Oppositionists had used earlier. One was that it entangled the nation with foreign powers, making independent, self-determined action impossible. Not only had Hamilton's system prevented the United States from siding with Revolutionary France against Britain in the early 1790s—which the Republicans believed to be the moral course, as well as the one most advantageous to the country—but it continually subjected America to alien influences because foreigners owned a large percentage of the public debt and the stock of the Bank of the United States. This involvement, in turn, gave rise to the second set of grounds for objection: foreign entanglements necessitated standing armies and navies, the support of which added to an already oppressive tax burden. The gentry and yeomanry, the Republicans believed, had been carrying more than their share of the tax load, even when taxes had been mainly in the form of import duties; and when excise taxes were levied specifically to support the military during the quasi war with France in 1798, the new burden fell almost exclusively on the landed. Taxes to support standing armies and navies were doubly galling because a professional military corps, as a class distinct from the people, was a threat to liberty in its own right, and it could also be unleashed to collect taxes by force, thus making the people pay for their own oppression. (English Oppositionists had been afraid of standing armies, but not of navies, for they had regarded a strong naval establishment as necessary for the protection of British commerce. The American Republicans' fear of standing armies was largely abstract, since they believed that the traditional American reliance on militias would prevent the rise of dangerous armies; but their hostility to navies was immediate and strong, for navies seemed most likely to involve the United States in fighting, and besides, navies cost a lot of money for upkeep even when they were not actively employed.)

Given all that, a revolution in the form of a return to first principles was called for. The several branches of government must be put back into constitutional balance, the moneychangers must be ousted from the temples, the gentry and yeomanry must be restored to supremacy, commerce must be returned to its subor-

dinate role as agriculture's handmaiden, and the values of the agrarian way of life must be cherished anew. In the undertaking, the Republicans had reason for hope—as, in reality, Bolingbroke and his circle had not—for it could all be done within the framework of the Constitution. The Constitution made it possible for the Republicans to gain control of the national government, and should they prove able to do so, only two major tasks needed to be done. The first was to purge government of extreme, irreconcilable monarchists. Jefferson believed that this could be done quickly and easily, for he thought that all but a handful of the people in government were men of sound and honorable principles. The second was to pay off the public debt as rapidly as possible, since that was the wellspring of the whole system of corruption. This would not be easy; but with good management, honest administration, and rigid economy, Jefferson believed that it could be accomplished within sixteen years.

That was the Republicans' ideology and the essence of their program: restore the separation of powers through the voluntary restraint of virtuous officials, cast out the monarchists and the money men, repeal the most oppressive of taxes, slash expenses, pay off the public debt, and thus restore America to the pristine simplicity of an Arcadian past.

It is to be observed that nothing has been said of strict construction of the Constitution and the extreme states'-rights doctrine of interposition, with which Jefferson was associated in his argument against the constitutionality of the Bank in 1791 and in his authorship of the Kentucky Resolutions against the Alien and Sedition Acts in 1798 and 1799. The fact is that only a handful of people knew of those documents or knew that Jefferson had written them; they were not a part of his public identity. Moreover, they were arguments that had been coined in the first instance as matters of political expediency—as means of heading off what Jefferson regarded as dangerous activity by the Federalists—and he never thought of them as sacred principles of constitutional government.

It is also to be observed that nothing has been said of the federal judiciary or of territorial expansion, two matters that consumed much of the energy and attention of the Jeffersonians when they came to power. The judiciary was of merely tangential consequence in the Jeffersonians' thinking; it became important to them only when it loomed as an unexpected stumbling block. Territorial expansion was an integral part of their program, but only implicitly: it went without saying that the nation should expand as the opportunity arose, to make room for generations of farmers yet unborn.

The Republicans gained control of the national government, after twelve years of Federalist domination, in a bitterly contested election that began in April of 1800 and was not completed until February of 1801. Their triumph was not a popular mandate for the implementation of the Republican ideology, nor was it a popular mandate for anything else. The presidential electors were, for the most part, chosen by the state legislatures, who also chose all the members of the United States Senate. The decision was in the hands of no more than a thousand men, and for practical purposes it turned on the activities of two or three dozen factional leaders. The supporters of Thomas Jefferson proved to be more skillful as political manipulators and masters of intrigue than were the sup-

porters of President John Adams—they had already proved, in capturing majorities in most legislatures, that they were better organized and more artful in arousing the voters—and that was the key to their success.

Nonetheless, their program had a broad basis of popular support, for it was peculiarly suited to the genius of the American people, and it appealed to their prejudices and interests as well. Moreover, there was no doubt that the Republicans had the talent, the energy, and the determination to carry the program into execution. But there was a question, a very large one. Republican theory was wondrous potent as an ideology of opposition. It remained to be seen whether it was a sound basis for administration.

Jeffersonian Republicanism was an ideology and an idea, a system of values and a way of looking at things; and as the aphorism goes, ideas and ideals have consequences. But it was also a program of action, carefully crafted and methodically executed; and as we are sometimes wont to forget, actions have consequences, too. To appraise Jefferson's presidency, it is therefore necessary to take both sets of criteria into account.

In the realm of ideas and ideology, Jeffersonian Republicanism was a body of thought that had been taken largely from the Oppositionist tradition of eighteenth-century England, principally as incorporated in the writings of Charles Davenant, John Trenchard, Thomas Gordon, James Burgh, and most particularly Henry St. John, Viscount Bolingbroke. This system of thought is explicated rather fully in the text, and it would be pointless to reiterate the effort here. It is useful, however, to remember that we are speaking of *oppositionist* thought: Bolingbroke and his predecessors and followers (whether calling themselves Tories or Commonwealthmen or Real Whigs) were condemning and seeking to undo the Financial Revolution and its attendant political corruption, as epitomized by the ministry of Sir Robert Walpole, In its stead, they proposed to restore a pristine and largely imaginary past in which life was rural, relationships were personal, the gentry ruled as a natural aristocracy, the main corpus of the citizenry was an honest yeomanry, commerce and craft-manufacturing existed only as handmaidens to agriculture, standing armies and privileged monopolies and fictitious paper wealth were all unknown, and government was limited—limited to an essentially passive function as impartial arbiter and defender of the existing social order, and limited by the unwritten but inviolable Constitution, dividing power among three separate, distinct, and coequal branches. In other words, the Jeffersonians' ideological forebears were reactionaries, swimming against the tide of history, for the world aborning was the depersonalized world of money, machines, cities, and big government.

The Jeffersonians, though castigated by their enemies as dangerous innovators and radicals, were likewise resisting the emergence of the modern world. They had seen the Hamiltonian Federalists attempting to transform and corrupt America, even as the Oppositionists had seen Walpole and the new monied classes transform and corrupt England, and they swallowed the Oppositionists' ideas and ideology whole. The Jeffersonians republicanized Bolingbroke, to be sure, developing the doctrine that absolute separation of powers, with a strictly limited presidency, was guaranteed by the written Constitution. In their hearts, however, they did not trust paper constitu-

tions, and their view of Jefferson's mission as president did not differ substantively and significantly from Bolingbroke's idea of a Patriot King: a head of state who would rally the entire nation to his banner, and then, in an act of supreme wisdom and virtue, voluntarily restrain himself and thus give vitality and meaning to the constitutional system. The Republicans also added the doctrine of states' rights, but that was mainly a tactical position which most of them abandoned—except rhetorically—once they came into control of the national government. The only genuine changes they brought to the ideology were two. One was to relocate its social base, from that of an Anglican gentry to that of southern slaveholders, Celtic-American back-country men, and evangelical Protestants. The other was to put the ideology into practice.

If who they were and what they were seeking are thus understood, it is evident that they remained remarkably true to their principles throughout Jefferson's presidency—despite charges to the contrary by a host of critics, ranging from Alexander Hamilton to Henry Adams to Leonard Levy. Moreover, they were remarkably successful in accomplishing what they set out to do. They set out to destroy the complex financial mechanism that Hamilton had built around the public debt, and they went a long way toward that goal—so close that if war could have been avoided for another eight years, their success might have been total. They also set out to secure the frontiers of the United States by expanding the country's territorial domain into the vast wilderness, and they succeeded so well that it became possible to dream that the United States could remain a nation of uncorrupted farmers for a thousand years to come.

And yet on the broader scale they failed, and failed calamitously—not because of their own shortcomings, but because their system was incompatible with the immediate current of events, with the broad sweep of history, and with the nature of man and society. As an abstract idea, Bolingbrokism *cum* Jeffersonian Republicanism may have been flawless, and it was certainly appealing. In the real world, it contradicted and destroyed itself.

At the core of the Republicans' thinking lay the assumption, almost Marxian in its naïveté, that only two things must be done to remake America as an ideal society and a beacon unto mankind. First, the public debt must be extinguished, for with it would die stock-jobbing, paper-shuffling, "monopoly" banking, excisemen, placemen, and all the other instrumentalities of corruption that the Walpole/Hamilton system "artificially" created. Second, governmental power must be confined to its constitutional limits, which implied reduction of the functions of government but also, and more importantly, meant adherence to the rules of the separation of powers—that being the only legitimate method, in their view, whereby a free government could exercise its authority. If ancient ways were thus restored, the Jeffersonians believed, liberty and independence would inevitably follow. In turn, liberty and independence—by which they meant the absence of governmental restraint or favor and the absence of effective interference from foreign powers—would make it possible for every man, equal in rights but not in talents, to pursue happiness in his own way and to find his own "natural" level in the natural order.

Things did not work out that way, especially in regard to relations with foreign powers: far from freeing the country from foreign interference, Republican policy sorely impaired the nation's ability to determine its own destiny. In their eagerness to retire the public debt, the Jeffersonians tried diligently to economize. Toward that end they slashed military and naval appropriations so much as to render the United States incapable of defending itself—at a time when the entire Western world was at war. Simultaneously, in their haste to destroy all vestiges of the Hamiltonian system, the Jeffersonians abolished virtually all internal taxes. This relieved the farmers and planters of an onerous tax burden and arrested the proliferation of hated excisemen, but it also made national revenues almost totally dependent upon duties on imports—which meant dependent upon the uninterrupted flow of international commerce, which in turn depended upon the will of Napoleon Bonaparte and the ministers of King George III.

For two or three years the Jeffersonians were extremely lucky. That is to say, during that period the kaleidoscope of events in Europe turned briefly and flukishly in their favor. They obtained Louisiana as a result of a concatenation of circumstances that was wildly improbable and was never to be repeated. They were able to pay off much of the public debt and to accumulate sizable treasury surpluses because Great Britain, out of consideration for its own interests, allowed the Americans to engage in a trade of debatable legality, thus swelling the volume of American imports and, concomitantly, the revenues flowing into the United States Treasury.

From 1803 onward, however, each turn of the international wheel was less favorable to the United States. By 1805 it was apparent that West Florida—for which the Jeffersonians hungered almost obsessively, since its strategic and economic value was considerably greater than that of all Louisiana excepting New Orleans—would not become American in the way that Louisiana had. In the same year it began to be clear that the British would not long continue to allow the United States to grow wealthy by trading with Britain's mortal enemies.

But for their ideology, the Jeffersonians could have reversed their earlier policy stance, embraced Britain, and become hostile toward France and Spain, thus enabling the nation to continue to prosper and expand. Given their ideological commitment, they could not do so. Moreover, given the consequences of their actions so far, they lacked the strength to make even a token show of force against Great Britain. Thus in 1807, when both Britain and France forbade the United States to engage in international commerce except as tributaries to themselves, the embargo—a policy of pusillanimity and bungling, billed as a noble experiment in peaceful coercion—was the only course open to them.

At home, as they became ever more deeply impaled upon the horns of their self-created international dilemma, the Jeffersonians became progressively less tolerant of opposition or criticism. From the beginning they had shown considerable disdain for the federal courts; as Jefferson's second term wore on, this disdain degenerated into contempt for due process of law and for law itself. Thus the embargo became a program of domestic tyranny in inverse ratio to its ineffectiveness as an instrument of international policy: the more the policy was found wanting, the more rigorously was it enforced.

The embargo, then, both as a bankrupt foreign policy and as a reign of domestic oppression, was not a sudden aberration but the logical and virtually certain outcome of the Jeffersonian ideology put into practice: the ideology's yield was dependence rather than independence, oppression rather than liberty.

One other aspect of the Jeffersonian experience wants notice, and that concerns the Republicans' conception of the presidency as a limited branch of government, absolutely separate from the legislative branch. In practice, adherence to that ideal was impossible because of the very nature of the presidential office. For one thing, though some presidential powers are relatively independent, others are intermeshed with those of Congress. For another, the American executive branch is "republicanized," or kept from being monarchical, by being made elective for a fixed term of years. To be sure, the Republicans' political machinery was so effective that Jefferson could doubtless have been elected to a third and even a fourth term, had he chosen. But Washington's two-term precedent was strong, and, what was more telling, the psychic cost of the presidential office was and is frightful; by the seventh or eighth year Jefferson, like Washington before him and like most two-term presidents who followed him, was physically, emotionally, and spiritually exhausted. The second term was therefore a lame-duck term, and that fact subtly but significantly altered the relationship between the president and Congress. Pure though Jefferson's motives and the motives of many Republican congressmen were, it was important to them that his popularity would cease to be of use to them in seeking reelection, and it was important to him that he would not need their political support in 1808. In the circumstances, Jefferson did what lame-duck presidents normally do—that is, he gravitated toward the arena in which he had less to do with Congress, the area of foreign relations; and Congress, and especially the Senate, also followed the norm by rising at the end to regain powers that it believed had been more or less usurped from it.

Still another crucial aspect of the American presidency, one with which the Republicans were not at all prepared to cope, is that the Constitution vests in one office and one person two distinct and nearly incompatible roles which under the British system had come to be divided between the king and his ministers. One is the truly monarchical function, that of serving as the ritualistic symbol of the nation. The other is the purely executive function, that of fashioning policy and directing its implementation. Success in the one hinges upon the president's charisma, his leadership, and his abstract appeal to the whole people; success in the other hinges upon the president's skill in tangible dealings with small groups and individual human beings. The Republicans' conception of the presidency was, in these terms, entirely unrealistic: they disavowed the first role and wanted the president to fill the second by standing as aloof from Congress as a proper king stands from his subjects.

Jefferson was superbly gifted at playing both roles, and he was able to play them without offending Republican sensibilities or prejudices. He ostentatiously disdained the pomp and pageantry that had marked the presidencies of Washington and Adams, but all the while he assiduously and effectively courted popularity. Foreign ministers and Federalist critics alike commented upon his inordinate love of popularity, and marked it as a weakness of character; perhaps it was, but it was also true wisdom, for reverence toward the Crown was a deep-rooted habit in the English-speaking world, and love of the president as king-surrogate was a crucial social adhesive for the diffuse and pluralistic infant United States. Indeed, in this respect Jefferson made a profound contribution toward the perdurance of the republic. Washington had been a veritable demigod and a symbol of the nation, and thus provided a sort of half-way house between monarchy and republicanism; Jefferson humanized the presidency and served as a symbol, not of the nation, but of the people, and thus made the transition complete.

In the role of policy-maker and administrator, Jefferson was even more skilled. After his inaugural he abandoned the monarchical practice of appearing in person before Congress; he never held court or levees, but invited congressmen in small groups for dinner, where he wore homespun and hosted them in the manner of a country squire; he never openly initiated legislation, and only deferentially suggested that Congress might look into one subject or another; he never vetoed a bill on policy grounds, and would not have dreamed of doing so. In sum, he allowed Congress to function with no overt presidential direction and with only the gentlest of presidential guidance. As to cabinet meetings, he conducted them as a democracy of equals. And yet, almost until the end, he ran Congress more successfully and more thoroughly than did any preceding president and precious few succeeding presidents, and the cabinet always reflected his will except when he had no firm opinions on a matter. Moreover, he did so without the use of bribery, patronage, corruption or coercion: it all flowed from the force of his intellect, his character, and his personality.

But, perversely, that too was a weakness of the Jeffersonian scheme of things: the system could be made to work only with a Thomas Jefferson at the helm. When Jefferson himself faltered, as he did on several occasions during his presidency, the government almost stopped functioning except in the routine operations of Galatin's Treasury machinery. When Jefferson left the office, all the shortcomings of his method of administration became manifest. The cabinet became a center of petty bickering and continuous cabalizing, and Congress split into irreconcilable factions and repeatedly asserted its will against the president.

For all these reasons, Jefferson's legacy to his successor was a can of serpents. Jefferson's second term was merely a calamity; Madison's first would be a disaster.

There is more to a presidency than the tangible events that happen during and in consequence of it: there are also the myths it inspires. For a time, of course, memories were too fresh, feelings were too strong, and events were too unpleasant to admit of the kind of romanticization that is a necessary prelude to myth-making. By 1826, however—when Jefferson along with John Adams died on the fiftieth anniversary of the Declaration of Independence—memories had mellowed, new rivalries had replaced the old, and artful and designing men were looking to the past for heroes whose lives could be used or misused to justify their own doings. Jefferson was admirably suited for such use and misuse, for he had written and acted in a greater variety of ways on a greater variety of sub-

jects than any of the other Founding Fathers, and he was more quotable than any of them save possibly Adams alone.

But the Jefferson legend developed along curiously divided lines. In the realm of formal historical writing, he fared poorly until well into the twentieth century. . . .

Meanwhile, in the realm of folklore and political rhetoric, which ordinary Americans heard and heeded more frequently and more trustingly than they did the staid pronouncements of historians, Jefferson was exalted as the patron saint of all good things. The range of causes for which his name was invoked is staggering: democracy and partisanship, states' rights and nationalism, slavery and abolitionism, egalitarianism and racism, imperialism and isolationism, populism and laissez-faire capitalism, the planned and the decentralized society. In the nineteenth century, so long as rural values continued to prevail in America despite the relentless march of industrialization, Jefferson continued to be identified with the agrarian tradition; in the twentieth, when the center of American life and values became the city, his connection with that ideal was all but forgotten, and instead he came to be regarded as the champion of the "have-nots" against the "haves," of the "common man" (or the "forgotten man" or the "little fellow") against aristocrats and plutocrats.

In the 1920s and 1930s the two strands of the legend began to come together. The Democratic politician-historian Claude G. Bowers and the more scholarly Gilbert Chinard began the process of beatification through the written word, and though the Jefferson they described was one he would scarcely have recognized, the process has continued. Franklin Roosevelt's New Deal depicted itself as thoroughly Jeffersonian, though given to the use of "Hamiltonian means to accomplish Jeffersonian ends"—and while building a federal bureaucracy almost as large as the population of the entire country had been during Jefferson's time and while extending its regulatory power apace, it built Jefferson a monument which declared his true mission to have been as a libertarian. In time, and in our own time, "Jefferson" and "Jeffersonian" came to mean merely "good," or "that which the nation aspires to be."

The real Jefferson—the one who once lived in Virginia and once worked in the President's House—was lost in the shuffle. So, too, was the America he wanted his country to become; and in a nation of crime-ridden cities and poisoned air, of credit cards and gigantic corporations, of welfare rolls and massive bureaucracies, of staggering military budgets and astronomical public debts, of corruption and alienation, that loss is the more poignant. He and his followers set out to deflect the course of History, and History ended up devouring them and turning even their memory to its own purposes. History has a way of doing that.

POSTSCRIPT

Did President Jefferson Outfederalize the Federalists?

It is interesting to note that neither Hofstadter nor McDonald dwell upon the apparent reversals of Jefferson's states' rights and strict constructionist views of the Constitution when he became president. Hofstadter does not mention this because he considers Jefferson a pragmatist. McDonald argues that while Jefferson considered Hamilton's proposal for a national bank and Adams's Alien and Sedition Acts unconstitutional, he never thought of them as sacred principles of constitutional government.

Both writers also agree that the embargo and the subsequent War of 1812 with Great Britain undermined the attempts of Jefferson and his successors Madison and Monroe to maintain America as primarily an agrarian society. Both authors also note that the war forced the Republicans to accept manufacturing as an integral part of the American economy. But the two authors stress different consequences of the war. Hofstadter maintains that although the Federalist party disappeared soon after the war, the Republicans had totally adopted its political and economic philosophy of high tariffs, a national banking system, and the promotion of an industrial economy. McDonald, on the other hand, stresses that the failed embargo against England and France made Jefferson's administration intolerant of dissent and contemptuous of the law itself. "Thus," says McDonald, "the embargo became a program of domestic tyranny in inverse ratio to its ineffectiveness as an instrument of international policy: the more the policy was found wanting, the more rigorously was it enforced." McDonald could also have pointed out that Jefferson would not be the last president to have a reform program thwarted by the repressed atmosphere that war creates. Twentieth-century presidents Woodrow Wilson, Franklin Roosevelt, and Lyndon Johnson also saw their domestic reforms undone when the country put its energies into waging war.

It is not surprising that Jefferson's two major biographers, both professors at the University of Virginia for many years, have written sympathetic portraits. Dumas Malone's magisterial *Jefferson and His Times*, 6 volumes (Little, Brown, 1948–1981) and Merrill Peterson's 900-page opus *Thomas Jefferson and the New Nation: A Bibliography* (Oxford, 1970) contain detailed accounts of most facets of his life and are very useful as reference works. Peterson's *The Jeffersonian Images in the American Mind* (Oxford, 1960) is a wonderful account of the use and misuse of Jefferson's image in American politics since his death. Widely acclaimed by general reviewers though not by historians is Fawn M. Brodie's psychobiography *Thomas Jefferson: An Intimate History* (Norton, 1974), which accepts as true the liaison between

Jefferson and Sally Hemings that led to five unacknowledged sons and daughters. A shorter version can be found in Brodie's "The Great Taboo," *American Heritage* (June 1972). There are few modern critical portraits of Jefferson. One is Leonard Levy, *Jefferson and Civil Liberties: The Darker Side* (Quadrangle, 1973), which occasionally reads like a lawyer's brief but points out the contradictions between Jefferson's philosophical principles and his actions as president. More balanced, though critical, is Forrest McDonald's *Thomas Jefferson* (Kansas, 1976). No student should miss McDonald's concise critical summary of Washington's and Jefferson's precedent-setting impact on the American presidency in "A Mirror for Presidents," *Commentary* (December 1976).

The 1980s continue to produce books about the third president. A solid work of reasonable length which represents a lifetime of scholarship is Noble E. Cunningham, Jr., *In Pursuit of Reason: The Life of Thomas Jefferson* (Louisiana State University Press, 1987). Those who want to sample *Thomas Jefferson's Writings* should consult the 1,600-page volume edited by Merrill Peterson for the Library of America in 1985. Peterson has also edited *Thomas Jefferson: A Reference Biography* (Scribner's, 1986), which contains 25 original essays that integrate the many interests of this Renaissance man. Finally, the Library of America has recently reissued Henry Adams's *History of the United States of America During the Administrations of Thomas Jefferson and James Madison*. Both volumes deserve the title "classic" and should be sampled by the serious student.

ISSUE 9

Did Women Achieve Greater Autonomy in the New Nation?

YES: Nancy Woloch, from *Women and the American Experience* (Alfred A. Knopf, 1984)

NO: Gerda Lerner, from "The Lady and the Mill Girl: Changes in the Status of Women in the Age of Jackson," *American Studies Journal* (Spring 1961)

ISSUE SUMMARY

YES: Nancy Woloch, a fellow of the National Endowment for the Humanities, describes the exercise of autonomy and authority in the domestic life of middle-class wives.

NO: Professor of history Gerda Lerner considers a spectrum of women's roles, emphasizing the subservient position of female industrial workers.

Social and economic changes after 1783 altered the economic status of women. Increased urbanization, the accumulation of wealth, and the imitation of European bourgeois values and habits combined to eliminate the androgynous workplace where previously women could display their skills alongside men. Perhaps a diminished concern over survival contributed to changes in behavior also. With the onset of industrialization, work which had been performed in homes was transferred to factories, and women usually worked only for a limited time, until they married. Residence and workplace were no longer one; the roles of wife, mother, and worker no longer could be juggled easily.

Most historians interpret the War for Independence as a negative influence on women's status. The opinions of foreign visitors, however, were mixed. Alexis de Tocqueville, acknowledged as the most acute of the early nineteenth-century observers of the United States, uncovered an interesting dichotomy. "In America," he wrote, "the independence of woman is irrevocably lost in the bonds of matrimony. If an unmarried woman is less constrained there than elsewhere, a wife is subjected to stricter obligations." Tocqueville was astonished because "Long before an American girl arrives at the marriageable age, her emancipation from maternal control begins; she has scarcely ceased to be a child when she already thinks for herself, speaks with freedom and acts on her own impulse."

Class distinctions separated American women into different groups. Moreover, different sources of family income—agriculture versus commerce or the professions—further complicate any generalizations. The sectional divisions of North, South, and West, which historians use to explain the alignment of general attitudes in the United States, must also be considered for a fuller understanding of women's behavior. The kind of household added still another dimension. For example, contrast the modest rural cottage, where the housewife prepared almost all the foodstuffs and much of the clothing on the premises, with the plantation, where the concerns of the mistress were similar but whose duties were largely supervisory, and, then, with the urban home, where the woman possessed the opportunity to purchase most necessities if she wished, instead of making them. Recognizing that women did not represent a monolithic entity, it is not surprising that historians should offer clashing interpretations of women's status in the antebellum period.

In the following selections, Nancy Woloch focuses upon middle-class women for whom the home became a private retreat from the outside commercial world. As controller of this social space, these women, Woloch claims, acquired an independent role that added to their social prestige and were able to exercise greater control over their everyday lives. For Gerda Lerner, antebellum women confronted shrinking opportunities in the professions and trades, partly because work outside the home came to be viewed as employment unbefitting a "lady." In addition, she points out, women were excluded from the wave of political democracy that swept through the nation while white adult males were gaining suffrage rights, leading to a state of "relative deprivation" for women in antebellum America.

YES   Nancy Woloch

THE HOME AND THE WORLD

When the *Ladies Magazine* first appeared in 1828, a transformation in domestic life was well under way, at least in the commercial, urbanizing Northeast. During colonial days, when most families lived on farms, the household was a productive unit. All family members engaged in work to sustain it, work that was done in or near the home. As part of the family labor force, women and children were subordinate to paternal authority. But during the early nineteenth century, as a market economy developed, old patterns of life started to vanish. Men who once would have been farmers or craftsmen were now working outside the home to earn the income that supported it. The home was no longer a center of production, nor did family members work together for family sustenance. Within the emerging middle class, "home" became a private enclave, a retreat from the "world" and a refuge from commercial life. And within the home, women assumed a distinctive role.

The middle-class wife, like the *Ladies Magazine* reader of 1828, remained at home while her income-earning husband went to work outside it, in office or store, business or profession. While the man ventured forth into the world, the woman at home gained an independent realm of her own, one that was no longer constantly under male domination. Domestic life was now under female control. Nor was the wife tied down to wheel and loom, hearth and dairy. Once home manufacture was transferred to workplace, the woman at home was responsible primarily for housekeeping, child rearing, and moral and religious life. Within her own domestic space, however, she had gained both a new degree of autonomy and a new degree of authority over others.

The doctrine of sphere, as expounded in the *Ladies Magazine, Godey's Lady's Book*, and countless other publications, celebrated the new status of the middle-class woman, along with her distinctive vocation, values, and character. It also described an unspoken bargain between middle-class women and men. While men were still heads of families, their real domain was now in the world—a world of business, professions, politics, and money making.

Family status depended on their earned income and public roles. Women were expected to devote themselves entirely to private life, to the "chaste circle of the fireside," and to maintain an alternate world with separate values. But their roles at home also helped to define family status. Moreover, within the home, they had gained new clout and respect. The bargain was based on mutual gain. If men had the opportunity to rise in the world, women had the opportunity to rise in the home.

The middle-class woman's role was of course a dependent one. Her authority expanded only as the family's productive functions contracted, and those functions contracted only when family income went up. Rising income was at the center of woman's sphere. Only with substantial support could a married woman adopt the nonproductive role once reserved for the very wealthy or the anti-economic attitudes propounded by the *Ladies Magazine*. In reality, few women could sever themselves completely from either home production or physical work. Middle-class women and those who aspired to that status remained active contributors to the family economy. Most women, moreover, were only remote beneficiaries of the middle-class bargain. In rural areas, on farms in New England, in the South, and in the Midwest, traditional ways of life persisted. Household production continued, women and children were still part of the family labor force, and paternal authority as head of that labor force remained in effect, if not entirely intact. A woman's clout did not increase if a family was poor, or if she was not attached to a dependable, income-producing man. In many cases, the perquisites of woman's sphere—influ-

ence, autonomy, and authority—were little more than shared aspirations.

Nor were women of any class able to ignore worldly concerns. Within the growing middle class, woman's sphere was as precarious an ideal as its counterpart for men—the opportunity to rise in the world. The early-nineteenth-century family was likely to be in both financial and geographical motion. Income rose or fell according to personal fate and twists and turns of the economy such as the depression that diminished *Ladies Magazine* subscriptions in 1834. Buffeted by panics or elevated by good fortune, Americans faced the possibility of downward mobility at every turn. The "vicissitudes" were particularly precarious for women, who had little ability to determine family finances. When a husband died or a father failed in business, consequences could be dire. Shifts in family fortune, moreover, were usually linked to shifts in locale, to constant waves of internal migration—from rural areas to towns and cities, or from crowded areas to vacant land. Hardly insulated by sphere, early-nineteenth-century women were continually adapting to new homes, communities, associations, and economic situations.

But in important ways, woman's sphere was also a reality with which many women could identify, because their everyday patterns of life and work were becoming increasingly different from those of men. Even on the family farm, that most traditional of settings, men were now attuned to the market economy while women's responsibilities remained tied to the household economy. In towns and cities, differences between male and female work patterns were even more marked. During colonial times, as historian Nancy Cott points out, the work of both men and women was closely tied to the land. It was seasonal, discontinuous, and task oriented. But during the early nineteenth century, as the economy changed and as wage labor replaced family labor, male work patterns became oriented to time, not task. Whatever a man did for a living—laborer, businessman, tradesman, or clerk—he now had a clearly defined working day. His work, accordingly, became separated from the rest of life. Household work, however, remained in a time warp of task orientation. Women's work day expanded and contracted to fit the jobs at hand, whether the washing of clothes, baking of bread, or care of children—activities that all merged into life. In short, women's work and homebound world remained premodern, whereas men's was changing. A distinctive rhythm of labor and life style also defined woman's sphere.

Finally, women of all regions and all social levels could hope to benefit from the new importance now attributed to their shared vocation. In traditional society, household work and child-care had never drawn much acclaim. During the early nineteenth century, however, they were found to have social significance, to contribute to the well-being of society at large. Women's sphere was in fact a new social space, one that had not been recognized before. On the one hand, it was an enclosed, limited, private space. On the other, it was an improvement over having no space at all. Woman's sphere, according to popular literature, encompassed a now important social institution, the home. It linked all women together in a valuable vocation—domesticity and child rearing. It fostered a positive consciousness of gender, one that had not existed in the colonial era. And it necessitated a redefinition of female

character, one appropriate to the middle-class woman's elevated domestic status.

During the early nineteenth century, the home took on new significance, material and emotional. By mid-century, the middle class home had become a substantial place, with pantries and drawing rooms, mirrors and pianos, and at least some of the items featured in *Godey's Lady's Book*—upholstered sofas, elaborate furniture, carpets, and draperies. Its center was no longer the hearth, where colonial women did much of their work, but the parlor, where the family assembled. Since middle-class Americans had not only far more possessions but rising standards of neatness and cleanliness, "housework" quickly replaced "housewifery." Even with hired help, the middle-class women was hardly idle, since home maintenance and management was now a more elaborate procedure.

The middle-class home was also viewed as an emotional space, a refuge from the competitive world, and a source of stability and order in a society that weemed to be losing both. And it was now under feminine sway. Increasingly, the home was idealized as a bastion of feminine values, of piety and morality, affection and self-sacrifice—commodities that were in short supply outside it. Literature directed at women, especially, lost no opportunity to define the home as a feminine fief. "The family state . . . is the aptest earthly illustration of the heavenly kingdom and woman is its chief minister," educator Catherine Beecher declared in her *Treatise on Domestic Economy* in the 1840s. "The duties of the woman are as sacred and important as any ordained by man." By midcentury, the home was depicted as an insulated, privatized, feminized shrine. "Our homes—what is their corner-stone but the virtue of a woman, and on what does social well-being rest but in our homes?" asked *Godey's Lady's Book* in 1856.

Must we not trace all other blessings of civilized life to the doors of our private dwellings? Are not our hearthstones guarded by holy forms, conjugal, filial and parental love, the corner-stone of church and state, more sacred than either, more necessary than both? Let our temples crumble and capitals of state be levelled with the dust, but spare our homes! Man did not invent, and he cannot improve or abrogate them. A private shelter to cover . . . two hearts dearer to each other than all in the world; high walls to exclude the profane eyes of every human being; seclusion enough for the children to feel that mother is a holy and peculiar name—this is home. . . . Here the church and state must come for their origin and support. Oh! spare our homes.

While the middle-class home expanded in size and significance, the family itself was getting smaller. Americans were having fewer children. In 1800, the national birth rate had been the highest in the world; but during the next few decades it rapidly fell, a process that would continue for the rest of the century. The mother of 7.04 in 1800 became the mother of 5.92 in 1850 and 3.56 by 1900. Although the decline was national, it was uneven. During the early nineteenth century, large families were still the rule in most agricultural regions, along the newly settled frontier and among immigrants and blacks. Rural fertility, in fact, was also falling, but urban fertility was consistently lower. The most precipitous drop was among the new middle class in towns and cities.

But as the family began to shrink, the value attached to motherhood rose. Though such mounting significance had already been suggested in post-Revolutionary rhetoric, during the early nineteenth century it increased dramatically. Once household production waned, child raising became the family's central focus and purpose. In the middle-class home, children were no longer family workers but rather *what* the family produced. More time was devoted to their upbringing, more resources to their education, more effort to instilling the values and traits that would keep them in the middle class. The increased importance of child rearing contributed to an authority shift in the family. Paternal power dropped a notch as maternal affection became the main psychological force at home. The mother was now the primary child rearer, the crucial dispenser of values and former of character. She could "generate those moral tendencies which cover the whole of existence," as a minister wrote in the *Ladies Magazine*. "Her character is felt throughout the intricate workings of society." By the 1830s, when the publishing industry began an era of rapid expansion, the mother's significance was celebrated on all sides.

Innumerable tracts and stories—like those in the *Ladies Magazine*—paid tribute to the mother of Washington. In prints and etchings, a new iconography of motherhood developed. Magazines featured scenes of mothers at home, surrounded by children, in affectionate poses. In literature directed at women, motherhood was celebrated as the ultimate opportunity for self-sacrifice and, simultaneously, the ultimate role of female power. "How entire and perfect is this dominion over the unformed character of your infant," *Ladies Magazine* author Lydia Sigourney exuded in her *Letters to Mothers* (1838). No opportunity was lost to celebrate the social utility of motherhood. It was mothers, as Lydia Maria Child declared in her popular *Mother's Book* (1831) "on whose intelligence and discretion the safety and prosperity of our nation so much depend."

Nor was the expansion of maternal influence just rhetorical. By midcentury, it began to be recognized in the law. Northern states started to alter the tradi̇tion of paternal custody in cases of separation and divorce. Courts began to consider the "needs" of young children and "parental fitness," as well as to award custody to the "innocent party." Women did not gain equal custody rights, to say nothing of preference, until the end of the century. But adulation of motherhood was not without some legal ramifications, at least in the North. In the antebellum South, where patriarchy remained intact, legal encroachments on paternal power were rejected.

While celebrations of woman's sphere stressed the significance of domestic roles and maternal influence, they also suggested a new and positive consciousness of gender. The polarity of spheres that segregated middle-class men and women was not without an emotional bonus. Since women shared a common vocation, values, and attitudes appropriate to the home, not the world, they did have more in common with one another than did men, as Sarah Hale contended in *Ladies Magazine*. And they profited from long-term, intense relationships with other women—relationships that continued for decades, despite marriage and geographical separation, often taking the form of lengthy visits and correspondence. Such correspondence, as historian Carroll Smith Rosenberg contends, reveals that "Women's sphere had an essential dignity and integrity that grew out of women's shared experiences and mutual affection." Within their self-contained female world—noncompetitive, empathetic, and supportive—women valued one another and thereby gained a sense of security and self-esteem. "Women, who had little status and power in the larger world of male concerns, possessed status and power in the lives of other women."

Historians disagree as to whether an intimate mother-daughter relationship lay at the heart of this female world, or whether the peer relationship was more important. In either case, early-nineteenth-century middle-class women assumed centrality in one another's lives, depended emotionally on one another, and appreciated their same-sex connections and friendships. The role of friendship as an outlet for shared "sentiments" was reflected in the New England letters and diaries analyzed by historian Nancy Cott. Men, in these documents, were usually remote, distant figures, often without names. Or they might be referred to, with muted sarcasm, as "the Lords of Creation," an expression favored by Sarah Hale in the *Ladies Magazine*. But affection among women was explicit. Friendship provided an opportunity to exchange "reciprocal views and feelings," wrote Eliza Chaplin to Laura Lovell in 1820. "To you I unfold my whole heart without apology." "I do not believe that men can ever feel so pure an enthusiasm for women as we can feel for one another," *Ladies Magazine* author Catherine Sedgwick revealed to her diary in 1834. "Ours is nearest to the love of angels."

The positive consciousness of gender suggested by personal documents reflected and supported a new assessment of female character. According to the doctrine of sphere, character traits, like social roles, were now divided between men and women. Men were expected to be competitive, assertive, individualistic, and materialistic so as to be able to make their way in the world. The woman at home needed a compensatory set of character traits. Dependent and affectionate, she was also pious, pure, gentle, nurturant, benevolent, and sacrificing. Such "softer" virtues had been filtering in throughout the eighteenth century, especially in advice tracts destined for the upwardly mobile. But during the early nineteenth century, the softer virtues became accepted as innate. Women, moreover, compared to men, were believed to have a firmer grip on religion and morals, a virtual monopoly on piety and purity, a positive sense of moral superiority. In traditional society, women were not assumed to be superior to men in any way. Now, piety and purity provided some leverage. They also involved a new set of bargains between women and men.

PIETY AND PURITY

During the early nineteenth century, ministers provided a vital bolster to the doctrine of woman's sphere. They opposed those forces antithetical to women's interests—materialism, immorality, intemperance, and licentiousness. They helped to formulate a new definition of female character. Christian virtues—such as humility, submission, piety, and charity—were now, they suggested, primarily female virtues. Most important, ministers confirmed female moral superiority. Women might be the weaker members of society, but they were now assured that they exceeded men in spiritual fervor and moral strength.

Religion was also one of the few activities beyond the home in which women might participate without abdicating their sphere. Their participation in the churches was in fact vital. Women formed the majority of congregants. Accordingly, female piety, and even activism, were heartily encouraged by their ministers. "We look to you, ladies, to raise the standard of character in our own sex," announced New England clergyman Joseph Buckminster in an 1810 sermon. "We look to you for the continuance of domestick purity, for the revival of domestick religion, for the increase of our charities, and the support of what remains of religion in our private habits and publick institutions." Under such circumstances, a mutually dependent relationship developed between Protestant clerics and their middle-class female parishioners. Both saw themselves as outsiders in a society devoted to the pursuit of wealth, as allies who strove for morality in a competitive world. It was no accident that women's publications such as the *Ladies Magazine* counted on ministers for articles exalting the character of women. Ministers in turn depended on women for their loyal support.

Despite clergymen's persistent fears that their authority was diminishing, religion was not on the wane. Protestantism flourished during the early nineteenth century. The Second Great Awakening of the first quarter of the century was surpassed by the great evangelical crusades of the second. Presbyterians and Congregationalists attracted members in New England, fiery waves of revivals swept over New York state, westerners flocked to camp meetings on the frontier, and Baptists and Methodists made gains nationwide. According to some estimates, formal church membership tripled. Throughout all this fervor, women remained prominent. Their affinity for piety became evident in a spate of revivals at the start of the century. The Second Great Awakening marked the beginning of the new alliance between women and ministers as well as of their unstated bargain: clerical endorsement of female moral superiority in exchange for women's support and activism.

Female converts outnumbered male converts three to two in the Second Great Awakening in New England, and women formed the bulk of congregations thereafter. They played an equally prominent role in revival-swept western New York. By 1814, for instance, women outnumbered men in the churches and religious societies of bustling Utica, and they could be relied on to urge the conversion of family members. A mother's conversion, ministers learned, could lead to those of her children and husband; a daughter's conversion might soon create a pious family. The most zealous activists of these early revivals, significantly, were women of the new middle class—the wives and daughters of men who worked outside the home. Church membership became a boost to upward mobility. But female religiosity also moved down the social scale, to wives of artisans and farmers, just as it spread to other regions. On the midwestern frontier, it was women who could be counted on to form congregations, join religious societies, and demand Sabbath observance. Piety had become female property. When Englishwoman Frances Trollope investigated American society in the 1830s, she claimed that she had never seen a country "where religion had so strong a hold upon the women, or a slighter hold upon the men."

If religion had a hold on women, however, they in turn had a hold on the clergy. Through weight of numbers, women gained a genuine influence in Protestant churches that they lacked elsewhere. They contributed, for instance, to a softening of doctrine: the old idea of infant damnation had little appeal to American mothers. Ministers, accordingly, granted that Christian nurture could outweigh original sin. Discarding predestination as an axiom, ministers now suggested that mothers, not God, were responsible for their children's souls. The "feminization" of religion and of child rearing went hand in hand. Ministers bolstered the authority not only of the pious mother but of any pious woman, even the once insignificant daughter. Evangelical magazines, for instance, celebrated female influence in tales of dying daughters who, to the end, sought the conversion of relatives and friends. Social weakness, even fatal illness, was no obstacle to spiritual strength.

While ministers accorded women a new degree of influence, religious commitment offered other advantages. It also provided a community of peers outside the home, among like-minded women in church-related associations. The passivity of the convert, once she was united with her sisters, could be transformed into activist zeal. Early-nineteenth-century women provided the constituency for a multitude of societies formed under clerical auspices. They joined Bible and tract societies, which distributed pious literature, and Sabbath school unions, such as those endorsed in the *Ladies Magazine*, and missionary societies, which raised funds for pious endeavors. They formed charitable associations to aid the indigent and maternal associations to foster Christian motherhood. Through voluntary religious groups, women gained one another's company, new routes to participation in the world, and clerical approval. "While the pious female . . . does not aspire after things too great for her," a minister told a women's charitable society in 1815, "she discovers that there is wide field opened for the exercise of all her active powers."

In many ways, the evangelical Protestant experience was loaded with potential for women. Conversion encouraged introspection and self-attention. Cooperative efforts in church groups inspired a conscious sense of sisterhood and mutual interest. And clerical assurance of moral superiority supported a new degree of authority over others. But religious activism also had built-in limitations; clerical support meant clerical control. In the heat of revivals, as female piety assumed new significance, ministers warned women to avoid leadership roles as, for example, revivalists. Their piety was to be limited to the private role of personal persuasion; "influence" was contingent on acceptance of limits. As long as a woman kept to her "proper place," a tract society pamphlet explained in 1823, she might exert "almost any degree of influence she pleases." This was part of the implicit bargain between clergymen and women parishioners. It was also a fundamental tenet espoused by Sarah Hale in the *Ladies Magazine*.

If piety became a vital component of female character, so did purity, a word with several meanings. One was passionlessness, or lack of sexual feeling. According to the doctrine of sphere, the sexes were distinguished by features that were not merely different but opposite. Lust and carnality were male characteristics, or liabilities. Women, less physical, more spiritual, and morally superior, were indeed closer to "angels." This was of course a new development. In traditional society, women, like men, were assumed to be sexual beings. Since weaker of will, they were often assumed to be even more lustful, licentious, and insatiable than men. But early in the nineteenth century, around the time of the Second Great Awakening, purity became a female bargaining point. Like piety, it was now a prerequisite for influence. Sermons often warned that if purity gave away, all of the perquisities of sphere were lost. "let her lay aside delicacy," a minister held in 1837, "and her influence over our sex is gone."

Though ministers were the first authorities to endorse the female virtue of purity, they were not the only ones. By mid-century, the medical profession also confirmed that passionlessness was an innate and commendable female characteristic. "The majority of women (happily for them)," physician William Acton stated in a much-quoted medical treatise, "are not much troubled with sexual feeling of any kind." There were dissenting opinions within the profession. But in medical manuals aimed at the upwardly mobile middle class, midcentury physicians usually emphasized the debilitating effects of sexual indulgence, recommended infrequent intercourse, opposed contraception, and confirmed female asexuality. They also assured women that their physical health, and social roles, were determined by their reproductive organs. Doctors explained that the uterus was linked to the female nervous system, and that any malfunction affected the entire body, causing a gamut of ailments—headaches, backaches, indigestion, insomnia, and nervous disorders. Women's unusual physiology, indeed, determined her emotions, character, and vocation. "Mentally, socially, spiritually, [woman] is more interior than a man," a Philadelphia physician concluded in the 1860s. "The house, the chamber, the closet, are the centers of her social life and power."

Like other components of woman's sphere, purity encompassed both sanctions and benefits. The sanctions were stressed in the advice literature directed at middle-class women. Etiquette manuals, for instance, counseled prudent behavior that would serve to deter male advances. "Sit not with another in a space that is too narrow," warned the *Young Ladies Friend*. Magazine fiction offered tales about girls who lacked discretion, were consequently victimized by male predators, and ended up ruined, impoverished, ostracized, or dead. Such proscriptions were related to significant changes in courtship customs, since incidence of premarital pregnancy sharply declined—from a high of almost 30 percent of first births in the late eighteenth century to a new low of under 10 percent in the mid-nineteenth century. This precipitous drop, historians contend, suggests the acceptance by both young men and women of a new ideology of sexual restraint. Convictions about female purity imposed limitations not only on women but men as well.

Purity was also a code word for a new degree of female sexual control within marriage. During the early nineteenth century, when the fertility of white women began its precipitous decline, the shrinking family became a hallmark of the new middle class. It may also have been a result of the new clout of wives within middle-class homes. Now imbued with moral superiority, wives gained a right of refusal, an escape from "submission," and power to limit the frequency of sexual relations. They also gained more control over the number of children they had. Available methods of family limita-

tion (beyond folk remedies and patent medicines) were abstinence, as recommended in medical literature, and withdrawal, which was condemned; abortion was also a possible last resort, at least until later in the century when it was outlawed. Although abstinence was not the sole effective means of curbing births, it probably was in widespread use. And female purity was probably an ideal on which middle-class men and women agreed, an asset for the family that wanted to rise in the world—a family in which children were no longer economic assets but, rather, liabilities. In the early nineteenth century, sexual restraint appeared to both serve family goals and enhance women's autonomy within the home.

Convictions about female purity also affected women's relation to the medical profession. Connections between women and doctors were hardly as clear-cut as the unstated bargain between women and ministers. Physicians were a far newer source of authority. Medicine became a recognized profession only after the turn of the century. By the 1820s, all states except three had laws requiring medical practitioners to be licensed, and most licensing laws required graduation from medical college. As a result, women were excluded from medical practice, and mid-wifery, once a female monopoly, began a slow decline. In rural areas and on the frontier, midwives continued to deliver babies, and also among the urban poor. The rural midwife, indeed, remained in business into the twentieth century. But the urbanizing East set the trend for the future. During the early nineteenth century, middle-class mothers in towns and cities turned to physicians. No longer a public female ritual, childbirth became a private event with two main participants, a woman and a male professional.

The physician's new role in childbirth brought both loss and gain. The entourage of women relatives and friends who had once played a supportive part gradually vanished. But middle-class women seemed to appreciate the use of the forceps (the physician's prerogative) as the means of a faster delivery with less suffering. Mothers, indeed, became the doctor's prime constituency, since a successful obstetric practice paved the way for a profitable family practice. Moreover, with the rise of the medical profession, female ill health assumed new visibility.

Middle-class women of the early nineteenth century were distinguished by their debilitating illnesses—nervousness, anemia, hysteria, headaches, backaches. The marked rise in female illness, much of it never diagnosed, may have been connected to physical causes—such as the spread of venereal disease—or psychological ones. Women's dependent status could have had debilitating effects on their health. Sickness might also have had a positive function, providing reprieve from domestic work. In any case, physical fragility became a female liability. When Catherine Beecher surveyed women's health across the nation in the 1850s, she concluded that sick women outnumbered the healthy three to one. Reporting from one Illinois town, Beecher gave her version of the terrible state of women's health.

> Mrs. H. an invalid. Mrs. G. scrufula, Mrs. W. liver complaint, Mrs. S. pelvic disorders, Mrs. B. pelvic deseases very badly. Mrs. B. not healthy. Mrs. T. very feeble. Mrs. G. cancer. Mrs. N. liver complaint. Do not know one healthy woman in the place.

If all the facts and details of women's diseases were known, Catherine Beecher claimed, "It would send a groan of terror and horror over the land."

Even when chronically ill, however, women did not completely trust their doctors. The professionalization of medicine did not ensure its competence. At midcentury, as historian Regina Morantz explains, medicine was in a state of crisis. "Heroic" medicine—bleeding and enormous doses of dangerous substances—was being discarded, but it had not yet been replaced by anything better. Not only were well trained doctors unlikely to be very effective, but few were well trained. During the 1830s, any profit-minded doctor could open a medical college and, however lax its standards, produce hundreds of graduates to be licensed. Women had especial reason to be wary. Since female complaints of all sorts were believed to stem from uterine malfunction, the woman patient might well be subjected to "local treatment"—a procedure involving uterine cauterization, injection of solutions, even the insertion of leeches. Not surprisingly, "local treatment" seemed a dire assault on female purity. And not surprisingly, middle-class women sought alternatives.

One set of alternatives were nonmedical remedies or fads—Grahamism (diet reform), water cures, animal magnetism, or phrenology. The *Ladies Magazine*, for instance, ran many features on phrenology, complete with huge charts of the human skull. Middle-class women also took refuge at spas, joined ladies' physiological societies, where health and medicine were discussed and accepted the views of health reformers. The latter usually favored preventive measures that would preclude the need to resort to physicians at all—such as exercise, fresh air, baths, and cereals. Similar measures were endorsed in the medical columns of *Godey's Lady's Book*, written by doctors. Women also turned to irregular practitioners—unlicensed dispensers of remedies and advice, who might well be women. Dr. Harriot Hunt, for instance, went into practice in Boston with her sister in the 1830s, after an apprenticeship with other irregulars. Opposed to the "heroic" methods of the licensed profession, which rejected her, she prescribed homeopathic, preventive measures and became interested in the psychological causes of women's ailments. An even less regular practitioner, Mary Gove Nichols, once a contributor to the *Ladies Magazine*, became a water cure therapist and health reformer, catering, like Hunt, to a female clientele. Although not committed to the female passionlessness, these leading irregulars were committed to the protection of women from male depravity.

Another response to the professionalization of medicine was explained in *Godey's Lady's Book*. Women, wrote Sarah Hale, should be allowed to enter the medical profession in order to minister to women and children. Her argument for women doctors was based on the sanctity of sphere. Propriety and morality dictated that women should be examined by women. The woman physician, moreover, would raise the moral tone of the profession and open to women new avenues for practicing their altruism, benevolence, and sympathy. Through the entry of women into medicine, woman's sphere would be not destroyed but preserved. Hale lent especial support to Elizabeth Blackwell, the first woman medical college graduate and licensed woman physician. Like Hunt and Nichols, Blackwell was hardly a subscriber to the doctrine of female asexuality. She was, however, a crusader against prostitution and obscenity, and a supporter of the moral purity movement.

The doctrine of woman's sphere, and its redefinition of female character, could therefore be used as a bargaining tool. Piety, purity, and moral superiority could be mobilized to increase women's authority at home and demand more influence outside it. The doctrine of sphere could also be used to bolster other demands, such as that for "advanced" education. Although only a small proportion of Americans had any education beyond the primary level, an increasing number of them were women. Sending a daughter to an academy or seminary was now a perquisite of the expanding middle class.

NO

Gerda Lerner

THE LADY AND THE MILL GIRL:
CHANGES IN THE STATUS OF WOMEN
IN THE AGE OF JACKSON

The period 1800–1840 is one in which decisive changes occurred in the status of American women. It has remained surprisingly unexplored. With the exception of a recent, unpublished dissertation by Keith Melder and the distinctive work of Elisabeth Dexter, there is a dearth of descriptive material and an almost total absence of interpretation. Yet the period offers essential clues to an understanding of later institutional developments, particularly the shape and nature of the woman's rights movement. This analysis will consider the economic, political, and social status of women and examine the changes in each area. It will also attempt an interpretation of the ideological shifts which occurred in American society concerning the "proper" role for women.

Periodization always offers difficulties. It seemed useful here, for purposes of comparison, to group women's status before 1800 roughly under the "colonial" heading and ignore the transitional and possible atypical shifts which occurred during the American Revolution and the early period of nationhood. Also, regional differences were largely ignored. The South was left out of consideration entirely because its industrial development occurred later.

The status of colonial women has been well studied and described and can briefly be summarized for comparison with the later period. Throughout the colonial period there was a marked shortage of women, which varied with the regions and always was greatest in the frontier areas. This (from the point of view of women) favorable sex ratio enhanced their status and position. The Puritan world view regarded idleness as sin; life in an underdeveloped country made it absolutely necessary that each member of the community perform an economic function. Thus work for women, married or single, was not only approved, it was regarded as a civic duty. Puritan town councils expected single girls, widows, and unattached women to be self-supporting and for a long time provided needy spinsters with parcels of land. There was no social sanction against married women working; on the contrary, wives were expected to help their husbands in their trade and won social approval for doing extra work in or out of the home. Needy children, girls as well as boys, were indentured or apprenticed and were expected to work for their keep.

The vast majority of women worked within their homes, where their labor produced most articles needed for the family. The entire colonial production of cloth and clothing and in part that of shoes was in the hands of women. In addition to these occupations, women were found in many different kinds of employment. They were butchers, silversmiths, gunsmiths, upholsterers. They ran mills, plantations, tan yards, shipyards, and every kind of shop, tavern and boarding house. They were gate keepers, jail keepers, sextons, journalists, printers, "doctoresses," apothecaries, midwives, nurses, and teachers. Women acquired their skills the same way as did the men, through apprenticeship training, frequently within their own families.

Absence of a dowry, ease of marriage and remarriage, and a more lenient attitude of the law with regard to women's property rights were manifestations of the improved position of wives in the colonies. Under British common law, marriage destroyed a woman's contractual capacity; she could not sign a contract even with the consent of her husband. But colonial authorities were more lenient toward the wife's property rights by protecting her dower rights in her husband's property, granting her personal clothing, and upholding pre-nuptial contracts between husband and wife. In the absence of the husband, colonial courts granted

women "femme sole" rights, which enabled them to conduct their husband's business, sign contracts, and sue. The relative social freedom of women and the esteem in which they were held was commented upon by most early foreign travelers in America.

But economic, legal, and social status tells only part of the story. Colonial society as a whole was hierarchical, and rank and standing in society depended on the position of the men. Women did not play a determining role in the ranking pattern; they took their position in society through the men of their own family or the men they married. In other words, they participated in the hierarchy only as daughters and wives, not as individuals. Similarly, their occupations were, by and large, merely auxiliary, designed to contribute to family income, enhance their husbands' business or continue it in case of widowhood. The self-supporting spinsters were certainly the exception. The underlying assumption of colonial society was that women ought to occupy an inferior and subordinate position. The settlers had brought this assumption with them from Europe; it was reflected in their legal concepts, their willingness to exclude women from political life, their discriminatory educational practices. What is remarkable is the extent to which this felt inferiority of women was constantly challenged and modified under the impact of environment, frontier conditions, and favorable sex ratio.

By 1840 all of American society had changed. The Revolution had substituted an egalitarian ideology for the hierarchical concepts of colonial life. Privilege based on ability rather than inherited status, upward mobility for all groups of society, and unlimited opportunities for individual self-fulfillment had become ideological goals, if not always realities. For men, that is; women were, by tacit consensus, excluded from the new democracy. Indeed, their actual situation had in many respects deteriorated. While, as wives, they had benefitted from increasing wealth, urbanization, and industrialization, their role as economic producers and as political members of society differed sharply from that of men. Women's work outside of the home no longer met with social approval; on the contrary, with two notable exceptions, it was condemned. Many business and professional occupations formerly open to women were now closed, many others restricted as to training and advancement. The entry of large numbers of women into low status, low pay, and low skill industrial work had fixed such work by definition as "woman's work." Women's political status, while legally unchanged, had deteriorated relative to the advances made by men. At the same time the genteel lady of fashion had become a model of American femininity, and the definition of "woman's proper sphere" seemed narrower and more confined than ever.

Within the scope of this essay only a few of these changes can be more fully explained. The professionalization of medicine and its impact on women may serve as a typical example of what occurred in all the professions.

In colonial America there were no medical schools, no medical journals, few hospitals, and few laws pertaining to the practice of the healing arts. Clergymen and governors, barbers, quacks, apprentices, and women practiced medicine. Most practitioners acquired their credentials by reading Paracelsus and Galen and serving an apprenticeship with an established practitioner. Among the semi-trained "physics," surgeons, and healers, the occasional "doctoress" was fully accepted and frequently well rewarded. County records of all the colonies contain references to the work of the female physicians. There was even a female Army surgeon, a Mrs. Allyn, who served during King Philip's war. Plantation records mention by name several slave women who were granted special privileges because of their useful service as midwives and "doctoresses."

The period of the professionalization of American medicine dates from 1765, when Dr. William Shippen began his lectures on midwifery in Philadelphia. The founding of medical faculties in several colleges, the standardization of training requirements, and the proliferation of medical societies intensified during the last quarter of the 18th century. The American Revolution dramatized the need for trained medical personnel, afforded first-hand battlefield experience to a number of surgeons and brought increasing numbers of semi-trained practitioners in contact with the handful of European-trained surgeons working in the military hospitals. This was an experience from which women were excluded. The resulting interest in improved medical training, the gradual appearance of graduates of medical colleges, and the efforts of medical societies led to licensing legislation. In 1801 Maryland required all medical practitioners to be licensed; in 1806 New York enacted a similar law, followed by all but three states. This trend was reversed in the 1830s and 40s when most states repealed their licensure requirements. This was due to pressure from eclectic, homeopathic practitioners, the public's dissatisfaction with the "heroic medicine" then practiced by licensed physicians, and to the distrust of state regulation, which was widespread during the Age of Jackson. Licensure as prime proof of qualification for the practice of medicine was reinstituted in the 1870s.

In the middle of the 19th century it was not so much a license of an M.D. which marked the professional physician as it was graduation from an approved medical college, admission to hospital practice and to a network of referrals through other physicians. In 1800 there were four medical schools, in 1850, forty-two. Almost all of them excluded women from admission. Not surprisingly, women turned to eclectic schools for training. Harriot Hunt, a Boston physician, was trained by apprenticeship with a husband and wife team of homeopathic physicians. After more than twenty years of practice she attempted to enter Harvard Medical school and was repeatedly rebuffed. Elizabeth Blackwell received her M.D. from Geneva (New York) Medical College, an eclectic school. Sarah Adamson found all regular medical schools closed against her and earned an M.D. in 1851 from Central College at Syracuse, an eclectic institution. Clemence Lozier graduated from the same school two years later and went on to found the New York Medical College and Hospital for women in 1862, a homeopathic institution which was later absorbed into the Flower-Fifth Avenue Hospital.

Another way in which professionalization worked to the detriment of women can be seen in the cases of Drs. Elizabeth and Emily Blackwell, Marie Zakrzewska, and Ann Preston, who despite their M.D.s and excellent training were denied access to hospitals, were refused recognition by county medical societies, and were denied customary referrals by male colleagues. Their experiences were similar to those of most of the pioneer

women physicians. Such discrimination caused the formation of alternate institutions for the training of women physicians and for hospitals in which they might treat their patients. The point here is not so much that any one aspect of the process of professionalization excluded women but that the process, which took place over the span of almost a century, proceeded in such a way as to institutionalize an exclusion of women, which had earlier been accomplished irregularly, inconsistently, and mostly by means of social pressure. The end result was an *absolute* lowering of status for all women in the medical profession and a *relative* loss. As the professional status of all physicians advanced, the status differential between male and female practitioners was more obviously disadvantageous and underscored women's marginality. Their vital exclusion from the most prestigious and lucrative branches of the profession and their concentration in specializations relating to women and children made such disadvantaging more obvious by the end of the 19th century.

This process of pre-emption of knowledge, of institutionalization of the profession, and of legitimation of its claims by law and public acceptance is standard for the professionalization of the sciences, as George Daniels has pointed out. It inevitably results in the elimination of fringe elements from the profession. It is interesting to note that women had been pushed out of the medical profession in 16th-century Europe by a similar process. Once the public had come to accept licensing and college training as guarantees of up-to-date practice, the outsider, no matter how well qualified by years of experience, stood no chance in the competition. Women were the casualties of medical professionalization.

In the field of midwifery the results were similar, but the process was more complicated. Women had held a virtual monopoly in the profession in colonial America. In 1646 a man was prosecuted in Maine for practicing as a midwife. There are many records of well-trained midwives with diplomas from European institutions working in the colonies. In most of the colonies midwives were licensed, registered, and required to pass an examination before a board. When Dr. Shippen announced his pioneering lectures on midwifery, he did it to "combat the widespread popular prejudice against the man-midwife" and because he considered most midwives ignorant and improperly trained.

Yet he invited "those women who love virtue enough, to own their Ignorance, and apply for instruction" to attend his lectures, offering as an inducement the assurance that female pupils would be taught privately. It is not known if any midwives availed themselves of the opportunity.

Technological advances, as well as scientific, worked against the interests of female midwives. In 16th-century Europe the invention and use of obstetrical forceps had for three generations been the well-kept secret of the Chamberlen family and had greatly enhanced their medical practice. Hugh Chamberlen was forced by circumstances to sell the secret to the Medical College in Amsterdam, which in turn transmitted the precious knowledge to licensed physicians only. By the time the use of the instrument became widespread, it had become associated with male physicians and male midwives. Similarly in America, introduction of the obstetrical forceps was associated with the practice of male midwives and served to their advantage. By the end of the 18th

century a number of male physicians advertised their practice of midwifery. Shortly thereafter female midwives also resorted to advertising, probably in an effort to meet the competition. By the early 19th century male physicians had virtually monopolized the practice of midwifery on the Eastern seaboard. True to the generally delayed economic development in the Western frontier regions, female midwives continued to work on the frontier until a much later period. It is interesting to note that the concepts of "propriety" shifted with the prevalent practice. In 17th-century Maine the attempt of a man to act as a midwife was considered outrageous and illegal; in mid-19th-century America the suggestion that women should train as midwives and physicians was considered equally outrageous and improper.

Professionalization, similar to that in medicine with the elimination of women from the upgraded profession, occurred in the field of law. Before 1750, when law suits were commonly brought to the courts by the plaintiffs themselves or by deputies without specialized legal training, women as well as men could and did act as "attorneys-in-fact." When the law became a paid profession and trained lawyers took over litigation, women disappeared from the court scene for over a century.

A similar process of shrinking opportunities for women developed in business and in the retail trades. There were fewer female storekeepers and business women in the 1830s than there had been in colonial days. There was also a noticeable shift in the kind of merchandise handled by them. Where previously women could be found running almost every kind of retail shop, after 1830 they were mostly found in businesses which served women only.

The only fields in which professionalization did not result in the elimination of women from the upgraded profession were nursing and teaching. Both were characterized by a severe shortage of labor. Nursing lies outside the field of this inquiry, since it did not become an organized profession until after the Civil War. Before then, it was regarded peculiarly as a woman's occupation, although some of the hospitals and the Army during wars employed male nurses. These bore the stigma of low skill, low status, and low pay. Generally, nursing was regarded as simply an extension of the unpaid services performed by the housewife—a characteristic attitude that haunts the profession to this day.

Education seems, at first glance, to offer an entirely opposite pattern from that of the other professions. In colonial days women had taught "Dame schools" and grade schools during summer sessions. Gradually, as educational opportunities for girls expanded, they advanced just a step ahead of their students. Professionalization of teaching occurred between 1820 and 1860, a period marked by a sharp increase in the number of women teachers. The spread of female seminaries, academies, and normal schools provided new opportunities for the training and employment of female teachers.

This trend, which runs counter to that found in the other professions, can be accounted for by the fact that women filled a desperate need created by the challenge of the common schools, the ever-increasing size of the student body, and the westward growth of the nation. America was committed to educating its children in public schools, but it was insistent on doing so as cheaply as possible. Women were available in great numbers, and they were willing to work cheaply. The result was another ideological adaptation: in the very period when the gospel of the home as woman's proper sphere was preached most loudly, it was discovered that women were the natural teachers of youth, could do the job better than men, and were to be preferred for such employment. This was always provided, of course, that they would work at the proper wage differential—30 to 50 percent of the wages paid male teachers was considered appropriate. The result was that in 1888 in the country as a whole 63 percent of all teachers were women, while the figure for the cities only was 90.04 percent.

It appeared in the teaching field, as it would in industry, that role expectations were adaptable provided the inferior status group filled a social need. The inconsistent and peculiar patterns of employment of black labor in the present-day market bear out the validity of this generalization.

There was another field in which the labor of women was appreciated and which they were urged to enter—industry. From Alexander Hamilton to Matthew Carey and Tench Coxe, advocates of industrialization sang the praises of the working girl and advanced arguments in favor of her employment. The social benefits of female labor particularly stressed were those bestowed upon her family, who now no longer had to support her. Working girls were "thus happily preserved from idleness and its attendant vices and crimes," and the whole community benefitted from their increased purchasing power.

American industrialization, which occurred in an underdeveloped economy with a shortage of labor, depended on the labor of women and children. Men were occupied with agricultural work and were not available or were unwilling to enter the factories. This accounts for the special features of the early development of the New England textile industry: the relatively high wages, the respectability of the job and relatively high status of the mill girls, the patriarchal character of the model factory towns, and the temporary mobility of women workers from farm to factory and back again to farm. All this was characteristic only of a limited area and of a period of about two decades. By the late 1830s the romance had won off: immigration had supplied a strongly competitive, permanent work force willing to work for subsistence wages; early efforts at trade union organization had been shattered, and mechanization had turned semi-skilled factory labor into unskilled labor. The process led to the replacement of the New England-born farm girls by immigrants in the mills and was accompanied by a loss of status and respectability for female workers.

The lack of organized social services during periods of depression drove ever greater numbers of women into the labor market. At first, inside the factories distinctions between men's and women's jobs were blurred. Men and women were assigned to machinery on the basis of local need. But as more women entered industry the limited number of occupations open to them tended to increase competition among them, thus lowering pay standards. Generally, women regarded their work as temporary and hesitated to invest in apprenticeship training, because they expected to marry and raise families. Thus they remained untrained, casual labor and were soon, by custom, relegated to the lowest paid, least skilled jobs. Long hours, overwork, and poor working conditions would characterize women's work in industry for almost a century.

POSTSCRIPT

Did Women Achieve Greater Autonomy in the New Nation?

Disenchanted with lost economic opportunities and a relative deterioration in their political status, many women in the "age of Jackson" began to channel their frustration into a variety of reform efforts. Causes such as the abolition of slavery and the prohibition of alcohol attracted numerous female participants and offered women opportunities to exercise their leadership abilities. Several outstanding women later turned their attention from temperance and racial injustice to the benefit of their own sex. Lucretia Mott, Sarah and Angelina Grimke, Susan B. Anthony, and Elizabeth Cady Stanton organized their sisters to pursue the rights of women. In light of the favorable conditions attributed to middle-class women by Woloch, it is significant that, according to Lerner, the women's rights movement was dominated by middle-class concerns. These concerns were clarified in 1848 by the Women's Rights Convention in Seneca Falls, New York. Here Elizabeth Cady Stanton presented the Declaration of Sentiments, which proclaimed that "all men and women are created equal" and which included a proposal for women's suffrage. That the struggle for voting rights would be a long, uphill battle was indicated by an article published in *Harper's Monthly Magazine* in 1853. Women's suffrage, the author wrote, "is avowedly opposed to the most time-honored propensities of social life; it is opposed to nature; it is opposed to revelation. . . . This unblushing female Socialism defies alike apostles and prophets. In this respect no kindred movement is so decidedly infidel, so rancorously and avowedly anti-biblical. . . . It is equally opposed to nature and the established order of society founded upon it."

There is a large and growing historiography of American women. In addition to the surveys by Sochen, Ryan, and Woloch cited in the postscript to Issue 3, students should consult Carl N. Degler, *At Odds: Women and the Family in America from the Revolution to the Present* (Oxford University Press, 1980). Barbara Welter, "The Cult of True Womanhood, 1820–1860," *American Quarterly* (Summer 1966), analyzes a concept addressed in both the Woloch and Lerner essays. Thomas Dublin, *Women at Work: The Transformation of Work and Community in Lowell, Massachusetts, 1826–1860* (Columbia University Press, 1979), and Alice Kessler-Harris, *Out to Work: A History of Wage-Earning Women in the United States* (Oxford University Press, 1982), focus upon the significant role played by working-class women. Hasia R. Diner, *Erin's Daughters in America: Irish Immigrant Women in the Nineteenth Century* (Johns Hopkins Press, 1983), is an important reminder that women outnumbered men in the Irish migration and, thus, deserve as much attention as their male counterparts have received from historians in the past. The lives of women in the South are assessed in two marvelous studies: Catherine Clinton, *The Plantation Mistress* (Pantheon, 1982), which attempts to overturn popular myths about this group, and Suzanne Lebsock, *The Free Women of Petersburg: Status and Culture in a Southern Town, 1784–1860* (Norton, 1984), which suggests a steady increase in the economic autonomy of Southern women, white *and* black. For another work treating the status of black women in the antebellum period, see Dorothy Sterling, ed., *We Are Your Sisters: Black Women in the Nineteenth Century* (Norton, 1984). For important studies related to the rise of the women's movement and the reform activities of antebellum women, see Barbara J. Berg, *The Remembered Gate: Origins of American Feminism—The Woman and the City, 1800–1860* (Oxford University Press, 1978); Gerda Lerner, *The Grimke Sisters from South Carolina: Pioneers for Women's Rights and Abolition* (Houghton Mifflin, 1967); Ellen C. DuBois, *Feminism and Suffrage: The Emergence of an Independent Women's Movement in America, 1848–1869* (Cornell University Press, 1978); and Barbara Leslie Epstein, *The Politics of Domesticity: Women, Evangelism, and Temperance in Nineteenth-Century America* (Wesleyan University Press, 1981).

San Jacinto Museum of History Association

PART 3

Antebellum America

Pressures and trends that began building in the early years of the American nation continued to gather momentum until conflict was almost inevitable. America had to respond to challenges from society members who felt alienated from or forgotten by the new nation because the ideals of human rights and democratic participation that guided the founding of the nation had been applied only to selected segments of the population. Changes in the nature of the voting population and the ways in which Americans viewed their place in the world had dramatic implications for the future.

Did the Election of 1828 Represent a Democratic Revolt of the People?

_____

Was Antebellum Reform Motivated Primarily by Humanitarian Goals?

_____

Was U.S. Foreign Policy in the Early Nineteenth Century Imperialistic?

_____

Did Slaves Exercise Religious Autonomy?

ISSUE 10

Did the Election of 1828 Represent a Democratic Revolt of the People?

YES: Robert V. Remini, from "Election of 1828," in Arthur M. Schlesinger, Jr., ed., *The Coming to Power: Critical Presidential Elections in American History* (McGraw-Hill, 1972)

NO: Richard P. McCormick, from "New Perspectives on Jacksonian Politics," *The American Historical Review* (January 1960)

ISSUE SUMMARY

YES: Professor of history Robert V. Remini argues that the 1828 presidential election symbolized the people's arrival at political responsibility and began a genuine, nationally organized, two-party system that came of age in the 1830s.

NO: Professor of history Richard P. McCormick maintains that voting statistics demonstrate that a genuine political revolution did not take place until the presidential elections of 1840, when fairly well balanced political parties had been organized in virtually every state.

According to conventional wisdom, Andrew Jackson's election to the presidency in 1828 began the era of the common man, in which the mass of voters, no longer restrained from voting by property requirements, rose up and threw the elite leaders out of our nation's capital. While recent historians are not quite sure what constituted Jacksonian democracy or who supported it, and they question whether there ever existed such an era of egalitarianism, American history textbooks still include the obligatory chapter on the age of Jackson.

There are several reasons why this old-fashioned view of the period continues to prevail. In part it is because it is still easier to generalize about political events, even in spite of the new scholarly interest in social history. Consequently, many texts continue to devote the major portion of their pages to detailed examinations of the successes and failures of various presidential administrations. Whether Jackson was more significant than other presidents is difficult to assess because "Old Hickory's" forceful personality, compounded with his use of strong executive authority, engendered constant controversy during his eight years in office.

Another reason the traditional concept of Jacksonian democracy has not been abandoned is because critics of the progressive interpretation have not been able to come up with an acceptable alternative view. Culminating with Arthur M. Schlesinger, Jr.'s Pulitzer Prize-winning *Age of Jackson* (Little, Brown, 1945), the progressive historians viewed Jackson's election in 1828 as the triumph of the common man in politics. Oversimplified as this interpretation may be, there is little doubt that a major change was taking place in the political system during these years. The death of both Thomas Jefferson and John Adams on July 4, 1826, the 50th anniversary of the U.S. Declaration of Independence from England, signified the end of the revolutionary generation's control over American politics. The first six presidents had been leaders or descendants of leaders in the revolutionary movement. At the Constitutional Convention in 1787, most of the time was spent discussing the powers of the presidency. Because of their experiences with the British king, the Founding Fathers were fearful of strong executive authority. Therefore, the presidency was entrusted only to those individuals whose loyalty remained unquestioned. Jackson was the first president of the United States who did not come from either Virginia or Massachusetts. Though Jackson was only a teenager at the time of the American Revolution, his career was similar to those of the early Founding Fathers. Like Washington and Jefferson, Jackson became a living legend before he was 50 years old. His exploits as an Indian fighter and the military hero of the Battle of New Orleans in the War of 1812 were more important than his western background in making him presidential material.

During the past two decades, a number of historians have studied the effects of presidential elections on the development and maintenance of the two-party system. Borrowing concepts and analytical techniques from political scientists and sociologists, the "new political" historians have demonstrated the effectiveness of the parties in selecting candidates, running campaigns, developing legislation, and legitimizing conflicts within the democratic system. By 1815, the first-party system of competition between the Federalists and the Republican-Democrats had broken down, in part because the Federalists had refused to become a legitimate opposition party. A second-party system developed during the Jackson era between Old Hickory's Democratic party and his Whig opponents. It lasted until the 1850s, when the slavery issue led to the formation of a new system of party competition between Republicans and Democrats.

The following selections disagree on the significance of the 1828 presidential race as a critical election in the development of the second-party system. Robert V. Remini agues that the 1828 presidential election symbolized the people's arrival at full political responsibility and began a genuine, nationally organized, two-party system that matured in the 1830s. Richard P. McCormick revises the traditional interpretation. His analysis of the voting statistics demonstrates that a genuine political revolution did not take place until the presidential election of 1840, when fairly well balanced parties had been organized in virtually every state.

YES

Robert V. Remini

JACKSON, CALHOUN, AND LIBERTY

Jackson's appearance on the national scene in larger-than-life size was indeed fortuitous. He arrived just as the country was undergoing profound economic and political changes, when a new generation of men was coming forward to seize leadership from an older social and political elite. These men saw in Jackson a symbol of their own ambitions; they also saw in him a living example of the self-made man. Surely if an orphan boy from the backwoods could make good, there was no reason why they too could not aspire to wealth and social status by relying on their own talents to get what they wanted.

Furthermore, this was an age of developing professionalism in all fields—including politics. In the 1820s, men were hard at work perfecting the techniques of winning elections. They built machines to manage the popular vote; they believed in organization; and they were determined to rule. As sharp-nosed professionals, like Van Buren, they were quick to sense the response the General's popularity produced among the "rising" classes of Americans and to realize that association with Jackson might be crucial to their future position in politics, both nationally and locally. Small wonder, then, that Van Buren decided in the winter of 1826-27 to move into the Jackson camp and to bring with him as many of the Old Republicans as he could influence. "If Gen Jackson & his friends will put his election on old party grounds," Van Buren wrote to one Radical, "preserve the old systems, avoid if not condemn the practices of the last campaign we can by adding his personal popularity to the yet remaining force of old party feeling, not only succeed in electing him but our success when achieved will be worth something."

Since Jackson had resigned his Senate seat after his House defeat and was therefore not in Washington, Van Buren went to Vice-President Calhoun, who was now openly allied to the General, and offered him Radical support for the election of Jackson in 1828. Van Buren promised to swing over the Richmond Junto, the Virginia political machine, through his influence with

From Robert V. Remini, "Election of 1828," in Arthur Schlesinger, Jr., ed., *The Coming to Power* (McGraw-Hill, 1972). Copyright © 1972 by McGraw-Hill Publishing Company. Reprinted by permission.

Thomas Ritchie, editor of the Richmond *Enquirer* and a leader of the Junto. He also promised to tour the South and do everything possible to bring the entire Old Republican faction into the new coalition, even to the extent of seeing Crawford and winning his support. During their conversation about this alliance, Calhoun and Van Buren also discussed the possibility of holding a national nominating convention to replace the outmoded caucus system, but nothing definite was decided at this time.

In a subsequent letter to Ritchie, Van Buren clearly stated that his concern for the political scene went further than a single election. He urged the Radicals to join him in this new coalition, not simply to defeat Adams but to achieve "what is of still greater importance, the substantial reorganization of the Old Republican party." He called for a revival of the two-party system and for a renewal of Jefferson's old North-South alliance, between what he termed the "planters of the South and the plain Republicans of the North." For Van Buren, like many other politicians of the day, recognized that the political system of the 1820s had failed to respond to a changing society and that unless something were done right away it might collapse altogether.

Because of the efforts of many men to restructure the system, the election of 1828 witnessed the reemergence of the two-party system, in American politics. The Jackson-Calhoun-Van Buren coalition eventually became known as the "Democratic" Republican party, or simply the Democratic party, while the Adams-Clay combination was called the "National" Republican party. With respect to party principles—not that they were much discussed in the campaign of 1828—the Democrats tended, when prodded, to restate the doctrines of Jefferson, particularly those emphasizing the rights of the states and the importance of the ordinary citizen. The National Republicans, on the other hand, affirmed the need for a strong central government in advancing the material well-being of the nation. Although there continued to be personal factions and cliques operating within the system, and while party organization did not advance in every state with equal rapidity, still in 1828 there was the beginning of a genuine, nationally organized, two-party system, a system that came of age in the 1830s. . . .

Balloting in the election extended from September to November. In most states, voting occurred over a period of several days. The states did not provide an official ballot; instead, the parties printed their own ballots, distributing them to friends and employing high-pressure party hacks at the polls to get the voter to accept the ticket. It was not unusual for a person to be accosted by several hawkers at once and threatened with bodily harm unless he accepted the proffered ballot.

The procedures for voting varied considerably throughout the twenty-four states. Delaware and South Carolina were the only states whose legislatures chose the electors. In all other states, they were chosen from a general or district ticket by an electorate that was roughly equivalent—except in Louisiana, Virginia, and Rhode Island—to the adult, white male population. Maryland, Maine, Illinois, Tennessee, and New York were the states using the district system, which meant that their electoral votes could be split between the candidates on a proportional basis. In all other states where the general ticket was employed, the candidate with the highest popular vote received all the electoral votes. Only Rhode

Island and Virginia continued to restrict suffrage with property qualifications, and Louisiana maintained tax payments as a voting requirement.

When the election ended and the ballots were counted, it was clear that Jackson had won a stupendous victory. Out of a total of 1,155,022 popular votes cast, John Quincy Adams received 507,730; Andrew Jackson won 647,292 or just a little better than 56 per cent of the entire vote. This was an extraordinary achievement by Jackson, a veritable landslide. In percentages it was unequalled in any presidential election during the nineteenth century. And his total represented substantial support from all sections of this country, including New England.

The total popular vote in the election represented an increase of nearly eight hundred thousand over the previous election in 1824. In Pennsylvania alone, the number rose from forty-seven thousand to 152,000 four years later. There were several reasons for this spectacular rise. In the first place, the two-party system had been reestablished, if unevenly, and where in 1824 there were several candidates running for the Presidency there were only two in 1828. Second, there was considerable interest in the election generated to a large extent by an exciting, if not scurrilous, campaign initiated by both the Democratic and National Republican parties. Third, there was a concerted effort on the part of many politicians to get out the vote at election time; and finally, four states, representing a considerable electorate, changed their laws and transferred the selection of electors from the legislature to the people.

In the Electoral College, Jackson's victory was even more impressive. He won a total of 178 electoral votes to 83 for Adams. He swept everything south of the Potomac River and west of New Jersey. Adams carried New England (except for a single electoral vote in Maine), Delaware, New Jersey, and most of Maryland. Adams and Jackson shared New York, with the General taking 20 of the state's 36 electoral votes. All the remaining states went to Old Hickory. The election was relatively close in New Hampshire, New York, New Jersey, Maryland, Kentucky, Louisiana, Ohio, and Indiana. In the final analysis, what made the difference in virtually every one of these states was superior party organization.

In the Vice-Presidential race, Calhoun won an easy reelection over Richard Rush, but received 7 fewer electoral votes than Jackson, because Georgia, which resented Calhoun's treatment of William H. Crawford when they sat in Monroe's Cabinet together, awarded 7 votes to Senator William C. Smith of South Carolina.

Aside from the importance of party in producing Jackson's triumph there was also his own popularity and charisma. He was a living, authentic legend, the victor of New Orleans, the man who won over the British, the greatest feat of arms in American history. Moreover, there was a dignity and bearing about him that bespoke leadership and authority. He was "presidential-looking," more so than any other public figure of the day. He inspired confidence among the largest mass of voters despite his lack of education and his reputation as an untamed westerner. In that sense Jackson himself was the essential issue in the campaign, just as he would be again in 1832, and the people in "vast numbers" crowded to his side.

Recently, however, some historians have questioned the vastness of the 1828 victory. Comparing the statistics of this election with previous state elections and future presidential elections, one historian has raised serious doubts as to whether the people poured out to the polls to express their confidence in Jackson. Perhaps it is possible to make meaningful comparisons between a presidential election and a state election for local officers held at different times or two presidential elections separated by a dozen or more years. And perhaps not. But in any event the fact remains that no matter how the statistics are analyzed or interpreted the people themselves who lived at the time believed that Jackson's election represented a great surge of popular support for the General. They believed that the ordinary citizen, the so-called "common man," who were farmers, workers, frontiersmen, and the like, had seized the opportunity to express their political opinion by voting for Jackson. And what is believed by the electorate is frequently more important than the objective reality. Many Democratic politicians, of course, saw the contest as one between "farmers & mechanics of the country" on one hand and the "rich and well born" on the other, "between the *aristocracy* and democracy of America." Thus when they read the returns from such states as Pennsylvania, Virginia, North Carolina, Ohio, and elsewhere they were astounded by the figures and therefore convinced of the truth of their own propaganda.

Not only did the Democrats see the election as a victory produced by the "vast numbers" of American people, but the National Republicans thought so too. That is what is even more astonishing. "Well," sighed one of them, "a great revolution has taken place. . . . This is what I all along feared but to a much greater extent." "It was the howl of raving Democracy" wrote another, "that

tiped /sic/ Pennsylvania & New York & Ohio—and this will be kept up here after to promote the ends of the /Democratic party./" "All our efforts," said one of Clay's friends, "have not withstood the Torrent." Hezekiah Niles in his newspaper credited Jackson's "triumphant victory" to the "ardor of thousands." And Edward Everett of Massachusetts, one of Adams' most dedicated supporters in Congress, explained to his brother that the General won "by a majority of more than *two* to *one*, an event astounding to the friends of the Administration and unexpected by the General himself and his friends. . . . /They/ are embarrassed with the vastness of their triumph and the numbers of their party."

Generations of historians, therefore, have interpreted Jackson's election in 1828 as the beginning of the "rise of the common man" in American history. Of course, such an easy and sweeping generalization does not take into consideration the fact that the "common man" had been rising for generations, and had made notable political advances long before Jackson appeared on the scene. Yet this election seemed to symbolize the people's arrival to political responsibility. Whether or not this was objectively true hardly mattered; what mattered was an expressed sense of participation in the electoral process experienced by ordinary citizens and that because of it a true "man of the people" had at last been elected President of the United States.

The notion of a popular "uprising" in Jackson's favor was strengthened by the scenes that occurred during his inauguration as President on March 4, 1829. Some twenty thousand people from all parts of the country converged on Washington to witness the triumph of their candidate. It was "like the inundation of the northern barbarians into Rome," wrote one, "save that the tumultuous tide came in from a different point of the compass." Daniel Webster was dumbfounded at the scene. "I never saw such a crowd here before," he said. "Persons have come five hundred miles to see General Jackson, *and they really seem to think that the country is rescued from some dreadful danger.*"

NO

Richard P. McCormick

NEW PERSPECTIVES
ON JACKSONIAN POLITICS

The historical phenomenon that we have come to call Jacksonian democracy has long engaged the attention of American political historians, and never more insistently than in the past decade. From the time of Parton and Bancroft to the present day, scholars have recognized that a profoundly significant change took place in the climate of politics simultaneously with the appearance of Andrew Jackson on the presidential scene. They have sensed that a full understanding of the nature of that change might enable them to dissolve some of the mysteries that envelop the operation of the American democratic process. With such a challenging goal before them, they have pursued their investigations with uncommon intensity and with a keen awareness of the contemporary relevance of their findings. . . .

That a "new democracy, ignorant, impulsive, irrational" entered the arena of politics in the Jackson era has become one of the few unchallenged "facts" in an otherwise controversial field. Differences of opinion occur only when attempts are made to account for the remarkable increase in the size of the active electorate. The commonest explanations have emphasized the assertion by the common man of his newly won political privileges, the democratic influences that arose out of the western frontier, or the magnetic attractiveness of Jackson as a candidate capable of appealing with singular effectiveness to the backwoods hunter, the plain farmer, the urban working-man, and the southern planter.

Probably because the image of "mighty democratic uprising" has been so universally agreed upon, there has been virtually no effort made to describe precisely the dimensions of the "uprising." Inquiry into this aspect of Jacksonian democracy has been discouraged by a common misconception regarding voter behavior before 1824. As the authors of one of our most recent and best textbooks put it: "In the years from the beginning of the government to 1824, a period for which we have no reliable election statistics, only small numbers of citizens seemed to have bothered to go to the polls."

Actually, abundant data on pre-1824 elections is available, and it indicates a far higher rate of voting than has been realized. Only by taking this data into consideration can voting behavior after 1824 be placed in proper perspective.

The question of whether there was indeed a "mighty democratic uprising" during the Jackson era is certainly crucial in any analysis of the political character of Jacksonian democracy. More broadly, however, we need to know the degree to which potential voters participated in elections before, during, and after the period of Jackson's presidency as well as the conditions that apparently influenced the rate of voting. Only when such factors have been analyzed can we arrive at firm conclusions with respect to the dimensions of the political changes that we associate with Jacksonian democracy. Obviously in studying voter participation we are dealing with but one aspect of a large problem, and the limitations imposed by such a restrictive focus should be apparent.

In measuring the magnitude of the vote in the Jackson elections it is hardly significant to use the total popular vote cast throughout the nation. A comparison of the total vote cast in 1812, for example, when in eight of the seventeen states electors were chosen by the legislature, with the vote in 1832, when every state except South Carolina chose its electors by popular vote, has limited meaning. Neither is it revealing to compare the total vote in 1824 with that in 1832 without taking into consideration the population increase during the interval. The shift from the legislative choice of electors to their election by popular vote, together with the steady population growth, obviously swelled the presidential vote. But the problem to be

investigated is whether the Jackson elections brought voters to the polls in such enlarged or unprecedented proportions as to indicate that a "new democracy" had burst upon the political scene.

The most practicable method for measuring the degree to which voters participated in elections over a period of time is to relate the number of votes cast to the number of potential voters. Although there is no way of calculating precisely how many eligible voters there were in any state at a given time, the evidence at hand demonstrates that with the exception of Rhode Island, Virginia, and Louisiana the potential electorate after 1824 was roughly equivalent to the adult white male population. A meaningful way of expressing the rate of voter participation, then, is to state it in terms of the percentage of the adult white males actually voting. This index can be employed to measure the variations that occurred in voter participation over a period of time and in both national and state elections. Consequently a basis is provided for comparing the rate of voting in the Jackson elections with other presidential elections before and after his regime as well as with state elections.

Using this approach it is possible, first of all, to ascertain whether or not voter participation rose markedly in the three presidential elections in which Jackson was a candidate. Did voter participation in these elections so far exceed the peek participation in the pre-1824 elections so as to suggest that a mighty democratic uprising was taking place? . . .

In the 1824 election not a single one of the eighteen states in which the electors were chosen by popular vote attained the percentage of voter participation that had been reached before 1824. Prior to that critical election, fifteen of those eighteen states had recorded votes in excess of 50 per cent of their adult white male population, but in 1824 only two states—Maryland and Alabama—exceeded this modest mark. The average rate of voter participation in the election was 26.5 per cent. This hardly fits the image of the "roaring flood of the new democracy . . . foaming perilously near the crest. . . ."

There would seem to be persuasive evidence that in 1828 the common man flocked to the polls in unprecedented numbers, for the proportion of adult white males voting soared to 56.3 per cent, more than double the 1824 figure. But this outpouring shrinks in magnitude when we observe that in only six of the twenty-two states involved were new highs in voter participation established. In three of these—Maryland, Virginia, and Louisiana—the recorded gain was inconsiderable, and in a fourth—New York—the bulk of the increase might be attributed to changes that had been made in suffrage qualifications as recently as 1821 and 1826. Six states went over the 70 per cent mark, whereas ten had bettered that performance before 1824. Instead of a "mighty democratic uprising" there was in 1828 a voter turnout that approached—but in only a few instances matched or exceeded—the maximum levels that had been attained before the Jackson era.

The advance that was registered in 1828 did not carry forward to 1832. Despite the fact that Jackson was probably at the peak of his personal popularity, that he was engaged in a campaign that was presumably to decide issues of great magnitude, and that in the opinion of some authorities a "well-developed two-party system on a national scale" had been established, there was a slight de-

cline in voter participation. The average for the twenty-three states participating in the presidential contest was 54.9 per cent. In fifteen states a smaller percentage of the adult white males went to the polls in 1832 than in 1828. Only five states bettered their pre-1824 highs. Again the conclusion would be that it was essentially the pre-1824 electorate—diminished in most states and augmented in a few—that voted in 1832. Thus, after three Jackson elections, sixteen states had not achieved the proportions of voter participation that they had reached before 1824. The "new democracy" had not yet made its appearance. . . .

When an examination is made of voting in other than presidential elections prior to 1824, the inaccuracy of the impression that "only small numbers of citizens" went to the polls becomes apparent. Because of the almost automatic succession of the members of the "Virginia dynasty" and the early deterioration of the national two-party system that had seemed to be developing around 1800, presidential elections did not arouse voter interest as much as did those for governor, state legislators, or even members of Congress. In such elections at the state level the "common man" was stimulated by local factors to cast his vote, and he frequently responded in higher proportions than he did to the later stimulus provided by Jackson.

The average voter participation for all states in 1828 was 56.3 per cent. Before 1824 fifteen of the twenty-two states had surpassed that percentage. Among other things, this means that the 1828 election failed to bring to the polls the proportion of the electorate that had voted on occasion in previous elections. There was, in other words, a high potential vote that was frequently realized in state elections but which did not materialize in presidential elections. The unsupported assumption that the common man was either apathetic or debarred from voting by suffrage barriers before 1824 is untenable in the light of this evidence. . . .

Down to this point the voter turnout in the Jackson elections has been compared with that in elections held prior to 1824. Now it becomes appropriate to inquire whether during the period 1824 through 1832 voters turned out in greater proportions for the three presidential contests than they did for the contemporary state elections. If, indeed, this "new democracy" bore some special relationship to Andrew Jackson or to his policies, it might be anticipated that interest in the elections in which he was the central figure would stimulate greater voter participation than gubernatorial contests, in which he was at most a remote factor.

Actually, the election returns show fairly conclusively that throughout the eight-year period the electorate continued to participate more extensively in state elections than in those involving the presidency. Between 1824 and 1832 there were fifty regular gubernatorial elections in the states that chose their electors by popular vote. In only sixteen of these fifty instances did the vote for President surpass the corresponding vote for governor. In Rhode Island, Delaware, Tennessee, Kentucky, Illinois, Mississippi, Missouri, and Georgia the vote for governor consistently exceeded that for President. Only in Connecticut was the reverse true. Viewed from this perspective, too, the remarkable feature of the vote in the Jackson elections is not its immensity but rather its smallness.

Finally, the Jackson elections may be compared with subsequent presidential elections. Once Jackson had retired to the Hermitage, and figures of less dramatic proportions took up the contest for the presidency, did voter participation rise or fall? This question can be answered by observing the percentage of adult white males who voted in each state in the presidential elections of 1836 through 1844. . . . Voter participation in the 1836 election remained near the level that had been established in 1828 and 1832, with 55.2 per cent of the adult white males voting. Only five states registered percentages in excess of their pre-1824 highs. But in 1840 the "new democracy" made its appearance with explosive suddenness.

In a surge to the polls that has rarely, if ever, been exceeded in any presidential election, four out of five (78.0 per cent) of the adult white males cast their votes for Harrison or Van Buren. This new electorate was greater than that of the Jackson period by more than 40 per cent. In all but five states—Vermont, Massachusetts, Rhode Island, Kentucky, and Alabama—the peaks of voter participation reached before 1824 were passed. Fourteen of the twenty-five states involved set record highs for voting that were not to be broken throughout the remainder of the ante bellum period. Now, at last, the common man—or at least the man who previously had not been sufficiently aroused to vote in presidential elections—cast his weight into the political balance. This "Tippecanoe democracy," if such a label is permissible, was of a different order of magnitude from the Jacksonian democracy. The elections in which Jackson figured brought to the polls only those men who were accustomed to voting in state or national elections, except in a very few states. The Tippecanoe canvass witnessed an extraordinary expansion of the size of the presidential electorate far beyond previous dimensions. It was in 1840, then, that the "roaring flood of the new democracy" reached its crest. And it engulfed the Jacksonians.

The flood receded only slightly in 1844, when 74.9 per cent of the estimated potential electorate went to the polls. Indeed, nine states attained their record highs for the period. In 1848 and 1852 there was a general downward trend in voter participation, followed by a modest upswing in 1856 and 1860. But the level of voter activity remained well above that of the Jackson elections. The conclusion to be drawn is that the "mighty democratic uprising" came after the period of Jackson's presidency. . . .

There remains to be considered the factor of Jackson's personal popularity. Did Jackson, the popular hero, attract voters to the polls in unprecedented proportions? The comparisons that have already been made between the Jackson elections and other elections—state and national—before, during, and after his presidency would suggest a negative answer to the question. Granted that a majority of the voters in 1828 favored Jackson, it is not evident that his partisans stormed the polls any more enthusiastically than did the Adams men. Of the six highest states in voter participation in 1828, three favored Adams and three were for Jackson, which could be interpreted to mean that the convinced Adams supporters turned out no less zealously for their man than did the ardent Jacksonians. When Van Buren replaced Jackson in 1836, the voting average increased slightly over 1832. And, as has been demonstrated, the real manifestation of the "new democracy" came not in 1828 but in 1840.

The most satisfactory explanation for the increase in voter participation between 1824 and 1828 is a simple and obvious one. During the long reign of the Virginia dynasty, interest in presidential elections dwindled. In 1816 and 1820 there had been no contest. The somewhat fortuitous termination of the Virginia succession in 1824 and the failure of the congressional caucus to solve the problem of leadership succession threw the choice of a President upon the electorate. But popular interest was dampened by the confusion of choice presented by the multiplicity of candidates, by the disintegration of the old national parties, by the fact that in most states one or another of the candidates was so overwhelmingly popular as to forestall any semblance of a contest, and possibly by the realization that the election would ultimately be decided by the House of Representatives. By 1828 the situation had altered. There were but two candidates in the field, each of whom had substantial sectional backing. A clear-cut contest impended, and the voters became sufficiently aroused to go to the polls in moderate numbers.

One final question remains. Why was the vote in the Jackson elections relatively low when compared with previous and contemporary state elections and with presidential votes after 1804? The answer, in brief, is that in most states either Jackson or his opponent had such a one-sided advantage that the result was a foregone conclusion. Consequently there was little incentive for the voters to go to the polls.

This factor can be evaluated in fairly specific quantitative terms. If the percentage of the total vote secured by each candidate in each state in the election of 1828 is calculated, the difference between the percentages can be used as an index of the closeness, or one-sidedness, of the contest. In Illinois, for example, Jackson received 67 per cent of the total vote and Adams, 33; the difference—thirty-four points—represents the margin between the candidates. The average difference between the candidates, taking all the states together, was thirty-six points. Expressed another way this would mean that in the average state the winning candidate received more than twice the vote of the loser. Actually, this was the case in thirteen of the twenty-two states. . . . Such a wide margin virtually placed these states in the "no contest" category. . . .

When Jacksonian democracy is viewed from the perspectives employed in this analysis, its political dimensions insofar as they relate to the behavior of the electorate can be described with some precision. None of the Jackson elections involved a "mighty democratic uprising" in the sense that voters were drawn to the polls in unprecedented proportions. When compared with the peak participation recorded for each state before 1824, or with contemporaneous gubernatorial elections, or most particularly with the vast outpouring of the electorate in 1840, voter participation in the Jackson elections was unimpressive. The key to the relatively low presidential vote would seem to be the extreme political imbalance that existed in most states as between the Jacksonians and their opponents. Associated with this imbalance was the immature development of national parties in connection with the Jackson elections. As balanced, organized parties subsequently made their appearance from state to state, and voters were stimulated by the prospect of a genuine contest, a marked rise in voter participation occurred. Such conditions did not prevail generally across the nation until 1840, and then at last the "mighty democratic uprising" took place.

POSTSCRIPT

Did the Election of 1828 Represent a Democratic Revolt of the People?

The two essays in this issue discuss the presidential election of 1828 from different approaches. The portion of Remini's essay which is reprinted here is an example of good, solid narrative history sprinkled with interpretations. Though a full-fledged, two-party system was not yet in effect in all parts of the country, Remini demonstrates that a well-organized coalition of supporters for Andrew Jackson existed in Congress and in a number of states in various sections of the country. Often holding different ideological perspectives, these politicians united around one common goal: the election of Andrew Jackson to the presidency. Remini's description of the staged rallies, the name-calling, the fudging of the issues, and the importance of organization over ideology sounds not unlike recent presidential campaigns.

McCormick, a veteran analyzer of nineteenth-century politics, views the 1828 election through the lens of quantitative history. He uses statistics to break down a number of generalizations about the significance of Jackson's election. The Rutgers University professor discounts the removal of property qualifications for voting, the influence of the western states, and the charisma of Jackson as the major reasons why twice as many voters turned out for the 1828 presidential race than they did four years earlier. He argues that in spite of such statistics, a higher percentage of voters had turned out for earlier gubernatorial and legislative elections in most states than for the 1828 presidential election. In McCormick's view, the key election was 1840, not 1828, because by this time, the two parties—Whigs and Democrats—were equally balanced in all sections of the country, and voters turn out in larger numbers when they perceive a closely contested presidential race.

McCormick's article raises a number of questions. Is he comparing apples and oranges, as Remini seems to imply? Using McCormick's data, is it possible for other historians to reach different conclusions? How does one explain a 50 percent increase in voter turnout between 1824 and 1828?

For more information, see Richard P. McCormick, "Political Development and the Second Party System," as well as the other essays in William Nesbet Chambers and Walter Dean Burnham, eds., *The American Party Systems: Stages of Political Development* (New York, 1967).

ISSUE 11

Was Antebellum Reform Motivated Primarily by Humanitarian Goals?

YES: Alice Felt Tyler, from *Freedom's Ferment: Phases of American Social History From the Colonial Period to the Outbreak of Civil War* (University of Minnesota Press, 1944)

NO: David J. Rothman, from *The Discovery of the Asylum: Social Order and Disorder in the New Republic* (Little, Brown, 1971)

ISSUE SUMMARY

YES: Professor of history Alice Felt Tyler argues that American reformers in the antebellum period were products of evangelical religion and frontier democracy who accepted the mission of perfecting human institutions.
NO: Professor of history David J. Rothman contends that antebellum reformers established orphan asylums and reformatories primarily to enforce strict discipline and to inculcate respect for authority and order among those seeking refuge in these institutions.

In the era following the War of 1812, several dramatic changes in the United States occurred. Andrew Jackson's military triumph over the British at the Battle of New Orleans generated a wave of nationalistic sentiment in the country, even though the victory had come two weeks *after* the Treaty of Ghent officially ended the conflict with England. The republic experienced important territorial expansion with the addition of new states in each of the half-dozen years following the end of the war. A "transportation revolution" produced a turnpike, canal, and railroad network that brought Americans closer together and enhanced the opportunities for economic growth. In politics, the demise of the nation's first two-party system, following the decline of the Federalists, was succeeded by the rise to prominence of the Democratic and, later, the Whig parties.

Although some historians have characterized this period as the "era of good feelings," it is important to remember that many Americans were aware that the nation was not without its problems. Drawing upon intellectual precepts associated with the Enlightenment, some citizens believed in the necessity of and potential for perfecting American society. Ralph Waldo Emerson captured the sense of mission felt by many nineteenth-century men and women when he wrote: "What is man for but to be a Re-former, a Re-maker of what man has made; a renouncer of lies; a restorer of truth and good, imitating that great Nature which embosoms us all, and which sleeps no moment on an old past, but every hour repairs herself, yielding to us every morning a new day, and with every pulsation a new life?" These ideas were reinforced by the encouragement for moral and spiritual perfection produced by the revivalistic movement known as the Second Great Awakening. Significantly, revivalists like Charles G. Finney combined a desire to promote salvation through faith and spiritual conversion with an active interest in social change.

This "age of reform" was a multifaceted and often interrelated movement. Reformers, most of whom were from the middle and upper classes, hoped to improve the condition of inmates in the country's prisons and asylums or to encourage temperance or even total abstinence from drinking. Some reformers emphasized the necessity of maintaining peace in the world, while others hoped to improve the educational system for the masses. Still others directed their energies into movements emphasizing dietary reform and clothing reform for women. Finally, large numbers of Americans sought to improve society through campaigns to improve the status of women and to eliminate slavery.

Thousands of Americans belonged to one or more of these antebellum reform societies, but some controversy exists as to the motivations of these reformers. Were they driven by humanitarian impulses that surfaced in the reinvigorated American republic after 1815? Or was it merely self-interest that encouraged middle- and upper-class Americans to attempt to order society in such a way as to preserve their positions of power?

Alice Felt Tyler's essay represents the traditional thesis that antebellum reformers were motivated largely by humanitarian ideals and desired primarily to perfect American society. These impulses, Tyler claims, stemmed from America's democratic spirit and the evangelical sentiment produced by the Second Great Awakening.

David J. Rothman, however, focusing upon the various child-care institutions (orphan asylums and reformatories, for example) that began to appear in the 1830s, suggests that the prevailing goal of the reformers involved in those endeavors was to impose a strict disciplinary routine that would ensure absolute respect for authority among the asylum's inmates. In fact, although the superintendents of these institutions frequently employed the metaphor of the family to characterize their operations, they were inclined to exercise over their charges a quasi-military control, which they deemed essential for preserving social and moral order in the United States.

YES

Alice Felt Tyler

FREEDOM'S FERMENT

THE FAITH OF THE YOUNG REPUBLIC

The time has come when the experiment is to be made whether the world is to be emancipated and rendered happy, or whether the whole creation shall groan and travail together in pain. . . . If it had been the design of Heaven to establish a powerful nation in the full enjoyment of civil and religious liberty, where all the energies of man might find full scope and excitement, on purpose to show the world by one great successful experiment of what man is capable . . . where should such an experiment have been made but in this country! . . . The light of such a hemisphere shall go up to Heaven, it will throw its beams beyond the waves; it will shine into the darkness there, and be comprehended—it will awaken desire, and hope, and effort, and produce revolutions and overturnings until the world is free. . . . Floods have been poured upon the rising flame, but they can no more extinguish it than they can extinguish the flames of Aetna. Still it burns, and still the mountain murmurs; and soon it will explode with voices and thunderings, and great earthquakes. . . . Then will the trumpet of jubilee sound, and earth's debased millions will leap from the dust, and shake off their chains, and cry, "Hosanna to the Son of David!"

With this vision of the future as a new and glorious epoch Lyman Beecher a hundred years ago voiced the exuberant optimism of the young American republic in which he lived. In that time, if ever in American history, the spirit of man seemed free and the individual could assert his independence of choice in matters of faith and theory. The militant democracy of the period was a declaration of faith in man and in the perfectibility of his institutions. The idea of progress so inherent in the American way of life and so much a part of the philosophy of the age was at the same time a challenge to traditional beliefs and institutions and an impetus to experimentation with new theories and humanitarian reforms.

The period was one of restless ferment. An expanding West was beckoning the hungry and dissatisfied to an endless search for the pot of gold.

From Alice Felt Tyler, *Freedom's Ferment: Phases of America's Social History from the Colonial Period to the Outbreak of the Civil War* (University of Minnesota Press, 1944). Copyright © 1944 by the University of Minnesota Press. Reprinted by permission.

Growing industrialization and urbanization in the East, new means of communication and transportation, new marvels of invention and science, and advance in the mechanization of industry, all were dislocating influences of mounting importance. And increasing immigration was bringing into the country thousands of Europeans who were dissatisfied with the difficult conditions of life in their native lands. Nor did religion place any restraint on the unrest; recurring revivals, emphasis on individual conversion and personal salvation, and the multiplicity of sects, all made religion responsive to the restlessness of the time rather than a calming influence upon it. The pious editors of the writings of a Shaker seeress asserted in their preface to her revelations.

Let any candid people, endowed with a common share of discernment seriously examine the signs of the times, and view the many wonderful events and extraordinary changes that are constantly taking place in the moral religious and political world, as well as in the natural elements, through the operations of Providence, and they cannot but consider the present age as commencing the most extraordinary and momentous era that ever took place on earth.

Each in his own way the citizens of the young republic recognized the ferment of the era and made answer to its challenge. Itinerant revivalists and the most orthodox of clergymen alike responded with missionary zeal. For an influential few transcendentalism proved to be a satisfying reconciliation between the rationalism of their training and the romanticism of the age, while among the less intellectual, adventism, spiritualism, Mormonism, and perfectionism each won adherents who founded churches and preached their creeds with fervor. To these sects were added the cults and communities transplanted from abroad. The combination of religious toleration, overflowing optimism, and cheap lands caused Europeans of unorthodox faith or unusual social ideas to seek asylum in America. Each such sect, each isolated religious community, each social utopia, was an evidence of the tolerant, eclectic spirit of the young republic, and each made its contribution to the culture of the land that gave it sanctuary.

The desire to perfect human institutions was the basic cause for each sect and community, and this same desire lay at the roots of all the many social reform movements of the period. The American reformer was the product of evangelical religion, which presented to every person the necessity for positive action to save his own soul, and dynamic frontier democracy, which was rooted deep in a belief in the worth of the individual. Born of this combination, the reformer considered reform at once his duty and his right, and he did not limit his activities to one phase of social betterment. Education, temperance, universal peace, prison reform, the rights of women, the evils of slavery, the dangers of Catholicism, all were legitimate fields for his efforts.

The American reformer knew that he did not work alone. He recognized that each cause he espoused was a part of a world of progress and aspiration, but peculiarly his was the freedom to experiment, for in his homeland there was room and hospitality for adventure. Happy in his privilege, he acknowledged his duty and accepted for his age the sign of his crusade. . . .

DYNAMIC DEMOCRACY

It was a long process of democratization, begun before the signing of the Declaration of Independence, accelerated by the Revolution, and continued through the influence of the frontier, that made American society, in the words of the French traveler, Michel Chevalier, in 1834, "essentially and radically a democracy, not in name merely but in deed." . . .

Frederick Jackson Turner, the historian whose name is identified with the frontier, has wisely said that the West is at bottom a form of society, rather than an area. From the beginning each colony had its frontier, its West: areas in which men of courage and vigor won new opportunities, where land was cheap or free and the struggle for existence, although severe, brought rewards commensurate with the effort expended. There the "cake of custom" was broken, old standards were discarded, new ideals and new institutions were set up. The back country was relatively near the Atlantic Coast in the early days, but it was pushed farther west, north, or south decade by decade. In 1790 one hundred thousand had reached the Mississippi Valley. The census of 1810 showed a Western population of a million, that of 1830 gave the West more than three and a half millions, and that of 1840 made the total six millions. . . .

From whatever background they came, no matter how diverse their motives or their equipment, the frontier shaped these settlers into its own pattern. And the type of American developed under frontier conditions set his mark upon the life of his nation so unmistakably that the philosophy of the frontier came to color the activities of the entire United States. Equality of condition was a fact, not a

theory, on the frontier; station, education, refinement, and even wealth mattered little. All must face the same perils and hardships, the same grueling labor in clearing the land, the same isolation, the same grueling labor in clearing the land, the same isolation, the same lack of the refinement of civilization. The weaklings move on, dropped back, or died of their failures, while the vigorous and self-reliant remained to become the leaders and the models of frontier achievement.

The same conditions produced the paradox of the frontier—a belief in equality so profound that the American almost confounded equality of opportunity with equality of ability, together with an intense, militant individualism that resented all restrictions and was restless, buoyant, self-assertive, and optimistic. The frontiersman had the utmost confidence in himself, his region, and his country, and he both craved and resented comparisons and criticisms. Acknowledging no debt to the past, he believed in progress and accepted change as the natural order. Hopeful and idealistic, he yet could not forget the necessity for commons sense and a realistic attitude, for the conquest of the wilderness was an arduous task, exacting, monotonous, and burdensome. . . .

The frontier's faith in democracy and freedom soon took on an element of crusading zeal as Americans became convinced of the glorious future ahead of them and came to consider themselves entrusted with the mission of portraying democracy to less favored nations. A magazine article in 1821, perhaps with some sense of humor, illustrated this confidence in the future with the statement:

Other nations boast of what they are or have been, but the true citizen of the

United States exalts his head to the skies in the contemplation of what the grandeur of his country is going to be. Others claim respect and honor because of the things done by a long line of ancestors; an American appeals to prophecy, and with Malthus in one hand and a map of the back country in the other he defies us to a comparison with America as she is to be, and chuckles his delight over the splendors the geometrical ratio is to shed over her story. This appeal to the future is his never-failing resource. . . .

Francis Grund, writing in 1836 for an English public, made the same sort of comment in his statement that Americans loved their country not for what it then was, but for what it was to be—not the land of their fathers, but the land their children were destined to inherit. The Scotsman, Alexander Mackay, heard the same idea from a South Carolina farmer in response to a question about genealogy: "We don't vally those things in this country. It's what's above ground, not what's under, that we think on." Whether or not the visiting Europeans approved of American democracy, and many did not, they all were agreed that Americans themselves were content with their institutions and believed them better than those of Europe.

This American solidarity was noted by the most famous foreign visitor of the period, Alexis de Tocqueville, in a letter from the United States in June 1831. After stating that he envied Americans the comfort of their common opinion, he went on to enumerate them: All the people believe that a republic is the best possible government and do not question that the people have a right to govern themselves. This belief is almost a *faith*, which is at basis a faith in the good

sense of human beings and in the perfectibility of human institutions. In order that those institutions may constantly improve, education and enlightenment must become as universal as suffrage. De Tocqueville found no evidence of ancient traditions and little effect of old customs or memories. Americans were a new people. He felt that the reason there was so great a respect for law was that the people made it themselves and could change it themselves. "It is really an incredible thing . . . to see how this people keeps itself in order through the single conviction that its only safeguard against itself lies in itself." Somewhat reluctantly, apparently, the young Frenchman admitted that on the whole the country presented "an admirable spectacle!" His great work published some years later, *Democracy in America*, reaffirmed this first impression, saying,

> In America, the principle of the sovereignty of the people is not either barren or concealed . . . it is recognized by the customs and proclaimed by the laws. . . . If there be a country in the world where the doctrine of the sovereignty of the people can be fairly appreciated, where it can be studied in its application to the affairs of society, and where its dangers and its advantages may be foreseen, that country is assuredly America.

The American's own view of his achievement in democracy was usually optimistic, sometimes complacent, but occasionally tempered by analysis and criticism. The novelist, James Fenimore Cooper, although professing belief in democracy, was a caustic critic of American life, attacking what he thought were its abuses and faults with a vehemence that won him many enemies. In his *America and the*

Americans: Notions Picked up by a Travelling Bachelor, published in 1836, he endeavored to explain his country to the outside world and to express his own faith. But in *The American Democrat,* designed for his own countrymen, he warned of the danger of the rise of a "vulgar tyrant" and repeatedly asserted that the leading principle of a republic must be that political power is a trust to be guarded with "ceaseless vigilance." Feeling that imperfect as popular government was, it was less dangerous than any other, Cooper came to the conclusion that men of intelligence and wealth, of education and station, must take their proper place in democratic society and aid in directing national policies.

The self-conscious democracy of the West, in conjunction with the laboring classes of the seaboard states, exercised its newly acquired manhood suffrage in 1828 to bring about the Jacksonian Revolution and install "Old Hickory," the hero of the land-speculating, Indian-fighting West, in the White house. . . .

With the election of Andrew Jackson the creed of the frontier won its victory in the arena of national affairs, and the Western interest in politics became national with the rise of the common man to political importance. While office-holders trembled and Washington official and social circles paled with anticipatory anguish, the President-elect prepared to act in accordance with a creed that summarizes well the essential faith of the young republic:

> I believe man can be elevated; man can become more and more endowed with divinity; and as he does he becomes more God-like in his character and capable of governing himself. Let us go on elevating our people, perfecting our institutions, until democracy shall reach such a point of perfection that we can acclaim with truth that the voice of the people is the voice of God.

EVANGELICAL RELIGION

The religious heritage of the young republic was as important in the development of nineteenth-century ideas as were the liberties won in the struggle with civil authorities. "When the common man has freed himself from political absolutism, he will become dissatisfied with theological absolutism." The cold and repressive doctrines of Calvinism could not win the hearts of those who escaped from its control when its dictatorial governmental power came to an end. Moreover, the rationalism of John Locke and the French philosophes had the same dislocating effect on religious thinking as on political ideas. Calvin's doctrine of total depravity might have sufficed an older generation as an explanation of the presence of evil in human society, but man's reason found other causes, and his common sense rejected the idea that he and his neighbor were utterly depraved. The idea of progress and of the importance of the individual undermined the old doctrines of election and predestination. The consequent dissatisfaction with Genevan dogma, coupled with the aridity and dullness of New England cultural life, caused the people to turn with eagerness to evangelical Protestantism. . . .

The frank and open adoption of emotionalism in religion and the sensational methods of revivalists did not go unnoticed by American and European contemporary commentators. Margaret Bayard Smith in describing a revival in Washington in 1822 stated that the preachers were introducing all the habits and hymns of the Methodists into our Presbyterian churches . . . that they were going through the highways and hedges, to invite guests . . . into every house exhorting the people, particularly into all the taverns, grog-shops, and other resorts of dissipation and vice. Whether all these excessive efforts will produce a permanent reformation I know not; but there is something very repugnant to my feelings in the public way in which they discuss the conversions and convictions of people and in which young ladies and children display their feelings and talk of their convictions and experiences. Dr. May calls the peculiar fever, the *night* fever, and he says almost all cases were produced by night meetings, crowded rooms, excited feelings, and exposure to night air.

A somewhat less naïve explanation of revivalistic phenomena was made by Bishop Hopkins of Vermont, who stated that revivalists secured conversions solely because of the terror induced by their exhortations. Disapproval of such tactics seems to have been prevalent among the Episcopalian clergy, one of whom Captain Marryat quoted as saying that revivals were

those startling and astounding shocks which are constantly invented, artfully and habitually applied, under all the power of sympathy, and of a studied and enthusiastic elocution, by a large class of preachers among us. To startle and to shock is their great secret power.

But the American clergy in general probably felt that the revival had come to stay and could be made a valuable part of the religious program of the Protestant churches.

European travelers almost invariably were taken to camp meetings, especially in the West, and reacted to the experi-

ence in accord with their own temperaments. Captain Marryat drew back in disgust from the preacher who began his prayer with the words "Almighty and diabolical God," and depreciated all the excesses and extravagances of evangelical religion. Frances Trollope made many caustic comments about both revivals and preachers. Always suspecting the worst, she felt sure that such sessions must turn at times into sex orgies, although the only ocular evidence she had was the sight of a preacher whispering consolation into the ear of a sobbing and distraught young feminine convert.

James Stuart was much impressed by the perfect decorum of the audience, the "faultless" sermons, and the magnificent singing. The revival he attended, however, was on Long Island; he was not exposed to the crudities of a genuine frontier camp meeting. It is more surprising to find the usually censorious Thomas Hamilton commending the camp meeting as an agency of civilization.

In a free community [he wrote] the follies of the fanatic are harmless. The points on which he differs from those around him are rarely of a nature to produce injurious effects on his conduct as a citizen. But the man without religion acknowledges no restraint but human laws; and the dungeon and the gibbet are necessary to secure the rights and interests of his fellow-citizens from violation. There can be no doubt, therefore, that in a newly settled country the strong effect produced by these camp-meetings and revivals is on the whole beneficial. The restraints of public opinion and penal legislation are little felt in the wilderness; and, in such circumstances, the higher principle of action, communicated by religion, is a new and additional security to society.

Two of the most detailed descriptions of camp-meeting revivals are those of Francis Lieber and Fredrika Bremer, written nearly twenty years apart and published in 1835 and 1853. Lieber was repelled by the emotionalism of the camp meeting he attended and was shocked by the "scenes of unrestrained excitement," but the Swedish traveler, Fredrika Bremer, was much impressed by the immense crowd of both white and colored people at the Georgia camp meeting she witnessed in the early 1850's. The grandeur of the night meeting in the forest, the eight fine altars, the campfires of resinous wood, the superb singing of the thousands of Negroes, the wails of the penitent, the thunder and lightning of an approaching storm—all, she said, combined to make the night one never to be forgotten.

The effects of the absence of state control and the consequent multiplicity of sects seemed to interest all foreign observers. Many of them mention the lack of religious intolerance in the United States and the easy "live and let live" philosophy apparent in the attitude of most men. Alexander Mackay, who traveled extensively in America in the 1840's, was so impressed that he wrote:

It is true that the insulting term "toleration" is but seldom heard in America in connexion with the religious system of the country. To say that one tolerates another's creed, implies some right to disallow it, a right that happens to be suspended or in abeyance for the time being. The only mode in which the American manifests any intolerance in reference to religion is that they will not tolerate that the independence of the individual should in any degree, be called in question in connexion with it.

On the more fundamental question of the connection between the American democratic faith and the emotional perfectionistic religion that had swept over the United States the observers seemed in agreement. Again and again missionaries and patriots identified democratic with religious faith and asserted that neither could stand alone, that combined they furnished an invincible bulwark for American freedom. Timothy Flint, writer and missionary preacher of the first decade of the century, emphasize always that missionary enterprise in the West was for the good of the whole country; the West must not fall into Godless anarchy, for the representative institutions of the East would then also perish. As the Western missionary told De Tocqueville, "It is, therefore, our interest that the New States should be religious, in order that they may permit us to remain free."

In an essay published in 1851, Mark Hopkins, president of Williams College, expressed the same feeling that democracy must be linked with Christianity:

Man himself is the highest product of this lower world, those institutions would seem to be the best which show, not the most imposing results of aggregated labor, but humanity itself, in its most general cultivation and highest forms. This idea finds its origin and support in the value which Christianity places upon the individual, and, fully carried out, must overthrow all systems of darkness and mere authority. Individual liberty and responsibility involve the right of private judgment; this involves the right to all the light necessary to form a correct judgment; and this again must involve the education of the people, and the overthrow of everything, civil and religious, which will not stand the ordeal of the most scrutinizing examination and of the freest discussion.

Regardless of their differences as to details, European and American observers alike were insistent upon the prominence of the part played by religion in the Western World. They saw that the same intensity of faith vivified both the democracy and the religious experience of many Americans, and they realized the potentialities of that combination. The mind and heart quickened by the "lively joy" of a vital religious experience were easily turned toward social reforms, and the spirit of inquiry and soul-searching that animated the revival had a dynamic social significance. The American faith in democratic institutions found its alter ego in the romantic evangelical spirit of American religious life. Together they gave to the Americans of the first half century of the republic their conviction that their institutions could be perfected and their national destiny be fulfilled.

NO

David J. Rothman

THE DISCOVERY OF THE ASYLUM

THE WELL-ORDERED ASYLUM

No reformers were more confident of the advantage and success of their program than the philanthropists who founded child-saving institutions. For proponents, the movement to incarcerate the orphan, the abandoned child, the youngster living in dire poverty, the juvenile vagrant, and the delinquent promised enormous benefits while entailing few risks. Like their colleagues sponsoring insane asylums and penitentiaries and almshouses, they shared an intense faith in the rehabilitative powers of a carefully designed environment and were certain that properly structured institutions would not only comfort the homeless but reform the delinquent.

Child-care institutions, new to Americans, fundamentally altered traditional practices. In the colonial period, overseers of the poor, in the absence of responsible relatives and friends, typically had apprenticed the orphan to a local householder. In unusual circumstances, when the child suffered from a major disability, they might have recourse in one of the larger towns to the almshouse. The orphan asylum was all but unknown in the eighteenth century. . . .

In the 1830's a basic transformation occurred as child-care institutions spread rapidly through the country. In this decade alone, twenty-three private orphan asylums began operating in various towns and cities, and the movement continued to grow in the 1840's with the founding of thirty more of them. They opened not only in New York, Boston, and Philadelphia—as usual, among the leaders in building institutions—but also in Bangor, Maine; Richmond, Virginia; Mobile, Alabama; Avondale and Cincinnati, Ohio; and Chicago, Illinois. By 1850, New York State alone had twenty-seven public and private child-care institutions. Within two decades they had become common structures, widespread and popular, with their own unique and important attributes, not just a last resort when apprenticeship was impossible. Indeed, their promise seemed so great that trustees quickly spread

From David J. Rothman, *The Discovery of the Asylum: Social Order and Disorder in the New Republic* (Little, Brown, 1971). Copyright © 1971 by Little, Brown & Co. Reprinted by permission. Notes omitted.

their nets to catch a wide variety of dependent children. They admitted the abandoned as well as the orphaned child, and those whose widowed or deserted mothers, hard pressed to make ends meet, had little time for supervision. They accepted minors whose parents were quite alive but very poor, and those from families that seemed to them morally, if not financially, inadequate to their tasks. From an administrator's perspective, there was no reason to penalize the unfortunate child for the fact of his parents' survival.

During these decades another type of caretaker institution became popular—the reformatory for disobedient children, the house of refuge. It took in several types of minors—the juvenile offender, convicted by a court for a petty crime, the wandering street arab, picked up by a town constable, and the willfully disobedient child, turned over by distraught parents. The reformatory, like the orphan asylum, maintained a flexible admissions policy, prepared to accept the commitment decisions of a judicial body, the less formal recommendations of overseers of the poor, or the personal inclinations of the head of a household. Its administrators expressed no fears about a possible miscarriage of justice and were disinclined to bring the protections of due process to these minors. A good dose of institutionalization could only work to the child's benefit.

Once again, the major eastern cities set the trend. New York philanthropists founded a house of refuge in 1825, and colleagues in Boston and Philadelphia followed suit within three years. The idea did not immediately spread to other urban areas, for most municipalities and state legislatures invested their funds first in multifunction orphan asylums.

But by the 1840's specialization increased and houses of refuge appeared in Rochester, Cincinnati, and New Orleans; during the 1850's they opened in Providence, Baltimore, Pittsburgh, Chicago, and St. Louis as well. By 1857 the movement was broad enough to hold a national convention of refuge superintendents in New York. Its first committee on statistics calculated that seventeen reformatories now operated, with a combined inmate population of over 20,000, a value in land and buildings of almost $2,000,000, and total annual expenditures of about $330,000. Here was another sizable investment in institutionalization.

Taken together, the admissions policies of child-care institutions were a catalogue of practically every misfortune that could befall a minor. The abject, the vagrant, the delinquent, the child of poverty-stricken or intemperate parents were all proper candidates for one or another asylum or refuge. Other practices did persist. One could still find minors confined to an almshouse or incarcerated in a local jail; smaller communities continued to rely upon apprenticeship to solve child-care problems. The new structures never won a monopoly. Nevertheless, they did become the model treatment for the homeless and delinquent. Like the mental hospital, penitentiary, and almshouse, they dominated the thinking of interested reformers, competing successfully for city-council, state-legislature, and philanthropic funds. The asylum and the refuge were two more bricks in the wall that Americans built to confine and reform the dangerous classes.

The founders of orphan asylums and houses of refuge shared fully with the proponents of other caretaker institutions a fear that anyone not carefully and diligently trained to cope with the open, free-wheeling, and disordered life of the community would fall victim to vice and crime. The orphan, robbed of his natural guardians, desperately needed protection against these dangers. Many children of the poor were in no better position, since their parents—at best too busy trying to eke out a living and at worst intemperate—provided no defense against corruption. The vagrant, by definition lacking in supervision, would certainly come under the sway of taverns, gambling halls, and theaters, the crowd of drunks, gamblers, thieves, and prostitutes. The nightmare come true, of course, was the juvenile delinquent, his behavior ample testimony to the speed and predictability of moral decline.

To counter these conditions, the asylum was shelter and sanctuary. Supporters pleaded vigorously and passionately for funds in order to snatch the child from the contagion of vice. The directors of the Orphan Society of Philadelphia asked patrons to endow a place where children of misfortune "are sheltered from the perils of want and the contamination of evil example." The Boston Children's Friend Society assumed the task of removing the sons and daughters of intemperate, depraved, and pauper parents as rapidly as possible "from those baleful influences which inevitably tend to make them pests to society, and ultimately the tenants of our prisons." A state reformatory in New Hampshire also defined its function in terms of "the separation of the young convict from society; his seclusion from vicious associates." And the managers of the Philadelphia House of Refuge, appealing for funds, boasted that visitors would find "the orphan, deserted or misguided child, shielded from the temptations of a sinful world."

But the asylum program had another, more important component—to train and rehabilitate its charges. It would not only shelter the orphan and delinquent, but discipline and reform them. Some philanthropic societies, it is true, limited their activities to rescuing the child from his poverty and giving him over to others, to a sea captain going on a lengthy whaling voyage, or to a country farmer needing another hand. For them, removal was a sufficient program. Many organizations, however, assumed a broader function, eager to carry out the tasks of child rearing. Starting afresh, they would organize a model routine, design and administer an upbringing that embodied the highest standards. In a manner clearly reminiscent of the mental hospital and the penitentiary, and to some degree of the almshouse as well, they expected to demonstrate the validity of general principles through the specific treatment of deviants and dependents. The experiment would rehabilitate the particular inmate and by exemplification spark the reform of the whole society.

This perspective dominated the asylum movement. Proponents insisted that the discipline at the Philadelphia House of Refuge would provide delinquents with "a healthy moral constitution, capable of resisting *the assaults of temptations,* and strong enough to keep the line of rectitude through *the stormy and disturbing influences by which we are continually assailed.*" This siege mentality united those attending the first national convention of house of refuge officials. They quickly formed a consensus around the sentiments expressed by Orlando Hastings, the delegate from the Rochester reformatory. Defining the fundamental purpose of the program, Hastings declared: "The object is not alone to make the boys behave well while in our charge; that is not difficult. . . . [But] any discipline . . . which does not enable the boy to *resist temptation* wherever and whenever he finds it, is ineffectual, and the whole object of houses of refuge is a failure." An even more elaborate rationale emerged in the reports of the Boston asylum. "There are," its managers explained, "two ways to aid in the redemption of society—one is to remove the sources of corruption, and the other is to remove the young from the temptations that exist." While some reformers chose to follow the first strategy, they were determined to adopt the second, "to enlighten their [inmates] minds, and aid them in forming virtuous habits, that they may finally go forth, *clothed as in invincible armour."* Let others try to weaken the force of vice in the society. They would gird the young to withstand temptation.

Once again, the analysis which diagnosed an ostensibly desperate state of things also promised a sure remedy. Since the root of the problem lay in a faulty environment, the means for improvement were ready at hand, and asylum proponents were even more confident than their counterparts in other caretaker institutions of the prospects for success. Although all reformers assumed a plasticity of human nature that gave a logic to their efforts, asylum supporters felt themselves singularly fortunate: their clientele was young, especially impressionable, and not fixed in deviant or dependent behavior. "Youth," happily reported the governors of the Philadelphia House of Refuge, "is particularly susceptible of reform. . . . It has not yet felt the long continued pressure, which distorts its natural growth. . . . No habit can then be rooted so firmly as to refuse

a cure." In the same spirit, the Boston Children's Friend Society looked forward to rehabilitating those "whose plastic natures may be molded into images of perfect beauty, or as perfect repulsiveness." And managers of the New York House of Refuge assumed that "the minds of children, naturally pliant, can, by early instruction, be formed and molded to our wishes." If the young were highly vulnerable to corruption, they were also eminently teachable.

Asylum proponents were not apprehensive about promoting the very vices they planned to eradicate. Overseers of the poor in this period anxiously wondered whether too comfortable an almshouse might inadvertently attract the lower classes, thereby promoting idleness; wardens also feared that a short sentence in a lax prison which coddled the criminal would increase recidivism. But child-care institutions were free of these concerns. Managers were confident that incarceration would not rob orphans of initiative—they were simply too young for that—or encourage their parents to avoid responsibility through commitment. And an indeterminate sentence to a house of refuge, for a term as long as the young offender's minority, could hardly be considered too lenient. Thus, without hesitation or qualification, they urged the new program.

At the core of the child-reformers' optimism was a faith completely shared by colleagues promoting other caretaker institutions: that a daily routine of strict and steady discipline would transform inmates' character. The asylum's primary task was to teach an absolute respect for authority through the establishment and enforcement of a rigorous and orderly routine. Obedience would bring reform. The function of the orphan asylum, according to Charleston, South Carolina, officials, was to train boys to a proper place in a community where "*systematic labor* of *order* and *regularity* established, and *discipline* enforced, are the social obligations." A strict training in accord with these virtues "disciplines them for . . . various walks of life," enabling them to become "practical men of business and good citizens, in the middle classes of society." The Boston Asylum and Farm School for destitute and vagrant children was dedicated to the same means and ends. These classes, managers told would-be donors, "have been received within the walls of a Christian asylum, where they have listened to good counsel, and acquired habits of *order, industry* and *usefulness*. . . . We know not how anyone interested in the preservation of order or stability of government . . . can withhold his sympathy." Its annual reports regularly replayed this theme, noting that "it is almost astonishing how readily boys, hitherto accustomed to have their own way, and to dispute supremacy with inefficient or indulgent parents, are brought into habits of respect and order by a system of *uniformly firm discipline*." The Boston asylum directors recognized fully the affinity between their program and that of other contemporary caretaker institutions. "A hospital for the insane," they announced, "has hardly greater superiority over the private family in regulating its inmates, in this respect, than the Farm School over the mis-government or no-government of the weak and careless parent."

The primacy of obedience and respect for authority in the process of rehabilitation was even more apparent in the institutions treating delinquents and vagrants. The New York Juvenile Asylum, serving

these groups, put the matter aggressively. "We do not believe," announced its superintendent, "in the mawkish, sentimental and infidel philosophy of modern days, which discards the Bible method of disciplining the child into obedience. . . . It is manifest that but little good can be effected with all our appliances, unless order and obedience to establishment rules are vigilantly maintained. . . . What is needed for the children whom the law entrusts to us is the government of a well-ordered Christian household." Their neighbors at the New York House of Refuge agreed. Let inmates, officials declared, "be made tractable and obedient . . . [through] a vigorous course of moral and corporal discipline." With fidelity to this principle, the refuge superintendent argued that "the most benevolent and humane method for the management of children, is, to require prompt and implicit obedience." And to support his point he presented some sample cases. For one typical delinquent, the "discipline of the House was all that was requisite to make him obedient." For another, an especially refractory youngster bent on escaping, "it was found necessary to apply severe and continued punishments, in order to break the obstinacy of his spirit." Ultimately success came: "The discipline enforced had a most happy effect. He became submissive and obedient."

All child-care institutions made this strategy basic to their procedures. In an 1826 prospectus, the founders of the Philadelphia House of Refuge promised to return delinquents to society after "a course of rigid but not cruel or ignominious discipline." There would be "unrelenting supervision, mild but certain punishments for any infraction of the rules, and habits of quiet and good order at all times." They described with obvious pleasure a recent tour through the New York House of Refuge, taking particular delight in one scene: the children silently marching in file into Sunday chapel, sitting attentively and quietly through the service, and then leaving in an orderly line. Here they found an achievement worth emulating. A similar perspective won the general approval of the refuge superintendents meeting in national conference. As Orlando Hastings, the Rochester delegate, expressed it: asylum mangers had to secure "the confidence and affection of those committed to their care"; otherwise they were not suitable governors. But this dictum had a very special meaning to Hastings and his audience, and he immediately explained it. "I am prepared further to say," he declared, "that the principle thing to be aimed at, and which must be secured, is obedience." Nothing was quite as pleasant to witness as "cheerful submission," compliance given with affection. However, there was no mistaking priorities; even if one had to resort regularly to punishing the child, obedience had to be won. And there was no need to worry about the possibly detrimental effects of such a policy. "After you establish the proposition in his mind that you are the ruler," Hastings complacently concluded, "he will look to you as his friend and benefactor, and you can cultivate his heart with ten-fold more effect." In this best of systems, authority bred friendship and admiration. . . .

If fidelity to a doctrine could have guaranteed success, the antebellum orphan asylums and houses of refuge would have enjoyed remarkable achievements. Like the other caretaker institutions of the era, they too made isolation and order central to the design. Trustees and managers systematically attempted to remove and protect inmates from the corrupting influences of the community, to impose an exact and demanding schedule, and to enforce rules and regulations with strict and certain discipline. To these ends, they arranged admission policies and visiting rights, established daily activities, and meted out punishments. They translated a good part of prevailing theory into institutional reality.

The first element in the asylum superintendents' program was to abrogate parental authority and substitute their own. To bring the inmate under as absolute a control as possible, trustees characteristically insisted that the parent transfer to them all legal rights upon the child's admission. The requirement was a new one; the occasional colonial benevolent society that had housed dependent children did not attempt to erect legal barriers against parental intervention. Should a family's fortune improve, eighteenth-century officials willingly returned the youngster, at most asking for repayment for past expenses. But nineteenth-century institutions typically would brook no actual or potential interference. The orphan asylum in Philadelphia, for example, compelled destitute parents wishing to institutionalize a child to sign a pledge declaring: "I do hereby surrender to the Orphan Society of Philadelphia, the child A.B. to be provided for. . . . I will not demand or receive any compensation . . . or in any way interfere with the views or direction of the said society." The District of Columbia asylum was just as rigid. Under its act of incorporation relatives and friends did not have the right to remove an inmate before he reached the age of twenty-one. Managers insisted upon having the time and the freedom to effect a reformatory program. . . .

The daily routine at the New York House of Refuge represented in slightly exaggerated form the kind of discipline and control that managers everywhere wished to exercise. Officials carefully organized a schedule for the 160 inmates, divided segments of time precisely, and used the house bells to announce each period. The first bells rang at sunrise to wake the youngsters, the second came fifteen minutes later to signal the guards to unlock the individual cells. The inmates stepped into the hallways and then, according to the managers' description, "marched in order to the washroom. . . . From the washroom they are called to parade in the open air (the weather permitting), where they arranged in ranks, and undergo close and critical inspection as to cleanliness and dress." Inmates next went in formation to chapel for prayer (it was the Sunday variant on this that so impressed the visitors from the Philadelphia refuge), and afterwards spent one hour in school. At seven o'clock the bells announced breakfast and then, a half hour later, the time to begin work. The boys spent till noon in the shops, usually making brass nails or cane seats, while the girls washed, cooked, made and mended the clothes. "At twelve o'clock," officials reported, "a bell rings to call all from work, and one hour is allowed for washing . . . and dinner. . . . At one o'clock, a signal is given for recommencing work, which continues till five in the afternoon, when the bell rings for the termination of the labor of the day." There followed thirty minutes to wash and to eat, two and one half hours of evening classes and, finally, to end the day, evening prayers. "The children," concluded the refuge account, "ranged in order, are then marched to the Sleeping Halls, where each takes possession of his separate apartment, and the cells are locked, and silence is enforced for the night." . . .

Precision and regularity dominated other aspects of asylum life. Many institutions habitually drilled their inmates, organizing them in parade ranks and marching them up and down the field. "In one place," noted Lydia Child after a visit to the Long Island asylum, "I saw a stack of small wooden guns, and was informed that the boys were daily drilled to military exercises, as a useful means of forming habits of order." She discovered that this drill-like quality had infected other parts of the institution, the infant school, and even the chapel. "I was informed," wrote Child, "that it was 'beautiful to see them pray; for at the first tip of the whistle, they all dropped on their knees.' " Her verdict on this asylum may well stand for the others: "Everything moves by machinery, as it always must with masses of children never subdivided into families."

The extraordinary emphasis of child-care institutions on obedience and authority was most apparent in their systems of classification and punishment. Houses of refuge in particular went to great lengths to enforce discipline, conceiving and administering elaborate programs. They depended first upon a highly intricate pattern of grading. Some institutions established four classes, others used seven—but the principle was constant. Superintendents assigned a new inmate to the bottom category and then, depending upon his subsequent behavior, promoted him. Every teacher, dormitory guard, and work supervisor had to file reports on each child's performance as a basis for rank, and the inmate wore a numbered badge on his arm to signify his standing. . . .

Fundamental to the institutions' discipline was habitual and prompt punishment, so that inmates' infractions not only brought a mark in the grading system, but an immediate penalty as well. Corrections ranged from a deprivation of a usual privilege to corporal punishment, with various alternatives along the way. There was the loss of a play period, increased work load, a diet of bread and water, Coventry—with no one permitted to talk with the offender—solitary confinement in a special prison cell, wearing a ball and chain, the whip—and any one or two of these penalties could be combined with yet another and inflicted for varying lengths of time.

Given their perspective on discipline and order, managers openly admitted and vigorously defended strict punitive tactics. They quoted with predictable regularity Solomon's warnings on spoiling the child, insisting that although the rod should be saved for a last resort, it still had to be used. A resolution of the convention of refuge superintendents set out the creed most succinctly: "The first requisite from all inmates should be a strict obedience to the rules of the institution; and where moral suasion fails to produce the desired result, the more severe punishments of deprivation of meals, in part, and of recreation, and the infliction of corporal punishment should be resorted to: the latter only, however, in extreme cases." The superintendent of the Western House of Refuge at Pittsburgh made the matter a precondition for remaining in his post. "I advocate the judicious use of the rod," he announced. "So well am I convinced of its efficacy . . . that I could not think of retaining my connection with such institutions, were the power of using it denied to me. . . . I never yet have seen the time when I thought the rod could be dispensed with." . . .

To follow the metaphors of superintendents of asylums and refuges, the family was the model for institutional organization. Whether serving the poor or the orphan or the delinquent, they repeatedly described their operations in household terms. The Baltimore Home of the Friendless, for example, announced a determination to "see that the order and decorum of a well regulated Christian family be strictly observed." The tougher the clientele, the more elaborate the family metaphor. The New York Juvenile Asylum insisted that "the government of the Institution has been strictly parental. The prominent object has been to give a home feeling and home interest to the children—to create and cultivate a family feeling . . . to clothe the Institution as far as possible with those hallowed associations which usually cluster about home." The manager of the St. Louis Reform School was just as committed to this language. The refuge, he insisted, would succeed "by assimilating the government in Reformatories, as nearly as possible, to that of the *time-honored* institution which guided the infancy of nearly all the truly great and good men and women—that model, and often humble institution— the *family* . . . 'God's University' . . . the well-ordered Christian family."

But as is readily apparent, rhetoric and reality had little correspondence. Except for these public declarations, one would not have considered the family to be the model for the asylum. Rather, from all appearances, a military tone seems to have pervaded these institutions. Managers imposed on their charges a routine that was to resemble an army camp. They grouped inmates into large companies under a central administration, rather than establishing small familylike units under the individual care of surrogate parents. Inmates slept in separate cells or on cots in large dormitories, all neatly spaced and arranged in ways more reminiscent of orderly military barracks than of households. They ate silently in large refectories, using hand signals to communicate their needs, in a style that was much closer to an army mess than a family meal. They marched about the institution, stood in formation for head counts and public quizzes, and carried wooden guns in parades for recreation. They followed an exact schedule, responding to bells like recruits to a bugler's call. They wore uniforms with badges for insignias and grades for ranks. They learned to drop to one knee at the sound of a whistle, even making prayer into a military exercise. They obeyed rules of silence or suffered punishment. They took the whip like disobedient soldiers being flogged. If anyone escaped, or went AWOL, the ball and chain awaited him upon his return.

As surprising as it may seem, the superintendents saw no contradiction between their language and actions, no opposition between parading children in ranks while paying homage to the family. For they believed that they were offering a critique of the conduct of the antebellum family, and an alternative to it. In their view the family had to emulate the asylum as constituted—that is, put a greater premium on order, discipline, and obedience, not on domestic affections, pampering the child, or indulging his every whim. The family did not need to march its members from bedroom to kitchen or keep children silent throughout a meal (although the adage did call for children to be seen and not heard), but parents were to exercise a firm and consistent authority and brook no willfulness. Thus, managers found no real divergence between the well-ordered asylum and the well-ordered family. The quasi-military quality of the institution was a rebuke and an example to the lax family. The problem was that parents were too lenient, not that the refuge or asylum were too strict. As long as the desideratum was order and discipline, as long as the virtues most in demand in child rearing were regularity and respect for authority, then the asylum was at least as effective a training center as the home. To the extent that the family neglected or overindulged or corrupted its members, the institution was a distinctly preferable setting.

POSTSCRIPT

Was Antebellum Reform Motivated Primarily by Humanitarian Goals?

The social-control school of thought, into which Rothman's essay could be placed, draws upon the works of Michel Foucault, Erving Goffman, Howard Becker, Thomas Szasz, and others. According to this interpretation, American reformers were more interested in serving their own interests than in providing assistance to mankind. As a result, middle- and upper-class reformers responding to momentous changes within their society imposed their standards of morality and order on the lower classes and, thus, denied the latter group freedom to act as a diverse set of individuals.

Ronald G. Walters, in *American Reformers, 1815–1860* (Hill and Wang, 1978), concludes that although many nineteenth-century reformers expressed sentiments that were self-serving and bigoted, their motivations were not based entirely upon a desire to control the lower classes. Rather, reformers were convinced that improvements could and should be made to help people. In this regard, the essays by Tyler and Rothman are in agreement.

The scholarly literature on the "age of reform" is extensive. Interested students should consult Timothy L. Smith, *Revivalism and Social Reform: American Protestantism on the Eve of the Civil War* (Harper & Row, 1957); Whitney R. Cross, *The Burned-Over District: The Social and Intellectual History of Enthusiastic Religion in Western New York, 1800–1850* (Cornell University Press, 1950); and Clifford S. Griffin, *Their Brothers' Keepers: Moral Stewardship in the United States, 1800–1865* (Rutgers University Press, 1960). David Brion Davis, ed., *Ante-Bellum Reform* (Harper & Row, 1967), is an excellent collection of readings. The social-control thesis can be traced for various reform endeavors in Joseph R. Gusfield, *Symbolic Crusade: Status Politics and the American Temperance Movement* (University of Illinois Press, 1966); Michael B. Katz, *The Irony of Early School Reform: Education and Innovation in Mid-Nineteenth Century Massachusetts* (Beacon Press, 1968); Joseph M. Harris, *Children in Urban Society: Juvenile Delinquency in Nineteenth-Century America* (Oxford University Press, 1971); and Gerald Grob, *Mental Institutions in America: Social Policy to 1875* (Free Press, 1973). For some of the aspects of American reform generally dismissed by Tyler as "fads," see John D. Davies, *Phrenology, Fad and Science: A Nineteenth-Century American Crusade* (Yale University Press, 1955), and Ronald L. Numbers, *Prophetess of Health: A Study of Ellen G. White* (Harper & Row, 1976).

ISSUE 12

Was U.S. Foreign Policy in the Early Nineteenth Century Imperialistic?

YES: Ramon Eduardo Ruiz, from "Manifest Destiny and the Mexican War," in Howard H. Quint et al., eds., *Main Problems in American History, vol. 1,* 5th ed. (Dorsey Press, 1988)

NO: Robert Hugh Ferrell, from *American Diplomacy, A History,* 2d ed. (W. W. Norton, 1969)

ISSUE SUMMARY

YES: Professor of history Ramon Eduardo Ruiz argues that, for the purpose of conquering Mexico's northern territories, the United States waged an aggressive war against Mexico from which Mexico never recovered.
NO: Professor of diplomatic history Robert Hugh Ferrell believes that, although the American government waged an aggressive war in Mexico, it remained the Manifest Destiny of the United States to possess Texas, New Mexico, and California.

The American government in the early 1800s greatly benefited from the fact that European nations generally considered what was going on in North America of secondary importance to what was happening in their own countries. In 1801, President Thomas Jefferson became alarmed when he learned that France had acquired the Louisiana territory from Spain. He realized that western states might revolt if the government did not control the city of New Orleans as a seaport for shipping their goods. Jefferson dispatched negotiators to buy the port. He pulled off the real estate coup of the nineteenth century when his diplomats caught Napoleon in a moment of despair. With a stroke of the pen and $15 million, the Louisiana Purchase of 1803 nearly doubled the size of the country. The exact northern, western, and southeastern boundaries were not clearly defined. "But," as diplomatic historian Thomas Bailey has pointed out, "the American negotiators knew that they had bought the western half of perhaps the most valuable river valley on the face of the globe, stretching between the Rockies and the Mississippi, and bounded somewhere on the north by British North America."

After England fought an indecisive war with the United States from 1812 to 1815, she realized that it was to her advantage to maintain peaceful relations with her former colony. In 1817, the Great Lakes, which border on the United States and Canada, were mutually disarmed. Over the next half-century, the principle of demilitarization was extended to the land, resulting in an undefended frontier line which stretched for more than 3,000 miles. The Convention of 1818 clarified the northern boundary of the Louisiana Purchase and ran a line along the 49th parallel from Lake of the Woods in Minnesota to the Rocky Mountains. Beyond that point there was to be a 10-year joint occupancy in the Oregon Territory. In 1819, Spain sold Florida to the United States after Secretary of State John Quincy Adams sent a note telling the Spanish government to keep the Indians on their side of the border or else to get out of Florida. A few years later, the Spanish Empire crumbled in the New World and a series of Latin American republics emerged.

Afraid that the European powers might attack the newly independent Latin American republics and that Russia might expand south into the Oregon Territory, Adams convinced President James Monroe to reject a British suggestion for a joint declaration and to issue instead a unilateral policy statement. The Monroe Doctrine, as it was called by a later generation, had three parts. First, it closed the western hemisphere to any future colonization. Second, it forbade "any interposition" by the European monarchs that would "extend their system to any portion of this hemisphere as dangerous to our peace and safety." And third, the United States pledged to abstain from any involvement in the political affairs of Europe. Viewed in the context of 1823, it is clear that Monroe was merely restating the principles of unilateralism and nonintervention. Both of these were at the heart of American isolationism.

While Monroe renounced the possibility of American intervention in European affairs, he made no such disclaimer toward Latin America, as was originally suggested by Great Britain. It would be difficult to colonize in South America, but the transportation revolution, the hunger for land which created political turmoil in Texas, and the need for ports on the Pacific to increase American trade in Asia encouraged the acquisition of new lands contiguous to the southwestern boundaries. In the 1840s, journalists and politicians furnished an ideological rationale for this expansion and said it was to the Manifest Destiny of Americans to spread democracy, freedom, and white American settlers across the entire North American continent, excluding Canada because it was a possession of Great Britain. Blacks and Indians were not a part of this expansion.

In the following selections, Ramon Eduardo Ruiz argues that the United States waged a racist and aggressive war against Mexico for the purpose of conquering what became the American southwest. In his view Manifest Destiny was strictly an ideological rationale to provide noble motives for what were really acts of aggression against a neighboring country. Robert Hugh Ferrell, on the other hand, justifies the U.S. government's expansionist policies in the 1840s in terms of the ideology of Manifest Destiny. Admitting that the American government started the war against Mexico, Ferrell still argues that it was inevitable for the United States to possess Texas, New Mexico, and California.

YES

Ramon Eduardo Ruiz

MANIFEST DESTINY
AND THE MEXICAN WAR

All nations have a sense of destiny. Spaniards braved the perils of unknown seas and the dangers of savage tribes to explore and conquer a New World for Catholicism. Napoleon's armies overran Europe on behalf of equality, liberty, and fraternity. Communism dictates the future of China and the Soviet Union. Arab expansionists speak of Islam. In the United States, Manifest Destiny in the nineteenth century was the equivalent of these ideologies or beliefs. Next-door neighbor Mexico first felt the brunt of its impact and suffered the most from it.

What was Manifest Destiny? The term was coined in December 1845 by John L. O'Sullivan, then editor and cofounder of the *New York Morning News*. Superpatriot, expansionist, war hawk, and propagandist, O'Sullivan lived his doctrine of Manifest Destiny, for that slogan embodied what he believed. O'Sullivan spoke of America's special mission, frequently warned Europe to keep hands off the Western Hemisphere, later joined a filibustering expedition to Cuba, and had an honored place among the followers of President James K. Polk, Manifest Destiny's spokesman in the Mexican War.

Manifest Destiny voiced the expansionist sentiment that had gripped Americans almost from the day their ancestors had landed on the shores of the New World in the seventeenth century. Englishmen and their American offspring had looked westward since Jamestown and Plymouth—confident that time and fate would open the vast West that stretched out before them. Manifest Destiny, then, was first territorial expansion—American pretensions to lands held by Spain, France, and later Mexico; some even spoke of a United States with boundaries from pole to pole. But Manifest Destiny was greater than mere land hunger; much more was involved. A spirit of nationalism was pervasive—the belief that what Americans upheld was right and good, and that providence had designated them the chosen people. In a political framework, Manifest Destiny stood for democracy as Americans conceived it; to spread democracy and freedom was the goal. Also included were ideals of regeneration: the conquest of virgin lands for the sake of their

From Ramon Eduardo Ruiz, "Manifest Destiny and the Mexican War," in Quint et al., eds., *Major Problems in American History*, vol. 1, 5th ed. (Dorsey Press, 1972). Copyright © 1972 by The Dorsey Press, a division of Wadsworth, Inc. Reprinted by permission.

development, and concepts of Anglo-Saxon superiority. All these slogans and beliefs played a role in the Mexican question that culminated in hostilities in 1846.

Apostles of these slogans pointed out that Mexicans claimed lands from the Pacific to Texas but tilled only a fraction of them, and did so inefficiently. "No nation has the right to hold soil, virgin and rich, yet unproducing," stressed one U.S. representative. "No race but our own can either cultivate or rule the western hemisphere," acknowledged the *United States Magazine and Democratic Review*. The Indian, almost always a poor farmer in North America, was the initial victim of this concept of soil use; expansionists later included nearly everyone in the New World, and in particular, Mexicans. For, Caleb Cushing asked: "Is not the occupation of any portion of the earth by those competent to hold and till it, a providential law of national life?"

Oregon and Texas, and the Democratic Party platform of 1844, kindled the flames of territorial expansion in the roaring forties. Millions of Americans came to believe that God had willed them all of North America. Expansion symbolized the fulfillment of "America's providential mission or destiny"—a mission conceived in terms of the spread of democracy, which its exponents identified with freedom. Historian Albert K. Weinberg has written: "It was because of the association of expansion and freedom in a means-end relationship, that expansion now came to seem most manifestly a destiny."

Americans did not identify freedom with expansion until the forties. Then, fears of European designs on Texas, California, and Oregon, perhaps, prompted an identity of the two. Not only were strategic and economic interests at stake, but also democracy itself. The need to extend the area of freedom, therefore, rose partly from the necessity of keeping absolutistic European monarchs from limiting the area open to American democracy in the New World.

Other factors also impelled Americans to think expansion essential to their national life. Failure to expand imperiled the nation, for as historian William E. Dodd stated, Westerners especially believed "that the Union gained in stability as the number of states multiplied." Meanwhile, Southerners declared the annexation of Texas essential to their prosperity and to the survival of slavery, and for a congressional balance of power between North and South. Other persons insisted that expansion helped the individual states to preserve their liberties, for their numerical strength curtailed the authority of the central government—the enemy of local autonomy and especially autonomy of the South. Moreover, for Southerners extension of the area of freedom meant, by implication, expansion of the limits of slavery. Few planters found the two ideas incompatible. Religious doctrines and natural principles, in their opinion, had ruled the Negro ineligible for political equality. That expansion favored the liberties of the individual, both North and South agreed.

In the forties, the pioneer spirit received recognition as a fundamental tenet of American life. Individualism and expansion, the mark of the pioneer, were joined together in the spirit of Manifest Destiny. Expansion guaranteed not just the political liberty of the person, but the opportunity to improve himself economically as well, an article of faith for the democracy of the age. Furthermore, when antiexpansionists declared that the territorial limits of the United States in 1846 assured all Americans ample room for growth in the future, the expansionists-turned-ecologists replied that some 300 million Americans in 1946 would need more land, a prediction that overstated the case of the population-minded experts. And few Americans saw the extension of freedom in terms other than liberty for themselves—white, Anglo-Saxon, and Protestant. All these concepts, principles, and beliefs entered into the expansionist creed of Manifest Destiny.

None of these was a part of the Mexican heritage, the legacy of three centuries of Spanish rule and countless years of pre-Columbian civilization. Mexico and the United States could not have been more dissimilar in 1846. A comparison of colonial backgrounds helps to bring into focus the reasons that the two countries were destined to meet on the field of battle. One was weak and the other strong; Mexico had abolished slavery and the United States had not; Americans had their Manifest Destiny, but few Mexicans believed in themselves.

Daughter of a Spain whose colonial policy embraced the Indian, Mexico was a mestizo republic, a half-breed nation. Except for a small group of aristocrats, most Mexicans were descendants of both Spaniards and Indians. For Mexico had a colonial master eager and willing to assimilate pre-Columbian man. Since the days of the conqueror Hernán Cortés, Spaniards had mated with Indians, producing a Mexican both European and American in culture and race. Offspring of the Indian as well as the Spaniard, Mexican leaders, and even the society of the time, had come to accept the Indian, if not always as an equal, at least as a member of the republic. To have rejected him would have been tantamount to the

Mexican's self-denial of himself. Doctrines of racial supremacy were, if not impossible, highly unlikely, for few Mexicans could claim racial purity. To be Mexican implied a mongrel status that ruled out European views of race.

Spain bequeathed Mexico not merely a racial attitude but laws, religious beliefs, and practices that banned most forms of segregation and discrimination. For example, reservations for Indians were never a part of the Spanish heritage. Early in the 16th century, the Spaniards had formulated the celebrated Laws of the Indies—legislation that clearly spelled out the place of the Indian in colonial society. Nothing was left to chance, since the Spanish master included every aspect of life—labor, the family, religion, and even the personal relations between Spaniard and Indian. The ultimate aim was full citizenship for the Indian and his descendants. In the meantime, the Church ruled that the Indian possessed a soul; given Christian teachings, he was the equal of his European conqueror. "All of the people of the world are men," the Dominican Bartolomé de las Casas had announced in his justly famous 1550 debate with the scholar Sepúlveda.

Clearly, church and state and the individual Spaniard who arrived in America had more than charity in mind. Dreams of national and personal glory and wealth dominated their outlook. Yet, despite the worldly goals of most secular and clerical conquerors, they built a colonial empire on the principle that men of all colors were equal on earth. Of course, Spain required the labor of the Indian and therefore had to protect him from the avarice of many a conquistador. Spaniards, the English were wont to say, were notorious for their disdain of manual labor of any type. But Spain went beyond merely offering the Indian protection in order to insure his labor. It incorporated him into Hispanic-American society. The modern Mexican is proof that the Indian survived: all Mexicans are Indian to some extent. That the Indian suffered economic exploitation and frequently even social isolation is undoubtedly true, but such was the lot of the poor in the Indies—Indian, half-breed, and even Spaniard.

Spain's empire, as well as the Mexican republic that followed, embraced not just the land but the people who had tilled it for centuries before the European's arrival. From northern California to Central America, the boundaries of colonial New Spain, and later Mexico, the Spaniard had embraced the Indian or allowed him to live out his life. It was this half-breed population that in 1846 confronted and fell victim to the doctrine of Manifest Destiny.

America's historical past could not have been more dissimilar. The English master had no room for the Indian in his scheme of things. Nearly all Englishmen—Puritans, Quakers, or Anglicans—visualized the conquest and settlement of the New World in terms of the exclusive possession of the soil. All new lands conquered were for the immediate benefit of the new arrivals. From the days of the founding of Jamestown and Plymouth, the English had pushed the Indian westward, relentlessly driving him from his homeland. In this activity, the clergy clasped hands with lay authorities, neither offered the red man a haven. Except for a few hardy souls, invariably condemned by their peers, Englishmen of church and state gave little thought to the Indian. Heaven, hell, and the teachings of Christ were the exclusive domain of the conquerors.

Society in the thirteen colonies, and in the Union that followed, reflected English and European customs and ways of life. It was a transplanted society. Where the Indian survived, he found himself isolated from the currents of time. Unlike the Spaniards, whose ties with Africa and darker skinned peoples through seven centuries of Moorish domination had left an indelible imprint on them, most Englishmen had experienced only sporadic contact with people of dissimilar races and customs. Having lived a sheltered and essentially isolated existence, the English developed a fear and distrust of those whose ways were foreign to them. The Americans who walked in their footsteps retained this attitude.

Many American historians will reject this interpretation. They will probably allege that American willingness to accept millions of destitute immigrants in the nineteenth century obviously contradicts the view that the Anglo-Saxon conqueror and settler distrusted what was strange in others. Some truth is present here, but the weight of the evidence lies on the other side. What must be kept firmly in mind is that immigration to the English colonies and later to the United States—in particular, the tidal wave of humanity that engulfed the United States in the post-Civil War era—was European in origin. Whether Italians, Jews, or Greeks from the Mediterranean, Swedes, Scots, or Germans from the North, what they had in common far outweighed conflicting traits and cultural and physical differences. All were European, offspring of one body of traditions and beliefs. Whether Catholics, Protestants, or Jews, they professed adherence to Western religious practices and beliefs. The so-called melting pot was scarcely a melting pot at all; the ingredients were European in origin.

All spices that would have given the stew an entirely different flavor were carefully kept out—namely, the Black and the Indian.

It was logical that Manifest Destiny, that American belief in a Providence of special design, should have racial overtones. Having meticulously kept out the infidel, Americans could rightly claim a racial doctrine of purity and supremacy in the world of 1846. Had not the nation of Polk's era developed free of those races not a part of the European heritage? Had the nation not progressed rapidly? Most assuredly, the answer was yes. When American development was compared to that of the former Spanish-American colonies, the reply was even more emphatically in the affirmative. After all, the latin republics to the south had little to boast about. All were backward, illiterate, and badly governed states. Americans had just cause for satisfaction with what they had accomplished.

Unfortunately for Latin America, and especially Mexico, American pride had dire implications for the future. Convinced of the innate racial supremacy which the slogan of Manifest Destiny proclaimed throughout the world, many Americans came to believe that the New World was theirs to develop. Only their industry, their ingenuity, and their intelligence could cope fully with the continental challenge. Why should half-breed Mexico—backward, politically a wasteland, and hopelessly split by nature and man's failures—hold Texas, New Mexico, and California? In Mexico's possession, all those lands would lie virgin, offering a home to a few thousand savage Indians, and here and there a Mexican pueblo of people scarcely different from their heathen neighbors. Manifest Destiny proclaimed what most Americans firmly believed—the right of Anglo-Saxons and others of similar racial origin to develop what Providence had promised them. Weak Mexico, prey of its own cupidity and mistakes, was the victim of this belief.

Manifest Destiny, writes Mexican historian Carlos Bosch García, also contradicts an old American view that means are as important as ends. He stresses that the key to the history of the United States, as the doctrine of Manifest Destiny illustrates, lies in the willingness of Americans to accept as good the ultimate result of whatever they have undertaken. That the red man was driven from his homeland is accepted as inevitable and thus justifiable. American scholars might condemn the maltreatment of the Indian, but few question the final verdict.

Equally ambivalent, says Bosch García, is the American interpretation of the Mexican War. Though some American scholars of the post-Civil War period severely censured the South for what they called its responsibility for the Mexican War, their views reflected a criticism of the slavocracy rather than a heartfelt conviction that Mexico had been wronged. Obviously, there were exceptions. Hubert H. Bancroft, a California scholar and book collector, emphatically denounced Polk and his cohorts in his voluminous *History of Mexico* (1883–88). Among the politicians of the era, Abraham Lincoln won notoriety—and probably lost his seat in the House of Representatives—for his condemnation of Polk's declaration of war against Mexico. There were others, mostly members of the Whig Party, which officially opposed the war; but the majority, to repeat, was more involved with the problem of the South than with the question of war guilt.

Most Americans have discovered ways and means to justify Manifest Destiny's war on Mexico. That country's chronic political instability, its unwillingness to meet international obligations, its false pride in its military establishment—all, say scholars, led Mexican leaders to plunge their people into a hopeless war. Had Mexico been willing to sell California, one historian declares, no conflict would have occurred. To paraphrase Samuel F. Bemis, distinguished Yale University diplomatic scholar, no American today would undo the results of Polk's war. Put differently, to fall back on Bosch García, American writers have justified the means because of the ends. Manifest Destiny has not only been explained but has been vindicated on the grounds of what has been accomplished in California and New Mexico since 1848. Or, to cite Hermann Eduard von Holst, a late nineteenth-century German scholar whose writings on American history won him a professorship at the University of Chicago, the conflict between Mexico and the United States was bound to arise. A virile and ambitious people whose cause advanced that of world civilization could not avoid battle with a decadent, puerile people. Moral judgments that applied to individuals might find Americans guilty of aggression, but the standards by which nations survive and prosper upheld the cause of the United States. Might makes right? Walt Whitman, then editor of the *Brooklyn Daily Eagle*, put down his answer succinctly:

> We love to indulge in thoughts of the future extent and power of this Republic—because with its increase is the increase in human happiness and liberty. . . . What has miserable Mexico—with her superstition, her burlesque upon freedom, her actual tyranny by

the few over the many—what has she to do with the great mission of peopling the New World with a noble race? Be it ours, to achieve that mission! Be it ours to roll down all of the upstart leaven of the old despotism, that comes our way.

The conflict with Mexico was an offensive war without moral pretensions, according to Texas scholar Otis A. Singletary. It was no lofty crusade, no noble battle to right the wrongs of the past or to free a subjugated people, but a war of conquest waged by one neighbor against another. President Polk and his allies had to pay conscience money to justify a "greedy land-grab from a neighbor too weak to defend herself." American indifference to the Mexican War, Singletary concludes, "lies rooted in the guilt that we as a nation have come to feel about it."

American racial attitudes, the product of a unique colonial background in the New World, may also have dictated the scope of territorial conquest in 1848 and, ironically, saved Mexico from total annexation. Until the clash with Mexico, the American experience had been limited to the conquest, occupation, and annexation of empty to sparsely settled territories, or lands already colonized by citizens of the United States, such as Oregon and Texas. American pioneers had been reincorporated into the Union with the annexation of Oregon and Texas and even with the purchase of Louisiana in 1803. The alien population proved small and of little importance in all three territories. White planters, farmers, and pioneers mastered the small Mexican population in Texas and easily disposed of the Indians and half-breeds in the Louisiana territory.

Expansionists and their foes had long considered both Indian and Black unfit for regeneration; both were looked on as inferior and doomed races. On this point, most Americans were in agreement. While not entirely in keeping with this view, American opinions of Latin Americans, and of Mexicans in particular, were hardly flattering. Purchase and annexation of Louisiana and Florida, and of Texas and Oregon, had been debated and postponed partly out of fear of what many believed would be the detrimental effect on American democracy resulting from the amalgamation of the half-breed and mongrel peoples of these lands. Driven by a sense of national aggrandizement, the expansionists preferred to conquer lands free of alien populations. Manifest Destiny had no place for the assimilation of strange and exotic peoples. Freedom for Americans—this was the cry, regardless of what befell the conquered natives. The location of sparsely held territory had dictated the course of empire.

James K. Polk's hunger for California reflected national opinion on races as well as desire for land. Both that territory and New Mexico, nearly to the same extent, were almost barren of native populations. Of sparsely settled California, in 1845, the *Hartford Times* eloquently declared that Americans could "redeem from unhallowed hands a land, above all others of heaven, and hold it for the use of a people who know how to obey heaven's behests." Thus, it was that the tide of conquest —the fruits of the conference table at Guadalupe Hidalgo—stopped on the border of Mexico's inhabited lands, where the villages of a people alien in race and culture confronted the invaders. American concepts of race, the belief in the regeneration of virgin lands—these logically ordered annexation of both California and New Mexico, but left Mexico's settled territory alone.

Many Americans, it is true, gave much thought to the conquest and regeneration of all Mexico, but the peace of 1848 came before a sufficiently large number of them had abandoned traditional thoughts on race and color to embrace the new gospel. Apparently, most Americans were not yet willing to accept dark-skinned people as the burden of the white man.

Manifest Destiny, that mid-nineteenth-century slogan, is now merely a historical question for most Americans. Despite the spectacular plums garnered from the conference table, the war is forgotten by political orators, seldom discussed in classrooms, and only infrequently recalled by historians and scholars.

But Mexicans, whether scholars or not, have not forgotten the war; their country suffered most from Manifest Destiny's claims to California. The war of 1846–48 represents one of the supreme tragedies of their history. Mexicans are intimately involved with it, unlike their late adversaries who have forgotten it. Fundamental reasons explain this paradox. The victorious United States went to a post-Civil War success story unequaled in the annals of Western civilization. Mexico emerged from the peace of Guadalupe Hidalgo bereft of half of its territory, a beaten, discouraged, and divided country. Mexico never completely recovered from the debacle.

Mexicans had known tragedy and defeat before, but their conquest by General Zachary Taylor and Winfield Scott represented not only a territorial loss of immense proportions, but also a cataclysmic blow to their morale as a nation and as a people. From the Mexican point of view, pride in what they believed they had mastered best—the science of warfare—was exposed as a myth. Mexicans could not even fight successfully, and they had little else to recall with pride, for their political development had enshrined bitter civil strife and callous betrayal of principle. Plagued by hordes of scheming politicians, hungry military men, and a backward and reactionary clergy, they had watched their economy stagnate. Guadalupe Hidalgo clearly outlined the scope of their defeat. There was no success story to write about, only tragedy. Mexicans of all classes are still engrossed in what might have been *if* General Antonio López de Santa Anna had repelled the invaders from the North.

Polk's war message to Congress and Lincoln's famous reply in the House cover some dimensions of the historical problem. Up for discussion are Polk's role in the affair, the responsibility of the United States and Mexico, and the question of war guilt—a question raised by the victorious Americans and their allies at Nuremberg after World War II. For if Polk felt "the blood of this war, like the blood of Abel, is crying to Heaven against him," as Lincoln charged, then both the war and Manifest Destiny stand condemned.

SUGGESTED READINGS

Bill, A. H. *Rehearsal for Conflict: The War with Mexico, 1846–1848.* New York: Alfred A. Knopf, 1947.

Billington, Ray A. *Westward Expansion: A History of the American Frontier.* New York: Macmillan, 1949.

Bulnes, Francisco. *Las Grandes Mentiras de Nuestra Historia.* Mexico: Editorial Nacional, 1969.

Castañeda, Carolos E., ed. *The Mexican Side of the Texas Revolution.* Dallas: P. L. Turner, 1928.

DeVoto, Bernard. *The Year of Decision, 1846.* Boston: Little, Brown, 1946.

Fuentes Mares, José. *Poinsett. La Historia de una Intriga.* Mexico: Editorial Jus, 1964.

Graebner, Norman A. *Empire on the Pacific.* New York: Ronald Press, 1955.

Merk, Frederick. *Manifest Destiny and Mission in American History: A Reinterpretation.* New York: Alfred A. Knopf, 1963.

Price, Glenn W. *Origins of the War with Mexico: the Polk-Stockton Intrigue.* Austin: University of Texas, 1967.

Ramirez, Jose Fernando. *Mexico during the War with the United States.* Columbia, MO.: University of Missouri Press, 1950.

Roa Barcena, José María. *Recuerdos de la Invasión Norteamericana, 1846–1848.* 3 vols., Mexico: Editorial Porrúa, 1947.

Santa Anna, Antonio López de. *Mi Historia Militar y Política, 1810–1874.* Mexico: Editorial Nacional, 1958.

Singletary, Otis A. *The Mexican War.* Chicago: University of Chicago Press, 1960.

Smith, Justin H. *The War with Mexico.* 2 vols. New York: Macmillan, 1919.

Stephenson, Nathaniel W. *Texas and the Mexican War.* New Haven, Conn.: Yale University Press, 1921.

Valades, Jose C. *Santa Anna y la Guerra de Texas.* Mexico: Imprenta Mundial, 1935.

Vasconcelos, José. *Breve Historia de México.* Mexico: Editorial Continental, 1980.

Vázquez, Josefina. *Mexicanos y Norteamericanos Ante la Guerra Del 47.* Mexico: Secretaría de Educación Pública, 1972.

Weinberg, Albert K. *Manifest Destiny: A Study of Nationalist Expansion in American History.* Baltimore: Johns Hopkins Press, 1935.

NO

MANIFEST DESTINY

In the history of American diplomacy few ideas have been more important than "manifest destiny"—the belief of the people of the United States that the North American continent, despite prior claims by France, Spain, Russia, Great Britain, and Mexico, was destined to become American territory. This mystic conviction translated itself into reality in the years from the beginning of the nineteenth century to the end of the Civil War. It was the presiding force behind the Mexican War of 1846–1848, the subject of the present chapter. French claims to North America vanished with the Louisiana Purchase of 1803. Spanish claims received settlement in the Adams-Onís Transcontinental Treaty of 1819, after which Spain's lands contiguous to the United States passed under control of the new government of Mexico. Russia's claims to Pacific territory withdrew northward to Alaska in a Russian-American agreement of 1824. British claims to Oregon territory disappeared in a treaty signed in 1846. And by 1848 Mexico's claims to Texas, New Mexico, and California were no more. "Away, away with all those cobweb tissues of rights of discovery, exploration, settlement, continuity, etc.," cried the New York editor, John L. O'Sullivan, who in the year 1845 coined the phrase "manifest destiny." It was, O'Sullivan claimed, "the right of our manifest destiny to overspread and to possess the whole of the continent which Providence has given us for the development of the great experiment in liberty and federative self-government entrusted to us."

Some exponents of manifest destiny believed that the United States should not confine its territorial ambitions to the continent of North America. According to one writer "Its floor shall be as a hemisphere, its roof the firmament of the star-studded heavens, and its congregation a Union of many Republics, comprising hundreds of happy millions . . . governed by God's natural and moral law of equality." Such hopes, of course, were never to be realized, and manifest destiny in its more practical vision limited itself to North America.

From Robert Hugh Ferrell, *American Diplomacy, A History*, 2d ed. (W. W. Norton, 1959). Copyright © 1959 by W. W. Norton & Company, Inc. Copyright renewed 1987 by Robert H. Ferrell. Reprinted by permission of the author and W. W. Norton & Company, Inc.

Two questions might arise at this point, the first of which can be stated as follows: Was manifest destiny nothing but imperialism, an American brand of a well-known nineteenth-century European practice? The nineteenth century was the age of imperialism in Europe, and although European nations undertook their vast colonial conquests in the latter part of the century, whereas the United States pursued its manifest destiny and continental ambition in earlier years, still it might well seem that there was little difference between imperialism and manifest destiny.

In actual fact there was a considerable difference. Manifest destiny was not imperialism if the latter term is properly defined as "rule over alien peoples." There were few Indians in the American West, hardly any at all if compared to the millions of inhabitants of Africa and the hundreds of millions of Asians. It is true that American policy toward the Indians frequently adhered to the frontier maxim that the only good Indians were dead Indians, and it is true that new diseases brought by the settlers decimated the Indians. But in view of the few Indians in the United States one must say that only in an extremely legalistic sense was the American nation imperialist during the early nineteenth century.

A second question in connection with manifest destiny concerns specifically the Mexican War: Was not this war, one of the most important chapters in American territorial expansion, a war of aggression—did not Americans pick a quarrel in 1846 with a weak and divided Mexico for the purpose of despoiling the Mexicans of New Mexico and California, and could not one therefore say that manifest destiny, at least as avowed in 1846–1848, was only an excuse for a war of conquest? . . .

MEXICO AND THE TEXAS REVOLUTION

At the turn of the nineteenth century the lands of Mexico belonged to Spain, and it was only after some years of uncertainty during the Napoleonic wars, after reconquest of Mexico by Spain at the end of the wars, that Mexico in 1821 became an independent nation. Twenty-five years of independence followed before the government in Mexico City had to face war with the United States.

The tasks of the Mexican government in its early years were, by any standard, large. The lands of Mexico began in Central America at the border of Guatemala. Mexican territory reached eastward through Yucatán, northward through the isthmus of Tehuantepec to spread like a gigantic fan across twelve hundred miles of virgin territory from the Sabine River in the east to California in the west. Over these distances the government in Mexico City had to exert its authority, distances that in the early nineteenth century rendered them much more remote from the Mexican capital than mid-twentieth century Fairbanks or Honolulu from Washington, D.C. The task of administering the territory of Mexico from the capital in Mexico City was therefore almost impossible. The northern Mexican provinces of Texas, New Mexico, and California were distinctly separated by geography from the populous region about Mexico City, and were oriented economically to the United States. From the Nueces River to the Rio Grande was a desert tract. South of the Rio Grande for hundreds of miles there was almost no cultivation. Westward for hundreds of miles stretched sheer wilderness and desert.

Was there any chance that with time Mexico might have peopled its northern empire? Not unless time were reckoned in terms of several decades, perhaps a century or more, and even this might not have sufficed. Some six million Indians and half-castes lived in Mexico—no one knows, of course, just what the population really was—and controlling this ignorant and poverty-stricken mass were only some 60,000 Spanish-speaking and Spanish-descended persons who were the government officials and landholders and priests and army officers. Nearly all of the 60,000 Spanish lived in the area now embraced within the republic of Mexico. They had little desire to migrate to the northern provinces, Texas and New Mexico and California. They remained in their comfortable towns and ranches, and only a trickle of people from Mexico proper entered the upper territories. This trickle could do little when the Yankee flood began coming across the Sabine shortly after signature of the Transcontinental Treaty in 1819.

One cannot stress sufficiently the point that Texas and the other northern territories of Mexico were virtually empty lands, lacking Mexican settlers, and because of distance lacking almost any control from Mexico City.

Mexican establishments in California, like those in Texas, were pitiful in their poverty and unimportance. If in Texas there were only about three thousand Mexicans of Spanish origin in the 1830s, there were little more than four thousand in California, a mere handful consisting chiefly of priests and monks about the missions, soldiers employed to keep the Indians submissive, and a few large landowners and cattle raisers. In California the area of Mexican control never extended north of San Francisco, nor inland beyond the coastal area. The first Mexican settlers had come at about the time of the American revolution, and few settlers followed them. Certainly there could be no comparison between the Mexican attempt to settle California and the effort by Englishmen a hundred and fifty years earlier to settle the province of New England, for in the Great Migration of 1630–42 some 16,000 Englishmen from the Old World came there, to say nothing of simultaneous English migrations to other parts of America.

Aside from the difficulty of holding the northern territories there was the more serious problem of the debility and incompetence of the Mexican government. The revolution against Spain had broken out in 1810, and the Mexicans triumphed conclusively over the forces of their mother country in 1821. In the next year a military adventurer, Augustín de Iturbide, made himself emperor of Mexico with the title of Augustus I. After a short time he fell from power, went abroad, returned, and was shot. The Mexicans in 1824 established a federal constitution on the United States model, and this constitution managed to stay in effect for five years, after which another military leader, Bustamante, subverted it and took office for three years. He was displaced by Antonio López de Santa Anna, the prince of Mexican adverturers, who was in and out of power several times in the next two decades. There was no peace in Mexico before 1877 when General Porfirio Díaz took the reins of government and held them with absolute authority until 1911, after which came a new time of trouble for government in Mexico.

It was nominally the effort of Santa Anna in 1835 to centralize the Mexican government that led to a revolt in Texas in 1835–1836, but behind the constitutional issue lay the weakness of Mexican control in Texas, the thinness of Mexican settlement, and—above all—the fact that in the fifteen years preceding the Texas revolution some thirty thousand Americans had moved into the Mexican province.

Land hunger had drawn American settlers to Texas during the years after the first group arrived in 1821 under the guidance of the *empresario* Stephen F. Austin. Austin had contracted with the Mexican government for many thousands of acres of land in return for bringing in families of settlers. The families paid about ten cents an acre for their land, with liberal arrangements of credit, at a time when inferior land was selling in the United States for $1.25 cash. The United States government, following a financial panic in 1819, had tightened its land policy, and the Bank of the United States, then the principal bank of credit in the country, had drastically reduced its loans and raised its rates of interest, so that settlers seeking cheap lands were driven by force of circumstance to accept the propositions of such men as Stephen Austin. Few of these early American settlers in Texas stopped to inquire as to the type of government they would encounter in their new country. Even the demand of Mexican authorities that they become converts to Catholicism did not disturb their consciences, and they accepted the forms of Catholicism as easily as they accepted other Mexican laws exercised through the Texas organs of the Mexican government—always provided that government, law, and religion did not interfere with their wholehearted search for cheap land.

Naturally the carefree attitude and abandon with which settlers moved into Texas changed when, after a few years, prosperity permitted leisure for thought and consideration. What in early days had proved acceptable began to irk. Especially the effects of frontier religious revivals must be considered, for as Methodist and Baptist preachers took up superintendence over the souls of American frontiersmen, there came advice from the new ministers that it was blasphemous for the settlers to participate in any way in the forms of the Catholic Church. By the latter 1820s, when signs of civilization were appearing at every hand and settlers were becoming annoyed by increased numbers of Mexican government officials, a new spirit of discontent swept the scattered communities of Texas. Settlers remembered their old allegiance to the United States. When General Andrew Jackson took office as president of the United States in 1829, a wave of enthusiasm and hope rose in the American West. No frontier settlement, even in Mexican Texas, could forget that the "Ginral" was a man of the people. Meanwhile life kept improving. "Within four miles of me," wrote one Texan settler in the mid-1830s, "there are more than one thousand inhabitants, chiefly new emigrants, and within the same distance we have four small stores, two blacksmith shops and two schools. We have a dancing frolick every week and preaching allmost [sic] every Sunday."

In a bare decade and a half more settlers came to Texas than in centuries of Spanish administration. This was the inescapable statistic of the Texas situation by the time of the Texas revolution. By the early 1830s the American settlers outnumbered the Spanish-Mexican population by ten to one. Mexican administrators in Mexico City and Texas took alarm. The Americans had been fairly happy under the short-lived constitution of 1824, the easy requirements of which were laxly enforced. The processes of Mexican government had not touched them to any important extent. But when the government of Santa Anna sought in 1835 to tighten the administration in Texas, trouble began, which might have been foreseen from the moment the first American immigrants entered Texas in 1821. It was not foreseen, and by 1835 time had run out on Mexican claims to Texas. There followed during the winter and early spring of 1835–1836 the chief events of the Texas revolution.

Some settlers in Texas had risen in November 1835 and in an unorganized but effective fashion had expelled the few Mexican soldiers and administrators then present on Texas soil. To quell this rebellion, Santa Anna led a large army of 3,000 men into Texas and began his assault with the famous attack on the Alamo. There the rapacious Mexican leader isolated 188 Americans under Colonel William B. Travis and raised from the cathedral the black flag of No Quarter. For seven or eight days the Texas held out, issuing a defiant call for help to "all Americans in the world." but no help arrived, and the Mexican troops closed in on the defenders and slaughtered them to the last man. The Alamo, to indulge in an understatement, incited Texans to fury. "Thermopylae had her messenger of defeat—the Alamo had none," roared General Edward Burleson when he heard the news of the tragedy. Foolishly Santa Anna followed up this slaughter by an even larger carnival at Goliad, where he shot down more than 300 American prisoners in cold blood. News of these massacres spread terror among thousands of the Texas settlers, and as Santa Anna advanced there began a wild flight to the border of the United States, the Sabine River. A long, suffering procession of refugees, women and children and Negro slaves, struggled to reach American territory. The exodus took place in cold weather, with incessant rain. Fortunately Santa Anna shortly thereafter met his downfall when General Sam Houston caught him encamped in a trap. Houston had only to attack. This the Texan leader vigorously did, to the embarrassment of the Head of the Mexican State, who at the crucial moment was taking a siesta. With the Battle of San Jacinto on April 21, 1836, the capture of Santa Anna and dispersal of his army, Texas became independent. . . .

The Texan revolution of 1835–1836 made no change in American policy. Andrew Jackson, consummate politician that he was, refused during his second administration to sponsor admission of Texas to the union. Desiring annexation, he refrained from making political capital of it, for fear that the Texas question if propelled into politics would reopen the slavery question, uneasily adjourned by the Compromise of 1820. Northern congressional leaders were certain that Texas upon admission to the union would be a slave state, and this would raise the inconvenient issue of balance of slave versus free states in the Senate, which then was exactly even, thirteen slave and thirteen free. Especially they thought of what might happen if Texas upon annexation should split itself into five or ten slave states, for this would ruin any hope of maintaining the sectional balance. Jackson was aware of Northern feeling on this matter. The most obtuse statesman—which Jackson assuredly was not—could hardly remain ignorant of the rising feeling between North and South. Jackson moved gingerly and with complete impartiality of action, if not of feeling, when the Texans in 1836 declared their independence. . . . Giving as excuse for his inaction the existence of a treaty between his country and Mexico, and the proprieties of international intercourse, Jackson had in mind the delicate political situation in the United States.

With the refusal of the Jackson administration to annex Texas after San Jacinto, relations between the two sovereign English-speaking states of North America settled down to a brief and quiet interlude. Jackson recognized Texan independence eleven months after San Jacinto, four months longer than the American government had waited to recognize Mexico after its successful revolution against Spain in 1821. The Mexicans nonetheless protested American recognition of Texas, and refused themselves to recognize Texan independence, a policy in which they persisted to the bitter end. Events continued in this course—Texan independence, American recognition, Mexican nonrecognition—until President John Tyler in 1844 sponsored in the Senate a treaty of annexation, and failing in that effort resorted early in 1845 to a joint resolution of annexation. . . .

To no avail were the antislavery arguments against annexation. The feeling of manifest destiny was too strong and too popular in 1845, antislavery sentiment not yet strong enough. Tyler's joint resolution passed Congress with a whoop. "You might as well attempt to turn the current of the Mississippi," Old Hickory declared in a letter given to the press at the crucial political moment, "as to turn the democracy from the annexation of Texas to the United States . . . obtain it

the U. States must—peaceably if we can, but forcibly if we must."

All but forgotten in the uproar were the pretensions of the Mexican government. Texas, Mexican diplomats had been claiming, was still part of Mexico, and annexation by the United States would be tantamount to a declaration of war. Upon passage of the joint resolution of March 1, 1845, the Mexican minister in Washington asked for and received his passports.

THE MEXICAN WAR

A year elapsed after the annexation of Texas before the war with Mexico began. There followed after Tyler's resolution of March 1845 a period of maneuvering and uncertainty during which President Polk waited to see what the Mexicans would do. The president was not averse to war. Still, he did not wish war if he could get its fruits without any fighting. He therefore sent a representative to Mexico City, John Slidell, in the hope of obtaining Mexican recognition of a Texas boundary at the Rio Grande, in exchange for which the United States would assume payments of claims of its nationals against the Mexican government. (Because Mexico had been in turmoil for thirty years and more, many Americans had found their properties confiscated and sometimes their lives endangered by the various revolutionary troubles; these claims had been settled by a mixed claims commission for approximately two million dollars, but the Mexicans had refused to pay the claims.) This was Slidell's minimum proposal: recognition of the Rio Grande boundary in return for American assumption of the claims payments. In addition the emissary was empowered to purchase New Mexico and California for

$25,000,000. Polk would have gone as high as $40,000,000. He especially desired California with its fine harbor of San Francisco.

The president's representative, Slidell, unfortunately for Mexico, met with rebuff. Before Slidell's journey to Mexico City Polk had received a stately in writing from the Mexican foreign minister to the effect that an American commissioner would find a friendly reception. The Mexican government upon Slidell's arrival refused to treat with him, on the technicality that his credentials were those of a minister plenipotentiary rather than a special *ad hoc* representative. What happened was that the Mexican government of the moment, led by General Mariano Paredes, was in imminent peril of being thrown from office, and could not face the hostility of popular opinion in the capital city, should it undertake to negotiate with the Americans. The Mexican people—when one spoke of a "people" of Mexico in the nineteenth century he meant little more than the literate inhabitants of the capital—were determined that annexation of Texas would be tantamount to war.

Whatever sort of government was in control, it was a fatuous act in 1846 to turn down an overture from the government of the United States. Mexico was in the position of refusing to sell territories that she could not keep anyway. Napoleon in 1803, seeing that he could not hold Louisiana, had sold it. There were no Napoleons in Mexico in 1846 but only factional politicians who found momentary power too sweet to relinquish, be the responsibilities of their decisions ever so serious for the future of their country.

And so John Slidell went away, and President Polk, tired of the irresolution of his adversary, disposed American troops

under Brigadier General Zachary ("Old Zach") Taylor in the disputed border area of Texas between the Nueces River and the Rio Grande. The local Mexican commander on April 25, 1846 surprised a company of American soldiers, killing or wounding sixteen and capturing the remainder, and the war was on. This even before news had reached the Mexican commander that the government in Mexico City had declared a "defensive war" against the United States. In Washington, Polk was preparing a war message to Congress when the welcome news arrived of the Mexican attack. War, Polk then could assert, had been forced upon the United States by act of Mexico. Congress declared on May 13, 1846 that "by the act of the Republic of Mexico, a state of war exists between the Government and the United States."

That this war with Mexico in the mid-nineteenth century was not a popular conflict soon became obvious to everyone. The war with Mexico of 1846–1848 never evoked the popularity that surrounded the first or second World Wars or the war with Spain in 1898. Not merely was there grumbling and disgruntledness in New England, but outright speeches against the war by such Western opponents as Congressman Abraham Lincoln of Illinois. The issue on which opposition arose was, of course, the extension of slavery. Northern opposition to the war found expression everywhere from pulpits, rostrums, and "stump" platforms. No sooner had the war begun than it received a name indicating its alleged origin—President Polk's War. . . .

President Polk in taking the country to war against Mexico did not, incidentally, act from proslavery motives. Polk was dismayed at the debates over the slavery issue, and became embittered after the war began by the reintroduction into Congress in January 1847 of the Wilmot Proviso to prevent the expansion of slavery into new territory. Slavery as an institution, the president always maintained, had no connection with the war or the peace. "Its introduction in connection with the Mexican War," he recorded in his diary, "is not only mischievous but wicked." Although a citizen of Tennessee and a slaveholder, like his predecessor Andrew Jackson, he had in mind first and foremost the territory and Pacific ports of California, and only after this goal was achieved would he concern himself over the slavery question. Economic interests, but of a territorial sort, moved Polk in his actions, peaceful and otherwise, toward Mexico. . . .

The Treaty of Guadalupe Hidalgo was concluded on February 2, 1848, and had a most interesting background. It was signed by Trist after his commission had expired. President Polk through Secretary of State James Buchanan had annulled Trist's commission, fearing that to have a negotiator accompanying Scott's army would seem to the Mexicans like a sign of American weakness. But Trist at this point began to fear that without an immediate peace there might develop a sentiment in the United States for taking all of Mexico. The Mexican government had been reconstituted through the efforts of General Scott, whose troops were billeted comfortably in the Mexican capital. The abject defeat of the Mexicans was so obvious that, as Trist knew, it might well encourage the more ambitious apostles of manifest destiny to stretch the American eagle's wings all the way to Guatemala. . . . Trist negotiated his treaty at the little village of Guadalupe Hidalgo just outside Mexico City

and sent the treaty off to Washington to see what Polk would do with it.

Polk was furious. The president, an able, conscientious, sincere man, was intensely suspicious of political plots during his administration—and he saw a plot in Trist's treaty.

Polk, it seems altogether fair to say, had begun the Mexican War not out of partisan but for national reasons. The president believed that his country's future demanded a border of Texas at the Rio Grande, and in addition he wanted to acquire New Mexico and especially California. This was a broadly national purpose, but as Whig opposition to the war became more vehement Polk found that matters of politics plagued his every move, that he had to be circumspect in his every act to fend off the Whigs and keep the war going to a victorious conclusion. He managed to do this, but only with difficulty, and one of his worst problems in the conduct of the war was that the two leading military commanders. Generals Taylor and Scott, were both Whigs and likely to profit personally from the war by being nominated on the Whig ticket for the presidency. . . .

Trist's treaty, despite the improprieties of its conclusion, was not unwelcome, for Polk's agent had secured New Mexico and California plus Mexican acceptance of the Texan boundary at the Rio Grande, and the United States was to pay $15,000,000 and assume the adjusted claims of its citizens against the Mexican government. These terms, Polk realized, were virtually the maximum that Slidell had been empowered to negotiate in the abortive mission of 1846, and despite his intense disgust with Trist for acting without commission the president sent the treaty to the Senate, which gave its advice and consent on March 10, 1848. After ratification by Mexico, Polk proclaimed the treaty in effect on the anniversary of American independence, July 4, 1848. By this stroke of war, following upon the stroke of diplomacy which had gained Texas in 1845, the United States had added altogether (including Texas) 1,200,000 square miles to its domain, an increase of more than sixty-six percent.

What could one say about manifest destiny, as it had found fulfillment in the events of 1845–1848? The peaceful process by which the United States of America had been expanding across the enormously valuable North American continent had been punctuated by a short and sharp and altogether victorious war. At the time, people were asking whether political leaders from the Southern portion of the United States had not forced the war with Mexico for the enlargement of their slave domains, for the miserable purpose of obtaining "more pens to cram slaves in." This fear, so far as concerned the reasoning of President Polk himself and probably many of his supporters, was unfounded. Even so, in the twentieth century when war led to the near-destruction of Western civilization, many people were again going to ask if the Mexican War were not an unjust war of aggression. Was, then, the Mexican War a conflict that for this latter reason should have been avoided? Should not the United States in 1846–1848 have trusted to its diplomacy and restrained its pursuit of manifest destiny, if that were possible?

The answer to this question is not easy. No American today would like to give up the territories secured from Mexico. Those expanses so varied in their riches gave us first gold, then oil, now uranium, and have increased enormously the power of the United States. If one may be permitted the luxury of reading the present into the past—assuredly a most unhistorical operation—he can easily see that at a time in the mid-twentieth century when the power of the United States and the Union of Soviet Socialist Republics is so neatly balanced, any large subtraction from American power might have changed the course of history. This is no fanciful notion, pleasantly speculated upon in these pages, but an idea that bears some considerable possibilities for thought. What might have happened if the United States during the second World War had not had enough economic and military strength to throw the victory to the Allies? Or for that matter, what might have happened in the gray spring of 1918 when the German offensive came within an ace of success, if the morale of Allied troops had not been bucked up by the prospect, soon to be realized, of two million American soldiers in France? If the nation had stopped at the Sabine River, if such statesmen as John Tyler and James K. Polk had taken Mexican complaints and protests as insuperable obstacles to realization of manifest destiny, the American people might today find their personal and public circumstances altogether unenviable.

POSTSCRIPT

Was U.S. Foreign Policy in the Early Nineteenth Century Imperialistic?

Ferrell presents an interesting defense of the United States' policy of Manifest Destiny towards Mexico in the 1840s. Admitting that the United States created conditions which pushed Mexico into starting the war, Ferrell nevertheless justifies the goals of the war, which were the acquisition of Texas, New Mexico, and California. Not everyone will agree with Ferrell's acceptance of the ideology of Manifest Destiny. Some historians, like Richard W. Van Alstyne, in *The Rising American Empire* (Quadrangle, 1965), and William Appleman Williams, in the very influential *The Tragedy of American Diplomacy*, 2d rev., enlarged ed. (Delta, 1972), are critical of the narrow definition of imperialism employed by writers like Ferrell. These radical historians believe that America created an economic empire during the nation's formative years which has continued into the present day.

Ruiz's essay offers a fresh approach when he considers the causes and effects of the war upon both sides. He rejects the ethnocentric approaches of earlier diplomatic historians like Justin Smith, Samuel F. Bemis, and Robert Ferrell, as well as the economic deterministic views of the radical historians. Ruiz tries to balance the North American and Latin American perspectives but in the end comes down hard upon the racist and aggressive policies of James K. Polk's administration. Students who would like to see the Mexican perspective more fully developed should read the passionate account by Rodolfo Acuna in "Legacy of Hate: The Conquest of the Southwest," in *Occupied America: A History of Chicanos*, 2d ed. (Harper & Row, 1981).

Though somewhat dated, the most accessible collection of interpretations can be found in *Mexican War: Was It Manifest Destiny?* (Holt, Rinehart & Winston, 1963) was edited by Ramon E. Ruiz. Ruiz's selections are well balanced in terms of their interpretations and include two translated essays from Carlos Bosch Garcia and Justo Sierra. Recent writings from American diplomatic scholars are also less ethnocentric and paternalistic in tone. Norman A. Graebner has continually refined his interpretations about the Mexican War period in a number of essays which have been conveniently reprinted in *The Foundation of American Foreign Policy* (Scholarly Resources, 1985). Reginald Horseman updates Alfred K. Weinberg's classic treatment in *Manifest Destiny* (Johns Hopkins Press, 1935) and refines his opinions in *Race and Manifest Destiny: The Origins of American Anglo-Saxonism* (Harvard University Press, 1981). Finally, in *The Diplomacy of Annexation* (University of Missouri Press, 1985), David M. Pletcher revives the needless war theory.

ISSUE 13

Did Slaves Exercise Religious Autonomy?

YES: Albert J. Raboteau, from "Slave Autonomy and Religion," *Journal of Religious Thought* (Fall–Winter 1981–82)

NO: John B. Boles, from "Introduction," in John B. Boles, ed., *Masters & Slaves in the House of the Lord: Race and Religion in the American South, 1740–1870* (University Press of Kentucky, 1988)

ISSUE SUMMARY

YES: Professor of history Albert J. Raboteau claims that the religious activities of American slaves were characterized by institutional and personal independence, which undermined the ability of the masters to exercise effective control over their chattel property.

NO: Professor of history John B. Boles recognizes that slaves often worshiped apart from their masters, but he asserts that the primary religious experience of Southern slaves occurred within a biracial setting in churches dominated by whites.

Since the mid-1950s, few issues in American history have generated more interest among scholars than the institution of slavery. Books and articles analyzing the treatment of slaves, comparative slave systems, the profitability of slavery, slave rebelliousness (or lack thereof), urban slavery, the slave family, and slave religion abound. This proliferation of scholarship, stimulated in part by the civil rights movement, contrasts sharply with the amount of historical literature written on slavery between the two world wars, a time that was monopolized by a single book—Ulrich B. Phillips's apologetic and blatantly racist *American Negro Slavery* (1918).

Phillips, a native Georgian who taught for most of his career at Yale, based his sweeping view of the Southern slave system upon plantation records left by some of the wealthiest slave owners. He concluded that American slavery was a benign institution controlled by paternalistic masters. These owners, Phillips insisted, rarely treated their bond servants cruelly but, instead, provided their childlike, acquiescent human property with food, clothing, housing, and other necessities of life.

Although black historians such as George Washington Williams, W. E. B. Du Bois, Carter G. Woodson, and John Hope Franklin produced scholarly works that emphasized the brutal impact of slavery, their views received almost no consideration from the wider academic community. Consequently, recognition of a "revisionist" interpretation of slavery was delayed until the post–World War II era when, in the wake of the *Brown* desegregation case, Kenneth Stampp, a white Northern historian, published *The Peculiar Institution* (1956). Stampp also focused primarily upon antebellum plantation records, but his conclusions were literally a point-by-point rebuttal of the Phillips thesis. The institution of slavery, he said, was a harsh, oppressive system in which slave owners controlled their servants through fear of the lash. Further, in contrast to the image of the passive, happy-go-lucky "Sambo" described by Phillips, Stampp argued that slaves were "a troublesome property" who resisted their enslavement in subtle as well as overt ways.

In 1959, Stanley Elkins synthesized these seemingly contradictory interpretations in his controversial study *Slavery: A Problem in American Institutional and Intellectual Life.* Elkins clearly accepted Stampp's emphasis on the harshness of the slave system by hypothesizing that slavery was a "closed" system in which masters dominated their slaves in the same way that Nazi concentration camp guards in World War II had controlled the lives of their prisoners. Such an environment, he insisted, generated severe psychological dysfunctions that produced the personality traits of Phillips's "Sambo" character type.

As the debate over the nature of slavery moved into the 1960s and 1970s, several scholars, seeking to provide a history of the institution "from the bottom up," began to focus upon the slaves themselves. Interviews with former slaves had been conducted in the 1920s and 1930s under the auspices of Southern University in Louisiana, Fisk University in Tennessee, and the Federal Writers Project of the Works Progress Administration. Drawing upon these interviews and previously ignored slave autobiographies, sociologist George Rawick and historians John Blassingame and Eugene D. Genovese, among others, portrayed a multifaceted community life over which slaves held a significant degree of influence. This community, which operated beyond the view of the "Big House," was, according to Genovese, "the world the slaves made."

These contrasting interpretive currents are reflected in the following essays on the nature of slave religion. In the first selection, Albert J. Raboteau describes the ways in which the acceptance of Christianity produced numerous opportunities for slaves to assume control over their own religious activities, which led to an autonomy that permitted slaves to resist some of the dehumanizing elements of the slave system. John B. Boles admits that slaves in the antebellum South worshiped in a variety of ways (in independent black churches, plantation chapels, or informal, secret gatherings), but he concludes that the typical site for slave religious activities was the church of their masters.

YES

Albert J. Raboteau

SLAVE AUTONOMY AND RELIGION

One of the perennial questions in the historical study of American slavery is the question of the relationship between Christianity and the response of slaves to enslavement. Did the Christian religion serve as a tool in the hands of slaveholders to make slaves docile or did it serve in the hands of slaves as a weapon of resistance and even outright rebellion against the system of slavery? Let us acknowledge from the outset that the role of religion in human motivation and action is very complex; let us recognize also that Christianity played an ambiguous role in the stances which slaves took toward slavery, sometimes supporting resistance, sometimes accommodation. That much admitted, much more remains to be said. Specifically, we need to trace the convoluted ways in which the egalitarian impulse within Christianity overflowed the boundaries of the master-slave hierarchy, creating unexpected channels of slave autonomy on institutional as well as personal levels. To briefly sketch out some of the directions which religious autonomy took among slaves in the antebellum South is the purpose of this essay.

INSTITUTIONAL AUTONOMY

From the beginning of the Atlantic slave trade in the fifteenth century, European Christians claimed that the conversion of slaves to Christianity justified the enslavement of Africans. For more than four centuries Christian apologists for slavery would repeat this religious rationalization for one of history's greatest atrocities. Despite the justification of slavery as a method of spreading the gospel, the conversion of slaves was not a top priority for colonial planters. One of the principal reasons for the refusal of British colonists to allow their slaves religious instruction was the fear that baptism would require the manumission of their slaves, since it was illegal to hold a fellow Christian in bondage. This dilemma was solved quickly by colonial legislation stating that baptism did not alter slave status. However, the most serious obstacle to religious instruction of the slaves could not be legislated

From Albert J. Raboteau, "Slave Autonomy and Religion," *Journal of Religious Thought*, vol. 38 (Fall 1981/Winter 1982), pp. 51–64. Copyright © 1981 by *Journal of Religious Thought*. Reprinted by permission. Notes omitted.

away. It was the slaveholder's deep-seated uneasiness at the prospect of a slave laying claim to Christian fellowship with his master. The concept of equality, though only spiritual, between master and slave threatened the stability of the system of slave control. Christianity, complained the masters, would ruin slaves by allowing them to think themselves equal to white Christians. Far worse was the fear, supported by the behavior of some Christian slaves, that religion would make them rebellious. In order to allay this fear, would-be missionaries to the slaves had to prove that Christianity would make better slaves. By arguing that Christian slaves would become obedient to their masters out of duty to God and by stressing the distinction between spiritual equality and worldly equality, the proponents of slave conversion in effect built a religious foundation to support slavery. Wary slaveholders were assured by missionaries that "Scripture, far from making an Alteration in Civil Rights, expressly directs, *that every Man abide in the Condition wherein he is called, with great Indifference of Mind* concerning outward circumstances."

In spite of missionary efforts to convince them that Christianity was no threat to the slave system, slaveowners from the colonial period on down to the Civil War remained suspicious of slave religion as a two-edged sword. Clerical assurances aside, the masters' concern was valid. Religious instruction for slaves had more than spiritual implications. No event would reveal these implications as clearly as the series of religious revivals called the Great Awakenings which preceded and followed the Revolution. The impact of revival fervor would demonstrate how difficult it was to control the egalitarian impulse of Christianity within safe channels.

The first Great Awakening of the 1740s swept the colonies with the tumultuous preaching and emotional conversions of revivalistic, evangelical Protestantism. Accounts by Whitefield, Tennent, Edwards, and other revivalists made special mention of the fact that blacks were flocking to hear the message of salvation in hitherto unseen numbers. Not only were free blacks and slaves attending revivals in significant numbers, they were taking active part in the services as exhorters and preachers. The same pattern of black activism was repeated in the rural camp meetings of the Great Awakening of the early nineteenth century.

The increase in slave conversions which accompanied the awakenings was due to several factors. The evangelical religion spread by the revivalists initiated a religious renaissance in the South where the majority of slaves lived. The revival became a means of church extension, especially for Methodists and Baptists. The mobility of the Methodist circuit rider and the local independence of the Baptist preacher were suited to the needs of the rural South. Among the Southerners swelling the ranks of these denominations, were black as well as white converts.

Moreover, the ethos of the revival meeting, with its strong emphasis upon emotional preaching and congregational response, not only permitted ecstatic religious behavior but encouraged it. Religious exercises, as they were termed, including fainting, jerking, barking, and laughing a "holy laugh," were a common, if spectacular, feature of revivals. In this heated atmosphere slaves found sanction for an outward expression of religious emotion consonant with their tradition of danced religion from Africa. While converting to belief in a "new"

God, slaves were able to worship in ways hauntingly similar to those of old.

Extremely important for the development of black participation in revival religion was the intense concentration upon individual inward conversion which fostered an inclusiveness that could become egalitarianism. Evangelicals did not hesitate to preach to racially mixed congregations and had no doubt about the capacity of slaves to share the experience of conversion to Christ. Stressing plain doctrine and emotional preaching, emphasizing the conversion experience instead of religious instruction, made Christianity accessible to illiterate slave and slaveholder alike. The criterion for preachers was not seminary training but evidence of a converted heart and gifted tongue. Therefore, when an awakened slave showed talent for preaching, he preached, and not only to black congregations. The tendency of evangelical Protestantism to level the souls of all men before God reached its logical conclusion when blacks preached to and converted whites.

By the last quarter of the eighteenth century a cadre of black preachers had begun to emerge. Some of these pioneer black ministers were licensed, some not; some were slaves, others free. During the 1780s a black man named Lewis preached to crowds as large as four hundred in Westmoreland County, Virginia. Harry Hosier traveled with Methodist leaders, Asbury, Coke, Garretson, and Whatcoat and was reportedly such an eloquent preacher that he served as a "drawing card" to attract larger crowds of potential converts, white and black. In 1792 the mixed congregation of the Portsmouth, Virginia Baptist Church selected a slave, Josiah Bishop, as pastor, after purchasing his freedom and also his family's. An-

other black preacher, William Lemon, pastored a white Baptist church in Gloucester County, Virginia, for a time at the turn of the century.

In 1798, Joseph Willis, a freeman, duly licensed as a Baptist preacher, began his ministry in southwest Mississippi and Louisiana. He formed Louisiana's first Baptist church at Bayou Chicot in 1812 and served as its pastor. After developing several other churches in the area, he became the first moderator of the Louisiana Baptist Association in 1818. Uncle Jack, an African-born slave, joined the Baptist church and in 1792 began to preach in Nottoway County, Virginia. White church members purchased his freedom and he continued to preach for over forty years. Henry Evans, a free black licensed as a local preacher by the Methodists, was the first to bring Methodist preaching to Fayetteville, North Carolina. Initially preaching to black people only, he attracted the attention of several prominent whites and eventually the white membership of his congregation increased until the blacks were crowded out of their seats. Evans was eventually replaced by a white minister, but continued to serve as an assistant in the church he had founded until his death.

That black preachers should exhort, convert, and even pastor white Christians in the slave South was certainly antithetical to the premise of slave control. Though such occasions were rare, they were the ineluctable result of the impulse unleashed by revivalistic religion. Of greater importance for the development of autonomy in the religious life of slaves was the fact that black preachers, despite threats of punishment, continued to preach to slaves and in some few cases even founded churches.

An early historian of the Baptists applauded the anonymous but effective ministry of these black preachers:

> Among the African Baptists in the Southern states there are a multitude of preachers and exhorters whose names do not appear on the minutes of the associations. They preach principally on the plantations to those of their own color, and their preaching though broken and illiterate, is in many cases highly useful.

Several "African" Baptist churches sprang up before 1800. Some of these black congregations were independent to the extent that they called their own pastors and officers, joined local associations with white Baptist churches, and sent their own delegates to associational meetings. Though the separate black church was primarily an urban phenomenon, it drew upon surrounding rural areas for its membership, which consisted of both free blacks and slaves. Sometimes these black churches were founded amidst persecution. Such was the case with the African Baptist Church of Williamsburg, Virginia, whose history was chronicled in 1810:

> This church is composed almost, if not altogether of people of colour. Moses, a black man, first preached among them, and was often taken up and whipped, for holding meetings. Afterwards Gowan Pamphlet . . . became popular among the blacks, and began to baptize, as well as to preach. It seems, the association had advised that no person of colour should be allowed to preach, on the pain of excommunication; against this regulation, many of the blacks were rebellious, and continued still to hold meetings. Some were excluded, and among this number was Gowan. . . . Continuing still to preach and many professing faith under his ministry, not

being in connexion with any church himself, he formed a kind of church out of some who had been baptized, who, sitting with him, received such as offered themselves; Gowan baptized them, and was moreover appointed their pastor; some of them knowing how to write, a churchbook was kept; they increased to a large number; so that in the year 1791, the Dover association, stat[ed] their number to be about five hundred. The association received them, so far, as to appoint persons to visit them and set things in order. These making a favourable report, they were received, and have associated ever since.

Several features of this narrative deserve emphasis as significant examples of black religious autonomy. Ignoring the threat of excommunication, not to mention physical punishment, blacks rebelled against white religious control and insisted on holding their own meetings, led by their own ministers. They gathered their own church, apparently according to the norms of Baptist polity, accepted their own members, kept their own minutes, and finally succeeded in joining the local association, all the while growing to a membership of five hundred by 1791!

In Savannah, Georgia, a slave named Andrew Bryan established an African Baptist Church, against white objection and persecution. In 1790, Bryan's church included two hundred and twenty-five full communicants and approximately three hundred and fifty converts, many of whom did not have their masters' permission to be baptized. In 1803, a Second African Church of Savannah was organized from the first, and a few years later a third came into being. Both of the new churches were led by black pastors. After Bryan's death, his nephew, Andrew Marshall, became pastor of the First African Church and by 1830 his congregation had increased in size to two thousand, four hundred and seventeen members.

The labors of these early black preachers and their successors were crucial in the formation of slave religion. In order to adequately understand the development of Christianity among the slaves, we must realize that slaves learned Christianity not only from whites but from other slaves as well. Slave preachers, exhorters, and church-appointed watchmen instructed their fellow slaves, nurtured their religious development, and brought them to conversion in some cases without the active involvement of white missionaries or masters at all. The early independence of black preachers and churches was curtailed as the antebellum period wore on, particularly in periods of reaction to slave conspiracies, when all gatherings of blacks for whatever purpose were viewed with alarm. For slaves to participate in the organization, leadership, and governance of church structures was perceived as dangerous. Surely it was inconsistent, argued the guardians of the system, to allow blacks such authority. As the prominent South Carolinian planter, Charles Cotesworth Pinkney, declared before the Charleston Agricultural Society in 1829, the exercise of religious prerogatives left slaves too free from white control. "We look upon the habit of Negro preaching as a widespreading evil; not because a black man cannot be a good one, but . . . because they acquire an influence independent of the owner, and not subject to his control. . . . when they have possessed this power, they have been known to make an improper use of it." No doubt, Pinkney and his audience had in mind the African Methodist Church of Charleston which had served as a seedbed of rebellion for the Denmark Vesey conspiracy of 1822. (Following discovery of the plot, whites razed the church to the ground.)

Regardless of periodic harassment by civil and ecclesiastical authorities, black preachers continued to preach and separate black churches continued to be organized. Just as Pinkney and others warned, in preaching and in church life some blacks found channels for self-expression and self-governance. To be sure, the exercise of such autonomy was frequently modified by white supervision, but it was nonetheless real. In various sections of the antebellum South, black churches kept gathering members, over the years swelling in size to hundreds and in a few instances thousands of members. Certainly, the vast majority of slaves attended churches under white control. However, even in racially mixed churches some black Christians found opportunities to exercise their spiritual gifts and a measure of control over their religious life. This was so especially in Baptist churches because Baptist polity required that each congregation govern itself. In some churches committees of black members were constituted to oversee their own conduct. These committees listened to black applicants relate their religious experience and heard the replies of members charged with moral laxity. Meeting once a month, committees of "brethren in black" conducted business, reported their recommendations to the general meeting and gave to black church members experience in church governance. This experience laid a foundation upon which freedmen would rapidly build their own independent churches after emancipation.

Hampered though it was, the exercise of religious autonomy among slaves was a fact of antebellum life. It was due to the nature of the revival fervor of the Great

Awakenings of the eighteenth and early nineteenth centuries which first brought the slaves to conversion in large numbers and also created a situation in which it became possible for black freemen and slaves to preach and even pastor. (By way of contrast, these avenues to spiritual authority would not open for blacks in either the Church of England or the Roman Catholic Church for a long time to come.) To the extent possible, then, black Christians proved not at all reluctant about deciding their own religious affairs and managing their own religious institutions. For the vast majority of slaves, however, institutional religious autonomy was not possible. This did not stop them from seeking religious independence from whites in more secretive ways.

PERSONAL AUTONOMY

Like their colonial predecessors, antebellum missionaries to the slaves had to face objections from whites that religion for slaves was dangerous. Beginning in the 1820s, a movement led by prominent clerics and laymen attempted to mold southern opinion in support of missions to the slaves. Plantation missionaries created an ideal image of the Christian plantation, built upon the mutual observance of duties by masters and by slaves. One leader of the plantation mission stated the movement's basic premise when he predicted that "religious instruction of the Negroes will *promote our own morality and religion.*" For, when "one class rises, so will the other; the two are so associated they are apt to rise or fall together. Therefore, servants do well by your masters and masters do well by your servants." In this premise lay a serious fallacy; for while the interests of master

and slave occasionally coincided, they could never cohere. No matter how devoted master was to the ideal of a Christian plantation, no matter how pious he might be, the slave knew that the master's religion did not countenance the slaves' freedom in this world.

Precisely because the interests of master and slave extended only so far and no further, there was a dimension of the slaves' religious life that was secret. The disparity between the master's ideal of religion on the plantation and that of the slaves led the slaves to gather secretly in the quarters or in brush arbors (aptly named hush harbors) where they could pray, preach, and sing, free from white control. Risking severe punishment, slaves disobeyed their masters and stole off under cover of secrecy to worship as they saw fit. Here it was that Christianity was fitted to their own peculiar experience.

It was the slaveholding gospel preached to them by master's preacher which drove many slaves to seek true Christian preaching at their own meetings. "Church was what they called it," recalled former slave Charlie Van Dyke, "but all that preacher talked about was for us slaves to obey our masters and not to lie and steal." To attend secret meetings was in itself an act of resistance against the will of the master and was punished as such. In the face of the absolute authority of the Divine Master, the authority of the human master shrank. Slaves persisted in their hush harbor meetings because there they found consolation and communal support, tangible relief from the exhaustion and brutality of work stretching from "day clean" to after dark, day in and day out. "Us niggers," remarked Richard Carruthers, describing a scene still vivid in his memory many years later, "used to have a prayin' ground down in the hollow and sometimes we come out of the field . . . scorchin' and burnin' up with nothin' to eat, and we wants to ask the good Lawd to have mercy. . . . We takes a pine torch . . . and goes down in the hollow to pray. Some gits so joyous they starts to holler loud and we has to stop up they mouth. I see niggers git so full of the Lawd and so happy they draps unconscious."

In the hush harbor slaves sought not only substantive preaching and spiritual consolation they also talked about and prayed for an end to their physical bondage. "I've heard them pray for freedom," declared one former slave. "I thought it was foolishness then, but the old time folks always felt they was to be free. It must have been something 'vealed unto 'em. Though some might be skeptical, those slaves who were confident that freedom would come, since God had revealed it, were able to cast their lives in a different light. Hope for a brighter future irradiated the darkness of the present. Their desire for freedom in this world was reaffirmed in the songs, prayers, and sermons of the hush harbor. This was just what the master—those who didn't believe in prayer, as well as those who did—tried to prevent. The external hush harbor symbolized an internal resistance, a private place at the core of the slaves' religious life which they claimed as their own and which, in the midst of bondage, could not be controlled.

For evangelical Christians, black or white, full admission into membership in the church required that the candidate give credible testimony about the inner workings of the Spirit upon his or her heart. The conversion experience, as described by ex-slaves, was typically a visionary one, inaugurated by feelings of sadness and inner turmoil. Frequently the individual "convicted of sin" envisioned Hell and realized that he was destined for damnation. Suddenly, the sinner was rescued from this danger and led to a vision of Heaven by an emissary from God. Ushered into God's presence, the person learned that he was not damned but saved. Awakening, the convert realized that he was now one of the elect and overwhelmed with the joyful feeling of being "made new" shouted out his happiness. For years afterwards, this "peak" experience remained a fixed point of identity and value in the convert's life. He knew that he was saved, and he knew it not just theoretically but experientially. Confident of their election and their value in the eyes of God, slaves who underwent conversion, gained in this radical experience a deeply rooted identity which formed the basis for a sense of purpose and an affirmation of self-worth—valuable psychic barriers to the demeaning and dehumanizing attacks of slavery.

Conversion, as an experience common to white and black Christians, occasionally led to moments of genuine emotional contact, in which the etiquette of racial relationships was forgotten. A dramatic instance of one such occasion was recounted by a former slave named Morte:

One day while in the field plowing I heard a voice . . . I looked but saw no one . . . Everything got dark, and I was unable to stand any longer . . . With this I began to cry, Mercy! Mercy! Mercy! As I prayed an angel came and touched me, and I looked new . . . and there came a soft voice saying, "My little one, I have loved you with an everlasting love. You are this day made alive and freed from hell. You are a chosen vessel unto the Lord." . . . I must have been in this trance more than an hour. I went on to the barn and found my master waiting for me. . . . I began to tell him of my experiences . . . My master sat watching and listening to me, and then he began to cry. He turned from me and said in a broken voice, "Morte I believe you are a preacher. From now on you can preach to the people here on my place . . . But tomorrow morning, Sunday, I want to preach to my family and my neighbors." . . . The next morning at the time appointed I stood up on two planks in front of the porch of the big house and, without a Bible or anything, I began to preach to my master and the people. My thoughts came so fast that I could hardly speak fast enough. My soul caught on fire, and soon I had them all in tears . . . I told them that they must be born again and that their souls must be freed from the shackles of hell.

The spectacle of a slave reducing his master to tears by preaching to him of his enslavement to sin certainly suggests that religion could bend human relationships into interesting shapes despite the iron rule of slavery. Morte's power over his master was spiritual and (as far as we know) it was temporary. It was also effective.

While commonality of religious belief might lead to moments of religious reciprocity between blacks and whites, by far the more common relationship, from the slaves' side, was one of alienation from the hypocrisy of slaveholding Christians. As Frederick Douglass put it, "Slaves knew enough of the orthodox theology of the time to consign all bad slaveholders to hell." On the same point, Charles Ball commented that in his experience slaves thought that heaven would not be heaven unless slaves could be

avenged on their enemies. "A fortunate and kind master or mistress, may now and then be admitted into heaven, but this rather as a matter of favour, to the intercession of some slave, than as a matter of strict justice to the whites, who will, by no means, be of an equal rank with those who shall be raised from the depths of misery in this world." Ball concluded that "The idea of a revolution in the conditions of the whites and blacks, is the cornerstone of the religion of the latter. . . ."

Slaves had no difficulty distinguishing the gospel of Christianity from the religion of their masters. Ex-slave Douglas Dorsey reported that after the minister on his plantation admonished the slaves to honor their masters whom they could see as they would God whom they could not see, the driver's wife who could read and write a little would say that the minister's sermon "was all lies." Charles Colcock Jones, plantation missionary, found that his slave congregation did not hesitate to reject the doctrine preached in a sermon he gave in 1833:

I was preaching to a large congregation on the *Epistle of Philemon*: and when I insisted upon fidelity and obedience as Christian virtues in servants and upon the authority of Paul, condemned the practice of *running away*, one half of my audience deliberately rose up and walked off with themselves, and those that remained looked any thing but satisfied, either with the preacher or his doctrine. After dismission, there was no small stir among them: some solemnly declared "that there was no such Epistle in the Bible:" others, "that I preached to please the masters;" others, "that it was not the Gospel;" others, "that they did not care if they ever heard me preach again!" . . There were some too, who had strong objections against me as a Preacher, because I was a *master*, and said, "his people have to work as well as we."

The slaves' rejection of white man's religion was clearly revealed in their attitudes toward morality. While white preachers repeated the command, "Do not steal," slaves simply denied that this precept allied to them since they themselves were stolen property. Josephine Howard put the argument this way: "Dey allus done tell us it am wrong to lie and steal, but why did de white folks steal my mammy and her mammy . . . Dat de sinfulles' stealin' dey is." Rachel Fairley demanded, "How could they help but steal when they didn't have nothin'? You didn't eat if you didn't steal." Henry Bibb declared that under slavery "I had a just right to what I took, because it was the labor of my hands." Other slaves concluded that it was not morally possible for one piece of property to steal another since both belonged to the same owner: it was merely a case of taking something out of one tub and putting it in another. This view of stealing referred only to master's goods, however, for a slave to steal from another slave was seriously wrong. As the saying went, "a slave that will steal from a slave is called *mean as master*." Or as one ex-slave remarked, "This is the lowest comparison slaves know how to use: 'just as mean as white folks.' "

Not all slaves, however, were able to distinguish master's religion from authentic Christianity, and were led to reject this religion totally. In 1839, Daniel Alexander Payne explained how this could happen:

The slaves are sensible of the oppression exercised by their masters; and they see these masters on the Lord's day worshipping in his holy Sanctuary. They year their masters professing Christianity; they see their masters preaching the gospel; they hear these masters praying in their families, and they know that oppression and slavery are inconsistent with the Christian religion; therefore they scoff at religion itself—mock their masters, and distrust both the goodness and justice of God.

Frederick Douglass too remembered being shaken by "doubts arising . . . from the sham religion which everywhere prevailed" under slavery, doubts which "awakened in my mind a distrust of all religion and the conviction that prayers were unavailing and delusive." Unable to account for the evil of slavery in a world ruled by a just God, some slaves abandoned belief. "I pretended to profess religion one time," recalled one former slave, "I don't hardly know what to think about religion. They say God killed the just and unjust; I don't understand that part of it. It looks hard to think that if you ain't done nothing in the world you be punished just like the wicked. Plenty folks went crazy trying to get that straightened out." There is no way of estimating how many slaves felt these doubts, but they indicate how keenly aware slaves were of the disparity between the gospel of Christ and what they termed "white man's religion."

At the opposite extreme from the agnostic slave was the slave who developed a life of exemplary Christian virtue which placed him in a position of moral superiority over his master. William Grimes, for example, was possessed of a sense of righteousness which led him to take a surprising attitude toward his master when punished for something he had not done:

It grieved me very much to be blamed when I was innocent. I knew I had been faithful to him, perfectly so. At this time I was quite serious, and used constantly to pray to my God. I would not lie nor steal. . . . When I considered him accusing me of stealing, when I was so innocent, and had endeavored to make him satisfied by every means in my power, that I was so, but he still persisted in disbelieving me, I then said to myself, if this thing is done in a green tree what must be done in a dry? I forgave my master in my own heart for all this, and prayed to God to forgive him and turn his heart.

Grimes is of course alluding to the sacrifice of Christ and identifying himself with the innocent suffering servant who spoke the words concerning green and dry wood on his way to death on Calvary. From this vantage point Grimes is able to forgive his master. Note however the element of threat implied in the question, "if this thing is done in a green tree (to the innocent) what must be done in a dry (to the guilty)?" Those who are guilty of persecuting the innocent, like Grimes's master, will be judged and punished. (The full context of the biblical allusion includes a terrifying prediction of the destruction of Jerusalem.) What did it mean to Grimes's self-image to be able to have moral leverage by which he might elevate his own dignity. A similar impulse lay behind the comment of Mary Younger, a fugitive slave in Canada, "if those slaveholders were to come here, I would treat them well, just to shame them by showing that I had humanity." To asset one's humanity in the face of slavery's power to dehumanize, perhaps explained Grimes's careful adherence to righteousness, a righteousness which might at first glance seem merely servile.

CONCLUSION

In the slave society of the antebellum South, as in most societies, the Christian religion both supported and undermined the status quo. On the one hand, Nat Turner claimed that God's will moved him to slaughter whites, on the other, "good" slaves protected their masters out of a sense of duty. Slave religion, however was more complex than these alternatives suggest. Institutionally, the egalitarian impulse of evangelical Protestantism, leveling all men before God and lifting some up to declare his word with power and authority, gave slaves and free blacks the opportunity to exercise leadership. Usually this leadership was not revolutionary and from the perspective of political strategy it was overwhelmingly conservative. Yet political action is not the only measure of resistance to oppression. Despite political impotence, the black preacher was still a figure of power as an unmistakable symbol of the talent and ability of black men, a fact which contradicted the doctrine of inherent black inferiority. As white slaveholders occasionally recognized, black preachers were anomalous, if not dangerous, persons under the system of slave control precisely because their authority could not be effectively limited by whites.

Nor were slaveowners able to control the spirit of religious independence once it had been imbibed by their slaves. Continually this spirit sought to break out of the strictures confining slave life. When possible, it sought expression in separate institutions controlled by blacks. When that proved impossible, it found expression in secret religious gatherings "out from under the eye of the master." In both cases, the internal autonomy of the slave's own moral will prove[d] impossible to destroy. Throughout the history of Christianity, earthly rulers (civil and religious) have been troubled by the claim that individuals owed obedience to a higher authority than their own. Antebellum slaveholders and missionaries faced the same problem. When slaves disobeyed their masters in order to obey God, a long tradition of Christian heroism validated their assertion of human freedom.

The emotional ecstasy of slave religion has been criticized as compensatory and otherworldly, a distraction from the evils of this world. And so it was. But it was much more. Individually, slaves found not only solace in their religion but, particularly in the conversion experience, a source of personal identity and value. Collectively, slaves found in the archetypical symbol of biblical Israel their identity as a community, a new chosen people bound for Divine deliverance from bondage. From this communal identity mutual support, meaning, and hope derived. In the ecstasy of religious performance individual and communal identity and values were dramatically reaffirmed time and time again. In the hand-clapping, footstomping, headshaking fervor of the plantation praisehouse, the slaves, in prayer, sermon, and song, fit Christianity to their own peculiar experience and in the process resisted, even transcended the dehumanizing bonds of slavery.

NO

John B. Boles

MASTERS & SLAVES IN THE HOUSE
OF THE LORD

Race and religion have probably always been controversial topics in the South, as elsewhere, particularly when their intersection has called into question widely accepted folkways about the place of blacks in southern society. Different interpreters have suggested that the South has been haunted by God and preoccupied with race, so perhaps we should not expect a scholarly consensus on how the two intertwined in the decades from the Great Awakening to Reconstruction. The last generation of our own times has witnessed a remarkable burst of scholarship on blacks and race relations in the region and a similar if not quite as prolific discovery of southern religious history. . . .

Most laypersons today seem completely unaware that a century and a half ago many churches in the Old South had significant numbers of black members: black and white co-worshipers heard the same sermons, were baptized and took communion together, and upon death were buried in the same cemeteries. Such practices seem inconceivable today, when the old cliché that Sunday morning at 11:00 A.M. is the most segregated hour in America still rings true. When I was a boy in the rural South thirty years ago, we all supported the Lottie Moon Christmas offering to send missionaries to convert the "heathen" in Africa and elsewhere, but the church deacons and the congregation would have been scandalized had one of the black converts traveled from Africa expecting to worship with us. Yet a century earlier biracial attendance at Baptist churches like ours was the norm in the rural South.

Blacks worshiped in a variety of ways, and some did not participate in any Christian worship, for, especially in the colonial period, a smattering of blacks practiced Islam and others clung tenaciously to traditional African religions. All non-Christian religious activity was discouraged by most slaveowners, who were as ethnocentric as they were concerned about the potential for unrest and rebellion they sensed in their slaves' participation in what to whites were strange and exotic rites. In addition, many slaveowners

John B. Boles, "Introduction," in John B. Boles, ed., *Masters & Slaves in the House of the Lord: Race and Religion in the American South, 1740-1870* (University Press of Kentucky, 1988). Copyright © 1988 by the University Press of Kentucky. Reprinted by permission of the publishers. Notes omitted.

in the seventeenth and eighteenth centuries were hesitant to attempt to convert their bondspeople to Christianity—if they themselves were Christians—out of fear that conversion might loosen the ties of their bondage. The English knew of slavery long before they had any New World settlements and had considered it a backward institution that might be promoted by Catholic Spain but not by the England of Elizabeth. Even so, the English believed that certain persons might be held in bondage—convicted felons, war prisoners, in some cases heathens, that is, nonbelievers in Christianity. It took several generations before Englishmen in the North American mainland colonies came to accept the practicality of African slavery, then argue the necessity of it, and finally surpass their Spanish rivals in its applications. To the extent that they needed any noneconomic justification, they assumed that the Africans not being Christians made it morally acceptable to enslave them. But if Africans' "heathenism" justified making them slaves, would not their conversion at the very least call into question the rightness of keeping them in bondage? On at least several occasions in the seventeenth century blacks had won their freedom in court by proving they had been baptized. Hence any moral uneasiness that might have existed among less-than-devout slaveowners for not sharing the gospel with their slaves was entirely overcome by their uneasiness about the stability of their work force should they do so. To clarify this ambiguity obliging laws were passed in the late seventeenth century specifying that a person's "civil state" would not be affected by his conversion to Christianity. . . .

Yet despite the difficulties inherent in converting the slaves—the whites' hesitancy to have their slaves hear Christian doctrines and no doubt a hesitancy on the part of some slaves to give up traditional beliefs, even if those beliefs had been attenuated by a long presence in the New World—in the middle decades of the eighteenth century increasing numbers of bondspeople became members of Christian churches. A dramatic shift was occurring in the history of black Americans, most of whom before 1750 had been outside the Christian church, for within a century the majority of slaves were worshiping in one fashion or another as Christians. After emancipation, freedpersons continued to find in their churches solace from the cares of the world and joy and a purpose for living in a society that continued to oppress black people. Everyone acknowledges the significance of the church in the black community after freedom; less understood is black worship during the antebellum era and earlier. Yet the half-century following 1740 was the critical period during which some whites broke down their fears and inhibitions about sharing their religion with the slaves in their midst, and some blacks—only a few at first—came to find in Christianity a system of ideas and symbols that was genuinely attractive. . . .

Several aspects of African traditional religion bore close enough parallels to Christianity that bondspeople who were initially disinterested in the white man's religion could—once they glimpsed another side to it—see sufficient common ground between the whites' Christianity and their own folk religions to merit closer examination. That willingness, that openness, on the part of blacks to the claims of Christianity was all the entrée white Christian evangelicals needed. Most West African religions assumed a tripartite hierarchy of deities—nature gods, ancestral gods, and an omnipotent creator god who was more remote though more powerful than the others. This conception was roughly transferable to the Christian idea of the trinity. West Africans understood that spirit possession was a sure sign of contact with the divine, an experience not totally dissimilar from the emotional fervor of evangelistic services. Before the mid-eighteenth century slaves had not come into contact with white evangelicals, who were also largely of the lower social order, who worshiped with emotional abandon, and who spoke movingly of being possessed by the Holy Spirit and knowing Jesus as their personal savior. But such evangelical Christians came increasingly to minister to slaves, and they would bridge the chasm between the races and introduce large and growing numbers of slaves to evangelical Christianity.

During the second quarter of the eighteenth century, Evangelicalism and Pietism swept across England and Europe, and the quickening of heartfelt religion soon leapfrogged to the New World in the person of George Whitefield. The resulting Great Awakening occurred primarily north of Maryland, but Whitefield's preaching and the example of his life gained disciples in South Carolina and Georgia. None of Whitefield's followers were more devout than members of the prominent Bryan family in Georgia, and . . . the two Bryan brothers sincerely believed Jesus' call for repentance was addressed to all persons, black and white, bond and free. Consequently, they undertook to promote Christianity among their own and neighboring slaves, but they did so in such a way as to support the institution of slavery. From today's perspective, their paternalistic efforts to-

ward the blacks under their control seem a truncated version of Christianity, but they did present the faith to the slaves in a way that was acceptable to the larger society. A subtle shift in rationales had occurred that would have a far-reaching influence on whites and blacks. At first it had been deemed appropriate to enslave Africans because they were considered heathens; by the mid-eighteenth century some Anglican clergy had begun to argue that it was appropriate to enslave Africans because they might thereby be converted to Christianity. In that sense this development foreshadowed an important tradition of elite white evangelism to blacks, and through such efforts then and in the future thousands of slaves came to know Christianity and, in various ways, to appropriate its message for their own ends.

Another development of the mid-eighteenth century was to be even more important for the growth of Christianity among the slaves than the limited Anglican awakening in the aftermath of Whitefield. In the quarter of a century following 1745 three evangelical Protestant groups planted their seeds in the colonial South—first the Presbyterians, then the Separate Baptists (later the term Separate was dropped as this species came almost completely to swallow all competing versions of believers in adult baptism), and finally the Methodists (first only a subset of the Church of England but after 1784 an independent denomination). These three churches grew at different rates and had different constituencies. The Presbyterians never experienced the extensive growth among rural southerners that the other two did but found increasing support from among those on the upper rungs of society, supplanting the erstwhile Anglican (the postrevolutionary

Episcopal) church in influence among the elite. Presbyterian church members, disproportionately wealthy, of course owned disproportionate numbers of slaves, and continuing the elite paternalism pioneered by the Anglican Bryans in colonial Georgia, they tended to minister to blacks by providing them special ministers and separate accommodations. A form of religious noblesse oblige motivated some of them to devise ways to bring the gospel message to their blacks, especially after abolitionists charged that southern whites neglected the spiritual well-being of their slaves. Moreover, the developing argument that slavery was a progressive institution designed by God to effect the Christianization of Africans gave slaveholders a moral obligation to consider the religious needs of their bondspeople. This sentiment, especially strong among Presbyterians and Episcopalians, produced the significant "mission to the slaves" movement of the late antebellum period. . . .

Although the Presbyterian church was to remain relatively small but influential beyond its numbers, the Baptists and Methodists experienced remarkable growth, especially after the Great Revival at the beginning of the nineteenth century. It would be inappropriate in this brief overview to rehearse the reasons for the success these two evangelical denominations had in the rural South; to an extraordinary degree they became the folk churches of the region. Certainly in their youthful decades, the 1750s through 1790s, when their appeal was even more emphatically to those whites who lived at the margins of society—poor, isolated, largely nonslaveholding—the Baptists and Methodists maintained a fairly consistent antislavery stance. Especially south of Maryland, both denominations recog-

nized the political explosiveness of such beliefs if preached incautiously. They tended to criticize slavery in the abstract, delineate its evils both to the slaves and even more to the whites, emphasize that slaves were persons with souls precious in the sight of God, and suggest that slavery be ended "insofar as practicable"—or words to that effect. This is not to argue that they were insincere or hypocritical. Rather, they understood the realities of the economic and social-control imperatives of the institution and occasionally stated explicitly that if they boldly attacked slavery, they would not be allowed to preach to the blacks, thereby—by their lights—causing the unfortunate bondspeople not to hear the gospel. It is easy from today's perspective, and probably incorrect, to see as self-serving such remarks as Methodist Francis Asbury's summation of his position in 1809: "Would not an *amelioration* in the condition and treatment of slaves have produced more practical good to the poor Africans, than any attempt at their *emancipation*? The state of society, unhappily, does not admit of this: besides, the blacks are deprived of the means of instruction; who will take the pains to lead them into the way of salvation, and watch over them that they may not stray, but the Methodists? . . . What is the personal liberty of the African which he may abuse, to the salvation of his soul; how may it be compared?"

The point is not the limited emancipationist impulse in the evangelical denominations and how it was thwarted over time by political and racial pressures. More appropriate here is the way the lower-class structure of the early Baptist and Methodist churches, most of whose members did not own slaves and felt estranged from the wealthier whites who did, enabled them to see blacks as potential fellow believers in a way that white worshipers in more elite churches seldom could. From the moment of their organization, typical Baptist or Methodist churches included black members, who often signed (or put their "X") on the founding documents of incorporation. Black membership in these two popular denominations was substantial from the last quarter of the eighteenth century through the Civil War. Without claiming too much or failing to recognize the multitude of ways slaves were not accorded genuine equality in these biracial churches, it is still fair to say that nowhere else in southern society were they treated so nearly as equals.

Because church membership statistics for the antebellum period are incomplete, and because churches varied in their definitions of membership, a quantitatively precise portrait of the extent to which blacks and white worshiped together is impossible to obtain. Historian John Blassingame has written that "an overwhelming majority of the slaves throughout the antebellum period attended church with their masters. Then, after the regular services ended, the ministers held special services for the slaves." Such special services were more typical of Episcopal and Presbyterian churches; Methodist and Baptist preachers would usually, sometimes toward the end of the service, call for something like "a special word for our black brothers and sisters" and then turn to them in the back pews or in the balcony and address them with a didactic sermon that often stressed obedience to their earthly masters. Sarah Fitzpatrick, a ninety-year-old former slave interviewed in 1983, recalled that "us 'Niggers' had our meetin' in de white fo'ks Baptist Church in de town o' Tuskegee. Dere's a place up in de loft dere now dat dey built fer de 'Nigger' slaves to 'tend church wid de white fo'ks. White preacher he preach to de white fo'ks an' when he git thu' wid dem he preach some to de 'Niggers.' Tell'em to mind dere Marster an' b'have deyself an' dey'll go to Hebben when dey die."

Slaves saw through these words and felt contempt for the self-serving attention they received. More important to them was the remainder of the service that they heard and participated in with the rest of the congregation. Here the slaves heard a more complete version of the gospel, and despite whatever social-control uses some ministers tried to put religion to in a portion of the Sunday service, most slaves found grounds for hope and a degree of spiritual liberation through their participation in these biracial churches. As Blassingame concluded, "Generally the ministers tried to expose the slaves to the major tenets of Christianity. . . . [And] only 15 percent of the Georgia slaves who had heard antebellum whites preach recalled admonitions to obedience."

Slaves worshiped apart from whites on some occasions, often with the knowledge of their owners and often without the white supervision the law called for. Some black churches were adjuncts to white churches, and completely independent and autonomous black churches existed in southern cities. Blacks worshiped privately and often secretly in their cabins and in the fields. Sometimes, and especially when their owner was irreligious, slaves had to slip away to hidden "brush arbors" deep in the woods to preach, shout, sing, and worship. But such practices should not lead us to forget that the normative worship experience of blacks in the antebellum South was in a biracial church. "Including black Sunday School scholars and catechumens," Blassingame writes, "there were probably 1,000,000 slaves under the regular tutelage of Southern churches in 1860." When David T. Bailey examined some 40 autobiographies of blacks and 637 interviews of slaves on the subject of religion, he discovered that 32 percent of the autobiographers who mentioned religion reported that they had gone to white churches, 14 percent said their master led the services for them, and another 14 percent attended worship services at special plantation chapels, whereas 36 percent mentioned that they had attended black prayer meetings. Of the former slaves interviewed, 43.5 percent mentioned attending white churches, 6.5 percent reported master-led services, 6.5 percent described plantation chapels, and only 24 percent discussed attendance at black prayer meetings.

Such substantial black participation in churches normally considered white indicates that white evangelicals, even in the late antebellum period, when they had moved up the social scale, joined the establishment, and come to support the institution of slavery, still felt a Christian responsibility to include slaves in the outreach of the church. Their idea of mission assumed that slaves were persons with souls precious in God's sight. In fact, many white evangelicals came to believe that part of their responsibility to God involved Christianizing the slave work force. It was to that end, they reasoned, that God had sanctioned slavery. . . . [A]bolitionist charges that the southern church ignored the slaves infuriated southern clergymen and caused them to redouble their efforts to bring slaves into the church. During the Civil War clergy feared that God was chastis-

ing the region for not sufficiently supporting the mission effort to the blacks, and religiously inspired attempts to amend slavery by correcting the worst abuses, teaching bondspeople to read (so the Scriptures would be accessible to them), and providing missionaries for them . . . almost reformed slavery out of existence in Confederate Georgia.

Devout white clergy often took seriously their responsibilities toward the blacks in their midst, and their paternalistic and racist assumptions should not blind us to their convictions that slaves too were God's children and that white slaveowners stood under God's judgment for the way they treated their bondspeople. It is difficult to understand today how devout whites could define blacks legally as chattel and yet show real concern for the state of their souls. Could genuine Christians so compartmentalize their charity? Apparently so, given their assumptions that blacks were a race of permanent children. A misguided sense of Christian responsibility led well-meaning, decent whites to justify slavery as the white man's duty to Africans, for it was, they argued, through the order and discipline bondage provided that slaves learned—sampled?—Christianity and Western civilization. Almost like whistling in the dark to drive away one's fears, white churchmen sometimes were particularly anxious to Christianize their slaves as though only thus could the institution be justified and their guilt be lessened.

Blacks too must have derived a substantial reward from their participation in the institutional churches or they would not have been involved with them to such an extent for so long. The manuscript records of hundreds of local Baptist churches across the South allow us to see a seldom-studied aspect of white-black interaction that helps explain the attraction biracial churches held for slaves. First, . . . blacks were accorded a semblance of equality when they joined antebellum Baptist churches. White members often addressed them as brother or sister, just as they did fellow white members. This equality in the terms of address may seem insignificant today, but in an age when only whites were accorded the titles of Mr. and Mrs., and it was taboo for a white to so address a black, any form of address that smacked of equality was notable. Behind it lay the familial idea, accepted by whites in principle if not always in practice, that in the sight of God all were equal and were members of His spiritual family. Incoming or outgoing members of Baptist churches were accepted or dismissed with "letters" attesting to their good standing, and slaves asking to join Baptist churches were expected to "bring their letter" just as prospective white members were. Churches seem to have routinely supplied such letters to their members of both races who moved to other locations. New members, black and white, were usually given the "right hand of fellowship" after their letters were accepted or after they came to the altar following the minister's sermon-ending call for conversion to "confess their sins and accept Christ's mercy." Individual churches often varied in this practice, as in much else in the South, where strict uniformity in anything was the exception.

Blacks usually sat in a separate section of the church, perhaps a balcony or a lean-to. There is evidence, however, that slaves sat scattered throughout Anglican churches in colonial Virginia and that sometimes they sat with or next to the pew of their master. Today, such segregated seating would seem to contradict the idea of spiritual equality, but the contradiction probably did not seem so stark to slaves, who were excluded from most other white-dominated functions. The white women often sat apart from the white men, too; in that age segregation by gender was almost as common as that by race, and the familiarity of such separation might well have lessened the negative connotation although it accentuated each subgroup's sense of separate identity. That is, the sense of both a separate women's culture and a separate black culture might have been inadvertently strengthened by the prevalent mode of segregated seating under a common roof. In fact, for some blacks who were isolated on farms and small plantations with no or only a few fellow slaves, the gathering together on Sunday at the church house with slaves from other farms may have been the primary occasion for experiencing a sense of black community. For such slaves the forced segregation in seating may have seemed both natural and desirable because they hungered for close interaction with persons of their own kind. The interaction may have been a stronger attraction than the worship itself. No doubt many bondspeople found their marriage partners through such social involvement at church—certainly much white courtship began there. Perhaps, then, for slaves dispersed on farms outside the plantation district, the slave community was largely created and vitalized in the one arena in which slaves belonging to different owners could freely mingle—the biracial church service.

As with church membership practices, there was an important but limited degree of equality in slaves' participation in antebellum church discipline. . . . [C]ertainly no one would want to argue that whites completely forgot or transcended the racial mores of a slave society in the confines of the church building, but it is significant that slaves were allowed to give testimony—sometimes even conflicting with white testimony—and that on occasion their witness overruled the charges of whites. This occurred in a society that did not allow blacks to testify against whites in civil courts. Moreover, blacks were not disciplined out of proportion to their numbers; on the whole, they were charged with infractions similar to those of whites; and they were held to the same moral expectations as whites with regard to profanity, drunkenness, lying, adultery, failure to attend church, and fighting. There surely were charges against blacks that had no parallel for whites—for example, blacks alone were charged with running away. But nowhere else in southern society were slaves and whites brought together in an arena where both were held responsible to a code of behavior sanctioned by a source outside the society—the Bible. The Scriptures were interpreted in culturally sanctioned ways, but whites as well as blacks were occasionally found wanting.

Blacks discovered in the church and in church discipline a unique sphere wherein to nurture (and be recognized by whites to have) moral responsibility and what Timothy L. Smith has called "moral earnestness." Through the church slaves found a meaning for their lives that could give a touch of moral grandeur to the tragic dimension of their bondage. Images of the children of Israel and the suffering servant provided ways to accept their life predicament without feelings of self-worthlessness. The church offered a spark of joy in the midst of pain, a promise of life-affirming forgive-ness to soften the hopelessness of unremitting bondage, an ultimate reward in heaven for unrewarded service in this world. Participation in the biracial churches was one of the ways slaves found moral and psychological strength to survive their bondage.

It is important to remember that social interaction does not necessarily imply social equality; in a variety of contexts outside the churches slaves and masters mingled closely without narrowing the gap between freedom and bondage. In many ways such interaction could even magnify the sense of enslavement. Yet it would be a mistake so to emphasize the belittling possibilities of white-black interaction that we fail to see the alternative possibilities inherent in the biracial churches. Slaves apparently had their image of being creatures of God strengthened by the sermons they heard—even when that was not the intention of the ministers—and the discipline they accepted. Their evident pleasure in occasionally hearing black preachers speak to biracial congregations no doubt augmented their sense of racial pride. Taking communion together with whites, serving as deacons or Sunday school teachers, being baptized or confirmed in the same ceremonies, even contributing their mite to the temporal upkeep of the church, could surely have been seen as symbolic ways of emphasizing their self-respect and equality before God. Slaves certainly were not dependent on white-controlled institutions to nurture their sense of self-worth, but neither were they adverse to seizing opportunities wherever they found them and using them for that purpose. In a society that offered few opportunities for blacks to practice organizational and leadership skills or hear themselves addressed and see themselves evaluated morally on an equal basis with whites, small matters could have large meanings. Blacks did not discover in the biracial churches an equality of treatment that spiritually transported them out of bondage, but they found in them a theology of hope and a recognition of self-worth that fared them well in their struggle to endure slavery.

As Robert L. Hall documents in his analysis of religion in antebellum Florida, blacks worshiped in a variety of ways in the antebellum South besides in biracial Protestant churches. In most southern cities and large towns there were completely independent black churches, with black ministers, black deacons or elders, and a panoply of self-help associations connected to and supported by the church. Usually such churches, like the St. James African Episcopal Church in Baltimore, were under the control of free blacks, although many if not most of the members were slaves. Although the surrounding white-dominated churches tended to ignore societal ills, emphasize conversion, and minister primarily to individuals, the black churches tended to minister to all the social and religious needs of their parishioners. There was a communal and social thrust in the independent black churches that was notably absent from the mainstream white churches of the South. (That difference even today sets many black churches apart from white.) Often the black churches had very large memberships, and sometimes their meeting places had the largest seating capacity in the city.

Blacks also worshiped in black churches that were adjunct to white churches. Such situations typically arose after the biracial church built a new sanctuary and, with the black members perhaps outnumbering the white, the blacks were allowed ("allowed" seems more accurate than "forced") to conduct separate services in the old structure. The motivation of the whites here is not clear; they often indicated that the blacks preferred their own services, but to what extent whites desired segregated white churches for essentially racist reasons is impossible to determine. In most cases when blacks were split off into separate "African" churches, as they were known, a committee of whites was assigned to oversee their services. The supervision seems to have been honored more in the breach, however. In a variety of other ways black church members were often given some autonomy in regulating portions of their worship life, again apparently more because the blacks desired such separation than because whites required it. These small islands of black autonomy within the biracial church were perhaps the beginning of the complete racial separation that would come after the Civil War.

Not all the organized churches in the South were Protestant, although Protestantism was far more dominant in the South than elsewhere in the nation. There were pockets of Catholic strength in Maryland, Kentucky, and Missouri, and in south Louisiana Catholicism was preponderant. Most southern cities had at least one Catholic church, usually attended primarily by immigrant workers. Louisiana and Maryland had rural Catholic churches as well, with numbers of black Catholic parishioners. Catholic masters sometimes required that their slaves worship as Catholics, though their bondspeople may have preferred the neighboring Baptist or Methodist churches either as a subtle form of rebellion against their masters or because of the appeal of the demonstrative emotionalism of the evangelical churches. In various ways the Catholic church ministered to bondspeople; separate black orders and sisterhoods were established and the sacraments extended. Because it was a minority church in a rabidly Protestant region and was concerned not to attract notoriety, the Catholic church never questioned the morality of slavery. An occasional Catholic institution or order might own slaves, as did the Jesuits in Maryland, though this property in humans was divested for reasons of ethics and economics. . . .

In addition to the various kinds of formal churches—biracial, adjunct, and independent black churches and plantation chapels—to which slaves had access, black worshipers also gathered in more informal, often secret settings. The evidence for this is to be found in black memoirs and slave narratives, although even these sources suggest that most blacks worshiped in one or another of the formal churches. There are many reasons why slaves would choose to worship in a manner less subject to white supervision or control. Some masters sought to prevent slaves from worshiping at all, which forced slaves to develop an underground religion and to meet secretly either in their cabins at night or in the brush arbors. Slaves who were allowed (or required) to attend a biracial church (or any formal service carefully monitored by whites) in which the minister placed too much emphasis on the "slaves-obey-your-master" homily and thereby neglected to preach the gospel in its fullness often sought an alternative worship experience. There must have been other times when slaves felt inhibited in the presence of whites and simply desired a time and a place to preach, sing, and shout without having to suffer the condescending glances of less emo-

tionally involved white churchgoers. Although slaves worshiping apart and secretively may have developed a distinctly black Christianity significantly different from that which they heard in the more formal institutions, there is no unambiguous evidence that they did so. More probably the services in the brush arbors were simply a longer, more emotionally demonstrative version of those in the biracial churches, with more congregational participation. No precise record exists of the theology implicit in such brush arbor meetings or of special emphases that might have developed, but the similarity in worship practice and ecclesiology of the autonomous black churches that emerged after the Civil War to the earlier biracial churches argues against the evolution of any fundamentally different system in the brush arbors.

A momentous change in the nature of church practice in the South took place at the beginning of Reconstruction. Blacks in significant numbers—eventually all of them—began to move out of the biracial churches and join a variety of independent black denominations. As Katharine Dvorak notes in her insightful essay, the blacks left on their own volition; they were not forced out. At first many white churchmen tried to persuade them to stay, but within several decades the degenerating racial climate of the region led these same churchmen on occasion to applaud the new segregated patterns of worship, so different from the common practice before the Civil War.

Of course, that freedpersons wanted to leave the biracial churches is a commentary on the less-than-complete equality they had enjoyed in them. Blacks had a strong sense of racial identity, reinforced by their having been slaves and, within the confines of the churches, by their segregated seating. The complete sermons they had heard for years, not just the self-serving words the white ministers directed specifically at them, had engendered in blacks a sense of their moral worth and equality in the sight of God. The biracial churches simultaneously nurtured this sense of moral equality and thwarted it by their conformity to the demands of the slave society. Black participation in the biracial churches—as preachers, deacons, stewards, and Sunday school teachers—had given them practical leadership and administrative experience, as had their islands of autonomy within the demographically biracial churches. Theologically and experientially blacks were ready to seize the moment offered by emancipation to withdraw from their old allegiances and create autonomous denominations. No better evidence of the freedom slaves had not enjoyed in the biracial churches exists than the rapidity with which blacks sought to establish separate denominations after the Civil War. And no better evidence exists of the extent to which slaves in the biracial churches accepted evangelical Christianity as their preferred expression of religious faith and molded their lives to its demands than the denominations they created after emancipation.

The worship services and institutional arrangements in the new black churches bore a very close resemblance to the biracial churches from which the blacks withdrew. In fact, black Baptist and Methodist services were closer to the early nineteenth-century post–Great Revival services of the evangelical churches than those of the postbellum all-white churches. Blacks had assimilated the theology and order of service in the biracial churches. Rejecting the modernizing tendencies of the white churches toward less emotion, shorter sermons, an emphasis on choir singing rather than congregational singing, and seminary-trained ministers, they more truly carried on the pioneer evangelical traditions. It should not have been surprising to anyone that when born-again Baptist presidential candidate Jimmy Carter wanted to appeal to blacks in 1976, he spoke to them in their churches. Despite the differences—black services are longer, the music is more expressive, emotions are more freely expressed, there is greater congregational participation—the kinship between the white and black Baptist churches of today is readily apparent, and it points back to a time more than a century ago when the religious culture of the South was fundamentally biracial.

POSTSCRIPT

Did Slaves Exercise Religious Autonomy?

One of the most intriguing issues for students of American slavery is the relationship between religion and resistance. Specifically, did slaves find in Christianity moderation that conditioned them to seek salvation only in God's heavenly kingdom, or did it steel their resolve to seek deliverance from their bondage in the earthly realm? To what extent is Karl Marx's dictum that religion is an "opiate of the masses" applicable to the slave experience?

Actually, there was a certain dualism evident in the slave's religious life. Some obviously were pacified by a fatalistic attitude that slavery was their permanent status, yet hopeful that salvation would be achieved in the heavenly afterlife. Slave owners, of course, attempted to ensure their bond servants' loyalty and passivity by reminding them of Paul's injunction to Philemon, the runaway servant, to return to his master. For their own part, slaves much preferred to hear Bible readings related to Moses' deliverance of the Israelites from Egypt. It should be remembered that Gabriel Prosser, Denmark Vesey, and Nat Turner all employed religious symbolism to foster their revolutionary conspiracies.

The nature of slave religion is an important topic in virtually every scholarly treatment of the institution of slavery. Albert Raboteau's conclusions are presented more fully in *Slave Religion: The "Invisible Institution" in the Antebellum South* (Oxford, 1978). John Boles's description of the "biracial church" was inspired in part by Kenneth Bailey's seminal article "Protestantism and Afro-Americans in the Old South: Another Look," *Journal of Southern History* (November 1975). Eugene D. Genovese, in *Roll, Jordan, Roll: The World the Slaves Made* (Pantheon, 1974), argues that the religion developed in the slave quarters represented a synthesis of African traditions and

Protestant Christianity, which fused Moses' promise of deliverance in this world with Jesus' promise of personal redemption. For the "dualism" of slave religion discussed above, see Vincent Harding, "Religion and Resistance Among Antebellum Negroes, 1800–1860," in August Meier and Elliott Rudwick, eds., *The Making of Black America: Volume I* (Atheneum, 1969). Lawrence Levine, *Black Culture and Black Consciousness* (Oxford, 1977), explores the latent and symbolic elements of protest contained in slave songs.

PART 4

Conflict and Resolution

The changing nature of the American nation and the demands of its own principles finally erupted into violent conflict. Perhaps it was an inevitable step in the process of building a coherent nation from a number of distinct and diverse groups. The leaders, attitudes, and resources that were available to the North and the South were to determine the course of the war itself, as well as the national healing process that followed.

Were the Abolitionists "Unrestrained Fanatics"?

Was the Antebellum South a Unique Section in American History?

Was Abraham Lincoln America's Greatest President?

Reconstruction: Could It Have Given Blacks Full Equality?

ISSUE 14

Were the Abolitionists "Unrestrained Fanatics"?

YES: Avery Craven, from *The Coming of the Civil War*, 2d ed. (University of Chicago Press, 1957)

NO: Irving H. Bartlett, from "The Persistence of Wendell Phillips," in Martin Duberman, ed., *The Antislavery Vanguard: New Essays on the Abolitionists* (Princeton University Press, 1965)

ISSUE SUMMARY

YES: Professor of history Avery Craven believes that the fanaticism of the abolitionist crusade created an atmosphere of crisis that resulted in the outbreak of the Civil War.

NO: Professor of American studies Irving H. Bartlett differentiates between agitation and fanaticism and claims that abolitionists like Wendell Phillips were deeply committed to improving the quality of life for all Americans, including those blacks held as slaves.

Opposition to slavery in the American colonies dates back to the seventeenth and eighteenth centuries, when Puritan leaders, like Samuel Sewall, and Quakers, such as John Woolman and Anthony Benezet, published a number of pamphlets condemning the existence of the slave system. The connection between religion and antislavery sentiment also is evident in the decision of the Society of Friends in 1688 to prohibit members from owning bond servants because slavery was contrary to Christian principles. These attacks, however, did little to diminish the institution. In fact, efforts to force emancipation gained little headway in the colonies until the outbreak of the American Revolution. Complaints that the English government had instituted a series of measures that "enslaved" the colonies in British North America also raised thorny questions about the presence of *real* slavery in those colonies. How could Americans demand their freedom from King George III, who was cast in the role of oppressive master, and at the same time deny freedom and liberty to black bondsmen in their midst? Such a contradiction inspired a gradual emancipation movement in the North, which often was accompanied by compensation for the former owners.

In addition, antislavery societies sprang up throughout the nation to continue the crusade against bondage. Interestingly, the majority were located in the South. Prior to the 1830s, the most prominent antislavery organization was the American Colonization Society, which offered a twofold program: (1) gradual, compensated emancipation of slaves, and (2) exportation of the newly freed former slaves to colonies outside the boundaries of the United States, especially to Africa.

In the 1830s, antislavery activity underwent an important transformation. As the colonizationists proved unable to eliminate either slavery or African Americans from the country, a new strain of antislavery sentiment expressed itself in the abolitionist movement. Drawing momentum from both the Second Great Awakening and the example set by England (which prohibited slavery in its imperial holdings in 1833), abolitionists called for an immediate end of slavery without compensation to masters for the loss of their property. Abolitionists viewed slavery not so much as a practical problem to be resolved but rather as a moral offense incapable of being resolved through traditional channels of political compromise. In January 1831, William Lloyd Garrison, who came to symbolize the abolitionist crusade, published the first issue of *The Liberator*, a newspaper dedicated to the immediate end to slavery. In his first editorial, Garrison expressed the self-righteous indignation of many in the abolitionist movement when he warned slaveholders and their supporters to "urge me not to use moderation in a cause like the present. I am in earnest—I will not equivocate—I will not excuse—I will not retreat a single inch—AND I WILL BE HEARD."

Unfortunately for Garrison, relatively few Americans were inclined to respond positively to his call. His newspaper generated little interest outside Boston, New York, Philadelphia, and other major urban centers of the North. This situation, however, changed within a matter of months. In August 1831, a slave preacher named Nat Turner led a rebellion of slaves in Southampton County, Virginia, resulting in the death of some 60 whites. Although the revolt was quickly suppressed and Turner and his supporters (along with many slaves not involved in the uprising) were executed, the incident spread fear throughout the South. Governor John B. Floyd of Virginia turned an accusatory finger toward the abolitionists when he concluded that the Turner revolt was "undoubtedly designed and matured by unrestrained fanatics in some of the neighboring states." The message was clear: Garrison and other abolitionist "fanatics" were responsible for generating discontent among slaves and attempting to undermine traditional Southern institutions. Moreover, it would be charged, these radicals contributed to a crisis environment that degenerated over the next generation and ultimately produced civil war.

Avery Craven accepts this view that abolitionist fanaticism led to political deterioration in the United States, which culminated in secession and war. He blames abolitionists for inciting volatile emotions by characterizing slaveholders as sinful aristocrats willing to distort the American dream of freedom to preserve their institution. Irving H. Bartlett, in contrast, surveys the abolitionist career of Wendell Phillips and concludes that he was not a fanatic but rather a practical agitator, an intellectual, and a committed philosopher of reform who clearly understood the difference between agitation and demagoguery.

YES

Avery Craven

THE NORTHERN ATTACK ON SLAVERY

The abolition movement . . . was part of the drive to unseat aristocrats and re-establish American democracy according to the Declaration of Independence. It was a clear-cut effort to apply Christianity to the American social order.

The anti-slavery effort was at first merely one among many. It rose to dominance only gradually. Fortunate from the beginning in leadership, it was always more fortunate in appeal. Human slavery more obviously violated democratic institutions than any other evil of the day; it was close enough to irritate and to inflame sensitive minds, yet far enough removed that reformers need have few personal relations with those whose interests were affected. It rasped most severely upon the moral senses of a people whose ideas of sin were comprehended largely in terms of self-indulgence and whose religious doctrines laid emphasis on social usefulness as the proper manifestation of salvation. And, what was more important, slavery was now confined to a section whose economic interests, and hence political attitudes, conflicted sharply with those of the Northeast and upper Northwest.

Almost from the beginning of the new anti-slavery movement, two distinct centers of action appeared, each with its distinct and individual approach to the problem. One developed in the industrial areas of New England. Its most important spokesman was William Lloyd Garrison, founder and editor of a Boston abolition paper called the *Liberator*. Garrison at first accepted the old idea that slavery was an *evil* to be pointed out and gradually eradicated by those among whom it existed, but he shifted his position in the early 1830's and denounced slavery as a damning crime to be unremittingly assailed and immediately destroyed. The first issue of his paper announced a program from which he never deviated: " . . . *I do not wish to think or speak or write with moderation. I will not retreat a single inch, and I will be heard.*" The problem, as Garrison saw it, was one of abstract right and wrong. The Scriptures and the Declaration of Independence had already settled the issue. Slavery could have no legal status in a Christian democracy. If the Constitution recognized

From Avery Craven, *The Coming of the Civil War* (University of Chicago Press, 1957). Copyright © 1957 by Avery Craven. Reprinted by permission of the University of Chicago Press.

it, then the Constitution should be destroyed. Slaveholders were both sinners and criminals. They could lay no claim to immunity from any mode of attack. . . .

The extreme and impractical nature of the Garrison anti-slavery drive served to attract attention and arouse antagonism rather than to solve the problem. It did, however, show how profoundly the conditions of the time had stirred the reform spirit and how wide the door had been opened to the professional reformers—men to whom the question was not so much "how shall we abolish slavery, as how shall we best discharge our duty . . . to ourselves." Garrison may be taken as typical of the group. His temperament and experiences had combined to set him in most relationships against the accepted order of things. His life would probably have been spent in protesting even if slavery had never existed. From childhood he had waged a bitter fight *against* obstacles and *for* a due recognition of his abilities. A drunken father had abandoned the family to extreme poverty before William was three years old, and the boy, denied all but the rudiments of an education, had first been placed under the care of Deacon Bartlett, and then apprenticed for seven years to one Ephraim Allen to learn the printing trade. His first venture after his apprenticeship was over failed. His second gave him the opportunity to strike back at an unfair world. He became an editor of the *National Philanthropist,* a paper devoted to the suppression of "intemperance and its Kindred vices." This publication served also as a medium through which to attack lotteries, Sabbath-breaking, and war. A new Garrison began to emerge. His personality, given opportunity for expression, asserted itself. . . .

Anti-slavery efforts entered the Garrison program when Benjamin Lundy, the pioneer abolitionist, invited him to help edit the *Genius of Universal Emancipation* in Baltimore. Hostile treatment there, climaxed by imprisonment for libel, together with the influence of extreme British opinion, changed a moderate attitude which admitted "that immediate and complete emancipation is not desirable . . . no rational man cherishes so wild a vision," into the extreme and uncompromising fanaticism expressed only two years later in the *Liberator.* From that time on Garrison was bothered only by the fact that the English language was inadequate for the expression of his violent opinions. Southerners in Congress were desperados.

> We would sooner trust the honor of the country . . . in the hands of the inmates of our penitentiaries and prisons than in their hands . . . they are the meanest of thieves and the worst of robbers. . . . We do not acknowledge them to be within the pale of Christianity, or republicanism, or humanity!

Hatred of the South had supplanted love for the Negro!

In such an approach as this, there could be no delay, no moderation. Right was right, and wrong was wrong. The Slaveholder could not be spared or given time to learn the evil of his ways. Action immediate and untempered was demanded. . . .

The second center of anti-slavery effort was in upper New York and the farther Northwest. Influences from this center included in their sweep, however, much of rural New England and the Middle States and the movement found liberal financial help in New York City. Benjamin Lundy and other Quaker leaders started the crusade, but it did not come to full and wide expression until Theodore Weld, already the ablest temperance orator in the Northwest, set about cultivating the great field prepared for social reform by the Finney revivals.

Weld was, like Garrison, unusual both in abilities and in personal characteristics. He was much given to "anti-meat, -butter, -tea, and -coffee, etc. -ism[s]." He indulged in excessive self-effacement and in extravagant confessions of selfishness, pride, impatience of contradiction, personal recklessness, and "a bad, unlovely temper." . . .

He wrote also of his contempt of opponents—"one of the *trade* winds of my nature [which] very often · . . *blows a hurricane,*" and he listed by name those "who strangely and stupidly idolize me . . . and yield themselves to my sway in all confidence and love." He boasted of his daring and told of how as a child a tremendous thunderstorm would send him whooping and hallooing through the fields like a wild Indian. He had the Puritan's love of enduring; the saint's "right" to intolerance. He was, in fact, always a revivalist—a man with a mission to perform in the great West—"the battlefield of the World."

The campaign which he launched was but an expansion of the benevolence crusade already a part of the Western revival effort. As W. C. Preston said: "Weld's agents made the anti-slavery cause 'identical with religion,' and urged men, by all they esteem[ed] holy, by all the high and exciting obligations of duty to man and God . . . to join the pious work of purging the sin of slavery from the land." The movement, as it developed, was generally temperate in tone, and tended to function through the existing agencies of religion and politics. Lane Theological Seminary, founded in Cincinnati to train leaders in the Finney tradition, became the center from which Weld worked. Here, in a series of debates, he shaped the doctrine of gradual immediatism which by insisting that *gradual emancipation* begin *at once,* saved the movement from Garrison's extremes; from here he went out to win a group of converts which included James G. Birney, Joshua Giddings, Edwin M. Stanton, Elizur Wright, and Beriah Green; and here he adapted the revival technique to the abolition crusade and prepared the way for his loyal band of Seventy to carry that crusade throughout the whole Northwest.

There was, however, another aspect to the movement in this region—a very hard-headed practical aspect. Its leaders believed in action as well as agitation. And action here meant political action. Western men had a way of viewing evil as something there ought to be a law against. They thought it was the business of government to secure morality as well as prosperity. They were even inclined to regard the absence of prosperity as the result of the existence of evil. Naturally, therefore, in spite of the revival-meeting procedure used to spread the gospel of abolition, action against slavery followed political precedent. This action began with petitions to Congress for such a practical end as the abolition of slavery in the District of Columbia. When Southern resentment of such a measure brought the adoption of gag rule methods, the contest was broadened into a fight on the floors of Congress for the constitutional rights of petition and free speech. This proved to be an excellent way to keep the slavery question before the public and to force slaveholders to reveal their undemocratic attitudes. Petitions arrived in such quantities as to clog the work of Congress. A Washington organization for agitation and lobbying became necessary. Weld himself went to Washington to advise with John Quincy Adams and his fellow workers. Slavery thus again entered national politics, this time by way of the Northwest. Anti-slavery politicians, such as Joshua Giddings and Salmon P. Chase of Ohio, quickly proved the value of the cause as a stepping-stone to public office. . . .

With the new growth and importance of the movement, the technique of its propaganda also reached new efficiency. Never before or since has a cause been urged upon the American people with such consummate skill and such lasting effects. Every agency possible in that day was brought into use; even now the predominating opinions of most of the American people regarding the antebellum South and its ways are the product of that campaign of education.

Indoctrination began with the child's A B C's which were learned from booklets containing verses like the following:

A is an Abolitionist
A man who wants to free
The wretched slave, and give to all
An equal liberty.
B is a Brother with a skin
Of somewhat darker hue,
But in our Heavenly Father's sight,
He is as dear as you.
C is the Cotton field, to which
This injured brother's driven,
When, as the white man's *slave*, he toils
From early morn till even.
D is the Driver, cold and stern,
Who follows, whip in hand,
To punish those who dare to rest,
Or disobey command.
· · ·
I is the Infant, from the arms

Of its fond mother torn,
And at a public auction sold
With horses, cows, and corn.
· · ·
Q is the Quarter, where the slave
On coarsest food is fed
And where, with toil and sorrow worn
He seeks his wretched bed.
· · ·
W is the Whipping post,
To which the slave is bound,
While on his naked back, the lash
Makes many a bleeding wound.
· · ·
Z is a Zealous man, sincere,
Faithful, and just, and true;
An earnest pleader for the slave—
Will you not be so too?

For children able to read, a wider variety of literature was written. One volume in verse urged "little children" to "plead with men, that they buy not slaves again." . . .

Juvenile story books, with some parts written in verse and printed in large and bold type and the rest written in prose and set in smaller type, were issued with the explanation that the verses were adapted to the capacity of the youngest reader, while the prose was well suited for being read aloud in the family circle. "It is presumed," said the preface, "that [with the prose] our younger friends will claim the assistance of their older brothers and sisters, or appeal to the ready aid of their mamma." Such volumes might contain pictures and stories from *Uncle Tom's Cabin* or they might consist of equally appealing tales of slave children cruelly torn from their parents or tortured by ingenious methods.

For adults the appeal was widened. No approach was neglected. Hymn books offered abolition songs set to familiar tunes. To the strains of "Old Hundred" eager voices invited "ye Yeomen brave" to rescue "the bleeding slave," or, to the "Missionary Hymn," asked them to consider

The frantic mother
Lamenting for her child,
Till falling lashes smother
Her cries of anguish wild!

Almanacs, carrying the usual information about weather and crops, filled their other pages with abolition propaganda. In one of these, readers found the story of Liburn Lewis, who, for a trifling offense, bound his slave, George, to a meat block and then, while all the other slaves looked on, proceeded slowly to chop him to pieces with a broad ax, and to cast the parts into a fire. Local, state, and national societies were organized for more efficient action in petitioning, presenting public speakers, distributing tracts, and publishing anti-slavery periodicals. The American Anti-Slavery Society "in the year 1837-38, published 7,877 bound volumes, 47,256 tracts and pamphlets, 4,100 circulars, and 10,490 prints. Its quarterly *Anti-Slavery Magazine* had an annual circulation of 9,000; the *Slave Friend*, for children, had 131,050; the monthly *Human Rights*, 189,400, and the weekly *Emancipator*, 217,000." From 1854 to 1858 it spent $3281 on a series of tracts discussing every phase of slavery, under such suggestive titles as "Disunion, our Wisdom and our Duty," "Relations of Anti-Slavery to Religion," and "To Mothers in the Free States." Its "several corps of lecturers of the highest ability and worth . . . occupied the field" every year in different states. Its Annual Reports, with their stories of atrocities and their biased discussion of issues, constituted a veritable arsenal from which weapons of attack could be drawn. Like

other anti-slavery societies, it maintained an official organ, issued weekly, and held its regular conventions for the generation of greater force.

Where argument and appeal to reason failed, the abolitionists tried entertainment and appeal to emotion. *Uncle Tom's Cabin* was written because its author, "as a woman, as a mother," was "oppressed and broken hearted, with the sorrows & injustice" seen, and "because as a Christian" she "felt the dishonor to Christianity—because as a lover of [her] country, [she] trembled at the coming day of wrath." It became a best seller in the most complete sense. Only the Bible exceeded it in numbers sold and in the thoroughness with which it was read in England and America. Editions were adapted to every pocketbook, and translations carried it throughout the world. Dramatized and put on the stage, it did more to make the theatre respectable in rural America than any other single influence. The fictitious Uncle Tom became the stereotype of all American Negro slaves; Simon Legree became the typical slaveholder. A generation and more formed its ideas of Southern life and labor from the pages of this novel. A romantic South, of planter-gentlemen and poor whites, of chivalry and dissipation, of "sweet but worthless" women, was given an imaginative reality so wide and so gripping that no amount of patient research and sane history writing could alter it. Other novels, such as *Our World: or the Slaveholder's Daughter*, built their plots about the love affairs of Southern planters with their Negro slaves. Jealousies between wives and mistresses, struggles between brothers for the possession of some particularly desirable wench, or the inner conflict of a master over his obligation to his mulatto bastards, constituted the main appeal in such works. The object was always the same: to reveal the licentious character of Southern men, the unhappy status of Southern homes, and the horrible violation of Negro chastity everywhere existing under slavery.

Reformed slaveholders and escaped slaves were especially valuable in the crusade. Under the warming influence of sympathetic audiences their stories of cruelty and depravity grew apace. Persecution and contempt from old friends increased their zeal. Birney, the Grimké sisters, Frederick Douglass, and many others influenced the movement and were influenced by it in a way comparable only to the relation of reformed drunkards to the temperance cause.

By means of such agencies and methods a well-defined picture of the South and slavery became slowly fixed in Northern minds. The Southern people were divided into two distinct classes—slaveholders and poor whites. The former constituted an aristocracy, living in great white-pillared houses on extended plantations. The latter, ignorant and impotent, made up a rural slum which clung hopelessly to the pine barrens or the worn-out acres on the fringes of the plantations. Planters, who lived by the theft of Negro labor, completely dominated the section. They alone were educated; they alone held office. Non-slaveholders were too poor to "buy an education for themselves and their children," and the planters, not wishing to "endanger their supremacy," refused to establish public schools. Few poor whites could either read or write. They gained their opinions and their principles from "stump speeches and tavern conversations." They were "absolutely in the slaveholder's power." He sent "them to the polls to vote him into office and in so

doing to vote down their own rights and interests. . . ." They knew "no more what they [were] about, than so many children or so many Russian serfs. . . ."

Social-economic conditions in the South were described as tumble-down and backward. The slave, lacking the incentive of personal gain, was inefficient. The master, ruined by power, self-indulgence, and laziness, was incapable of sound management. . . . Others went so far as to charge the panic of 1837 to Southern profligacy. "The existence of Slavery," resolved the American Anti-Slavery Society in 1840, "is the grand cause of the pecuniary embarrassments of the country; and . . . no real or permanent relief is to be expected . . . until the total abolition of that execrable system." Joshua Leavitt called the slave system "a bottomless gulf of extravagance and thriftlessness." Another explained its "withering and impoverishing effect by the fact that it was the "rule of violence and arbitrary will. . . . It would be quite in character with its theory and practice," he said, "if slave-drivers should refuse to pay their debts and meet the sheriff with dirk and pistol." Leavitt estimated that the South had "taken from the North, within five years, more than $100,000,000, by notes which will never be paid," and quoted an English writer to the effect that "planters are always in debt. The system of society in a slaveholding community is such as to lead to the contraction of debt, which the system itself does not furnish the means of paying. . . ."

Nor did the Southern shortcomings, according to the anti-slavery view, end with things material. Moral weaknesses were even more offensive. Sexual virtue was scarcely known. "The Slave States," wrote an abolitionist, "are Sodoms, and almost every village family is a brothel." Another writer declared that "in the slaveholding settlements of Middle and Southern Mississippi . . . there [was] not a virtuous young man of twenty years of age." "To send a lad to a male academy in Mississippi," he said, "is moral murder." An anti-slavery pamphlet told of "a million and a half of slave women, some of them without even the tinge of African blood . . . given up a lawful prey to the unbridled lusts of their masters." Another widely circulated tract described a slave market in which one dealer "devoted himself exclusively to the sale of young mulatto women." The author pictured the sale of "the most beautiful woman I ever saw," without "a single trace of the African about her features" and with "a pair of eyes that pierced one through and through" to "one of the most lecherous-looking old brutes" that he had ever seen. The narrative closed with the shrieking appeal: "God shield the helpless victim of that bad man's power—it may be, ere now, that bad man's lust!" The conclusion was inescapable. Slavery and unrestrained sexual indulgence at Negro expense were inseparable.

In such a section and in the hands of such men, abolitionists assumed that slavery realized its most vicious possibilities. Anti-slavery men early set themselves to the task of collecting stories of cruelty. These were passed about from one to another, often gaining in ferocity as they travelled. Weld gathered them together in a volume entitled *American Slavery As It Is* and scattered them broadcast over the North. The annual reports of the anti-slavery societies, their tracts and periodicals, also revelled in atrocities, asking no more proof of their absolute truth than the word of a fellow fanatic.

The attempt to picture slavery "as it was," therefore, came to consist almost entirely of a recital of brutalities. Now and then a kind master and seemingly contented slaves were introduced for the purpose of contrast—as a device to deepen shadows. But, as a rule, Southerners, according to these tracts, spent their time in idleness broken only by brutal cock-fights, gander pullings, and horse races so barbarous that "the blood of the tortured animal drips from the lash and flies at every leap from the stroke of the rowel." Slavery was one continual round of abuse. The killing of a slave was a matter of no consequence. Even respectable ladies might cause "several to be *whipped to death*." Brandings, ear cropping, and body-maiming were the rule. David L. Child honestly declared: "From all that I have read and heard upon the subject of whipping done by masters and overseers to slaves . . . I have come to the conclusion that some hundreds of cart whips and cowskin instruments, which I am told make the skin fly like feathers, and cut frequently to the bone, are in *perpetual daily motion* in the slave states." John Rankin told of Negroes stripped, hung up and stretched and then "whipped until their bodies [were] covered with blood and mangled flesh," some dying "under the lash, others linger[ing] about for a time, and at length die[ing] of their *wounds*. . . ." The recital was indeed one of *"groans, tears, and blood."*

To abuse was added other great wrongs. Everywhere slaves were overworked, underfed, and insufficiently clothed and sheltered. Family ties were cut without the slightest regard for Negro feelings—infants were torn from the mother's breast, husbands separated from their wives and families. Marriage was unknown among slaves, and the right to worship God generally denied. Strangely enough, little was said of slave-breeding for market. That charge was largely left to the politicians of the next decades and to the historians of a later day.

Two principal assumptions stood out in this anti-slavery indictment of the slaveholder. He was, in the first place, the arch-aristocrat. He was the great enemy of democracy. He was un-American, the oppressor of his fellow men, the exploiter of a weaker brother. Against him could be directed all the complaints and fears engendered by industrial captains and land speculators. He, more than any other aristocrat, threatened to destroy the American democratic dream.

In the second place, he was a flagrant sinner. His self-indulgence was unmatched. His licentious conduct with Negro women, his intemperance in the use of intoxicating liquors, his mad dueling, and his passion for war against the weak were enough to mark him as the nation's moral enemy number one! The time for dealing moderately had passed. Immediate reform was imperative.

Thus it was that the slaveholder began to do scapegoat service for all aristocrats and all sinners. To him were transferred resentments and fears born out of local conditions. Because it combined in itself both the moral and the democratic appeal, and because it coincided with sectional rivalry, the abolition movement gradually swallowed up all other reforms. The South became the great object of all efforts to remake American society. Against early indifference and later persecution, a handful of deadly-in-earnest men and women slowly built into a section's consciousness the belief in a Slave Power. To the normal strength of sectional ignorance and distrust they added all the force of Calvinistic morality and American democracy and thereby surrounded every Northern interest and contention with holy sanction and reduced all opposition to abject depravity. When the politician, playing his risky game, linked expansion and slavery, Christian common folk by the thousands, with no great personal urge for reforming, accepted the Abolition attitudes toward both the South and slavery. Civil war was then in the making.

NO

Irving H. Bartlett

THE PERSISTENCE OF WENDELL PHILLIPS

Wherever Wendell Phillips walked on the Harvard campus he carried the aura of Beacon Hill with him. He was as well born as any Winthrop or Saltonstall and had been brought up in an imposing brick mansion on Beacon Hill only a few steps from the State House. The son of Boston's first mayor, a man universally respected for sound conservative principles, young Phillips seemed intent on following in his father's footsteps. He gained a reputation as being "the pet of the aristocracy," and in orations at the college exhibitions went out of his way to attack reformers and defend the standing order. One of his friends later recalled that Phillips would probably have been chosen by his classmates as the man "*least likely* to give the enthusiasm and labor of [his life] to the defense of popular rights."

Fifteen years after he left Harvard Phillips was asked by the secretary of the class of 1831 to fill out a questionnaire. He noted that he was in good health but growing bald. Under occupation he said he had prepared for the law "but grew honest and quitted what required an oath to the Constitution of the United States." Asked to note any other remarks that might be interesting to his classmates, he wrote: "My main business is to forward the abolition of slavery. I hold that the world is wrong side up and maintain the propriety of turning it upside down. I go for Disunion and have long since abjured that contemptible mockery, the Constitution of the United States."

To understand Phillips' career as an abolitionist and free-lance radical it is first necessary to account for his transformation from gentility to "fanaticism." Certainly it was not a natural development. After graduating from Harvard College Phillips entered the Harvard Law School. His career there and later as a practicing attorney was uneventful. Like most of the other sons of the old Federalists, he was happy to follow Daniel Webster into the Whig party which continued to serve the bulwarked conservatism of Massachusetts. He shared an office at this time with a man who later led a mob against abolitionists, and most of his social contacts were with the old aristocratic families who, if they knew anything about William Lloyd Garrison, naturally "supposed him to be a man who ought to be hung," and were unanimously determined to outlaw

From Irving H. Bartlett, "The Persistence of Wendell Phillips," in Martin Duberman, ed., *The Antislavery Vanguard: New Essays on the Abolitionists* (Princeton University Press, 1965). Copyright © 1965 by Princeton University Press. Reprinted by permission.

anyone, even the saintly William Ellery Channing, for expressing the slightest sympathy with his principles.

Phillip's first personal encounter with the antislavery movement came in October 1835, when he stood on a Boston street corner and watched a jeering mob drag Garrison through the street at the end of a rope. A few weeks later he met Ann Terry Greene, one of Garrison's disciples, and in less than a year, to the consternation of his mother and most of Boston society, married her. A few months later he made his first antislavery speech.

As with most of the early abolitionists, religion played a dominant role in making Phillips an abolitionist. We will never know how successful he might have been in law or politics, but his advantages in family background and education, his intelligence, and his remarkable oratorical talent suggest that the achievements of a Webster, Choate, or Sumner were not beyond his reach. The fact is, however, that between the time he graduated from college and met his wife, Phillips appears to have been in a melancholy state of mind largely because he lacked a sense of vocation. He had been brought up as a devout Calvinist, and it was a fundamental article in his belief that a man must make his life count for something. Like all new lawyers he found it slow going to get a practice started, but even more important he found no great satisfaction in the profession. He needed to find a calling. As it turned out he fell in love and found his calling at the same time. His bride introduced him to William Lloyd Garrison and other Boston abolitionists, and in the early days of their marriage, when her health permitted, accompanied him to antislavery meetings. Phillips had undergone religious conversion years before under the powerful preaching of Lyman Beecher. As he joined hands with the abolitionists he felt he was being born a third time. "None know what it is to live," he wrote in 1841, "till they redeem life from its seeming monotony by laying it a sacrifice on the altar of some great cause."

Phillips never forgot the importance of religion to the antislavery movement. "Our enterprise is eminently a religious one," he said, "dependent for success entirely on the religious sentiment of the people." When Phillips refused to take an oath to support the "proslavery constitution" of the United States, he thought of himself as following in the tradition of his forbear, the Reverend George Phillips, who had come to America in 1630 to put the Atlantic Ocean "between himself and a corrupt church." He did not think of himself as an ordinary lecturer or orator, but as a kind of minister to the public, preaching the gospel of reform. When he was called to fill Theodore Parker's pulpit in the Boston Music Hall in 1860, it was natural for him to begin a sermon by announcing that "Christ preached on the last political and social item of the hour; and no man follows in his footsteps who does not do exactly the same thing." Phillips' sermons before Parker's congregation were the same sermons that he preached in Faneuil Hall before antislavery meetings, and he was convinced that he did his duty to God in both places by flaying the public sinners of the day whether their names were Webster, Everett, Jefferson Davis, or Abraham Lincoln.

The idealism of the American revolutionary tradition also played a decisive role in shaping Phillips' career. When he was a boy, he remembered later, the Boston air still "trembled and burned with Otis and Sam Adams." He had been born practically next door to John Hancock's mansion, within site of Bunker Hill and only a few steps from the site of the Boston massacre. When he was thirteen years old and a student at the Boston Latin School he stood for hours in a crowd on the Common to catch a glimpse of Lafayette upon his visit to the city. Two years later, while poring over his lessons at the school, the sound of tolling bells came through the open windows announcing the deaths of Thomas Jefferson and John Adams.

Phillips never doubted that the revolutionary fathers were on his side. His first antislavery speech was given to support John Quincy Adams in his fight to get the Congress to hear petitions attacking slavery. Phillips argued that the right of petition was a traditional right for free men and that in attacking it the South threatened the freedom of all men. "This is the reason we render to those who ask us why we are contending against southern slavery," he said, "*that it may not result in northern slavery* . . . it is our own rights which are at issue."

The speech which made Phillips famous in Boston was given at a Faneuil Hall meeting to honor the memory of Elijah Lovejoy who had been killed by a mob in Alton, Illinois. The meeting was called to pay tribute to Lovejoy, but the abolitionists almost lost control of it when James Austin, the Attorney General for Massachusetts, stood up and made a violent speech attacking Lovejoy for having published an incendiary antislavery newspaper. Austin likened the mob which destroyed Lovejoy and his press to the patriots responsible for the Boston Tea Party. Phillips was able to get the floor after Austin, and overcome the hooting and jeering of the proslavery faction in the audience with an eloquent defense of Lovejoy. Again Phillips was defending a traditional American right, freedom of the press, and he insisted that the spirit of the American revolution supported him. . . .

In his reliance on religion and the spirit of the Declaration of Independence, Phillips was like most other abolitionists. As an orator, however, despite the fact that he was part of a movement full of celebrated speakers, his uniqueness is unchallenged. . . .

By far the most sensational characteristic of Phillips as a speaker was the contrast between his perfectly controlled, poised, almost dispassionate manner, and the inflammatory language he employed. It was the apparent effortlessness of his delivery that impressed many listeners most. "Staples said the other day that he heard Phillips speak at the State House," wrote Thoreau in his *Journal*. "By thunder! he never heard a man that could speak like him. His words come so easy. It was just like picking up chips." In an effort to explain how the speaker remained somehow detached from his own eloquence, another observer compared him to "a cold but mysteriously animated statue of marble." Time and time again when Phillips was on tour, talking before new audiences, the reporter would register the audience's surprise. "They had conceived him to be a ferocious ranter and blustering man of words. They found him to be a quiet, dignified and polished gentleman and scholar, calm and logical in his argument."

One of the reasons why abolitionist meetings in the middle and later 1850's began to draw impressively large crowds, as the critics of the abolitionists pointed out, was that for many people an antislavery meeting had all the elements of a theatrical performance. The star performer was usually Wendell Phillips, and his stock in trade, according to the unconverted, was "personal abuse." To the abolitionists themselves he was, as his publisher remarked, the greatest "master of invective" in the nineteenth century. With sublime confidence, almost as if he were reading from a sheaf of statistics or reciting a series of scientific facts, Phillips would take the platform to announce that Daniel Webster was "a great mass of dough," Edward Everett "a whining spaniel," Massachusetts Senator Robert C. Winthrop "a bastard who had stolen the name of Winthrop," and the New England churches an ecclesiastical machine to manufacture hypocrisy "just as really as Lowell manufactures cotton." It was the way Phillips uttered his epithets that fascinated most critics. The shrewd Scottish traveler David Macrae who had been led "from the ferocity of his onslaughts on public men and public measures . . . to form a false conception of his delivery" noted with surprise that vehemence and declamation were replaced by sarcasm, "cold, keen, withering." Macrae was impressed by the relentless manner in which Phillips pursued his opponents. "He follows an enemy like an Indian upon the trail. . . . When he comes to strike, his strokes are like galvanic shocks; there is neither noise nor flash but their force is terrible."

A writer for an English paper who was contrasting Phillips' speeches with "the rounded periods of Mr. Seward" and "the finished artistic rhetoric of the patriotic Mr. Everett" noted one quality which grated on European ears, and that was "the concentrated bitterness, the intense spirit of hatred with which they are frequently suffused." Because Phillips did not like to talk in general terms about issues, because he always took dead aim on personalities and heaped "the concentrated bitterness" of his rhetoric upon the heads of men prominent in public life, and because the people turned out in droves to hear him, Robert C. Winthrop believed that Phillips had "gradually educated our people to relish nothing but the 'eloquence of abuse.' "

A good many later critics have been much harsher than Winthrop in criticizing Phillips. Theodore Roosevelt called him a wild-eyed fanatic and Professor Randall has dismissed his speeches as "a kind of grandiloquent, self-righteous raving." A careful reading of his career shows these estimates to be incorrect. What distinguishes Phillips from the other abolitionists more significantly than anything else is that he was an intellectual, a philosopher of reform as well as a practical agitator. It is impossible to understand him, therefore, without knowing more about his political ideas and his conception of the role of the reformer in America.

Like other abolitionists Phillips believed in the Higher Law and judged every public question from an absolute moral standard. He believed that a man's first duty was to God, and that men should do their duty at whatever cost. He was convinced that anything right in principle had to be right in practice. He accepted Garrison's demand for immediate emancipation without question. Phillips' Calvinism, his belief in Divine Providence, made it possible for him to dismiss whatever doubts he might have had about the practicality of this radical solution. "No matter if the charter of emancipation was written in blood," he said in one of his early speeches, "and anarchy stalk abroad with giant strides—if God commanded, it was right." Phillips' Calvinism reinforced his radicalism. He did not have to worry about the consequences of his agitation. A man could only do his duty and let God do the rest.

As the most eloquent and intellectual of all the radicals, Phillips was called upon to defend the position that abolitionists should not support a constitution or government which supported slavery. Although the refusal of the radical abolitionists to vote or hold office, and their continued agitation to get the North to secede from the union seemed incomprehensible to most people, the position was perfectly consistent with Phillips' principles. Slavery was evil and this evil was supported by a Federal government which protected slave states from insurrection, undertook to return their fugitives and gave them special representation in Congress. Therefore anything voluntarily done in support of this government (i.e. taking an oath to support the Constitution or voting for a candidate who would be required to take such an oath), supported slavery also and was evil.

Despite the fact that his position was condemned in the public mind from the beginning, Phillips, through pamphlets and lectures, did as much as anyone could do to persuade people of its worth. He never once doubted its soundness. When friends like Charles Sumner argued that the course he advocated would impede the struggle for emancipation, he replied that "honesty and truth are more important than even freeing slaves." When Sumner asked how he could consistently pay taxes or even remain in the country, he reminded him that a man's choices were always limited by the social and historical situation in which God placed him. A man had to live in the world, but he did not have to collaborate with the devil, which is what Sumner and all other "loyal citizens" were doing. "To live where God sent you and protest against your neighbor—this is certainly different from *joining him* in sinning, which the office holder of this country does."

Phillips' moralism supplied the ballast for his career. His solutions to difficult problems were both "right" and simple. When he continued to badger the government long after Garrison and other abolitionists had retired from the field after the war, it was because he sought "*justice*—absolute, immediate, unmixed justice to the negroe." He did not, however, live by shibboleths alone, and his tactics as a reformer were based on a surprisingly sophisticated conception of American politics and society.

Phillips recognized that slavery was a threat to the freedom of all Americans. This conviction developed gradually out of his early experiences. He had the grisly reminiscences of the Grimké sisters to remind him of the evils of slavery in the south—the whippings and mutilations, the ruthless separation of husband and wife, of parent and child. Closer to his personal experience was what slavery had done to supposedly free American citizens. It had jailed Prudence Crandall for opening a school for Negro girls. It had publicly whipped Amos Dresser for daring to distribute antislavery literature. It had tried to gag John Quincy Adams in Congress, had mobbed Garrison within the shadow of Faneuil Hall, and had finally killed Lovejoy. The pattern seemed always to be the same; principle was overcome by power. For the first time Phillips sensed the demonic possibilities of a slave power supported by public opinion in America. . . .

Having recognized the importance of public opinion in America Phillips began to examine American institutions more closely. He distinguished a fundamental tension between the American ideal, a society based on the rights of man, and an American political system based on numbers. "The majority rules, and law rests on numbers, not on intellect or virtue," thus "while theoretically holding that no vote of the majority can authorize injustice, we practically consider public opinion the real test of what is true and what is false; and hence, as a result, the fact which Tocqueville has noticed, that practically our institutions protect, not the interest of the whole community but the interests of the majority." . . .

Although Phillips knew that in some nations public opinion was shaped by political leaders, he could find nothing to show that this was true in the American experience. Theoretically every American male citizen was supposed to be eligible for office, but in practice, "with a race like ours, fired with the love of material wealth," the best brains were drawn into commerce. As a result politics took up with small men, "men without grasp enough for large business . . . men popular because they have no positive opinions." Even if an occasional man of the first rank (a Charles Sumner for example), did emerge in politics, he would be lost to the reformer because the whole art of politics in America was based on the ability to compromise. "The politician must conceal half his principles to carry forward the other half," Phillips said, "must regard, not rigid principle and strict right, but only such a degree of right as will allow him at the same time to secure *numbers.*"

These considerations led Phillips to conclude that the reformer in America had to confront the people directly. "Our aim," he said in his lecture *The Philosophy of Abolitionism*, "is to alter public opinion." Slavery endured and abolitionists were mobbed because a majority of Americans refused to face the moral issues involved. Phillips was too much of a realist to believe that he could suddenly convert the nation, but he did feel that he could force the issue and change the public attitude toward slavery.

Phillips knew that most people in the North disliked slavery, but he also knew that it was to their self-interest to leave it alone. To stir up controversy was dangerous: no one wanted to be known as a troublemaker; mill owners were concerned for their capital; mill hands were concerned for their jobs; the respectable middle class was concerned for its reputation. The easy thing for everyone was to turn away from the problem. The abolitionist's job was to scatter thorns on the easy road by dramatizing the moral issue and insisting that every man who did not throw his whole influence into the scales against slavery was as guilty as the slaveholder. . . .

Phillips was not a fanatic. He used the most violent language dispassionately as a surgeon uses the sharpest steel. He could not actually cut away the diseased tissue with his rhetoric, but he could expose it. Thus when he called Lincoln a "slave hound" he was reminding his listeners and readers that as a Congressman Lincoln had supported a bill which would have enforced the return of fugitive slaves escaping into the District of Columbia. This was the man who expected to get the antislavery vote. Phillips' intention in attacking Lincoln so savagely was simply to dramatize the rottenness of the American conscience by showing that only a "slave hound" could be elected President. His reply to those who accused him of extravagance and distortion was that "there are far more dead hearts to be quickened, than confused intellects to be cleared up— more dumb dogs to be made to speak than doubting consciences to be enlightened. We have use, then, for something beside argument."

The easiest way to treat nettlesome reformers like the abolitionists is to dismiss them as cranks. Nothing irritated Phillips more than the attempts of his opponents to thrust him outside the mainstream of American life. The antislavery agitation, he insisted, was "an essential part of the machinery of the state . . . not a disease nor a medicine . . . the normal state of the nation."

The preceding statement takes us to the heart of Phillips' philosophy of reform. He recognized that American ideals could ultimately be translated into practice only through politics. At the same time he knew that the American politician's ability to gain and hold power was largely determined by his ability to effect compromises that appealed to numbers rather than to principle. He added to these corruptive tendencies the fact that people in a democracy always tend to have as high an opinion of themselves as possible—always tremble on the edge of national idolatry. . . . A democratic society that trusted to constitutions and political machinery to secure its liberties never would have any. "The people must be waked to a new effort," he said, "just as the church has to be regenerated in each age." In the middle of the nineteenth century the abolitionist was the agency of national regeneration, but even after he had vanished his function in the American system would still remain. . . .

It should be clear now that Phillips believed the radical abolitionist to be justified as much by his radicalism as by his abolitionism. Phillips preferred the word agitator to radical, and since he himself was frequently accused of demagoguery,

he took pains to point out the difference between the demagogue and agitator. A demagogue (he used Robespierre as an example), "rides the storm; he has never really the ability to create one. He uses it narrowly, ignorantly, and for selfish ends. If not crushed by the force which, without his will, has flung him into power, he leads it with ridiculous miscalculation against some insurmountable obstacle that scattters it forever. Dying, he leaves no mark on the elements with which he has been mixed." Quoting Sir Robert Peel, Phillips defined agitation as "the marshalling of the conscience of a nation to mould its laws." Daniel O'Connell who, after thirty years of "patient and sagacious labor," succeeded in creating a public opinion and unity of purpose to free Ireland from British tyranny was one of Phillips' models as a successful agitator.

It was because Phillips thought of himself primarily as an agitator and Garrison thought of himself primarily as an abolitionist that the two came to a parting of the ways in 1865. With the war over and slavery prohibited by the passage of the thirteenth amendment, Garrison felt that the "covenant with death" had been annulled. The American nation had become "successor to the abolitionists," and the American Anti-Slavery Society had lost its excuse for being. Phillips did not agree. He argued that the nation needed "the constant, incessant discriminating criticism of the abolitionists as much as ever." The debate grew rancorous and resulted in Garrison's quitting the Society. Phillips was elected President in his place, and for the next five years continued to agitate as fiercely for Negro suffrage as he had for emancipation. Only after the fifteenth amendment was passed did he allow the organization to be dissolved.

Even then Phillips did not relax his efforts. He denounced the decision to remove Federal troops from the South as vehemently as he had the Fugitive Slave Law, and predicted that a " 'solid south'— the slave power under a new name" would soon control national politics. Most of the other surviving abolitionists had long since gone over to the Republican party lock, stock, and barrel, but Phillips saw through the moral pretensions of the Republicans as clearly as anyone in the country. They had waved the bloody flag with regularity, but had been unwilling to make the sacrifices and the long-term commitments in reconstruction that were necessary if the moral legacy of the war was not to be squandered away. Accusing the Republicans of "a heartless and merciless calculation" to exploit war memories and Ku Klux Klan atrocities for party purposes, Phillips claimed that no party in history had ever "fallen from such a height to such a depth of disgrace."

The rhetoric was the same but the response was not. The people had grown tired of the war, and newspapers that would have praised him in the sixties now wrote about "Mr. Phillips' Last Frenzy" and called him "the apostle of unforgiving and relentless hate."

Meanwhile, even as he decried the growing popularity of the illusion that the Negro might be safe in the hands of his old master, Phillips turned his attention to the struggle of free labor in the North. "While this delusion of peace without purity persists," he was saying in 1878, "labor claims every ear and every hand." And so, in the declining years of his life, Wendell Phillips, true to his belief that agitation was "an essential part of the machinery of the state," poured his whole influence into the struggle for social justice in an industrial society. His solutions were still simple—passage of an eight-hour law—the unlimited issuance of Greenbacks. His tactics were the same. "The only way to accomplish our object," he said, "is to shame greedy men into humanity. Poison their wealth with the tears and curses of widows and orphans. In speaking of them call things by their right names. Let men shrink from them as from slave dealers and pirates." And the response was the same he had received during the hard, bitter years before the war. If anything Phillips was even more of an outsider now than he had been then. His support of unions, the right to strike, shorter hours of work, a graduated income tax, and his derision of laissez-faire ("the bubble and chaff of 'supply and demand' ") offended even the old abolitionists. If Phillips had acted "with ordinary common sense and good temper when slavery was abolished and had gone into politics," Edmund Quincy thought, "he might have been the next Senator . . . but he is 'played out' as we say, and will be merely a popular lecturer and a small demagogue for the rest of his life."

Quincy was a retired reformer. Like most of his contemporaries and most of the American historians who have followed, he could not appreciate Wendell Phillips, a gentleman who understood the difference between agitation and demagoguery, and knew that the radical in America could never retire.

POSTSCRIPT

Were the Abolitionists "Unrestrained Fanatics"?

One of the weaknesses of most studies of abolitionism, which is reflected in both of the preceding essays, is that they are generally written from a monochromatic perspective. In other words, historians typically discuss whites within the abolitionist crusade and give little, if any, attention to the roles African Americans themselves played in the movement. Instead, whites are the active agents of reform while blacks are the passive recipients of humanitarian efforts to eliminate the scourge of slavery. Students should be aware that African Americans, enslaved and free, also rebelled against the "peculiar" institution both directly and indirectly.

Benjamin Quarles, in *Black Abolitionists* (Oxford University Press, 1969), describes a wide range of roles played by blacks in the abolitionist movement. For example, as Garrison's *Liberator* struggled to survive in the early months of 1831, black subscribers in the North kept the paper afloat. In addition, black Americans organized themselves into local antislavery societies, became members of the national abolitionist organizations (especially the American Anti-Slavery Society and the American and Foreign Anti-Slavery Society), contributed funds to the operations of those societies, made black churches available for abolitionist meetings, and promoted abolitionism through pamphleteering and speaking engagements. Between 1830 and 1835, the Negro Convention Movement sponsored annual meetings of blacks during which protests against slavery were a central feature.

David Walker, a free black from North Carolina who resided in Boston, published his famous *Appeal* in 1828. In vitriolic language rivaling that of Garrison, Walker urged slaves to rebel against their bondage. Frederick Douglass, who had escaped from slavery in Maryland, became one of the most popular speakers on the abolitionist circuit.

The black challenge to the slave system is also evident in the network known as the underground railroad. Traditionally, the heroes of this means of abetting black fugitives from Southern bondage are the white abolitionists who "conducted" runaways to freedom in the Northern United States or Canada. Larry Gara, however, in *The Liberty Line: The Legend of the Underground Railroad* (University of Kentucky Press, 1961), concludes that the real heroes of the underground railroad were not white abolitionists but the slaves themselves who depended primarily upon their own resources or assistance they received from other blacks.

Other studies treating the role of black abolitionists in the antislavery movement include Jane H. and William H. Pease's, *They Who Would Be Free: Blacks' Search for Freedom, 1830–1861* (Atheneum, 1974) and James M. McPherson's, *The Struggle For Equality: Abolitionists and the Negro in the Civil War and Reconstruction* (Princeton University Press, 1964). Walker's pamphlet can be read in Charles M. Wiltse, ed., *David Walker's Appeal* (Hill & Wang, 1965). Frederick Douglass's contributions are evaluated in Benjamin Quarles, *Frederick Douglass* (Atheneum, 1968; originally published 1948); Nathan Irvin Huggins, *Slave and Citizen: The Life of Frederick Douglass* (Little, Brown, 1980); Waldo E. Martin, Jr., *The Mind of Frederick Douglass* (University of North Carolina Press, 1984); and William McFeeley, *Frederick Douglass* (W. W. Norton, 1991).

Various interpretations of the abolitionists are presented in Richard O. Curry, ed., *The Abolitionists: Reformers or Fanatics?* (Holt, Rinehart & Winston, 1965), and Lewis Perry and Michael Fellman, eds., *Antislavery Reconsidered: New Perspectives on the Abolitionists* (Louisiana State University Press, 1979). For general discussions of the abolitionist movement, see Merton L. Dillon, *The Abolitionists: The Growth of a Dissenting Minority* (Northern Illinois Press, 1974); Gerald Sorin, *Abolitionism: A New Perspective* (Praeger, 1972); James Brewer Stewart, *Holy Warriors: The Abolitionists and American Slavery* (Hill & Wang, 1976); Ronald G. Walters, *The Antislavery Appeal: American Abolitionism After 1830* (Johns Hopkins, 1978); and Lawrence J. Friedman, *Gregarious Saints: Self and Community in American Abolitionism, 1830–1870* (Cambridge University Press, 1982). The lives of individual white participants in the abolitionist movement are discussed in Russell B. Nye, *William Lloyd Garrison and the Humanitarian Reformers* (Little, Brown, 1955); Gerda Lerner, *The Grimke Sisters from South Carolina: Pioneers for Woman's Rights and Abolition* (Schocken Books, 1967); and Stephen B. Oates, *To Purge This Land With Blood: A Biography of John Brown* (Harper & Row, 1970).

ISSUE 15

Was the Antebellum South a Unique Section in American History?

YES: Eugene D. Genovese, from *The Political Economy of Slavery* (Pantheon Books, 1965)

NO: Edward Pessen, from "How Different From Each Other Were the Antebellum North and South?" *The American Historical Review* (December 1980)

ISSUE SUMMARY

YES: Professor of history Eugene D. Genovese believes "that slavery gave the South a social system and a civilization with a distinct class structure, political community, economy, ideology and set of psychological patterns."
NO: Professor of history Edward Pessen argues that a comparison of Northern and Southern states in the three decades before the Civil War reveals common political, economic, and social practices.

"The South is not quite a nation within a nation but it is the next thing to it," began the North Carolinian journalist Wilbur J. Cash in his classic statement on *The Mind of the South* (Knopf, 1941). Cash wrote his book on the eve of World War II, shortly before he committed suicide (some say because he dared to tell the truth about the South). Cash's death created a myth within a myth and helped solidify the popular image of the "tragic" South.

Since *The Mind of the South* first appeared, novelists, journalists, and historians from all sections of the country and of various political persuasions have tried to explain the myths and realities of the American South. When the reader cuts through the multitude of adjectives used to describe the South, he or she concludes that there are actually only two types—positive and negative.

An earlier generation of Southern historians—Louis Wright, Clement Eaton, and Rollin G. Osterweis—have taken the myths of the plantation South seriously enough to claim that, with additional small doses of realism, such a place did in fact exist before the Civil War. Louis Wright claims that the first gentlemen of Virginia had established an aristocracy of large land-owning farmers who developed great wealth from the profits on their tobacco estates. Although they were not descendants of British nobility, these planters lived in considerable splendor and developed a pattern of life

312

modeled after the mother country's gentry. Dominating the colony's assemblies from its earliest years, the Virginia planter produced generations of leaders who, in the late eighteenth century, would be in the forefront of the American Revolution. Clement Eaton describes how the descendants of the coastal aristocrats carried the ideal of the country gentlemen with them as they migrated to other portions of the southwest in the early nineteenth century. Rollin G. Osterweis argues that the cult of chivalry permeated the South's romantic image of itself in the plantation system and that the institution of slavery shaped Southern nationalism, eventually leading to secession and civil war.

Howard Zinn, a white radical historian who spent many years teaching at a black Southern college in Atlanta while actively participating in the civil rights movement in the 1960s, has turned these epitaphs on their heads. In his book *The Southern Mystique* (Knopf, 1964), he defines "Southernism" as merely being an extension of the nation's worst qualities. There is no distinct South, he argues. Non-Southerners have merely projected onto the South those qualities which they least like about the American nation. Zinn points out that more violence occurred in clashes between settlers and Indians on our western frontier than between masters and slaves in the antebellum South.

In the following selections, Eugene D. Genovese, author of the best modern study of slavery, disagrees with Howard Zinn. Employing a sophisticated Marxian class analysis, Genovese argues that the antebellum South was a unique precapitalist society dominated by "quasi-aristocratic landowners who had to adjust their economy and ways of thinking to a capitalist world market." In contrast, Edward Pessen contends that the similarities between the Northern and Southern sections in the three decades before the Civil War were more important than their differences. Pessen summarizes much of the recent scholarly literature on the pre–Civil War political, social, and economic structures of both the North and South and he finds that an unequal distribution of wealth between the upper and lower classes continued to widen in both sections. At the same time, planter-aristocrats and urban merchants dominated the economies and the two major political parties in their respective sections as well.

YES

Eugene D. Genovese

THE SHAPING OF A UNIQUE SOCIETY

The uniqueness of the antebellum South continues to challenge the imagination of Americans, who, despite persistent attempts, cannot divert their attention from slavery. Nor should they, for slavery provided the foundation on which the South rose and grew. The master-slave relationship permeated Southern life and influenced relationships among free men. A full history would have to treat the impact of the Negro slave and of slaveless as well as slaveholding whites, but a first approximation, necessarily concerned with essentials, must focus on the slaveholders, who most directly exercised power over men and events. The hegemony of the slaveholders, presupposing the social and economic preponderance of great slave plantations, determined the character of the South. These men rose to power in a region embedded in a capitalistic country, and their social system emerged as part of a capitalistic world. Yet, a nonslaveholding European past and a shared experience in a new republic notwithstanding, they imparted to Southern life a special social, economic, political, ideological, and psychological content.

To dissolve that special content into an ill-defined agrarianism or an elusive planter capitalism would mean to sacrifice concern with the essential for concern with the transitional and peripheral. Neither of the two leading interpretations, which for many years have contended in a hazy and unreal battle, offers consistent and plausible answers to recurring questions, especially those bearing on the origins of the War for Southern Independence. The first of these interpretations considers the antebellum South an agrarian society fighting against the encroachments of industrial capitalism; the second considers the slave plantation merely a form of capitalistic enterprise and suggests that the material differences between Northern and Southern capitalism were more apparent than real. These two views, which one would think contradictory, sometimes combine in the thesis that the agrarian nature of planter capitalism, for some reason, made coexistence with industrial capitalism difficult.

The first view cannot explain why some agrarian societies give rise to industrialization and some do not. A prosperous agricultural hinterland has

From Eugene D. Genovese, *The Political Economy of Slavery* (Pantheon Books, 1961).

generally served as a basis for industrial development by providing a home market for manufactures and a source of capital accumulation, and the prosperity of farmers has largely depended on the growth of industrial centers as markets for foodstuffs. In a capitalist society agriculture is one industry, or one set of industries, among many, and its conflict with manufacturing is one of many competitive rivalries. There must have been something unusual about an agriculture that generated violent opposition to the agrarian West as well as the industrial Northeast.

The second view, which is the more widely held, emphasizes that the plantation system produced for a distant market, responded to supply and demand, invested capital in land and slaves, and operated with funds borrowed from banks and factors. This, the more sophisticated of the two interpretations, cannot begin to explain the origins of the conflict with the North and does violence to elementary facts of antebellum Southern history. . . .

CAPITALIST AND PSEUDO-CAPITALIST FEATURES OF THE SLAVE ECONOMY

The slave economy developed within, and was in a sense exploited by, the capitalist world market; consequently, slavery developed many ostensibly capitalist features, such as banking, commerce, and credit. These played a fundamentally different role in the South than in the North. Capitalism has absorbed and even encouraged many kinds of precapitalist social systems: serfdom, slavery, Oriental state enterprises, and others. It has introduced credit, finance, banking, and similar institutions where they did not previously exist. It is pointless to suggest that therefore nineteenth-century India and twentieth-century Saudi Arabia should be classified as capitalist countries. We need to analyze a few of the more important capitalist and pseudo-capitalist features of Southern slavery and especially to review the barriers to industrialization in order to appreciate the peculiar qualities of this remarkable and anachronistic society.

The defenders of the "planter-capitalism" thesis have noted the extensive commercial links between the plantation and the world market and the modest commercial bourgeoisie in the South and have concluded that there is no reason to predicate an antagonism between cotton producers and cotton merchants. However valid as a reply to the naive arguments of the proponents of the agrarianism-versus-industrialism thesis, this criticism has unjustifiably been twisted to suggest that the presence of commercial activity proves the predominance of capitalism in the South. Many precapitalist economic systems have had well-developed commercial relations, but if every commercial society is to be considered capitalist, the word loses all meaning. In general, commercial classes have supported the existing system of production. As Maurice Dobb observes, their fortunes are bound up with those of the dominant producers, and merchants are more likely to seek an extension of their middlemen's profits than to try to reshape the economic order.

We must concern ourselves primarily with capitalism as a social system, not merely with evidence of typically capitalistic economic practices. In the South extensive and complicated commercial relations with the world market permitted the growth of a small commercial bourgeoisie. The resultant fortunes flowed into slaveholding, which offered prestige and economic and social security in a planter-dominated society. Independent merchants found their businesses dependent on the patronage of the slaveholders. The merchants either became planters themselves or assumed a servile attitude toward the planters. The commercial bourgeoisie, such as it was, remained tied to the slaveholding interest, had little desire or opportunity to invest capital in industrial expansion, and adopted the prevailing aristocratic attitudes.

The Southern industrialists were in an analogous position, although one that was potentially subversive of the political power and ideological unity of the planters. The preponderance of planters and slaves on the countryside retarded the home market. The Southern yeomanry, unlike the Western, lacked the purchasing power to sustain rapid industrial development. The planters spent much of their money abroad for luxuries. The plantation market consisted primarily of the demand for cheap slave clothing and cheap agricultural implements for use or misuse by the slaves. Southern industrialism needed a sweeping agrarian revolution to provide it with cheap labor and a substantial rural market, but the Southern industrialists depended on the existing, limited, plantation market. Leading industrialists like William Gregg and Daniel Pratt were plantation-oriented and proslavery. They could hardly have been other.

The banking system of the South serves as an excellent illustration of an ostensibly capitalist institution that worked to augment the power of the planters and retard the development of the bourgeoisie. Southern banks functioned much as did those which the British introduced into Latin America, India, and Egypt during the nineteenth century. Although the British banks fostered dependence on British capital, they did not directly and willingly generate internal capitalist development. They were not sources of industrial capital but "large-scale clearing houses of mercantile finance vying in their interest charges with the local usurers."

The difference between the banking practices of the South and those of the West reflects the difference between slavery and agrarian capitalism. In the West, as in the Northeast, banks and credit facilities promoted a vigorous economic expansion. During the period of loose Western banking (1830-1844) credit flowed liberally into industrial development as well as into land purchases and internal improvements. Manufacturers and merchants dominated the boards of directors of Western banks, and landowners played a minor role. Undoubtedly, many urban businessmen speculated in land and had special interests in underwriting agricultural exports, but they gave attention to building up agricultural processing industries and urban enterprises, which guaranteed the region a many-sided economy.

The slave states paid considerable attention to the development of a conservative, stable banking system, which could guarantee the movement of staple crops and the extension of credit to the planters. Southern banks were primarily designed to lend the planters money for outlays that were economically feasible and socially acceptable in a slave society: the movement of crops, the purchase of land and slaves, and little else.

Whenever Southerners pursued easy-credit policies, the damage done outweighed the advantages of increased production. This imbalance probably did not occur in the West, for easy credit made possible agricultural and industrial expansion of a diverse nature and, despite acute crises, established a firm basis for long-range prosperity. Easy credit in the South led to expansion of cotton production with concomitant overproduction and low prices; simultaneously, it increased the price of slaves.

Planters wanted their banks only to facilitate cotton shipments and maintain sound money. They purchased large quantities of foodstuffs from the West and, since they shipped little in return, had to pay in bank notes. For five years following the bank failures of 1837 the bank notes of New Orleans moved at a discount of from 10 to 25 percent. This disaster could not be allowed to recur. Sound money and sound banking became the cries of the slaveholders as a class.

Southern banking tied the planters to the banks, but more important, tied the bankers to the plantations. The banks often found it necessary to add prominent planters to their boards of directors and were closely supervised by the planter-dominated state legislatures. In this relationship the bankers could not emerge as a middle-class counterweight to the planters but could merely serve as their auxiliaries.

The bankers of the free states also allied themselves closely with the dominant producers, but society and economy took on a bourgeois quality provided by the rising industrialists, the urban middle classes, and the farmers who increasingly depended on urban markets. The expansion of credit, which in the West financed manufacturing, mining, transportation, agricultural diversification, and the numerous branches of a capitalist economy, in the South bolstered the economic position of the planters, inhibited the rise of alternative industries, and guaranteed the extension and consolidation of the plantation system.

If for a moment we accept the designation of the planters as capitalists and the slave system as a form of capitalism, we are then confronted by a capitalist society that impeded the development of every normal feature of capitalism. The planters were not mere capitalists; they were precapitalist, quasi-aristocratic landowners who had to adjust their economy and ways of thinking to a capitalist world market. Their society, in its spirit and fundamental direction, represented the antithesis of capitalism, however many compromises it had to make. The fact of slave ownership is central to our problem. This seemingly formal question of whether the owners of the means of production command labor or purchase the labor power of free workers contains in itself the content of Southern life. The essential features of Southern particularity, as well as of Southern backwardness, can be traced to the relationship of master to slave.

THE BARRIERS TO INDUSTRIALIZATION

If the planters were losing their economic and political cold war with Northern capitalism, the failure of the South to develop sufficient industry provided the most striking immediate cause. Its inability to develop adequate manufactures is usually attributed to the inefficiency of its labor force. No doubt slaves did not easily adjust to industrial employment, and the indirect effects of the slave system impeded the employment of whites.

Slaves did work effectively in hemp, tobacco, iron, and cotton factories but only under socially dangerous conditions. They received a wide variety of privileges and approached an elite status. Planters generally appreciated the potentially subversive quality of these arrangements and looked askance at their extension.

Slavery concentrated economic and political power in the hands of a slaveholding class hostile to industrialism. The slaveholders feared a strong urban bourgeoisie, which might make common cause with its Northern counterpart. They feared a white urban working class of unpredictable social tendencies. In general, they distrusted the city and saw in it something incongruous with their local power and status arrangements. The small slaveholders, as well as the planters, resisted the assumption of a heavy tax burden to assist manufacturers, and as the South fell further behind the North in industrial development more state aid was required to help industry offset the Northern advantages of scale, efficiency, credit relations, and business reputation.

Slavery led to the rapid concentration of land and wealth and prevented the expansion of a Southern home market. Instead of providing a basis for industrial growth, the Southern countryside, economically dominated by a few large estates, provided only a limited market for industry. . . .

THE IDEOLOGY
OF THE MASTER CLASS

The planters commanded Southern politics and set the tone of social life. Theirs was an aristocratic, antibourgeois spirit with values and mores emphasizing family and status, a strong code of honor, and aspirations to luxury, ease, and accomplishment. In the planters' community, paternalism provided the standard of human relationships, and politics and statecraft were the duties and responsibilities of gentlemen. The gentleman lived for politics, not, like the bourgeois politician, off politics.

The planter typically recoiled at the notions that profit should be the goal of life; that the approach to production and exchange should be internally rational and uncomplicated by social values; that thrift and hard work should be the great virtues; and that the test of the wholesomeness of a community should be the vigor with which its citizens expand the economy. The planter was no less acquisitive than the bourgeois, but an acquisitive spirit is compatible with value antithetical to capitalism. The aristocratic spirit of the planters absorbed acquisitiveness and directed it into channels that were socially desirable to a slave society: the accumulation of slaves and land and the achievement of military and political honors. Whereas in the North people followed the lure of business and money for their own sake, in the South specific forms of property carried the badges of honor, prestige, and power. Even the rough parvenu planters of the Southwestern frontier—the "Southern Yankees"—strove to accumulate wealth in the modes acceptable to plantation society. Only in their crudeness and naked avarice did they differ from the Virginia gentlemen. They were a generation removed from the refinement that follows accumulation.

Slavery established the basis of the planter's position and power. It measured his affluence, marked his status, and supplied leisure for social graces and aristocratic duties. The older bourgeoisie of New England in its own way struck an aristocratic pose, but its wealth was rooted in commercial and industrial enterprises that were being pushed into the background by the newer heavy industries arising in the West, where upstarts took advantage of the more lucrative ventures like the iron industry. In the South few such opportunities were opening. The parvenu differed from the established planter only in being cruder and perhaps sharper in his business dealings. The road to power lay through the plantation. The older aristocracy kept its leadership or made room for men following the same road. An aristocratic stance was no mere compensation for a decline in power; it was the soul and content of a rising power.

Many travelers commented on the difference in material conditions from one side of the Ohio River to the other, but the difference in sentiment was seen most clearly by Tocqueville. Writing before the slavery issue had inflamed the nation, he remarked that slavery was attacking the Union "indirectly in its manners." The Ohioan "was tormented by wealth," and would turn to any kind of enterprise or endeavor to make a fortune. The Kentuckian coveted wealth "much less than pleasure or excitement," and money had "lost a portion of its value in his eyes."

Achille Murat joined Tocqueville in admiration for Southern ways. Compared with Northerners, Southerners were frank, clever, charming, generous, and liberal. They paid a price for these advantages. As one Southerner put it, the North led the South in almost everything because the Yankees had quiet perseverance over the long haul, whereas the Southerners had talent and brilliance but no taste for sustained labor. Southern projects came

with a flash and died just as suddenly. Despite such criticisms from within the ranks, the leaders of the South clung to their ideals, their faults, and their conviction of superiority. Farmers, said Edmund Ruffin, could not expect to achieve a cultural level above that of the "boors who reap rich harvests from the fat soil of Belgium." In the Northern states, he added with some justification, a farmer could rarely achieve the ease, culture, intellect, and refinement that slavery made possible. The prevailing attitude of the aristocratic South toward itself and its Northern rival was ably summed up by William Henry Holcombe of Natchez: "The Northerner loves to make money, the Southerner to spend it."

At their best, Southern ideals constituted a rejection of the crass, vulgar, inhumane elements of capitalist society. The slaveholders simply could not accept the idea that the case nexus offered a permissible basis for human relations. Even the vulgar parvenu of the Southwest embraced the plantation myth and refused to make a virtue of necessity by glorifying the competitive side of slavery as civilization's highest achievement. The slaveholders generally, and the planters in particular, did identify their own ideals with the essence of civilization and, given their sense of honor, were prepared to defend them at any cost.

This civilization and its ideals were antinational in a double sense. The plantation offered virtually the only market for the small nonstaple-producing farmers and provided the center of necessary services for the small cotton growers. Thus, the paternalism of the planters toward their slaves was reinforced by the semipaternal relationship between the planters and their neighbors. The planters, in truth, grew into the closest thing to feudal lords imaginable in a nineteenth-century bourgeois republic. The planters' protestations of love for the Union were not so much a desire to use the Union to protect slavery as a strong commitment to localism as the highest form of liberty. They genuinely loved the Union so long as it alone among the great states of the world recognized that localism had a wide variety of rights. The Southerners' source of pride was not the Union, nor the nonexistent Southern nation; it was the plantation, which they raised to a political principle.

NO

Edward Pessen

HOW DIFFERENT FROM EACH OTHER WERE THE ANTEBELLUM NORTH AND SOUTH?

How different from each other were the North and South before the Civil War? Recent work by historians of antebellum America throws interesting new light on this old question. Since some of these studies deal with individual communities, others with single themes of antebellum life, they are in a sense Pirandelloan pieces of evidence in search of an overarching synthesis that will relate them to one another and to earlier findings and interpretations. My modest hope is that the discussion that follows will be useful to historians in pursuit of such a synthesis.

The terms "North" and "South" are, of course, figures of speech that distort and oversimplify a complex reality, implying homogeneity in geographical sections that, in fact, were highly variegated. Each section embraced a variety of regions and communities that were dissimilar in climatic, topographical, demographic, and social characteristics. If, as Bennett H. Wall has written, "there never has been the 'one' South described by many historians," neither has there been the one North. Historians who have compared the antebellum South and North without referring to the diversity of each have not necessarily been unaware of this diversity. Their premise, in speaking of the North and South, is that the Mason-Dixon line divided two distinctive civilizations, the basic similarities within each of which transcended its internal differences. . . .

Here were two sections containing roughly equal areas for human settlement. Yet on the eve of the Civil War the population of the North was more than 50 percent greater than that of the South. The most dramatic disparity concerned racial balance: roughly one-quarter of a million Northern blacks comprised slightly more than 1 percent of the Northern population; the more than four million blacks in the South constituted one-third of the Southern population. And almost 95 percent of Southern blacks were slaves. Although the value of agricultural products in the two sections was almost equal,

From Edward Pessen, "How Different From Each Other Were the Antebellum North and South?" *American Historical Review* (December 1980). Copyright © 1980 by Edward Pessen. Reprinted with permission. Notes omitted.

Northern superiority in manufactures, railroad mileage, and commercial profits was overwhelming, far surpassing the Northern advantage in population. Similarly, Northern urban development outdistanced Southern, whether measured by the number of cities or by the size and proportions of the population within them. What did these and other, harder to measure, differences signify? To what extent were they balanced out by important sectional similarities? These are among the questions this essay will consider. . . .

A comprehensive comparison of the two sections would overlook nothing, not even the weather, which, according to Phillips, "has been the chief agency in making the South distinctive." In the space available here I shall focus on what our sociological friends might call three social indicators: (1) the economy, (2) the social structure, and (3) politics and power. In selecting these matters for examination, I do not mean to suggest that they are more important than values, ideals, the life of the mind, or any number of other features of antebellum life. Tangible phenomena may be easier to measure than intangible, but they offer no better clue to the essential character of a place and a people. I emphasize economic, social, and political themes because all of them are clearly important, the evidence on them is substantial, and each has recently been re-examined to interesting effect.

The economic practices of each section—one hesitates to call them economic "systems" in the face of the contradictory and largely planless if not improvisatory nature of these practices—were similarly complex. Northerners and Southerners alike made their living primarily in agriculture. Guided by the unique weather and the unequal length of the growing seasons in their sections, Northern and Southern farmers increasingly specialized, but in dissimilar crops. Tobacco and, above all, rice, sugar, and cotton were largely unknown to the North. Yet in the South, as in the North, farmers—whether large or small—sought and, for the most part achieved, self-sufficiency. They produced more grains and corn than anything else and in both sections raised and kept domestic animals roughly equal in quantity and, it has recently been claimed, comparable in quality. In view of the regularity with which Northern farmers brushed aside the lonely voices in their midst who urged subordination of profits to the "long-range needs of the soil," their money-mindedness in planting wheat (their own great dollar earner) year after year, and their unsentimental readiness to dispose of "family land" so long as the price was right, what Stanley L. Engerman had said about Southern planters seems to apply equally well to Northern agriculturists: they were certainly not "noncalculating individuals not concerned with money." . . .

The most distinctive feature of the antebellum Southern economy, as of Southern life as a whole, was, of course, its "peculiar institution." Slavery had not been unknown in the North, flourishing through much of the seventeenth and eighteenth centuries and persisting in New Jersey until 1846. But it had involved relatively few blacks and had had slight effect on Northern life and thought. Northern public opinion, better represented by the authors of the Federal Constitution in 1787 and the Missouri Compromise in 1820 than by the abolitionists of the antebellum decades, accepted slavery, approved of doing business with those who controlled it, abhorred its black victims, and loathed Northern whites who agitated against it. Northern acquiescence in Southern slavery does not erase this most crucial difference between the sections, but it does argue for the complementarity and economic interdependence of North and South. . . .

Several trade unionists in the antebellum North agreed with slavery's apologists that not only the working and living conditions but in some respects the "liberty" enjoyed by Northern hirelings compared unfavorably with the situation of slaves. These were patently self-serving arguments, designed to put the lot of the Northern worker in the worst possible light. The fact remains that the economic gap between enslaved black and free white workers in antebellum South and North was narrower than historians once thought. Evidence bearing on the conditions of white Northern as well as black Southern labor demonstrates that during the middle decades of the nineteenth century the real wages of Northern workingmen declined and their living conditions remained bleak, their job security was reduced, their skills were increasingly devalued, and in many respects their lives became more insecure and precarious.

At mid-century industrial workers in the South as in the North worked primarily in small shops and households rather than in factories. Trade unionists in Baltimore, Louisville, St. Louis, and New Orleans were with few exceptions skilled and semi-skilled white artisans, precisely as they were in Philadelphia, New York, Boston, and Pittsburgh. In Southern as in Northern towns and cities, the least skilled and prestigious

jobs were those done preponderantly by Catholic immigrants rather than by older Protestant, ethnic groups. Significantly, the South attracted far fewer of the antebellum era's "new immigrants"—that is, Germans and Irish—than did the North. For all of their smaller numbers in the South, European immigrants played an economic and social role there that was not dissimilar to what it was in the North. Diverse measurable evidence indicates that the pattern of immigrant life in the United States was national, rather than distinctly regional, in character. A similar point can be made about Southern urbanism and manufacturing—namely, quantitative distinctiveness (or deficiency), qualitative similarity to the North. Although the value of Southern manufactured products was usually less than one-fifth of the national total during the antebellum decades, the South was hardly a region devoid of industrial production. Articulate Southerners "crusade[d] to bring the cotton mills to the cotton fields," and, whether due to their exhortations or to the play of market forces, the amount of capital the slave states invested in cotton manufacturing doubled between 1840 and 1860, surpassing their rate of population growth. Because the South nevertheless lagged far behind the Northeast in manufacturing, one influential school of historians has described the antebellum economy—and, for that matter, Southern society as a whole—as noncapitalist, prebourgeois, or "seigneurial."

Some historians have criticized Southern deficiences in commerce, finance, transportation, and manufacturing as manifestations of economic wrongheadedness and irrationality and have attributed to these deficiencies the South's defeat in the Civil War. A number of modern economic historians, cliometricians for the most part, have interpreted the evidence somewhat differently. Invoking the old argument of "comparative advantage," they have noted that heavy investment in cotton, the nation's great dollar earner in international trade, was hardly irrational, since it enabled the South to equal the national rate of profit during the era. Southerners who did invest in Southern factories got a return that compared favorably with industrial profits elsewhere. (Why, ask the critics, didn't they invest more of their capital that way?) If Southern manufacturing was outdistanced by that in the Northeast, it compared favorably with industrial production in the Northwest and, for that matter, in Continental Europe in the mid-nineteenth century. If the South suffered inordinately in the wake of the financial panics of 1837 and 1839, it was, as Reginald C. McGrane noted long ago, precisely because the South had speculated excessively in transportation projects and land acquisition as well as other investments. The South's "unusually favorable system of navigable streams and rivers" has been cited to explain its lag in railroads. Yet in the 1840s Southern railroads "equalled or exceeded the national average capitalization per mile." The views of many scholars are expressed in Gavin Wright's recent observation that "before the War the South was wealthy, prosperous, expanding geographically, and gaining economically at rates that compared favorably to those of the rest of the country.

Antebellum Northern investors, like their counterparts in the South and in Europe, put their money into American products, industrial and agricultural, solid and flimsy, drawn almost entirely by the profit margin likely to result from their investment. Investors in all latitudes appear to have been indifferent to possible long-range consequences of their financial transactions, acting rather on the principle that the "rational" investment was the one likely to pay off. That the railroads, the diversified industry, and the commercial superiority of the North turned out to have important military implications in the 1860s could hardly have been anticipated by earlier profit-seekers. . . .

Historians have long known that a society's social structure offers an important clue to its character. The kind of social classes that exist, the gulf between them, their roles in society, the ease or difficulty of access to higher from lower rungs on the social ladder, and the relationships between the classes tell as much about a civilization as do any other phenomena. What distinguishes modern from earlier historians in their treatment of social class is the extent to which they have borrowed from social scientists both in theorizing about class and in the methodology used for measurement. Employing these new approaches, historians have drastically modified earlier notions of antebellum society.

The ancient belief that the white antebellum South consisted of two classes, wealthy planters at the top and a great mass of poor whites below, may continue to command some popular acceptance. That belief has been so long dead among historians, however, that as early as 1946 Fabian Linden could remark that "the debunking of the 'two class' fallacy" had "become the tedious cliché." For, beginning in 1940 and continuing steadily thereafter, Frank L. Owsley and a group of scholars influenced by his work utilized hitherto neglected primary sources to reveal that the most typical white Southerners by far were small farmers working the modest acreage they owned with few, if any, slaves.

The too neat portrait that the Owsley school drew of the white Southern social structure was quite similar to the picture of *Northern* society accepted by historians less than a generation ago. The white population was ostensibly composed primarily of the great "middling orders," hard-working, proud, and not unprosperous farmers for the most part, whose chance to rise even higher socially matched the opportunities an increasingly democratic society gave them to exert political influence and power. Small groups of rich men—great planters in the one clime and merchants and industrialists in the other—occupied the highest social plateau; professionals who served the rich were slightly above the middle, which was occupied by small business people and independent farmers, skilled artisans, and clerks; and below them stood industrial and landless agricultural laborers. Since class is determined not by bread alone, blacks—whether slave or free and regardless of how much individuals among them had managed to accumulate—were universally relegated to the lowest levels of the social structure, scorned even by white vagrants and frequently unemployed workers, urban and rural, who constituted America's equivalent of a propertyless proletariat.

The achievement of recent research is its transformation of what was a rather blurred image of social groups, whose membership and possessions were both unclear, into a more sharply focused picture. By digging deeper, particularly in nineteenth-century data on wealth and property, historians have come close to knowing the numbers of families belonging to different wealth strata and the amount of wealth these families owned.

The beauty of the new evidence on who and how many owned what and how much is that in the antebellum era wealth appears to have been the surest sign of social, as well as economic, position. Antebellum wealth was almost invariably made in socially acceptable ways. Modern scholars have found that "the social divisions of antebellum America were essentially wealth-holding categories." The upper class did not comprise so much the families who "controlled the means of production" as it did the families who "controlled the vast wealth created largely through the exchange of goods produced." Degree of wealth was the surest sign of the quality of housing, furnishings, and household goods a family could afford, of its style of living and uses of leisure, and of the social circle within which it moved and its individual members married. Gathering from the manuscript census schedules, probate inventories, and tax assessors' reports statistically valid samples or, in some cases, evidence on every family in the community under study, modern scholars have been able to arrange the antebellum Southern and Northern populations on a wealth-holding scale. While it is close to a statistical inevitability that the distribution of wealth in the South and North would not be precisely the same, the most striking feature of the evidence is how similarly wealth was distributed—or maldistributed—in the two sections.

On the eve of the Civil War one-half of the free adult males in both the South and the North held less than 1 percent of the real and personal property. In contrast, the richest 1 percent owned 27 percent of the wealth. Turning from the remarkable similarity in sectional patterns of wealthholding at the bottom and the very top, the richest 5 to 10 percent of propertyowners controlled a somewhat greater share of the South's wealth, while what might be called the upper middle deciles (those below the top tenth) held a slightly smaller share in the North. The South also came close to monopolizing wealthy counties, the per capita wealth of which was $4,000 or more and, despite its smaller population, the South, according to the 1860 census, contained almost two-thirds of those persons in the nation whose worth was at least $110,000. According to Lee Soltow, the leading student of this evidence, these sectional disparities "could be attributed almost entirely to slave values. . . . If one could eliminate slave market value from the distribution of wealth in 1860 . . . , the inequality levels in the North and South were similar."

In view of the centrality of slavery to the antebellum South, it is idle to speak of "eliminating the market value" of slaves from the sectional comparison. Northern free labor, rural and industrial, also represented a form of "sectional wealth," if a much overlooked form. Although as individual human beings they did not add to their own private wealth or to the wealth of the employers they served, their labor created wealth for themselves and for these same capitalists at rates of productivity that, I believe, even Robert W. Fogel and Stanley L. Engerman would concede compared favorably with the rates of the most efficient slaves. In other words, the North had access to a form of wealth, free labor, that was roughly as valuable per capita as was slave wealth, however absent this Northern wealth was from the reports prepared by census takers and assessors. Given the known habits of these officials to overlook small property holdings—precisely the kind of holdings that would have been owned by Northern working people—and to accept as true the lies people swore to as to their worth, it is likely that the fairly substantial cumulative wealth owned by small farmers and modest wage earners was almost entirely omitted from the wealth equation. Such groups were far more numerous in the North than in the South. Had slaves been treated as part of the potential property-owning Southern population to which they actually belonged, instead of being treated as property pure and simple, the total wealth of the antebellum South would have been diminished by several billion dollars: the product of multiplying the number of slaves by the average market price of almost $1,000 per slave. The addition of nearly four million very poor black people to the number of potential propertyowners in the South would have increased its rate of inequality (and the Gini coefficient of concentration that measures it), although not everywhere to the same extent.

Wealth in both sections was distributed more equally—perhaps the more apt phrase is less unequally—in the countryside than in towns and cities. While the rural North has been less intensively investigated than its Southern counterpart, enough research has been completed to disclose that the North was hardly a haven of egalitarian distribution of property. Rural Wisconsin (which had a Gini coefficient of inequality as high as that of antebellum Texas), the Michigan frontier, and northwestern New York State were centers of inequality and poverty. At mid-century, the proportion of white men who owned land in any amount was substantially lower in the Northwest than in the South. The percentage of free males owning land in the North as a whole was slightly smaller than in the South. Owing to the absence of slaves and to the relative paucity of very large farms, wealth was somewhat less unequally distributed in the rural North than in the South.

In investigating the distribution of wealth in the antebellum rural South, scholars have probed data on different states, counties, and regions. The patterns throughout are remarkably similar, whether for wealth in general, land and real estate, or personal and slave property. Accentuating the maldistribution of landed wealth—whether in Alabama, Mississippi, Louisiana, Texas, the "cotton South," or the agricultural South as a whole—was a fact of life that the Owsley school neglected: the dollar value per acre of large farms owned by slave-owning planters was substantially greater than the value per acre of the small farm. And yet, regardless of the nature of the soil or the proportion of large farms in a given region, the rates of wealth concentration were remarkably similar as well as constant during the decades before the war. Paralleling the recent finding that in antebellum Texas, no matter what the differences were "in climate, soil, and extent of settlement, the most striking fact is . . . the high degree of concentration in wealthholding across all the regions," another recent study reports no great differences in "the degree of inequality" between the cotton South and the other "major agricultural regions" of grain, tobacco, sugar, and rice production in 1860.

The distribution of slave wealth closely followed the pattern of other forms of Southern wealth. During the decade before the war, slaveownership was confined to between 20 and 25 percent of white families, and maldistribution of this form of property was the rule within the slave-owning population. Half of all slaveowners owned five or fewer slaves, with only one-tenth owning the twenty or more slaves that by Ulrich B. Phillips's definition made them "planters." Less than one-half of 1 percent owned one hundred or more slaves. As with other forms of wealth, the concentration of slave wealth increased slightly between 1850 and 1860.

While the South had long lagged behind the North in urban development, recent scholarship has unearthed evidence that Southern cities grew at a remarkable rate during the antebellum decades. If the Southern rate of urban expansion still did not match the Northern quantitatively, Southern cities, old and new, were qualitatively not unlike their Northern counterparts. Antebellum cities in all latitudes were amazingly similar in the roles they played in the political, administrative, financial, economic, artistic, and intellectual affairs of their regions. Antebellum cities were also alike in the types of men who ran them, in the underlying social philosophies guiding those men, and in their "social configurations." Not the least of the similarities of cities in both great sections was in their distribution of wealth.

Three things can be said about the distribution of wealth in the towns and cities of the Old South. Property ownership was even more concentrated there than in rural areas. Riches became more unequally distributed with the passage of time, with the proportion of the propertyless increasing sharply between 1850 and 1860. There was an increase too in the proportion of urban wealth owned by the largest wealthholders—at least for the dozen communities measured to date. And the patterns of wealth distribution in Southern cities were very much like those that were obtained in the North. . . .

Throwing important, if indirect, light on the relatively slight opportunities for upward social and economic movement antebellum America offered to poor or economically marginal men is the era's high rate of physical or geographical mobility. In rural as well as urban communities, in large cities and small, and on both sides of the Mason-Dixon line, armies of footloose Americans were on the move, following trails never dreamed of in the Turner thesis. One-half of the residents, primarily the poorer and propertyless, left those communities from one decade to another in their search for a more acceptable living. I have no doubt that future research will yet disclose that, during what was a period of economic expansion in both sections, significant numbers of Americans improved their lot, even if modestly. To date, however, the data reveal equally slight rates of social mobility and high rates of geographical mobility on both sides of the Mason-Dixon line.

Carl Degler has recently observed that Southern society "differed from northern in that the social hierarchy culminated in the planter, not the industrialist." At mid-century, great Northern fortunes, in fact, owned more to commerce and finance than to manufacturing. What is perhaps more important is that a sharply differentiated social hierarchy obtained in both sections. In Degler's phrase, planter status was "the ideal to which other white southerners aspired." A good case can be made for the equally magnetic attraction that exalted merchant status had for Northerners. If the fragmentary evidence on Virginia, Georgia, and the Carolinas, which Jane H. Pease has so effectively exploited, is any indica-

tion, then great planters lived less sybaritically and consumed less conspicuously than historians had previously thought. If Philip Hone's marvelous diary—two dozen full-to-the-brim volumes of life among the swells during the antebellum decades—had broader implication, then the Northeastern social and economic elite commanded a lifestyle of an elegance and costliness that, among other things, proved irresistably attractive to the aristocratic Southerners who graced Hone's table, pursued diversion with other members of Hone's set, and married into its families—the Gardiners, Coolidges, Coldens, Bayards, Gouverneurs, and Kortrights. . . .

Influence, power, and, above all, politics in antebellum America have been the subjects of massive recent research. Most discussions of antebellum politics have stressed differences between the major parties. The literature takes on new meaning peculiarly germane to this discussion when it is recast and its focus shifted to a comparison of politics in the North and South. . . .

By mid-century the American political system was everywhere formally democratic. Notorious exceptions to and limitations on democracy persisted, but they persisted in both North and South and for largely the same reasons. If blacks could not vote in the Old South, with rare exceptions neither could they vote in the Old North, where they were barred by statute, subterfuge, custom, and intimidation. The South initiated the movement to limit the powers and terms of office of the judiciary and substitute popular elections for the appointment of judges. When Fletcher M. Green reminded us a generation ago that antebellum Southern states created new, and modified old, constitutions that were fully as democratic as those in Northern states, he concluded that by this "progressive expansion in the application of the doctrine of political equality . . . , the aristocratic planter class had been shorn of its political power." Power, he claimed, had now been transferred to "the great mass of whites." As Green's critics were quick to point out, popular suffrage and theoretical rights to hold office are not synonomous with popular power. Yet these are not empty or hollow rights. That they have often been made so testifies not to their insignificance but rather to the importance of the larger context in which democratic political gains are registered. It remains neither a small matter nor a small similarity that on the constitutional level the antebellum North and South were similarly democratic and republican.

At least as important as society's system for selecting political officeholders is the kind of men who are regularly selected and their characteristic performance in office. . . .

Abundant data have been accumulated on the occupations, wealth and property ownership, church affiliations, education, and other social indicators not only of antebellum officeholders in several dozen cities equally divided between South and North and in counties in every Southern state but also of state officials in all of the Southern and most of the Northern states and of Congressmen from most of the states in the Union. The resultant picture inevitably is not uniform. Humble county and town officials, for example, were less likely to be drawn from the highest levels of wealth and from the most prestigious occupations than were men who occupied more exalted state and federal positions. Aldermen and councilmen usually did not

match the mayor either in wealth or in family prestige. But the relatively slight social and economic differences found between men at different levels of government or between men nominated by the parties that dominated American politics from the 1830s to the 1850s were not differences between the North and South. In the South as in the North, men similar in their dissimilarity to their constituencies held office and exercised behind-the-scenes influence. In contrast to the small farmers, indigents, laborers, artisans, clerks, and shopkeepers—the men of little or no property who constituted the great majority of the antebellum population—the men who held office and controlled the affairs of the major parties were everywhere lawyers, merchants, businessmen, and relatively large property owners. In the South they were inordinately men who owned slaves and owned them in unusually large numbers. It may well be that a society that is stratified economically and socially will confer leadership on those who have what Robert A. Dahl has called substantial material "advantages." It is not clear that this is an iron law. What is clear is that the Old South and the North awarded leadership to precisely such men.

More important than the social and economic backgrounds of political leaders are their public behavior and the ideologies or "world views" underlying this behavior. Not that the thinking or action of powerful men is totally unaffected by their material circumstances. But, in view of the complexity of any individual's ideology and of the diverse elements that help shape it, the effect of these circumstances cannot be assumed and is likely to vary from one individual to another. Although the political philosophies of men do not lend themselves to quantitative or precise measurement, the burden of recent scholarship is that most Southern and Northern political activists were similarly ambitious for worldly success, opportunistic, materialistic, and disinclined to disturb their societies' social arrangements. Men with values such as these were ideally suited to lead the great pragmatic parties that dominated antebellum politics.[1]

Many parties flashed across the American political horizon during the antebellum decades. That the Antimasonic Party, the Liberty Party, and the Free Soil Party almost entirely bypassed the South is an important difference between the sections. The South was not hospitable to organized political dissent, particularly dissent hostile to the expansion of slavery. . . .

The Democrats and Whigs were national parties drawing their leaders and followers from both sections. They could usually count on intersectional support for the national tickets they presented quadrennially to the nation at large. Interestingly, the presidency—whether occupied by Southerners Jackson, Tyler, Polk, and Taylor and the Southern-born Harrison or Northerners Van Buren, Fillmore, Pierce, and Buchanan—was in the 1830s, 1840s, and 1850s in the hands of Whigs and Democrats who displayed great sensitivity toward the political and economic interests of the slave-owning South. In the 1840s Congressmen voted not by region as Northerners or Southerners but primarily as Whigs and Democrats. Party rather than sectional interest prevailed in the roll calls on most issues reaching the national political agenda. In the 1850s, as Thomas B. Alexander has reported, "forces greater than party discipline . . . were evidently at work . . . ,

forcing party to yield to section on a definable number of issues." Yet, even in the 1950s, "both major parties maintained a high level of cohesion of intersectional comity" with regard to the range of issues not bearing on slavery and its right to expansion.

The great national issues of antebellum politics, culminating as they did in Sumter and the ensuing war, were of transcendant importance to Americans. A good case can nonetheless be made that local and state politics touched the lives of people more often and more directly than did national politics, particularly during an era when the men in the nation's capital were inclined to treat laissez faire as an article of faith. State governments in North and South, by contrast, engaged in vigorous regulation of a wide range of economic activities. Local governments taxed citizens and, if with limited effectiveness, sought to provide for their safety, regulate their markets and many of their business activities, look after the poor, maintain public health, improve local thoroughfares, dispose of waste, pump in water, light up the dark, and furnish some minimal cultural amenities though the exercise of powers that characteristically had been granted by state government. States chartered banks, transportation companies, and other forms of business enterprise, determined the scope of such charters, themselves engaged in business, disposed of land, and regulated local communities. The great question is how did the actual operations of local and state governments in the North and South compare during the antebellum decades.

Antebellum state government was almost invariably controlled by either Whigs or Democrats. The major parties were essentially state parties, bound together in the most loosely organized national confederations. Citizens divided not by geographical section but by party preference within each state. The parties were in all latitudes characteristically controlled by tight groups of insiders that sometimes monopolized power, sometimes shared it with rival factions, in the one case as in other controlling nominations and conventions, hammering out policy, disseminating and publicizing the party line, organizing the faithful to support it, enforcing strict discipline, and punishing those who dared challenge either the policies or the tactics pursued by the leadership. While party policies could conceivably have been infused with the noble principles proclaimed in party rhetoric, such infusion rarely appears to have been the case. The "Albany Regency," the "Richmond Junto," the "Bourbon Dynasty" of Arkansas, and similar cliques in control elsewhere have been described as realists rather than idealists.

In towns and cities, unlike the states, party counted for little. Candidates for the mayor's office and the local council or board of aldermen did not fail to remind voters of the moral superiority of their own parties. But, as students of antebellum urban politics have noted, it mattered little whether this major party or that won the election or whether the town was located north or south of the Mason-Dixon line. . . .

Perhaps in no other milieu was governmental policy so permeated with class bias. Whether it was Natchez or Springfield, Charleston or Brooklyn, New Orleans or Boston, the lawyers, merchants, and large propertyowners who occupied city hall ran things in the interests of the "wealthier inhabitants." Tax rates were everywhere miniscule and property flagrantly underassessed, at the insistence of large taxpayers. Valuable lots were leased to rich men at ridiculously low rates, if not sold to them for a song. Funds provided by the niggardly budgets typical of the time were spent most freely to improve or widen streets used by businessmen rather than to clean streets in the neighborhoods of the poor. Improved public facilities for disposing of waste or carrying fresh water into the city were usually introduced first in upper-class residential districts. The "indisputable connection between the policies of the city council and the interests of the wealthier inhabitants" that Richard Wade discerned in Cincinnati early in the era could be found in most other cities.

Power is not, of course, confined to control of government. Control over banks, credit, capital, communications, and voluntary associations, which in an era of laissez faire often exercised more influence than did public authorities over education and culture, crime and punishment, social welfare and poverty, gave to those who had it a power that was barely matched by those who held the reins of government. The burden of recent research is that small social and economic elites exercised a degree of control over the most important institutions in the antebellum North that bears close resemblance to the great power attributed to the great planter-slaveowners by William E. Dodd a half century ago and by Eugene D. Genovese more recently. Influential voluntary associations and financial institutions appear to have been run by similarly atypical sorts on both sides of the Mason-Dixon line.

Shortly after secession, Governor Joseph E. Brown told the Georgia legislature that in the South the "whole social system is one of perfect homogeneity of interest, where every class is interested in sustaining the interest of every other class." Numerous Southerners agreed with him, and many scholars concur. In their failure to challenge planter supremacy, small farmers—slaveowners and nonslaveowners alike—ostensibly demonstrated the unique identity of interest that was said to bind all whites together in the antebellum South. The interest of a group is a normative term, known only to God (and perhaps to Rousseau in his capacity as authority on the General Will), in contrast to its perceived interests, as stated in its words and implicit in its actions. There are, therefore, as many interpretations of the "true interests" of Southern—or, for that matter, of Northern—small farmers as there are historians writing on the subject. The South's large enslaved black population doubtless affected the perceptions of all Southern whites, if in complex and unmeasurable ways. Recent research indicates that poorer and nonslave-owning Southern whites were, nevertheless, sensitive enough to their own social and economic deprivation to oppose their social superiors on secession and other important matters. Whether the acquiescence of the mass of antebellum Northerners in their inferior social and economic condition was in their own interest will be decided differently by conservative, reformist, and radical historians. Our admittedly insubstantial evidence on the issue suggests that the degree of social harmony coexisting with subtle underlying social tensions was, racial matters apart, not much different in the North and the South.

Limitations of space permit no more than a swift allusion to a number of other matters that are fascinating either because, like religiosity and values, they are intangible or, like crime and violence, they resist precise measurement. Scholars of a revisionist bent can have a field day with these themes, for the growing literature on them yields tantalizing evidence that appears to overturn the traditional view of a distinctive antebellum South. Legal briefs can thus be written attesting the near similarity of the South and North in their achievements in science, medicine, public health, and other aspects of intellectual and cultural life, in their ideals of womanhood, in their racial attitudes, in their violence and attitudes toward violence, in their materialism as in other values, in aspects of humanitarian reform, and in religion, particularly in the roles played by evangelicalism and the Benevolent Empire in the Protestant denominations that were predominant in both sections. Much of this literature implicitly promotes the concept of sectional convergence either by upgrading Southern or by downgrading Northern achievements. But, since historians—unlike embattled attorneys—cannot content themselves with evidence that is both insubstantial and contradicted by evidence pointing in an opposite direction, they are best advised to reserve judgment. Wisdom consists in re-examining and re-evaluating the earlier literature on these themes, weighing carefully the merits of the recent contributions, and, above all, probing for additional evidence.

Having examined economic developments, social structure, and politics and power in the antebellum sections, let me now return to the question of capitalism in the Old South. Several historians have recently argued that Southern planters constituted a "seigneurial" class presiding over a "pseudocapitalistic" society, a class whose "world view" ostensibly set them "apart from the mainstream of capitalistic civilization." By this analysis, the Old South, though influenced by modern capitalism, belonged (as do early modern India and Saudi Arabia, among others) to the category of "premodern" societies that have been the economic and political dependencies of the dynamic industrial world that exploits them. The antebellum South's banking, commercial, and credit institutions did not in this view manifest the section's own capitalistic development so much as they served to facilitate the South's exploitation by the "capitalistic world market." This argument can be accepted uncritically only by accepting Eugene D. Genovese, Barrington Moore, Jr., and Raimondi Luraghi as the arbiters and interpreters of what represents "every normal feature of capitalism."

Capitalism is not a rigid system governed by uniform economic practices, let alone inflexible definitions. The economy of the antebellum United States, like capitalistic economies in Victorian England and other nations, was composed of diverse elements, each playing a part in a geographical and functional division of labor within the larger society. As Lewis C. Gray and Thomas P. Govan long ago and other scholars more recently have observed, Southern planters had the attitudes and goals and were guided by the classic practices of capitalistic businessmen. The antiurbanism and antimaterialism that Genovese has attributed to the great planters is unconvincing because thinly documented and contradicted by much other evidence. Some people, including planters themselves, may have likened the planter class to a seigneurial

aristocracy. Unlike the lords of the textbook manor, however, Southern planters depended heavily on outside trade, participated enthusiastically in a money economy, and sought continuously to expand their operations and their capital. Marx once said that the limits of the serf's exploitation were determined by the walls of the lord's stomach. The limits of the slave's exploitation were determined by the expanding walls of the world cotton market.

That slavery is not the classic labor system associated with a Marxist definition of capitalism is, of course, true. The problem with Marx as pundit of capitalism, for all the undeniable brilliance of his interpretation, is that he was, as he conceded, more interested in changing the system than in explaining it. Those of us content with merely understanding so complex a phenomenon as capitalism know that, whether in its labor system or in other respects, it is a flexible and constantly shifting order, susceptible of diverse definitions. The Southern economy did differ in important respects from the Northern, developing special interests of its own. Yet, far from being in any sense members of a colony or dependency of the North, the Southern upper classes enjoyed close ties with the Northern capitalists who were, in a sense, their business partners. The South was an integral component of a wealthy and dynamic national economy, no part of which conformed perfectly to a textbook definition of pure capitalism. In part because of the central place in that economy of its great export crop, cotton, the South from the 1820s to the 1860s exerted a degree of influence over the nation's domestic and foreign policies that was barely equalled by the antebellum North. India within the Empire indeed! The

South's political system of republicanism and limited democracy, like its hierarchical social structure, conformed closely to the prevailing arrangements in the North, as they also did to the classic features of a capitalistic order.

The striking similarities of the two antebellum sections of the nation neither erase their equally striking dissimilarities nor detract from the significance of these dissimilarities. Whether in climate, diet, work habits, uses of leisure, speech and diction, health and disease, mood, habits, ideals, self-image, or labor systems, profound differences separated the antebellum North and South. One suspects that antebellum Americans regarded these matters as the vital stuff of life. The point need not be labored that a society, one-third of whose members were slaves (and slaves of a distinctive "race"), is most unlike a society of free men and women. An essay focusing on these rather than on the themes emphasized here would highlight the vital disparities between the antebellum South and North. And yet the striking dissimilarities of the two antebellum sections do not erase their equally striking similarities, nor do they detract from the significance of these similarities.

The antebellum North and South were far more alike than the conventional scholarly wisdom has led us to believe. Beguiled by the charming version of Northern society and politics composed by Tocqueville, the young Marx, and other influential antebellum commentators, historians have until recently believed that the Northern social structure was far more egalitarian and offered far greater opportunity for upward social movement than did its Southern counterpart and that white men of humble position had far more power in the Old North than they did in the Old South. In disclosing that the reality of the antebellum North fell far short of the egalitarian ideal, modern studies of social structure sharply narrow the gulf between the antebellum North and South. Without being replicas of one another, both sections were relatively rich, powerful, aggressive, and assertive communities, socially stratified and governed equally—and disconcertingly—oligarchic internal arrangements. That they were drawn into the most terrible of all American wars may have been due, as is often the case when great powers fight, as much to their similarities as to their differences. The war owed more, I believe, to the inevitably opposed but similarly selfish interests—or perceived interests—of North and South than to differences in their cultures and institutions.

Late in the Civil War, William King of Cobb County, Georgia, reported that invading Union officers had told him, "We are one people, [with] the same language, habits, and religion, and ought to be one people." The officers might have added that on the spiritual plane Southerners shared with Northerners many ideals and aspirations and had contributed heavily to those historical experiences the memory and symbols of which tie a people together as a nation. For all of their distinctiveness, the Old South and North were complementary elements in an American society that was everywhere primarily rural, capitalistic, materialistic, and socially stratified, racially, ethnically, and religiously heterogeneous, and stridently chauvinistic and expansionist—a society whose practice fell far short of, when it was not totally in conflict with, its lofty theory.

NOTES

1. By pragmatic parties I mean, as do most historians and political scientists who have used the term, parties largely but not solely concerned with electoral success, parties not devoid of principles so much as parties of flexible or shifting principles.

POSTSCRIPT

Was the Antebellum South a Unique Section in American History?

While Genovese's view of a unique South is widely accepted, his theoretical framework of a precapitalistic South dominated by a class-oriented group of paternalistic slaveholders has been challenged in several ways. First, Pessen charges that Genovese's definition of capitalism is too rigid and underestimates the entrepreneurial motivations of the plantation owners. Part of the reason for his precapitalist views of the South can be attributed to the fact that Genovese, like earlier Southern historians such as Ulrich B. Phillips, believed that slavery was not only an inefficient system but was also unprofitable. Employing contemporary methods of economic analysis, Alfred H. Conrad and John R. Meyer, in their classic article "The Economics of Slavery in the Antebellum South," *The Journal of Political Economy* (April 1958), conclude that slavery was profitable. The slave owners, they argue, were market-oriented capitalists who operated in a two-tier economy. Those with the less productive land in the upper South and border states continued to produce slaves and sell them to the staple crop areas in the deep South, which needed the labor to grow cash crops such as cotton, sugar, and indigo.

Other historians, like James Oakes in *The Ruling Race: A History of American Slaveholders* (Knopf, 1982), challenge Genovese's argument "that slavery was a precapitalist form of social organization whose 'logical outcome' was a paternalistic world view." Denying that the antebellum South was of one view, Oakes "found major divisions within a diverse slaveholding class, along with a general tendency away from paternalism and toward an acceptance of liberal democracy and free-market commercialism."

In *Place Over Time: The Continuity of Southern Distinctions* (LSU Press, 1977), Pulitzer Prize-winning historian Carl N. Degler accepts the argument that the South was a unique society, but he challenges Genovese's Marxian class-oriented analysis. Degler denies that the planters were able to impose "their" values onto the other classes of Southern society. He rejects a class analysis in favor of a social consensus analysis, which maintains that "on fundamental social values and goals the slaveholders and nonslaveholders were in agreement. . . ." "Nonslaveholders," continues Degler, "not only accepted slavery as a means of control over labor and over black people, but also aspired to become slaveholders themselves and to perpetuate the world slavery made."

In making the argument that the North and South were more similar than dissimilar, Pessen has presented the reader with a synthesis of the political, social, and economic characteristics of pre–Civil War American society. He has based his findings on a number of local mobility studies that employ quantitative evidence of census data, including his own works about New

York City during the Jacksonian era. According to Pessen, the two-party system of competition between Democrats and Whigs was operating in both sections; upper-class merchants and planters controlled the wealth and dominated the leadership of the major political and social organizations; and finally, both North and South were agrarian in nature with the majority of the population engaged in farming.

Pessen's views have not gone unchallenged. The well-known economic historian Stanley L. Engerman, in an *American Historical Review* Forum, points out that attitudes toward race and slavery and the influence of the planter-slaveholders on the economic policies of the nation certainly differentiated the antebellum North and South. "However similar the motivations of planter capitalists and industrial capitalists," says Engerman, "However efficiently each section followed its comparative advantage, and however rapidly both sections were growing economically, one section included a slave-based agriculture and the other had, in addition to a commercial agriculture based on family farms, a developing industrial sector based upon wage labor. One section was more influenced by planter–slave owners, the other more by merchants and industrial capitalists."

Cliometricians, those economic historians who rely very heavily on statistical analysis, have also questioned the validity of Pessen's portrait of a highly stratified, class-dominated, Jacksonian America. The sophisticated reader might want to compare Robert E. Gallman's critique of "Professor Pessen On the 'Egalitarian myth'," *Social Science History* (Winter 1978) with Pessen's response "On a Recent Cliometric Attempt to Resurrect the Myth of Antebellum Egalitarianism," *Social Science History* (Winter 1979). In comparing British and American wealth before the Civil War, Gallman believes that "America must have produced new fortunes at an extraordinarily high rate and that the *relative* economic standing of the idle rich must have been eroded at a *relatively* rapid pace." It was this new money, concludes Gallman, that provided the impetus for the early stages of our industrial revolution.

If the reader wishes to pursue Pessen's approach further, see *Riches, Class and Power Before the Civil War* (Heath, 1973). Genovese also published a number of influential works, including *Roll, Jordan, Roll: The World the Slaves Made* (Pantheon, 1974), which is considered one of the best accounts of nineteenth-century slavery. Two important collections of his essays, many of which were written for a general audience, are *In Red and Black: Marxian Explorations in Southern and Afro-American History* (Pantheon, 1971) and *Fruits of Merchant Capitalism* (Oxford, 1983), written with Elizabeth Fox-Genovese.

In their efforts to reveal the true South, James Oakes attempts to synthesize the "unique" and "American" South in his most recent book *Slavery and Freedom: An Interpretation of the Old South* (Knopf, 1990), while Charles Reagan Wilson and William Ferris, eds., in the *Encyclopedia of Southern Culture* (University of North Carolina Press, 1989), give focus to the heart of Dixie.

ISSUE 16

Was Abraham Lincoln America's Greatest President?

YES: Stephen B. Oates, from *Abraham Lincoln: The Man Behind the Myths* (Harper & Row, 1984)

NO: M. E. Bradford, from *Remembering Who We Are: Observations of a Southern Conservative* (University of Georgia Press, 1985)

ISSUE SUMMARY

YES: Professor of history Stephen B. Oates insists that Abraham Lincoln's greatness as president of the United States stemmed from a moral vision that had as its goal the protection and expansion of popular government.

NO: Professor of English literature M. E. Bradford characterizes Lincoln as a cynical politician whose abuse of authority as president and commander in chief during the Civil War marked a serious departure from the republican goals of the Founding Fathers and established the prototype for the "imperial presidency" of the twentieth century.

The American Civil War (1861–1865) produced what historian Arthur Schlesinger, Jr., has called "our greatest national trauma." To be sure, the War Between the States was a searing event that etched itself on the collective memory of the American people and inspired an interest that has made it the most thoroughly studied episode in American history. During the last century and a quarter, scholars have identified a variety of factors (including slavery, economic sectionalism, cultural distinctions between the North and South, the doctrine of states' rights, and the irresponsibility of abolitionists and proslavery advocates) that contributed to sectional tensions and, ultimately, war. Although often presented as "sole causes," these factors are complicated, interconnected, and controversial. Consequently, historians must consider as many of them as possible in their evaluations of the war, even if they choose to spotlight one or another as the main explanation.

Most historians, however, agree that the war would not have occurred had eleven Southern states not seceded from the Union to form the Confederate States of America following Abraham Lincoln's election to the presidency in 1860. Why was Lincoln viewed as a threat to the South? A Southerner by birth, Lincoln's career in national politics (as a congressman representing his adopted state of Illinois) apparently had been short-circuited by his unpopular opposition to the Mexican War. His attempt to emerge from political obscurity a decade later failed when he was defeated by Stephen Douglas in a bid for an Illinois Senate seat. This campaign, however, gained for Lincoln a reputation as a powerful orator, and in 1860 Republican party managers passed over some of their more well known leaders, such as William Henry Seward, and nominated the moderate Mr. Lincoln for the presidency. His victory was guaranteed by factionalism within Democratic ranks, but the election results revealed that the new president received only 39 percent of the popular vote. This fact, however, provided little solace for Southerners, who mistook the new president's opposition to the extension of slavery into the territories for evidence that he supported the abolitionist wing of the Republican party. Despite assurances during the campaign that he would not tamper with slavery where it already existed, Lincoln could not prevent the splintering of the Union.

Given such an inauspicious beginning, few observers at the time could have predicted that future generations would view Lincoln as our nation's greatest president. What factors have contributed to this assessment? The answer would appear to lie in his role as commander in chief during the Civil War. Is this reputation deserved? The essays that follow assess Lincoln's presidency from dramatically different perspectives.

Stephen B. Oates, a recent biographer of Lincoln, sees greatness in the leadership of the nation's 16th chief executive. Lincoln possessed a moral vision that served as his inspiration for ending oppression and enlarging the rights of the people. Oates's Lincoln is a practical politician who held the Union together and played a prominent role in formulating the strategy for the North's military victory.

M. E. Bradford offers a sharp critique of the conclusions reached by Oates. By pursuing an anti-Southern strategy, Bradford argues, President Lincoln perverted the republican goals advanced by the Founding Fathers and destroyed the Democratic majority which was essential to the preservation of the Union. Furthermore, he abused his executive authority by cynically expanding the scope of presidential powers to an unhealthy extent. Finally, Bradford charges that Lincoln was uncommitted to the cause of black Americans.

YES

Stephen B. Oates

THE MAN BEHIND THE MYTHS

THE BEACON LIGHT OF LIBERTY

In presidential polls taken by *Life* Magazine in 1948, the *New York Times Magazine* in 1962, and the *Chicago Tribune Magazine* in 1982, historians and political scholars ranked Lincoln as the best chief executive in American history. They were not trying to mythologize the man, for they realized that errors, vacillations, and human flaws marred his record. Their rankings indicate, however, that the icon of mythology did rise out of a powerful historical figure, a man who learned from his mistakes and made a difference. Indeed, Lincoln led the lists because he had a moral vision of where his country must go to preserve and enlarge the rights of all her people. He led the lists because he had an acute sense of history—an ability to identify himself with a historical turning point in his time and to articulate the promise that held for the liberation of oppressed humanity the world over. He led the lists because he perceived the truth of his age and embodied it in his words and deeds. He led the lists because, in his interaction with the spirit and events of his day, he made momentous *moral* decisions that affected the course of humankind. . . .

THE CENTRAL IDEA

In the flames of civil war, Lincoln underwent seemingly endless crises that might have shattered a weaker man. Here he was—a President who lacked administrative experience, suffered from chronic depression, hated to fire inept subordinates and bungling generals (he had never liked personal confrontations anyway)—thrust into the center of a fratricidal conflict. Here he was, forced to make awesome decisions in a war that had no precedent in all American history, a war without constitutional or political guidelines for him to follow. At the same time, Lincoln had to live with the knowledge that he was the most unpopular President the Republic had known up to that time. . . .

From Stephen B. Oates, *Abraham Lincoln: The Man Behind the Myths* (Harper & Row, 1984). Copyright © 1984 by Stephen B. Oates. Reprinted by permission of Harper & Row, Publishers, Inc.

From all directions came cries that Lincoln was unfit to be President, that he was too inexperienced, too inept, too stupid and imbecilic, to reunite the country. Even some of his Cabinet secretaries, even some of his friends, feared that the war was too much for him.

Melancholy and inexperienced though he was, unsure of himself and savagely criticized though he was, Lincoln managed nevertheless to see this huge and confusing conflict in a world dimension. He defined and fought it according to his core of unshakable convictions about America's experiment and historic mission in the progress of human liberty. The central issue of the war, he told Congress on Independence Day, 1861, was whether a constitutional republic—a system of popular government—could preserve itself. There were Europeans who argued that anarchy and rebellion were inherent weaknesses of a republic and that a monarchy was the more stable form of government. Now, in the Civil War, popular government was going through a fiery trial for its very survival. If it failed in America, if it succumbed to the forces of reaction represented by the slave-based Confederacy, it might indeed perish from the earth. The beacon of hope for oppressed humanity the world over would be destroyed. . . .

In short, the war and Lincoln's response to it defined him as a President. Here is a classic illustration of how the interaction of people and events shapes the course of history. As the war grew and changed, so Lincoln grew and changed. At first, he warned that the conflict must not turn into a "remorseless revolutionary struggle," lest that cause wide-scale social and political wreckage. As a consequence, his initial war strategies were cautious and limited. But when the conflict ground on with no end in sight, Lincoln resorted to one harsh war measure after another to subdue the rebellion and save popular government: he embraced martial law, property confiscation, emancipation, Negro troops, conscription, and scorched-earth warfare. These turned the war into the very thing he had cautioned against: a remorseless revolutionary struggle whose concussions are still being felt.

And it became such a struggle because of Lincoln's unswerving commitment to the war's central idea.

DEATH WARRANT FOR SLAVERY

Nowhere was the struggle more evident than in the nagging problem of slavery. How Lincoln approached that problem—and what he did about it—is one of the most written about and least understood facets of his presidency. As we examine this dramatic and complicated story, recall that what guided Lincoln in the matter of emancipation was his commitment, not just to the Union, but to what it represented and symbolized. Here, as in all war-related issues, Lincoln's devotion to the war's central idea—to preserving a system that guaranteed to all the right of self-government—dictated his course of action. . . .

At first, Lincoln rejected a presidential move against slavery. "I think Sumner and the rest of you would upset our applecart altogether if you had your way," he told some advanced Republicans one day. "We didn't go into the war to put down slavery, but to put the flag back; and to act differently at this moment would, I have no doubt, not only weaken our cause, but smack of bad-faith. . . . This thunderbolt will keep."

In short, as President he was accountable to the entire country, or what remained of it in the North and West, and the vast majority of whites there remained adamantly opposed to emancipation.

Still, Lincoln was sympathetic to the entire range of arguments Sumner and his associates rehearsed for him. Personally, Lincoln hated slavery as much as they did, and many of their points had already occurred to him. On certain days he could be seen like them in the lecture hall of the Smithsonian Institution, listening quietly and intently as antislavery orators damned slavery for the evil that it was. Under the combined and incessant demands that he act, Lincoln began wavering in his hands-off policy about slavery; as early as November and December, 1861, he began searching about for some compromise—something short of a sweeping emancipation decree, which he still regarded as "too big a lick." Again he seemed caught in an impossible dilemma: how to remove the cause of war, keep Britain out of the conflict, solve the refugee problem, cripple the Confederacy, and suppress the rebellion, and yet retain the allegiance of northern Democrats and the critical border. . . .

On July 22, 1862, Lincoln summoned his Cabinet members and read them a draft of a preliminary Emancipation Proclamation. Come January 1, 1863, in his capacity as Commander-in-Chief of the armed forces in time of war, Lincoln would free all the slaves everywhere in the rebel states. He would thus make it a Union objective to annihilate slavery as an institution in the Confederate South.

Contrary to what many historians have said, Lincoln's projected Proclamation went further than anything Congress had done. True, Congress had just enacted (and Lincoln had just signed) the second confiscation act, which provided for the seizure and liberation of all slaves of people who supported or participated in the rebellion. Still, most slaves would be freed only after protracted case-by-case litigation in the federal courts. Another section of the act did liberate certain categories of slaves without court action, but the bill exempted loyal slaveowners in the rebel South, allowing them to keep their slaves and other property. Far short of a genuine emancipation measure, the act was about as far as Congress could go in attacking slavery, for most Republicans still acknowledged that Congress had no constitutional authority to remove bondage as a state institution. Only the President with his war powers— or a constitutional amendment—could do that. Nevertheless, the measure seemed a clear invitation for the President to exercise his constitutional powers and abolish slavery in the rebellious states. And Stevens, Sumner, and others repeatedly told Lincoln that most congressional Republicans now favored this.

In contrast to the confiscation act, Lincoln's Proclamation was a sweeping blow against slavery as an institution in the rebel states, a blow that would free *all* slaves there—those of secessionists and loyalists alike. Thus Lincoln would handle emancipation himself (as congressional Republicans wanted him to do), avoid judicial red tape, and use the military to vanquish the cornerstone of the Confederacy. Again, he justified this as a military necessity to save the Union— and with it America's experiment in popular government. . . .

THE MAN OF OUR REDEMPTION

When he won the election of 1864, Lincoln interpreted it as a popular mandate for him and his emancipation policy. But in reality the election provided no clear referendum on slavery, since Republican campaigners had played down emancipation and concentrated on the folly of the Democrats in running General George McClellan on a peace plank in the midst of civil war. Nevertheless, Lincoln used his reelection to promote a constitutional amendment that would guarantee the freedom of all slaves, those in the loyal border states as well as those in the rebel South. Even before issuing his Proclamation, Lincoln had worried that it might be nullified in the courts or thrown out by a later Congress or a subsequent administration. Consequently he wanted a constitutional amendment that would safeguard his Proclamation and prevent emancipation from ever being overturned.

Back in December, 1862, Lincoln himself had called on Congress to adopt an emancipation amendment, and advanced Republicans had introduced one in the Senate and guided it through, reminding their colleagues that nobody could deny that all the death and destruction of the war stemmed from slavery and that it was their duty to support this amendment. In April, 1864, the Senate adopted it by a vote of thirty-eight to six, but it failed to muster the required two-thirds majority in the House.

After that Lincoln had insisted that the Republican platform endorse the measure. And now, over the winter of 1864 and 1865, he put tremendous pressure on the House to approve the amendment, using all his powers of persuasion and patronage to get it through. He buttonholed conservative Republicans and opposition Democrats and exhorted them to support the amendment. He singled out "sinners" among the Democrats who were "on praying ground," and informed them that they had a lot better chance for the federal jobs they desired if they voted for the measure. Soon two Democrats swung over in favor of it. In the House debates, meanwhile, Republican James Ashley quoted Lincoln himself that *"if slavery is not wrong, nothing is wrong,"* and Thaddeus Stevens, still tall and imposing at seventy-two, asserted that he had never hesitated, even when threatened with violence, "to stand here and denounce this infamous institution." With the outcome much in doubt, Lincoln and congressional Republicans participated in secret negotiations never made public—negotiations that allegedly involved patronage, a New Jersey railroad monopoly, and the release of rebels related to congressional Democrats—to bring wavering opponents into line. "The greatest measure of the nineteenth century," Stevens claimed, "was passed by corruption, aided and abetted by the purest man in America."

On January 31, 1865, the House adopted the present Thirteenth Amendment by just three votes more than the required two-thirds majority. At once a storm of cheers broke over House Republicans, who danced around, embraced one another, and waved their hats and canes. "It seemed to me I had been born into a new life," recalled one advanced Republican, "and that the world was overflowing with beauty and joy."

Lincoln, too, pronounced the amendment "a great moral victory" and "a King's cure" for the evils of slavery. When ratified by the states, the amendment would end human bondage everywhere in America. Lincoln pointed across the Potomac. "If the people over the river had behaved themselves, I could not have done what I have." . . .

He had come a long distance from the harassed political candidate of 1858, opposed to emancipation lest his political career be jeopardized, convinced that only the distant future could remove slavery from his troubled land, certain that only colonization could solve the ensuing problem of racial adjustment. He had also come a long way in the matter of Negro social and political rights, . . . The Proclamation had indeed liberated Abraham Lincoln, enabling him to act more consistently with his moral convictions.

He had none of the racial prejudice that infected so many whites of that time, even advanced Republicans like Benjamin Wade. Frederick Douglass, who interviewed Lincoln in 1863, said he was "the first great man that I talked with in the United States freely who in no single instance reminded me of the difference between himself and myself, of the difference of color." Other blacks also testified that the President treated them as they wanted to be treated—as human beings with feelings. He did not tell dialect jokes in their presence, did not condescend to them, did not spell out his thoughts in imbecilic one-syllable language, as did many other whites when speaking to Negroes. He opened the White House doors to black visitors as no other President had ever done before and as few would do after. At his New Year's reception in 1865, he shook hands with a parade of Negro men and women, some in their Sunday finest, others in patched overalls, who had come to pay their respects to the man who signed "the Freedom bill."

During his inaugural reception that March, the President learned that Frederick Douglass was at the front door of the executive mansion, but was having trouble getting past the police because he was a Negro. Lincoln had him shown in at once, hailed him as "my friend Douglass," and asked what he thought of the Inaugural Address. "There is no man in the country whose opinion I value more than yours," Lincoln said. Douglass replied that he was impressed, that he thought it "a sacred effort." "I am glad you liked it!" Lincoln said. In truth, he strongly identified with this proud black man, referring to "the similarity with which I had fought my way up, we both starting off at the lowest round of the ladder."

Douglass, reflecting back on Lincoln's presidency, recalled how in the first year and a half of the war, Lincoln "was ready and willing" to sacrifice black people for the benefit and welfare of whites. But since the preliminary Emancipation Proclamation, Douglass said, American blacks had taken Lincoln's measure and had come to admire and some to love this complicated man. Though Lincoln had taxed Negroes to the limit, they had decided, in the roll and tumble of events, that "the how and the man of our redemption had somehow met in the person of Abraham Lincoln."

NECESSITY KNOWS NO LAW

Lincoln became a tough wartime President, flexing his executive muscles and expanding his war powers whenever necessity demanded. "Necessity," he argued, "knows no law." In the exigency of domestic insurrection, he would do whatever he thought imperative to save the country and all it represented. Yet he did not intend to establish a precedent for an "imperial presidency," one that would allow subsequent chief executives to meddle in the internal affairs of other nations, under the pretext of saving the world. In short, we cannot blame Lincoln for Lyndon Johnson's disastrous policy in Vietnam. Except for emancipation, Lincoln regarded all of his severe war measures as temporary necessities to end the rebellion and preserve the American experiment, the central idea of the war.

Consider his emergency measures during the eighty days between the outbreak of war and the convening of Congress on Independence Day, 1861. Since rebel forces were threatening to occupy Washington and the nation was on the brink of disintegration, Lincoln met with his Cabinet, and they all decided that they must assume broad emergency powers or let the government fall. Accordingly, Lincoln directed that Secretary of the Navy Gideon Welles empower several individuals—among them his own brother-in-law—to forward troops and supplies to embattled Washington. The President allowed his Secretary of War to authorize the governor of New York and one Alexander Cummings to transport troops and acquire supplies for the public defense. Since Lincoln believed that government departments brimmed with traitors, he himself chose private citizens known for "their ability, loyalty, and patriotism" to spend public money for arms and military preparations. Perhaps these emergency measures were "without authority of law," Lincoln told Congress later, but he deemed them absolutely necessary to save popular government itself. And his Cabinet unanimously agreed.

With Cabinet approval, Lincoln also declared a blockade of the southern coast, added 22,000 men to the regular army and 18,000 to the navy, called for 42,000 three-year volunteers, and put national armories into full production. As Lincoln subsequently informed Congress, "These measures, whether strictly legal or not, were ventured upon, under what appeared to be a popular demand, and public necessity; trusting, then as now, that Congress would readily ratify them." When Congress convened in July, it did indeed ratify "all the acts, proclamations, and orders of the President" relating to the army and navy and the volunteers, "as if they had been issued and done under the previous express authority and direction of Congress." In short, if Lincoln went beyond the letter of the law to save the government, Congress sanctioned his actions.

Generally Congress did the same in the area of martial law and military arrests. From the outset, Lincoln dealt harshly with "the enemy in the rear"— with what he called "a most efficient corps of spies, informers, suppliers, and aiders and abettors" of the rebellion who took advantage of "Liberty of speech, Liberty of the press and *Habeas corpus*" to disrupt the Union war effort. Consequently, he suspended the writ of habeas corpus—which required that a citizen be told why he was being held—and authorized army commanders to declare martial law in various areas behind the lines and to try civilians in military courts without juries. Lincoln openly defended such an invasion of civil liberties, contending that strict measures were essential if the laws of the Union—and liberty itself—were to survive the war.

Lincoln's suspension of the writ of habeas corpus infuriated Roger B. Taney, Chief Justice of the U.S. Supreme Court, who accused the President of usurping power. Taney argued that only Congress could legally suspend the writ, and he admonished Lincoln not to violate the very laws he had sworn to defend. "Are all the laws, but one, to go unexecuted,"

Lincoln asked Congress, in reference to habeas corpus, "and the government itself go to pieces lest that one be violated?" Moreover, the Constitution did not specify which branch of the government could suspend the writ, so that Lincoln did not think he had broken any laws or violated his oath of office.

Still, he invoked his presidential powers in heretofore undreamed-of-ways, as we have seen in the matter of emancipation. Recall, though, the novelty of the war. Nothing like this had ever occurred in America, and there were no guidelines in dealing with dissent and national security in the midst of a giant domestic insurrection that imperiled the nation itself. As in most war matters, Lincoln and his Cabinet found themselves in uncharted legal territory.

In 1862 the President centralized jurisdiction over internal-security matters in the War Department. To deal with such matters, the department created a corps of civilian provost marshals, but allowed them too much independence in policing and jailing alleged disloyalists. Their zealous, far-ranging operations led to widespread criticism of the Lincoln administration. At the same time, Lincoln's War Department empowered army officers to apprehend anybody who discouraged volunteering or otherwise helped the enemy. And the department got up dragnets in which state militia, home guards, police chiefs, and vigilantes all participated. In all, they seized and imprisoned at least 14,000 people—many of them antiwar Democrats—under Lincoln's authority. The outcry against arbitrary arrests became so strident that Lincoln tried to restrain excessive use of power whenever he could. He speedily ordered the release of people unwarrantedly arrested, especially political prisoners.

Also, when General Ambrose E. Burnside suspended the Chicago *Times* for virulent outbursts against the administration, Lincoln promptly revoked the order. . . .

Lincoln admitted that internal security in the midst of civil war was a complex problem and that errors and excesses had occurred. It pained him that government agents often confused antiwar rhetoric with disloyal designs and that innocent people suffered. That was why he tempered military arrests with generous pardons and refused to suppress popular assemblies and antiwar newspapers. Yet throughout the conflict he maintained a severe line on disloyalty; and most Republicans supported him. Without military law, they all feared, the rebellion would rage into the North and consume the government from within.

Lincoln was a tough warrior in other ways, too. He fully endorsed military conscription—which Congress authorized in April, 1863—and saw to it that the War Department rigorously enforced the measure. No matter what some historians have claimed, the President also enforced the confiscation of enemy property, believing as he did that "the traitor against the general government" should forfeit his farms, plantations, and other property as just punishment for the crime of insurrection.

Still, Lincoln was no dictator—the very idea appalled him, for it violated everything he held sacred in government. In fact, one of the major reasons he remains our best President is that he shunned a dictatorship, even when some Americans thought it the only way to save the country. But what kind of country would remain if popular government itself were sacrificed? Was it not for this that the war was being fought? Consider Lincoln's stand on the presidential election of 1864. With Union fortunes still uncertain, some men urged Lincoln to cancel the contest lest it result in the victory of antiwar Democrats who would sell out the Union cause. Lincoln refused. "The election," he said later, "was a necessity. We can not have free government without elections; and if the rebellion could force us to forego, or postpone a national election, it might fairly claim to have already conquered us." So he ran against George B. McClellan and the peace plank of the Democratic party, and he won in a fair and open contest.

Later he told a group of White House serenaders what this meant to him. Above all, it meant that the American system still worked, that the people could still choose their leaders even in the middle of domestic rebellion. By holding the contest, Lincoln and the northern people had preserved their popular government and demonstrated how strong they were. And Lincoln was glad, he told the serenaders, that most voters had gone for him, the candidate most devoted to the Union and opposed to treason.

Harriet Beecher Stowe, who interviewed Lincoln in 1864, thought him the most trusted leader the country could have in war. "Surrounded by all sorts of conflicting claims," she wrote, "by traitors, by half-hearted, timid men, by Border States men, and Free States men, by radical Abolitionists and Conservatives, he has listened to all, weighed the words of all, waited, observed, yielded now here and now there, but in the main kept one inflexible, honest purpose, and drawn the national ship through." Had he been "a reckless, bold, theorizing, dashing man of genius," she said, he "might have wrecked our Constitution and ended us in a splendid military despotism."

THE WARRIOR

He was, then, a warrior for the American dream, prepared to do whatever was necessary to save it short of abandoning the dream itself. This ends-justifies-the-means philosophy was blazingly clear in Lincoln's approach to military strategy. Here he faced some perplexing questions: How could he utilize the Union's vast superiority in manpower and war matériel to stamp out the rebellion? Should he battle only the armies of the insurrectionists, or their institutions and resources as well?

At first, Lincoln elected to fight only the rebel military forces, a decision that would alter drastically as the war roared on and necessity demanded a harsher strategy. But almost from the start Lincoln had the whole military picture in mind, which was to be expected of a man who saw the struggle itself in a world dimension. Before any of his generals or advisers, Lincoln understood that the only way to whip the hard-fighting Confederates was to hit them with coordinated attacks in all theaters. Only that way could the Union bring to bear its tremendous advantage in manpower and war resources.

Yet it took Lincoln a long time to translate his strategic insights into action. He made mistakes. He gave too many important commands to "political" generals or to incompetent professionals who impressed him simply because they were generals. Who was he, a mere civilian, to question their military expertise? When his chosen commanders failed to fight as he wanted, he could lose his temper and cry "damn" or "hell" or even throw his stovepipe hat on the floor, as he did on one battlefront visit in 1862. Too many of his early generals, as he put it himself, had the "slows" when it came to fighting. Yet it was Lincoln who had chosen them. . . .

During the summer and autumn of 1863, Lincoln kept prodding his generals to fight in concert, to move against Confederate forces with coordinated attacks. He wanted to "hurt this enemy," to "whip these people." But it took Lincoln until 1864 before he found in Grant and William Tecumseh Sherman the right combination to implement his big-picture strategy. In the spring of that year, Lincoln made Sherman overall commander in the West and called Grant to the East as General-in-Chief of all Union armies. Now Lincoln had a command set-up that he hoped would produce victories. With Grant as General-in-Chief, Halleck functioned officially as chief of staff, integrating information and giving out advice. Grant, electing to travel with Meade and the Army of the Potomac, would coordinate its movements with those of armies in other theaters.

A terse, slight man who chewed cigars and walked with a lurch, Grant worked out with Lincoln a Grand Plan that called for simultaneous offensive movements on all battlefronts. In the East, Grant and Meade would attempt to obliterate Lee's force while Sherman's powerful army would punch into Georgia, seize Atlanta and its crucial railway nexus, and destroy rebel resources in the Atlanta area. In sum, the Union war machine would now utilize its vastly superior manpower and smash the Confederacy with concerted blows in all theaters.

Lincoln was delighted. The Grand Plan entailed exactly the kind of concerted action he had advocated since 1861. And though it was basically Grant's design, Lincoln helped forge it in weekly strategy sessions in the White House. So

in May, 1864, Union armies on all fronts moved forward in the mightiest offensive of the war, battering the Confederacy from all directions and thrusting toward "a common center." Alas, in East and West alike, the offensive mired down and Union casualties, especially in Virginia, were staggering. Yet Lincoln never lost hope. Even when Lee escaped to the redoubts of Petersburg and Grant settled in for a protracted seige, Lincoln urged him to "hold on with bull-dog grip, and chew & choke, as much as possible."

The Grand Plan worked better in the western theater, where Sherman captured and burned Atlanta, and General George "Old Pap" Thomas smashed the Confederate Army of Tennessee, destroying it so completely that it could never fight again. What Lincoln had long desired had finally been accomplished.

In the late fall of 1864 red-haired Bill Sherman, a tall, lean man who spoke in picturesque phrases, proposed to take Lincoln's strategic notions a step further. Even more than Grant, Sherman realized that modern wars were won not simply by fighting enemy armies, but by destroying the very ability of the enemy to wage war—that is, by wrecking railroads, burning fields, and eradicating other economic resources. "We are not only fighting hostile armies," Sherman reasoned, "but a hostile people, and must make old and young, rich and poor, feel the hard hand of war." "There is many a boy here who looks on war as all glory," Sherman later told his veterans, "but, boys, it is all hell."

Those were Lincoln's sentiments exactly. And since war was hell, it should be ended as swiftly as possible, by whatever means were necessary. Thus, when Sherman proposed to visit total war on the people of the Deep South, Lincoln approved. With ruthless efficiency, Sherman's army stormed through Georgia and the Carolinas, tearing up railroads, pulverizing corn and cotton fields, assassinating cows and chickens, wiping out all and anything that might sustain Lee's army and all other rebel forces. At the same time, Union cavalry in Virginia's Shenandoah Valley burned a broad path of destruction clear to the Rapidan River. The Union's scorched-earth warfare earned Lincoln and Sherman undying hatred in Dixie, but it paid off: within five months after Sherman started his march through Georgia, the war was over.

It cannot be stressed enough that Lincoln, then deeply involved in matters of reconstruction, fully endorsed Sherman's scorched-earth policy. If Sherman was "a total warrior," so was his Commander-in-Chief. Putting aside his own aversion to bloodshed and violence, Lincoln ended up pounding all his southern foes into submission—civilians and soldiers alike. And he did so because that was the surest way he knew to shorten the conflict, end the killing, and salvage his American dream.

NO

M. E. Bradford

THE LINCOLN LEGACY: A LONG VIEW

With the time and manner of his death Abraham Lincoln, as leader of a Puritan people who had just won a great victory over "the forces of evil," was placed beyond the reach of ordinary historical inquiry and assessment. Through Booth's bullet he became the one who had "died to make men free," who had perished that his country's "new birth" might occur: a "second founder" who, in Ford's theater, had been transformed into an American version of the "dying god." Our common life, according to this construction, owes its continuation to the shedding of the sacred blood. Now after over a century of devotion to the myth of the "political messiah," it is still impossible for most Americans to see through and beyond the magical events of April 1865. However, Lincoln's daily purchase upon the ongoing business of the nation requires that we devise a way of setting aside the martyrdom to look behind it at Lincoln's place in the total context of American history and discover in him a major source of our present confusion, our distance from the republicanism of the Fathers, the models of political conduct which we profess most to admire. . . .

Of course, nothing that we can identify as part of Lincoln's legacy belongs to him alone. In some respects the Emancipator was carried along with the tides. Yet a measure of his importance is that he was at the heart of the major political events of his era. Therefore what signifies in a final evaluation of this melancholy man is that many of these changes in the country would never have come to pass had Lincoln not pushed them forward. Or at least not come so quickly, or with such dreadful violence. I will emphasize only the events that he most certainly shaped according to his relentless will, alterations in the character of our country for which he was clearly responsible. For related developments touched by Lincoln's wand, I can have only a passing word. The major charges advanced here, if proved, are sufficient to impeach the most famous and respected of public men. More would only overdo.

The first and most obvious item in my bill of particulars for indictment concerns Lincoln's dishonesty and obfuscation with respect to the nation's future obligations to the Negro, slave and free. It was of course an essential ingredient of Lincoln's position that he make a success at being anti-Southern or anti-slavery without at the same time appearing to be significantly impious about the beginnings of the Republic (which was neither anti-Southern nor antislavery)—or significantly pro-Negro. He was the first Northern politician of any rank to combine these attitudes into a viable platform persona, the first to make his moral position on slavery in the South into a part of his national politics. It was a posture that enabled him to unite elements of the Northern electorate not ordinarily willing to cooperate in any political undertaking. And thus enabled him to destroy the old Democratic majority—a coalition necessary to preserving the union of the states. Then came the explosion. But this calculated posturing has had more durable consequences than secession and the Federal confiscation of property in slaves. . . .

In the nation as a whole what moves toward fruition is a train of events set in motion by the duplicitous rhetoric concerning the Negro that helped make Abraham Lincoln into our first "sectional" president. Central to this appeal is a claim to a kind of moral superiority that costs absolutely nothing in the way of conduct. Lincoln, in insisting that the Negro was included in the promise of the Declaration of Independence and that the Declaration bound his countrymen to fulfill a pledge hidden in that document, seemed clearly to point toward a radical transformation of American society. Carried within his rejection of Negro slavery as a continuing feature of the American regime, his assertion that the equality clause of the Declaration of Independence was "the father of all moral principle among us," were certain muted corollaries. By promising that the peculiar institution would be made to disappear if candidates for national office adopted the proper "moral attitude" on that subject, Lincoln recited as a litany the general terms of his regard for universal human rights. But at the same time he added certain modifications to this high doctrine: modifications required by those of his countrymen to whom he hoped to appeal, by the rigid racism of the Northern electorate, and by "what his own feelings would admit." The most important of these reservations was that none of his doctrine should apply significantly to the Negro in the North. Or, after freedom, to what he could expect in the South. It was a very broad, very general, and very abstract principle to which he made reference. By it he could divide the sheep from the goats, the wheat from the chaff, the patriot from the conspirator. But for the Negro it provided nothing more than a technical freedom, best to be enjoyed far away. Or the valuable opportunity to "root, hog, or die." For the sake of such vapid distinctions he urged his countrymen to wade through seas of blood.

To be sure, this position does not push the "feelings" of that moralist who was our sixteenth president too far from what was comfortable for him. And it goes without saying that a commitment to "natural rights" which will not challenge the Black Codes of Illinois, which promises something like them for the freedman in the South, or else offers him as alternative the proverbial "one-way-ticket to nowhere" is a commitment of empty words. It is only an accident of political history that the final Reconstruction settlement provided a bit more for the former slave—principally, the chance to vote

Republican; and even that "right" didn't last, once a better deal was made available to his erstwhile protectors. But the point is that Lincoln's commitment was precisely of the sort that the North was ready to make—while passing legislation to restrict the flow of Negroes into its own territories, elaborating its own system of segregation by race, and exploiting black labor through its representatives in a conquered South. Lincoln's double talk left his part of the country with a durable heritage of pious self-congratulation. . . .

The second heading in this "case against Lincoln" involves no complicated pleading. Neither will it confuse any reader who examines his record with care. For it has to do with Lincoln's political economy, his management of the commercial and business life of the part of the Republic under his authority. This material is obvious, even though it is not always connected with the presidency of Abraham Lincoln. Nevertheless, it must be developed at this point. For it leads directly into the more serious charges upon which this argument depends. It is customary to deplore the Gilded Age, the era of the Great Barbecue. It is true that many of the corruptions of the Republican Era came to a head after Lincoln lay at rest in Springfield. But it is a matter of fact that they began either under his direction or with his sponsorship. Military necessity, the "War for the Union," provided an excuse, an umbrella of sanction, under which the essential nature of the changes being made in the relation of government to commerce could be concealed. Of his total policy the Northern historian Robert Sharkey has written, "Human ingenuity would have had difficulty in contriving a more perfect engine for class and sectional exploration: creditors finally obtaining the upper

hand as opposed to debtors, and the developed East holding the whip over the underdeveloped West and South." Until the South left the Union, until a High Whig sat in the White House, none of this return to the "energetic government" of Hamilton's design was possible. Indeed, even in the heyday of the Federalists it had never been so simple a matter to translate power into wealth. Now Lincoln could try again the internal improvements of the early days in Illinois. The difference was that this time the funding would not be restrained by political reversal or a failure of credit. For if anything fell short, Mr. Salmon P. Chase, "the foreman" of his "green printing office," could be instructed "to give his paper mill another turn." And the inflationary policy of rewarding the friends of the government sustained. The euphemism of our time calls this "income redistribution." But it was theft in 1864, and is theft today.

A great increase in the tariff and the formation of a national banking network were, of course, the cornerstones of this great alteration in the posture of the Federal government toward the sponsorship of business. From the beginning of the Republican Party Lincoln warned his associates not to talk about their views on these subjects. Their alliance, he knew, was a negative thing: a league against the Slave Power and its Northern friends. But in private he made it clear that the hidden agenda of the Republicans would have its turn, once the stick was in their hand. In this he promised well. Between 1861 and 1865, the tariff rose from 18.84 percent to 47.56 percent. And it stayed above 40 percent in all but two years of the period concluded with the election of Woodrow Wilson. Writes the Virginia historian Ludwell H. Johnson, it would "facilitate a massive transfer of wealth, satisfying the dreariest predictions of John C. Calhoun." The new Republican system of banking (for which we should note Lincoln was directly accountable) was part of the same large design of "refounding." The National Banking Acts of 1863 and 1864, with the earlier Legal Tender Act, flooded the country with $480 million of fiat money that was soon depreciated by about two-thirds in relation to specie. Then all notes but the greenback dollar were taxed out of existence, excepting only United States Treasury bonds that all banks were required to purchase if they were to have a share in the war boom. The support for these special bonds was thus the debt itself—Hamilton's old standby. Specie disappeared. Moreover, the bank laws controlled the money supply, credit, and the balance of power. New banks and credit for farms, small businesses, or small town operations were discouraged. And the Federalist model, after four score and seven years, finally achieved.

As chief executive, Lincoln naturally supported heavy taxes. Plus a scheme of tax graduation. The war was a legitimate explanation for these measures. Lincoln's participation in huge subsidies or bounties for railroads and in other legislation granting economic favors is not so readily linked to "saving the Union." All of his life Lincoln was a friend of the big corporations. He had no moral problem in signing a bill which gifted the Union Pacific Railway with a huge strip of land running across the West and an almost unsecured loan of $16,000 to $48,000 per mile of track. The final result of this bill was the Credit Mobilier scandal. With other laws favoring land speculation it helped to negate the seemingly noble promise of the Homestead Act of 1862—

under which less than 19 percent of the open lands settled between 1860 and 1900 went to legitimate homesteaders. The Northern policy of importing immigrants with the promise of this land, only to force them into the ranks of General Grant's meatgrinder or into near slavery in the cities of the East, requires little comment. Nor need we belabor the rotten army contracts given to politically faithful crooks. Nor the massive thefts by law performed during the war in the South. More significant is Lincoln's openly disgraceful policy of allowing special cronies and favorites of his friends to trade in Southern cotton—even with "the enemy" across the line—and his calculated use of the patronage and the pork barrel. Between 1860 and 1880, the Republicans spent almost $10 million breathing life into state and local Republican organizations. Lincoln pointed them down that road. There can be no doubt of his responsibility for the depressing spectacle of greed and peculation concerning which so many loyal Northern men of the day spoke with sorrow, disappointment, and outrage. . . .

A large part of the complaint against Lincoln as a political precedent for later declensions from the example of the Fathers has to do with his expansion of the powers of the presidency and his alteration of the basis for the Federal Union. With reference to his role in changing the office of chief magistrate from what it had been under his predecessors, it is important to remember that he defined himself through the war powers that belonged to his post. In this way Lincoln could profess allegiance to the Whig ideal of the modest, self-effacing leader, the antitype of Andrew Jackson, and, in his capacity as Commander-in-Chief, do whatever he wished. That is, if he could do it in the name of preserving the Union. As Clinton Rossiter has stated, Lincoln believed there were "no limits" to his powers if he exercised them in that "holy cause." Gottfried Dietze compares Lincoln in this role to the Committee of Public Safety as it operated in the French Revolution. Except for the absence of mass executions, the results were similar. War is of course the occasion for concentration of power and the limitation of liberties within any nation. But an internal war, a war between states in a union of states, is not like a war to repel invasion or to acquire territory. For it is an extension into violence of a domestic political difference. And it is thus subject to extraordinary abuses of authority—confusions or conflations of purpose which convert the effort to win the war into an effort to effect even larger, essentially political changes in the structure of government. War, in these terms, is not only an engine for preserving the Union; it is also an instrument for transforming its nature. But without overdeveloping this structure of theory, let us shore it up with specific instances of presidential misconduct by Lincoln: abuses that mark him as our first imperial president. Lincoln began his tenure as a dictator when between April 12 and July 4 of 1861, without interference from Congress, he summoned militia, spent millions, suspended law, authorized recruiting, decreed a blockade, defied the Supreme Court, and pledged the nation's credit. In the following months and years he created units of government not known to the Constitution and officers to rule over them in "conquered" sections of the South, seized property throughout both sections, arrested upwards of twenty thousand of his political enemies and confined them without trial in a North-

ern "Gulag," closed over three hundred newspapers critical of his policy, imported an army of foreign mercenaries (of perhaps five hundred thousand men), interrupted the assembly of duly elected legislatures and employed the Federal hosts to secure his own reelection—in a contest where about thirty-eight thousand votes, if shifted, might have produced an armistice and a negotiated peace under a President McClellan. To the same end he created a state in West Virginia, arguing of this blatant violation of the explicit provisions of the Constitution that it was "expedient." But the worst of this bold and ruthless dealing (and I have given but a very selective list of Lincoln's "high crimes") has to do with his role as military leader per se: as the commander and selector of Northern generals, chief commissary of the Federal forces, and head of government in dealing with the leaders of an opposing power. In this role the image of Lincoln grows to be very dark—indeed, almost sinister.

The worst that we may say of Lincoln is that he led the North in war so as to put the domestic political priorities of his political machine ahead of the lives and the well-being of his soldiers in the field. The appointment of the venal Simon Cameron of Pennsylvania as his secretary of war, and of lesser hacks and rascals to direct the victualing of Federal armies, was part of this malfeasance. By breaking up their bodies, the locust hoard of contractors even found a profit in the Union dead. And better money still in the living. They made of Lincoln (who winked at their activities) an accessory to lost horses, rotten meat, and worthless guns. But all such mendacity was nothing in comparison to the price in blood paid for Lincoln's attempts to give the nation a genuine Republican hero. He had a problem with this project throughout the entire course of the war. That is, until Grant and Sherman "converted" to radicalism. Prior to their emergence all of Lincoln's "loyal" generals disapproved of either his politics or of his character. These, as with McClellan, he could use and discharge at will. Or demote to minor tasks. One thinks immediately of George G. Meade—who defeated Lee at Gettysburg, and yet made the mistake of defining himself as the defender of a separate Northern nation from whose soil he would drive a foreign Southern "invader." Or of Fitz John Porter, William B. Franklin, and Don Carlos Buell—all scapegoats thrown by Lincoln to the radical wolves. In place of these heterodox professionals, Lincoln assigned such champions of the "new freedom" as Nathaniel P. ("Commissary") Banks, Benjamin F. ("Beast") Butler, John C. Fremont, and John A. McClernand. Speaking in summary despair of these appointments (and adding to my list, Franz Sigel and Lew Wallace), General Henry Halleck, Lincoln's chief-of-staff, declared that they were "little better than murder." Yet in the East, with the Army of the Potomac, Lincoln make promotions even more difficult to defend, placing not special projects, divisions, and brigades but entire commands under the authority of such "right thinking" incompetents as John Pope (son of an old crony in Illinois) and "Fighting Joe" Hooker. Or with that "tame" Democrat and late favorite of the radicals, Ambrose E. Burnside. Thousands of Northern boys lost their lives in order that the Republican Party might experience rejuvenation, to serve its partisan goals. And those were "party supremacy within a Northern dominated Union." A Democratic "man-on-horseback" could not serve those ends, however faithful to "the Constitution as it is, and the Union as it was" (the motto of the Democrats) they might be. For neither of these commitments promised a Republican hegemony. To provide for his faction both security and continuity in office, Lincoln sounded out his commanders in correspondence (much of which still survives), suborned their military integrity, and employed their focus in purely political operation. Writes Johnson:

> Although extreme measures were most common in the border states, they were often used elsewhere too. By extreme measures is meant the arrest of anti-Republican candidates and voters, driving anti-Republican voters from the polls or forcing them to vote the Republican ticket, preventing opposition parties from holding meetings, removing names from ballots, and so forth. These methods were employed in national, state and local elections. Not only did the army interfere by force, it was used to supply votes. Soldiers whose states did not allow absentee voting were sent home by order of the President to swell the Republican totals. When voting in the field was used, Democratic commissioners carrying ballots to soldiers from their state were . . . unceremoniously thrown into prison, while Republican agents were offered every assistance. Votes of Democratic soldiers were sometimes discarded as defective, replaced by Republican ballots, or simply not counted.

All Lincoln asked of the ordinary Billy Yank was that he be prepared to give himself up to no real purpose—at least until Father Abraham found a general with the proper moral and political credentials to lead him on to Richmond. How this part of Lincoln's career can be reconciled to the myth of the "suffering savior" I cannot imagine.

We might dwell for some time on what injury Lincoln did to the dignity of his office through the methods he employed in prosecuting the war. It was no small thing to disavow the ancient Christian code of "limited war," as did his minions, acting in his name. However, it is enough in this connection to remember his policy of denying medicines to the South, even for the sake of Northern prisoners held behind the lines. We can imagine what a modern "war crimes" tribunal would do with that decision. There may have been practicality in such inhumane decisions. *Practicality* indeed! As Charles Francis Adams, Lincoln's ambassador to the Court of St. James and the scion of the most notable family in the North, wrote in his diary of his leader, the "President and his chief advisers are not without the spirit of the serpent mixed in with their wisdom." And he knew whereof he spoke. For practical politics, the necessities of the campaign of 1864, had led Lincoln and Seward to a decision far more serious than unethical practices against prisoners and civilians in the South. I speak of the rejection by the Lincoln administration of peace feelers authorized by the Confederate government in Richmond: feelers that met Lincoln's announced terms for an end to the Federal invasion of the South. The emissary in this negotiation was sponsored by Charles Francis Adams. He was a Tennessean living in France, one Thomas Yeatman. After arriving in the United States, he was swiftly deported by direct order of the government before he could properly explore the possibility of an armistice on the conditions of reunion and an end to slavery. Lincoln sought these goals, but only on his terms. And in his own time. He wanted total victory. And he needed a still-resisting, impenitent Confederacy to justify his re-election. We can only speculate as to why President Davis allowed the Yeatman mission. We know that he expected little of such peace feelers. (There were many in the last stages of the conflict.) He knew his enemy too well to expect anything but subjection, however benign the rhetoric used to disguise its rigor. Adam's peace plan was perhaps impossible, even if his superiors in Washington had behaved in good faith. The point is that none of the peace moves of 1864 was given any chance of success. Over one hundred thousand Americans may have died because of the Rail-Splitter's rejection of an inexpedient peace. Yet we have still not touched upon the most serious of Lincoln's violations of the Presidential responsibility. I speak, finally, of his role in bringing on the War Between the States.

There is, we should recall, a great body of scholarly argument concerning Lincoln's intentions in 1860 and early 1861. A respectable portion of this work comes to the conclusion that the first Republican president expected a "tug," a "crisis," to follow his election. And then, once secession had occurred, also expected to put it down swiftly with a combination of persuasion, force, and Southern loyalty to the Union. The last of these, it is agreed, he completely overestimated. In a similar fashion he exaggerated the force of Southern "realism," the region's capacity to act in its own pecuniary interest. The authority on Lincoln's political economy has remarked that the Illinois lawyer-politician and old line Whig always made the mistake of explaining in simple economic terms the South's hostile reaction to anti-slavery proposals. To that blunder he added the related mistake of attempting to end the "rebellion" with the same sort of simplistic appeals to the prospect of riches. Or with fear of a servile insurrection brought on by his greatest "war measure," the emancipation of slaves behind Southern lines, beyond his control. A full-scale Southern revolution, a revolution of all classes of men against the way he and some of his supporters thought, was beyond his imagination. There was no "policy" in such extravagant behavior, no human nature as he perceived it. Therefore, on the basis of my understanding of his overall career, I am compelled to agree with Charles W. Ramsdell concerning Lincoln and his war. Though he was no sadist and no war-monger, and though he got for his pains much more of a conflict than he had in mind, Lincoln hoped for an "insurrection" of some sort—an "uprising" he could use.

The "rational" transformation of our form of government which he had first predicted in the "Springfield Lyceum Speech" required some kind of passionate disorder to justify the enforcement of a new Federalism. And needed also for the voting representatives of the South to be out of their seats in the Congress. It is out of keeping with his total performance as a public man and in contradiction of his campaigning after 1854 not to believe that Lincoln hoped for a Southern attack on Fort Sumter. As he told his old friend Senator Orville H. Browning of Illinois: "The plan succeeded. They attacked Sumter—it fell, and thus did more service than it otherwise could." And to others he wrote or spoke to the same effect. If the Confederacy's offer of money for Federal property were made known in the North and business relations of the sections remained unaffected, if the Mis-

sissippi remained open to Northern shipping, there would be no support for "restoring" the Union on a basis of force. Americans were in the habit of thinking of the unity of the nation as a reflex of their agreement in the Constitution, of law as limit on government and on the authority of temporary majorities, and of revisions in law as the product of the ordinary course of push and pull within a pluralistic society, not as a response to the extralegal authority of some admirable abstraction like equality. In other words, they thought of the country as being defined by the way in which we conducted our political business, not by where we were trying to go in body. Though once a disciple of Henry Clay, Lincoln changed the basis of our common bond away from the doctrine of his mentor, away from the patterns of compromise and dialectic of interests and values under a limited, Federal sovereignty with which we as a people began our adventure with the Great Compromise of 1787-1788. The nature of the Union left to us by Lincoln is thus always at stake in every major election, in every refinement in our civil theology; the Constitution is still to be defined by the latest wave of big ideas, the most recent mass emotion. Writes Dietze:

> Concentrations of power in the national and executive branches of government, brought about by Lincoln in the name of the people, were processes that conceivably complemented each other to the detriment of free government. Lincoln's administration thus opened the way for the development of an omnipotent national executive who as a spokesman for the people might consider himself entitled to do whatever he felt was good for the Nation, irrespective of the interests and rights

of states, Congress, the judiciary, and the individual. . . .

But in my opinion the capstone of this case against Lincoln . . . is what he had done to the language of American political discourse that makes it so difficult for us to reverse the ill effects of trends he set in motion with his executive fiat. When I say that Lincoln was our first Puritan president, I am chiefly referring to a distinction of style, to his habit of wrapping up his policy in the idiom of Holy Scripture, concealing within the Trojan horse of his gasconade and moral superiority an agenda that would never have been approved if presented in any other form. It is this rhetoric in particular, a rhetoric confirmed in its authority by his martyrdom, that is enshrined in the iconography of the Lincoln myth preserved against examination by monuments such as the Lincoln Memorial, where his oversized likeness is elevated above us like that of a deified Roman emperor.

POSTSCRIPT

Was Abraham Lincoln America's Greatest President?

As Oates reveals in his essay, Abraham Lincoln, at the time of his assassination, was perhaps the most hated president in history. Still, virtually no scholars in recent times have launched the type of assault exhibited by Bradford. Instead, since Arthur Schlesinger, Jr., first polled experts on the subject in 1948, historians consistently have rated Lincoln the nation's best chief executive. Another president, Harry Truman, also ranked Lincoln in the category of "great" chief executives. In words that are echoed by Oates, Truman wrote of Lincoln: "He was a strong executive who saved the government, saved the United States. He was a president who understood people, and when it came time to make decisions, he was willing to take the responsibility and make those decisions, no matter how difficult they were. He knew how to treat people and how to make a decision stick, and that's why his is regarded as such a great Administration."

Lincoln also is the most written-about president. Students should consult Carl Sandburg, *Abraham Lincoln*, 6 vols. (Harcourt, Brace & World, 1926–1939), a poetic panorama which focuses upon the mythic Lincoln. Benjamin Thomas, *Abraham Lincoln: A Biography* (Knopf, 1952), and Stephen B. Oates, *With Malice Toward None: The Life of Abraham Lincoln* (Harper & Row, 1977), are both excellent one-volume biographies. David Donald, *Lincoln Reconsidered: Essays on the Civil War Era* (Knopf, 1956), and Richard N. Current, *The Lincoln Nobody Knows* (McGraw-Hill, 1958), offer incisive interpretations of many aspects of Lincoln's political career and philosophy. Psychoanalytical approaches to Lincoln are offered by George B. Forgie, *Patricide in the House Divided: A Psychological Interpretation* (Norton, 1979), and Dwight G. Anderson, *Abraham Lincoln: The Quest for Immortality* (Knopf, 1982). The events leading up to the Civil War are presented best in David M. Potter, *The Impending Crisis, 1848–1861* (Harper & Row, 1976). Lincoln's responsibility for the precipitating event of the war is explored in Richard N. Current, *Lincoln and the First Shot* (Lippincott, 1963). T. Harry Williams, *Lincoln and His Generals* (Knopf, 1952), looks at Lincoln as commander in chief and remains one of the best Lincoln studies. Peyton McCrary, *Abraham Lincoln and Reconstruction: The Louisiana Experiment* (Princeton University Press, 1978), examines Lincoln's plan for restoring the Southern states to the Union. For his role as "the Great Emancipator" and his attitudes toward race and slavery, see Benjamin Quarles, *Lincoln and the Negro* (Oxford University Press, 1962), and LaWanda Cox, *A Study in Presidential Leadership* (University of South Carolina Press, 1981). Gabor S. Boritt, ed., *The Historian's Lincoln: Pseudohistory, Psychohistory, and History* (University of Illinois Press, 1988), is a valuable recent collection.

ISSUE 17

Reconstruction: Could It Have Given Blacks Full Equality?

YES: Eric Foner, from "The New View of Reconstruction," *American Heritage* (October/November 1983)

NO: C. Vann Woodward, from *The Future of the Past* (Oxford University Press, 1988)

ISSUE SUMMARY

YES: Professor of history Eric Foner believes that, although Reconstruction was nonrevolutionary and conservative, it was a splendid failure because it offered blacks a temporary vision of a free society.

NO: Professor of history C. Vann Woodward argues that there was very little hope that African Americans would receive their basic freedoms under Reconstruction. Taking a comparative approach and examining the treatment of freedmen in other societies, as well as the failure of U.S. land distribution policies toward poor whites and Native Americans, Woodward is skeptical about the promises of Reconstruction.

The Reconstruction era (1865–1877) contains a mythological history which has been impossible for professional historians to dislodge. While the Civil War has been portrayed as a heroic era for both sides, Reconstruction has been categorized as a tragedy for all Americans—Northerners, Southerners, whites, and blacks. According to the mythology, a vengeful Congress, dominated by radical Republicans, imposed military rule upon the Southern states. Carpetbaggers from the North, along with traitorous white scalawags and their ignorant black accomplices, rewrote the state constitutions, disenfranchised former Confederate whites, controlled the legislature, passed laws which enabled them to raise taxes, looted the government treasuries, and stole the possessions of the good white Northerners. This farce came to an end in 1877 when a deal was struck to allow Rutherford B. Hayes to assume the presidency. Hayes received 15 disputed electoral college votes (which enabled him to defeat his opponent Samuel J. Tilden by one vote). In return, Hayes agreed to end Reconstruction by withdrawing federal troops from the Southern states.

Between the years 1890 and 1930, this portrait of Reconstruction dominated the historical profession. The reasons for this are obvious. White

Southerners who wrote about this period made two basic assumptions: (1) that the South was capable of solving its own problems without federal government interference, and (2) that African Americans were intellectually inferior to whites and incapable of running a government (much less one in which whites would be their subordinates).

The traditional interpretation of Reconstruction has been under attack by professional white historians since the 1930s, but three decades earlier the brilliant African American historian W. E. B. Du Bois established many of the basic arguments used by the revisionists against the standard view of Reconstruction. In *The Souls of Black Folk* (1903, Reprint, Fawcett Publications, 1961) and "Reconstruction and Its Benefits," *American Historical Review* (July 1910), Du Bois presented treatments which placed the role of the black voter and the corruption of the Southern state governments in their proper historical context.

In response to the critics of Reconstruction, revisionists have argued that, although there was a great deal of corruption in the Republican governments of the South, the looting of state treasuries also took place in the Northern states and in Washington, D.C. While taxes increased in the Southern states, this looting was necessary because the pre–Civil War tax structure was regressive and public monies were necessary to rebuild roads and finance new systems of railroads and public schools.

Revisionist historians sharply attacked the notion that African Americans dominated the politics of the Reconstruction South. They pointed out that there were no black governors, only 2 black senators, and 15 black congressmen during this period. In no Southern state did blacks control both houses of the legislature. Black politicians were usually better educated than their constituents and, contrary to legend, generally followed moderate policies favoring black equality.

In brief, revisionist historians have painted a more positive picture of Reconstruction. New state constitutions were written during this era that outlasted the politicians who wrote them, improvements were made in local administrations, the court systems were revised, and state-supported public schools were established for both whites and blacks.

In the 1980s a third group of historians, the postrevisionist writers, have given a gloomier and more conservative portrait of the era. The first selection by Eric Foner, for example, summarizes the earlier writings on the period and at the same time searches for a new synthesis which moves beyond the negative postrevisionist studies. Foner concedes that Reconstruction was not very radical and much less revolutionary. Nevertheless, it was a "splendid failure" because it offered blacks a vision of how a free society could look. C. Vann Woodward, however, offers an ironic counterfactual analysis and argues that there was little hope for African Americans to secure equality. In addition, he thinks the idea of redistributing land confiscated from former white planters to former slaves was unrealistic.

YES

Eric Foner

THE NEW VIEW OF RECONSTRUCTION

In the past twenty years, no period of American history has been the subject of a more thoroughgoing reevaluation than Reconstruction—the violent, dramatic, and still controversial era following the Civil War. Race relations, politics, social life, and economic change during Reconstruction have all been reinterpreted in the light of changed attitudes toward the place of blacks within American society. If historians have not yet forged a fully satisfying portrait of Reconstruction as a whole, the traditional interpretation that dominated historical writing for much of this century has irrevocably been laid to rest.

Anyone who attended high school before 1960 learned that Reconstruction was an era of unrelieved sordidness in American political and social life. The martyred Lincoln, according to this view, had planned a quick and painless readmission of the Southern states as equal members of the national family. President Andrew Johnson, his successor, attempted to carry out Lincoln's policies but was foiled by the Radical Republicans (also known as Vindictives or Jacobins). Motivated by an irrational hatred of Rebels or by ties with Northern capitalists out to plunder the South, the Radicals swept aside Johnson's lenient program and fastened black supremacy upon the defeated Confederacy. An orgy of corruption followed, presided over by unscrupulous carpetbaggers (Northerners who ventured south to reap the spoils of office), traitorous scalawags (Southern whites who cooperated with the new governments for personal gain), and the ignorant and childlike freedmen, who were incapable of properly exercising the political power that had been thrust upon them. After much needless suffering, the white community of the South banded together to overthrow these "black" governments and restore home rule (their euphemism for white supremacy). All told, Reconstruction was just about the darkest page in the American saga.

Originating in Anti-Reconstruction propaganda of Southern Democrats during the 1870s, this traditional interpretation achieved scholarly legitimacy around the turn of the century through the work of William Dunning and his

From Eric Foner, "The New View of Reconstruction," *American Heritage,* vol. 34, no. 6 (October/November 1983). Copyright © 1983 by American Heritage, a division of Forbes, Inc. Reprinted by permission.

students at Columbia University. It reached the larger public through films like *Birth of a Nation* and *Gone With the Wind* and that best-selling work of myth-making masquerading as history, *The Tragic Era* by Claude G. Bowers. In language as exaggerated as it was colorful, Bowers told how Andrew Johnson "fought the bravest battle for constitutional liberty and for the preservation of our institutions ever waged by an Executive" but was overwhelmed by the "poisonous propaganda" of the Radicals. Southern whites, as a result, "literally were put to the torture" by "emissaries of hate" who manipulated the "simple-minded" freedmen, "inflaming the negroes' egotism" and even inspiring "lustful assaults" by blacks upon white womanhood.

In a discipline that sometimes seems to pride itself on the rapid rise and fall of historical interpretations, this traditional portrait of Reconstruction enjoyed remarkable staying power. The long reign of the old interpretation is not difficult to explain. It presented a set of easily identifiable heroes and villains. It enjoyed the imprimatur of the nation's leading scholars. And it accorded with the political and social realities of the first half of the century. This image of Reconstruction helped freeze the mind of the white South in unalterable opposition to any movement for breaching the ascendancy of the Democratic party, eliminating segregation, or readmitting disfranchised blacks to the vote.

Nevertheless, the demise of the traditional interpretation was inevitable, for it ignored the testimony of the central participant in the drama of Reconstruction—the black freedman. Furthermore, it was grounded in the conviction that blacks were unfit to share in political power. As Dunning's Columbia colleague John W.

Burgess put it, "A black skin means membership in a race of men which has never of itself succeeded in subjecting passion to reason, has never, therefore, created any civilization of any kind." Once objective scholarship and modern experience rendered that assumption untenable, the entire edifice was bound to fall.

The work of "revising" the history of Reconstruction began with the writings of a handful of survivors of the era, such as John R. Lynch, who had served as a black congressman from Mississippi after the Civil War. In the 1930s white scholars like Francis Simkins and Robert Woody carried the task forward. Then, in 1935, the black historian and activist W. E. B. Du Bois produced *Black Reconstruction in America*, a monumental reevaluation that closed with an irrefutable indictment of a historical profession that had sacrificed scholarly objectivity on the altar of racial bias. "One fact and one alone," he wrote, "explains the attitude of most recent writers toward Reconstruction; they cannot conceive of Negroes as men." Du Bois's work, however, was ignored by most historians.

It was not until the 1960s that the full force of the revisionist wave broke over the field. Then, in rapid succession, virtually every assumption of the traditional viewpoint was systematically dismantled. A drastically different portrait emerged to take its place. President Lincoln did not have a coherent "plan" for Reconstruction, but at the time of his assassination he had been cautiously contemplating black suffrage. Andrew Johnson was a stubborn, racist politician who lacked the ability to compromise. By isolating himself from the broad currents of public opinion that had nourished Lincoln's career, Johnson created an impasse with

Congress that Lincoln would certainly have avoided, thus throwing away his political power and destroying his own plans for reconstructing the South.

The Radicals in Congress were acquitted of both vindictive motives and the charge of serving as the stalking-horses of Northern capitalism. They emerged instead as idealists in the best nineteenth-century reform tradition. Radical leaders like Charles Sumner and Thaddeus Stevens had worked for the rights of blacks long before any conceivable political advantage flowed from such a commitment. Stevens refused to sign the Pennsylvania Constitution of 1838 because it disfranchised the state's black citizens; Sumner led a fight in the 1850s to integrate Boston's public schools. Their Reconstruction policies were based on principle, not petty political advantage, for the central issue dividing Johnson and these Radical Republicans was the civil rights of freedmen. Studies of congressional policy-making, such as Eric L. McKitrick's *Andrew Johnson and Reconstruction*, also revealed that Reconstruction legislation, ranging from the Civil Rights Act of 1866 to the Fourteenth and Fifteenth Amendments, enjoyed broad support from moderate and conservative Republicans. It was not simply the work of a narrow radical faction.

Even more startling was the revised portrait of Reconstruction in the South itself. Imbued with the spirit of the civil rights movement and rejecting entirely the racial assumptions that had underpinned the traditional interpretation, these historians evaluated Reconstruction from the black point of view. Works like Joel Williamson's *After Slavery* portrayed the period as a time of extraordinary political, social, and economic progress for blacks. The establishment of public school systems, the granting of equal citizenship to blacks, the effort to restore the devastated Southern economy, the attempt to construct an interracial political democracy from the ashes of slavery, all these were commendable achievements, not the elements of Bower's "tragic era."

Unlike earlier writers, the revisionists stressed the active role of the freedmen in shaping Reconstruction. Black initiative established as many schools as did Northern religious societies and the Freedmen's Bureau. The right to vote was not simply thrust upon them by meddling outsiders, since blacks began agitating for the suffrage as soon as they were freed. In 1865 black conventions throughout the South issued eloquent, though unheeded, appeals for equal civil and political rights.

With the advent of Radical Reconstruction in 1867, the freedmen did enjoy a real measure of political power. But black supremacy never existed. In most states blacks held only a small fraction of political offices, and even in South Carolina, where they comprised a majority of the state legislature's lower house, effective power remained in white hands. As for corruption, moral standards in both government and private enterprise were at low ebb throughout the nation in the postwar years—the era of Boss Tweed, the Credit Mobilier scandal, and the Whiskey Ring. Southern corruption could hardly be blamed on former slaves.

Other actors in the Reconstruction drama also came in for reevaluation. Most carpetbaggers were former Union soldiers seeking economic opportunity in the postwar South, not unscrupulous adventurers. Their motives, a typically American amalgam of humanitarianism and the pursuit of profit, were no more insidious than those of Western pioneers. Scalawags, previously seen as traitors to the white race, now emerged as "Old Line" Whig Unionists who had opposed secession in the first place or as poor whites who had long resented planters' domination of Southern life and who saw in Reconstruction a chance to recast Southern society along more democratic lines. Strongholds of Southern white Republicanism like east Tennessee and western North Carolina had been the scene of resistance to Confederate rule throughout the Civil War; now, as one scalawag newspaper put it, the choice was "between salvation at the hand of the Negro or destruction at the hand of the rebels."

At the same time, the Ku Klux Klan and kindred groups, whose campaign of violence against black and white Republicans had been minimized or excused in older writings, were portrayed as they really were. Earlier scholars had conveyed the impression that the Klan intimidated blacks mainly by dressing as ghosts and playing on the freedmen's superstitions. In fact, black fears were all too real: the Klan was a terrorist organization that beat and killed its political opponents to deprive blacks of their newly won rights. The complicity of the Democratic party and the silence of prominent whites in the face of such outrages stood as an indictment of the moral code the South had inherited from the days of slavery.

By the end of the 1960s, then, the old interpretation had been completely reversed. Southern freedmen were the heroes, the "Redeemers" who overthrew Reconstruction were the villains, and if the era was "tragic," it was because change did not go far enough. Reconstruction had been a time of real progress and its failure a lost opportunity for the South and the nation. But the legacy of Reconstruction—the Fourteenth and Fifteenth Amendments—endured to inspire future efforts for civil rights. As Kenneth Stampp wrote in *The Era of Reconstruction*, a superb summary of revisionist findings published in 1965, "If it was worth four years of civil war to save the Union, it was worth a few years of radical reconstruction to give the American Negro the ultimate promise of equal civil and political rights."

As Stampp's statement suggests, the reevaluation of the first Reconstruction was inspired in large measure by the impact of the second—the modern civil rights movement. And with the waning of that movement in recent years, writing on Reconstruction has undergone still another transformation. Instead of seeing the Civil War and its aftermath as a second American Revolution (as Charles Beard had), a regression into barbarism (as Bowers argued), or a golden opportunity squandered (as the revisionists saw it), recent writers argue that Radical Reconstruction was not really very radical. Since land was not distributed to the former slaves, they remained economically dependent upon their former owners. The planter class survived both the war and Reconstruction with its property (apart from slaves) and prestige more or less intact.

Not only changing times but also the changing concerns of historians have contributed to this latest reassessment of Reconstruction. The hallmark of the past decade's historical writing has been an emphasis upon "social history"—the evocation of the past lives of ordinary Americans—and the downplaying of strictly political events. When applied to Reconstruction, this concern with the "social" suggested that black suffrage and officeholding, once seen as the most radical departures of the Reconstruction era, were relatively insignificant.

Recent historians have focused their investigations not upon the politics of Reconstruction but upon the social and economic aspects of the transition from slavery to freedom. Herbert Gutman's influential study of the black family during and after slavery found little change in family structure or relations between men and women resulting from emancipation. Under slavery most blacks had lived in nuclear family units, although they faced the constant threat of separation from loved ones by sale. Reconstruction provided the opportunity for blacks to solidify their preexisting family ties. Conflicts over whether black women should work in the cotton fields (planters said yes, many black families said no) and over white attempts to "apprentice" black children revealed that the autonomy of family life was a major preoccupation of the freedmen. Indeed, whether manifested in their withdrawal from churches controlled by whites, in the blossoming of black fraternal, benevolent, and self-improvement organizations, or in the demise of the slave quarters and their replacement by small tenant farms occupied by individual families, the quest for independence from white authority and control over their own day-to-day lives shaped the black response to emancipation.

In the post-Civil War South the surest guarantee of economic autonomy, blacks believed, was land. To the freedmen the justice of a claim to land based on their years of unrequited labor appeared self-evident. As an Alabama black convention put it, "The property which they [the planters] hold was nearly all earned by the sweat of our brows." As Leon Litwack showed in *Been in the Storm So Long,* a Pulitzer-Prize-winning account of the black response to emancipation, many freedmen in 1865 and 1866 refused to sign labor contracts, expecting the federal government to give them land. In some localities, as one Alabama overseer reported, they "set up claims to the plantation and all on it."

In the end, of course, the vast majority of Southern blacks remained propertyless and poor. But exactly why the South, and especially its black population, suffered from dire poverty and economic retardation in the decades following the Civil War is a matter of much dispute. In *One Kind of Freedom,* economists Roger Ransom and Richard Sutch indicted country merchants for monopolizing credit and charging usurious interest rates, forcing black tenants into debt and locking the South into a dependence on cotton production that impoverished the entire region. But Jonathan Wiener, in his study of postwar Alabama, argued that planters used their political power to compel blacks to remain on the plantations. Planters succeeded in stabilizing the plantation system, but only by blocking the growth of alternative enterprises, like factories, that might draw off black laborers, thus locking the region into a pattern of economic backwardness.

If the thrust of recent writing has emphasized the social and economic aspects of Reconstruction, politics has not been entirely neglected. But political studies have also reflected the postrevisionist mood summarized by C. Vann Woodward when he observed "how essentially nonrevolutionary and conservative Reconstruction really was." Recent writers, unlike their revisionist predecessors, have found little to praise in federal policy toward the emancipated blacks.

A new sensitivity to the strength of prejudice and laissez-faire ideas in the nineteenth-century North has led many historians to doubt whether the Republican party ever made a genuine commitment to racial justice in the South. The granting of black suffrage was an alternative to a long-term federal responsibility for protecting the rights of the former slaves. Once enfranchised, blacks could be left to fend for themselves. With the exception of a few Radicals like Thaddeus Stevens, nearly all Northern policymakers and educators are criticized today for assuming that, so long as the unfettered operations of the marketplace afforded blacks the opportunity to advance through diligent labor, federal efforts to assist them in acquiring land were unnecessary.

Probably the most innovative recent writing on Reconstruction politics has centered on a broad reassessment of black Republicanism, largely undertaken by a new generation of black historians. Scholars like Thomas Holt and Nell Painter insist that Reconstruction was not simply a matter of black and white. Conflicts within the black community, no less than divisions among whites, shaped Reconstruction politics. Where revisionist scholars, both black and white, had celebrated the accomplishments of black political leaders, Holt, Painter, and others charge that they failed to address the economic plight of the black masses. Painter criticized "representative colored men," as national black leaders were called, for failing to provide ordinary freedmen with effective political leadership. Holt found that black officeholders in South Carolina mostly emerged from the old free mulatto class of Charleston,

which shared many assumptions with prominent whites. "Basically bourgeois in their origins and orientation," he wrote, they "failed to act in the interest of black peasants."

In emphasizing the persistence from slavery of divisions between free blacks and slaves, these writers reflect the increasing concern with continuity and conservatism in Reconstruction. Their work reflects a startling extension of revisionist premises. If, as has been argued for the past twenty years, blacks were active agents rather than mere victims of manipulation, then they could not be absolved of blame for the ultimate failure of Reconstruction.

Despite the excellence of recent writing and the continual expansion of our knowledge of the period, historians of Reconstruction today face a unique dilemma. An old interpretation has been overthrown, but a coherent new synthesis has yet to take its place. The revisionists of the 1960s effectively established a series of negative points: the Reconstruction governments were not as bad as had been portrayed, black supremacy was a myth, the Radicals were not cynical manipulators of the freedmen. Yet no convincing overall portrait of the quality of political and social life emerged from their writings. More recent historians have rightly pointed to elements of continuity that spanned the nineteenth-century Southern experience, especially the survival, in modified form, of the plantation system. Nevertheless, by denying the real changes that did occur, they have failed to provide a convincing portrait of an era characterized above all by drama, turmoil, and social change.

Building upon the findings of the past twenty years of scholarship, a new portrait of Reconstruction ought to begin by viewing it not as a specific time period, bounded by the years 1865 and 1877, but as an episode in a prolonged historical process—American society's adjustment to the consequences of the Civil War and emancipation. The Civil War, of course, raised the decisive questions of America's national existence: the relations between local and national authority, the definition of citizenship, the balance between force and consent in generating obedience to authority. The war and Reconstruction, as Allan Nevins observed over fifty years ago, marked the "emergence of modern America." This was the era of the completion of the national railroad network, the creation of the modern steel industry, the conquest of the West and final subduing of the Indians, and the expansion of the mining frontier. Lincoln's America—the world of the small farm and artisan shop—gave way to a rapidly industrializing economy. The issues that galvanized postwar Northern politics—from the question of the greenback currency to the mode of paying holders of the national debt—arose from the economic changes unleashed by the Civil War.

Above all, the war irrevocably abolished slavery. Since 1619, when "twenty negars" disembarked from a Dutch ship in Virginia, racial injustice had haunted American life, mocking its professed ideals even as tobacco and cotton, the products of slave labor, helped finance the nation's economic development. Now the implications of the black presence could no longer be ignored. The Civil War resolved the problem of slavery but, as the Philadelphia diarist Sydney George Fisher observed in June 1865, it opened an even more intractable problem: "What shall we do with the Negro?" Indeed, he went on, this was a problem *"incapable of* any solution that will satisfy both North and South."

As Fisher realized, the focal point of Reconstruction was the social revolution known as emancipation. Plantation slavery was simultaneously a system of labor, a form of racial domination, and the foundation upon which arose a distinctive ruling class within the South. Its demise threw open the most fundamental questions of economy, society, and politics. A new system of labor, social, racial, and political relations had to be created to replace slavery.

The United States was not the only nation to experience emancipation in the nineteenth century. Neither plantation slavery nor abolition were unique to the United States. But Reconstruction was. In a comparative perspective Radical Reconstruction stands as a remarkable experiment, the only effort of a society experiencing abolition to bring the former slaves within the umbrella of equal citizenship. Because the Radicals did not achieve everything they wanted, historians have lately tended to play down the stunning departure represented by black suffrage and officeholding. Former slaves, most fewer than two years removed from bondage, debated the fundamental questions of the polity: What is a republican form of government? Should the state provide equal education for all? How could political equality be reconciled with a society in which property was so unequally distributed? There was something inspiring in the way such men met the challenge of Reconstruction. "I knew nothing more than to obey my master," James K. Greene, an Alabama black politician later recalled. "But the tocsin of freedom sounded and knocked at the door and we walked out like free men and we met the exigencies as they grew up, and shouldered the responsibilities."

"You never saw a people more excited on the subject of politics than are the negroes of the South," one planter observed in 1867. And there were more than a few Southern whites as well who in these years shook off the prejudices of the past to embrace the vision of a new South dedicated to the principles of equal citizenship and social justice. One ordinary South Carolinian expressed the new sense of possibility in 1868 to the Republican governor of the state: "I am sorry that I cannot write an elegant stiled letter to your excellency. But I rejoice to think that God almighty has given to the poor of S.C. a Gov. to hear to feel to protect the humble poor without distinction to race or color. . . . I am a native borned S.C. a poor man never owned a Negro in my life nor my father before me. . . . Remember the true and loyal are the poor of the whites and blacks outside of these you can find none loyal."

Few modern scholars believe the Reconstruction governments established in the South in 1867 and 1868 fulfilled the aspirations of their humble constituents. While their achievements in such realms as education, civil rights, and the economic rebuilding of the South are now widely appreciated, historians today believe they failed to affect either the economic plight of the emancipated slave or the ongoing transformation of independent white farmers into cotton tenants. Yet their opponents did perceive the Reconstruction governments in precisely this way—as representatives of a revolution that had put the bottom rail, both racial and economic, on top. This perception helps explain the ferocity of the attacks leveled against them and the per-

vasiveness of violence in the postemancipation South.

The spectacle of black men voting and holding office was anathema to large numbers of Southern whites. Even more disturbing, at least in the view of those who still controlled the plantation regions of the South, was the emergence of local officials, black and white, who sympathized with the plight of the black laborer. Alabama's vagrancy law was a "dead letter" in 1870, "because those who are charged with its enforcement are indebted to the vagrant vote for their offices and emoluments." Political debates over the level and incidence of taxation, the control of crops, and the resolution of contract disputes revealed that a primary issue of Reconstruction was the role of government in a plantation society. During presidential Reconstruction, and after "Redemption," with planters and their allies in control of politics, the law emerged as a means of stabilizing and promoting the plantation system. If Radical Reconstruction failed to redistribute the land of the South, the ouster of the planter class from control of politics at least ensured that the sanctions of the criminal law would not be employed to discipline the black labor force.

An understanding of this fundamental conflict over the relation between government and society helps explain the pervasive complaints concerning corruption and "extravagance" during Radical Reconstruction. Corruption there was aplenty; tax rates did rise sharply. More significant than the rate of taxation, however, was the change in its incidence. For the first time, planters and white farmers had to pay a significant portion of their income to the government, while propertyless blacks often escaped scot-free.

Several states, moreover, enacted heavy taxes on uncultivated land to discourage land speculation and force land onto the market, benefiting, it was hoped, the freedmen.

As time passed, complaints about the "extravagance" and corruption of Southern governments found a sympathetic audience among influential Northerners. The Democratic charge that universal suffrage in the South was responsible for high taxes and governmental extravagance coincided with a rising conviction among the urban middle classes of the North that city government had to be taken out of the hands of the immigrant poor and returned to the "best men"— the educated, professional, financially independent citizens unable to exert much political influence at a time of mass parties and machine politics. Increasingly the "respectable" middle classes began to retreat from the very notion of universal suffrage. The poor were no longer perceived as honest producers, the backbone of the social order; now they became the "dangerous classes," the "mob." As the historian Francis Parkman put it, too much power rested with "masses of imported ignorance and hereditary ineptitude." To Parkman the Irish of the Northern cities and the blacks of the South were equally incapable of utilizing the ballot: "Witness the municipal corruptions of New York, and the monstrosities of Negro rule in South Carolina." Such attitudes helped to justify Northern inaction as, one by one, the Reconstruction regimes of the South were overthrown by political violence.

In the end, then, neither the abolition of slavery nor Reconstruction succeeded in resolving the debate over the meaning of freedom in American life. Twenty years before the American Civil War,

writing about the prospect of abolition in France's colonies, Alexis de Tocqueville had written, "If the Negroes have the right to become free, the [planters] have the incontestable right not to be ruined by the Negroes' freedom." And in the United States, as in nearly every plantation society that experienced the end of slavery, a rigid social and political dichotomy between former master and former slave, an ideology of racism, and a dependent labor force with limited economic opportunities all survived abolition. Unless one means by freedom the simple fact of not being a slave, emancipation thrust blacks into a kind of no-man's land, a partial freedom that made a mockery of the American ideal of equal citizenship.

Yet by the same token the ultimate outcome underscores the uniqueness of Reconstruction itself. Alone among the societies that abolished slavery in the nineteenth century, the United States, for a moment, offered the freedmen a measure of political control over their own destinies. However brief its sway, Reconstruction allowed scope for a remarkable political and social mobilization of the black community. It opened doors of opportunity that could never be completely closed. Reconstruction transformed the lives of Southern blacks in ways unmeasurable by statistics and unreachable by law. It raised their expectations and aspirations, redefined their status in relation to the larger society, and allowed space for the creation of institutions that enabled them to survive the repression that followed. And it established constitutional principles of civil and political equality that, while flagrantly violated after Redemption, planted the seeds of future struggle.

Certainly, in terms of the sense of possibility with which it opened, Reconstruction failed. But as Du Bois observed, it was a "splendid failure." For its animating vision—a society in which social advancement would be open to all on the basis of individual merit, not inherited caste distinctions—is as old as America itself and remains relevant to a nation still grappling with the unresolved legacy of emancipation.

NO

C. Vann Woodward

RECONSTRUCTION:
A COUNTERFACTUAL PLAYBACK

The ruins of two great failures dominate the landscape of American history. They stand close together in the middle distance, back to back, but separate and distinct. One is the ruins of the Confederacy, the South's failure to gain independence. The other is the ruins of Reconstruction, the North's failure to solve the problem of the black people's place in American life. The South's failure was the North's success and vice versa. Each can be and, of course, has been described by its opponents as simply the wreckage wrought in preventing acknowledged wrong. But from the standpoint of their supporters and champions there can be no doubt that each of these ruins represents a great American failure. . . .

The achievements of the revisionists are impressive. But as a contribution to explaining the failure of Reconstruction they tend rather to complicate than to solve the enigma. For if, as they have demonstrated, the statesmanship of the Radicals was all that inspired and their motivation all that pure, if the freedmen were so responsive and capably led, if government by the Scalawag-Carpetbagger-freedmen coalition was all that constructive, and if the opposition were indeed headed by a misfit in the White House who was out of touch with the electorate, then success would seem more indicated than failure. The paradox reminds me of the first historical problem I confronted as a boy. It went something like this: If Marse Robert was all that noble and intrepid, if Stonewall was all that indomitable and fast on his feet, if Jeb Stuart was all that gallant and dashing, and if God was on our side, then why the hell did we *lose* that war?

This is not to write off the accomplishments of the revisionists. I hope the record is clear that I have aided and abetted and egged them on, presumed to teach some of them, read many of their manuscripts and all their monographs, praised what I could and encouraged when I could. What they did in the main much needed doing. I do believe that they have produced many works with better prospects of durability than the school of the 1900s or that of the 1930s.

I am more interested in what comes next and what problems remain unsolved. This brings me back to the old problem of failure. As I have remarked earlier, Americans have rather a thing about failure—about confronting it, confessing it, and accepting it, as well as about explaining it. It is noteworthy that the great bulk of work done by the revisionists has been on Andrew Johnson's administration, not on the two Grant administrations, that is, on the period where, paradoxically, the ephemeral successes and triumphs multiplied, not the period of twice that length when the failures piled up or became unavoidably conspicuous. This may be mere coincidence, but my guess is that it is more than that. Another tendency might be called the deferred success approach, the justification (or dismissal) of failure in the First Reconstruction on the ground that it prepared the way for success in the Second Reconstruction, or maybe a Third yet to come. Thus one historian writes that the failures of the First Reconstruction diminish to insignificance in comparison with successes of the Second in advancing equal civil and political rights for blacks and promise of further progress to come. This is a generational shift of the burden of responsibility. But it must be recognized as essentially another strategy of evasion.

One habit of mind that has complicated American ways of dealing with failure, apart from a relative unfamiliarity with the experience, has been the isolation of American history from comparative reference. Comparisons have indeed been used with regard to Reconstruction, but they have been inter-nalized. Lacking foreign comparisons, or indifferent to them, Americans have turned inward to compare professed ideals with actual practice. This has encouraged a strong moralistic tendency in our historical writing and controversy. Since the nation has advertised a commitment to some very lofty ideals and principles, the contrast between performance and principle has always been painful, and the application of absolute and abstract standards of judgment often sets up moral disturbance that clouds issues and distorts perspectives.

For more realistic perspective on the American experience of Reconstruction we need to turn to comparison with foreign experiences, including but not limited to those of the other twenty-odd slave societies in the New World that went through the post-emancipation ordeal. To avoid repetition, since I have sampled those comparisons before, I must be content with summarizing conclusions of the best informed authorities. The most important finding is that wherever slavery was widespread, emancipation was invariably followed by resort to drastic measures, including use of force, to put the freedmen back to work. The old masters of the American South were by no means alone in resorting to black codes and chain gangs. Old masters everywhere—West Indies, Latin America, Africa, Asia—took forceable steps to drive the freedmen back to work.

Furthermore, in those lands undergoing emancipation where the process of reconstruction was subject to outside control or supervision, whether from the crown, the mother country, an imperial or metropolitan administration, or as in the South the federal government under Northern control, such authorities proved quite ineffective in protecting the lives and rights of the emancipated. The universality of failure by authorities and oppression by old masters does not excuse or justify either the governments or the masters anywhere—especially not a government that had just fought a bloody civil war in the name of freedom. Reconstruction left a lasting blot on the American conscience and national history and continues to breed moral recrimination between regions and races. But at least the comparative context removes the stigma of uniqueness and places moral issues in a broader setting. That, I believe, is a legitimate use of history—not only to recover the past but to enable us to live with it.

Another type of comparison has often been used in interpreting Reconstruction, but not always with sufficient caution. To place a historical event in a category of events is to make a comparison. Thus, when Reconstruction is spoke of as a revolution, we are compelled to think of it in comparison with other revolutions. If we reserve the term "revolution" for the classic phenomena of England in the seventeenth century, America and France in the eighteenth century, and Russia and China in the twentieth century, then it is certainly misused when applied to the American Reconstruction of the nineteenth century. For in the last instance there were no mass executions, no class liquidations. No heads rolled. There were constitutional changes, to be sure, but they were insignificant compared with those in England, France, Russia, and China, and they were mainly effected through constitutional forms. The South's so-called Bourbons or Redeemers did not become proscribed and outlawed émigrés. They remained at home, retained their estates, took over from the ephemeral radical governments,

and after their so-called counter-revolution they did not find it necessary to make very drastic changes in the system left them by the so-called revolution. All things considered, it would be better to abandon both the concept of revolution and that of counter-revolution in writing of Reconstruction as it *was*.

But in writing of what it *might* have been, what many hoped it would be, and of why Reconstruction failed, the concept of revolution seems indispensable. It should be fairly obvious that in order to succeed with the professed aims of full civil rights, equality, and justice for the freedmen, Reconstruction would have had to go much further in the way of revolutionary measures than it ever did. Even then it might have failed, for revolutions are not invariably successful nor are their innovations always lasting. It is not very helpful to prescribe revolution in the abstract without specifying the revolutionary program. Nor is it very realistic to imagine a revolutionary program without regard to the nature of the party and the people who would carry it out and the historical context in which they would have worked. Only by that means can we test the hypothesis that the failure of Reconstruction is to be explained by the lack of revolutionary measures.

One revolutionary measure, a favorite for the speculation over a century, is the confiscation of rebel estates and redistribution of them among the freedmen. This deserves serious consideration for a number of reasons. In the first place such a proposal was seriously made and had an able and powerful advocate in Thaddeus Stevens. The Stevens plan called for the confiscation of all rebel estates over $10,000 or over 200 acres. He estimated that this would result in the taking over of some 394 million out of 465 million acres in the rebel states. The redistribution would give 40 acres to each adult male freedman. This would take 40 million acres, and the remaining 254 million would be sold to the highest bidder and the proceeds allocated to pensions for Union veterans, damages and reparations, and enough left to retire three-quarters of the national debt. The plan was defeated, of course, but it has had advocates such as W. E. B. Du Bois and various other Marxists.

Americans need no Marxist precedents, however, for there was ample precedent for the wholesale confiscation of the estates of disloyal elements of the population in the treatment of Tories during the American Revolution, and there was a spectacular contemporary example abroad in the distribution of some of the confiscated lands to emancipated serfs by the Czar of All the Russias in 1861. The American freedmen surely had as great a moral claim on the land on which they had toiled for 250 years. Furthermore if the federal government could overcome the legal and constitutional problems of confiscating the slave property of the planters, it surely could have justified confiscating their landed property as well. The planters would have objected strenuously, of course, but they would have been powerless to prevent the action had Congress been determined. Let us assume, then, that the Stevens Land Confiscation Bill actually passed, that President Ben Wade signed it in the White House after President Johnson's removal by successful impeachment, and that the Fortieth Congress then brought to bear all its experience and wisdom in refining the legislation and President Wade marshalled the best talents for administering the land act. What would have been the consequences

for the outcome of Reconstruction? Would this have converted a failure into a reasonable success?

No one can possibly say for sure, of course. What one *can* describe with some assurance, however, is the record of the same federal government, the same Congresses under the control of the same party in administering and distributing public lands elsewhere. Again we resort to the comparative approach, though this time the comparisons are drawn from domestic rather than foreign instances. The Reconstruction period coincided with the great era of public land distribution by the federal government according to the provisions of the Homestead Act of 1862 and other federal land laws placed on the books between 1862 and 1878. The public domain available for distribution under the Homestead and subsequent acts amounted to some 1,048,000,000 acres, more than half the total area of the nation and more than two and a half times the 394 million acres of confiscated rebel estates that would have been added to the public domain by the Stevens Act. This fabulous opportunity, without precedent in history, appeared to be the fruition of the American dream, the most cherished dream of reformers—free land for those who tilled the land.

What came of that dream in the administration of the Homestead Act is a matter of public record. We know that as things turned out the homesteaders got short shrift and proved to be the least favored of the various groups attracted to the western lands. The land-grant railroads alone got four times as much land as the homesteaders in the first four decades of the Homestead Act. In that period 84 percent of the new farms brought under cultivation were purchased or subdivided from larger holdings. Of the patents actually granted to homesteaders a great number were handed to pawns of speculators and monopolists, so that in all probability little more than one-tenth of the new farms were free in the homestead sense. Furthermore, the bona fide homesteader was typically shunted off into the poorest land and least desirable tracts, while the speculators pre-empted tracts closest to settlement and transportation and held them for resale at prices beyond the means of the class the Homestead Act was presumably designed to help. It is the opinion of Fred Shannon that, "In its operation the Homestead Act could hardly have defeated the hopes of the [land-reform] enthusiasts . . . more completely if the makers had drafted it with that purpose uppermost in mind."

While many of the same people who drafted and administered the Homestead Act for the West would in all probability have drafted and administered the Stevens Act for the South, it is only fair to remember that the Western land problem was complicated by variables absent from the Southern picture—granting that the latter had its own complications. But at least the South lay within the humid, forested longitudes, conditions that were far more familiar to Eastern lawmakers than Walter Webb's Great Plains, and also the rebel estates provided a larger proportion of arable land, much more conveniently located in relation to the prospective homesteaders. Because of these advantages and the idealism said to have motivated Radicals in their dealings with freedmen (however inoperative it was in the same men's dealings with Western homesteaders) it is possible that the Stevens Act would have had a happier history than the Homestead Act and that the black freedmen would have

actually entered into the promised land, peacefully and cheerfully, each one secure in the possession of his forty acres. And let us throw in an army mule apiece for good measure.

That outcome is conceivable and one would hope even probable. But in calculating the degree of probability one is forced to take into account certain other conditioning and relevant factors in addition to the western homestead experience. For one thing the Stevens Act as detailed by the Pennsylvania Radical set aside nine-tenths of the 394 million acres of confiscated rebel land for sale to the highest bidder—an open invitation to the speculator and monopolist. It is possible that these types might have behaved toward the black homesteaders of the South in much the same way they behaved toward the white homesteader in the West. If so the probability of success for the philanthropic part of the Stevens Act is appreciably diminished.

Prospects of success for the Stevens Act are also illuminated by the history of a Southern Homestead Act that actually *was* adopted by Congress. There were 47,700,000 acres of public land in five of the Confederate states in 1861, more than the amount of rebel estates set aside for freedmen by the hypothetical Stevens Act. In 1866 the Radicals pushed through a drastic bill applying exclusively to these lands, reserving them to homesteaders at 80 acres per holding, and favoring freedmen by excluding ex-Confederates from homesteading privileges. These lands were generally less accessible and less desirable than those of confiscated estates might have been, and as in the case of the Western act no provision was made for furnishing credit and transportation to homesteaders. These conditions probably explain why extremely few blacks seized upon this opportunity to double the elusive 40 acres. In that respect the act was a failure and, at any rate, Congress reversed the policy in 1876 and threw open this rich Southern empire to unrestricted speculation. There ensued a scramble of monopolists that matched any land rush of the Wild West, and the freedmen were thrust aside and forgotten. Admittedly this episode offers further discouragement for the chances of the revolutionary Stevens Act.

Determined revolutionists are not disheartened by reverses, however. They merely press forward with more heroic measures. Perhaps Thaddeus Stevens was not revolutionary enough. There is the problem of the rebel resistance to Radical Reconstruction and federal authority in the defeated states. My own researches have impressed me deeply with the seriousness of this resistance. It was often open, defiant, organized, and effective. White Southerners repeatedly insulted, persecuted, and sometimes murdered federal officials, army officers included. They scoffed at the law and ridiculed the courts. They did everything to black citizens the law forbade their doing and invented mistreatments that law never thought of. How any self-respecting government put up with such defiance unless, indeed, it was at least subliminally sympathetic with the resistance, it is difficult to understand. With overwhelming power in his hands, even an ordinary respectable non-revolutionary government could have done better than this.

Let me remind you, however, that this is a revolutionary program that we are pursuing. Here Thad Stevens lets us down. He raises the question whether any Republican, Senator Charles Sumner included, really deserved the name

"Radical." It is true that his rhetoric against the "proud, bloated, and defiant rebels" was violent enough, that he promised to "startle feeble minds and shake weak nerves," that he ridiculed "the prim conservatives, the snobs, and the male waiting maids in Congress," that he asked, "How can republican institutions, free schools, free churches . . . exist in a mingled community of nabobs and serfs," and that he thundered the promise to "drive her nobility into exile," or worse. But when it came right down to it he confessed that he "never desired bloody punishments to any extent." This admission of bourgeois softness proves that Stevens has exhausted his usefulness as a guide to revolutionary solutions.

It is becoming a bit tiresome (and it is entirely unnecessary) to be flanked on the left in speculative audacity. Armchair bloodbaths can be conducted with impunity by anyone, even a professor emeritus. Let us then pursue the logic of the revolutionary process on past Stevens and Sumner, past the Old Left and the New Left, and out to the wild blue—or rather infra-red—yonder. Let us embrace in our revolutionary program, along with the Stevens Act, an act for the liquidation of the enemy class. There is ample precedent for this in the history of revolutions. Even the American Revolution drove the Tories into exile. Mass deportation, considering the merchant marine's state of total disrepair in 1865, is unfortunately not a practicable option. That leaves available only the messier alternatives. It is true that the Alaska purchase from Russia made providentially available an American Siberia in 1867, but that would take care of relatively few, and again there is the tedious problem of transportation. The numbers are formidable, for the counter-revolutionary resistance extended beyond the planter class through a very large percentage of Southern whites. A few hundred thousand Northern Copperheads can be handled in concentration camps, but in Dixie harsher measures are indicated. Let no true revolutionary blanch at the implications. Remember that we must be cruel in order to be kind, that we are the social engineers of the future, that we are forestalling future bloodbaths, race riots, and relieving our Northern metropolitan friends of problems that trouble their thoughts and for a time threatened to destroy their cities. If our work is bloody our conscience is clear, and we do all that we do—compassionately.

Having liquidated the white resistance down to the last unregenerate lord of the lash and the last bed-sheeted Ku Kluxer, let us proceed unencumbered to build the true Radical Reconstruction. We will find it expedient to import managerial talent in large numbers to replace the liquidated white resistance, and place them in charge of agriculture, industry, railroads, and mines. They will doubtless come from the same states the carpetbaggers hailed from, but they must be carefully screened to eliminate the more objectionable types and certified as non-racists and non-Copperheads. We will also establish a permanent Freedmen's Bureau, perhaps modeled on the Indian Bureau, and place in command of it the very finest talent. If not General O. O. Howard, perhaps we can get the nomination of Frederick Douglass through a miraculously radicalized U.S. Senate, after a radicalized U. S. Grant had executed a Pride's Purge of half the members.

After these Draconian, Cromwellian, Stalinist measures had removed all resistance and interference from Southern and Northern racists and Kluxers and nightriders, silenced all Confederate orators, and shut down the last obstructionist press, the revolutionists should have had a perfectly free hand. What then would have been the consequences for fulfillment of Reconstruction purposes? Would these additional measures have converted failure into success? One would surely hope so after paying such a bloody price.

But again, no one can say for sure. And again we turn to the comparative method for possible illumination. I hope that I am sufficiently alert to the dangers of these comparisons. I realize that no analogy is complete, that no two historical events are identical, and that the risks of drawing conclusions by such reasoning are most formidable. I have tried to guard against such risks and to be very tentative about drawing conclusions, but I suspect I have already outraged respected historians by mentioning Grant in the same breath with Cromwell or Stalin. Nevertheless I shall take heart and venture one last excursion into the treacherous field of comparative or counterfactual history.

Once again the comparison is close to home and contemporaneous with the Reconstruction period. Moreover, the same electorates, the same congressmen, the identical presidents and judiciary, the same editorial chorus and clerical censors are involved in the one as in the other—one cast for two dramas. The second drama also has as its plot the story of reformers using the federal government to bring justice and rights and decent lives to men of color. This time the theater is in the West instead of the South and the colored minority is red instead of black. Since we have "controlled the variable" (as the quantifiers say) of Confederate slave owners' resistance in the South—with a regrettable amount of bloodshed to be sure—the two theaters are more readily comparable. For while the reformers in the West had their own problems, they were not encumbered by die-hard Confederate reactionaries, former owners and masters of the red people, and not dogged at every step by determined and desperate nightriders. In these respects they had a relatively free hand.

The personnel and policies of the white guardians of the blacks and the white guardians of the reds were often interchangeable. General W. T. Sherman moved from command of the Southern District to command of the Western District in 1867, from the final arbiter of the black freedman's destiny to final arbiter of the redskin's fate. Many other military officers including General O. O. Howard moved back and forth from South to West. While General Howard, who had been head of the Freedmen's Bureau, was serving as president of an all-black Howard University in 1872 he was dispatched by Grant to conclude a treaty with the Apaches; in 1874 he was placed in command of the Department of Columbia, and in 1877 he led a punitive expedition against the Nez Perce Indians. Black regiments served in West and South under the same white officers. In the educational field Samuel Armstrong of Hampton Institute, Booker Washington's mentor and model, took Richard Henry Pratt, the great Indian educator, as disciple and assistant, and the two of them integrated and taught black and red students at Hampton. Later Pratt took the Armstrong-Booker Washington gospel to Indian schools. The same missionaries, preachers, editors, and reformers often concerned themselves with the problems and destinies of both colored minorities.

What can be said, in view of the relatively free hand they had in the West, of the performance of the American reformers toward the Indian, as compared with their performance toward the Negro, when they did not have the free hand I have imagined for them? Was it any better? As a matter of fact the two problems were solved in much the same way. The red man like the black man was given to understand that the white man's will was supreme, that he had few rights the white man was bound to respect. He was promised land and the land was taken away. He was promised integration and then segregated, even more completely than the black man. He was degraded, exploited, humiliated, and because he offered more resistance he was cut down ruthlessly by military force or vigilante action. Idealists like Richard Henry Pratt who operated in both South and West were as frustrated in their efforts for red man as they were with the black man. White supremacy forces were as triumphant over Eastern "Indian lovers" in Arizona and Colorado as they were over Northern "nigger lovers" in Mississippi and Alabama.

But this comparison is an outrage against established compartmentalizations of historical thought, a preposterous violation of respected conventions. Everyone knows what a "good Indian" was. And what but confusion of the undergraduate mind can possibly come from comparing Colorado and Alabama? I apologize for this travesty against sound canons of the profession. Nevertheless, I confess that these irresponsible speculations have raised such doubts in the mind of one dedicated revolutionary arm-chair ultra-radical as to palsy his hand and sickly over with the pale cast of thought the native hue of resolution. Almost am I persuaded to countermand belatedly the order for the Confederate liquidation.

I owe further apologies. Having invited you to consider the causes of the failure of Reconstruction, I have produced nothing but negative results. While applauding the revisionists for their excellent work, I have questioned the emphasis on the idealism and sincerity of the Radicals and their ephemeral triumphs as an adequate indication of their ultimate failure. In the second place, I have raised doubts about moralistic and uniquely American explanations for post-emancipation failure in the protection of freedmen on the ground that much the same pattern of forced labor occurred everywhere in the world as a sequel to abolition. Thirdly, having embraced the Stevens policy of rebel land confiscation and redistribution, I am forced to admit that contemporaneous experience with federal administration of public lands discourages optimism about the freedman's chances. And finally, after eliminating Confederate resistance with bloody measures I am overcome with doubts, caused by belated reflections on the fate of the poor red man, that even these drastic steps would ensure success. With the candor I have urged upon other historians I am obliged to confess a failure of my own, the failure to find a satisfactory explanation for the failure of Reconstruction.

The problem remains unsolved. The assignment still goes begging. It deserves high priority among the unfinished tasks of American historiography. Those who next undertake the task will not, I hope, rely too uncritically on the received ideas, the shared moral convictions and political values of their own time to sanction their premises. They should give scrupulous attention to uniquely American conditions, but remember that the post-emancipation problem they attack was not unique to America. They may well profit from consideration of allegedly idyllic race relations on happy islands in the Caribbean sun, but remember that their home problem was environed by Protestant Anglo-American institutions of a temperate zone unblessed by Pope or tropical sun. They should give due weight to constitutional issues without fruitlessly pining for an English-type constitution to deal with states' rights, a Russian-type Czar to distribute land among the emancipated, or a Soviet-type commissar of security to liquidate mass resistance.

I hope those who accept this challenge will not take these reflections as the counsel of despair, or as intimation that Reconstruction was doomed to failure, or that our ancestors might not have done better by their experiment than they actually did. Nor should other historians be discouraged from revolutionary speculations by the inconclusive results of my own. Let them be as far-out left as is currently fashionable. But in the transports of revolutionary imaginings, armchair edicts, and dreams of glory, they would do well to keep in mind the human materials and the historic context of their problem. If they do this, they will face up to the fact that nineteenth-century Americans (and some in the twentieth century as well) were fatefully stuck with a perverse mystique of squatter sovereignty. The tenets of this perversion of the democratic dogma, this squatter sovereignty, were that whatever the law or the Constitution or the Supreme Court or world opinion or moral codes said to the contrary notwithstanding, the will of the dominant white majority would prevail. And where whites were not in the majority it would prevail anyway. How it was, and how early, we got stuck with a commitment to this caricature of democ- racy is a long story, a very long story, and the story did not begin in 1865, and the commitment was not confined to the South.

POSTSCRIPT

Reconstruction: Could It Have Given Blacks Full Equality?

Both the traditional and revisionist writers of Reconstruction history have treated African Americans in a passive manner. Traditionalists like J. G. Randall and E. Merton Coulter, who assumed that African Americans were intellectually inferior to whites, argued that African American politicians were the junior partners of the white carpetbaggers and scalawags in robbing the Reconstruction governments. Revisionists like Kenneth M. Stampp, who believed in the biological equality of all human races, maintained that the African American politicians did not constitute a majority in the Reconstruction governments, were not totally corrupt, and did not want to disenfranchise whites. African Americans, he insisted, only desired their civil and political constitutional rights. Writing at the peak of the civil rights movement in 1965, Stampp was trying to assure his readers that African Americans only wanted to become good Americans and obtain (in this "second Reconstruction") what had been denied them a century earlier.

Foner's conclusions are more upbeat than those of most postrevisionists. "However brief," he argues, "the United States was the only society which offered the freedman a measure of political control over their own destinies. It transformed their lives in ways not measurable by statistics. It raised their expectations and aspirations . . . and established constitutional principles of civil and political equality that . . . planted the seeds of future struggle."

In *Nothing But Freedom: Emancipation and Its Legacy* (Louisiana State University Press, 1984), Foner advances his interpretation by comparing the treatment of American ex-slaves with those newly emancipated in Haiti and the British West Indies. Only in America, he claims, were the freedmen given voting and economic rights. Although these rights had been stripped away from the majority of black Southerners by 1900, Reconstruction had, nevertheless, created a legacy of freedom which inspired succeeding generations of African Americans.

C. Vann Woodward is more pessimistic about the outcome of Reconstruction than Foner. For all the successes listed by the revisionists, he claims that the experiment failed. Woodward makes clever use of both counterfactual ("what if") history and comparative history to destroy the optimistic assumption of some of the earlier revisionists that, if the national government had engaged in extensive land reforms and enforced laws protecting the civil rights of African Americans, Reconstruction would have worked. In contrast to Foner, Woodward argues that former slaves were as poorly treated in the United States as they were in other countries. He also believes that the confiscation of former plantations and the redistribution of land to the former slaves would have failed in the same way that the Homestead Act of 1862 failed to generate equal distribution of government lands to poor white settlers. Finally, Woodward claims that the reformers who worked with African Americans during Reconstruction and with Native Americans a decade or two later were often the same people who failed in both instances because their goals were out of touch with the realities of the late nineteenth century.

Much research still remains to be done on the Reconstruction period. State and local studies which employ modern social science frameworks yield new perspectives. Thomas Holt's *Black Over White* (Illinois, 1977) is a sophisticated study of African American political leadership in South Carolina during Reconstruction. Combining traditional sources, such as old letters, military service records, and newspapers, with sophisticated quantitative analyses of voting records, Holt gives a complex picture of that reconstructed state. Reconstruction failed in South Carolina, says Holt, not because of corruption but because African American leaders failed to develop a clear and unifying ideology to challenge whites who wanted to restore white supremacy.

Willie Lee Rose's *Rehearsal for Reconstruction: The Port Royal Experiment* (Bobbs Merrill, 1964) is an earlier study by a former Woodward student that describes the difficulties of enacting a land reform policy. Ten thousand slaves in the South Carolina sea islands took over lands abandoned by their owners in 1861 and ran them as self-sufficient farmers. When the national government sold off most of the lands to Northern speculators and cotton companies, the former slaves were forced to sign labor contracts or leave the lands.

Foner has provided us with a major postrevisionist summary in *Reconstruction: America's Unfinished Revolution, 1863–1867* (Harper & Row, 1988), a 600-page text which contains the most extensive bibliography on the subject. Before tackling Foner, students should read Michael Perman's *Emancipation and Reconstruction, 1862–1879* (Harlan Davidson, 1987), or earlier summaries of revisionism by John Hope Franklin, *Reconstruction* (University of Chicago, 1961), and Kenneth M. Stampp, *The Era of Reconstruction, 1865–1877* (Knopf, 1965). Traditional accounts of Reconstruction can be sampled in William Archibald Dunning's biased classic *Reconstruction: Political and Economic* (Harper & Row, 1907); the 1937 edition of J. G. Randall's *The Civil War and Reconstruction* (D. C. Heath); and E. Merton Coulter, *The South During Reconstruction, 1865–1877* (LSU Press, 1947), the last major work written from the Dunning (or traditional) point of view. A scathing critique of Coulter's work can be found in John Hope Franklin's "Whither Reconstruction Historiography," which is conveniently reprinted along with a number of other articles that deserve attention, in *Race and History: Selected Essays, 1938–1988* (LSU Press, 1989). Finally, Staughton Lynd's *Reconstruction* (Harper & Row, 1967) is an older but valuable edited collection of the main viewpoints on Reconstruction.

CONTRIBUTORS
TO THIS VOLUME

EDITOR

JAMES M. SORELLE, a native Texan, received a Bachelor of Arts (1972) and a Master of Arts (1974) degree from the University of Houston and a Ph.D. from Kent State University (1980). He has taught at Ball State University and currently is an assistant professor of history at Baylor University. In addition to introductory courses in Western civilization and American history, he teaches upper-level sections in African American, urban, and late nineteenth- and twentieth-century United States history. His scholarly articles have appeared in the *Houston Review, Southwestern Historical Quarterly,* and a forthcoming anthology, *Black Dixie: Essays in Afro-Texan History in Houston.* He also has contributed entries to *The Handbook of Texas.*

LARRY MADARAS was born in Bayonne, New Jersey, in 1937. He attended Xavier High School in New York City and received his Bachelor's degree from Holy Cross College in 1959, an M.A. from New York University in 1961, and a Ph.D. from New York University in 1964. He has taught at Spring Hill College, the University of South Alabama, and the University of Maryland at College Park. He is currently teaching history and political science full-time at Howard Community College in Columbia, Maryland. he has been a Fulbright Fellow and has held two fellowships from the National Endowment for the Humanities. He is the author of dozens of journal articles and book reveiws.

STAFF

Marguerite L. Egan   Program Manager
Brenda S. Filley   Production Manager
Whit Vye   Designer
Libra Ann Cusack   Typesetting Supervisor
Juliana Arbo   Typesetter
David Brackley   Copy Editor
David Dean   Administrative Assistant
Diane Barker   Editorial Assistant
David Filley   Graphics

AUTHORS

IRVING H. BARTLETT is the John F. Kennedy Professor of American Civilization at the University of Massachusetts-Boston. His publications include *Wendell and Ann Phillips: The Community of Reform, 1840–1880* (W. W. Norton, 1982).

JOHN B. BOLES is a professor of history at Rice University and the managing editor of *The Journal of Southern History*.

M. E. BRADFORD is a professor of English literature at the University of Dallas in Irving, Texas.

JON BUTLER is a professor of religious studies and American studies at Yale University.

LOIS GREEN CARR is an adjunct professor at the University of Maryland at College Park and is also associated with the St. Mary's City Historic Commission.

The late **AVERY CRAVEN** was a professor of history at the University of Chicago.

ROBERT HUGH FERRELL is a historian and a professor emeritus of history at Indiana University, where he has taught since 1953.

DAVID HACKETT FISCHER is the Earl Warren Professor of History at Brandeis University, where he has taught since 1962. His publications include *Historians' Fallacies: Toward a Logic of Historical Thought* (Harper & Row, 1970).

ERIC FONER is a professor of history at Columbia University and the author of *Nothing But Freedom: Emancipation and Its Legacy* (Louisiana State University Press, 1983). He has also recently published a major synthesis of the post–Civil War period, *Reconstruction: America's Unfinished Revolution, 1863–1867* (Harper & Row, 1988).

EUGENE D. GENOVESE is a scholar-in-residence at the University Center in Georgia. His publications include *Roll, Jordan, Roll: The World the Slaves Made* (Random House, 1976) and *The Political Economy of Slavery: Studies in Economy and Society of the Slave South* (Random House, 1967).

JAMES A. HENRETTA is the Priscilla Alden Burke Professor of American History at the University of Maryland at College Park.

RICHARD HOFSTADTER (1916–1970) was a professor of history at Columbia University and is considered to be among the best of the post–World War II generation of American historians. His publications include the two classics—*The American Political Tradition and the Men Who Made It* (Alfred A. Knopf, 1948) and *The Age of Reform: From Bryan to F.D.R.* (Alfred A. Knopf, 1955).

LYLE KOEHLER received his Ph.D. in history from the University of Cincinnati and works there in an administrative position.

ALLAN KULIKOFF is a professor of history at Northern Illinois University in DeKalb, Illinois.

KAREN ORDAHL KUPPERMAN is a professor of history at the University of Connecticut in Storrs, Connecticut.

JEAN BUTENHOFF LEE is an associate professor of history at the University of Wisconsin-Madison.

JAMES T. LEMON is a professor of geography at the University of Toronto.

GERDA LERNER is the Robinson-Edwards Professor of History at the University of Wisconsin-Madison. Her publications include *The Creation of Patriarchy* (Oxford University Press, 1986).

RICHARD P. McCORMICK is a professor emeritus of history at Rutgers University, where he has taught since 1945. He is the author of *The Presidential Game: The Origins of American Presidential Politics* (Oxford, 1982).

FORREST McDONALD is a historian and research professor at the University of Alabama in Tuscaloosa, Alabama. He is the 1980 recipient of the George Washington medal from Freedom's Foundation in Valley Forge, Pennsylvania, and the author of *Novus Ordo Seclorum: The Intellectual Origins of the Constitution* (University Press of Kansas, 1985).

WILLIAM G. McLOUGHLIN is a professor of history at Brown University in Providence, Rhode Island.

GARY B. NASH is a professor of history and the dean of undergraduate curriculum development at the University of California, Los Angeles, where he has been on the faculty since 1966. He is a member of the editorial board for *American Indian Culture and Research Journal* and the author of *Forging Freedom: The Formation of Philadelphia's Black Community, 1720–1840* (Harvard University Press, 1988).

STEPHEN B. OATES is a professor of history and the Paul Murray Kendall Professor of Biography at the University of Massachusetts-Amherst. He is the author of *Let the Trumpet Sound: The Life of Martin Luther King, Jr.* (Harper & Row, 1982) and *William Faulkner: Storyteller of the Heart* (Harper & Row, 1987).

MICHAEL PARENTI is a political scientist, lecturer, and social commentator. He is the author of *Inventing Reality: Politics and the Mass Media* (St. Martin's Press, 1985) and *The Sword and the Dollar: Imperialism, Revolution, and the Arms Race* (St. Martin's Press, 1989).

EDWARD PESSEN is a professor of history at City University of New York's Baruch College and Graduate Center, where he has received Professor of the Year awards for 1983, 1984, and 1985.

ALBERT J. RABOTEAU is a professor of history and African American studies at the University of California, Berkeley.

ROBERT V. REMINI is a professor of history and the director of the Institute of Humanities at the University of Illinois, where he has taught since 1965. He received a number of awards for his trilogy on the life of Andrew Jackson, including the American Book Award for Nonfiction in 1984.

DAVID J. ROTHMAN is a professor of history at Columbia University.

RAMON EDUARDO RUIZ is a professor of Latin American history and the director of the public programs division at the University of California, San Diego. He is the author of *The Great Rebellion: Mexico, Nineteen Five to Nineteen Twenty-Four* (W. W. Norton, 1980), which won the Herbert C. Herring Prize.

The late ALICE FELT TYLER was a professor of history at the University of Minnesota.

ALDEN T. VAUGHAN is a professor of history at Columbia University.

LORENA S. WALSH is a fellow with the Colonial Williamsburg Foundation and has written several key articles on seventeenth-century Maryland.

NANCY WOLOCH has taught at several universities and has been a fellow of the National Endowment for the Humanities.

GORDON S. WOOD is a professor of history at Brown University, where he has taught since 1969, and the chairman of the board of advisors for the National Historical Society.

C. VANN WOODWARD, considered by many of his contemporaries to be the greatest living American historian, is Sterling Professor Emeritus of History at Yale University. He won the Pulitzer Prize in 1982 for *Mary Chestnut's Civil War* (Yale University Press, 1981).

INDEX